REPORTS OF CASES

ADJUDGED IN THE

Court of King's Bench

Since the Time of LORD MANSFIELD's Coming to preside in it:

By JAMES BURROW Esq;

With TABLES,
Of the NAMES of the CASES,
AND
Of the MATTER contained in them.

VOLUME the SECOND:

Beginning with *Michaelmas* Term 32 *G*. 2. 1758.
AND
Ending with *Trinity* Term 1 *G*. 3. 1761, (inclusive).

LONDON:
Printed by His Majesty's Law-Printers;
For J. WORRALL and B. TOVEY, at the *Dove* in *Bell-Yard*, near *Lincoln's Inn*.
MDCCLXVI.

NOTWITHSTANDING what has been *hinted* in the *Preface*, and *expressly declared* in the *Advertisement* prefixed to the former Volume, in Excuse at least, if not in Justification of reporting *fully and circumstantially* such Cases as may deserve it; Yet *some* Gentlemen (choosing to take their Cases by *Tale* rather than by *Weight*) have complained "that the former Volume "does not contain a sufficient NUMBER of them, in "Proportion to it's Size."

The present Volume is less liable to the same Objection. It must be confessed, that two of the Cases in the preceding Volume are *very* long; perhaps, unreasonably so. In *this* Volume, I recollect but One, of any considerable Length: And I flatter My self that Few would wish to have had it much curtailed.

Inner Temple:
28*th June* 1766.

Errors

Errors of the Prefs.

In the *preceding* Volume—
In the Margin of *Page* 426,
For § 41. r. § 18.

Page	Line	In this Volume—
1035	24.	For *on* r. *in*
1052	20.	For " Caufe why r. Caufe " why
1090	41.	For $\frac{1}{4}$ r. $\frac{1}{2}$
1136	3.	In Margine—r. 15th *April*
1149	24.	In Margine—For 6th r. 16th
1233	19.	For arrefted. r. arrefted—

In the Table to it—
5. Title " Policy of Infurance"—place a) after Land-Man

A *Chrono-*

A *Chronological* TABLE of the NAMES of the CASES contained in this Volume, according to the Order of their Determination.

A Chronological Table, &c.

Trinity Term 1759, 32 & 33 *Geo.* 2.

Michaelmas Term 1759, 33 *Geo.* 2.

Hilary Term 1760, 33 *Geo.* 2.

Easter Term 1760, 33 *Geo.* 2.

Trinity Term 1760, 33 & 34 *Geo.* 2.

A Chronological Table, &c.

Michaelmas Term 1760, 1 *Geo.* 3.

Hilary Term 1761, 1 *Geo.* 3.

Easter Term 1761, 1 *Geo.* 3.

Trinity

A Chronological Table, &c.

An

An *Alphabetical* TABLE of the NAMES of the CASES comprised in this Volume.

An Alphabetical Table, &c.

Rex

An Alphabetical Table, &c.

S.

An Alphabetical Table, &c.

Michaelmas

Michaelmas Term

32 Geo. 2. B.R. 1758.

Rex *verſ.* Athay Eſq;

Monday 6th November 1758.

ON ſhewing Cauſe Why a Rule ſhould not be made abſolute, for an Information againſt a Juſtice of Peace, for a Miſdemeanour in *refuſing to grant a Licence* to One *Francis Simes* (who had been licenſed for ſeveral preceding Years) to ſell Ale, as uſual; and afterwards convicting him, WITHOUT any previous *Summons*, for having ſold it without a Licence; It appeared that the *pretended Grounds* upon which this Rule had been applied for and obtained, were either falſe or fallacious. The firſt was, That the *only* Reaſon why the Licence was refuſed him, was his declining to *pay a Sum of Money* (5 *l.*) which was claimed of him upon a diſtinct and collateral Account, and which he denied to be due from him: The Payment of which Sum of Money was (as He alledged) inſiſted upon by the Juſtice, as a Condition precedent to his granting the Man a Licence. The ſecond pretended Ground of the Motion was "that the Juſtice had "convicted him of the Offence, without any previous Summons."

As to the firſt—The COURT were unanimous that the Allegation appeared to be falſe in Fact: But, at the ſame Time, they declared explicitly, "That Juſtices of Peace have *no Sort of Autho*-"*thority* to annex any ſuch *Conditions* to the Grant of theſe Licences.

As to the ſecond—They eſteemed it to be fallacious, as the Fact came out upon ſhewing Cauſe: For the Man was actually *preſent* before the Juſtice (who *had ſent for him*;) and was ſo far from offering at making any Defence, that he rather ſeemed to apply for Mercy; declaring, however, "that if the Juſtice did convict him, "he would not pay the Penalty."

Thirdly. The COURT observed that the Man had *not* any where *alledged* "*That he was* INNOCENT of the Offence:" Which they thought it *incumbent upon him* to have done, to intitle himself to make this Application against the Justice of Peace.

RULE DISCHARGED.

Tuesday 7th November 1758.

Rex *vers.* Fielding Esq;

ON shewing Cause why an Information should not be granted against Mr. *Fielding*, for a Misdemeanour in his Office of a Justice of the Peace, the Complaint appeared to be frivolous and vexatious; so that the Justice ought to have the Costs he had been put to in defending himself against it: The only Question was, *Who* should *pay* them.

The Complaint was made upon a Joint-Affidavit made by the Prosecutor (one *Taylor*) *and his Attorney* (Mr. *Callaghan*:) Which *Attorney* was also sworn to have *declared*, (and in rude and virulent Terms too,) "That *if it should cost* HIM 100 *l*, He would lay "*Fielding* by the Heels."

It was strongly urged, on Behalf of Mr. *Callaghan*, that it would be a very great Discouragement to Attornies, in the Course of their Practice, if THEY were to be made *personally liable to Costs*, in Case their Clients Motions should not succeed; which Motions they had engaged in at the Application of their Clients, and upon Facts *represented to them by* their Clients, as being true and candidly stated; and which they themselves could not know or suspect to be otherwise: And that it would be still more hard upon them, to do this *without hearing* what they could urge in their own Defence.

But the COURT (*viz.* Lord *Mansfield*, Mr. Just. *Foster*, and Mr. Just. *Wilmot*) were clear and unanimous, that in *this* Case, they might and ought to do it; because Mr. *Callaghan* not only appeared *as* PROSECUTOR, *by* JOINING *in the Original Affidavit* of Complaint; but had also expresly declared "That if it should cost HIM "100 *l.* he would lay *Fielding* by the Heels." Therefore they

DISCHARGED the Rule; with Costs, to be *paid* by Mr. *Taylor* AND MR. CALLAGHAN.

Pomp

Pomp *verſ.* Ludvigſon.

Saturday 11th *November* 1758.

A Rule for diſcharging the Defendant upon *Common* Bail, was made abſolute; the Affidavit to hold him to Special Bail, *not* being POSITIVE: Which it is the * eſtabliſhed Rule of the Court, "that it *muſt* be."

* So was the Reſolution in *Innys* v. *Sinclaire, P.* 1733, 6 *G.* 2. *B. R.* and in *Holmes et al'* v. *Mendes Coſta et al'. Tr.* 1733. 6 & 7 *G.* 2. *B. R.* and in *Leverland* v. *Baſnet, Tr.* 16 *G.* 2. *B. R.* and in *Claphamſon* v. *Bowman, P.* 18 *G.* 2. *B. R.* and in *Rios* v. *Beliſante, P.* 17 *G.* 2. *B. R.* and in *Coillot* v. *Hague, Tr.* 1747, 21 *G.* 2. *B. R.* and in *Van Moorſell* v. *Jullien, M.* 1748, 22 *G.* 2. *B. R.* and in *Kelly* v. *Devereux, M.* 1752, 26 *G.* 2. *B. R* and in *Prior* v. *Scott, H.* 1753, 26 *G.* 2. *B. R.* To which Reſolutions, the preſent One being added, This Point ſeems to be moſt fully ſettled.

Lord MANSFIELD ſaid that the Act of Parliament required a *poſitive* Oath of the Debt: Which poſitive Oath may not be contradicted by the Defendant.

But Mr. Juſt. FOSTER ſaid He Himſelf had always thought the Rule *too ſtrict*; And that He had *never complied* with it at his Chambers, though He would not go *againſt* it.

The preſent Caſe was that of a Merchant in *London*, whoſe Correſpondent in *Sweden* had ſent him over the Accounts from *Sweden, where the Debt aroſe*: And conſequently the Plaintiff, the Merchant here, could only ſwear to *his* BELIEF, with a *Reference* to the Accounts ſent to him from *Sweden*; the Fact itſelf not being within his own *perſonal* Knowledge. So that the Affidavit could not have been more poſitive than it was; unleſs the Correſpondent in *Sweden* had come over hither, to ſwear it: (For an Affidavit *ſworn there* could not have been read here.)

See the Act of Parliament of 12 *G.* 1. *c.* 29. § 2. intitled "An "Act to prevent frivolous and vexatious Suits:" Which enacts "That no Perſon ſhall be held to ſpecial Bail, upon any Proceſs "iſſuing out of any Superior Court, where the Cauſe of Action ſhall not amount to the Sum of 10*l.* or upwards; nor "out of any Inferior Court, where the Cauſe of Action ſhall "not amount to the Sum of Forty Shillings or upwards." Then the ſecond Clauſe directs the Method, in Caſes where the Cauſe of Action *does* amount to thoſe reſpective Sums.

And the Words of this Second Clauſe of the Act are—"That in "all Caſes where the Plaintiff or Plaintiff's Cauſe of Action "ſhall amount to the Sum of Ten Pounds or 40*s.* or upwards, "as aforesaid, *Affidavit* shall be made and filed, OF *such Cause* "*of Action*; And the Sum or Sums specified in such Affidavit, "shall be indorsed on the Back of such Writ or Process: *For* "*which* Sum or Sums so indorsed, the Sheriff or other Officer "to whom such Writ or Process shall be directed, shall take "Bail; and *for no more*."

The present Defendant was discharged on Common Bail.

Brucklesbank *vers.* Smith Esquire.

Tuesday 14th *November* 1758.

THIS was a Special Verdict from *Northumberland* Assizes, upon an Action of Trespass for breaking and entering the Plaintiff's Ship in the River *Tyne*, at *Newcastle* upon *Tyne*, and taking and carrying away an Anchor—: To which the Defendant pleaded "Not guilty."

The Special Verdict finds that the Defendant was a Justice of the Peace of and for the Town and County of *Newcastle* upon *Tyne*; And that the Plaintiff was Master of a Ship called the *Leeds-Merchant*, floating &c. in the River *Tyne*, being a navigable River: That 3 Tons of Ballast and more were unloaded *out of* the said Ship, INTO a Machine or Vessel called a *Hopper*, in the said River, *with Intent* that it should be carried therein, into the High and open Seas; And that it *was accordingly carried out of* the said River, *into the high and open Seas*, and was *there* cast out of the said Hopper, where the Water was more than 14 Fathom deep, at a Distance from any Port, Haven, Channel or navigable River. It finds that *Thomas Field* before the Time of the supposed Trespass, *viz.* on such a Day &c. came before the Defendant being a Justice of Peace &c, and laid Information of the Facts of "putting the Ballast *into* "*the Hopper* with an *Intent that it should be dropped* out of the said "Hopper INTO *the* WATER, and NOT *be cast* &c *upon the* LAND "*where the Tide and Water never flows or runs*;" *contrary* to the Statute. It finds that the Plaintiff was summoned to appear, and that he did appear before the said Justice; and that *Proof* was then and there made, by his Confession, "That it was so put *on Board the* "*Hopper*, in the said River, *with Intent* that it should be therein "carried out of the said River *into the High and open Sea*, and cast "*therein* at the Depth of 14 Fathom and upwards, at a Distance "from any Haven &c (*ut supra*) where the Tide or Water never "flows or runs." It is found That the Defendant thereupon *convicted* the Plaintiff, and adjudged him to be an Offender against the Statute of 19 *G.* 2. *c.* 22. Then it finds the Conviction before the

 Justice,

Justice, *in hæc verba*; and that the then Defendant (the now Plaintiff) was adjudged to forfeit 2*l.* 10*s.* for the said Offence.

It finds that the Justice of Peace (the now Defendant) issued his Warrant under his Hand and Seal, to levy the same by Distress &c; And that *William Bruce* a Serjeant at Mace (to whom the Warrant was directed,) by Virtue of the said Warrant, took the said Anchor &c.

This Case was first argued on *Friday* the 9th of *June* last, by Mr. *Winn* for the Plaintiff; and Mr. Serjeant *Poole* for the Defendant.

Mr. *Winn*—rehearsed the Statute of 19 *G.* 2. *c.* 22. § 1, 2. And said That the Fact found to have been *proved*, is *no Offence within* this Act: And consequently, the Defendant was a Trespasser, in levying the Penalty. Nothing is found to have been proved but a *mere* INTENTION.

This is a *pœnal* Law, and must be construed *strictly*.

34, 35 *H.* 8. *c.* 9. § *ult.* gives the Penalty for casting Rubbish into Havens, Roads, Channels &c. Then 19 *G.* 2. *c.* 22. describes the Offence to be casting throwing out or unlading any Ballast, Rubbish &c, " BUT ONLY *upon the* LAND, where the Tide or " Water never flows or runs." And the Preamble describes the Mischief to be " Casting, throwing out, and unlading their Bal- " last, either on the Shore, or on the Side, and *below* the usual and " full Sea-Mark, and doing other Annoyances, *to the Detriment* " *and Obstruction of Navigation.*

In the *Thames*, this Method of disposing of the Ballast is never treated as an Offence: And that is under the Care and Inspection of the *Trinity-house*.

The Mischief which the Legislature had in View, was throwing the Ballast &c either on the Shore, or on the *Sides of Rivers*, and below the full Sea-Mark.

But this was in the open and high Sea, above 14 Fathom deep; at a Distance from any Port, Haven, Channel, or River.

He relied upon the *Intention* and *Spirit* of this Law, rather than upon the *Letter* of it: Which Intention of the Act, he said, would plainly appear from the Proviso at the End of it, (*V. Sect. penult.*) and that it was intended solely to prevent Prejudice to the Navigation in Havens, Ports, Roads, Channels or Rivers, and for no other

other Purpoſe. But Nothing is ſtated here of any Sort of Prejudice actually done to the Navigation or even of any ſuch Intention to prejudice the Navigation of the Haven, Port, Road, Channel or River.

The Ballaſt was carried *out of* the River, into the high and open Sea; and *there* caſt out, at above 14 Fathom Depth, and at a Diſtance from any Port Haven Channel or River.—And the *Intention only* is laid accordingly.

And the Confeſſion is of Nothing more than *ſuch* an Intention. But there is neither Proof nor Confeſſion of any *Fact* whatſoever: Nor was any *actual* Injury done.

Mr. Serjeant *Poole contra*, for the Defendant—It was impoſſible for Us, in the Nature of the Thing, to *prove* "That the Ballaſt "*was* ACTUALLY dropped in the River:" For this is done privately from the Bottom of the Hopper. It was neceſſary therefore for Us to charge the *Intent* as the Offence. And this Intent the Defendant has *confeſſed*. And the *Offence, as* We have charged it, is within the Act; *viz.* "Putting the Ballaſt into the Hopper, "with Intent &c."

This is a *poſitive Law*, "That no Perſon ſhall caſt, throw out, "or diſcharge out of &c. any Ballaſt &c; BUT ONLY *upon the* "*Land*, where the Tide or Water *never flows or runs*." To which poſitive Law, the Fact charged is *directly contrary*. The preſent Act of 19 *G.* 2. was made to inforce and make more eaſy the proſecuting Offences againſt the former Statute of 34, 35 *H.* 8: upon which, it was difficult to proſecute the Offender, in ſome Caſes. And here are proper Exceptions, upon proper Occaſions: In all other reſpects it is a general Law.

It is ſaid indeed, on the Part of the Plaintiff, "that here is no "actual Prejudice done to the Navigation." But what the Plaintiff has done, *may*, by ſome Means or other, prejudice the Navigation of the River: It is in their Power, to drop the Ballaſt out of this Hopper, in the *Channel* of the River, without any Poſſibility of being diſcovered.

And this Statute is in Negative Words, *viz.* "BUT ONLY upon "the *Land*." *Co. Lit.* 115. affirms that there is a Diverſity between an Act of Parliament in the Negative, and One in the Affirmative; and ſhews ſuch Diverſity.

Therefore he prayed Judgment for the Defendant.

 Mr.

Mr. *Winn*, in Reply—This Act ought to be conftrued *ftrictly*; As it is a Reftraint of a Common-Law Right which a Man has to lay his Ballaft where he pleafes; provided he be not Guilty of a Nufance, in fo doing.

And this is no Offence againft the *Spirit* and *Intention* of this Law. Nothing is charged, but an *Intent:* Which Intent was not, even if it had been *executed*, a *fubftantial* Offence againft this Law.

Lord MANSFIELD—This is a *General* Queftion, which goes farther than this particular Cafe.

Mr. Juft. FOSTER afked if the Corporation of *Newcaftle* were not Confervators of the River *Tyne*.

It was anfwered "That they were."

Mr. Juft. FOSTER—Corporations ought to be protected in their juft and ancient Rights.

The COURT did not upon this firft Argument, give any Opinion: But it was ordered to ftand for a further Argument.

ULTERIUS CONCILIUM.

And now, Mr. *Clayton* argued on Behalf of the Plaintiff, as before, "that this Fact found was *not* an Offence within the Act."

Mr. *Norton* was going to anfwer Him, on the Part of the Defendant. But

Lord MANSFIELD ftopped him, from entering into it at all; It being a very plain Cafe, and clearly againft the *exprefs* Prohibition of the Act: Which provides that it fhall *not* be thrown BUT *upon the Land*. Whereas this Man fays that he has found a better Way, than that which the Act has *exprefly* prefcribed.

But here is fuch an Opening to Fraud, in this Way that he has thought a better One, that it would be dangerous to truft to this Method, though it were not prohibited. However, it is enough, that it is contrary to the *direct* and *exprefs* Provifion of the Act.

Indeed if it was put upon the Hopper, *in Order merely to carry it upon the* LAND; that would only be the proper Means of doing it, and therefore would not be an Offence againft the Act. But this is with Intent to lay it in the WATER.

And

And there can be no Security as to the *Place where* the Hopper may *drop it*. It is mighty easy, from the Construction of the Hopper, to drop it privately: And it is also the Interest of the Person who carries it in the Hopper, to drop it assoon as he can; that he may come the sooner again, to fetch more.

The Shifting it out of one Ship into another, WITHOUT *Intention to drop it* ANY *where*, would not be a Case within the Act: For that would not be a *Casting or throwing out* at all, *within* the Meaning of the Act.

The Other THREE JUDGES agreed, in Terms, with Lord *Mansfield*; And All of them spoke explicitly to the same Effect.

Per Cur. unanimously,
JUDGMENT for the DEFENDANT.

Michell *verſ.* Cue et Ux'.

ON shewing Cause against setting aside an Execution for Irregularity (which Irregularity was the Suing out the *Execution above a Year after the Judgment* obtained, WITHOUT *any Scire facias* to revive it,) it appeared that the *whole Delay* had arisen from the Part of the *Defendants*, by Bills in Chancery for *Injunctions*, and by obtaining *Time for Payment &c.*

And though the Cases of *Winter* v. *Lightbound* in 1 *Strange* 301. and of *Booth* v. *Booth* in 1 *Salk.* 322, were urged as Authorities in Point on the Part of the Defendants; Yet

The COURT were unanimous that this Rule of "reviving a Judgment of above a Year old, by a *Scire facias*, before suing out Execution upon it," which was *intended* to prevent a SURPRIZE *upon the Defendant*, ought not to be taken Advantage of by a Defendant who was so far from being *surprized* by the *Plaintiff's* Delay, that *He himself* had been trying all Manner of Methods whereby HE *might delay the Plaintiff*: And therefore they not only discharged the Rule, but discharged it with *Costs* too.

Thomas Baſkett and *Robert Baſkett*, Adminiſtrators (with the Will annexed) of *John Baſkett*, Plaintiffs: The Chancellor, Maſters, and Scholars of the Univerſity of *Cambridge*, *Joſeph Bentham*, and *Charles Bathurſt*, Defendants.

THE Plaintiffs brought a Bill in the Court of Chancery, for an *Injunction* to reſtrain the Defendants from *Printing* or *Selling* a *Book* intitled " An exact *Abridgment* of all the *Acts* of " *Parliament* relating to the Exciſe on Beer *&c.*" And on the " Hearing of this Cauſe, the 24th of *January* 1743, the Lord Chancellor ordered that a Caſe ſhould be ſtated, for the Opinion of the Judges of the Court of King's Bench, upon the ſeveral Acts of Parliament Letters-Patent and Grants of the Crown inſiſted on by either Side, and any other Letters-Patent appearing upon Record relating to the Matters in queſtion between the Parties.

The ſeveral Letters-Patent inſiſted on by the Plaintiffs in Support of their Claim, as the *King's Printer*, to the *Sole* and *excluſive* Right of printing and publiſhing all *Acts* of *Parliament* or *Abridgments* of *Acts* of *Parliament &c*, bear Date the 22d of *April* 1 *Edw.* 6. the 29th of *December* 1 *Mariæ*, the 24th of *March* 1 *Eliz.* the 27th of *September* 19 *Eliz.* the 8th of *Auguſt* 31 *Eliz.* the 10th of *May* 1 *J.* 1. the 11th of *February* 14 *J.* 1. the 20th of *July* 3 *C.* 1. the 26th of *September* 11 *C.* 1. the 24th of *December* 27 *Car.* 2. and the 13th of *October* 12 *Ann:* Which Letters-Patent are ſeveral Grants of the Office of King's Printer of all and ſingular Statutes Acts of Parliament *&c.* The Letters-Patent of the 12th of Queen *Ann* are a Grant, in Reverſion, of the ſaid *Office*, for the Term of 30 Years, to commence after the Determination of a former Grant then in being: They expreſly grant the *Sole* Power of printing all and all Sorts of Abridgments of all and ſingular Statutes and Acts of Parliament, and *prohibit* all other Perſons to print any Volume Book or Work of which the Printing was thereby granted. The Eſtate and Intereſt granted by the ſaid Letters-Patent commenced upon the 10th of *January* 1739; and afterwards became veſted in *John Baſkett*, the Father of the now Plaintiffs; and is now veſted in the *Plaintiffs*, as Adminiſtrators to their ſaid Father with his Will annexed: And the Plaintiffs have been ſworn and admitted into the ſaid Office of *his Majeſty's Printer*.

The Caſe further ſtated that the Plaintiffs and Other Printers to his Majeſty and his Royal Predeceſſors have, by Virtue of the ſaid ſeveral Letters-Patent to them reſpectively granted, from Time to Time printed All Acts of Parliament and Abridgments of Acts of Parliament, Bibles, New Teſtaments, and other Books mentioned in the ſaid Letters-Patent. And the Plaintiffs claim the SOLE *Right* of printing *All* Acts of Parliament, EXCLUSIVE of *All other Perſons*, during the Term granted by the ſaid Letters-Patent of the 12th of Queen *Ann.*

The *Defendants* founded their Claim upon the ſeveral Letters-Patent and Act of Parliament following.

King *Henry* the 8th by his Letters-Patent bearing Date the 20th of *July* in the 26th Year of his Reign, for Him and his Heirs, granted *Licence* to the Chancellor Maſters and Scholars of the Univerſity of *Cambridge*, that They and their Succeſſors for ever, by their Writing under the Seal of the ſaid Chancellor, from Time to Time might aſſign and chooſe and for ever have among themſelves and within the Univerſity aforeſaid always remaining and inhabiting, *Three Stationers and Printers* or Venders of Books, as well Aliens and born without as Natives and born within his ſaid Majeſty's Obedience, having and holding as well hired Houſes as Houſes of their own: Which ſaid Stationers or Printers in Form aforeſaid aſſigned, and Any of them, *might lawfully there print All Manner of Books approved* or which thereafter ſhould be *approved* by the ſaid Chancellor or his Vice-Chancellor and three Doctors there; And as well *thoſe Books* as *other Books* printed whereſoever, as well within his ſaid Majeſty's Realm as without, *ſo as aforeſaid approved* or to be *approved*, might *put to Sale*, as well within this Kingdom whereſoever they ſhould pleaſe &c; and that, without Penalty.

The Statute of 13 *Eliz. c.* 29. confirms All Letters Patent &c, granted to the ſaid Univerſity.

By Letters-Patent dated 6th *February* 3 *Car.* 1. reciting the ſaid Letters-Patent of 26 *H.* 8. and the ſaid Act of Parliament of 13 *Eliz.* And alſo reciting "that ſince the ſaid Act of Parliament, "divers Letters-Patent had been made, by Queen *Elizabeth*, King "*James* the Firſt, and his then Majeſty, granting Authority to "print divers and ſundry Books, and prohibiting generally All "other Perſons to print the ſame; and alſo reciting a Decree in the Court of Star-Chamber, of the 23d *June* 28 *Eliz.* and a Proclamation of the 25th of *September* 21 *Jac.* 1. inforcing the ſame; The King *confirms* the Right granted by the ſaid Letters-Patent of 26 *H.* 8. to the Univerſity of *Cambridge*, *notwithſtanding* any Grant or Prohibition contained in the ſubſequent Letters-Patent or any of them.

The

The Questions upon this Case are—

1st. *Whether* the Plaintiffs are intitled to the *Sole Right* of printing *Acts* of *Parliament* and *Abridgments* of *Acts* of *Parliament*, *exclusive* of *All* other Persons, during the Term granted by the said Letters-Patent dated the 13th of *October* in the 12th Year of the Reign of Queen *Ann*.

2d. *Whether* the Defendants, the Chancellor Masters and Scholars of the University of *Cambridge*, by Virtue of the Grants and Acts of Parliament insisted on by the said Defendants, or any of them, *have* the *Right* or *Privilege* of printing *Acts* of *Parliament* or *Abridgments* of *Acts* of *Parliament*.

This Case was first argued in *Michaelmas* Term 1745, by Mr. *Comyns* for the Plaintiffs, and Mr. *Noel* for the Defendants. It was argued a second Time in *Michaelmas* Term 1747, by Mr. *Gundry* for the Plaintiffs, and Sir *Richard Lloyd* for the Defendants. It was argued a third Time in *Hilary* Term 1749, by Mr. *Hume* for the Plaintiffs, and Mr *Henley* for the Defendants. It then stood for the Certificate of the Judges; Which having been put off for several Years during the Life of the Lord Chief Justice *Lee*, the Parties did not apply to have it argued again, whilst the Lord Chief Justice *Ryder* lived: But in *Trinity* Term 1758, they applied to have it set down for further Argument, in the next *Michaelmas* Term.

Before it came on, The Court ordered Copies of all the abovementioned Letters-Patent Acts of Parliament and Instruments to be left with them: They also ordered Copies of the Charter to the Stationers of *London*, of the 4th of *May* 3 & 4 *Ph.* & *Mar*; the Grant to the University of *Oxford*, " to print Books," dated the 13th of *March* 8 *Car.* 1; and the Grant " to print Law-Books," dated the 12th of *August* 9 *Geo.* 2; and the Proclamation of the 25th of *September* 21 *Jac.* 1. against the disorderly printing of Books; and the several Decrees of the Court of Star-Chamber relative thereto.

On the 17th of *November* 1751, It was argued by Mr. *Comyns* for the Plaintiffs, and Mr. Solicitor General *(Yorke)* for the Defendants.

And very soon after this last Argument, the following Certificate was made.

" *Having* heard Counſel on both Sides, and conſidered of this " Caſe, We are of Opinion that during the Term granted by " the Letters-Patent dated the 13th of *October* in the 12th " Year of the Reign of Queen *Ann*, the Plaintiffs are intitled " to the Right of printing Acts of Parliament and Abridgments " of Acts of Parliament, excluſive of all other Perſons not " authorized to print the ſame by Prior Grants from the " Crown.

" *But* We think that by Virtue of the Letters-Patent bearing " Date the 20th Day of *July* in the 26th Year of the Reign " of King *Henry* the 8th, and the Letters-Patent bearing Date " the 6th of *February* in the 3d Year of the Reign of King " *Charles* the Firſt, The Chancellor Maſters and Scholars of " the Univerſity of *Cambridge* are intruſted with a *concurrent* " *Authority* to print Acts of Parliament and Abridgments of " Acts of Parliament, within the ſaid *Univerſity*, upon the " Terms in the ſaid Letters-Patent.

" MANSFIELD.
" T. DENISON.
" M. FOSTER.
" E. WILMOT.

" 24th *November* 1758."

Friday 17th *November* 1758.

Dr. Burton *verſ.* Thompſon.

ON ſhewing Cauſe againſt a Rule for a NEW TRIAL, which had been moved for by the Plaintiff, upon an Allegation " That the Verdict (which was found for the Defendant) was given " *contrary to Evidence*;"

Mr. Juſt. FOSTER (who tried the Cauſe) now reported, That it was an Action for a Libel; that the Charge *was proved* by the Plaintiff; but that the *Injury* done to him thereby, appeared upon the Evidence to be *ſo* VERY INCONSIDERABLE, that if the Jury had found for the Plaintiff, He ſhould have thought a *Half-Crown*, or even a *much ſmaller Sum*, to have been *ſufficient* Damages: But that the Jury had gone too far; and inſtead of giving the Plaintiff very ſmall Damages, had found a Verdict *againſt* him; which was certainly a Verdict AGAINST *Evidence*.

Lord

Lord Mansfield—It does not follow by neceſſary Conſequence, that there muſt ALWAYS be a new Trial granted, in *all* Caſes whatſoever, where the Verdict is *contrary to Evidence:* For it is poſſible that the Verdict *may ſtill* be on the Side of the *real* Juſtice and Equity of the Caſe. And of this, there are ſeveral Inſtances in the * printed Books; particularly the Dutcheſs of *Mazarine*'s Caſe in 2 *Salk.* 646. [*Deerly* v. the Dutcheſs of *Mazarine:* Which is directly in Point.]

* See Title *Trial* in 2 *Salk. pl.* 2, 3, 4, 5, 11, 18, 34. See before, *Farewell* Eſquire v. *Chaffey et al'.* Pa. 54.

Here, the Jury have found for the Defendant, whereas my Brother *Foſter*, who tried the Cauſe (which the Plaintiff has brought hither out of *Yorkſhire*) ſays that "He thinks *Half a Crown or leſs* "would have been Damages ſufficient, IF *they had given their Verdict* "*for the Plaintiff.*" He muſt pay the *Coſts*, before he *can* have a new Trial. Therefore I do not think that We ought to interfere, merely to give the Plaintiff an Opportunity of harraſſing the Defendant at a great Expence to Himſelf; where there has been *no Real* Damage, and where the Injury is ſo *trivial* as not to deſerve above a Half-Crown Compenſation. Beſides, the Plaintiff has brought the Action to be tried at a great Diſtance from the proper County. The Cauſe of Action is in the Nature of a *Crime:* The implied Damages are, in ſome Meaſure, by Way of *Puniſhment*. An Indictment or Information would lie. And in *criminal* Caſes, where the Defendant is acquitted, a New Trial cannot be granted.

Mr. Juſt. *Deniſon*, Mr. Juſt. *Foſter*, and Mr. Juſt. *Wilmot*, All ſpoke in very explicit Terms to the ſame Effect.

Per Cur. unanimouſly,
The Rule to ſhew Cauſe why there ſhould be a new Trial was DISCHARGED.

Aſlin *verſ.* Parkin.

Saturday 18th *November* 1758.

THIS was an Action of *Treſpaſs*, for the MESNE PROFITS of a Houſe in *Sheffield* in *Yorkſhire*, brought in the NAME of the *Leſſee* or NOMINAL *Plaintiff* in Ejectment, againſt the Tenant in Poſſeſſion, after Judgment obtained againſt the CASUAL EJECTOR, *by* DEFAULT. The *Coſts* of the Ejectment were alſo included and inſerted in the Declaration, *as conſequential* Damages of the Treſpaſs therein complained of.

On the Trial of this Cauſe before Lord *Manſfield* at the Summer Aſſizes 1758, at the City of *York*, the Plaintiff gave in Evidence, the

the Judgment in Ejectment, the Writ of Possession with the Return of Execution upon it, The Defendant's Occupation of the Premisses, the Value of them during that Time (which was proved to be 20 *l.*) and the Costs of the Ejectment (amounting to 12 *l.* more.)

On the Part of the Defendant, it was *objected*, That as the Judgment in the Ejectment was *by Default*, against the CASUAL *Ejector*, this Action could *not* be legally maintained in the NAME of the *nominal* Plaintiff; but ought to have been brought by the Plaintiff's LESSOR: And they ought to have proved the Plaintiff to have been in *Possession*, when the Defendant committed the Trespass for which the Action is brought.

In support of this Objection, It was argued that though the Law allows *fictitious* Proceedings in Ejectment, *for the trying of* TITLES; Yet in Actions *for* MESNE PROFITS, NO *such Fiction* prevails: But the *Suit*, the *Injury*, and the *Defendant* are REAL; and the Action *in* NO *respect differs* from any *other* Action of Trespass.

That this was a *Possessory* Action; which could in no Case be maintained, unless the *Plaintiff's* POSSESSION was either *proved* or *admitted*: And as, in the present Case, the Plaintiff *could not* POSSIBLY *prove* an *actual* Entry, there was NO *Evidence* of HIS *Possession*, that could *affect*, or be *received against* the *present* Defendant.

It was *admitted* that an Action of this Kind might be brought in the Name of the nominal Plaintiff in Ejectment, where the *Tenant had appeared and confessed* Lease Entry and Ouster; because being thereby become a PARTY *to the Record* in Ejectment, and *having confessed* the Entry of the Plaintiff, He is ESTOPPED *by that Confession and by the Judgment against him*, from controverting afterwards the Plaintiff's Possession: But where the Judgment in Ejectment was by *Default, against the* CASUAL Ejector, there was NO *such Confession of the* TENANT, NO *Matter of Record to* ESTOPP *him*; but He was *equally at Liberty to deny* the Plaintiff's Possession, and to put him upon *proving it*, as in *any other* Action of Trespass; And having *never been a* PARTY *to the Judgment* in Ejectment, *neither* that Judgment nor the Writ of Possession upon it, (as they were *merely between* the *nominal* Plaintiff and a *third* Person, the Casual Ejector,) could be any Conclusion or Evidence *against* the *present* Defendant:

It was therefore insisted that this Action *ought* to have been brought by the *Lessor* of the Plaintiff, *in his* OWN *Name*; who might have

have proved an *actual* Entry under the Writ of Poffeffion; and by that Entry, the Poffeffion he thereby obtained would *relate back* to the *Commencement* of his Title: But being brought in the Name of the *nominal* Plaintiff, and the Defendant being a *Stranger to the Judgment* in Ejectment, the Plaintiff had *failed* of maintaining his Action.

In Support of this Objection, The Defendant's Counfel urged That although the Diftinction was carried no farther, in the Cafe of *Jefferies* v. *Dyfon* (2 *Strange* 960, *H.* 7 *G.* 2. *B. R.*) than to admit the Tenant in Poffeffion (where the Judgment was againft the Cafual Ejector, by Default,) to controvert the *Title* of the Plaintiff, upon an Action for the mefne Profits; Yet both Parts of that Cafe had been fince contradicted; and it had been fince holden "that "the Defendant fhould *not* controvert the Plaintiff's Title:" But (where the Tenant has not entered into the Common Rule) "the "Plaintiff *muft prove* his own *actual Poffeffion*; and can only re-"cover Damages from *that* Time." For this, they cited a Cafe of *Stanynought* v. *Cofins*, *H.* 19 *G.* 2. *C. B.* (2 *Barnes* 367.) and fome Circuit-Traditions of Nonfuits for want of the Plaintiff's proving his Poffeffion, where the Judgment was by Default, againft the Cafual Ejector.

Lord MANSFIELD *referved* the Point, at the Affizes; and afterwards propofed it to *All* the Judges, and had their Opinion: Which He thought fit now publickly and particularly to *declare*.

Upon Principles, His Lordfhip faid, He was clearly of Opinion againft the Objection, on the Trial, without hearing the Counfel for the Plaintiff. But, as *Authorities* were then referred to, and as the Point related to the *Effect* of that *Proceeding* which is *now* almoft the *only* Remedy, in Practice, for recovering Land wrongfully with-held; He thought it of great Confequence that the Matter fhould be confidered by All the Judges. He therefore referved the Cafe, declaring "He did it with that View; and that He would "endeavour to get their Opinion without any Delay or Expence to "the Parties."

Accordingly, His Lordfhip laid it before them upon the firft Day of Term; And They took till laft *Thurfday*, the 16th of *November*, to look into the Cafes, fo far as they could, with any Accuracy, be traced. And befides thofe that are in print, They had feen fome in Manufcript, *different Ways*; which were now, He faid, totally immaterial to be mentioned:

Becaufe All the Judges are unanimoufly of Opinion "That the "Nominal Plaintiff, and the Cafual Ejector, are judicially to be

 "confidered

" confidered as the *fictitious Form* of an Action *really* brought by " the *Leffor* of the Plaintiff againft the *Tenant in Poffeffion*; invent- " ed, under the Control and Power of the Court, for the Ad- " vancement of Juftice in many refpects; and to force the Parties " to go to Trial on the Merits, without being intangled in the " Nicety of Pleadings on either Side."

" That the *Leffor* of the Plaintiff, and the *Tenant in Poffeffion*, " are, fubftantially, and in Truth, *the Parties*, and the *only* Parties " to the Suit. The Tenant in Poffeffion muft be duly ferved: And " if He is not, He has a Right to fet afide the Judgment. If, after " he is duly ferved, He does not appear, but lets Judgment go by " Default; fuch Judgment is carried into Execution againft him by " a Writ of Poffeffion."

" That there is *no* Diftinction between a Judgment in Ejectment " upon a *Verdict*; and a Judgment by *Default*. In the firft Cafe, " the Right of the Plaintiff is tried and determined againft the " Defendant: In the laft Cafe, It is *confeffed*."

" An Action for the *mefne Profits* is *confequential* to the Recovery " in Ejectment. It may be brought by the Leffor of the Plaintiff " in his *own* Name, or in the Name of the *nominal Leffee*; And in " either Shape, it is equally *his* Action."

" The Tenant is *concluded* by the Judgment, and cannot con- " trovert the *Title*. Confequently, He cannot controvert the Plain- " tiff's *Poffeffion*; becaufe his Poffeffion is *Part* of his Title: For " the Plaintiff, to intitle himfelf to recover in an Ejectment, muft " fhew a poffeffory Right not barred by the Statute of Limitations."

" This Judgment, like all others, only concludes the Parties, as to " the *fubject Matter* of it. Therefore, *beyond* the Time laid in the " Demife, it proves Nothing at all: Becaufe, beyond that Time, " the Plaintiff has alledged no Title, nor could be put to prove " any."

" As to the *Length of Time the Tenant has occupied*, the Judg- " ment proves Nothing; nor as to the *Value*. And therefore, it " was *proved* in this Cafe (and muft be in all) *How long* the De- " fendant enjoyed the Premiffes; and what the *Value* was: And it " appeared that the Time of fuch Occupation by the Defendant, " was *within* the Time laid in the Demife."

This unanimous Refolution of all the Judges, upon fhort plain Principles, will not only be a certain and uniform Rule, upon Actions for mefne Profits; but may tend to put this fictitious Remedy by Ejectment, upon a true and liberal Foundation; to attain speedily and effectually the complete Ends of Justice, according to the real Merits of the Case.

My Brother WILMOT tells me, that he had the very same Question made before Him, upon the *Oxford* Circuit, the last Assizes: But the Cause went off upon another Point.

I am therefore glad that the general Rule is now settled; and that the Settling it, has occasioned no Expence or Delay to the particular Parties in this Cause.

The RULE consequently was, That the *Postea* be delivered to the PLAINTIFF, that He might have Judgment.

Heylyn and Others *vers.* Adamson.

Monday 20th *November* 1758.

THIS was an Action on the Case, upon Promises. And the first Count in the Declaration was upon an INLAND *Bill of Exchange, drawn* by *Robert Carrick* and directed to *William Dods*, dated the 13th Day of *March* 1756; Whereby the said *Robert Carrick* required the said *William Dods* to pay to the Defendant or his Order 100 *l.* at 40 Days after Date, Value received, as advised by the said *Robert Carrick*: Which said Bill was *indorsed* by the said Defendant (*Eleanor Adamson*) to the said Plaintiffs, and was accepted by the said *Dods*, but not paid by by Him.

Upon the Trial of this Cause, before Lord *Mansfield*, at the Sittings after last *Hilary* Term at *Guildhall*, It was proved on the Part of the Plaintiffs, That the said *Robert Carrick* made the Bill; And that the Defendant *indorsed it to the Plaintiffs*; And that the said *William Dods accepted* it, but afterwards *refused Payment*; And that the Plaintiffs thereupon, on the Day it became payable, carried it to be *protested for the Non-payment*; and soon afterwards brought their Action thereon, against the Defendant: But it did not appear, on the Trial, that the DRAWER of the Bill had any *Notice* of such Non-payment; or that any *Demand* of the Money was ever made on HIM before the Commencement of the Suit.

It was thereupon Objected by the Defendant's Counsel, "That "the Action would not lie against the Defendant (the Indorser,) "UNTIL a *Demand* of Payment had been made upon the DRAW-"ER:" And as no such Demand was proved to have been made on the Drawer, the Plaintiffs ought therefore to be nonsuited.

Lord Mansfield directed a Verdict to be given upon the said first Count, for the Plaintiffs, for 100 *l.* Damages and 40 Shillings Costs; subject to the Opinion of the Court, " Whether, upon this " Case, the Plaintiffs were intitled to recover."

A Case was accordingly stated for the Opinion of the Court, and signed by Sir *Richard Lloyd* for the Plaintiffs, and by Mr. *Norton* for the Defendant.

The only Question was, Whether, in an Action brought upon an *Inland* Bill of Exchange, by the Indorsee against an *Indorser*, This *Objection*, " That No Evidence was given at the Trial, of " *Notice* to the Drawer of the Bill, or even of making *any Inquiry* after *Him*," was a Ground of nonsuit.

It was argued on *Tuesday* last, (the 14th Instant,) by Mr. Serjeant *Davey* for the Plaintiff, and Mr. *Rooke* for the Defendant.

Serjeant *Davey* made a *Distinction* between *Inland* Bills of Exchange, and *Notes of Hand*. In the latter, the *Drawer* is to be the Payer: In the former, the *Drawee*, (the Acceptor of the Bill) is to pay it. So that upon a *Note* of Hand, the *Drawer* of the *Note* is the *first* Person to be resorted to, for Payment: But upon an *Inland Bill of Exchange*, the *Acceptor* of the Bill, *not* the Drawer is the *first* Person to be resorted to, for Payment; (though the Drawer shall indeed stand as a collateral Security for his so doing.) Therefore Cases upon promissory Notes are *not applicable* to Cases on Inland Bills of Exchange. The Bill-holder can't come upon the Drawer of the *Bill*, till the Person upon whom it is drawn shall either refuse to accept it, or refuse Payment after he has once accepted it.

Every Indorsement of a Bill of Exchange is in the Nature of a *new Bill* of Exchange: And if there are several Indorsers, they All undertake " that the Drawee (the Acceptor of the Bill,) " shall pay it."

The Indorsee is a *Stranger to the* Drawer of a Bill of Exchange: He is only concerned with the *Acceptor*.

A Bill of Exchange may happen not to be dated from any certain Place; or it may be dated from a Place where the Drawer does not reside; as where a Traveller, calling at an Inn, takes up Money there, and gives a Bill indorsed by his Landlord.

And

And it would be vastly inconvenient to all the Parties, if it should be holden necessary for the Indorsee to find out or even search for the *Drawer* of an Inland Bill of Exchange, to give him Notice "that "the acceptor has refused Payment." For the Security may be lost, in the Interim, whilst such Search is making: The Indorser may break, before he may be able to find Him. But the Indorser may know where to find him, or how to apply to Him.

Six Chief Justices have been of different Opinions on this Point: Three of them, of one Opinion; Three, of another.

The 9 & 10 *W.* 3. *c.* 17. was the first Act that gives Protests for Non-*Payment* of Inland Bills of Exchange: And the 3 & 4 *Ann. c.* 9. §. 4. 5. extends the Protest, to the Case of Non-*Acceptance*. The Words of both these Acts are remarkable; *viz.* "That the "Protest shall be notified to the Party FROM WHOM *the Bill* "*was* RECEIVED; *Who* shall repay the same with Interest and "Charges."

The Inconvenience may be the same (as to this Matter) upon an *Inland* Bill, as upon a *foreign* Bill. Yet upon a *foreign* Bill, it certainly is not necessary. In 1 *Strange* 441. *Bromley* v. *Frazier*, *Tr.* 7 *G.* 1. on a *foreign* Bill of Exchange, The Court, on mature Deliberation held, "That a Demand upon the Drawer is *not* ne-"cessary, to make a Charge upon the Indorser; but the Indorsee "has Liberty to resort to *Either*." It was a Point then unsettled. In 1 *Salk.* 131, 133. there are, as it is said in *Strange* 441. contradictory Opinions upon it; Which are professedly settled by that Case of *Bromley* v. *Frazier*, as the Book declares: But those contradictory Opinions are upon *Inland* Bills of Exchange. Indeed the Case of *Bromley* v. *Frazier* (then directly under Consideration) was upon a *foreign* One: But the Book goes on thus, (Which is *general*, and equally applicable to *both* Sorts,) And as to the Notion that has prevailed, "that the Indorser warrants *only* in Default of "the Drawer," there is *no Colour for it*: 'For every Indorser is in 'the *Nature of a new Drawer*; and at *Nisi prius* the Indorsee is '*never* put to *prove the Hand* of the *first* Drawer, where the Ac-'tion is against an Indorser. The Requiring a Protest for Non-'Acceptance, is *not* because a Protest amounts to a *Demand*: For 'it is no more than a giving Notice to the Drawer, to get his Ef-'fects out of the Hands of the Drawee; who, by the Other's 'Drawing, is supposed to have sufficient wherewith to satisfy the 'Bill.' So that this Notion is here exploded, "That the In-"dorser of a Bill of Exchange warrants *only in Default* of the "*Drawer*." But Every Indorser warrants against the Default of the *Payer*.

In

‡ The Serjeant called it *Richardson* v. *Mackerel*: But I took it by this Name of *Hamerton*.

In the Case of ‡ *Hammerton* v. *Mackrell*, *M.* 10 *G.* 2. *B. R.* (which was subsequent to the Case in 1 *Strange* 441.) In an Action by the Indorsee of a promissory Note against the Indorser, The Objection was that it was not alledged in the Declaration, " That a Demand " was made upon the *Drawer* of the Note." And it was there holden *not* necessary to be alledged in the *Declaration*. But Lord *Hardwicke* mentioned the Opinions of *Holt*, *Macclesfield*, *Pratt*, *Raymond*, *Eyre*, and *King*. *Holt*, *Eyre*, and * *Raymond* held it to be necessary: *Macclesfield*, *Pratt*, and *King* were of a contrary Opinion *viz.* " that it was not necessary."

* Lord Raymond first held the Opinion of *Macclesfield* and *Pratt*; but came over afterwards to that of *Holt* and *Eyre*; (as Lord *Hardwicke* said he had been informed.)

These Opinions seem to relate only to *Notes of Hand*: But upon a *Bill of Exchange*, the Indorsers are All only Promisers and Undertakers for the *Payer*, (the *Accepter*,) of the Bill; and are not obliged to look after the Original Drawer. And Fact and Experience in Business are agreeable to this Position.

Mr. *Rooke*, for the Defendant, insisted that upon an Action brought by the Indorsee against an Indorser of an INLAND *Bill* of Exchange, the Plaintiff ought, at the Trial, to *prove Notice to and Demand of Payment* from the DRAWER of the Bill.

The *Indorser* is only a *conditional* Undertaker for the DRAWER of the Bill, who is the first Contractor: He stands as a *Surety* only; and can not be called upon, *unless* the *Drawer makes Default*. It is like the Case of Principal and Accessary; where the Accessary cannot be tried before the Principal: So here, the Indorser cannot be liable, TILL the *Original* Contracter has failed in performing his Contract.

And great Inconvenience might follow, if this was otherwise.

There are several Authorities which fully prove that it is necessary. Cases in *B. R. Temp. W.* 3. 244. *Lambert* v. *Oakes* at *Guildhall*; and 1 *Ld. Raym.* 443. *Lambert* v. *Oakes*, S. C. is directly in Point. 1 *Salk.* 126, *pl.* 6. *Anon.* († probably S. C.) accordingly. 1 *Strange* 649. *M.* 12 *G.* 1. *Syderbottom* v. *Smith*. Upon an Action against the Indorser of a promissory Note, at *Guildhall*, *C. B.* Ld Ch. Just. *Eyre*'s Opinion was, accordingly, " That the Plaintiff " *must prove* Diligence to get the Money of the Drawer; the In- " dorser *only* warranting on *his Default*." And for want of such Proof, he directed the Jury to find for the Defendant. 2 *Strange*

† *Lambert* v. *Pack* 1 *Salk.* 127. *pl.* 9. seems clearly S. C. Indeed they are, All Four, probably, the same Case; though two of them are placed under *M.* 10. And the other two under *P.* 11 *W.* 3.

1087. *Collins* v. *Butler*, at *Guildhall*, *per Lee*, Ch. Juſt. It was ruled accordingly; who cited a Caſe determined on great Debate; in *C. B.* in *P.* 4 *G.* 2.—*Due Diligence* muſt be ſhewn to have been uſed in inquiring after the Drawer of the Bill of Exchange, *before* the Money can be recovered againſt the Indorſer.

And there is NO *Difference* between a *Note* of Hand, and a *Bill* of Exchange; other than that the Drawer of the Note is the *expreſs* Promiſer, and (as it were) *both* Drawer and Drawee: Whereas on a *Bill* of Exchange, he is only an *implied* Promiſer. Indeed on a *foreign* Bill of Exchange this Notice and Demand is not neceſſary; becauſe the *foreign* Drawer is *not amenable* to Juſtice *here*.

As to the Words of the Statutes of 9, 10 *W.* 3. & 3, 4 *Ann.* they do *not exclude* the Neceſſity of giving Notice to the Drawer: Though they add an *additional* Caution, "of giving Notice to the Perſon "from whom the Bill was received."

Mr. *Serjeant's* Caſe, wherein Mention is made of the Six Chief Juſtices differing in Opinion, ſeems to be taken from the 3d Volume of the *Abridgment of the Law* *.

* See *New Abridgment*, Vol. 3. Title, *Merchant* and *Merchandiſe*, *Pa.* 608. Note b. (which is undoubtedly the *ſame* Caſe cited by the Serjeant.)

Serjeant *Davey*, in Reply—I agree that the Drawer of a Bill of Exchange is only a *Conditional* Undertaker for the *Drawee:* And ſo alſo is the Indorſer of a Bill of Exchange a Conditional Undertaker for the *Drawee*: But it does not follow, that the Indorſer of a Bill of Exchange is only a Conditional Undertaker for the *Drawer*.

The Caſe of *Lambert* v. *Oakes* was upon a *Note of Hand* (according to Ld. *Raymond*:) And Ld. Ch. J. *Holt's* Opinion upon a *Bill of Exchange*, was upon a Caſe not before him.

In the Caſe of *Hammerton* v. *Mackrell*, Ld. *Hardwicke* † held it *not* neceſſary.

† The Serjeant had been miſinformed: For Lord *Hardwicke* (as appears by my Note of that Caſe) did not give or even intimate his own Opinion upon that Point.

The *Drawee's* Place of Abode is always known upon a Bill of Exchange; but not the *Drawer's*.

The COURT gave no Opinion at the Time of this Argument; but poſtponed it, in Order to ſettle the Point with Preciſion and Certainty.

Lord MANSFIELD obſerved, That the Confuſion ſeemed to have ariſen from it's not being ſettled, " WHO is the *Original* " *Debtor.*"

Mr. Juſt. DENISON ſaid, The Caſe of *Hammerton* v. *Mackrell* was upon a Writ of Error; and the Judgment was affirmed, upon the Allegation contained in the Declaration, of a PROMISE *made by the Indorſer*, which (upon a Writ of Error,) they conſidered as an *expreſs* Promiſe: But Lord *Hardwicke* did *not* give his *own* Opinion at all, upon what is now the preſent Queſtion.

CUR. ADVIS'.

Lord MANSFIELD now delivered the Reſolution of the Court.

His Lordſhip ſaid He could not perſuade himſelf that there had really been ſuch a Variety of Opinions upon this Queſtion, at *Niſi prius*, as had been mentioned at the Bar. But however that may be, It muſt now be determined upon the Nature of the Tranſaction, General Convenience, and the Authority of deliberate Reſolutions in Court.

A *Bill of Exchange* is an Order, or Command, to the Drawee who has, or is ſuppoſed to have, Effects of the Drawer in his Hands, to *pay*. When the Drawee has accepted, *He* is the *Original Debtor*; and due Diligence muſt be uſed in applying to *him*. The Drawer is only liable in *Default* of Payment by *him*, due Diligence having been uſed: And therefore if the Acceptor is not called upon, within a reaſonable Time after the Bill is payable, and happens to break, the Drawer is not liable at all.

Every Man therefore who takes a Bill of Exchange muſt know where to call upon the Drawee; and undertakes to demand the Money of *Him*.

When that Bill of Exchange is *indorſed*, by the Perſon to whom it was made payable; as between the Indorſer and Indorſee, it is a *new* Bill of Exchange; and the Indorſer ſtands in the *Place of the Drawer*.

The *Indorſee* undertakes to demand the Money of the *Drawee*: If He neglects, and the Drawee becomes inſolvent, the Loſs falls upon himſelf. If the Indorſee is diligent, and the Drawee refuſes Payment; his *immediate Remedy* is againſt the *Indorſer*: And it was very properly obſerved, that the Act of 9, 10 *W.* 3. requires Notice of the Proteſt to be given " to the Perſon *from whom the* " *Bill*

" *Bill was received*." He may have *another* Remedy againſt the firſt Drawer; as aſſignee to, and ſtanding in the Place of the Indorſer.

The Indorſee does not truſt to the Credit of the Original Drawer: He does not know whether ſuch a Perſon exiſts, or where he lives, or whether his Name may have been forged. The Indorſer is *his* Drawer, and the Perſon to whom he originally truſted in Caſe the Drawee ſhould not pay the Money. There is no Difference in this reſpect between *foreign* and *Inland* Bills of Exchange, except as to the Degree of Inconvenience: All the Arguments from Law, and the Nature of the Tranſaction, are exactly the ſame in both Caſes.

As to *foreign* Bills of Exchange, The Queſtion was ſolemnly determined by this Court, upon very ſatisfactory Grounds, in the Caſe of * *Bromley* v. *Frazier*—That was ' An Action upon the *Caſe* upon " a *foreign* Bill of Exchange, by the Indorſee againſt the Indorſer:' and on General Demurrer, It was objected, " that they had *not* " *ſhewn a Demand upon the Drawer*, in whoſe Default only it is " that the Indorſer warrants." And becauſe ' this was a Point un- ' ſettled, and on which there are contradictory Opinions in *Salkeld* ' 131 & 133. the Court took Time to conſider of it. And on the ' ſecond Argument, They delivered their Opinions, " That the " Declaration was well enough: For the Deſign of the Law of " Merchants in diſtinguiſhing theſe from all other Contracts, by " making them aſſignable, was for the Convenience of Commerce, " that they might paſs from Hand to Hand in the Way of Trade, " in the ſame Manner as if they were Specie. Now to require " a Demand upon the Drawer, will be laying ſuch a Clog upon " theſe Bills, as will deter every Body from taking them. The " Drawer lives abroad, perhaps in the *Indies*, where the In- " dorſee has no Correſpondent to whom He can ſend the Bill for " a Demand; or if he could, yet the Delay would be ſo great that " no Body would meddle with them. Suppoſe it was the Caſe of " ſeveral Indorſements, muſt the laſt Indorſee travel round the " World, before he can fix his Action upon the Man from whom " he received the Bill? In common Experience, every Body knows " that the more Indorſements a Bill has, the greater Credit it bears: " Whereas if thoſe Demands were all neceſſary to be made, it muſt " naturally diminiſh the Value, by how much the more difficult it " renders the Calling in the Money. And as to the Notion that " has prevailed, that the Indorſer warrants *only in Default of the* " *Drawer*, there is no Colour for it: For every Indorſer is in the " Nature of a *new* Drawer: And at *Niſi prius*, the Indorſee is never " put to prove the *Hand* of the *firſt* Drawer, where the Action is " againſt an Indorſer. The Requiring a *Proteſt* for Non-acceptance,

* 1 Strange 441. Tr. 7 G. 1. B. R.

" is not becauſe a Proteſt amounts to a *Demand:* For it is no more " than a giving Notice to the Drawer to get his Effects out of the " Hands of the Drawee, who, (by the Other's Drawing,) is ſup- " poſed to have ſufficient wherewith to ſatisfy the Bill."

Upon the whole, They declared themſelves to be of Opinion, " That in the Caſe of a *foreign* Bill of Exchange, a Demand upon " the Drawer is *not* neceſſary, to make a Charge upon the Indorſer; " but the Indorſee has his Liberty to reſort to *Either*, for the " Money: Conſequently, the Plaintiff (they ſaid), muſt have Judg- " ment."

Every Inconvenience *here ſuggeſted* holds to a *great Degree*, and *every other* Argument holds *equally*, in the Caſe of Inland Bills of Exchange.

We are therefore All of Opinion, " That to intitle the Indorſee " of an Inland Bill of Exchange to bring an Action againſt the " Indorſer, upon Failure of Payment by the Drawee, it is *not* ne- " ceſſary to make any Demand of, or Inquiry after, the firſt " *Drawer*."

The Law is exactly the ſame, and fully ſettled, upon the Analogy of *Promiſſory Notes* to Bills of Exchange; which is very clear, when the *Point of Reſemblance* is once fixed.

While a Promiſſory Note continues in its *original* Shape of a Promiſe from One Man to pay to another, it bears *no* Similitude to a Bill of Exchange. *When* it is *indorſed*, the *Reſemblance* begins: For *then*, it is an *Order*, by the Indorſer, *upon* the *Maker* of the Note, (*his Debtor*, by the Note,) *to pay to the Indorſee*. This is the very Definition of a Bill of Exchange.

The Indorſer is the Drawer; the Maker of the Note is the Acceptor; and the Indorſee is the Perſon to whom it is made payable. The Indorſer only undertakes, *in Caſe* the Maker of the Note does not pay. The Indorſee is bound to *apply to the Maker* of the Note: He takes it upon *that Condition*; and therefore muſt, in all Caſes, know who he is, and where he lives; And if, after the Note becomes payable, He is guilty of a Neglect, and the Maker becomes inſolvent, He loſes the Money and cannot come upon the Indorſer at all.

Therefore, before the *Indorſee of a Promiſſory Note* brings an Action againſt the *Indorſer*, He muſt ſhew a Demand, or due Diligence to get the Money from the *Maker* of the Note;—juſt as the Perſon to whom the Bill of Exchange is made payable muſt ſhew

a

a Demand, or due Diligence to get the Money from the *Acceptor*, before he brings an Action against the *Drawer*. This was determined by the whole Court of Common Pleas, upon great Consideration, in *Pasch.* 4 *G.* 2; as cited by my Ld. Ch. J. *Lee* in the Case of * *Collins* v. *Butler*.

* 2 *Strange* 1087. 11 *G.* 2.

So that the Rule is exactly the *same* upon Promissory *Notes*, as it is upon *Bills* of Exchange; and the Confusion has, in part, arisen from the *Maker* of a Promissory Note being called the *Drawer*: Whereas, by Comparison to Bills of Exchange, the *Indorser* is the *Drawer*.

All the Authorities, and particularly Ld. *Hardwicke*, in the Case of *Hammerton* v. *Mackerell*, *M.* 10 *G.* 2. (according to my Brother *Denison*'s State of what his Lordship said,) put *Promissory Notes* and *Inland Bills of Exchange* just upon the † *same* Footing: And the ‡ Statute expressly refers to Inland Bills of Exchange.

† My Note of that Case is exactly agreeable; viz. "Promissory Notes seem to me to be put upon the same Foot as Inland Bills of Exchange."
‡ *V.* 3, 4 *Ann. c.* 9.

But the same Law must be applied to the same Reason; to the *Substantial Resemblance* between Promissory Notes, and Bills of Exchange; and not to the same *Sound*, which is equally used to describe the Maker of Both.

My Ld. Ch. J. *Holt* is quoted as being of Opinion, "that in Actions upon Bills of Exchange, it is necessary to prove a Demand upon the Drawer." For Proof of this, the principal Case referred to, is that of *Lambert* v. *Oakes*, reported in three Books: 1 *Ld. Raym.* 1 *Salk.* and 12 *Mod.*

In 1 *Ld. Raym.* 443, It appears manifestly, that the Question arose upon a *Promissory Note*. "*R.* signed a NOTE under his Hand, payable to *Oakes*, or his Order; *Oakes* indorsed it to *Lambert*; upon which, *Lambert* brought the Action for the Money against *Oakes*. *Per Holt*, Ch. J. He ought to prove that he had demanded or done his Endeavour to demand this Money of *R*, before he can sue *Oakes* upon the Indorsement. The *same Law*, if the *Bill* was drawn upon any *other* Person, payable to *Oakes* to Order." That is, A Demand must be made of the Person UPON WHOM the Bill is drawn. And other Parts of the Case manifestly shew *this* to have been the *Meaning*. For my Ld. Ch. J. *Holt* is reported to have said, "The Indorsement will subject the Indorser to an Action; because it makes a new Contract, *in Case the Person* UPON WHOM *it is drawn does not pay it*." § Again, "If the Indorsee does not demand the Money payable by "the

§ *Pa.* 444.

" the Bill, *of the Person* UPON WHOM *it is drawn, in convenient* " *Time, and afterwards he fails*, the Indorser is *not* liable."

* 1 *Salk.* 127. (there called *Lambert* v. *Pack*,) *pl.* 9.

In * *Salkeld*, the Case is confounded: It is stated to be a *Bill of Exchange*, and " that the Demand must be made upon the *Drawer*, " *or him* upon whom it was drawn." My Ld. Ch. J. *Holt* had said that a Demand must be made of the *Maker* of a Promissory Note, (calling him the *Drawer*;) And in the Case of a Bill of Exchange, of *him* upon whom the Bill is *drawn*. The Report jumbles both together, as applied *only* to a Bill of Exchange; misled, I dare say, by the Equivocal Sound of the Term *Drawer*, and by the Chief Justice's Reasoning in the Case of a Promissory Note, from the Law upon Bills of Exchange. †

† Note. The Report in 1 *Salk.* 126. *pl.* 6. is much more strong and explicit: But it is short, anonymus, and a mere loose Scrap, by the same Reporter, who was manifestly unclear about the Case, (being S. C. with *pl.* 9.)

In 12th *Modern* 244. The Case is mistaken too; and stated as upon a *Bill of Exchange*, and as a Determination " that there must " be a Demand upon the *Drawer of the Bill of Exchange*:" And yet the Report itself shews demonstrably, that what was said by my Lord Ch. J. *Holt* was applied to the Maker of a *Promissory Note*, (calling him the *Drawer*.) For the Report makes Him argue— " —So if the Bill was drawn on any *other* Person, payable to *Oakes* " or Order:" Which shews that the Case in Judgment was *not* a Bill drawn upon *another* Person, but payable only to *Oakes*, *by R.* HIMSELF.

It seems to Me, as if my Ld. Ch. J. *Holt*, in that Case, had considered the *Drawee of a Bill* of Exchange in the same Light as the *Maker of a Promissory Note*: But loose and hasty Notes, misled by Identity of Sound, have misapplied what was said of the Drawer of a *Promissory Note* to the Drawer of a *Bill of Exchange*; and to such a Degree misapplied it, that two Reports out of the ‖ three have stated the Question as arising upon a Bill of Exchange, which is manifestly otherwise.

‖ There seem to be *four* Reports of S. C. or at least of S P (*V.* Note on *pa* 672. and on *pa.* 678)

But be this Conjecture as it may, We are All of Opinion " That " in Actions upon *Inland Bills of Exchange*, by an Indorsee against " an Indorser, the Plaintiff *must prove* a Demand of, or due Dili- " gence to get the Money from, the *Drawee* (or ACCEPTOR;) " but need *not prove* any Demand of the DRAWER: And that in " Actions upon *Promissory Notes*, by an Indorsee against the Indor- " ser, the Plaintiff must prove a Demand of, or due Diligence to " get the Money from the MAKER of the Note."

Accordingly, The RULE was, That the *Postea* be delivered to the PLAINTIFF.

Rex

Rex *verſ.* Mallinſon.

Wedneſday 22d November 1758.

THIS was upon a Conviction for killing ten Trouts.

The Conviction ſets forth that One *John Keap*, of &c, came before the Juſtice of Peace, and gave Information that the Defendant *Thomas Mallinſon*, of &c, Taylor; *not having any Lands* and Tenements or other Eſtate of *Inheritance* in his own Right nor in the Right of his Wiſe, of the clear yearly Value of 100*l*, or for Term of Life; *nor having any Leaſe or Leaſes* of 99 Years or for any longer Term, of the clear yearly Value of 150*l*; *nor being the Son and Heir* apparent of an Eſquire or other Perſon of higher Degree; *nor being Owner or Keeper* of any Foreſt Park Chaſe or Warren being ſtocked with Deer or Conies, for his own neceſſary Uſe, in reſpect of ſuch Foreſt Park Chaſe or Warren; *nor being Lord of any Manor* or Royalty, *nor Game-keeper* of any Lord or Lady of any Lordſhip or Manor, duely made conſtituted or appointed, with Power or Authority to take kill or deſtroy the Game in or upon any ſuch Lordſhip or Manor; *nor being a Maker or Seller* of any Nets Angles Leaps Piches or other Engines for the taking of Fiſh; NOR BEING OWNER *of any River or Fiſhery*; *nor being a Fiſherman* lawfully authorized to fiſh with Nets in navigable Rivers or Waters, *nor an Apprentice* to any ſuch Fiſherman; *nor in* ANY WISE WHATSOEVER *impowered authorized or qualified* by the Laws of this Realm, either to take kill or deſtroy any Sort of Fiſh Fowl or other Game whatſoever, *either for himſelf or for any other* Perſon or Perſons whomſoever, nor to keep or uſe any Greyhound Setting-Dog Hays Lurchers Tunnels Nets or any other Engine to kill and deſtroy the Game; on the 27th of *June* 31 *G.* 2. at *Golcarr* aforeſaid within the ſaid Riding, Did, *with* a certain *Net*, UNLAWFULLY *take and kill ten Fiſh*, that is to ſay *ten Trouts, contrary to the Form of the Statute* in ſuch Caſe made and provided. *Whereupon* the ſaid *Thomas Mallinſon*, afterwards, on the ſaid 27th Day of *June* in the Year aforeſaid, had Notice of the ſaid Information and of the Offence therein charged upon him as aforeſaid; and was then and there in due Manner ſummoned to be and appear before the ſaid Juſtice at his Dwelling-houſe in *M.* aforeſaid in the ſaid Weſt-Riding, IMMEDIATELY *upon his* Receipt of that Summons, to make his Defence againſt the ſaid Charge contained in the ſaid Information: But the ſaid *Thomas Mallinſon neglecteth to appear*, and doth not appear before the ſaid Juſtice, nor make any Defence againſt the ſaid Charge; but *maketh Default* therein. Wherefore the ſaid Juſtice, afterwards, that is to ſay on the 12th Day of *July* 31 *G.* 2. at his above-mentioned Dwelling-houſe in *M.* aforeſaid in the ſaid Weſt-Riding,

Riding, the ſaid *Thomas Mallinſon having* so *been ſummoned*, and having hitherto *neglected to appear or make any Defence* againſt the ſaid Charge, doth proceed to examine the Truth of the Charge aforeſaid in the ſaid Information contained. And hereupon *John Whiteley* of *Golcarr* aforeſaid Cordwainer, being a credible Witneſs, cometh before the ſaid Juſtice in his proper Perſon, and before the ſaid Juſtice upon his Corporal Oath upon the Holy Evangeliſts of God to him then and there adminiſtered by the ſaid Juſtice, depoſeth ſweareth and upon his ſaid Oath affirmeth and ſaith That the ſaid *Thomas Mallinſon*, not having any Lands and Tenements or other Eſtate of Inheritance in his own Right nor in the Right of his Wife, of the clear yearly Value of 100*l*, or for Term of Life; nor having any Leaſe or Leaſes of 99 Years or for any longer Term, of the clear yearly Value of 150*l*; nor being the Son and Heir apparent of an Eſquire, or other Perſon of higher Degree; nor being Owner or Keeper of any Foreſt Park Chaſe or Warren being ſtocked with Deer or Conies for his own neceſſary Uſe in reſpect of ſuch Foreſt Park Chaſe or Warren; nor being Lord of any Manor or Royalty, nor Game-keeper of any Lord or Lady of any Lordſhip or Manor, duely made conſtituted or appointed with Power or Authority to take kill or deſtroy the Game in or upon any ſuch Lordſhip or Manor; nor being a Maker or Seller of any Nets Angles Leaps, Piches or other Engines for the taking of Fiſh; *nor being Owner or Occupier of any River or Fiſhery*; nor being a Fiſherman lawfully authorized to fiſh with Nets and Engines in navigable Rivers or Waters; nor an Apprentice to any ſuch Fiſherman; *nor in* ANY WISE WHATSOEVER *impowered authorized or qualified by the Laws of this Realm, either to take kill or deſtroy* any Sort of Fiſh Fowl or other Game whatſoever, *either for himſelf or for any other* Perſon or Perſons whatſoever, nor to keep or uſe any Greyhound Setting-Dog Hayes Lurchers Tunnels Nets or any other Engine to kill and deſtroy the Game; on the 27th Day of *June* in the 31ſt Year aforeſaid, in *Golcarr* aforeſaid in the ſaid Riding, did, with a certain Net, *unlawfully* take and kill ten Fiſh, that is to ſay, ten Trouts, contrary to the Form of the Statute in ſuch Caſe made and provided. And thereupon the ſaid *Thomas Mallinſon*, on the 12th Day of *July* aforeſaid in the Year aforeſaid, *is duely convicted* before the ſaid Juſtice, of the *Offence aforeſaid* in the ſaid Information contained and therein charged upon him, by the Oath of one credible Witneſs, the aforeſaid *John Whiteley*, according to the Form of the Statute in ſuch Caſe made and provided. It is therefore adjudged by the ſaid Juſtice, That the ſaid *Thomas Mallinſon* is guilty of the *Offence aforeſaid* in the ſaid Information contained; and is hereby convicted thereof, according to the Form of the Statute in ſuch Caſe made and provided; *And* that the ſaid *Thomas Mallinſon* hath *forfeited* the Sum of Five Pounds for his *Offences aforeſaid*; that is to ſay Ten Shillings a piece for every and each

 of

of the abovementioned Fish so taken and killed by the said *Thomas Mallinson* as aforesaid, amounting together to the said Sum of 5*l*; to be levied and distributed according to the Form of the Statute in such Case made and provided. *In Witness, &c.*

Mr. *Norton*, on Behalf of the Defendant, made several Objections to this Conviction.

1st. The *Summons* is *bad*, as set out, (though indeed it was not necessary to have set it out at all.) It is "to appear IMMEDIATELY;" which is *not* a *reasonable* Summons. 1 *Strange* 261. *Rex* v. *Johnson*. An Objection of this Sort was taken to a Summons "to appear on the *same Day*." It received indeed a satisfactory Answer, from a Fact; *viz.* the Defendant's having there actually *appeared* to it, and made a Defence: Which Appearance and Defence *cured* all Defects in the Summons.

2d. Objection. Here is *not a full negative* Adjudication of the Defendant's WANT *of Qualification*: For here it is *not* stated "That the Defendant *had not the License or* CONSENT *of the Owner*." And as this essential Circumstance is omitted, the *General* Allegation, of his "taking and killing the Fish *unlawfully and against* "*the Statute*," is not sufficient. *V. ante Pa.* 154, 155. *Rex* v. *Jarvis, H.* 30 *G.* 2.

3d Objection. It might be his *own* Fish and in his *own* Pond, for Aught that appears to the contrary: For it is only alledged "That he killed ten Trouts *at* such a Place."

The Conviction seems to be intended upon * 4, 5 *W.* 3. *c.* 23. §. 3.

* It seems clearly to have been intended to be grounded on 22, 23 *C.* 2. *c.* 25. §. 7: And not upon 4, 5 *W.* & *M.*

Mr. *Yates contra*, for the Prosecutor.

1st. *No precise* Time of Appearance is requisite to be fixed by the Summons: And *this* gives a larger Latitude, than if a Day and Hour had been fixed; for it means only, "*as soon as he can*."

2dly. Though this Omission of his not having the Consent of the Owner, cannot be supported upon the Statute of 22, 23 *C.* 2. *c.* 25. §. 7; Yet it may, upon that of 4, 5 *W.* & *M. c.* 23; which says only—"If any Person *not qualified* by the Laws of this Land." (*V.* § 3.) And the Court will *not presume* a Qualification. As in a Conviction upon the Gin-Act, in the Case of *Rex* v. *Brian*, 2 *Strange* 1101, The Court would not presume that the Gin was

 sold

ſold *to be uſed in Medicine.* *Rex* v. *Theed, M.* 11 *G.* 1. in 2 *Lord Raym.* 1375. and in 1 *Strange* 608. The Conviction was preſumed to be *right*; as it did *not appear to be wrong.*

3dly. The ſame Anſwer holds; *viz.* " That the Court will " *not preſume* that the Fiſh were the Defendant's *own*," or " That " he killed them in his *own* Pond."

Lord MANSFIELD—This Conviction is clearly bad.

The Offence provided againſt by the Act of 22, 23 *C.* 2. *c.* 25. is *Stealing* Fiſh; Taking it *without* the Licence or Conſent of the Owner. The Juriſdiction given to the Juſtice of Peace is over every *ſuch* Offender or Offenders in *ſtealing* taking or killing Fiſh: (*V.* §. 7.) Taking and Killing, in the Intention of this Statute, means STEALING. But this Man is not convicted of ANY Offence. For he is not charged with *Stealing*, nor even with taking and killing the Fiſh *of* ANOTHER *Perſon*, or in ANOTHER *Perſon's Pond.* The Offence ſpecified in the Statute is Taking it " with- " out the Licence or Conſent of the Lord or Owner of the Water." But it may be his *own* Pond, and his *own* Fiſh, for any Thing that appears to the contrary, in the preſent Caſe.

Therefore, *if* there was no *other* Fault in it, it is eſſentially bad, for *this Reaſon alone.*

Mr. Juſt. DENISON—It is *full of Faults:* But *this alone* would be fatal. It does not appear that the Fiſh he killed, were not his *own*, or killed in his *own* Ponds.

Mr. Juſt. FOSTER—The Offence intended by the Act is the *Invading* ANOTHER *Man's Property.* But there is *no ſuch* Charge here upon this Man, as invading the Property of *Another.*

Mr. Juſt. WILMOT—This Conviction is bad, for the *Faults that have been mentioned*, and for a *great many others:* It is bad *throughout.*

Per Cur. unanimouſly,
CONVICTION QUASHED.

Goſs

Goſs and Another *verſ.* Withers.
Iidem *verſ.* Eundem.

THIS was a ſpecial Caſe, from the Sittings in *London*, upon two Actions, on two diſtinct Policies of Inſurance; one, upon a Ship; and the other, upon the Loading.

The former was an Inſurance upon the *David and Rebeccah*, at and from *Newfoundland* to her Port of Diſcharge in *Portugal* or *Spain*, without the *Streights*, or *England*; to commence from the Time of her beginning to load at *Newfoundland*, for either of the abovenamed Places: And it was upon the *Body*, Tackle, Apparel, Ordnance &c. &c. of the *Ship*; beginning the Adventure at *Newfoundland*; and to continue during her Abode there, and until the ſaid Ship, with all her Ordnance, Tackle &c. ſhould be arrived at her Port of Diſcharge as aforeſaid, and until She ſhould have been moored at Anchor 24 Hours in Safety. It was to be lawful for the Ship to touch at and ſtay in any Port whatſoever, without Prejudice to the Inſurance. The Ship was, by Agreement, to be valued at the Sum ſubſcribed, without further Account. And in Caſe of Loſs or Misfortune, it was to be lawful for the Aſſured, their Servants &c, to ſue labour and travel, for in or about the Defence Safeguard and Recovery of the Ship, or any Part thereof, without Prejudice to the Inſurance: To the Charges whereof the Inſurers were to contribute, *pro Rata*. The Inſurance was to be at 10 Guineas *per Cent*. And in Caſe of Loſs, to abate 2 *l. per Cent.* and in Caſe of Average-Loſs not exceeding 5 *l. per Cent.* to allow Nothing towards ſuch Loſs. And if the Veſſel diſcharged *without* the *Streights*, excepting the Bay of *Biſcay*, 2 Guineas *per Cent.* was to be returned: And if She failed with Convoy, and arrived, 2 Guineas more *per Cent.* was to be returned. The Plaintiffs declared upon a *total* Loſs, by Capture by the *French*.

The Policy declared upon, in the other Action, was an Inſurance upon any kind of lawful *Goods* and *Merchandizes*, loaden or to be loaden on board the aforeſaid Ship: Which, for 7 *l.* 7 *s.* inſured 70 *l.* And the Declaration alledged that divers Quantities of Fiſh and other lawful Merchandizes to the Value of the Money inſured were put on board, to be carried from *Newfoundland* to her Port of Deſtination, and ſo continued, (except ſuch as were thrown overboard as is aftermentioned,) till the Loſs of the Ship and Goods. The Declaration then avers that ¼ of the ſaid Goods were neceſſarily thrown overboard, in a Storm, to preſerve the Ship and the Reſt of the Cargo: After which *Jettizon*, the Ship and the Remainder of the Goods was taken by the *French*.

There

There was another Count in this Declaration, for Money had and received to the Use of the Plaintiffs.

The Case states That the Ship departed from her proper Port; and was *taken* by the *French* on the *23d of December* 1756; And that the *Master Mates* and *all the Sailors, except* an Apprentice and Landman, were *taken out and carried to France*. That the Ship remained in the HANDS OF THE ENEMY 8 *Days*; and was *then retaken* by a *British* Privateer, and brought in on the 18*th of January* to *Milford-Haven*; And that *immediate Notice* was given by the Assured to the Assurers, with *an Offer to* ABANDON the Ship to their Care. It was also proved at the Trial, That before the Taking by the Enemy, a violent Storm arose at Sea; which first separated the Ship from her Convoy, and afterwards *disabled her so far* as to render her incapable of proceeding on her destined Voyage, without going into Port to refit.

It was also proved, That part of the *Cargo* was thrown overboard in the Storm; and the Rest of it was *spoiled* whilst the Ship lay at *Milford-Haven*, *after* the Offer to abandon, and before She could be refitted. And the Assured proved their Interest in the Ship and Cargo, to the Value insured.

Several Questions arising upon the Trial of the first of the said Causes, It was agreed that the Jury should bring in their Verdict, in both Causes, for the Plaintiffs, as for a *total* Loss; Subject however, to the Opinion of the Court on the following Questions, *viz.*

1st. Whether *this Capture* of the Ship by the Enemy, was or was not SUCH a Loss as that the Insurers became *liable* thereby:

2dly. Whether, under the several Circumstances of this Case, the Assured had or had not a RIGHT TO ABANDON *the Ship to the Insurers, after* She was carried into *Milford-Haven*.

This Case was twice argued; viz. first, on *Tuesday* 6th *June* 1758, by Mr. *Morton pro Quer'*, and Mr. Serjeant *Davy pro Def'*: And again, on *Friday* 10th *November* 1758, by Mr. *Norton pro Quer'*, and Sir *Richard Lloyd pro Def'*.

Mr. *Morton* and Mr. *Norton*, on Behalf of the Plaintiffs, argued for the Affirmative, in both Questions.

They previously distinguished between Cases disputed *between Insurers and Insured*, and those *between Owners and Recaptors*; and observed that *This* is a mere Contract between the *Parties*.

First Point—This is such a *total Loss*, as renders the Insurers liable to answer for it. First Point.

They said they would consider (1st.) *What* an *Insurance is*; and (2dly.) *What* a *Capture by an Enemy*, is.

1st. The *Definition of an Insurance* is in *Bynkershoek's Quæstiones publici Juris, Lib.* 1. *cap.* 21.

2dly. A *Capture* is, when there is *no just Ground of Hope of recovering* the Ship; *Then* it becomes the Property of the Captor. *Grotius L.* 3. *c.* 6. *pa.* 814. *De jure belli & pacis.* "*Tunc enim* "*desperari incipit Recuperatio &c.*"

And the Period of *Time of the Detention* is another Rule; *viz.* being 24 *Hours in Potestate hostium.* Indeed subsequent Writers do not fix it so precisely: But they are then treating only upon * *Salvage. Bynkershoek*, indeed, differs in the *Premisses, Lib.* 1. *c.* 4. *Quæstiones juris publici*: But *both agree* in the *Conclusion*; For he also puts it upon the Despair of the Recovery of the Ship. And this Hope, or Despair, must be a reasonable and just One; not a whimsical and arbitrary Fancy, or a mere Wish.

* V. 29 G. 2. c. 34. p. 572. § 24. (the Prize-Act,) which directs, "that retaken Ships shall be restored to the Owners, they paying a Salvage in Proportion to the Time they were in the Possession of the Enemy."

This Vessel was 8 Days in Possession of the Enemy; near a Month, out of the Power of the Owners, (the Insured;) and almost all the Hands taken out. So that, by the Terms and Intent of the Insurance (which must be taken favourably for the Insured,) this Voyage must be taken to have been totally defeated to the Insurers; the Adventure totally stopt; and consequently, the Condition broken, *as between the Insurers and the Insured.*

And this is different from Cases of Salvage, where the *Property is not altered*; but the Marine Law only determines what shall be paid by the Owner, for the Salvage.

This is a *total* Loss: It was so long in Possession of the Enemy that the *Spes recuperandi* was *gone.*

Though this Ship was not carried *into Port*, nor *within the Enemy's Fleet*, yet it was 8 Days *in Possession* of the Enemy; and it might have been as many Months. And the *Spes recuperandi* would be as absolutely gone, as if it had been carried into the Enemy's Fleet: Out of which, it might possibly be immediately retaken.

Therefore the being carried *infra Præsidia* of the Enemy cannot be the *true* Rule. But the *true and certain Rule* must, in reason be, where the *Spes recuperandi is gone.* Indeed the being carried *infra Præsidia* may, in many Cases, be an Evidence of this.

Now upon the State of the present Case, all Hope of Retaking was totally lost and gone.

However, the *Principle* of this Case is not new. For by *Common Law*, the Thing taken from the Owner in War is *gone*, unless the Owner makes fresh Pursuit: And the Property of the Thing so taken in War belongs to the Captor. And the Common-Law Rule is— That in a War, the Captor of a Ship has a Right to the Ship and Goods taken; *unless* the Owner makes fresh Pursuit *ante Occasum Solis.* 7 *E.* 4. 14. * *Vavisour* said, that it was adjudged in the Time of that same King, "*q un q prist tiel Meason des Enemies quel il* "*avoit prise devant dun Englishe*, *que* il averoit ceo *come chose gaigne* "*en batel &c: Et nemy le Roy, ne l'Admiral,* ne le Partie a qui le "Property fuit devant &c; *Pur ceo q le Partie* ne vient freshment, "mesme le jour *q il fuit prise de luy, et ante Occasum Solis, Et* "*claime ceo.*" And this Determination has never been shaken by any *Common Law* Resolution: It has rather been confirmed and recognised.

* *Vavisour* was not then a Judge, nor even a Serjeant.

And the Determinations of the *Admiralty*-Courts will not affect this Case: For they have determined either upon particular Acts of Parliament, or upon the Principles of *other* Laws than the Common Law.

But this Court will follow the Determination of the Common Law. And the 3 Acts of Parliament made in the present Reign (which are All, upon this head) are built upon the same Principle. The † Saving-Clause in 29 *G.* 2. *c.* 34. supposes the Right of the Owner to be extinguished and gone; and that the Captor had a Right to the Thing taken: Otherwise, the Parliament had no Right to impose upon the Original Owners such Terms of Payment for Salvage. The Act itself even calls them the *former* Owners: And it is the *Bounty* of the Act, to restore to them *any Part* at all.

† § 24.

No Mischief can arise from this Construction: Many Inconveniences will flow from a contrary One. And Courts of Law will put liberal Constructions upon Policies of Insurance.

This Principle was recognised by Ld. Ch. J. *Lee* in the Case reported in 2 *Strange* 1250. *Denn* v. *Dicker:* Where the being carried into the Enemy's Port and detained 8 Days was esteemed a total Loss of the Voyage; and the Property of the Owners gone.

This

This is a Question *only between* the *Insurer* and the *Insured:* And the Insurer had undertaken against *all Sorts* of Perils, for a Premium received. And here the Voyage was totally lost; and the Cargo entirely perished. So that there can be no Doubt as to the *real Justice* of this Case.

Second Point—The Insured had a *Right to* ABANDON the Ship to the Insurers, after her Coming into *Milford Haven.* For the *Property insured* was irrecoverably *destroyed.* And here was *immediate Notice* given to the Insurers, of the abandoning of it to them. 2d Point.

Molloy Lib. 2. *c.* 7. *pa.* 278. and *Maline's Lex Mercatoria* 111. lay down the Rules of abandoning. *Maline's Lex Mercatoria* 115. puts it "where there is no Probability of putting to Sea, with the Thing insured."

Now here, the Ship was freighted with a *perishable* Commodity, (Fish, from *Newfound-land,*) bound to hot Countries, (*Portugal* or *Spain*;) was taken, and afterwards re-taken, and brought into *Milford Haven* without sufficient Hands of her own; and requiring so much Refitment as was impossible to be finished before the Cargo would and must be spoiled: And Part of the Cargo was thrown over-board, too. To what Purpose then should the Insurer be at the Expence of refitting the Ship, to carry a *spoiled* and *useless* Cargo?

Little is to be found in our Books, about Abandoning. The Rule laid down was, "That the Insured has a Right to abandon "to the Insurers, where there are *no Hopes of Saving the perishable* "*Cargo:* Provided there be no Fraud.

This Ship was in Port; the Hands all in *France,* in Prison. Besides, here was a total Loss: For the Costs of Salvage exceeded the Value of the Thing saved. Therefore they had a Right to abandon.

Sir *Richard Lloyd* and Mr. Serjeant *Davey* on Behalf of the Defendant, argued upon the same two Points; but made very different Deductions.

First—The Insurers could *not* be liable as for a TOTAL Loss: (Though they agreed it was an Average-Loss.) 1st Point.

The *Capture* of the Ship was *not* a *total* Loss. The *Property* was *not* divested out of the Owners: *A mere Capture,* without being

2 carried

carried *infra Præsidia*, or some other *such Circumstance*, will *not* alter the Property. The *Taking out the Mariners*, and putting in the Enemy's Crew, is *not enough* to do it. Nor is the Detaining it 8 *Days*: For it has been holden that 9 Days will not alter the Property. In *Lucas's Rep.* 77. *Assievedo* v. *Cambridge*, The Court held *this* to be * very plain, " That the Property was *not* there al- " tered by the Taking."

* They did so. But there is no Determination of the Case itself, in *Lucas*: He reports it to be adjourned for further Argument. N. B. Mr. Justice *Foster* said " That *Lucas*'s Report of that Case (of which He Himself had a Note,) was a pretty good One."

Yet in that Case there was 9 Days Possession by the Enemy. And Dr. *Henchman* in arguing for the Defendant, said That the Question would not have born a Dispute in the *Admiralty*-Court: For that the Law is clear, " That not Length of Time, but the " bringing *infra Præsidia*, is that which divests the Property." And He even cited a Case of 4 Years Possession not altering the Property; and also a great many other Authorities, to prove " That the Pro- " perty is not divested without bringing the Ship *Infra Præsidia*." *Bynkershoek*''s *Quæstiones Juris publici*, *Lib.* 1. *c.* 4. is contrary to *Grotius*'s Opinion; and says " That Length of Time alone is *not* " sufficient to divest the Property." Therefore this was *only* an Average-Loss; not a *total* Loss, or a Divesting of Property: And if so, the Insurer cannot be intitled to Recover.

The Statute of 29 *G.* 2. *c.* 34. §. 24. directs Ships taken and retaken to be restored to the Owners, on paying *Salvage*. This was an Insurance *with Benefit of Salvage*: So that the VOYAGE was *not* insured; but ONLY *the Ship and Cargo*.

The Distinction is between such Insurances as this (*with Benefit of Salvage*,) and Insurances *Interest or no Interest*. In the former Case, no Prevention of the *Voyage* can make the Insurers liable.

There are 3 Cases on this Head.

Pond v. *King*, *H.* 21 *G.* 2. *B. R*: Where the Interruption and Loss of the *Voyage* was holden to be the Thing insured against, by *that* Policy; which was without Benefit of Salvage, and interest or no Interest, and free of Average: And this was holden not to be an Average-Loss; but a *total* Loss, within the Terms and Extent of that Policy.

De Paiba v. *Ludlow*, *Tr.* 5 *G.* 1. *C.B.* reported in *Comyns* 360. An Assumpsit upon a Policy whereby the Defendant insured the Plaintiff, Interest or no Interest; and merely a *Wager*-Policy: And the Ship was taken by a Pirate, detained 9 Days, and then retaken. This was determined for the Plaintiff; because he received a Damage by the Interruption of the *Voyage*.

Fitzgerald v. *Pole*, *P.* 23 *G.* 2. Where the Plaintiff's Intereſt was by the Policy ſettled at 1000 *l.* And there was Benefit of Salvage. The Crew mutinied: Whereby the *Cruiſe* was totally interrupted and loſt. It was holden *not* to be a *total* Loſs; though the Voyage was obſtructed by a Mutiny.

Here, neither the Obſtruction of the Voyage, nor the Loſs of the Mariners, makes it a total Loſs: And if not, the Inſurer is not liable.

Many Things may be thrown out of the Caſe, as to the firſt Point, the Loſs of the Ship: *viz.* the Cargo being *Fiſh*; the *Tempeſt*; the Saving *Part of the Cargo.*

They denied the * Principle laid down by their Opponents as the Rule of the Common-Law, to have been ever determined: On the contrary, there has been a vaſt Variety of Opinions about it. Nor indeed can any Determination be made, on the Principles of *our Municipal* Laws: For the Queſtion concerns *Foreigners*, as well as Natives; and is a Queſtion of *general* Law, not of any particular and local Law. * *V. ante* 686.

The Acts of Parliament that have been mentioned, are not built upon the Principle that has been aſſigned, (*V. ante* 686;) but upon right Reaſon Juſtice and Equity. "Whether this was a "total "Loſs or not," muſt be determined by the Laws of War, and by the Law of Nature, that is, of right Reaſon.

The Captor has, for a Time, *only the poſſeſſory Right*; *not* the *abſolute* Right. The Right to *take*, is not the *perſonal* Right of the Taker; but the Right of the Subject of that Nation of which He is a Subject. So, the Right of Re-*taking*, is not *perſonal* to the Re-*taker*; but *national*, to any Subject of the Re-taker's Nation. At firſt, Each is *only poſſeſſory:* Neither *Taking* nor *Re-taking* give an *abſolute* Property.

The *freſh Purſuit* muſt depend upon *Circumſtances:* It cannot be confined to any *limited exact* Time; (as *ante Occaſum Solis.*) *Burlamaqui's Principles of natural Law, Lib.* 1. *c.* 6. *Lib.* 2. *c.* 7. A *freſh Purſuit* carried on as ſoon as may be, will prevent the mere *poſſeſſory* Property from becoming an *abſolute* Property. Our Ships of War and Privateers are in a CONSTANT *State of Purſuit:* They cruiſe, in order to *re-take*, as well as to take.

Indeed there muſt be a *fixed Limit* of the Time of this Poſſeſſory Property *becoming abſolute.* And this Limit is, When the right

Owner may be ſaid to GIVE UP his Claim, his *Spes recuperandi*. It is agreed, that Carrying *infra Præſidia, merely*, will not be a ſufficient Limit: Neither can the *mere Effluxion of Time*. This *fixed Limit* has never been preciſely ſettled by Writers. Therefore the *Spes recuperandi* is and muſt be the CRITERION.

The Queſtion indeed will not be ſo eaſily ſettled, "*When* this "*Spes recuperandi is* GONE, and *when* it SUBSISTS." But in our Seas, where our Ships are in a conſtant State of Purſuit, this Hope of Recovery can never be ſaid to be gone ſo ſoon as *within* 8 DAYS; Eſpecially, when in *Fact* and *Realty*, this Ship WAS *actually retaken* at the *End* of 8 Days.

The Court or a *Jury* are the proper Judges of this *Probability* or *reaſonable Hope* of Recovery. *Till* that is gone, the *abſolute* Property is *not* veſted in the Captor.

The Acts of Parliament do not mean to conſider the Point of *Property*.

2d Point.

Second Point, The Circumſtances ſtated do *not* intitle the Inſured to *abandon* the Ship to the Inſurers. This Right to abandon ſuppoſes a *total* Loſs.

They diſputed the Poſition, "That the Inſured are to be *fa*"*voured*." The Words of the Policy are calculated to prevent their abandoning. This Doctrine of abandoning, is a very inconvenient One to Inſurers.

As to *Molloy* and *Malines*—Almoſt any Thing may be proved by Citations from them *.

* Lord *Manſfield* ſpoke extremely well of *Bynkerſhoek*'s Writings (who was later than all the reſt except *Coccrius*;) and recommended eſpecially, as well worth reading, his Book of Prizes (*Quæſtiones publici juris*.)

The Under-Writer can never be ſuppoſed to inſure againſt theſe *accidental* Perils in diſtant Ports; but only againſt the *general* Perils of the EXISTENCE of the Cargo: The Inſurance is not upon the *beneficial Sale* of the Goods, upon the *Sanity* of them; but only upon the SAFETY of them.

There are ſeveral Caſes, where the Ship was totally loſt, and there was an End of all Claim and Right.

As to Inſurances upon a *Cruiſe*, All thoſe Caſes are cut up by the Roots, by the Caſe of *Fitzgerald* v. *Pole*: Which determined "that the Object of Inſurance, is the BODY *of the Ship, not* the "Cruiſe."

Bynkerſhoek's

Bynkershoek's Opinion is, "That there neither *is* nor *can be* any "*general* Rule laid down for a Limit: But every Case must depend upon its own Circumstances. *"

* Lord *Mansfield*. He does say so: And he combats the Opinion of *Grotius*, (supported by many other Writers,) "that 24 hours *quiet* "Possession is the fixed Rule."

There is a Common Law Case, in *March* 110. *pl.* 188. "That "the Property is *not* altered, unless the Ship be brought *infra* "*Præsidia* of the Enemy."

The Counsel for the Plaintiff in Reply—As to the Cases that have been cited— Reply—

1st. The only Case which may seem against Us, is the Case abridged by *Viner*, in *Vol.* 16. *Pa.* 405, 406. Title *Policy of Insurance Letter* A. *pl.* 13. *Assievedo* v. *Cambridge*, reported in *Lucas* 77. (called 10 *Mod.*) "That being 9 *Days in Possession of the Enemy* "(without being carried *infra Præsidia*) does *not* alter the Pro"perty." But there was *no Determination* upon that Case. Besides, that was upon a Policy *Interest or no Interest*; and the *Voyage* was the Thing there insured. 1st Point.

The 3 Cases of *Pond* v. *King*, *De Paiba* v. *Ludlow*, and *Fitzgerald* v. *Pole*, are no Proofs of their Point.

Pond v. *King* was Interest or no Interest. And the Court gave no opinion about the *Property*: They founded their Judgment on the *Cruise* being insured.

De Paiba v. *Ludlow* was an *Average*-Loss. There was no Determination upon the *Property*: For there also, the *Voyage* was interrupted.

Fitzgerald v. *Pole* was also an Insurance of a 4 Month's *Cruise*. So that too was upon the *Voyage* *.

* N. B. This Judgment was for the Plaintiff in *B. R.* who supposed this to be the *same* Point with the Case of *Pond* v. *King*: But the House of Lords reversed the Judgment, because they thought it *distinguishable* from *Pond* v. *King*.

The *Totality* of Capture depends upon the *Spes recuperandi*: And here was *none*. The *Average*-Loss here stipulated for, is where the Voyage is performed *without Interruption*.

They do not dispute our Principle "of the *Spes recuperandi* "being the *true Criterion*." But they say, "Our Ships are in *con*"*stant Pursuit*, in Seas frequented by our Men of War and "Privateers."

Now

Now it is hard to conceive a Purfuit WITHOUT *an* OBJECT, or even a *Knowledge* of any particular Ship's being taken. *Frefh Purfuit* means the going in Queft of *that particular individual* Ship, which is taken.

This Rule would carry it much too far, and proves too much: For if 8 Days be not fufficient, it might be carried to 8 or 10 Months, or to any *indefinite* Time: So that there would be *no Limit at all* left. This is a Queftion that *our* Courts muft determine according to *our* Laws. We only contend for the Time of a *reafonable* Hope or Recovery: Not for a *wanton* or *groundlefs* Hope. Now *no* fuch *reafonable* Hope can remain, after the Ship's continuing 8 Days in Poffeffion of the Enemy.

Grotius, in *Lib.* 3. *c.* 6. *pa.* 285. fays—" Sed recentiori jure " Gentium inter Europæos populos introductum videmus, ut talia " capta cenfeantur, ubi per horas viginti quatuor in poteftate hoftium " fuerint."

2d Point.

2dly. It has been urged, that the Infured can in *no* Cafe *abandon*. On the contrary, All provincial Laws allow the Power of abandoning, in *fome* Cafes *.

* Lord *Manf-field*—It goes fo far back, as the *Rhodian* Law and the Laws of *Oleron*.

This Cafe falls within the *Reafon* of the Cafes that have been already cited: And the Inconveniences that have been fuggefted, are altogether imaginary.

Lord MANSFIELD obferved, in general, that a large Field of Argument had been entered into; and that it would be neceffary to confider the Law of Nations; our own Laws, and Acts of Parliament; and alfo the Law and Cuftom of Merchants, which makes a *Part of* our Laws.

CUR. ADVIS'.

On *Thurfday*, 23d of *November* 1758—

His Lordfhip delivered the Refolution of the Court, (after having firft ftated the Cafe and Queftions, very particularly.)

Lord MANSFIELD,

It is not neceffary to confine what fhall be faid, to the two diftinct Queftions that are ftated.

The General Queftion is, Whether the Plaintiffs were, on the 18th of *January* 1757, intitled to recover againft the Infurers, *as upon a* TOTAL *Loss*; Under an Offer "to *abandon* the Ship and "Cargo to the Insurers, for them to make what Advantage of "Salvage they could." (For an Offer "to abandon" was *then* made: And nothing has happened since that Time, to alter the Case.)

There is one Point which We are All of Opinion is immaterial *as between the* INSURERS *and the* INSURED; *viz.* "Whether by this "Capture, the PROPERTY was or was not *transferred to the Ene-*"*my*, by the Law of Nations." *That Question* can happen but in *two* Cases: namely, (1st.) Between the Owner and a Neutral Person who has *bought* the Capture from the Enemy; (2d.) Between the Owner and a *Re-Captor*.

If the Ship taken by an Enemy *escapes* from the Enemy, or is *retaken*; or if the Owner *redeems* (ransoms) the Capture; his Property is thereby *revested*: Which Property in the Ship taken was by the Law of Nations obtained by the Captor.

The General Proposition of Writers upon this Subject is, That "*quæ ab hostibus capiuntur*, statim *Capientium fiunt*:" Which is to be understood, when the *Battle is over*. Indeed, Nothing can be said to be *taken*, *till* the Battle is *over*: And the Battle is *not over*, *till* all immediate Pursuit has ceased, and all Hope of Recovery is gone. This is the Definition of a Capture referred to by our Prize-Act 29 *G.* 2. *c.* 34. of a Ship taken by the Enemy. And accordingly, *Voet*, in his Commentary upon the *Pandects*, *Lib.* 49. Tit. 15. *Vol.* 2*d.* 1155. and many Authors he refers to, maintain, with great Strength, "per *solam* OCCUPATIONEM *dominium prædæ* "*hostibus acquiri*."

One Argument used to prove it, is, "that the Instant the Captor "has got *Possession*, no Friend, Fellow-Soldier, or Ally, can take "it from him; because it would be a *Violation of his Property*."

But *other* Writers and States have drawn *other* Lines, by arbitrary Rules; and partly from *Policy*, to prevent *too easy* Dispositions to *Neutrals*; and partly from *Equity*, to extend the *Jus Postliminii* in Favour of the *Owner*. No wonder there is so great Incertainty and Variety of Notions amongst them, about fixing a positive Boundary *by the mere force of Reason*; where the subject Matter is *arbitrary*, and not the Object of *Reason alone*.

Some have said from the *Roman* Law (which was introduced in Favour of the Liberty and Condition of a *Roman* Citizen taken Captive,) "that the Prize must be brought *infra Præsidia*. But, "*what* Custody *at Sea* should be equal to *Præsidia* at *Land*," is a new Fund of Dispute, and leaves the Matter just where it was.

The Writers whom *Grotius* follows, and many more who follow him, and some * Nations, have made 24 *Hours* quiet Possession by the Enemy, the Criterion. But *this*, † *Bynkershoek* and other Writers whom he follows, and several Nations absolutely *deny*. *Some* have said that the Ship must be carried into the *Enemy's Port*, *condemned* there, sail *out again*, and arrive in a *Friend's Port*. All these Circumstances are very arbitrary: And therefore *this* is generally *exploded*.

* V. The Ordinances of Lewis 14th.
† Quæst. Jur. pub. L. 1. c. 4.

I have taken the Trouble to inform Myself of the Practice of the Court of *Admiralty in England*, before any Act of Parliament commanded Restitution, or fixed the Rate of Salvage: And I have talked with Sir *George Lee*, who has examined the Books of the Court of Admiralty, and informs me That *they* held the *Property* NOT *changed*, so as to bar the Owner, in Favour of a Vendee or Recaptor, *till* there had been a *Sentence of Condemnation*; and That in the Reign of King *Charles* the 2d. Sir *Richard Floyd* (Father of the late Sir *Nathaniel*) gave a solemn Judgment upon the Point, and decreed Restitution of a Ship retaken by a Privateer, after she had been 14 *Weeks* in the Enemy's Possession, *because She had* NOT *been* CONDEMNED. Another Case, upon the *same Principle*, against a Vendee, is cited at the End of *Assievedo* v. *Cambridge*, in 1695. *Lucas* 79.) after a *long Possession*, *two Sales*, and *several Voyages*.

But whatever Rule ought to be followed, in Favour of the *Owner*, against a RECAPTOR or VENDEE, it can no way affect the Case of an *Insurance*, between the INSURER and INSURED. (Upon an Action against the Hundred for a Robbery, a Question might as well be started, " Whether the Property of the Goods, as against " the Owner, was changed by the Sale.")

The Ship is *lost*, by the Capture; though She be never condemned at all, nor carried into any Port or Fleet of the Enemy: And the Insurer must pay the Value. If, *after* Condemnation the Owner recovers or retakes her, the Insurer can be in no other Condition than if She had been recovered or retaken *before* Condemnation. The Reason is plain from the Nature of the Contract. The Insurer runs the Risque of the Insured, and undertakes to indemnify: He must therefore bear the Loss *actually* sustained; and can be liable to *no more*. So that if *after Condemnation*, the Owner recovers the Ship in her complete Condition; but has paid Salvage, or been at any Expence in getting her back; the Insurer must bear the Loss so *actually sustained*.

A Capture by a *Pirate*, (and in *Spain*, *Venice*, and *England*, the Goods go to the Captor of the Pirate, against the Owner; as there can be no Condemnation to intitle the Pirate;) or a Capture *under a Commission* where there is *no War*; do not change the Property: Yet, as between the *Insurer* and *Insured*, they are just upon the *same* Foot as Captures by an *Enemy*.

This Point never would have been started in Policies *upon real Interest*; because it never could have varied the Case: (And in *this* Cause, the Question could not have been material, if the Parties had not suffered the Cargo to perish, while they squabbled *Who* should take it.) But *Wager Policies* gave Rise to it: It was necessary to set up a total Loss as between third Persons, for the Purpose of their *Wager*; though *in Fact* the Ship was safe, and restored to the Owner.

In the Case of *Assievedo* v. *Cambridge*, the Man of War which retook the Ship, brought her into the Port of *London*, and restored her to the Owner upon reasonable Redemption: (That appears from the Special Verdict; though not stated in *Lucas*.) And then, the *Owner*, not abandoning the Ship, could only have come upon the Insurers for the *Redemption*; and no question could have arisen upon the *Change of Property*. But the Policy being *Interest or no Interest*, *without Benefit of Salvage*, the Question arose upon the Terms and Meaning of the *Wager*. That Case was not determined.

In the Case of *Spencer* v. *Franco*, before Ld. *Hardwicke* at *Guildhall* 1735, The *South-Sea* Ship, Prince *Frederick*, had returned safe to the Port of *London*, with her Cargo: The *Wagerers* contended "She was totally lost at *La Vera Cruz*," from this Notion of a Change of Property; but failed.

De Paiba v. *Ludlow* was also a *Wager*-Policy; and the Property could not be changed, because there was then no War, nor even a Declaration of War: But the Court held "that as the Ship was "once taken in Fact, the Event had happened, though She was "afterwards recovered." So, in the Case of *Pond* v. *King*; which was also a *Wager*-Policy.

But in the Case of *Pole* v. *Fitzgerald*, the Majority of the Judges and the House of Lords (in 1754, by the Name of *Fitzgerald* v. *Pole*,) held, "that though the Ship might be deemed *for a Time*, "as lost; yet, as She was afterwards recovered, the Event of a "total Loss had *not finally* happened according to the Construction "of the Wager."

These are all the Cases where this Question has been debated. But *this* is a Policy upon REAL INTEREST.

The fingle Queftion therefore upon which *this* Cafe turns, is, "Whether the Infured had, under all the Circumftances, upon "the 18th of *January* 1757, an *Election* to ABANDON."

The Lofs and Difability was in it's Nature *total*, at the *Time* it happened. *During Eight Days*, the Plaintiff was certainly *intitled* to be paid by the Infurer as for a *total* Lofs: And in Cafe of a *Re-capture*, the Infurer would have *ftood in his Place*. The fubfequent Re-capture is, at beft, a Saving only of a *fmall Part: Half* the Value muft be paid for *Salvage*. The Difability to *purfue the Voy-age*, ftill continued. The Mafter and Mariners were *Prifoners*. The Charter-party was *diffolved*. The Freight, (except in Proportion to the Goods faved,) was *loft*. The Ship was neceffarily brought into an *Englifh Port*. What could be faved, might *not be worth the Expence* attending it:) Which is proved by the Plaintiff's Offer to abandon.)

The *fubfequent* Title to *Reftitution* arifing from the Re-capture, at a great Expence, of the Ship difabled to purfue her Voyage cannot take away a Right *vefted* in the Infured at the Time of the Capture. But becaufe he cannot recover more than he has fuffered, he muft abandon what may be faved.

The better Opinion of the Books fays—"*Sufficit* femel extitiffe "*conditionem, ad beneficium affecurati, de amiffione navis*; etiam "*quòd poftea fequeretur* recuperatio: *Nam per talem recuperationem* "non *poterit prœjudicari affecurato.*" I cannot find a fingle Book, antient or modern, which does not fay, "that in Cafe of the Ship "being taken, the Infured may demand as for a *total* Lofs, *and* "*abandon.*" And what proves the Propofition moft ftrongly, is, That by the *general* Law, he may abandon in the Cafe merely of an *Arreft*, or an *Embargo*, by a Prince *not* an Enemy. Pofitive Regulations in different Countries have fixed a precife Time before the Infured fhould be at Liberty to abandon in that Cafe. The Fixing a precife Time proves the general Principle.

Every Argument holds *ftronger*, in the Cafe of the *other Policy* with Regard to the GOODS. The CARGO was in it's Nature *perifh-able*; deftined from *Newfoundland* to *Spain* or *Portugal*; And the Voyage as *abfolutely defeated*, as if the Ship had been wrecked, and a third or fourth of the Goods faved.

No Capture by the Enemy, though condemned, can be fo total a Lofs as to leave *no Poffibility* of a Recovery. If the Owner him-
* V. § 24. felf fhould retake at *any* Time, he will be intitled: and, by the * Act of Parliament, if an *Englifh* Ship retakes at *any* Time, (*before*

 Condemna-

Condemnation or *after*,) the Owner is intitled to Reſtitution, upon ſtated Salvage. This Chance does not ſuſpend the Demand, for a *total* Loſs, upon the *Inſurer*: But Juſtice is done, by putting him in the *Place* of the *Inſured*, in Caſe of a Recapture.

In Queſtions upon Policies, the Nature of the Contract, as an *Indemnity*, and *nothing elſe*, is always *liberally* conſidered. There *might* be Circumſtances, under which a Capture would be but a *ſmall temporary* Hindrance to the Voyage; perhaps, *none* at all: As, if a Ship was taken, and in a Day or two, eſcaped *entire*, and *purſued her Voyage*. There are Circumſtances, under which it would be deemed an *Average*-Loſs: If a Ship taken is *immediately ranſomed* by the Maſter and *purſues* her Voyage, there the Money paid is an *Average* Loſs. And in ALL Caſes the Inſured may chuſe "NOT *to abandon*."

In the ſecond Part of the "*Uſages and Cuſtoms of the Sea*" (a *French* Book tranſlated into *Engliſh*,) a Treatiſe is inſerted called "GUIDON:" Where * after mentioning the Right to abandon upon a Capture, he adds, "or any other *ſuch* Diſturbance as *defeats the Voyage*, or makes it *not worth while*, or worth the *Freight*, to *purſue* it." * C. 7. § 1.

I know that in *late* Times, the Privilege of *abandoning* has been *reſtrained* for fear of letting in Frauds: And the Merchant can *not* elect to turn what, at the Time when it happened, was in it's Nature but an *Average* Loſs, into a total One, by abandoning. But there is no Danger of Fraud, in the *preſent* Caſe. The Loſs was *total*, at the *Time* it happened. It *continued total*, as to the Deſtruction of the *Voyage*. A *Recovery* of any Thing could be had, *only* upon paying more than half the Value (including the Coſts.) What could be ſaved of the Goods, might *not be worth the Freight* for ſo much of the Voyage as they had gone when they were taken. The *Cargo*, from it's Nature, muſt have been ſold *where* it was brought in. The Loſs, as to the *Ship*, could not be eſtimated, nor the Salvage of *half* be fixed, by a *better* Meaſure, than a *Sale*. In ſuch a Caſe, there is no Colour to ſay, that the Inſured might not *diſentangle himſelf* from unprofitable Trouble and further Expence, and leave the *Inſurer* to ſave what he could. It might as reaſonably be argued, that if a Ship *ſunk* was *weighed up again* at a great Expence, the Crew having *periſhed*, the Inſured could not abandon, nor the Inſurer be liable, becauſe the *Body* of the Ship was ſaved.

We are therefore of Opinion, that the Loſs was TOTAL, by the Capture; and the Right which the Owner had, after the Voyage was defeated, "to obtain Reſtitution of the Ship and Cargo, pay-

" ing great Salvage to the Re-captor," *might* be ABANDONED to the Insurers, after She was brought into *Milford Haven*.

Let the *Postea* be delivered to the PLAINTIFF, in both Causes.

Friday 24th *November* 1758.

Hawks *vers.* Crofton.

ERROR upon a Judgment of *B. R.* in *Ireland*, in an Action of Trespass *vi et Armis* for an Assault and Battery, brought there above 15 Years ago (in 16 *G.* 2.) charging Special Damages for a violent Battery upon the Plaintiff, whereby he lost an Arm. The Defendant pleaded " Not guilty," as to *Vi et Armis*; and Issue was joined thereon. As to the Special Damages, he pleaded, " son " Assault demesne." To which, the Plaintiff replies " De injuria " suâ propriâ, absque tali causâ :" On which Issue is joined likewise. Upon Trial of these Issues, the Verdict finds the Defendant, GENERALLY, " *Guilty of the* TRESPASS *within written*;" and gives the Plaintiff 850*l*, Damages. Judgment for the Plaintiff.

Mr. *Nares*, for the Plaintiff in Error, Objected " That this *Ver-* " *dict is* INCOMPLETE; and the *Court cannot give Judgment upon* " *it:* It is no Verdict at all, as to the *material* Issue, which affects " the true Question between the Parties or the *Merits* of the Cause." Whereas a Verdict ought to be sufficient, both in Point of *Matter* and of *Form*.

Here are two Issues (1.) " Whether Guilty, or Not guilty;" On which Issue is joined; (2.) " Whether the Defendant beat the " Plaintiff, *without the alledged Cause*." And the Verdict is, " That " the Defendant is guilty of the Trespass, GENERALLY:" Which is no more than the mere Fact which the Defendant has acknowledged; but has insisted, at the same Time, that he had a *Cause* for it. *Style* 150. *Jennings* v. *Lee*: *Style* 210. S. C. 1 *Siderf.* 341. *Burton* v. *Chapman*. 2 *Keble* 278, 280. S. C.

And this bad Finding can *not be aided* by any Statute, or by any other Method. *Style* 167. *Hobbs* v. *Blanchard* is in Point with the present Case: Where the Defendant was clearly found Guilty generally; (though he is *there* * *said* to have been found *Not* guilty.)

* It is plainly an Error of the Press: The Word " *not*" is put for the Word " *Him*."

An *immaterial Issue* cannot be aided by any Verdict: Neither can an *immaterial Verdict* be aided by *any* Means whatever. This Verdict ought to have been, " Guilty as to the first Issue;" And, as to the second Issue—" That the Defendant beat the Plaintiff AS " *in the Declaration is alledged*;" (as in *Lilly's Entries* 516.)

Mr. *Ashurst contra*, for the defendant in Error.

The Question is "Whether this Verdict be *decisive* between the "Parties." The general Rule is "That Verdicts shall be *favour*-"*ably* construed." And "if a Verdict can be concluded out of the "Finding, to the Point in Issue, the *Court* shall work it into *Form*, "and make it serve." *Hob.* 54. is so expresly. 47 *E.* 3. 19. *a.* there cited. *Trials per Pais*, 394 to 400.

These Damages are no less than 850*l.* And the Plaintiff is *precluded in Time*, from bringing a *new* Action: (For this is an Action of near 20 Years standing, by Reason of the Defendant's having absconded.)

This Trespass must be intended an Assault *without* Cause: Else, it would not be a *Trespass*. And the Finding is, "That he is guilty "of *the Trespass within written*:" Which is sufficient. *Cro. Eliz.* 854. *Burper* v. *Baker* proves it to be so.

It has been argued, "that this is Finding Nothing more than the "Defendant has already *acknowledged*."

But the Defendant does not here acknowledge the *Trespass*: He only acknowledges the meer *Fact* of the *Assault*.

Style 150 & 210. is a very slight Authority; and not to the Point of a Finding by Verdict, so much as to the Joining of the Issue.

Mr. *Nares*, in Reply—*Cro. Eliz.* 854. is Right: For there the Finding was right as to the *essential* Part, and only defective in *Form*. Here, it is *essentially* incomplete. Nor do Mr. *Ashurst*'s other Cases affect this present Case. The Defendant admits the Fact indeed: But he *adds* an Excuse, sufficient to justify it.

Lord MANSFIELD—The Question is, "Whether this Verdict "is *so* uncertain, that the Court *can not give Judgment* upon it; "but must award a *Venire facias de novo*."

I think Mr. *Ashurst*'s Principle is true, and just; namely "That "where the Intention of the Jury is manifest and beyond Doubt, "the Court will *set right* Matters of *Form*, and the mere Act of "the *Clerk*."

And I think that the present Case is such a clear Case, that the Court *may* here give Judgment upon the *substantial* Finding; though the

the *Clerk* may have been irregular and faulty in Point of *Form*: It is very clear what the Jury *meant*.

Mr. Just. DENISON—Certainly, The Court ought not to award a *Venire facias de novo*, where the Verdict is *only* faulty in *Form*. And this here is no more than an Omission of the Clerk in Point of *Form*, in not being more particular than it is. But the MEANING of the Finding is plain.

* *Toe, qui tam &c, v. Adlam*, was the Name of the Cause, in *this* Court.

He mentioned a Case *Temp.* Lord *Hardwicke* * *Adlam* v. *Toe*—A Writ of Error out of *Stepney Court*, *P.* 11 *G.* 2. *B. R.* Where the Issue was upon the Cause of Action arising within the Jurisdiction of the Court; (the Defendant having pleaded "that it arose *without*," and the Plaintiff having replied "that it arose within it;") And the Jury found "that the Defendant promised in Manner and "Form *prout* the Plaintiff had alledged &c." Which was objected "not to be *ad idem*." There, indeed, the Judgment was reversed upon *another Objection*: But in speaking to the Objection which I have mentioned, the General Principle was allowed, from the Bench, "That Verdicts are not to be taken strictly (like Pleadings;) but "that the *Court will collect* the *Meaning* of the Jury, if they give "such a Verdict that the Court can understand them."

I am satisfied, upon the *Reason* of the Law, that this is sufficient.

Hobart 54. lays down a very just Rule, "That though the "Verdict may not conclude formally or punctually in the Words "of the Issue, Yet if the Point in Issue can be concluded out "of the Finding, the Court shall work the Verdict into Form, "and make it serve."

Mr. Just. FOSTER—I think this is sufficient. The Jury could not have found thus, *unless* the Defendant had failed in *proving* his Justification.

Mr. Just. WILMOT held accordingly—Every Body knows that this Sort of Trial, turns upon the Proof of the Justification: And *if* the Defendant *bad*, in this Case, *proved* his Justification, the Verdict *could not* have been found as it is.

Hob. 54. lays down a very right and just Rule—"That if a "Verdict can be concluded out of the Finding, to the Point in "Issue, the Court shall work and mould it into *Form*, according "to the *real Justice* of the Case:" And *what* is the real Justice of the Case? That the Defendant has not proved his Justification; and therefore that there ought to be Judgment against him, not-

4 withstanding

withstanding any Irregularity or Want of Form in *Wording* the Verdict.

Therefore I am very well satisfied that the Judgment is right.

Per Cur. unanimously,
JUDGMENT AFFIRMED.

Lucas, *ex dimiss.* Dr. Markham *et al'*, *vers.* Dr. Wilson.

UPON shewing Cause why an Attachment should not issue against Dr. *Wilson*, for refusing to perform an Award made pursuant to a Submission entered into by Rule of this Court IN *the abovementioned Cause then there depending*, It became Part of the Question, "Whether *this* was *within* the Act of 9, 10 *W.* 3. *c.* 15. "for determining Differences by Arbitration."

And the Court thought that it was *not*; but that it stood upon the Common Law, independent of the Act; which was made, to put Submissions to Arbitrations in Case where there was *no* Cause depending, upon the *same Foot* as those where there *was* a Cause depending. But here *was* a Cause depending at the Time of the Submission: And therefore the Case was *not* within the Provision of this Act.

And Lord MANSFIELD held this Act to be *only declaratory* of what the Law was before, in Cases where there was a Cause depending in the Court.

He added, that the Court will *not enter* at all into the MERITS of the *Matter* referred to Arbitration; but only take into Consideration such legal Objections as appear upon the Face of the Award, and such Objections as go to the *Misbehaviour of the Arbitrators.*

In the present Case, the Rule for the Attachment was
MADE ABSOLUTE.

Rex *vers.* Inhabitants of Shenston.

Tuesday 28th *November* 1758.

TWO Justices removed *Isaac Green* and *Mary* his Wife from *Aldridge* to *Shenston*: And the Sessions confirmed their Order.

The Special State of the Caſe was as follows—The Pauper, with *Mary* his *firſt* Wife, who was the Daughter of one *Robert Chamberlain*, came with a *Certificate*, in the Year 1717, from *Shenſton* to *Aldridge*, and there lived with *Robert Chamberlain*, in a Houſe of the ſaid *Robert*'s, till his Death. The ſaid *Robert Chamberlain by his Will* dated 23d *September* 1724, *gave to* his Daughter *Mary Green, then the Pauper's Wife*, All that his Houſe Barn Garden Croft and Shred with the Appurtenances IN ALDRIDGE aforeſaid, To hold to Her *for* HER *Life*; And from and after her Deceaſe, unto *Robert Green* Son of the ſaid *Mary Green*, the ſaid *Robert Green* paying *Mary* his Siſter 5*l*. The Teſtator died ſoon after making his ſaid Will. The *Pauper and his Wife Mary* (*the Deviſee for Life* under the ſaid Will) ENTERED *upon* the Premiſſes ſo deviſed, *and enjoyed* the ſame, (the ſaid Houſe being then new built, and the Premiſſes all together worth *Forty Shillings a Year,*) *from the Death* of *Robert Chamberlain*, *until the Death of Mary* his firſt Wife, which happened Six Months after the Death of her ſaid Father; and CONTINUED *in the Poſſeſſion* of the ſaid Premiſſes, *till removed* by the preſent Order; without paying Rent to any Perſon.

The Pauper's firſt Wife left Iſſue by him, One Son named *Robert*, (the Remainder-Man in the ſaid Will;) who, many Years ſince went for a Soldier; and whether living or dead, not known; and One Daughter, named *Mary*, now living.

The Pauper, after the Death of the ſaid *Mary* his firſt Wife, married *Mary* his preſent Wife.

Mr. *Aſton* had moved to quaſh this Order; and had objected to it, " That this *Iſaac Green* the Pauper had a *Right* to this Eſtate, " *when he entered* upon it; and had continued a peaceable and *un-* " *interrupted Poſſeſſion of it, for above* 30 *Years*, and was IRRE- " MOVABLE from it, notwithſtanding his Coming originally into " the Pariſh under a *Certificate*."

And He then mentioned the Caſes of *Aſhbrittle* and *Wiley*, *M.* 11 G. 1. 1 *Strange* 608. *Burclear* and *Eaſt-Woodhay*, 1 *Strange* 163, 164. *Rex* v. *Inhabitants of Marwood*, *H.* 29 *G.* 2. *B. R.* *Rex* v. *Inhabitants of Duns Tew*, *Tr.* 29, 30 G. 2. * *Rex* v. *Inhabitants of Cold Aſhton*, *H.* 31 G. 2. *B. R.*

* *V. ante* 507, 508.

And now, Mr. *Morton*, who was to have ſhewn Cauſe againſt quaſhing theſe Orders, candidly owned that he could not undertake to ſupport them againſt † ſeveral expreſs Reſolutions.

† *V.* 2 *Salk.* 524. *inter Ryſlip* and *Harrow* Pariſhes. 1 *Strange* 502. *Cranley* and *St. Mary Guildford*. 1 *Strange* 97. *Murſley and Grandborough*. 2 *Strange* 983, 984. *Rex* v. *Inhabitants of Sundriſh*.

2 Lord

Lord MANSFIELD—So it ſeemed to Us, upon the Original Motion.

Whereupon the RULE was made ABSOLUTE.

Rex *verſ.* Earl Ferrers.

ON Mr. *Aſton's* Motion for the Earl, and on reading the Act of Parliament made laſt Seſſions for the Separation of the Earl and Counteſs; And on the *Conſent* of Mr. *Campbell,* on Behalf of the Counteſs;

The Earl's * RECOGNIZANCE WAS DISCHARGED. * *V. ante* 656.

The End of *Michaelmas* Term 1758.

Hilary Term

32 Geo. 2. B. R. 1759.

Friday 26th *January* 1759.

Doe, ex dimiss. Odiarne, *vers.* Whitehead.

H. 30 *G.* 2. *Rot'lo* 988.

THIS was a Special Case, from *Warwick* Lent-Assizes 1757,

In Ejectment, on the Demise of *Wentworth Odiarne* Esquire, for divers Messuages and Lands in *Allesley* in that County.

It appeared in Evidence, at the Trial, as follows; *viz.*

That *Timothy Stoughton* Gent. being seised in Fee of the Premisses in question, by Indentures of Lease and Release, (the Release being dated the 1st of *March* in the first Year of Queen *Anne*,) in Consideration of the Marriage of *Antony Stoughton* his eldest Son with *Frances* his Wife, and other the Considerations in the said Release mentioned, did convey to *Basil St. Nicholas* and *Thomas Skeffington* Esquires the Premisses in question, *To hold* to them their Heirs and Assigns, to the several Uses following, that is to say, *To the Use* of the said *Timothy Stoughton* for Life, with Remainder to Trustees during the Life of the said *Timothy Stoughton*, to preserve contingent Remainders; Remainder to the said *Antony Stoughton* for 99 Years if he should so long live, with Remainder to Trustees during the Life of the said *Antony Stoughton*, to preserve contingent Remainders; Remainder to the Use of the *first and other Sons* of the Body of the said *Antony*, on the Body of the said *Frances* lawfully begotten or to be begotten, *in Tail Male*; Remainder to the Use of *Mary Odiarne*, Wife of *Charles Odiarne*, *Sole Daughter of the said Timothy Stoughton*, for 99 Years if She should so long live, with Remainder to Trustees and their Heirs during the Life of the said *Mary Odiarne*, to preserve contingent Remainders; And from and immediately after the Death of the ſaid *Mary Odiarne*, *To the Uſe* of the *firſt and eldeſt Son of the Body of the ſaid Mary Odiarne* lawfully begotten or to be begotten, and of the Heirs Male of the Body of ſuch firſt and eldeſt Son iſſuing; with divers Remainders over, and with a Remainder or Reverſion to the right Heirs of the ſaid *Timothy Stoughton.*

The ſaid *Timothy Stoughton* died, (many Years ago,) in the Life-time of his Son *Antony*. *Antony Stoughton*, his Son, had by the ſaid *Frances* his Wife only One Son, named TIMOTHY.

Antony died in *July* 1734; leaving by the ſaid *Frances* (who died in his Life-time) the *ſaid Timothy* his only Son and Heir.

Timothy Stoughton, the Son of *Antony*, died in *June* 1753, without Iſſue.

The ſaid *Mary Odiarne* died in *January* 1735; leaving Iſſue (by *Charles Odiarne* her Huſband) *Wentworth Odiarne*, her firſt and eldeſt Son; who is the *Leſſor of the Plaintiff.*

It appeared alſo, That the ſaid *Timothy Stoughton* the *Grandſon*, in his Life-time, being *in Poſſeſſion* of the ſaid Premiſſes *under* the before-mentioned Indentures of Leaſe and Releaſe, by Indentures of *Leaſe and Releaſe* dated the *26th and 27th of January* 1735, PREVIOUS *to his Marriage* with *Anne Samwell*, Spinſter, and in Conſideration of the ſame Marriage and of a Marriage Portion, granted and releaſed (amongſt other Lands and Tenements) the Premiſſes in queſtion, to Sir *Thomas Samwell* and *Thomas Samwell* Eſq; and their Heirs, *To hold* to the Uſes following, to wit, *To the Uſe* of the ſaid *Timothy Stoughton* the Grandſon and his Heirs, until the intended Marriage between him and the ſaid *Anne Samwell*; And then to the Uſe of Truſtees for 500 Years; Remainder to the ſaid *Timothy Stoughton for Life*; Remainder to Truſtees, to preſerve contingent Remainders; Remainder to the ſaid *Anne Samwell* for Life, as Part of her Jointure; Remainder to the Uſe of the firſt and other Sons of the ſaid *Timothy Stoughton* on the Body of the ſaid *Anne Samwell*, in Tail Male; with Remainder to the ſaid *Timothy Stoughton* in Fee.

IN *which Indenture of Releaſe*, is a Covenant, by the ſaid *Timothy Stoughton*, "TO LEVY A FINE *ſur conuſance de droit come ceo &c*, "*with Proclamations, (inter al')* of the Premiſſes in queſtion, to "the ſaid Sir *Thomas Samwell* and *Thomas Samwell* and the Heirs "of the ſaid Sir *Thomas*."

And it is *declared by the ſaid Indenture of Releaſe*, "that the ſaid "*Fine ſhould enure* to the ſeveral Intents and Purpoſes *and for the* "*ſeveral Eſtates in the ſaid Indenture of Releaſe contained*"; (and which are herein before-mentioned.)

It appeared, That the ſaid *Marriage took Effect*; and that, AFTERWARDS, the ſaid *Timothy Stoughton, being in Poſſeſſion*, did in *Hilary Term* 1735, LEVY A FINE *according to his ſaid Covenant*, with a *General Warranty* in the ſaid Fine, by the ſaid *Timothy Stoughton*, for him and his Heirs, "That they would warrant to "the aforeſaid Sir *Thomas* and *Thomas* and the Heirs of the ſaid Sir "*Thomas*, the ſaid Premiſſes in queſtion, againſt him the ſaid "*Timothy* and his Heirs, for ever." And it appeared that the ſaid *Anne* his Wife, after his Death, entered upon and poſſeſſed herſelf of the Premiſſes in queſtion.

It alſo appeared That the ſaid *Wentworth Odiarne*, (the Leſſor of the Plaintiff,) before the Time of bringing this Ejectment, and of making the Demiſe by him in his Declaration mentioned, duly made an *actual Entry* into and upon all the Premiſſes in queſtion, TO AVOID *the ſaid Fine*.

It appeared alſo That the ſaid *Wentworth Odiarne*, the Leſſor of the Plaintiff, was *Heir at Law to the ſaid Timothy Stoughton the Grandſon*, at the Time of his Death; that is to ſay, only Son of *Mary Odiarne*, who was the only Siſter and Heir of *Antony Stoughton* the Father of the ſaid laſt mentioned *Timothy*.

On the Trial, a Verdict was found for the Plaintiff, ſubject to the Opinion of the Court of King's Bench upon this Queſtion— "Whether the ſaid *Wentworth Odiarne* Eſq; the Leſſor of the "Plaintiff, is intitled to the Premiſſes in queſtion, and ought to "recover the ſame in this Cauſe; notwithſtanding the ſaid FINE "*ſo levied* by the ſaid *Timothy Stoughton* the Grandſon, *and the* "WARRANTY therein."

This Caſe was firſt argued in *Trinity* Term 1758; by Mr. *Knowler*, for the Plaintiff; and Mr. *Caldecott*, for the Defendant.

The Objections on the Part of the Plaintiff were founded on *Seymor*'s Caſe, 10 *Rep*. 95. The Sum of them was, "That the "Leſſor of the Plaintiff might maintain an Ejectment, (as an ac-"tual Entry had been made to avoid the Fine) unleſs a DISCON-"TINUANCE could be proved, or that the WARRANTY ſtood in "his Way as a *Bar* to his Title.

In Order to ſhew "that there had been NO *Diſcontinuance*;" and conſequently, "That the Remainder of the Leſſor was *not di-*"*veſted*;"

" *vested*;" Mr. *Knowler* said it would be necessary to consider the *Operation* of the *Lease and Release*, and of the *Fine*: Which were, in the present Case, quite *distinct* Conveyances.

A *Lease and Release* made by a Tenant in Tail has the *same* Sort of Operation, as if Tenant in Tail conveys by *Bargain and Sale inrolled*: No greater Estate passes, by either, than the Tenant in Tail can *lawfully* convey. *Litt.* § 606. And *if* it be the Property of the Conveyance made use of by the Tenant in Tail, to pass NO *greater* Estate than the Tenant in Tail can *lawfully* convey; SUCH Conveyance does NOT *discontinue* the Estate Tail, *nor divest* the Remainder. Now, when Tenant in Tail conveys by Bargain and Sale, or by Lease and Release, (which has the same Operation,) THAT Conveyance makes NO Discontinuance of the Estate Tail; *neither* doth it divest the Remainders: Because NO *greater* Estate passes by it, than a *base* Fee, *determinable* upon the Death of the Tenant in Tail; which is *all* the Estate he can *lawfully* convey.

It is true, that a *Feoffment*, or a *Fine*, or a *Common Recovery*, will make a Discontinuance; because a *Fee-Simple* passes by *them*; which is a *greater* Estate than the Tenant in Tail can lawfully convey.

It cannot therefore be denied or disputed, " That a *Fine* " which *passes a Freehold* will discontinue an Estate Tail." But in *this* Case, the *Fine* passed NO *Freehold*; the Freehold having been, *before* the levying of the Fine, conveyed by the *Lease and Release*. This Fine, levied *after* the Marriage, being a DISTINCT *Conveyance*, executed subsequent to the Lease and Release, All that it did or could do, was to *confirm* and *corroborate* the *base Fee* which passed by the Lease and Release, and make it *more durable*: The Estate which passed by the Lease and Release, was determinable on the *Death* of the Tenant in Tail; But the Fine made it more durable, namely, not to be determinable *till* the Death of the Tenant in Tail *without Issue Male*. Which Event being now come to pass, and the Estate Tail being now spent by the Death of *Timothy Stoughton* without Issue, The Lessor of the Plaintiff, *as the next Remainder-Man*, is intitled to the Estate, *unless* the WARRANTY stands in his Way, as a Bar to his Title.

But the *Warranty* has *no* Effect to bar or prejudice the Lessor of the Plaintiff's Title; because it *never* EXTENDED to his Remainder, and is now itself *determined*. A Warranty never bars a VESTED Estate, in Possession, Reversion, or Remainder: Before the Descent of the Warranty can *operate*, the Estate must be *devested and turned to a Right*; and this must be the Case before, or at the Time when the Warranty falls. *Co. Litt.* 388. *b.* And a *Remainder expectant* on an Estate Tail can *never be devested*, unless the Estate *on which*

 it

it is expectant, be *discontinued*. But the Estate Tail which was in *Timothy Stoughton was not* discontinued, for the Reason already mentioned. Therefore the Warranty did *not extend* to the Lessor's Remainder: But the Remainder continued undisturbed in Him, to the Time of the Death of *Timothy Stoughton* without Issue Male. *This* having happened; the Warranty, which depended solely on the Estate created by the Lease and Release, hath *lost* it's *Support*, and is therefore now determined, and no longer exists. Consequently, it had no Operation on the Estate of the Lessor, nor can be any Bar to his Title.

Mr *Knowler* relied on the before mentioned Case in 10 *Co.* 95, as in Point to prove All these Positions, upon which he had founded his Argument.

It came into Judgment upon a Special Verdict in an Ejectment on the Demise of *Edward Seymor*: And the Case was * this—

* *V.* 1 *Bulstr.* 162 S. C. (there called *Heywood* v. *Smith.*)

Sir *Thomas Cheney*, devised the Premisses in Question to his Son *Henry Cheney* and the Heirs of his Body; Remainder to *John Cheney* and the Heirs Male of his Body; Remainder to his own right Heirs. Sir *Thomas* died. And after his Death, *Henry* entered; And (being seised in Tail, Remainder in Tail, Remainder to himself in Fee,) conveyed by *Bargain and Sale inrolled*, to *William Higham* and his Heirs; who entered and became seised accordingly. *Henry Cheney afterwards* levied a Fine with Proclamations, to *William Higham* and his Heirs; with general Warranty. *William Higham* conveyed to *Henry* Lord *Seymor* in Fee. *John Cheney*, the Remainder-Man in Tail, had Issue *Thomas Cheney*. And then *Henry Cheney* died without Issue; *Thomas*, the Issue of *John* the Remainder-Man, being his Heir at Law. Upon the Death of *Henry*, *Thomas* entered, claiming the Premisses by Force of the Remainder limited to his Father: Upon which, *Edward Seymor*, who claimed under *Henry* Lord *Seymor*, entered and made the Lease to the Plaintiff: Who, being ejected by *Thomas Cheney*, brought the Ejectment. And the *Point* submitted by the Jury to the Judgment of the Court, was, "If the Entry of *Thomas* was lawful, or not." And the Case having been argued at the Bench as well as at the Bar, The *Court* were unanimously of Opinion—

"That the *Fine* levied by *Henry Cheney* to *William Higham* "the Bargainee, did NOT DIVEST *the Remainder* limited to *John* "*Cheney*;

"That *no Estate of Freehold passed by the Fine*; but that the "Fine, being with Proclamations, *corroborated* the Estate of the "Bargainee, and made it *more durable*, by making it determinable

3 "on

" on the Death of *Henry Cheney without Issue Male*, where before it, " was determinable *on his Death*;

" That if the Fine had been levied *before* the Bargain and Sale, " it *would* have made a *Discontinuance*; but being levied AFTER " it, it operated on the *Estate which passed by the Bargain and Sale*, " and was guided by *it*;

" That the WARRANTY created by the Fine did *not extend* to " the Estate of *John Cheney* in Remainder; because it was *not displaced*, but *continued in him*;

" That when the *Estate to which the Warranty was annexed*, de- " termined by the Death of *Henry Cheney* without Issue Male, the " *Warranty was determined* for *Want of an Estate* to support it:"

He urged that this Authority concurs, in *every* Point, with the Case now before the Court; And that there is no material Difference between them. *Seymor*'s Case arose indeed upon a Bargain and Sale inrolled: The present Case arises upon a Lease and Release. But *their Operation* is *the* SAME, as to the Estate and Interest which *pass* by them: For they *pass no greater Estate* than the Party who executes them, can *lawfully convey*. And in *that* Respect, they *Both* differ from a *Feoffment* and from a *Fine*. And Lord Chief Justice *Holt*, in the Case of *Machil* v. *Clark*, 2 *Salkeld* 619. ranks them together, *as* Conveyances which have the *same Operation*, as to the Quantity of Estate passing by them, when made by Tenant in Tail. And *Seymor*'s Case was there holden for Law, by Him: Which adds greatly to its Weight and Authority.

Mr. *Caldecott*'s Argument tended to answer these Objections, and to prove that at the Time of the Fine levied, there was a *Discontinuance* of the Estate Tail.

He insisted, that even supposing these to be *distinct* Conveyances, Yet *Timothy Stoughton* the Grandson was *Tenant in Tail in Possession*, with Remainder over in Fee: For He had an Estate for Life in Him, and also the Old Intail; and they must be consolidated.

However, this Lease and Release and Fine are *not distinct* Conveyances; but All *One entire* Conveyance; All done at the same Time, upon the same Occasion, and to the same Purpose, and under the same Deed: Whereas in *Seymor*'s Case, the Bargain and Sale were completed; and the Fine was a Twelve-month after; And the Person who levied it, had no Freehold in Him. And to

 prove

prove that all this was only One entire Conveyance, He cited 5 *Co.* 26. Countess of *Rutland*'s Case. 2 *Co.* 72. *b.* Lord *Cromwell*'s Case, the 2d Resolution. 3 *Bulstr.* 256. *Havergill* v. *Hare*, (what was said by Ch. Just. *Montague.*)

Mr *Knowler* conceded " That the Fine would discontinue the " Estate Tail and devest the Remainder (*i. e.* drive the Party in Re- " mainder to his Formdon,) if the Person who levied the Fine " was at that Time Tenant in Tail in Possession."

Lord Mansfield put Mr. *Knowler* upon shewing that this was not One Conveyance or *Assurance*; and that it was not the Intention and Agreement of the Parties " that all the Uses should " arise at *one and the same Time*, and be directed by the *same* " *Deed.*"

Mr. *Knowler*—*After* the Marriage and *before* the executing the Fine, *Timothy Stoughton* had *only* an Estate *for* Life in him; (For the Lease and Release had no other Operation:) Therefore, being only *Tenant for* Life, he could *not discontinue the Estate.*

There are but four Discontinuances of Estates Tail.

The State of the Case shews the *Order* in which the Deeds were executed.

It is said " That the Lease Release and the Fine are *but One* " *Conveyance.*" I say, they are *Three distinct Conveyances.* And after *the Lease and Release had taken their Effect,* then comes the Fine. Now *what Operation* could that have? *Not* to pass the *Freehold:* For *that* was done before. And *without that,* it could *never* work a *Discontinuance* of the Estate Tail.

Lord Mansfield—I take it to be an exceeding plain Case, upon Mr. *Caldecott*'s second Point.

If you could *distinguish* these Conveyances, and suppose *Timothy Stoughton* to have been only Tenant for *Life*, at the Time of his levying the Fine, it would be the *Forfeiture* of his Estate for Life. So that you see the *Consequence* of *this Position.*

But undoubtedly these are *All but* One Assurance, and shall *operate as such:* And the Fine is *Part* of it. This has been so holden in former Cases; *Stapylton* v. *Stapylton*, and the Case of the *Mansel* Family: It was in both these Cases, considered and taken that they were *all* but in the Nature of *One* Conveyance or *Assurance* (if you had rather call it so) and shall *operate as* such. But the

the *Fine* ſhall never operate *contrary* to the Intention of the Parties, and ſo as to *defeat* it. And this is agreeable to the Doctrine laid down in Lord *Cromwell's* Caſe, 2 *Co.* 72. *b.* And in the Counteſs of *Rutland's* Caſe, 5 *Co.* 26. And in many modern Caſes.

If One was to argue on *Fictions*, the Fine would, by *Relation*, *precede* the other Conveyance; and the Leaſe and Releaſe might be conſidered but as a Declaration of the Uſes of the Fine.

But this Conſtruction that is now attempted, would confound every Settlement made upon Marriage or other Events in Families; and would be of exceedingly inconvenient Conſequence. As to it's being one *Conveyance*, or one *Aſſurance*, there is no great Matter of Difference between them, except merely in the Name.

I do not meddle with the WARRANTY: For *that* is out of the Caſe. I look upon *all* this as ONE ASSURANCE. If they were diſtinct Conveyances or Aſſurances, this Fine would be a Forfeiture of his Eſtate for Life under the new Settlement. Which plainly ſhews that they were *never underſtood or intended* as diſtinct, but as One and the ſame.

Mr. Serjeant *Hewitt* would have had a ſecond Argument: He was on Mr. *Knowler's* Side; and had taken Notes for a ſecond Argument on Behalf of the Plaintiff.

But Lord *Mansfield* did not care to delay it, *merely* for aſking. And both he and Mr. Juſt. *Wilmot* aſked the Serjeant if he had any *Doubt* " Whether a *Fine with Proclamations* levied by Tenant in " Tail in Poſſeſſion, will not *diſcontinue the Reverſion* in Fee, as " well as *deveſt the Remainder* in Tail, ſo as to put the Remainder-" Man to his Formdon."

Mr. Juſt. *Foſter* expreſſed Himſelf to the ſame Effect with his his Lordſhip and Mr. Juſt. *Wilmot*. And I ſuppoſe that Mr. Juſt. *Deniſon* communicated to his Brethren " that He alſo con-" curred;" For

Lord *Mansfield* ſaid, " We are *All* ſatisfied that the *Poſtea* be " delivered to the DEFENDANT."

But on the Day following (*Saturday* 10th *June* 1758,) Mr. Serjeant *Hewitt*, on Behalf of the Defendant, moved that this Caſe might be argued again: For that he thought he ſhould be able to maintain " That the Fine does *not* work a *Diſcontinuance*."

The

The COURT having offered this Yesterday, provided the Serjeant, upon considering of it, would say "that He really thought he "could maintain this Position;" and He now declaring "that "He was * *really* of this Opinion"—

[* So also was Mr. *Knowler*: As the Release *conveyed an Estate*; and therefore differed (as he apprehended) from a Covenant to levy a Fine, which conveys *no Estate*.]

The *Postea* was *ordered* to be stayed; And that it should be set down again in the Paper, in the following Term, for farther Argument.

And after such further Argument by Mr. Serjeant *Hewit*,—

Mr. *Norton* for the Defendant rested it upon the Serjeant's *own* Argument: Which both He and the Court agreed to have been fair and candid, by Reason of his having stated all the * Cases which were against him, as well as for him, fully and at large.

* 1 *Mod.* 109. *Benson* v. *Hodson*. *Littlet.* §. 614. 1 *Inst.* 327. *a. b. Cro. Car.* 109, 110. *Isham* v. *Morrice*. *Litt.* §. 618. *Co. Litt.* 332. *Seymor's Case*. Lord *Cromwell's Case*. 2 *Ro. Rep.* 245. 2 *Lev.* 52. 4 *Mod.* 266. 3 *Bulstr.* 250. 5 *Co.* 26. *Cro Car.* 320. 1 *Ventr.* 280. and *Herring* v. *Brown*, in *Skinner* 35, 52, 71, 184. and *Carth.* 24. 1 *Inst.* 42. *a. b.* 10 *Co.* 39, 42. *a. Hob.* 261. *Noy* 66.

Lord MANSFIELD,—

The *strict* legal regular Form that should have been pursued, would certainly have been a *Common Recovery*: But though a different Form has been pursued, yet it was plainly *meant* by *Timothy Stoughton* (the Grandson,) that the Uses of the Marriage Settlement should be *supported by this Fine*.

And all was *executory* at the Time of making the Lease and Release, which were executed *previous* to the Marriage; And the Covenant contained in the Release, was "to levy a Fine thereupon, "*in Order* to carry them into Effect." All these are to be considered *as but* ONE *Conveyance*; and they *operate as a Declaration of Uses*: Which Uses all arise *out of the Fine*.

It would be a very strange Thing, that *the* FORM of the Conveyance should *destroy* the very INTENT of it; and that the Fine itself should *destroy* the *Estate* of the Tenant for Life, by occasioning a *Forfeiture* it. Instead of this, *All* the preceding Transaction is *only* EXECUTORY: And the Operation is only as a *Declaration of the Uses* of the Fine. 'Tis like a Case of a Tenant to the Præcipe: Who is considered merely as an Instrument, and not as the strict real Owner of the Land. This Release is but a Deed to lead the Uses of the Fine.

Seymor's Cafe goes upon quite *different Grounds* from the prefent. There, *Henry Cheney* upon the 18th of *December* 22 *Eliz.* by Indenture of Bargain and Sale inrolled, fold to *Higham* and his Heirs: By Force of which, *Higham entered* and was *feifed* accordingly. And AFTERWARDS in *Michaelmas* Term 22 *Eliz.* almoft a *Year* after the Bargain and Sale, *Henry Cheney* levied a Fine with Proclamations, to the faid *Higham* and his Heirs, with general Warranty. So that the Bargain and Sale in that Cafe was totally UNCONNECTED with the Fine: And *Higham* is exprefsly found to have *entered* and been *feifed*, by *Force of the Indenture* of Bargain and Sale. Whereas in the prefent Cafe, the Whole is ONE *Affurance*.

As to the Objections—This Leafe and Releafe was not a complete Agreement; but *executory*. The *Intent* was to make good by a Fine, as far as they could be made good by a Fine, the Ufes of the Family-Settlement which *Timothy Stoughton* the Grandfon was making upon his Marriage with *Anne Samwell*: And the Intent was certainly *lawful*, though there is a Blunder in the Manner of doing it.

It would be an Occafion of the utmoft confufion in Families, all over the Kingdom, if in every Settlement or Conveyance, the feveral Deeds were to be *divided* in Point of Time; and the *ftrict* legal Operation of each was to be confidered *diftinctly* and *feparately* from all the reft, and from the general View and Intention of the whole Tranfaction. It would be juft as reafonable, to take the *feparate Claufes* in one and the fame Deed; and to hunt after fuch different Conftructions as the Words of them might bear, if they ftood unconnected with the reft of the Claufes in the Deed, or in Deeds of quite another Import: Whereas in Point of Law and Reafon, the *whole Tranfaction* and its *General Intention* ought to be taken together in *one* View.

Mr. Juft. *Denifon* was of the fame Opinion.

Here are two Queftions upon the Operations of this Conveyance; which was by Leafe and Releafe and a Fine: (1ft.) "Whether it "made a Difcontinuance of the Eftate Tail;" (2d.) "Whether "it devefted the Remainder or Reverfion." And both thefe Queftions feem to Me fo very clear, that I think there could be no Doubt, but this which has been endeavoured to be raifed upon *Seymor*'s Cafe 10 *Co.* 95. *b.* 96: Which Cafe has been urged and relied upon as an Authority "That the Eftate Tail is *not* difcontinued, nor the Remainder devefted." Yet it feems to me otherwife, notwithftanding what has been argued from that Cafe; which is *very diftinguifhable* from the prefent.

The Estate passes BY *the Fine*, Whether the Uses be declared *prior*, or *subsequent* to the Fine. The Deeds must be considered as *executory*, till the Fine is levied; And *then* the Estate passes *by* the *Fine*.

The Comparison of this Case to *Seymor*'s Case is founded upon a *Mistake*. For there the Bargainee was found "to have *entered by* "*Force* of the Indenture of Bargain and Sale, and to have been "*seised according* to it," *before Henry Cheney* levied the Fine to him: And the Judges were *obliged* to take the Fact to be as it was found by the Verdict; They were not at Liberty to look upon it as One and the same Conveyance or Assurance, (whatever they might really think it to be, in it's Nature or Intention;) They were bound down by the *express and particular Finding*. He was *found* to be *seised according to the Indenture* of Bargain and Sale: And therefore the Fine could, in that Case, *only confirm and corroborate* it. But if that Fine had been levied to the Bargainee *within the Six Months*, I think the Estate would, in *that* Case, have passed *by the Fine*. That Case therefore turns merely upon the *Finding* of the Fact by the Special Verdict. But even there, if it had been found "That "the Fine was levied *to the Uses* of the Bargain and Sale," I believe the Court would have looked upon the whole, as One and the same Assurance; and would consequently have been of a different Opinion. Therefore That Case of *Seymor* is nothing to the Purpose of the present Case: For here, *All* the Deeds and the Fine are to be taken TOGEHER; and *All* of them, so taken together, make *but* ONE *Assurance*.

There can be no Sort of Doubt but that a Fine *with* Proclamations will work a Discontinuance, and consequently devest a Remainder, as well as a Fine *without* Proclamations.

Mr. Just. FOSTER—It is admitted "That the Deeds and Fine "shall operate as *one* Conveyance or Assurance, *if* the Intention of "the Parties be *clear* and *lawful*:" Now it was clearly the *Intention* of *Timothy Stoughton*, the Grandson, to work a Discontinuance: And this Intention was certainly *lawful*. I wish that Gentlemen of Learning and Ingenuity would rather turn their Thoughts towards endeavouring to *support* lawful Estates, than to search out such nice Distinctions as would *overturn* All the Settlements in the Kingdom.

Mr. Just. WILMOT was of the same Opinion.

He considered these Deeds, *as* a *Covenant to levy a Fine*: And therefore the Fine and they ought to be considered as *One and the same Assurance*.

This

This was most undoubtedly a *lawful* Intention; though the *Mode* of accomplishing it is indeed mistaken. The previous Agreement was what the Tenant in Tail had a *Right* to do; namely, to make this Family-Settlement of the Estate: And the Parties concerned covenant to levy a Fine, for that Purpose. The *Fine* is the *principal* Act: And the *Deeds* operate to lead the *Uses* of it.

Seymor's Case *materially differs* from this Case: For it does not appear there, that any Fine was *intended* to be levied, at the *Time* of making the Indenture of Bargain and Sale. But All these Transactions in the Case now before Us are to be considered as ONE AND THE SAME CONVEYANCE OR ASSURANCE: And the Deeds and the Fine shall *all* be taken *together*; And the Deeds shall be considered as leading the *Uses* of the Fine.

Per Cur. (unanimously and most clearly)
Let the *Postea* be delivered to the DEFENDANT.

Lamego *vers.* Gould.

Tr. 30 & 31 *G.* 2. *Rot'lo* 932.

THIS was an Action on the Case upon a Special Promise " to " pay the Plaintiff 20 Guineas on the Death of the Defen- " dant's Wife;" in Consideration of 2 Guineas in Hand paid by the Plaintiff to the Defendant. The Note was in these Words,—

" Memorandum—In Consideration of Two Guineas received of " *Aaron Lamego* Esquire &c; I promise to pay him 20 Guineas, " upon the Decease of my present Wife, *Anne Gould*."

The only Question now made was " Whether this Contract was " *usurious*; (the Woman, at the Time of making it, being then 70 Years of Age.)

Mr. *Gascoigne*, for the Plaintiff, argued that it was *not* so.

The Statute of 12 *Ann. c.* 16. only says " No Person shall take " above the Value of Five Pounds, for the *Forbearance* of One " Hundred Pounds for a Year; and so, after that Rate, for a greater " or lesser Sum, or for a shorter or longer Time;" in Pain that all Bonds and Contracts shall be void.

Now

Now here is *no Forbearance*; nor any *Certainty* of receiving either Principal or Interest: It is a MERE CONTINGENCY; and is like the Case put in *Cro. Eliz.* 643. in the Case of *Button* v. *Downham*, of a "Wager betwixt Two, to have 40 *l.* for 20 *l.* if One "be alive at such a Day:" Which, as there holden, is *not Usury*.

Lord MANSFIELD stopt him, under a Doubt how it is possible to *come at* this Question about *Usury*. For here is nothing at all stated about the *Loan* of Money: It might, for aught that appears to the contrary, be a *voluntary Gift*, to be made to him upon this Event. The Matter of *Usury* was never thought of at the Trial.

Mr. *Gascoigne*—The Truth of the Fact was, really, RUNNING the Life of the Plaintiff's *Horse*, against that of the Defendant's *Wife*; And nothing more.

Mr. Just. DENISON—We can *not intend* this to be an *usurious* Contract, (which is a Crime.) For which, He cited 1 *Lutw.* 273. *Yeoman* v. *Barstow*. It is a *foolish* Bargain; but not usurious. Here are *no Facts stated*, upon which We can say it is *usurious*.

Mr. Just. FOSTER and Mr. Just. WILMOT—*ad idem*.

And Mr. Just. WILMOT added, that the *true Distinction* was laid down in that Case in *Cro. Eliz.* 643. between a *real bona fide* WAGER, not at all * intended as a Loan; and a Transaction which is *really* an usurious LOAN, but *disguised* as a Wager, with Intent to have a *Shift*.

* *V.* 1 *Lutw.* 464, 465, 466. *Geang* v. *Swaine*.

Per Cur. unanimously,
Let the *Postea* be delivered to the PLAINTIFF.

Tudway *vers.* Bourn.

THIS was a Case from the Court of Chancery.

Elizabeth Collins, by her Will, gave a Legacy of 200 *l.* to One *Coward*, then a *Bankrupt*; Whose *Certificate* had, at the Time of her Death, been then signed by 4/5 of his Creditors in Number and Value, and also by the Commissioners; but the Testatrix's Death happened *before* it's being CONFIRMED *and* ALLOWED by the Lord Keeper.

The Commissioners, soon after her Death, and *before the Allowance* of the Certificate, assigned this Legacy to the Defendant

Bourn, for the Use of the Creditors. AFTER *which*, the Certificate was confirmed and allowed by the Lord Keeper, without Opposition. After the Allowance of the Certificate by the Lord Keeper, the Bankrupt Himself died; and made *Tudway*, the now Plaintiff, his Executor.

Tudway, the Bankrupt's Executor, brought his Bill in Equity against the Executor of the Testatrix and against *Bourn* the Assignee of the Commissioners; Claiming this 200 *l.* Legacy, as belonging to the *Bankrupt*, by Reason of his Certificate's having been signed before the Death of the Testatrix, and afterwards allowed and confirmed by the Lord Keeper.

But the Creditors insisted that it belonged to *them*; as it was assigned to their Use and Benefit, by the Commissioners, *before the Allowance and Confirmation* of the Certificate by the Lord Keeper.

The Question referred to this Court, was "Whether it belonged "to the *Bankrupt's* EXECUTOR, or to his *Creditors*."

Mr. *Gould* argued for the Plaintiff, (the Bankrupt's Executor.) *Bankrupts*, He said, were originally considered as *Criminals*. The Statute of 4, 5 *Ann. c.* 17. was the first Act of Parliament which was made for their Benefit: And by this Act, the * *Commissioners* ONLY (without the Creditors) were to sign the Certificate: Which was to be allowed by the Lord Chancellor or Keeper unless &c. Then the 5 *Ann. c.* 22. added the *Creditors*; *viz.* four Fifths in Number and Value. And 5 *G.* 1. *c.* 24. continued it upon the same Foot. But 5 *G.* 2. *c.* 30. directs that the Commissioners shall not sign it, *till* † *after* the Creditors have signed, and Affidavit be made thereof &c.

* V. Sect. penult. of that Act.

† § 10.

No Objection, but for *Fraud*, or for *unfairly obtaining it*, will lie against it before the Lord Chancellor or Lord Keeper: And if *no such* Objection is then made, the Allowance and Confirmation will RELATE TO THE ORIGINAL DATE of it, and will operate *as a* RELEASE from the Creditors.

It is like the Inrolment of Deeds of Bargain and Sale: Which has such Relation. 2 *Inst.* 674. *Hob.* 165. And consequently, the Allowance *over-reaches* the Assignment made to *Bourn*, by the Commissioners.

It is also like the Surrender of Copyholds into the Hands of a Tenant of the Manor who dies before Presentment. He cited a Case in *Mich.* 17 *G.* 2. in Chancery, *Bromley* v. *Child*. A Commission of Bankruptcy had issued against Sir *Stephen Evans*, in 1711.

The whole Debts were received, with Interest to the Time of the Commission. The Certificate was not allowed till after the Death of Sir *Stephen Evans*; when there was a Surplus of 35000 *l.* in the Assignee's Hands. The Question was concerning the Interest which accrued subsequent to the Date of the Commission: To which Time, the Certificate discharged him. The Certificate was not *allowed* till Lord *Harcourt*'s Time. Lord *Hardwicke* held that it was *well allowed*, though after the Bankrupt's Death: And He said the End of requiring the *Chancellor*'s Allowance of the Certificate was to prevent Surprize; and that it takes it's *Effect*, (when allowed,) *from the Signing of it by the Creditors.*

Mr. *Norton*, *contra*, argued that The Bankrupt can not be intitled to *subsequent* Effects, come to him after his Bankruptcy and *after the Signing* of his Certificate by the Creditors and Commissioners, but *prior to it's Allowance* by the Lord Chancellor or Lord Keeper.

Till the Statute of 4, 5 *Ann.* the Bankrupt's Person and Goods continued *always* liable to his Creditors. And the Bankrupt ought to be holden *strictly* to the bringing himself *within the later* Acts that have been mentioned; by shewing that he has performed *All* the Requisites of them.

Now the Allowance of the Certificate by the Lord Chancellor or Keeper is the most *essential* Part of those Requisites. The Creditors are not confined to the particular Objections mentioned by Mr. *Gould*; but are at Liberty to make *any Sort* of Objections to such Allowance: And as well Creditors who *have* signed, as those who have not signed, may be heard against the Allowance. For the Act says "*Any* Creditors" may "object to it:" And they are *not* confined by any restrictive Words whatsoever, to Matters of *Fraud* and *Unfairness*; but left quite * at large.

* *V.* 5 G. 2. c. 30, § 10.

Lord MANSFIELD—Certainly they are *not* so confined, either by Law, or by Practice: And *any* Creditor whatsoever may then object to the Allowance. And the Allowance has been sometimes refused, and sometimes adjourned, even where there has been *no* Opposition. Many Years may intervene between the Signing, and the Allowance of the Certificate; And large Effects may, in the mean Time, come to the Bankrupt: And the *future Allowance* ought not to over-reach them.

Here, the Commissioners had *actually assigned* this Legacy: And for *that* Reason, the Creditors might not perhaps think it worth their while to object to the Certificate.

It

It is not like the Relation of a Bargain and Sale, or the Surrender of a Copyhold; to which, it has been compared. Poſſibly, in this Caſe, the Money may have been actually *divided out*; (For here is no Application made for the Allowance of the Certificate, till even after the Death of the Bankrupt:) And it would be very unreaſonable, that all the Creditors ſhould *refund* their Dividends.

Mr. Juſt. FOSTER was of the ſame Opinion: But He did not proceed to declare it at large, neither did the Other two Judges declare theirs; becauſe, it being a Caſe out of Chancery, The Judges of this Court were to give a Certificate. And immediately after this Argument,

The COURT certified, as follows—

Having heard Counſel on both Sides, upon this Caſe, (which the Parties did not apply to be ſet down in the Paper, to be argued, ſooner than this Term,) We are of Opinion that the ſaid Two hundred Pounds veſted in the *Aſſignee* of the Bankrupt, and now belongs to him, for the *Benefit* of the Bankrupt's CREDITORS.

Rex *verſ.* Fielding Eſq;

Monday 29th January 1759.

UPON ſhewing Cauſe againſt an *Information* which had been moved for by One Mr. *Barnard*, againſt the Defendant for a Miſdemeanor committed by Him in his Office of a *Juſtice of the Peace*; relating to the Committing and Detaining *William Barnard* (the Son) in Priſon &c, on a *verbal* Charge by the Duke of *Marlborough*, "that this Young Man had ſent Him threatning Letters "&c."

Mr. Serj. *Davy*, on Behalf of the Defendant, objected to the Proſecutor's proceeding any further in this *Criminal* Application, till He had *previouſly made his* ELECTION "Whether to proceed in "this *Criminal* Method, Or in a CIVIL *Action* which he had ac"tually commenced."

Mr. *Norton*, for Mr. *Barnard* the Proſecutor, anſwered that this Caſe was quite *different* from *Common* ordinary Caſes; becauſe it was abſolutely neceſſary here, as the Defendant was a Juſtice of Peace, to give *Notice of*, and even actually to *commence* the Civil Action againſt the *Juſtice of Peace*, *within Six Months* after the Time when the Cauſe of Action aroſe: Which particular Circumſtance, he ſaid, was the only Reaſon of their acting thus. And he alledged that

that they had no Intention to proceed *both* Ways; And offered to *relinquish the Civil Action*, IN CASE the Court SHOULD *grant the Information.*

But The whole COURT were of Opinion that He ought to make this *Election* DIRECTLY, and *before* they entered into the Criminal Complaint: For that this was the *constant Rule*; and the particular Circumstance of the Civil Action being confined to be brought within Six Months, made *no Sort of Difference*.

The *Justice* of the Thing equally required, they said, in *this* Case as well as in the *Common* Case, that the Defendant should not be called upon in a Criminal Way, by *this discretionary Method*, of an *Information*, which would oblige him to *discover* the Matter of his Defence and his Evidence; unless the Prosecutor would give up the Right which he might otherwise have, to make Use of this very Discovery of the Defendant's Evidence, *against* the Defendant, in his *Civil* Action: Which would be giving him a most *unfair and unreasonable Advantage* over the Defendant.

They added, That *if* the Prosecutor had proceeded in the Method which he had a strict and undeniable *Right* to proceed in, namely, by way of *Indictment*; and if such Indictment had been actually *found*; Yet the Attorney General would (upon Application made to him) have granted a *Nolle prosequi* upon such Indictment, in Case it appeared to Him that the Prosecutor was determined to carry on a *Civil* Action at the *same Time*. And if this be so, where the Party is proceeding in a Method which he had a strict *legal Right* to proceed in; Surely it is much more reasonable for this Court to refuse to give him this *extraordinary* Assistance (which they ought to dispense with Caution and Discretion,) unless he would first consent to *wave* the Civil Action which he had commenced for the very same Matter.

Mr. *Norton*, nevertheless, struggled extremely hard, to *distinguish* this Case (of being thus *fixed to* 6 *Months* for bringing the Civil Action,) from the *Common* Case, where the Prosecutor was *not at all restrained* in Time: And he remonstrated (with great Vehemence) against laying down this as a GENERAL *Rule*; as it might be a great Prejudice to Parties injured by Justices of Peace, who oftentimes might not be able completely to obtain any Remedy by Way of Information, *within* the 6 Months.

He was answered—"That the *present* Application for an Information was not made near *so early* as it *might* have been: Which was the *Prosecutor's own Laches*."

2 Mr.

Mr. *Norton* acknowledged that *if* this was really the Caſe, it would materially weaken his Argument as to *this particular* Caſe: And, in fine, He deſired Time to adviſe Whether they ſhould inſiſt upon their Civil Action, or not. Whereupon it was *adjourned* from *Wedneſday* the 22d of *November*, to the *Saturday* following.

And then the Proſecutor's Counſel agreed to *diſcontinue* their Civil Action, and proceed upon the Criminal Rule: Which they accordingly did, till it grew ſo late in the Day that the Court was obliged to *adjourn* it to the *Monday* following.

The Caſe then proceeded: But ended in an Adjournment to the preſent *Hilary* Term, in order to get further Elucidation of Facts, by procuring the Affidavits of the Earl of *Litchfield* and Mr. *Pierce*, who (though Both preſent) had not made any Affidavits at all hitherto.

On *Thurſday* the firſt Day of this Term, this Matter came again before the Court; the Earl of *Litchfield*'s and Mr. *Pierce*'s Affidavits being then obtained: And being then read, the Counſel confined themſelves to Obſervations upon *them*; All *other* Circumſtances having been fully diſcuſſed before. CUR' ADVIS.

The COURT now delivered their Opinion, by the Mouth of the Chief Juſtice. In which Opinion, Lord *Mansfield* declared Himſelf and his Brothers *Foſter* and *Wilmot* to be unanimous: But He ſaid that His Brother *Deniſon*, not happening to be preſent at the Time of the Motion and Defence, had a Delicacy in forming an Opinion from the mere Reading of the Affidavits, without having heard the Obſervations which the Counſel on both Sides had made upon them; and for that Reaſon, declined interfering in the Matter.

His Lordſhip went through the ſeveral Parts of the Charge (which conſiſted of no leſs than ſeven Particulars) and alſo of the Defence, and the ſeveral Affidavits in Support of both, with the utmoſt Accuracy and Exactneſs; and examined them moſt minutely, in Order to diſcover whether Mr. *Fielding* had acted with a bad and oppreſſive Intention, and whether the Perſons complaining of his Behaviour had been *Sufferers* or received any *Injury* or *Inconvenience*, in *Conſequence* of it: (For it was agreed that it was not, in two or three of it's Parts, ſuch as could be *ſtrictly juſtified*.)

Upon the whole, They were unanimous in Opinion, That the main and principal Charge which was the Ground and Foundation of the Reſt, and indeed the Key to the whole Nature and Complexion of Mr. *Fielding*'s Behaviour, appeared to be *falſe in Fact* and quite *misrepresented* to the Court by *Barnard* the Father and *Barnard* the Son; and that the Justice of Peace appeared to have acted in this Affair, *without any bad* or *oppressive* or *injurious Intention*, though (in some Respects) *irregularly*: And therefore, though the present Complaint appeared to be so ill grounded, that the Complainants deserved to be *punished in Costs* for making it; Yet as the Justice had made the Commitment without previously taking the Duke of *Marlborough's Oath*, and had also neglected to take his Grace's *Recognizance* to prosecute, (both which Parts of his Conduct were irregular,) He had no Right to *receive* Costs.

The *Rule* therefore was expressly directed to be taken thus—It is *Ordered* that the Rule made "That *John Fielding* Esq; and *George* "*Box* should shew Cause why an Information should not be ex-"hibited against them for certain Misdemeanours," be discharged: But in regard to the Warrants of Commitment and Detainer of the said *William Barnard*, made by the said *John Fielding* Esq; This Court doth *not* think fit to discharge the said Rule, with *Costs* to be paid to the said Mr. *Fielding*.

Douglass, Widow and Administratrix, *vers.* Yallop Esq;

A Neglect of entering a Judgment, and a Loss of the Roll, having been sufficiently shewn to the Court;

A Rule was made, "That the Clerk of the Judgments shall "*sign a new Roll*, whereon is entered the Judgment signed in this "Cause, in *Michaelmas* Term 1729; And that the same be "numbered as Roll 256, and filed amongst the Rolls of that "Term; A Special Entry being first made, expressing the *Day of* "*docketting* the same:" And it is further Ordered, "that this Judg-"ment shall not be made Use of against the *Administrator* of the "Defendant."

Note. Lord Mansfield intimated that it very much concerned the *Chief Clerk*, to take Care that Judgments be *actually entered up* upon the Roll in due Time, and *docketted*: For that, after he has received his Fees for making such Entry, He would be liable to an Action upon the Case, to be brought by a Purchaser who should have become liable to it, and had searched the Roll without finding it entered up. And He said that the Attorney who had undertaken to do this, and neglected it, would be liable indeed to the Chief Clerk: But still, the *Chief Clerk* would be liable to the *Purchaser* who had suffered by this Neglect.

N. B. The present Course is, for the Attorney for the Plaintiff to undertake to make this Entry upon the Roll: For doing which, the Chief Clerk (who is intitled to 8 *d. per* Sheet) allows him 5 *d. per* Sheet. So that the Attorney in this Case, acts *as* one of the *Clerks of the Chief Clerk:* Which would render the *Chief Clerk* liable to the *Party's Action*; though the *Attorney* would be *answerable over* to him. (In Fact, the Attornies are very apt to be negligent in bringing in these Entry Rolls.)

(The *Chief Clerk*, perceiving the Inconvenience to which this Practice renders him liable, determines to put the Matter upon a *safer* Foot, for the future.)

Rex *vers.* Mayor Bailiffs and Common Council of the Town of Liverpool.

Wednesday 31st January 1759.

THIS came on, in the Crown-Paper, upon the Return to a *Mandamus* to restore *Joseph Clegg* into the Place and Office of One of the *Common Council* of the said Town.

Return—That the Town of *Liverpool* is and from Time immemorial has been an ancient Town and Borough *&c*, consisting of a Mayor and two Bailiffs and a Common Council, *&c.* That they were incorporated by Letters Patent dated 4th *July* 2 *Car.* 1: Which Letters Patent they accepted and agreed to. Then they set forth other Letters Patent, of 26th *September* 7 *W.* 3. confirming their former Franchises, and further constituting granting and declaring that thence forward and for ever there might and should be within the said Town the Officers and Ministers following, to wit, 41 honest and discreet Men of the Burgesses of the Town aforesaid, who should be and be called the *Common Council* of the said Town *&c.* And the same King, by the said Letters Patent, named the first and then modern Common Council of the said Town, *to continue* in the Office of Common Council of the said Town *so long* as they should behave themselves well; UNLESS some or any of them should happen, for a REASONABLE Cause, to be removed, BY *the Mayor Bailiffs and Common Council* of the said Town or the greater Part of them for the Time being. Which same Letters Patent of King *William* the 3d the then Mayor Bailiffs and Burgesses of the said Town, in due Manner, accepted and agreed to: And ever since the Granting of the same Letters Patent, the Common Council of the said Town have of Right consisted, and have used and of Right ought to consist of 41 Persons and no more.

Then

Then they admit *Joseph Clegg*'s Election and Admission into the said Office of One of the said Common Council, as by the Writ is suggested.

But they alledge, that from Time whereof the Memory of Man is not to the contrary, the Mayor Bailiffs and Common Council of the said Town for the Time being, or the greater part of them in Common Council assembled within the same Town, *have of Right removed*, and during all the Time aforesaid have used and been accustomed and of Right ought to *remove* any One or more of the Common Council of the said Town, from the Place and Office of One of the Common Council of the said Town, *for any* REASONABLE *and* LAWFUL *Cause*; And that the Person or Persons *so* removed therefrom, have accordingly been and continued absolutely and effectually discharged and removed from the said Place and Office.

They further certify and return, That the Mayor Bailiffs and Burgesses of the said Town are and Time immemorially have been *seised* in their Demesne as of Fee, in their Corporate Right and Capacity, of divers Messuages Lands Rents and Hereditaments, and lawfully intitled for themselves and their Successors to many large and valuable Tolls Duties and Customary Payments; And also now are, and for 50 Years and upwards now last past have been lawfully *possessed*, in their Corporate Right as aforesaid, of divers other Lands and Tenements for certain long Terms of Years yet to come and unexpired; And that the several *Estates Hereditaments Duties Rents Revenues* and *Possessions* of and belonging to the Mayor Bailiffs and Burgesses of the said Town, in their Corporate Right and Capacity as aforesaid, now are and at the Time of the Removal of the said *Joseph Clegg* therein after mentioned were, and for a great Number of Years now last past have been of *great yearly Value*, to wit, of the yearly Value (together) of 2000*l. and upwards*; And that the Office of one of the Common Council of the said Town now is and during all the Time aforesaid hath been an Office of *great Trust and Power*, with respect to the *Management*, *Receipt*, *Control*, and *Application* of the *Issues Rents* and *Profits* of the Estates Hereditaments Duties Revenues Tenements and Possessions of and belonging to the Mayor Bailiffs and Burgesses of the same Town, and in the *appointing* of proper Officers to collect the same.

Then the Return proceeds to alledge, that before the Removal of the said *Joseph Clegg* in the Return after mentioned, the said *Joseph Clegg* sought his Trade of Living, by buying and selling; and *became and was a* BANKRUPT within the Meaning and Intent of some or one of the Statutes made and in Force concerning Bankrupts; And that afterwards, and before the said Removal of the same *Joseph Clegg* in the Return after mentioned, to wit on the 27th Day of *July* in the Year of our Lord 1756, a certain COMMISSION *of Bankruptcy in due Manner* ISSUED *against the said Joseph Clegg*, under His Majesty's Great Seal of *Great Britain*, bearing Date at *Westminster* the said 27th Day of *July* in the 30th Year of his Reign, directed to *R. T. &c*, (the Commissioners in that Commission named,) authorizing them &c, (as therein mentioned;) And that afterwards, and before the Removal of the said *Joseph Clegg* in the Return after specified, that is to say, on the 5th Day of *August* in the Year last mentioned, the said *R. M. R. E. and R. R.* being the greater Part of the Commissioners in the Commission named, did duly put the same Commission in Execution, and by Virtue thereof in due Manner FOUND *and* DECLARED *the said Joseph Clegg* TO BE A BANKRUPT within the true Intent and Meaning of some or One of the Statutes made and in Force concerning Bankrupts; And that he the said *Joseph Clegg* afterwards, and before his Removal in the Return after mentioned, did (pursuant to public Notice for that Purpose given in the *London Gazette*,) submit himself to the aforesaid Commission so issued against him as aforesaid; And that the said *Joseph Clegg* at the *Time of his Removal* in the Return after mentioned *had not nor hath yet* OBTAINED from the above mentioned Commissioners in the said Commission named, or from the greater Part of them, a CERTIFICATE of his having conformed himself to the Directions of the Statutes or any of them made and in Force concerning Bankrupts: Whereby the said *Joseph Clegg then* BECAME and *was*, and from thenceforth hitherto *hath been and still is* UNFIT for the said Place and Office of One of the Common Council of the said Town, so being an Office *of great Trust and Power* with respect to the Management Receipt Control and Application of the Issues Rents and Profits of the Estates Hereditaments Duties Revenues Tenements and Possessions of and belonging to the Mayor Bailiffs and Burgesses of the said Town as aforesaid.

The Return proceeds—That afterwards and before the Removal of the said *Joseph Clegg* in the Return aftermentioned, (that is to say) *on the 1st Day of February* in the Year of our Lord 1758, the then Mayor and Bailiffs and the then greatest Part of the then Common Council of the said Town, that is to say, 26 of the same Common Council, to wit, *W. G. &c*, being all of them then of the Common Council of the said Town, whereof the then Mayor and Bailiffs were Three, at *Liverpool* IN DUE MANNER *met and assembled in Common Council* within the said Town of *Liverpool*, in the Council-Chamber of the said Town, and then and there *duly held a Common Council* of the said Town, CONCERNING *divers Matters and Businesses relating to the said Town and the good Regulation and Government thereof*; And that the said *Joseph Clegg* was *then* and *there*

there PRESENT at that Aſſembly: And that in the *ſame* Aſſembly ſo held and met in Common Council as aforeſaid, an INFORMATION *and* CHARGE *were in due Manner exhibited* to *that* Aſſembly, againſt the ſaid *Joſeph Clegg*, "*of his aforeſaid* BANKRUPTCY, and "of the Iſſuing of the ſaid COMMISSION of Bankrupt againſt him, "and of his NOT *having then obtained* his CERTIFICATE as afore-"ſaid;" as a REASONABLE *and* LAWFUL *Cauſe* for the Removal of the ſaid *Joſeph Clegg* from his aforeſaid Office of One of the Common Council of the ſaid Town, ſo being an Office of great Truſt and Power as aforeſaid. And that the ſaid *Joſeph Clegg* had, THEN AND THERE, *perſonal Notice* of the ſaid Information and Charge againſt him; and HEARD *the ſame made* againſt him; and was *then and there aſked* by that Aſſemby ſo met in Common Council as aforeſaid, "Whether he the ſame *Joſeph Clegg* was the Perſon againſt "whom the ſaid Commiſſion of Bankrupt had ſo iſſued as aforeſaid;" And "Whether he the ſaid *Joſeph Clegg* was then a Bankrupt, and "had obtained his Certificate in that Behalf, or not:" And thereupon, the ſaid *Joſeph Clegg then and there* CONFESSED and ACKNOWLEDGED to the *ſame* Aſſembly ſo met in Common Council as aforeſaid, "That he the ſaid *Joſeph Clegg was the Perſon* againſt "whom the ſaid Commiſſion of Bankrupt had ſo iſſued as afore-"ſaid; And that he *was then a Bankrupt*, and had *not then obtained* "*his Certificate* in that Behalf."

Then the Return ſays, That the ſaid *Joſeph Clegg having ſo confeſſed the Truth of the abovementioned Charge* againſt him, as aforeſaid, He the ſaid *Joſeph Clegg* was then and there *further aſked* by the ſaid Aſſembly of the Mayor Bailiffs and the greater Part of the Common Council of the ſaid Town, "*What he the ſaid Joſeph Clegg had to ſay in his Defence*, Why he ſhould not be removed from "the ſaid Office of One of the Common Council of the ſaid Town "for the Cauſe aforeſaid;" And the ſaid *Joſeph Clegg* did NOT *then, or at any other Time* before his Removal in the Return after mentioned, *deſire any* FURTHER *Time* to be allowed him, to make his Defence to the Information and the Charge aforeſaid: And the ſaid *Joſeph Clegg did not*, either then or at any Time before his Removal in the Return after mentioned, *alledge* or *offer* to *that* Aſſembly ANY CAUSE WHATSOEVER why he ſhould not be diſcharged and removed from his ſaid Place or Office of One of the Common Council of the ſaid Town as aforeſaid. And *being rendered and become, by his aforeſaid Bankruptcy* and *by his not having obtained his Certificate* in that Behalf, UNFIT for the ſaid Place or Office of one of the Common Council of the ſaid Town, *being an Office* of great Truſt and Power as aforeſaid, It was then and there moved in the ſaid Aſſembly, *in the Preſence and Hearing of the ſaid Joſeph Clegg*, by One of the Common Council ſo aſſembled as aforeſaid, that is to ſay, by *F. G. &c*, "That the ſaid *Joſeph Clegg* ſhould be "removed

" removed from his ſaid Place or Office of one of the Common " Council of the ſame Town, for the Cauſe aforeſaid:" Whereof the ſaid *Joſeph Clegg* had then, and before his Removal from Office in the Return aftermentioned, due Notice. And the ſaid *Joſeph Clegg did not*, then or at any Time before his ſaid Removal therefrom in the Return after ſpecified, *alledge or offer* to the *ſame* Aſſembly *any Cauſe whatſoever* why he ſhould not be removed and diſcharged from his ſaid Place or Office. *Wherefore* the ſaid Aſſembly so *met* in Common Council as aforeſaid, and conſiſting of the ſaid then and now Mayor and Bailiffs and the greater Part of the then Common Council of the ſaid Town as aforeſaid, having heard and duly weighed and conſidered the Information and Charge aforeſaid, and what was alledged and admitted by the ſaid *Joſeph Clegg*, did *then and there* duly diſcharge and remove the ſaid *Joſeph Clegg* from the ſaid Place and Office of one of the Common Council of the ſaid Town, FOR THE CAUSE AFORESAID: And by reaſon thereof, he hath ever ſince remained and ſtill is and continues removed and diſcharged therefrom. And *therefore* they cannot reſtore Him or cauſe him to be reſtored, as by the ſaid Writ they are commanded.

Mr. *Winn* on Behalf of *Clegg*, the Proſecutor of the *Mandamus*, Objected to this Return: To which, he took two Exceptions; or in Effect, three, as the former was divided into two diſtinct Parts.

1ſt. The Aſſembly who amoved him was *not legally* CONVENED, for want of NOTICE, either to the *Reſt* of the Common Council, or to *Mr. Clegg himſelf*: who ought to have had Notice of it, both as One of the Members compoſing that Body, and alſo as the Member to be amoved.

2d Objection. The CAUSE of Amotion is inſufficient.

Firſt—Notice ought to have been given to *all* the Members; And conſequently *Mr. Clegg* ought to have had Notice, as He was *One of the conſtituent Members* of this Corporate Body. For EVERY individual *Member* of the Body ought to be *ſpecially* ſummoned, previous to the *Amotion* of any Member; A *General* Summons being always inſufficient, *wherever any extraordinary* Buſineſs is to be done.—Whereas this Return does *not ſhew any* Summons *at all*, to *any* of the conſtituent Members: And it is incumbent upon them to *ſhew* their own Juriſdiction; as it is a ſummary One, founded upon Charter, and not upon the Common Law.

The Words " in *due* Manner met and aſſembled *&c*," are only a *Concluſion of Law*: But the Court can *not intend* any *Facts* not alledged; For Returns muſt be taken *ſtrictly*. " Nothing is to be " intended

" intended in a Return to a *Mandamus*," is the Declaration of Ld. Ch. J. *Holt*, in 1 *Shower* 282. *Rex* v. *Evans*: Where the Court would not make even a very obvious Intendment. And ſo it is, in *all ſummary* Juriſdictions: As upon the Game-Laws, and ſuch like Caſes. So, upon Indictments alſo: As in 5 *Mod.* 96. *Rex* v. *Harper*; which was an Indictment for not taking upon him the Office of Conſtable, being qualified, and having been *debito modo* elected thereto; And the Objection was that the Indictment ought to have ſet out Particularly *how* he was choſen, and that he had Notice; Or elſe, the Indictment ought to be quaſhed.

The next Objection is, " That Mr. *Clegg* Himſelf, as the *Mem-* " *ber to be amoved*, was *not ſummoned to anſwer* to the particular " Charge, *upon which* He was to be amoved." 4 *Mod.* 337. *The City of Exeter* v. *Glide*, is expreſs, " That he muſt and ought to " have a *particular* Summons *for a particular Charge*: And it is " *not* ſufficient to ſummon him *generally*; and then to alledge parti- " cular Crimes againſt him, which he may not be prepared to an " ſwer." And *if* a *previous* particular Summons to Mr. *Clegg*, " To " anſwer the *particular Charge*," was neceſſary; his *Appearance* in the *ordinary* Courſe of his Duty will NOT *cure* this Defect.

And the very Nature of *this* Charge (of Bankruptcy) more eſpecially *requires a particular* Summons " to anſwer to it," becauſe it depends upon a great Number of *complicated* Facts. Here, he is not charged with any *particular* ACT of Bankruptcy; Nor is it alledged, that the Commiſſion even *ſubſiſted long enough* for him to have obtained a Certificate under it.

Second Point—The CAUSE of Amotion is *inſufficient*.

It imports Nothing of *Infamy* or *Offence*, for which he was *indictable*; Nor any the leaſt Neglect of or Offence againſt the *Duty of his Office* as a Corporator. *Every Trader* is liable to Bankruptcy; which may happen to him by Accident and Misfortune, and without any *Fault* of his own. Becoming Bankrupt is a *Misfortune*; *not a Crime*: It does not even neceſſarily import *Inſolvency*; Nor if it did, would *that* diſqualify him from remaining a Corporator.

There is only one Caſe to be met with, of an Amotion for Bankruptcy: Which was in *M.* 8 *G.* 2. *B.R. Rex* v. *Mayor and Aldermen of King's Lynn*, on a *Mandamus* to reſtore one *Stephen Allen* to the Office of Common Council Man; and was in the Time of Ld. *Hardwicke*: But Indeed, this particular Point did not come to be *determined*; becauſe the Return was held clearly inſufficient on *another* Foot, *viz.* for *want of Summons*, or even an *Attempt* to ſummon.

Here

Here, It appears that Mr. *Clegg* was *neither an Object of their Jurisdiction*; Nor was the *Cause of his Amotion sufficient.*

Therefore this Return being insufficient, He prayed a Peremptory *Mandamus* to restore him to the Office.

Mr. *Clayton contra*—Three Objections are made to this Return: *viz.*

1st. That it is not said that ALL the Members of this select Corporate Body were *summoned*;

2d. That *Clegg himself* had not previous *particular Notice of the Charge*, which was to be made upon him;

3d. That the *Cause* of Amotion is insufficient.

Answer. 1st The Corporate Body who had the Right to amove, is alledged to be " in DUE *Manner met and assembled.*" Now this Assembly possibly *might* be upon a *Charter* Day: And *then* No Special Summons was necessary.

Or if in Fact it was *not duly* holden, they might have *traversed* it: As was done in the Case of *Green* v. *Mayor of Durham, H.* 1757. 30 *G.* 2. (*V. ante, Pa.* 127.) There was a Case similar to the present, *P.* 8 *G.* 2. *B. R. Kynaston* v. *Mayor and Aldermen of Shrewsbury* * Where the Facts were *traversed* and tried. So here, *if* they were *not* duly summoned, or the Assembly *not* duly holden, they might have traversed these Allegations of the Facts, and taken Issue.

* *V.* 2 *Strange* 1051.

The *General* Summons is *sufficient*, I cannot find any Return which *avers* " That ALL the constituent Members *were summoned*, " or *had Notice* of the Assembly." And it is *unnecessary to aver it*; because since the *Mandamus* † Act, they may traverse it, and before the Act they might have had an Action for a false Return.

† 9 *Ann. c.* 20.

To 2d Objection—(of Want of Notice to *Clegg* Himself,) The Answer is, That his *Appearance* CURED the Defect, if there was One. 2 *Salk.* 428. *Rex* v. *Mayor and Burgesses of Wilton*, on a *Mandamus* to restore *Elias Chalk* to the Place of Burgess, is in Point, " That where the Person amoved has been *heard*, the Want of " Summons is *no* Objection." So it is, in Convictions upon the Game Laws. And here, Mr. *Clegg was heard*, and *admitted* all the Facts; and desired *no further Time.*

As to the 3d Objection—Here *is* a *reasonable Cause* of Amotion. This is *not* an Amotion from his FREEDOM of the Corporation; but only from being One of the COMMON COUNCIL: In *which* Character, he had the *Management* of very great *Revenues* of the Corporation, *viz.* 2000 *l. per Annum.*

In *Rex* v. *Mayor of King's Lynn, M.* 8 *G.* 2. *this* Point about the Bankruptcy being a sufficient Cause of Amotion, or not, was NOT * *entred into:* It went off upon the want of *Stephen Allen's* being summoned, or even of any Endeavour to summon him.

* It was objected to, by *Allen's* Counsel; but no further discussed; The Court having put it upon the Counsel Who endeavoured to support the Amotion of *Allen*, to answer, in the first Place, to the Want of Summons.

It is objected, "That the *particular Acts* of Bankruptcy are not stated."

Answer—This Defect also (if it be any) is *cured* by his Appearance and Confession "That he *was* a Bankrupt, and had not obtained his Certificate."

Mr. *Winn*, in Reply—

1st. We are *not obliged* to take Issue upon the being "duly assembled." They ought to *shew* their own Jurisdiction: And therefore as the Assembly *does not appear* to have been holden upon a *Charter*-Day, they ought to have shewn either a *Special*, or at least a *General* Summons to the *several constituent Members* of it.

2dly. Mr. *Clegg* could not be *prepared* to defend himself against this complicated Charge, without previous Notice; although he *happened* to be *casually* present, in the Discharge of his General Duty to the Corporation.

3dly. It does not appear that Mr. *Clegg* was not *intitled* to his Certificate, though he had not had Time to obtain it.

And as to any *personal* Trust or Power as to the Revenue of the Corporation—He was not, *as* Common Council Man, PERSONALLY to receive and disburse the Estate of the Corporation, or to finger any of their Cash.

The Commission does not at all affect him in his *Corporate* Capacity.

Lord MANSFIELD said He had no Doubt at present: Though He would not preclude a further Argument if the Parties should not agree to his Reasons.

It is certainly true, He said, that where an Amotion is returned, the Return must set out *all the necessary Facts, precisely*; to shew that the Person is removed in a legal and proper Manner, and for a legal Cause. It is *not* sufficient to set out *Conclusions* only: They must set the *Facts themselves* out, precisely; that the Court may be able to judge of the Matter. And so it is also, as to the *Cause* of Amotion: *This* must be set out in the same Manner; that the Court may judge of it.

Here, Three Objections have been made.

1st. That supposing this *select* Body of the Corporation to have Authority to remove, (and to which no Exception is taken,) and abstractedly from the particular Cause of the present Amotion, yet it does not appear that the *Constituent Members* of the Body who made the Amotion were *summoned at all*, to this Meeting: Whereas, it not appearing to be a Meeting directed by the Charter, there ought to have been a *Special*, or at least a *General* NOTICE given to *each individual Member* of it, "That there was to be such a Meeting."

2dly. That it is also absolutely necessary, that *Mr. Clegg*, the Person intended to be amoved, should have had a *particular Summons*, "To answer to the particular Charge." To which it is answered, "That this is *cured*, by his * Appearance and * Confession and "not desiring further Time. I will say Nothing at all about *this* Matter; the 1st and 3d Objections being clear, full, and fatal. * *V. post.*

3dly. That the *Cause* of Amotion is insufficient.

Now as to the first. It is certain that no Summons of any of the Members is alledged in the Return: Whereas, if a *select* Number of a Corporation have Power to remove, and do amove at a Meeting holden upon a *Day not directed by Charter &c*, ALL that are within Summons, must be summoned. And so was Mr. *Kynaston*'s Case determined in *Tr.* 8, 9 *G.* 2. in this Court.

And it is not sufficient to alledge, "That they were *duly*, or in "*due Manner*, met and assembled:" It ought to be *expresly* alledged, "that they were ALL *summoned*,"

The Traverse, therefore, which it is said might have been here taken, would not go to the *Fact itself*, but only to the *legal Consequence*: And therefore they could not be obliged to traverse, in the present Case.

There-

Therefore this is a flat Objection.

As to the 2d I will ſay Nothing.

But as to the 3d Objection—*This* Point has never yet been determined.

The Caſe of *King's Lynn* turned upon the Want of Summons.

No Cauſe is *reaſonable*, unleſs it be *juſt* and *legal:* A *juſt*, a *legal*, a *ſufficient*, a *reaſonable* Cauſe, All mean the ſame thing; The only Difference is in the different Epithets.

* *V. ante* 538. S. P. (rather more at large) *Rex* v. *Richardſon*, *P.* 1758. 31 G. 2. *B.R.*

The * 3 Cauſes of Amotion of a Corporator, are (1ſt.) Offences againſt the *Duty of his Office*, as a Corporator; (2dly.) Crimes in their *own Nature* heinous and atrocious, and againſt the Offender's *general* Duty, *as a Subject*; yet not particularly relating to his Corporate Office or Duty; and (3dly.) Such as are of a *mixt* Nature.

Let Us therefore conſider the preſent Cauſe alledged for the Amotion, in theſe three Views.

1ſt. His mere being a Bankrupt is *no* Objection to his continuing a *Corporator:* It is no Offence againſt the *Duty of his Office*. He may become Bankrupt, *without his own Fault*. And there is no *Cenſus* requiſite as a Qualification to be a Corporator. Indeed ſome one or more of the *Conſequences* of Bankruptcy may *eventually become* a Cauſe of Amotion: But the Bankruptcy itſelf is not ſo. A Man may be able to pay above 20 Shillings in the Pound, notwithſtanding his being in Strictneſs a Bankrupt: Or he may very ſoon obtain a Certificate, after the Commiſſion has iſſued.

* *V. ante, pa.* 717.

2dly. It is *no* Offence againſt the *Law of the Land*. Bankrupts are *not now* conſidered as Criminals; whatever the * Old Acts may intimate of this kind. A Man may certainly be a Bankrupt, without being guilty of any *Crime* whatſoever; and may really be worth a large Surplus on a Balance: Sir *Stephen Evans*, and the *Woodwards*, and many Others have been Inſtances of this.

And this Diſ-franchiſing for becoming Bankrupt might be made a very bad Uſe of, by Juntoes in Corporations, or under particular Circumſtances, and with particular Views. A Run upon a Man of great Fortune and Credit may be artfully managed, ſo as to reduce him to Bankruptcy. And there is no Difference between a *Common-Council*-Man's becoming a Bankrupt, and an *ordinary* Freeman's becoming ſo.

As to the Truſt and Power over the *Revenues* of the Corporation— *This* Man is only One Member of the Number of *One and forty*, who have amongſt them, a Power of voting Corporate Acts: But he has nothing to do with the Receipt, or Truſt, or Management, or Fingering of the MONEY; nor *can* have any thing to do with it, unleſs the Reſt ſhould, by a Corporate Act of their *own*, truſt him with it.

Therefore the having become a Bankrupt, and not having obtained his Certificate under the Commiſſion awarded againſt him, is not, of itſelf, *alone*, ſufficient to diſqualify him from being a Member of the Common Council of this Town; whatever *might* have been the Caſe, if certain eventual Conſequences had happened to follow therefrom.

Therefore the 1ſt and 3d Objections are fatal: Which renders it unneceſſary to enter at all into the Diſcuſſion of the 2d Objection, and of the Anſwer that has been given to it.

Mr. Juſt. DENISON concurred with His Lordſhip in Opinion.

This Return is by no Means a ſufficient Return. Bankruptcy *alone* is no ſufficient Cauſe of Removal. There muſt have been, in Fact, many Inſtances of ſuch Bankruptcies of Corporators. I ſuppoſe the Queſtion was never determined, becauſe the Fact of it was * never made a Queſtion.

* In the Caſe of *King's Lynn*, there were other Cauſes of Amoving *Allen*, beſides his being a Bankrupt; namely, Non-Reſidence, Abſence, and Neglect of Duty.

In the Caſe of *Lynn*, they had never even endeavoured to ſummon him: And not a Word was ſaid about the Bankruptcy, by the *Court*, on determining the Caſe.

As to the 1ſt Objection in the preſent Caſe—They ſhould have ſhewn, in their Return, *which* were their *general* Days of Meeting, fixed by the Charter. But here it is an Amotion by a Meeting of a *ſelect* Number; Who ought *Every one of them* to have Notice, when they are to proceed on *particular* Buſineſs: Whereas it is not here pretended, by any direct Allegation, that they had any Notice at all. It is ſaid indeed, "That they were in *due Manner* "met and aſſembled." But a Return ought to be *certain*; and it ought as much to be ſo, *ſince* the Act of Parliament, as before.

They were *not obliged* to traverſe this Allegation of the Meeting being "duly aſſembled:" And indeed it would have been a Traverſe of *Conſequences*, not of *Facts*.

All the Members of the ſelect Body ought to have had *particular* Notice.

* *V. post.* 738. *Rex v. Mayor &c. of Doncaster.*

As to the 2d Objection—I think the * *Party Himself ought* to have had previous Notice. But, however, there are many *other* Objections to the Return: And therefore I will not meddle with *that*.

3dly. The *Cause* of this Amotion is certainly *insufficient*. For surely a Man may become a Bankrupt, without being guilty of *any Offence* at all; either against his *private* Office and Duty of a Common Council-Man, or against the Law of the *Land*. I have no Notion that being a Bankrupt will disqualify a Man from being a Common Council-Man or a Corporator. And the not obtaining his Certificate is an immaterial Circumstance: It was not in his Power; or he might not have had Time to do it.

And he had not the *Management of the Revenues* of the Corporation, so as to have any Concern in the *collecting* them. It does not appear that he had any thing to do with fingering the *Cash* of the Corporation; or that their pecuniary Interests could at all *suffer* by his having become a Bankrupt.

Upon the Whole therefore, it seems very clear that this is a bad Return, and ought to be quashed; and that a Peremptory *Mandamus* ought to issue.

Mr. Just. Foster declared Himself of the same Opinion. They ought, He said, either to have set out an Assembly upon a *Charter*-Day, or a *general* Summons to the component Members of this *select* Body who amoved. He added, I cannot go so far as to say that a *Special* Summons was necessary, setting forth the *particular* Business upon which they were to treat: But I think a *General* Summons, to *every* Member, was necessary.

As to the 2d Objection—I shall not say much upon it. But a Man ought not to be dispossessed of his Freehold, without having a *proper* Opportunity of making a *Defence* to the Charge upon which He is removed from it. He could not be prepared, in the present Case, to defend himself against *this particular* Charge: He ought to have been apprised what it was to be. There might be an Opportunity taken, when there was a thin Meeting, and when all his Friends were absent, who would perhaps have been present, if he had any Notice of *this* or even of *any* Charge against him.

As to the 3d Objection—The *Cause* of Amotion is *not* sufficient. *Bankruptcy alone* is *not* so. And the not having obtained his Certificate is not at all material: He might not have had Time or Opportunity to obtain it; or it might have been opposed, on purpose.

Bankruptcy does not neceſſarily import *Inſolvency*. But *Inſolvency itſelf* is no Cauſe of Amotion, where the Corporator is *not intruſted* with the Receipt of the Corporation's *Money*. And here he is not intruſted with a Penny of their Money: It is not alledged that he had any thing to do with their *Caſh*.

Therefore, upon the whole, This Return is bad, and ought to be quaſhed; and a Peremptory *Mandamus* ought to go.

Mr. Juſt. Wilmot was of the ſame Opinion.

He confined himſelf, (as Lord *Mansfield* had done,) to the firſt and third Objections, only.

1ſt. If the Aſſembly is not holden upon a *Charter*-Day or a *general* Day of Meeting, there muſt be a previous Summons to *every* Member; either *General*, or *Special*: I rather think, it ought to be *Special*; that every Member may come *prepared*, and have an Opportunity to give his Reaſons to his Brethren; which may perhaps alter their Opinion. But clearly there ought to be *a* previous Summons, *either* general, *or* ſpecial; and this, to every individual Member.

The Allegation of their being "duly *met and aſſembled*," is a *Complication* of Fact and Law; and therefore *not properly traverſable*: The *particular Facts* ought to be alledged upon the Record. The Act of 9 *Ann*. *c*. 20. makes no Difference at all: It is juſt the ſame *ſince*, as it was before this Act.

As to the 3d Objection—*Bankruptcy alone* is *no* ſufficient Cauſe of Amotion. He had nothing to do with the *Money* of the Corporation. Indeed *no Inſolvency* at all appears: Nor, if it did, is it an *Offence*. Bankruptcy alone is no Offence either againſt the Duty of his *Office* as a Corporator, nor any Offence or Crime rendering him infamous at *Common* Law.

Therefore this Return is inſufficient, and ought to be quaſhed; And there ought to be a peremptory *Mandamus*.

Per Cur. unanimouſly,
Let there be a Peremptory Mandamus.

Rule to quaſh the Return; and that a Peremptory *Mandamus* do iſſue.

Bailey

Thursday 1st February 1759.

Bailey *verſ.* Dillon.

MR. *Williams* ſhewed Cauſe why the Defendant ſhould not be *diſcharged upon* COMMON *Bail.*

The Caſe was this—The Defendant, *being indebted to the Plaintiff*, became a *Bankrupt*. The Commiſſion iſſued on the 7th of *May* 1754. The Bankrupt obtained his *Certificate:* Which was ſigned on the 30th of *Auguſt* 1754, and allowed in the *September* following, In *September* or *November* 1755, the now Plaintiff, who was One of this Bankrupt's Creditors as aforeſaid, and did not appear to have come in under the Commiſſion, produced to the Defendant an Account between them (prior to the Commiſſion;) upon which Account, there was a Ballance due to the Plaintiff from the Defendant, of 74 *l.* and upwards, remaining *due at the* TIME *of the Bankruptcy*. The Defendant deſired Time to examine it: And then acknowledged that this Ballance was due to the Plaintiff, and PROMISED "*to pay* it to the Plaintiff, WHEN *He ſhould be* "ABLE."

So that the GENERAL *Queſtion* ariſing upon this Caſe, will hereafter be "Whether a Perſon indebted to Another, and afterwards "becoming *Bankrupt*, and then being *regularly diſcharged*, by having duly conformed himſelf to the Bankrupt-Acts, and having "obtained his Certificate; but afterwards making a *new Acknowledgment* of the ſame Debt being due, and alſo a *new* PROMISE *to* "*pay it*, ſhall or ſhall not be LIABLE *to the Payment* of it:" But

The *particular* Queſtion *now* before the Court was ſingly, "Whether he ought to be *diſcharged* upon COMMON *Bail*, or *holden* to "SPECIAL *Bail*." For this alone was the Motion which Mr. *Norton* had made, and againſt which Mr. *Williams* now ſhewed Cauſe.

Mr. *Williams* argued, on Behalf of the Plaintiff, That this is a *new Debt*, founded upon a Promiſe made on a good and ſufficient Conſideration, *viz.* on a CONSCIENTIOUS *Obligation.*

He compared it to Caſes of new Promiſes made after the Expiration of the Six Years; which ſhall *revive* Debts barred by the Statute of Limitations: As that of *Dean* v. *Crane*, in 6 *Mod.* 309; and *Andrews* v. *Brown et Ux'*, in *Precedents in Chancery* 385. And ſo, the Bankrupt Acts muſt be taken favourably for Creditors.

A much ſtronger Inſtance, is the Caſe of an Infant, who *after full Age*, ratifies a Contract for Goods, not being Neceſſaries, by his

his Promiſe to pay for them. For which, he cited *Southerton* v. *Whitlock*, in 1 *Strange* 690: Where Ld. *Raymond*, at *Guildhall*, held "that the Infant was *bound*, in ſuch a Caſe." Yet the Infant was full as much diſcharged of the Contract, in that Caſe, as this Bankrupt was, in the preſent Caſe.

But * this Act which gives the Diſcharge by Certificate, was made for the *Benefit* of the Bankrupt; and therefore he may *wave* this Benefit: Which here he has done. Conſequently, it is not at all *within* the Act of Parliament. * *V. ante* 717.

As to the Caſe of *Turner* v. *Schomberg*, in 2 *Strange* 1233. there was *no good Conſideration* to found the Promiſe. The Defendant had there given his Note for 36 *l.* and was afterwards *diſcharged* on the Inſolvent Debtors Act: Afterwards, he promiſed to pay the Debt, at 2 Guineas *per* Month; Part whereof, he paid; and was arreſted for the Remainder. There, he was diſcharged indeed on Common Bail: And it was holden to be no new Conſideration, but the *old* Debt. And ſo it was.

Mr. *Norton* was ſtopt by the Court, from proceeding to argue, on Behalf of the Defendant, in anſwer to what Mr. *Williams* had urged. For

The Court held it quite unneceſſary to enter into the *general* and *principal* Queſtion, or to enter at all into the *Merits* of the Caſe, upon this preſent Motion: Since it would be very improper to determine ſuch a Point in this Method, upon a Queſtion about Special or Common Bail. Therefore they ſaid they would not meddle with the Merits, nor give any Opinion at all upon the *general* Queſtion. But

As to the *particular* Queſtion, which was the Subject of the preſent Motion, they were unanimous "that he ought to be diſ-" charged upon *Common* Bail." For

Lord Mansfield obſerved that the preſent Queſtion is no more than "Whether this Promiſe made by the Defendant under the "Circumſtances ſtated, and founded only upon a *conſcientious* Obli-" gation ſhall intitle the Plaintiff to keep him *in Priſon*." This would be taking Advantage of his *Conſcientiouſneſs*, to uſe it *againſt* Conſcience.

Mr. Juſt. Foster added, that the Caſe in 2 *Strange* 1233 determines, directly in Point, the Queſtion as to *Bail*. And

Mr. Just. WILMOT thought that Case to be even stronger than this.

Per Cur. unanimously,

RULE made absolute, to discharge the Defendant upon COMMON Bail.

Saturday 3d February 1759.

Rex *vers.* Mayor Aldermen and Burgesses of Doncaster.

A *Mandamus to restore Theosebius James Buckley Wilsford* to the Office of One of the *Capital Burgesses* of the Corporation of *Doncaster*.

The Mayor Aldermen and Burgesses return that they were a Burrough by Prescription, and were incorporated by Charter on the 2d of *May* 16 *C.* 2. with Power to make By-Laws *&c*, and to inforce them by Fines *&c*: Which Charter fixed *the Thursday next after Bartholomew-Day*, yearly, for the Mayor Aldermen and Capital Burgesses to meet together, for the Election of a Mayor; who should take his Oath of Office on the *Thursday* next before *Michaelmas*; and made Provision for a new Election, in Case of Death or Amotion, and also for filling up the vacant Places of deceased or amoved Aldermen and Burgesses. Then it alledges the Acceptance of these Letters Patent. Then it shews that the said *Theosebius James Buckley Wilsford*, on the 6th of *September* 1737 was elected chosen sworn and admitted a Capital Burgess. Then it alledges, that after the making and Acceptance of the Letters Patent, and before the issuing of this Writ of *Mandamus*, by Indenture made the 21st of *July* 1745, between the Mayor Aldermen and Burgesses of *Doncaster* of the one Part, and One *Thomas Smith* of the other Part, for the Considerations therein mentioned, the said Mayor Aldermen and Burgesses *did* DEMISE AND TO FARM LET *to the said* THOMAS SMITH divers Lands and Tenements of the said Mayor Aldermen and Burgesses, situate and being, or therein mentioned to be situate and being, at *Balby* in the said County of *York*; To hold to the said *Thomas Smith* his Executors Administrators and Assigns, from the 29th Day of *September* then last past before the Date thereof, for and during the full Term of ten Years from thenceforth next ensuing, at and under the Yearly Rent of 26*l.* 10*s.* payable half-yearly at *Lady-day* and *Michaelmas* by even and equal Portions.

Then they return That the said Mayor Aldermen and Burgesses, for a great Number of Years last past, have had and kept, and now have and keep a PUBLIC BOOK *for the use of the said Mayor Aldermen and Burgesses*, AS *a Corporation or Body Politic:* In which

Book, the *Orders and Resolutions* of the Mayor Aldermen and Burgesses of the said Burrough, for the Time being, AS *a Body Politic, relating to the said Burrough, and the Orders and Resolutions of the Common Council* of the said Burrough for the Time being, and also the *Accounts of the Estates* of the said Mayor Aldermen and Burgesses as a Body Politic, from Time to Time have been *written and entered for the Use of the said Body Corporate*; and *to which public Book, Each Capital Burgess* of the said Burrough, as a Member of the Common Council of the said Burrough, has, from Time to Time, at all reasonable Times, *had Access*.

They further certify and return That after the Making and Acceptance of the said Letters Patent, and before the Issuing of the *Mandamus*, to wit, on the 5th of *March* 1747, *at a Common Council* of and for the said Burrough duly assembled and held in the said Burrough, it was *Resolved and Ordered by the said Common Council* then and there so assembled, *amongst other Things*, "That at the "Expiration of the then present Lease made by the said Corpora-"tion to the said *Thomas Smith*, the Lands thereby demised should "be let to *some Other Person*:" And which Resolution and Order was afterwards, to wit, on the 6th Day of *March* in the said Year 1747, duly written and entered in the said public Book of the said Mayor Aldermen and Burgesses of the said Burrough.

And they further certify and return That after the making and Acceptance of the said Letters Patent, and before the Issuing of the Writ, to wit, on the 10th Day of *February* 1756, at the said Burrough of *Doncaster*, He the said *Theosebius James Buckley Wilsford*, then and there being One of the Capital Burgesses of the said Burrough, and also a Member of the Common Council of the same Burrough, and then and there well knowing that the last mentioned Resolution and Order was then written and entered in the said Public Book. He the said *Theosebius James Buckley Wilsford did unlawfully knowingly* and *wilfully*, and CONTRARY to the *Duty of his said Office* of one of the Capital Burgesses of the said Burrough, and *without the* CONSENT of the then Mayor Aldermen and Burgesses of the said Burrough, and also *without the* CONSENT of the then Common Council of the said Burrough, DEFACE AND OBLITERATE *the* ENTRY of the last mentioned Resolution and Order so written made and entered in the said Public Book as aforesaid; *To the* GREAT *Damage* of the Mayor Aldermen and Burgesses of the said Burrough.

They further return that afterwards, at an *Assembly* of the Mayor Aldermen and Burgesses of the said Burrough, held in and for the said Burrough of *Doncaster* in the *Guildhall* of the same Burrough, on the *7th Day of March* in the Year of our Lord 1757, They being

* *Vide ante* 731, 733, 734, 735. *Rex* v. *Mayor* &c. *of Liverpool* (Clegg's Case.)

being so * DULY assembled for the good Rule and Government of the said Burrough; and *George Waterer* Esq; the then Mayor of the same Burrough, and also the said *Theosebius James Buckley Wilsford*, then One of the Capital Burgesses of the said Burrough, being then and there *present*; He the said *Theosebius James Buckley Wilsford* was then and there, *at and in the* SAME *Assembly*, *charged and accused* "That He had defaced and obliterated the said Entry of the "last mentioned Resolution and Order so written made and entered "in the said Public Book as aforesaid:" And the said *Charge and Accusation* was thereupon *read to* the said *T. J. B. W.* then and there, at and in the *same Assembly*; And he was *asked*, by *Richard Sheppard* Gent. then the Common Clerk of the Mayor Aldermen and Burgesses of the said Burrough of *Doncaster* then and there present, and then and there the proper Officer on that Behalf, and by the Command of the said *George Waterer* then the Mayor of the same Burrough, "If "he had or knew any thing to say for himself, in his Defence against "the Charge aforesaid." And the said *T. J. B. W.* thereupon, at and in the *same* Assembly then and there DID CONFESS AND ACKNOWLEDGE "That he *did deface and obliterate the said Entry* of "the said Resolution and Order so written made and entered in the "said Public Book as aforesaid, and with which he was then and "there charged as aforesaid:" And he did *not then or there shew* any sufficient Cause why he should not *therefore be removed and displaced* from his said Office of One of the Capital Burgesses of the said Burrough of *Doncaster*; Nor *did then or there require or desire to have any further Day or Time* to be allowed him to make a Defence to the said Charge, or to shew Cause why he should not be removed and displaced from his Place and Office of One of the Capital Burgesses of the said Burrough, for the said Offence. Whereupon *the* SAID *Assembly* of the Mayor Aldermen and Burgesses of the said Burrough, having taken the Case of the said *T. J. B. W.* into Consideration, and having fully and deliberately weighed the same, did then and there Order that the said *T. J. B. W.* FOR *his* SAID *Offence*, should be REMOVED AND DISCHARGED from his said Place and Office of One of the Capital Burgesses of the said Burrough: And the said *T. J. B. W. was then and there accordingly*, by the said Mayor Aldermen and Burgesses of the same Burrough so *assembled as aforesaid*, then and there *removed and discharged* from his said Place and Office of One of the Capital Burgesses of the said Burrough of *Doncaster*.

They also further return the said *T. J. B. W.* at any Time since his being so removed as aforesaid, hath not been nominated elected sworn admitted or restored to or into the Place and Office of One of the Capital Burgesses of the said Burrough of *Doncaster*.

And for these Reasons, They cannot restore or cause to be restored the said *T. J. B. W.* into the aforesaid Place and Office of One of the Capital Burgesses of the Burrough aforesaid, with all the Liberties and Franchises to the said Place and Office belonging and appertaining, as by the said Writ they are commanded to do.

N. B. Mr. *Wilsford* had at first *traversed* the several Facts alledged in the Return; and Seven Issues were joined thereupon: But he afterwards deserted his Traverses, and set the Return down in the *Paper*, to be argued upon it's Validity in Law.

Qu. concerning the *Regularity* of this, if it had been objected to.

Mr. *Gould*, on Behalf of the Prosecutor, objected to this Return.

1st. That the ASSEMBLY which made this Amotion does *not* appear to have been *legally holden*; for want of it's being stated that *particular Notice* was given previously, to the *Members* of the Corporation, "That this *particular Business, of the Amotion* of this Capital Burgess, was *intended* to be thereat proceeded upon."

2dly. That *no sufficient Cause* of Amotion is *properly set out*: For the Sole Foundation of the Amotion is rested upon his *Confession* of a *Charge* which is *itself defective*; As the Charge itself, after giving a Narrative of the Fact, *only in general* alledges it to have been done "to the *great Damage* of the Corporation," but does NOT SPECIFY *any* PARTICULAR Damage, that they suffered in Consequence of it.

3dly. That the Corporation had no Power to amove him for an *Offence such* as THIS *is*, WITHOUT *a previous Conviction* at Common Law.

But before he entered particularly into these Objections, He first *premised in general*, That Returns to *Mandamuses* ought to be *certain*; And that every Thing ought to be intended *against* such Return. To prove which He cited 6 *Mod.* 309. *Queen* v. *Mayor of Hereford.* 2 *Salk.* 432. *Rex* v. *Mayor of Abingdon*, (the 2d Point of it.) 1 *Shower* 364. *Glyde*'s Case; *Rex* v. *Mayor and Aldermen of Exeter*. And this Precision is *equally necessary*, * *since* the 9 *Ann.* c. 20. *as before* that Act. * *V. ante, pa.* 733, 734.

He then enlarged upon his 3 Objections.

First—This Amotion was made by the *whole* Body Politic, *not* by a select Part of it; on a * *By*-Day, *not* upon the Charter-Day; and upon a * GENERAL *Summons* to meet to transact the Business of the Corporation, *not* upon a particular Notice to meet upon *this particular Affair*.

* *V. ante, pa.* 731 to 736.

Every Corporation has an Interest in Each of its Members: Which is proved by the Case of the Burrough of *Wigan*. *Tr.* 27 *G.* 2. *B. R.*

And a Resignation of a Corporate Interest cannot be made to a select Body. *Rex* v. *Powell B. R.* 5 or 6 Terms ago.

In the Case of *Kynaston* v. *Mayor and Aldermen of Shrewsbury*, It was settled, that upon an Amotion on a Day which is *not* the Gene-" ral Charter-Day, *Every* Member must be summoned."

Second Objection—The Lease mentioned in the Return was made by the *whole* Corporation. He observed also that the Expression was " amongst other Things:" And cited 2 *Salk.* 417. *Rex* v. *Bear.* This is *not an Offence sufficient* to ground an Amotion from his Freehold upon; there being *no particular Damage* to the Corporation specified or even alledged. 11 *Co.* 99. *James Bagg*'s Case. *Carthew* 176. Sir *Thomas Earle*'s Case.

Third Objection—Admitting (for Argument's Sake) the Cause of Amotion to be in it's own Nature sufficient, Yet neverthelesss there ought to have been a PREVIOUS *Conviction* at Common Law; As this Offence is both an Offence against the Duty of his Office as a Corporator, *And also* indictable at Common Law.

He cited *Rex* v. *Mayor of Derby*, *Tr.* 8, 9 *G.* 2. *B. R:* Where Ld. *Hardwicke* fully explained this Subject, and cited the Case of *Rex* v. *Mayor of Wilton*, (which Case is imperfectly reported in *Comberb.* 396. by the Name of *Rex* v. *Chalk*; and is the same Case with *Rex* v. *Mayor and Burgesses of Wilton* in 5 *Mod.* 257, and in 2 *Salk.* 428. *Pl.* 2.) Where the Offence was striking out One Name and putting in another: And his Lordship also cited *Parrot*'s Case, *Queen* v. *Mayor of Newcastle*, *M.* 8 *Ann. B. R.* and *M.* 8 *G.* 1. *B. R.* the Case of *Carlisle*, " for corrupting a Member of the Corpora-" tion to give a Vote;" where the Court were equally divided. Which Cases, Mr. *Gould* said, were cited by Ld. *Hardwicke*, to shew the *uncertain* State wherein this Matter then stood; and which His Lordship and the Court left to be determined and settled, when a proper Case should come directly in Judgment to require it.

Mr. *Gould* therefore urged that if the present Offence be of such a Magnitude as to amount to a sufficient Cause of Amotion, there ought to have been a *previous Conviction* at Common Law: because it might otherwise happen, that he might afterwards (subsequently to his Amotion) be indicted *and* ACQUITTED, in which Case there would be *contrary Judgments* upon the same Fact.

And this Objection is not answered by comparing such contrary Judgments to Cases where the Temporal and Spiritual Courts are *both* permitted to proceed upon the same Fact; because *they* proceed *diverso intuitu*. For in this Case, the *Corporation* would be obliged to look upon the Temporal Verdict as *Evidence*; Whereas the *Spiritual* Court do *not* receive a Verdict as Evidence, at least not as *conclusive*.

Mr. *Luke Robinson contra*, for the Return.

As to what Mr. *Gould* had in general premised, He observed that the *Reason* of requiring such precise Certainty in a Return to a *Mandamus* is *at an End*, * since the Statute of 9 *Ann. c.* 20: Since which Act, the Law may be ascertained by a Demurrer; or the Fact tried by Traverses. * *Sed V. ante* 733, 734.

The Reason given by the Ch. J. in 2 *Salk.* 432. is *now* a Reason *against* requiring such Precision: And Mr. Just. *Eyres* goes too far in *Glyde*'s Case, in saying "That *every* Thing shall be intended "against a Return."

The three Objections are (1st.) To the Want of previous *Notice* of the *particular Business* to be transacted at the Corporate Assembly; (2dly.) To the *Cause* of Amotion; Which is urged to be insufficient; (3dly.) To the Want of a previous *Conviction*.

First—*No* such *Special Notice* is at all necessary: And besides, this Mr. *Wilsford* was † *present*, and *confessed* the Charge. And neither the Case of *Wigan*, nor that of *Shrewsbury*, are applicable to the present Case. † *V. ante* 731, 734.

Secondly—The Offence charged *is* a *sufficient Cause* of Amotion: And it is *not necessary* to specify HOW, *in particular*, the Corporation has been damnified by it; it being alledged to be "to the Damage "of the Corporation," which is enough. And neither *Bugg*'s Case, nor *Carthew* 176. will support Mr. *Gould*'s Objection.

Thirdly—It would not have been easy to describe this Offence so as to get the Party convicted of it at Common Law. However, a a previous Conviction is NOT *neceſſary* in *this* Caſe; which is that of a Miſdemeanour contrary to his Oath and to the Duty of his Office, but is *not* an *infamous* Offence.

As to the Caſes of *Derby*, of *Wilton*, and of *Newcaſtle*, they are no Authorities: For Mr. *Gould* admits the Point to have been uncertain, and to have been left ſo by Ld. *Hardwicke*. But

In 1 *Keb.* 597. *The Town of Wigan* v. *Pilkington*, an Alderman of that Burrough, The Amotion was holden good on a *Mandamus*; *without* any previous Conviction; for that, contrary to his Oath, he *ſpoliavit et dilaceravit quædam Recorda* of ſuch a Court.

Mr. *Gould* in Reply—As to the general Poſitions premiſed—

Mr. *Robinſon* allows that *Preciſion* was neceſſary in a Return to a *Mandamus*, *before* the 9 *Ann. c.* 20. But that Act does *not excuſe* the Neceſſity of ſuch Preciſion in the Return; though it gives a Traverſe to the Material Facts alledged in it.

1ſt Objection. If Notice had been given of this intended Amotion, ſome Member or other who had thereupon attended, might perhaps have given ſuch Reaſons to the Aſſembly, as might have altered their Opinions. And this Argument holds equally ſtrong, in the Caſe of a Corporate Aſſembly of the *whole* Body, upon a Day which is *not* a Charter or Preſcription Day, as it does in the Caſe of a * *Select* Body.

* *Vide ante* 731, 733, 734, 735. *Rex* v. *Mayor &c. of Liverpool.*

2d Objection. It ought to be ſuch an Offence as tends to the *Deſtruction*, or *Injury* at leaſt, of the Corporation. And *Bagg*'s Caſe, and *Carthew* 176. prove this.

3dly. Ld. *Hardwicke* conſidered this Point of a previous Conviction as *unſettled*, in *Tr.* 8, 9 *G.* 2.

Lord MANSFIELD obſerved that Corporation-Law ought to be *well* ſettled: And therefore He was willing to hear it argued again. ULTERIUS CONCILIUM.

This former Argument, juſt now recited, was on *Saturday* the 25th of *November* laſt; And it now ſtood in the Paper for further Argument. But

Mr. *Yates*, who was to have argued for the Corporation, gave up the Return; The firſt Objection taken to it, being the ſame Point as was determined on *Wedneſday* laſt, in the Caſe of † *Rex* v. *Mayor* *Bailiffs*

† See the 1ſt Point of that Caſe.

Bailiffs and Common Council of Liverpool (*Clegg*'s Case) *ante pa.* 723 to 736.

Whereupon the like Rule was taken, as was made in that Case; *viz.* That the RETURN be quashed, And that a Peremptory *Mandamus* do issue.

Rex *verf.* Hartshorn et al'.

MR. *Caldecot* moved in *Trinity* Term last, (*Wednesday* 31st of *May* 1758,) to quash an Order made (*originally*) at the *General* Quarter Sessions, upon the Surveyors of the Highways of *Roston* for the Years 1751, 2, 3, 4, 5 and 6. "to pass their Ac-"counts respectively, and pay over the Money assessed and col-"lected &c, to the present Overseer &c."

He took 2 Exceptions: *viz.*

1st. The *original Application* ought to have been to a *Special* Sessions: For the *General* Quarter Sessions have no Authority *originally*, but ONLY *upon Appeal.* To prove which, he alledged 3, 4 *W.* & *M. c.* 12. § 9. 1 *Hawk. P. C.* 218. § 80.

2d Exception—This Order "for Overseers *so long out of Office*, "as 1751, 2, 3, &c, to pay over to the *present* Overseers," is not right: For Each ought to pay over to his *immediate* Successor.

A Rule having been afterwards obtained by the other Side, to shew Cause "Why the *Certiorari* should not be quashed."

Mr. *Caldecott*, on *Monday* 27th of *November* last, shewed Cause against the * *Certiorari* being quashed: Which Cause was "That "the *Prosecutors had enlarged* the Rule for shewing Cause why the "*Order* should not be quashed." Which

The COURT held to be a *sufficient Cause*; And that it was *too late*, *after* having *themselves enlarged that Rule*, to object to the *issuing* of the *Certiorari*.

Which being determined against the Prosecutors, The former Rule (to shew Cause why the *Order* should not be quashed,) was enlarged to the present Term.

Now, Mr. *Lee*, who shewed Cause against quashing the *Order*, first cited † *Rex* v. *Wakefield et al'*, *H.* 1758. 31 *G.* 2. *B. R.* to

* *V.* § 23 of 3, 4 *W.* & *M. c.* 12. "that No Order made *by Virtue* of that Act, shall be removed by *Certiorari*" Yet if the *Quarter* Sessions make an *original* Order, a *Certiorari* will lie; *per Hawkins*, *lib.* 1, *c.* 76. § 80.

† *V. ante* 485.

ſhew that the *Certiorari* and Return would not ſtand in his Way: And then proceeded to anſwer the Objections that had been made to the Order.

He began with the firſt; namely, to the Juriſdiction of the General Quarter Seſſions, as there had been *no previous Application* to a Special Seſſions. His Anſwer to this Objection was, that This was by *Conſent*.

Mr. Juſt. FOSTER obſerved, that *Conſent* cannot GIVE *Juriſdiction* to a Court that has *none*: And here the Objection is, "that this Court "of General Quarter Seſſions had NO *Original* Juriſdiction.

Per Cur.
ORDER of the Quarter Seſſions QUASHED.

Chauvet and Another *verſ.* Alfray.

MR. *Baynham*, on Behalf of the Defendant in Error, ſhewed Cauſe, why the *Fieri facias* ſhould not be ſet aſide, and the Goods levied be reſtored.

This was an Action of Debt upon a Bond, given to the Plaintiff and Another, being Creditors of One *Sutton*, by a third Perſon, as Security for a partial Payment of the Debt of the ſaid *Sutton* (which was thereby liquidated and aſcertained,) to his ſeveral Creditors; *viz.* 15 *s.* in the Pound, by Inſtalments: Which Bond was to be forfeited, if *Sutton* ſhould make Default in the ſaid Payment. The Plaintiffs having obtained Judgment againſt the Defendant, He brought a Writ of Error, but gave no Bail upon it. Whereupon, the Plaintiffs took out Execution: Which the Plaintiff in Error complained of, as being irregular. So that the Queſtion was, Whether this Bond, given by a third Perſon, and made to third Perſons for Payment of a Sum certain, by Inſtalments, (the laſt whereof was ſtill future,) be an Obligation conditioned for the *Payment of Money only*, within 3 *J.* 1. *c.* 8. (made to avoid unneceſſary Delays of Executions.)

Mr. *Norton* and Mr. *Field*, for the Plaintiff in Error, urged that a Counter-Bond, or a Collateral Security for the Debt of another Perſon, is *not* a Bond for *Payment of Money only*; nor within the Meaning of the Act of 3 *J.* 1. *c.* 8. And they cited *Yelv.* 227. *Gilling* v. *Baker*. 2 *Bulſtr.* 53. S. C. *Carthew* 28. *Gerrard* v. *Danby*, 1 *Shower* 14. S. C. *Comberb.* 105. S. C. 2 *Strange* 1190. *Thrale* v. *Vaughan*. *Lucas* 281. *Hammond* v. *Webb*.

3 Lord

Lord MANSFIELD—The Court will not contract the Conſtruction of that *beneficial* Act, beyond any Precedent. And this Bond is clearly for the *Payment of Money* ONLY; and liquidated as to the Sum too: All the Debts are liquidated. The Money is only to be *paid* by *another Perſon*.

Mr. Juſt. DENISON concurred—And the being payable *by Inſtalments* makes no Difference.

Mr. Juſt. FOSTER and Mr. Juſt. WILMOT declared their Concurrence in this Opinion.

Per Cur'—The Rule upon the Plaintiffs to ſhew Cauſe "Why "the Writ of *Scire facias* ſhould not be ſet aſide for Irregu-"larity, and the Goods levied be reſtored," (which Rule had been obtained upon Mr. *Field*'s Motion,) was now DISCHARGED.

Williams *verſ.* Rougheedge, (A *Priſoner* in Execution.)

Monday 5th February 1759.

THE Queſtion was "Whether the Priſoner, in Execution under Proceſs out of this Court, was *within Time* to lodge a Petition for his being brought up to the Aſſizes for the County Palatine of *Lancaſter*."

The Caſe was this—A Priſoner in Execution under Proceſs iſſuing out of *this* Court, had (for want of rightly underſtanding the proper Juriſdiction to which he ought to have applied) *totally omitted* to petition *this* Court *within due Time*, "that He might be brought "up to the Aſſizes &c, in order to his being diſcharged upon the "Inſolvent Debtors Acts:" Although he had preſented a Petition to another (*improper*) Juriſdiction, within Time; *viz.* to the Judges of Aſſize for the County Palatine.

The Doubt was "Whether he was now *precluded* from making "his Application to *this* Court; And Whether the *explanatory* Acts "of 3 *G.* 2. *c.* 27. and 8 *G.* 2. *c.* 24. and 14 *G.* 2. *c.* 34. and "21 *G.* 2. *c.* 33. are revived by 29 *G.* 2. *c.* 28:" Or "Whether "the Act of 2 *G.* 2. *c.* 22. be ALONE revived; And the *explana-*"*tory* Ones, of that very Act, *remain expired.*"

The COURT (having looked into All theſe ſeveral Acts of Parliament,) Declared that ALL *theſe* Acts explaining and amending that of 2 *G.* 2. are revived by 29 *G.* 2; *as well* as the Act of 2 *G.* 2. itſelf; And

And particularly, that that of 8 *G*. 2. *c*. 24. (upon which the present Question depends,) is now in Force: Consequently, that in Order to give this Court Jurisdiction, the Prisoner must come and apply to *this* Court by Petition, BEFORE the End of the *next Term* after his being charged in Execution; Otherwise, this Court has *no Jurisdiction* vested or attached in it; As was determined in a Case (remembered by Mr. Just. *Denison*) of * *Smallwood* v. *Grant*, *H*. 21 *G*. 2. *B*. *R*. Which Case was distinguishable from that of Sir *William Pool* v. *Lane*, in *Tr*. 16 *G*. 2. *B*. *R*; Where the Petition was *lodged in due Time*, and all was regular, except that 28 Days Notice only had been given instead of 30 Days. There indeed the Defendant was suffered to give a new Notice: But the Reason was, because the Jurisdiction was in *that* Case *attached*, by the Original Petitions having been lodged *within* due Time. Whereas, in the *present* Case the Court have *no Jurisdiction* at all.

* I believe, the proper Name of it, was *Goold* v. *Clarke*.

As to the Revival of the *explanatory* Acts, as well as the principal One, which had been at different times explained and amended by these several temporary Acts,—The COURT held that these, being all attendant upon it, were in Effect *revived along with it*: For that it would be absurd (as Mr. Just. *Foster* observed) to revive, *unamended*, an Act which *wanted so many Amendments* as this Act had received.

Mr. Just. FOSTER observed also the particular Course of these Explanations and Amendments; *viz*. that the Acts of 2 & 3 *G*. 2. are continued by 8 *G*. 2. Then 14th continues the 8th with the Amendments. Then 21st continues 2 *G*. 2. *only*, without expressly naming the explanatory Ones. And the 29th implicitly follows the Precedent of the 21st. Which Act of 29th will itself expire the next Sessions: When, He hoped, he said, that more † Accuracy would be observed.

† *V*. *post*, *pa*. —*Tr*. 1759. 32, 33 *G*. 2. *B*. *R*. The Prisoners Case.

Mr. Just. DENISON said that notwithstanding the Inaccuracy of the Penning, ALL the former Acts were *revived* by the 29 *G*. 2.

And this Matter was taken *equitably*, in Petitions offered to the Court after the Expiration of these Acts: For upon the Revival of them, the Court equitably held, "That the Prisoners should "have *another* Term after the then first Term, allowed them to "lodge their Petitions."

Rex

Rex *verſ.* Gwynne et al'.

Thurſday 8th *February* 1759.

LORD *Mansfield* being abſent in the Dutchy-Court,

The Three Other Judges (on a defended Motion) granted a *Procedendo*, at the Inſtance of the Defendant, to the Quarter Seſſions of *Brecon*, upon an Indictment for an Aſſault removed up hither; Becauſe the *Certiorari* had not iſſued till AFTER the Defendants had *confeſſed* the Aſſault below: Though the Conviction was not after a Trial, and though ſeveral of the Juſtices were ſworn to be near Relations of Mr. *Gwynne*, one of the Defendants; namely, his Father, two Brothers, and an Uncle.

Rex *verſ.* Inhabitants of Weſtbury.

Friday 9th *February* 1759.

TWO Juſtices removed *William Sheers* and *Sarah* his Wife from *St. Cuthbert*'s in *Wells*, to *Weſtbury*: And the Seſſions confirmed this Order.

The Special Caſe was this—*William Sheers*, the Pauper, being ſettled in *St. Cuthbert*'s in *Wells*, was bound an Apprentice on the 4th of *December* 1753, by Indenture of that Date, to *John Collier*, who then and for ſeveral Years before reſided in *Weſtbury*, but whoſe legal Settlement was at *Harptree*, a neighbouring Pariſh: And accordingly, the ſaid *William Sheers* entered into the Service of the ſaid *John Collier*, on the ſaid 4th of *December*. The ſaid *John Collier having been ſome Years before applied to* by the Pariſh Officers of *Weſtbury*, to obtain a Certificate from *Harptree*, (which he then promiſed to do,) did *afterwards*, on the 26th Day of the *ſame Month of December*, obtain a CERTIFICATE *from Harptree*, acknowledging him to be their Inhabitant legally ſettled: Which Certificate was, the ſame Day, delivered to the Overſeers of *Weſtbury*.

William Sheers, the Pauper, *continued with and ſerved* the ſaid *John Collier*, UNDER *the ſaid Indenture* of Apprenticeſhip, from the ſaid 4th Day of *December*, for and during the Space of *three Years*; and *reſided* all that Time, with his ſaid Maſter *John Collier* in the ſaid Pariſh of *Weſtbury*; and then married the ſaid *Sarah* his Wife.

Mr. *Gould* who had moved, in laſt Term, to quaſh theſe Orders, had Objected to them, "That *William Sheers* gained no Settlement in "*Weſtbury*, by this Apprenticeſhip:" He relied on 12 *Ann. Stat.* 1. c. 18.

c. 18. § 2; Which directs, "that no one shall gain a Settlement by serving a *Certificate-Person*, as a hired Servant or *Apprentice*."

On *Wednesday* last, Mr. *Burland* and Mr. *Popham* shewed Cause Why this Order should not be quashed: And they stated the Question thus—" Whether the Pauper should be *defeated* of his Settlement, " by a SUBSEQUENT Act of the *Master*, (an *ex post facto Act*,) *without* the Apprentice's Consent; AFTER the Apprentice had not only *begun his Service*, but even actually served 22 *Days* of it. They argued that he shall *not* be defeated of it, by this *subsequent* Act of the Master.

If he had served 40 Days, it is clear that his Settlement (being thereby completely gained) should not be defeated by such an *ex post facto* Act of the Master.

This Question depends on 12 *Ann. Stat.* 1. *c.* 18. § 2: Which Act, and also it's Preamble, they urged very particularly; and argued that this Case is neither within the *Words* nor *Meaning* of it; which shall not be taken strictly. So on 3, 4 *W. & M. c.* 11. § 7. A Person *having* a Child or Children, is *not strictly* within it; yet this has not been strictly kept to.

Suppose a Corporator should be disfranchised, (perhaps only in Order to become a legal Witness in a Cause,) would that disable his Apprentice from claiming his Freedom?

Similar Cases are, Bankruptcy Cases under 1 *J.* 1. *c.* 15: Where A prior Settlement, fairly made by a Man upon his Children, shall *not* be invalidated by *subsequent* Bankruptcy. *Cro. Car.* 550. in the Case of *Crisp* v. *Pratt*. 3 *Peere Williams* 298. *Lilly* v. *Osbborn*. In which Cases, the Reason was, because the Person was not in Debt nor a Trader at the *Time* of making the Settlement. So here, the Master was *not* a Certificate-Man, at the *Time* of the Binding.

This Right was *in Part vested*; and therefore shall remain unaffected by a *subsequent* Act. The Right of Dower, in a Feme Covert, is not complete till the Death of the Husband: Yet She shall claim *&c. Perkins* § 9.

On 3, 4 *W. & M. c.* 11 § 7. And 8, 9 *W.* 3. *c.* 30. § 4. A Person unmarried at the *Time* of the Hiring, *though married afterwards*, shall not be precluded from gaining a Settlement. And here can be *no Retrospect or Relation*: For Relations cannot do a *Wrong to Strangers*. And the prior Application of the Parish of *Westbury*, to the Master, to procure a Certificate from *Harptree*, makes no Difference: Or if it does, it is on our Side; for it shews their Acquiescence in his remaining there without any Certificate. And the Parish of *Westbury* could not be hurt; because it was in their Power to have removed the Master, *at any Time* before he had procured his Certificate.

Mr. *Gould* and his Brother, *contra*, against the Orders.—The Parish of *Westbury* might have removed the Master, and his Apprentice, and all the Master's Family, *within the* 22 *Days*, 'tis true: But there still remained 18 *Days*, after the Delivery of the Certificate, wherein they were *bound down* to receive them all. So that they would receive a great Injury, if there should be no Retrospect at all, in this Case.

This Pauper cannot be said to have performed an Apprenticeship with a Master who *resided* in this Parish *without* a Certificate. And this would give a great Opening to *Imposition* upon Parishes: Whereas the Parishes *to* which Persons come with Certificates, are to be favoured.

As to the intermediate *Marriages* of Servants between the Beginning and Completion of their Service; it has been so ruled, in favour of, or at least not to discourage *Matrimony*.

This Case is within the *Words* of 12 *Ann.* if they are fully considered and attended to: But it is certainly within it's *Meaning*. And the Preamble of an Act does not use to specify *all* the Mischiefs which the enacting Clauses intend to obviate.

Every intended Certificate-Man might, at this Rate, take Apprentices, and fix them upon other Parishes, by doing it without Notice, and then procuring a Certificate as soon as the Parish make any Objection to his Residence.

Lord MANSFIELD—This is a new Question; and there is no Case in Point. It seems to Me, at present, that the Apprentice can *not* have here gained a Settlement in *Westbury*.

Before the Act, Serving under an Apprenticeship to a Certificate-Man for 40 Days in the Parish where the Master lived would have gained a Settlement to the Apprentice in the Parish where the Certificate-Man resided.

But the * Act says, "That if any Person whatsoever, who shall "be Apprentice bound by Indenture to any Person whatsoever, who "did *come* into, OR SHALL RESIDE in any Parish, by Means or "Licence of such Certificate, (and not afterwards having gained a "legal Settlement in such Parish,) Such Apprentice, by Virtue of "such

* 12 *Ann.* *Stat.* 1. *c.* 18. § 2.

"such Apprenticeship, Indenture or Binding, to *such* Person, shall "*not* gain any Settlement in such Parish, by reason of such Apprenticeship or Binding."

Now here is *no Service for* 40 Days, under an Apprenticeship to a Master who did not come into OR RESIDE in this Parish by Means or Licence of a Certificate. And this is a *precedent* Condition, "That the Apprentice must be bound to and serve *for* 40 *Days*, "a Master *not residing by Licence of a Certificate*:" Or else, the Apprentice shall not be intitled to a Settlement. Whereas the "being "*unmarried*" is only a *subsequent* Condition; which shall *not destroy* a Right already *incboate*. Therefore it is not like *that* Case. And this Method of acquiring a Settlement might be attended with great Inconvenience, both to Parishes and Apprentices.

It had been a very different Case, I should think, if the Apprentice had actually *served* 40 *Days*, and regularly *completed* his Settlement thereby, *before* the Master became certificated.

This, He said, was his present Opinion: But he had no Objection to considering further of it.

Mr. Just. DENISON desired to think of it, for a Day or two.

Mr. Just. FOSTER and Mr. Just. WILMOT were silent.

Lord MANSFIELD—We will let You know our Opinions in a Day or two. CUR' ADVIS.

Lord MANSFIELD now delivered the Opinion of the Court; Which He said was agreeable to their Sentiments intimated upon the Argument: For

Their Opinion, He said, upon this Binding so circumstanced as is stated, and a Service of *only* 22 *Days* under it, by the Apprentice in *Westbury*, was, "That he has gained *no* Settlement there." For it is in the Nature of a *Condition* PRECEDENT to the Gaining any Settlement at all, "That the Apprentice must have been bound to, "and served *for* 40 *Days*, a Person who did *not* come into OR "RESIDE IN the Parish by Means or Licence of a Certificate:" And as in the present Case, this *precedent* Condition has never been performed, he *cannot* have gained a Settlement.

And it is distinguishable from the Case to which it has been compared, of a Servant *bired when unmarried*, and *marrying* before his Year is expired, (which has been holden "not to prevent his Settle-"ment;") because there the Event was *subsequent* to the Contract, which was complete and strictly regular when *entered into*, and required no precedent Condition of that kind; it being only necessary to be unmarried *when hired:* So that in that *Case*, it is in the Nature of a Condition *subsequent*.

But *this* is a Condition *precedent*; And the Apprentice is under an *absolute Disability* of gaining a Settlement, *unless* he is bound *and serves* 40 *Days* to a Man who did *not* come into OR RESIDE in the Parish, by Means or Licence of a Certificate: Which this Pauper has not done; And consequently, he has gained no Settlement by *this* Service.

Both ORDERS QUASHED.

Cooke *vers.* Peter Sayer.

ON the Master's Report (made two Days ago)—The Question was, "*What* COSTS should be allowed; and *to whom*;" upon the following Facts stated; (in Consequence of a Motion for a *Direction* to the Master, how to tax them.)

In an Action upon the Case for a Criminal Conversation with the Plaintiff's Wife, The Defendant, by Leave (pursuant to the Statute for Amendment of the Law, 4, 5 *Ann. c.* 16.) pleaded two Pleas; (1st.) Not Guilty; (2dly.) Not guilty within 6 Years. On the former Plea of "Not guilty," *Issue* was joined: To the latter Plea, there was a *Demurrer* put in by the Plaintiff. It so happened, that the *Issue* was tried *first*, and found for the *Plaintiff*, with 50 *l.* Damages; *Then* the Demurrer was *afterwards* argued, and overruled, and determined for the *Defendant*: And *Each* Party had *Judgment*; *viz.* the Plaintiff, on his Verdict; and the Defendant, on the Demurrer. The Plaintiff taxed his Costs upon the *Postea:* Then the Defendant came to tax his Costs on *his Judgment* upon the *Demurrer*.

N. B. By 8, 9 *W.* 3. *c.* 11. (For the better preventing frivolous and vexatious Suits,) § 2. *Defendants* shall have Costs against Plaintiffs, on Judgments given *for them*, upon any Demurrer put in by either Side. And

By 4, 5 *Ann. c.* 16. (For the Amendment of the Law,) which * enables Defendants to plead several Matters, It is provided, "(§ 5.) That if any such Matter (pleaded by a Defendant,) "shall, upon a Demurrer joined, be judged *insufficient*, Costs "shall be given at the *Discretion* of the Court." But there is *no particular* Direction in *this* Act, in Case of it's being judged

* V. § 4.

judged *sufficient*; (Which was the present Case:) So that *this* stands, I suppose, upon the former Act of 8, 9 *W.* 3. *c.* 11.

Master *Clarke* said He *never* had known an Instance of this kind.

Lord MANSFIELD—Perhaps the particular *Circumstances* of *this* Case may be considered, so as to determine it upon *them*, without entering into the *General* Question. But, however, lest the *General Question* should be involved, more or less, in this particular One, I would take a little Time to consider of it. CUR' ADVIS.

Lord MANSFIELD now delivered the Resolution of the Court.

The two Pleas pleaded by the Defendant have received different Determinations: One, is found against the Defendant; the Other has been adjudged for him. So that the Plaintiff, *upon the whole*, has *no* Cause of Action.

I said, at the Time when this Matter was before Us, that the particular Circumstances of *this* Case, might appear to be such, when considered, as might be a sufficient Foundation for our determining the Matter *now* in Dispute, *upon* those particular Circumstances, without entering into the General Question: But the *General* Question is a Point that might require a good deal of Consideration.

And upon looking into these Circumstances here, We are All of Opinion, "That the *particular Circumstances* of this present Case "*are* such as may very well suffice for our determining it *upon* "these Circumstances alone, *without* going into the *General* Question."

Now, upon the present Circumstances, it is clear,—That the Defendant must certainly have the Costs of the DEMURRER, which has been adjudged for him.

But as to the Costs of the TRIAL—We think that the Plaintiff ought *not* to have them, *though* he has obtained a Verdict upon *this* Issue: For *upon the* WHOLE, he had *no* Cause of Action. The Demurrer is decisive, as to *that*. And he has acted unadvisedly, in carrying this Issue down to Trial, before the Determination of the Demurrer.

We cannot say "That the Defendant did *wrong*, in pleading Not "guilty, *as well as* Not guilty within Six Years:" We cannot determine that he had no Pretence for so doing.

2

It

It has been objected, "That this was *unnecessary*, and that it was "*implied* in the Plea of not guilty within Six Years." But it *may* be necessary: And it is *not implied* in the other Plea of "Not guilty "within Six Years;" as that Plea *might* have been managed in the Course of Pleading. For the Plaintiff *might* have replied "That "he sued out an Original Writ within the Six Years;" and put the Defendant to answer to that Allegation; and so carried it off *from the Merits*, to a *collateral* Point: In *which* Case, it could never have come to be tried, upon this *second* Issue, "Whether he was "or was not *guilty of the Fact*."

Consequently, it is not true, "that upon this second Issue, the "former was *necessarily* included and implied."

Therefore We cannot say that the Defendant was *so* in the wrong in pleading Not guilty, generally, that he ought to PAY *Costs for so doing*. And yet, on the other hand, that Plea being found *false*, he ought not to RECEIVE Costs of the Plaintiff, upon the Trial of that Issue which has been found *against* him.

But nevertheless, though it is found against the Defendant; yet the Plaintiff cannot have *Damages* upon it; because, *upon the* WHOLE, Judgment must be *against* him: And therefore, neither can he have *Costs* upon it. So that the *Judgment* must be for the *Defendant*, clearly; And he also must have *Costs of the* DEMURRER: But upon the *Trial*, there are to be NO *Costs on* EITHER *Side*; But Each Party is to sit down by his own Costs.

N. B. There was no Rule drawn up in Form; this Declaration of the Court being only by way of *Direction to the Master*, in what Manner to tax these Costs.

Alder *vers.* Chipp.

Saturday 10th *February* 1759.

MR. *Hussey* shewed Cause against a Rule of Mr. *Gould*'s, "Why "the Plaintiff should not be at Liberty to *withdraw his Replication*, and *reply de novo*."

The Case was, that the Plaintiff had (by the Mistake of his former Attorney) traversed a Lease under which He himself claimed.

The COURT made the Rule absolute.

And

And Lord MANSFIELD said He considered this as an *Amendment*; and that the proposing it in this Method, of withdrawing the Replication and replying *de novo*, was only to prevent the defacing and obliterating the Roll. And He observed, that the Court had not used the same *Strictness* of late Years, with regard to *Amendments*, as they formerly did: And he said, it was much better for the Parties that they should not. However, the Court would always take Care that if One Party obtained Leave to amend, the *other* Party should not be *prejudiced nor delayed* thereby.

* V. 2 Strange 1002.

And He observed that the Case of the * Bank of *England* v. *Morrice* turned upon it's own particular Circumstances, and was the Case of an *Executrix* too.

Note—The Length of Time in the present Case, had been objected; *viz.* 6 Terms. But it was answered, "that in many "Cases, Amendments had been made after a *much longer* "Time."

RULE made ABSOLUTE.

Monday 12th *February* 1759.

George, *ex dimiss.* Bradley *et al'*, *vers.* Wisdom.

MR *Norton* shewed Cause against, And

The COURT, (consisting, at present, of Ld. *Mansfield* and Mr. Just. *Denison*,) discharged a Rule which had been made on Mr. Serj. *Nares*'s Motion, "to shew Cause Why a Writ of "*Habere* "*facias Possessionem*, should not be set aside, as being *irregularly* "*issued and executed*, with Costs; And why *Possession* of the Pre- "misses in Question should not be *restored* to the Defendant."

This was an *Ejectment*, in which, *Wisdom* (the *Landlord*) had (upon the Tenant's refusing to appear) made himself Defendant, in the Place of the Casual Ejector; against whom Judgment was signed, for want of Appearance.) And the Plaintiff, having obtained Judgment against *Wisdom* the Landlord, had afterwards moved for LEAVE *to take out Execution* against the Casual Ejector: From doing which *without* Leave, He stood restrained by the *Conditional Rule* "for "a Stay of Execution against the Casual Ejector *till further Order*," always made in Consequence of a Clause in the Act of 11 *G.* 2. *c.* 19. (which * Clause gives Leave for making the Landlord Defendant in the Room of the Non-appearing Casual Ejector, *upon* THESE *Terms*.)

* § 13th.

But

But a *Writ of Error* had in Fact been regularly sued out by the new Defendant *Wisdom* the Landlord, *before* the Plaintiff had made this Motion "for Leave to take out Execution against the Casual Ejector." Yet Nothing of this Matter of the Writ of Error was shewn for Cause, by the new Defendant *Wisdom* the Landlord, against the Plaintiff's said Motion "for Leave to take out Execution against the "Casual Ejector;" But that Rule was made absolute, *without any Cause* whatever being shewn against it.

Now The COURT, upon the whole State of this Affair, were of Opinion, That the *Day of shewing Cause* against *that* Rule was the *proper* Time for the Landlord to have made his *Stand* against the Plaintiff's taking out Execution and getting into *Possession*; And that he should have *then* shewn his Writ of Error, *as Cause* why the Plaintiff ought *not* to have had Leave to take out Execution; and why it ought still to have been further stayed: But that, as he had OMITTED to do so, when he had this * *proper Opportunity*, the Execution was *regular*, and consequently ought not now to be set aside.

RULE DISCHARGED.

Note—It was agreed on all Hands, that a Writ of Error could *not* have been taken out in the *Name* of the *Casual* Ejector.

* In the Case of *Jones, ex dimiss. Edwards, v. Edwards, M.* 1745. *B R.* It *was* so shewn for Cause, and allowed to be a good One.

Rex *vers.* Roger Philipps.

ON a Motion made on the Part of the Prosecutor, for my reviewing a *Taxation of Costs*, The Case was, That the Defendant had had leave to *amend his Plea*, † on Payment of Costs: But the Amendments made in it were not essential to the real Merits, nor such as DEFACED *the Record* (there being much more *struck out* than put in.) *The Allowances* made to the Prosecutor upon the Amendments of the PLEA itself, and of the *subsequent Pleadings* dependant upon it, had been only made, in *Proportion* to the *actual* Amendments made therein; and not as for a quite new Plea: Which was agreed on all Hands, to be the right Method.

† *V. ante* 306.

But the Dispute originally before Me, and now brought before the Court, was Whether the REPLICATION and *its* Dependencies ought to be *fully and wholly allowed* to the Prosecutor, as an ABSOLUTE *Replication* DE NOVO; Or *only partially*, in Proportion to the *real* and *necessary* Alterations which were fairly and unavoidably occasioned to Him, by the Defendant's Amendment of his Plea: Which *latter* Method I had pursued, in taxing these Costs.

Lord MANSFIELD—The Principle is certainly right, That where the Defendant has Leave to amend his Plea, the Profecutor ought, in Juftice, to have *Liberty* to reply *quite de novo*, IF he judges proper; And alfo that in *all* Events, he ought to be allowed the Expence of attending and confulting and feeing Counfel, in Order to *advife* whether it be prudent or proper to reply *de novo*, or not.

But where he does NOT judge proper to depart from his former Replication and reply *de novo*; but *only* makes fuch Alterations in it, as *merely* purfue and are the natural and neceffary Confequences of the Alterations made in the Plea by the Defendant, and which Alterations in the Replication do NOT *deface the Record*, (which, He took Notice, was the prefent Cafe;) Nothing more ought to be allowed, than *in* PROPORTION for fuch *neceffary* Alterations and Amendments in the Replication and it's feveral Dependencies: For it muft not be left in the Profecutor's Power to load the Defendant *unneceffarily*; either out of Spite or Vexation, or for any other Reafon exceeding the bare Neceffity of the Thing.

Mr. Juft. *Denifon* (the only other Judge in Court) was of the fame Opinion.

Confequently, As I had acted agreeably to this Reafoning, The Profecutor's Counfel took Nothing by their MOTION.

Cox *verf.* Hart.

MR. Serj. *Nares*, on behalf of the Defendant below, who had removed the Caufe hither by a *Habeas Corpus cum Caufa*, fhewed Caufe why a *Procedendo* fhould not go, to the Sheriff's Court in *London*.

Mr. *Norton*, who was for the Plaintiff below, had moved for, and obtained, this Rule, "to fhew Caufe Why a *Procedendo* fhould "not iffue;" And had founded his Motion upon this Fact, "that "the *Habeas Corpus cum Caufa* was *not delivered till after an* INTER-"LOCUTORY *Judgment* had been figned in the Court below, and "Notice given of executing a Writ of Enquiry;" and therefore, as He alledged, came too late, And ought not to have been received or allowed. And in Support of his Objection, He urged and relied on the *Spirit* and *Intention* of 21 *Jac* I. *c.* 23. § 1, 2: Which *Intention* He infifted to be clear and beyond Doubt, againft the Reception and Allowance of the Writ; though he acknowledged that the prefent Cafe was *not* within the WORDS of that Act.

The Serjeant's Anſwer to this Objection was, That the *Words* of the Act are, "That the *Habeas Corpus*, *Certiorari* &c, ſhall *not be* "*received or allowed*, but that the Inferior Judge may *proceed*; Ex- "cept the Writ be *delivered* to ſuch Inferior Judge &c, BEFORE "*Iſſue or Demurrer* joined in the Cauſe: (So as it be not joined "within Six Weeks after the Arreſt or Appearance of the De- "fendant.")

And He produced Affidavits from ſome of the Officers of the Sheriff's Court, (which were likewiſe confirmed by Maſter *Clarke*,) atteſting that the * PRACTICE is, "to allow the *Habeas Corpus*, "provided it be delivered at ANY *Time* BEFORE THE † JURY "IS SWORN."

* This Practice muſt have taken it's Riſe from the Act of 43 *Eliz.* c. 5. which fixes this Criterion; and ſo have been continued on, without attending to the Alteration made by 21 *Jac.* 1. c. 23.

† But that is directly contrary to the expreſs Words of the Preamble; which ſpecifies "*Suits ready for Trial*," as what ought *not* to be removed.

Lord MANSFIELD—The preſent Caſe is *not* within the *Words* of the Act: That is plain. And it appears that the PRACTICE has gone *much farther* than the Words of the Act: For *that* has been, to allow it at any Time before the *Jury be ſworn*.

Therefore Let the RULE be DISCHARGED.

The End of *Hilary* Term 1759.

Eaſter

Easter Term

32 Geo. 2. B. R. 1759.

Wednesday 9th *May* 1759.

Rex *verſ.* Inhabitants of Shenſton.

TWO Juſtices removed *Thomas Lymer*, Labourer, and *Anne* his Wife from the Pariſh of *Gratwich* to *Shenſton*, (both in the County of *Stafford* :) And the Seſſions confirmed this Order.

The Special Caſe, as agreed by the Court and Counſel at Seſſions, was this—That the Pauper *Thomas Lymer* having gained a Settlement at *Shenſton*, by a Year's Hiring and Service, afterwards, to wit about Fifteen Years ago, took a Houſe in the Pariſh of *Gratwich*, at *Thirty Shillings* a Year, which he has enjoyed ever ſince, till removed by this Order; and, five Years ago, took two Acres of Land in the Pariſh of *King's Bromley* in the County of *Stafford*, for the *growing of* POTATOES, FROM CANDLEMAS TO MICHAELMAS, for *Nine Pounds*; and at the ſame Time, and from the ſame Perſon took, in the ſaid Pariſh of *King's Bromley*, half an Acre of Land, at *Forty Shillings*, for the *like Term*; and paid his Rent for all the Premiſſes, which *were of the* VALUE *aforeſaid.* The Pauper entered upon and enjoyed the Lands during the Term: And, the latter Part of the Time of his enjoying the ſame, to wit, between *Midſummer* and *Michaelmas*, He *lodged above forty Days* in the Pariſh of *King's Bromley*, where the Lands lay, for the Convenience of digging up and diſpoſing of the Potatoes.

Mr. *Aſton*, who moved to quaſh theſe Orders, obſerved that the Act of 13, 14 *C.* 2. *c.* 12. does not require a Taking *for* A YEAR: Which the Juſtices ſeem to have thought neceſſary.

The Words of the Act (13, 14 *C.* 2. *c.* 12. § 1.) are "That upon "Complaint *&c*, to any Juſtice of Peace, within Forty Days after "any ſuch Perſon or Perſons coming ſo to ſettle as aforeſaid, in

" any Tenement UNDER *the* YEARLY VALUE of Ten Pounds, it " shall be lawful for any two Justices &c, to remove &c."

Mr. *Morton* and Mr. *Leigh* shewed Cause against quashing the Orders.

This Question depends on 13, 14 *C.* 2. *c.* 12.

It is agreed that the Pauper was *originally* and indisputably settled at *Shenston*. Therefore *if* he has not legally gained a *new* Settlement, either at *Gratwich* or at *King's Bromley*, He is *still* legally settled at *Shenston*.

But the Taking in *Gratwich* was *only* 30*s*. a Year; and there was not an *Occupation for a Year*, of a Tenement *taken for a Year*, in *King's Bromley*; Both of the Tenements in *King's Bromley* having been taken *only for* 8 *Months*. Therefore he had not gained a new Settlement in *either* of those Places.

North Nibley v. *Wotton Under-edge* is the Case, that they will rely upon: It is in *Cases of Settlement*, *Pa*. 66. Case 86. *Foley* 90, 91. And in *Vol*. 1. of *Sessions Cases*, *Pa*. 80. Case 73.

By the Case of *Rex* v. *Inhabitants* of *Sandwich*, *P*. 8 & *Tr*. 8, 9 *G*. 2. *B. R.*—No *Residence* is requisite upon the Tenement of the *greater* Value: Where the 10 *l*. *per Annum* arises from two Takings (of 10*l*. Value together,) in two different Parishes: In such Case, the Man is settled where he *resides*, if he resides in either of them.

But it ought to be a Taking *for a Year*: Which this is not. Therefore it gains no Settlement.

This Land was hired for a *particular Purpose*, for a *Potatoe-Ground*: Where *no Stock* is requisite. And the Residence in *King's Bromley* was for the mere Purpose of looking after the Potatoes. Therefore it is not within the *Intent* of the Act of Parliament.

Mr. *Aston* and Mr. *Norton*, *contra*, admitted that the Question depended on 13, 14 *C*. 2. *c*. 12: But insisted that *if* the Pauper *had* gained a subsequent Settlement, either in *Gratwich or* in *King's Bromley*, the Removal *to Shenston* was wrong; And that here was a clear Settlement gained in *King's Bromley*, *or* in *Gratwich*.

 The

The *being trusted with a Taking of* 10 *l. per Annum* shews the Person *not* to be within the Meaning and Description of 13, 14 *C.* 2. *c.* 12.

The Case of *Sandwich* was a Tenement of 10 *l. per Annum* lying in two different Parishes: And the Court went upon the *Ability* of the Man to rent above 10 *l. per Annum*; which excludes any Presumption or Likelihood of becoming chargeable. And Lord *Hardwicke* † said "That *that* was the *Ground* of these Resolutions."

† He *did* say so.

The Case of *North Nibley, M.* 1. *G.* 1. *B.R.* is in Point. It was a Taking for *less* than a Year; And the VALUE, (not the Tenure) was principally respected. Therefore though the Tenure was here for *less* than a Year, Yet the VALUE being *above* 10 *l. per Annum*, the Man was *not within the Purview* of the Act of 13, 14 *C.* 2. *c.* 12.

The Case of *Minchinghampton* v. *Bisley*, mentioned in 2 *Strange* 874. *Tr.* 4 *G.* 2. *B. R.* turned upon it's being only the || *Pasture* of the Land, or being *Pasture Ground*. Here, the Pauper has taken 12 *l.* 10 *s.* in all.

|| The Words in that Case were, "And the *Pasture* of a Piece of Land, from *All Saints* Day, till *Candlemas*." The yearly Value of it was 6 *l. per Annum*: And the Man was to pay 12 *s.* for it.

He has gained a Settlement *either* in *Gratwich or* in *King's Bromley*: It is immaterial to us, in *which* it is.

The Act of 13, 14 *C.* 2. only means to prevent Vagrancy in such poor Persons as are UNABLE *to rent* 10 *l. per Annum*. This is the clear Intent of the Statute. And these Statutes have been *liberally* construed, in Favor of Settlements: And the Court have *always* regarded the ABILITY of the Person to rent 10 *l. per Annum*, as the Ground of their Determinations. Now the whole of this is of much greater Value than 10 *l. per Annum*.

The Justices usually consider this taking of Potatoe Grounds for the whole *profitable* Part of the Year, as a Taking FOR *a Year*.

There is a Case in 2 *Strange* 502. *Between the Parishes of Cranley* and *St. Mary Guilford*, which proves that upon the Certificate Act of 8, 9 *W.* 3. *c.* 11. (where the Words are "Unless He or they shall "really and *bonâ fide* take a Lease of a Tenement of the yearly "Value of Ten Pounds,") A Taking *at Will*, by a Certificate-Man, is sufficient to satisfy that Act. Much more shall a Taking for Nine Months, (the *whole profitable* Season,) satisfy the 13, 14 *C.* 2. And here is *no Fraud*, or Possibility of Fraud.

Lord

Lord *Mansfield* asked Mr. *Morton* if he had any Case to prove "That a Taking *for a Year* has been holden necessary."

Mr. *Morton* owned, He had *not*.

Lord MANSFIELD—The first Matter, about the *Residence in the Parish*, is out of the Case: For Mr. *Morton* agrees that *if* the Taking be sufficient, it would be a Settlement in the Parish where the Man *resided*.

It stands therefore singly upon the Question, "Whether this "Man's Taking above 10*l.* a Year in the *Manner* stated, is a Set-"tlement." And there has been no Determination that it is necessary that there should be a Taking FOR *a Year*.

This Act of 13, 14 *C.* 2. *c.* 12. And the Certificate Act of 8, 9 *W.* 3. *c.* 11. ought to be considered *together*, being in *pari Materia*.

There being no Determination to the contrary, I have no Doubt but that this is a Settlement, upon the Facts here stated.

This Man has done that which the Act of 13, 14 *C.* 2. has made the *Criterion* of his Substance: The Taking One Tenement of 10*l. per Annum* or more Tenements *amounting together* to that Value, in the *same* Parish, or in *different* Parishes, in the *Manner here stated*, is sufficient to prevent him from being considered as a VAGRANT.

And here is *no Fraud* stated; nor is there any Suspicion of Fraud. If there was any Fraud in the Taking, *that* would make a different Case. But here, the Man has *bonâ fide* taken Ground of the yearly Value of 12*l.* 10*s.* if We are to judge by computing the proportional Rent: And in the Nature of *this Species of Culture*, It is a Taking for the *whole Year's Profits* of the Land.

In some *other* Cultures besides this, (as Woad, Rape &c,) it requires only a *Part* of the Year, to get the Crop: And it is *stronger*, where the Rent for *Part* of the Year *only* is above 10*l.* than where the 10*l.* is payable for the *whole* Year.

Mr. Just. *Denison* concurred.

The Reason why there has been no determined Case upon the *Duration* of the Tenure, is because the Act does *not mention* any such Thing as a Taking for a Year, or for any particular Time.

The

The Act goes upon the *Credit* of the Perfon and his *Ability* to rent 10 *l. per Annum*. *Such* a Man was not confidered by the Legiflature as a Vagrant, or as *likely* to become chargeable to the Parifh. And the *Nature of this Land* makes the prefent Cafe ftronger.

I think there is no Neceffity to require a Taking *for a whole Year*. It is like the Cafe of a Taking *at Will* fatisfying the *Certificate Act*: Where the Words are the fame, "the *Yearly Value* of Ten "Pounds."

The *Refidence* of 40 Days upon this Taking, gains the Settlement.

Mr. Juft. FOSTER—It is agreed by the Counfel for the Orders, that Refidence upon the Tenement of the *greater* Value is not neceffary. Then, taking that for granted; I have no Doubt that this is a *bonâ fide* renting a Tenement of 10 *l. per Annum* VALUE.

Potatoe-Grounds, (as every Gardener knows,) produce their *whole* Profit in one particular Part or Seafon of the Year; and *no* Profit at all in the remaining Part of it. Therefore this is in Effect, and as to *this particular Culture*, much the fame thing as Taking fuch Ground to be fo made Ufe of, for the *whole* Year.

Mr. Juft. WILMOT concurred.

That former Point, which Mr. *Morton* very candidly and rightly gave up, being fettled, "That the *Refidence upon a Part* of the dif-"ferent Takings is fufficient to gain the Man a Settlement in the "Parifh were he *refides*," I have no Doubt as to the Other, That the *Taking here ftated* is *fufficient* to anfwer the Meaning and Intention of the Legiflature in 13, 14 *C.* 2. *c.* 12. For it turns upon the *Credit* and *Ability* of the Perfon, who is capable of hiring and is judged proper to be trufted with a Taking of the Yearly *Value* of Ten Pounds.

But neither the Act of Parliament, nor any Determination upon it, have faid "That it muft be a Taking *for a whole Year*." And if it were to be efteemed neceffary to take fuch a Tenement for a *whole* Year, it might be attended with great Inconveniences: In fo much that a Man might be removed from a Houfe even of 100*l. per Annum* Value, which he fhould take only for half a Year.

And the Cafe of a Leafe *at Will* under the Certificate Act of 8, 9 *W.* 3. *c.* 11. is very like the prefent Cafe: For the Words of both Acts are almoft exactly the fame.

I

I hold it to be clear, upon this Act of Parliament, " That it " *needs not* to be a Taking for a *whole* Year.

Per Cur. unanimously,
Rule made absolute for quashing both Orders.

Rex *verf.* Barnard Schiever, a Swede.

Mr. *Stowe* moved for a *Habeas Corpus* to be directed to *Richard Rigby*, Keeper of the Town-Gaol of *Liverpool*, to bring up the Body of *Barnard Schiever*, a Subject of a *neutral Power*, taken *on Board of an Enemy's Ship*; but forced, as it was alledged, *into the Enemy's Service*.

The Substance of the Affidavit upon which he grounded his Motion, was, That this *Barnard Schiever* was *born* in the Dominions of the King of *Sweden*; and his Father was now in that King's Service. That this *Barnard Schiever*, being bred to the Sea, and understanding Navigation, was *desirous of entering into the Service of the Merchants of England*; and for *that Purpose* and for *no other Design* or Intent whatsoever, shipped himself as a Passenger from *Gottenburg* to *Elsineur*, in order there to enter on Board some *English* Merchant's Ship. That when he arrived at *Elsineur*, he applied to the *English* Consul there, who shipped him, *as a Mariner*, on Board an *English* Merchant's Vessel bound on a Voyage from *Hull* to *Dublin*: With which Ship he set sail. That in prosecuting the said Voyage, in the said Ship, He was *taken by a French Privateer*, and carried into *Norway*; Where there was another Privateer. That he, together with all the Prisoners taken on Board the *English* Vessel, were put on Board the latter Privateer, called the *Mareschal de Bellisle*, Captain *Thurot* Commander. That the Day after he was removed into the *Bellisle*, the *English* Prisoners were, by the Command of Captain *Thurot*, set ashore at their Liberty: But all the Persons belonging to the said *English* Vessel, who were Subjects of *Neutral* Powers, were *detained* to *serve on Board* the said Privateer, (the *Bellisle*.) Upon which, this *Schiever* applied to Captain *Thurot* to set *him* ashore likewise; Alledging " He was " *intitled* to his Liberty as being a *neutral* Person." But *Thurot* told him " That for *that* Reason He should not go on Shore: For " that he might as well *serve him*, as serve the *English*; and that " He would *make* him *serve Him*;" or Words to that Effect. And accordingly *Thurot detained him*, against his Will *and Inclination*, *on Board of* the said *Mareschall de Bellisle Privateer*, and treated him with so much Severity, that he would not suffer him to go on Shore when in Port, upon his necessary Occasions; but closely confined him to Duty, on Board the said Privateer. That the said Privateer commanded by *Thurot*, being on a Cruise, took two little Briggs: On Board of One of which, this *Schiever*, with some Others, were put, with Orders from *Thurot* "to navigate the said "Brigg into any Harbour in *Norway*." That the said last mentioned Brigg was, in going to *Norway*, re-taken by the *Fame* Letter-of-Mark Ship, and carried into *Liverpool*: Where this *Barnard Schiever* was sent to the Town-Gaol of *Liverpool*, as a *Prisoner of War*, under the Custody of the said *Richard Rigby* Keeper of the said Gaol; and is now, and ever since has been detained there for no other Cause than the Cause aforesaid. *Schiever* swears that his *Intention still is* (could he obtain his Liberty) to enter as a Mariner into the *English Merchants Service*; and that he *would not* nor should have *served on Board the said Privateer*, had he not been FORCED *thereto* and *detained* as aforesaid by the said Captain *Thurot*.

One *Oluf Grundell*, who was on Board the *Bellisle* Privateer when *Schiever* was put on Board of it, swears that *Schiever* was FORCED *against his Inclination*, by the said Captain *Thurot*, to serve on Board of it, in the Manner as *Schiever* has above deposed; And that All the Persons taken in the said Vessel, belonging to *Neutral* Powers, were forced by *Thurot*, in the like manner, to serve on Board the said Privateer.

Mr. *Stowe* urged that it would be very hard upon this Man, to be kept in Prison here, till exchanged by Cartel; and then sent back to *France*, where he would be forced into their Service again.

But the COURT thought this Man, upon his own shewing, clearly a Prisoner of War, and lawfully detained as such. Therefore they DENIED the MOTION.

Tuesday 15th *May* 1759.

Rex *vers.* Pigram.

ON shewing Cause against a Rule, ordering the Defendant, Mayor of the ancient Town of *Rye*, to shew Cause "Why he "does not replace and put all the *Records and Books* of the said "Town, in the *proper and usual Place* of keeping the said Books "and Records;"

The COURT, without entering into the *General Question* "How "far An Officer who has the Custody of public Corporation-Books, "has Power to take them from their proper and usual Place, for "certain particular Times and Uses, or upon particular Occasions "or

" or Accidents; or how far He might be compellable in this summary Way, to replace them;" were clear and unanimous that in the *particular Instance* now before them, as it stood circumstanced by reason of Disputes which had in this Case arisen between the Mayor and the Town-Clerk, The Mayor had given a *satisfactory Excuse* for a *temporary* Securing them from falling into his Adversary's Hands, who had already made an improper Use of One of them: And therefore they held it improper for them, in *this Case so circumstanced*, to interfere in this summary Way, to oblige him to replace them. In Consequence of which Opinion, They Ordered the present Rule to be

DISCHARGED.

Strong, ex dimiss. Cummin, vers. Cummin and Another.

Friday 18th May 1759.

Hil. 30 *G.* 2. *Rot'lo* 374.

THIS was a Special Case reserved for the Opinion of the Court, at *Winchester* Assizes.

It was an Ejectment brought by *William Cummin*, against his Eldest Brother *Robert*, for Lands called *Smart* and *Picked Lands*; being Copyhold Lands, of which the Devisor was, (amongst divers other Copyhold Lands) seised in Fee. He devised the Chief Part of all his Copyhold Lands to his said Eldest Son *Robert* and his Heirs, after the Decease of his (the Testator's) Wife; and *these*, to his second Son *John*, and eventually to the Plaintiff.

The Words of the Will are as follow—Whereas by the Power and Authority in me invested according to the Custom of the Manor of *East Woodbay* aforesaid, by several Surrenders by me made of my Copyhold Land in the said Meanor, I can dispose of them to the Use of my last Will; I do hereby give and bequeath Singular my Copyhold Land and Tenements in *East Woodbay* aforesaid hould by *seven* Copies of Court Roll, be the same more or less, to *my Eldest Son Robert and his Heirs, according to the Custom, after his Mother Decease*. *Item* I give to my Son *John*, All that belong to *Smart and Picked* Lands, and *to his Heirs, after his Mother's Decease*; and also that my Son *Robert* shall pay to my Eldest Daughter *Mary*, the Sum of *One hundred* Pounds of lawful Money, when She shall attain the Age of 21 Years; As also the like Sum of 100 *l.* to my Daughter *Ester*, as soon as She shall attain the Age of 21 Years; and the like Sum of 100 *l.* to my Daughter *Ann*, when she shall attain the Age of 21 Years; And also to my Son *Willem*, the Sum of *One hundred* Pounds, to be payd unto Hem when he shall attain the Age of

2 twenty

twenty one Years: Provided alway that if my said Daughter *Mary* or any of my other Children dye before he she or they are one and twenty Years old, that in that Case he shall divide amongst the Surviving Younger Children the Sum of One hundred Pounds. And IN CASE THAT YOUR SON *Robert or John dy, then your Son Willem is to have all that belong to Smart and Picked Lands, and to his Heirs.* and in Case that your Son *Willem* ingoye *Smart* and *Picked* Lands, then to pay to his Sister, the Sum of one hundred Pounds. Item, as to my wordly Goods, I give and Stock, I give to the Use of my Wife during her natural Life, and Liberty to dispose of them at her Death as She shall think fit; provided it be amongst my Children and their Issus. and his Wife to have the Freehold during her Life. Item, I do hereby make and appoint my dear Wife *Mary*, and my Son *Robert*, to be Exeators of this my last Will and Testament.

The Testator afterwards died seised in Fee &c. At the Time of his Death, the personal Estate amounted to 200*l.* and no more: And at that Time, All his Children were *under Age*; *viz. Robert*, the Eldest Son, Fifteen Years old; *John*, the Second Son, Three; *William*, the third Son, (the Lessor of the Plaintiff,) One Year old; And all the Daughters, under Twenty one.

The Widow was admitted, as Devisee under the Will: And it is stated to be the Custom, "for the Widow to enjoy during Widow-"hood." *John* died in the Life-time of his Mother, *viz.* on the 21st of *April* 1756, *without* Issue, and intestate; being then UPWARDS *of* 21 Years of Age.

The Widow died very soon after her Son *John*, *viz.* on the 25th of *April* 1756, without having ever married again.

Mr. Serj. *Davy* for the Plaintiff (*viz. William* the third Son.)

The General Question is, Whether upon the Event of *John* the second Son's dying without Issue, in the Life-time of his Mother, the Testator's third Son *William* became intitled to the Premisses in Question, by Force of these Words in the Will, "In Case that your Son "*Robert* or *John dy*, Then your Son *Willem* is to have all that "belong to Smart and Picked Lands:" Or whether the Eldest Son *Robert* is, upon *John*'s Death, to take the same, as Heir at Law to the Testator.

He insisted on the *Testator's Meaning* "That his Son *William* "should have this Estate upon *some* Event or Other." But this could not be, in Case of *John's leaving* Issue. Therefore it was in Case *John* should die *without* Issue.

The

The Eftate was firft given to "*John* and his *Heirs*, after his Mo-"ther's Death: Which the Teftator meant for an Eftate *Tail*; intending "Heirs of his *Body*."

N. B. There had been an Offer from the Defendant, to *divide* thefe Premiffes in queftion with his Brother: Which Offer the Plaintiff *rejected*. But

Lord *Mansfield* having inquired "*What* this Offer had been, and "how it was received;" and feeming to think that it had been much more prudent to have accepted it;

Serj. *Davy* faid He had already, but in vain, advifed his Client to accept it; and very ftrongly hinted how fmall hopes he himfelf had of his Client's Succefs, upon a *legal* Determination. After which, He proceeded to make the beft of his Cafe that he could. And He faid that the *whole* Claufe could not be rejected; however difficult it was to be underftood.

Mr. *Gould*, *contra*, for the Defendant *Robert*, (the Heir at Law of the Teftator, and alfo Heir at Law to his deceafed Brother *John*.)

The *Intention* of the Teftator is *totally* obfcure, dark and uncertain in the prefent Cafe. Therefore, the Heir fhall have it. In 2 *Bulftr.* 179, 180. *Mirrill* v. *Nichols*—It is laid down by Ld. *Coke*, That "Intentio *cæca* is not to be taken; nec *Intentio mutila*, "nec *manca*: In all *fuch* Cafes, We are to give Judgment for the "*Heir*." Which Ld. *Coke* confirms by feveral Cafes which He there cites.

The Devife "to *John* and his Heirs" cannot be meant for an Eftate *Tail*. For he devifes to his Eldeft Son *Robert*, in the fame Words: Which plainly, in *that* Devife, mean the *abfolute Ownerfhip* to be given to *Robert*. Neither can it be an *Executory* Devife; There being no Mention of dying without Iffue at all; nor any Reftriction to the doing fo *within the Life-time* of his Mother.

Mr. Serj. *Davy* in Reply, Chiefly urged that the Teftator muft have *meant* an Eftate *Tail* to *John*.

Lord *Mansfield* thought it better, as it was a Family-Affair, to ftand over for the Chance of a Compromife.

It therefore ftood over, by the Direction of the Court, till the *Friday* Seven-night.

On which Day, The Cause standing in the Paper; And the Lessor of the Plaintiff, (*viz. William*, the third Brother,) absolutely refusing any Compromise with the Defendant (*Robert* his Eldest Brother:)

Lord MANSFIELD delivered the Resolution of the Court, having first very minutely stated the Case.

It is very plain, from the Spelling and Phraseology of this Will, That it is a rough Draught, of the Testator's *own* making or dictating, without Assistance from any Person capable of advising him.

It appears that He was seised, and died seised in Fee, of these Copyhold Lands; And it appears that the whole Amount of his *personal* Estate was at the Time of his Death 200*l.* and *no more:* So that the Legacies given by his Will must be *Charges upon his* REAL Estate. And it likewise appears that *All* his Children were *under* Age at the time of his Death.

I thought that No *Argument* could make this Case plainer than it was upon the *Will itself*. But I readily listened to a Compromise; that the Elder Brother might have an Opportunity (as he seemed disposed to do so) of making some Provision for his younger Brother, in Conformity to his Father's Intention, out of that full Provision which He himself now had. The Elder Brother offered him Half of the Premisses now in Question: The Younger refused it. The Elder still adheres to his former Proposal: And the Younger, to his Rejection of it. Therefore We must now determine the Case according to *Law*.

The Rule of Construction of Wills is, "That *no Technical Form* "is necessary, to convey the Testator's Meaning."

The Words and Form of the Will are plainly the Testator's own, without any proper Advice or Assistance.

The Testator's *Meaning* must be *collected from the Will itself*; by attending to the several Parts of it, and comparing and considering them together.

* *V. ante* S. C. cited.

In the Case of * *Coriton* v. *Hollier*, where there was a Slip in penning the Will, Lord *Hardwicke* did not conduct Himself by making an *arbitrary* Construction of it; but was induced by a strong and violent Presumption arising from the several Parts of it compared and taken together with the Whole, to determine "That "the first Limitation to the Ancestor meant to be for 99 Years, if "he should so long live."

In

In the present Case, it is not difficult to discover what the Testator *intended*. He certainly did *not* mean *mere* Estates for *Lives*, to his two Eldest Sons: And if he did not mean to give them mere Estates for their Lives, it necessarily follows, " That He must mean " a Dying upon SOME *Contingency*." The only Question is, " WHAT *Contingency?*" For he has *not expressed it*. He only expresses himself, " That in Case *Robert* or *John* DY, *then Willem* is " to have all that belong to Smart and Picked Lands, and to his " Heirs." *One* Part of the Contingency plainly is " That if they " die *without Issue*."

He provides for his Eldest Son, by his best Copyhold Estate; for his second Son, by his next best Copyhold Estate; and for the Rest of his Children, by pecuniary Portions: *All* which Children were *under Age*. Now *if Robert had died under Age*, He could not have disposed of his Estate: but it must have gone to *John*, if *Robert* had left no Issue. So also, *if John had died under Age*, his Share must have gone to *Robert*, if *John* had left no Issue. In *either* Case, that Son which remained the Eldest, would be very well provided for. Therefore the Testator meant that in *either* Event, *Smart and Picked Lands* should go to *William* his third Son, who would *then* have become the *Second*.

But He could *not* mean that *John*'s Provision should *otherwise* go over to *William*. He could never mean it to do so, if *John* Himself left Issue, or if *Robert* left Issue: For he certainly never intended to provide for the Surviving Brother, and leave the Issue of the deceased One quite *unprovided for*. Nor did He mean to tie down his two Eldest Sons, so as to preclude them from *disposing* of their respective Estates, *after* they should attain 21 Years of Age: It is clear that He meant their " Dying *under the Age of* 21 " to be *another Part* of the Contingency." And the *Context* of the Will shews that this was his Meaning: For the other Provisions (for the younger Children) expresly relate to their Living to 21, or dying under that Age. But this Contingency happens, *currente calamo*, to be *slipped* in this Part of the Will. IF *John* had died *before* 21, then *this* part of the Contingency would have taken Effect: But as that has *not* happened, his Brother *William* can have no pretence to claim.

Therefore We can only be sorry that the Plaintiff has stood in his own Light, in rejecting the fair Offer made to him by his Brother.

We are All clear for the Defendant: And therefore the *Postea* must be delivered to Him.

RULE for the *Postea* to be delivered to the DEFENDANT.

I Cornwallis

Cornwallis *verſ.* Savery.

THIS was an Action of Debt upon a Bond, brought *for the Penalty*, (which was 1500 *l.*)

The Defendant prayed Oyer of the Bond and Condition. Which Condition appears to be, That, Whereas One *William Wilkinſon* was appointed (by Earl *Cornwallis*) to be Agent to Colonel *Edward Cornwallis*'s Regiment; If the ſaid *William Wilkinſon* ſhould well and duly pay to the ſaid Colonel and to all the Commiſſioned and Non-Commiſſioned Officers and Soldiers of the Regiment, All ſuch Sum and Sums of Money as He ſhould receive from the Pay-Maſter-General for the Uſe of the Regiment; and faithfully account either to the Earl or to Colonel *Cornwallis &c*; and indemnify the Colonel *&c*; Then the Bond to be void *&c:* Otherwiſe *&c.*

Then the Defendant pleaded, That the ſaid *William Wilkinſon* continued Agent of the Regiment, from *&c* to *&c*; And that he did well and truly pay *&c*, (in the Words of the Condition;) And that he faithfully accounted *&c*, during all the Time that he continued Agent; And that the Colonel was not at all damnified.

The Replication aſſigned a Breach; *viz.* That during the Time that the ſaid *William Wilkinſon* continued Agent of the ſaid Regiment, He received from the Paymaſter-General, for the Uſe of the ſaid Regiment, *ſeveral Sums of Money amounting in the Whole* to 1400 *l.* for and on Account of the ſaid Regiment, and of the Commiſſioned and Non-Commiſſioned Officers and Soldiers of the ſame, according to their reſpective Proportions; All which He ought to have paid *&c:* But avers that the ſaid *William Wilkinſon* had not paid, and refuſed to pay a great Part thereof, to and amongſt the ſaid Colonel and the Commiſſioned and Non Commiſſioned Officers and Soldiers of the ſaid Regiment, according to the ſeveral Proportions of their Pay.

To this Replication, the Defendant demurred; And ſhewed for Cauſe, " That it is uncertain, multifarious, confuſed, perplexed, " complicated, argumentative, double," and many other ſuch Epithets.

Mr. *Caldecott*, for the Defendant, objected to the Replication—

1ſt. That the Plaintiff ought to have *confined* Himſelf to ONE *particular Breach*; As this is an Action of Debt upon the Bond, to recover the *Penalty*, and *not* an Action for *Damages*. For the Act of 8, 9 *W.* 3. *c.* 11. § 8. does not extend to Actions of Debt brought for the *Penalty* of a Bond: It only relates to Actions for *Damages* for Non-performance of Covenants; and in *such* Cases, enables the Plaintiff to assign as many Breaches as he shall think fit.

In the Case of *Symms* v. *Smith*, *Cro. Car.* 176. The Distinction is laid down, " That in Covenant, the Plaintiff may assign as many " Breaches as he will; But *not* in Debt upon an Obligation for " Performance of Covenants."

Now here, it is charged that the Agent received *several Sums* of Money, amounting to 1400*l:* Great Part of which he has not paid to the Colonel Officers and Soldiers &c, according to the several Proportions of their Pay.

In the Case of the *Royal African Company* v. *Mason* (which is cited in 1 *Strange* 227.) *P.* 13 *Ann. B. R.* The Action was of Debt on a Bond. The Condition was " That *Mason* (who was recited to be Agent for the Company at *Bristol*) " should when required, pay " to the Use of the Company, All the Sums of Money in his " Hands and Possession, received by him for the Company, to whom " he was Agent at *Bristol*." The " Defendant pleaded Performance " of the Condition, generally; *viz.* That he had paid to the Com- " pany all that he had received for them." The Plaintiff, in his Replication, assigned for Breach, " That *Mason* did receive *of Ja-* " *cob Reynolds and divers others*, for the Use of the Company, *seve-* " *ral Sums* of Money amounting to 630*l:* Which he was reques- " ted to pay, but had not paid." This Replication was holden ill; because *many Breaches* were assigned; Whereas the Plaintiff ought to have assigned *only One:* And the Plaintiff discontinued. (He cited this from a Manuscript Note of Ld. Ch. J. *Reeves*.) *

* See it also in *Lucas* 227.

2d Objection to the Replication. It says that the Money was to be paid " to the Colonel and all the Commissioned and Non-Com- " missioned Officers and Soldiers of the Regiment, according to the " several Proportions of their Pay." Which is *uncertain* and *complicated*; and *no Issue* can be taken upon it.

3d Objection to the Replication—It concludes with an *Averment:* Whereas it ought to conclude to the *Country*; there being an Affirmative and a Negative. For the Defendant pleads " That *Wilkin-* " *son*, the Agent, *did pay all that he had received* of the Paymaster- " General &c." Then the Replication alledges " That he had " received 1400*l.* of him, and had *not* paid it." Which is an Affirmative and a Negative: And therefore the Replication ought to have concluded to the *Country*.

Mr. Serj. *Nares*, for the Plaintiff, was prevented from answering these Objections: because the Court did not think that they required any Answer.

Lord MANSFIELD—Mr. *Caldecott's Principles* are right: And the Case cited by Him may be so too. But his *Application* of them is wrong.

It is true, that where there are Alternative Parts of the Condition, the Plaintiff in an Action *upon the Bond*, FOR THE PENALTY, must confine himself to a *particular* Breach. But here *is only One* Breach assigned in this Case.

The Colonel is answerable for his Agent, whom He has appointed: And the Breach here assigned, is singly this, "That the Agent "received 1400*l*, from the Paymaster-General, which he has not "paid to the Colonel, Officers *&c.*"

If he has omitted to pay *any Part* of it, it is a Breach of the Condition.

The Case cited from Ld. Ch. J. *Reeves*'s Notes is not like the present Case. That was Money received from *several different* Persons: Here, it was *from One single* Person only. And the Defendant has incurred a Breach of the Condition, if the Agent has received a certain Sum of Money from the Paymaster-General for the Use of the Regiment, and has omitted to pay *any Part* of it to the Colonel and Officers *&c.*

And as to the 2d Objection—The Pay of a Regiment is a Thing very well known and notorious. The Agent must be perfectly well acquainted with the respective Proportions belonging to the Colonel Officers *&c*: And there was no Need to spin out the Proceedings to a great Prolixity, by entering into the Detail and stating the various Deductions out of the whole Pay, upon various Accounts and in different Proportions.

3dly. The Replication is rightly concluded with an Averment. For though the Plea avers generally "That *William Wilkinson* did "pay *All* that he had received of the Paymaster-General," Yet the Replication narrows this to a *particular Sum*, which it specifies in certain to be 1400*l*. So that although there be an Affirmative and a Negative, Yet they are *not* applied to the *same* Thing; and therefore not within the Rule.

Mr. Just. DENISON was of the same Opinion.

In

In an Action of Debt on a Bond, *for the Penalty*, it is true that the Plaintiff is to assign *only one single* Breach: And the Breach here assigned *is a single* Breach. The Plea is Performance of Covenants, generally; and that the Plaintiff was not damnified. The Replication shews that the Agent received from the Paymaster-General several Sums *amounting to* so much; Which it avers, "He has not "paid over:" Which is a *single* Breach. The Case cited was of several Receipts *from several Persons*.

It was not necessary to set out all the several Days and Times and Circumstances, and thereby render the Record prolix, to no Purpose.

The Replication is a good Replication; and not double, nor complicated, nor uncertain, nor multifarious, nor any of the numerous Epithets that are given to it in the Demurrer.

3dly. The Objection to it's Conclusion is only *Form*: And it is *not shewn for Cause*, "That it does want a proper Conclusion." However, if it did, it would not avail: For this Conclusion, with an Averment, in the *present* Case, is *not* wrong.

Mr. Just. Foster and Mr. Just. Wilmot concurred in the same Opinion.

Per Cur. unanimously,
Judgment for the Plaintiff.

Ballard and Another, Chamberlains of Worcester, *vers.* Bennett: The same *vers.* Clement.

MR. *Norton*, on behalf of the Defendants in both Causes, shewed Cause against the Issuing of a *Procedendo*, to the Court below.

On *Friday* the 2d of *June* last, Mr. Serj. *Nares* had moved for a Procedendo, to the Mayor Aldermen and Citizens of the City of *Worcester*, to proceed in these Actions; (which were Actions of Debt brought there, in the Name of the Chamberlains, and had been removed hither by *Habeas Corpus cum Causa*;) To which they had returned a *By-Law*, made by the Corporation, "*to restrain the Sale "of Flesh Meat* to certain proper Places, and that it should not be "sold in the public Streets, under a Penalty:" For which Penal-

 ty,

ty, the reſpective Actions were brought, in the Court of Pleas holden for the ſaid City.

The Words of the By-Law are "That All Sorts of Fleſh-Meat "ſold within the ſaid City on the Market Days or Fair-Days, "by Butchers and other Perſons not being Inhabitants and "keeping open Shops within the ſaid City, ſhould be publicly expoſed to Sale in ſuch new-erected *Shambles*, and *not* "*elſewhere* within the ſame City; And that no Perſon or Perſons whatever ſhould erect put or place, or cauſe to be erected put or placed, or aſſiſt in the erecting putting or placing "any Stall Standing Bench Table or other Thing, in any of "the Streets Lanes or Alleys within the ſaid City or the Liberties thereof, for the Selling or expoſing to Sale, by any "foreign Butcher or other Stranger reſorting to ſuch Markets or Fairs, any Sort of Fleſh Meat whatſoever: And "that every Perſon offending in the Premiſſes ſhould for every "ſuch Offence forfeit and pay to the Chamberlains of the ſaid "City for the Time being, the Sum of Three Pounds, to be "*recovered by Action of Debt*, in the Name of ſuch Chamberlains, in the Court of Pleas held for the ſaid City, *and* "*not elſewhere*, with full Coſts of Suit, and to be applied by "them to the Uſe and Benefit of the Poor belonging to the "ſeveral Alms-houſes erected within the ſaid City."

This By-Law the Serjeant alledged to be a good One; And cited in Proof of it, 1 *Siderſ.* 284. *Player* v. *Jenkins.*

Mr. Juſt. *Wilmot*, at the time of the original Motion, recollected that there was a * Caſe in the Year-Books, (the Prior of *Dunſtable*'s Caſe,) about a Man's being reſtrained from Selling Meat in his own Houſe.

* 'Tis in 11 *H.* 6. *fo.* 19. *pl.* 13. and *fo.* 25. *pl.* 2.

And Mr. Juſtice *Deniſon* and Himſelf (the only Judges then in Court) made a Rule to ſhew Cauſe why there ſhould not go a *Procedendo.*

On 5th *May* 1759, Mr. *Norton* ſhewed Cauſe againſt the *Procedendo*; and objected to the Validity of the *By-Law.*

But a PRELIMINARY *Doubt* was made by the Court, (originally ſtarted by Mr. Juſt. *Deniſon*,) "Whether the Court would ſuffer "a *By-Law to be objected to* in this *ſummary* Way, upon a *Motion* "on the Return of a *Habeas Corpus*; in any other Caſes EXCEPT "thoſe from the *City of* LONDON."

They

They agreed that this Method had been always practised upon By-Laws returned into this Court, to Writs of *Habeas Corpus cum Causa*, directed to the Courts of the City of LONDON: But they did not recollect any Instances where the same Thing had been permitted, in the Case of *any* OTHER City or Corporation.

Mr. Just. *Denison* said that such a *Distinction* between the City of *London*, and *all other* Cities and Corporations, might perhaps arise from particular Methods of Recovery being established and allowed by the *Customs* of *London*, which cannot be pursued in this or any other Court: So that the shewing that to be the Cause, is a good Cause of Detainer. For upon * these Writs of *Habeas Corpus*, the Persons to whom they are directed must shew a good Cause of Detainer: And if this Court cannot proceed, as the Customs of *London* authorize their Courts to proceed; it is a good Cause of Detainer. Therefore the Court will there enter into the Validity of the By-Law, to see whether that be the Case or no: And if the By-Law appears to be bad, the Party shall be discharged, as being detained without Cause.

* These Writs issue on the *Civil* Side, out of the King's Bench Office. They only order the *Person* of the Defendant to be brought up; without mentioning the Removal of the *Cause*.

And *no Writ of Error* lies *hither* from the Courts of the City of † LONDON. But in *all other* Cities and Corporations, if a *Habeas Corpus cum Causa* issues, and a By-Law is returned as the Foundation of the Action below, the *Method is not*, for the Defendant to object to the By-Law *upon Motion*; But the Plaintiff is to begin *de novo*, and to ‖ declare over again, here in this Court: And therefore the Question is Whether He ought not to do so here.

† In *other* Corporations, a Writ of Error does lie, returnable in this Court.

‖ *V.* 6 *Mod.* 177.

The COURT agreed with Mr. Justice *Denison*, that it was incumbent upon the Counsel for the *Procedendo* to shew that in any *other* Corporation *besides London*, the Court had ever entered into the Question concerning the Validity of the By-Law, *upon* MOTION.

But they urged, That the Action given by *this* By-Law is restrained to be brought in that Court, "*and* NOT *elsewhere*:" Consequently, no Action can proceed in *this* Court, founded upon *this* NEGATIVE By-Law: Nor can the Plaintiff declare *here*, upon the present By-Law.

The only Cases in the Books, upon any By-Law containing such *Negative* Words, (And all of them, in *London*;) they said, were 1 *Lev.* 14. *Mayor and Commonalty of London* v. *Bernardiston*. 2 *Siderf.*

derf. 178. S. C. *Chamberlain of London* v. *Barnardiston.* 1 *Keble* 32. S. C. *Player* v. *Barnardiston.* * 6 *Mod.* 123. *Cuddon, Chamberlain of London* v. *Provost*; and 6 *Mod.* 177. *Fazakerly* v. *Baldoe:* Both, on the same By-Law as *Barnardiston's* Case. They also cited a Case of the *Chamberlain of London* v. *Grosvenor* 14 *G.* 2. *C. B.* and a later One of *Harris* v. *Wakeman* 28 *G.* 2. *B. R.* a Writ of Error upon a Judgment given in an Action founded on a By-Law in this very City of *Worcester.*

* Mr. *Norton* said that 1 *Lev.* 14. was erroneously reported: For the By-Law had been searched; And there were *no* such negative Words in it.

But Mr. Serj. *Nares,* Mr. *Morton* and Mr. *Aston,* of Councel for the *Procedendo,* desired further Time to look into this *Preliminary* Question: For which, they said they were not prepared, as they were not at all apprized of an Objection of this Sort.

The Court granted it. But They observed, that if these *Negative* Words should be *allowed to prevail,* All the Cities and Corporations in *England,* and even All the little Burroughs who had Courts of Record, would put negative Words into their By-Laws, and *exclude* this Court.

The Rules were therefore, at that Time, enlarged.

And these Causes being now mentioned again,

Mr. Serj. *Nares,* Mr. *Morton,* and Mr. *Aston* acknowledged that they could *not find any Instance* where the Court had entered into the Validity of the By-Law returned, in a *summary* Way, upon *Motion*; Except in those which had been returned from *London.*

But they argued that there was *no reason* to distinguish between *London* and *other* great Cities; And that the Hands of the Inferior Court ought not to be tied up, where *this* Court cannot do the Plaintiff the *same Justice* that the Inferior Court (by Virtue of their local Customs) can. They urged the great Inconvenience of obliging the Parties residing in Corporations in the Country, to sue in *this* Court for Penalties of very small Value and upon local By-Laws: And they said it would be very hard, if the Plaintiffs should be excluded from entering into the Question here, *upon Motion,* when it was impossible for them to support a *Declaration here.*

They cited 1 *Ra. Rep.* 232. *Sterling's* Case, as being within the same Reason as this Negative By-Law: Which Case was upon a Charter, which had the exclusive Words " And not elsewhere;" And would have been a Ground for a *Procedendo,* if it had been returned.

And they also mentioned *Wade* and *Bemboe's* Case, in 1 *Leon.* 2. *Pl.* 3. and *Cro. Eliz.* 894. *Grice* v. *Chambers*; and 1 *Mod.* 96. Anony-

Anonymous: Which two latter Cases are upon *Cognovit Actionem, et petit quod inquiratur de debito*; under Customs prevailing in *Norwich* and in *Bristol*.

Mr. *Norton, contra*—This is a *mere personal Action*: It is *not* an Action grounded upon a *Custom*. And it is a Case where *this* Court *can* give the like Remedy and do the same Justice that the Inferior Court may.

Lord Mansfield—This is an Action upon a By-Law, and comes removed hither from a Corporation in the Country, upon the Return of a *Habeas Corpus*: And the whole Question, at present is, "Whether the Court can enter into the Consideration of the *Validity* of the By-Law, *upon the* Return."

There is a *settled Course and Form of Proceeding* in Cases of this Nature; Of which there are many thousand Instances: And yet, though there be such Numbers of Instances of this kind, there is *not a single One*, where the Court has ever determined the Validity of the By-Law, upon the Return, excepting in *London*.

As to the Validity of this *particular* By-Law, If it be true, "that there *never was such a One*," that is a strong Argument against it's being a good One. However, the *Validity* of it is not to be disputed *upon the* Return; but in the *ordinary Course* of Proceeding in the like Cases, *viz.* by the Plaintiff's *declaring* here, and the Defendant's demurring to it, if he thinks proper. It never has been done, in this *summary* Way, upon the *Return*; nor ever attempted or thought of before: And therefore We ought not to do it now. The proper Course is settled; It must be by *declaring* here: And the Defendant may demur, if He has any Objection to the By-Law.

As to *Sterling*'s Case in 1 *Ro. Rep.* 232. It is not an Authority in *this* Case: *Charters of Exemption* are very different from By-Laws of Corporations.

Mr. Just. Denison was of the same Opinion. He said that this had never been done, but upon Returns from the City of *London*: And this was an Attempt to get the Opinion of the Court extrajudicially.

Mr. Just. Foster—Let the Plaintiff *declare here*.

Mr. Just. Wilmot said He had searched very diligently; but could *not find* any Instance, *except in London*, where the Court had ever entered into a Question about the Validity of a By-Law, *upon the*

the RETURN: And therefore He was clear "that the Court were "not authorized to do so."

Per Cur. unanimously,
The RULE "to shew Cause why a *Procedendo* "should not issue," was DISCHARGED.

And The like RULE was also made in the other Cause.

Rex *vers.* Richard Waite.

THE COURT *rejected Articles of the Peace,* which One *Thomas Burrough*, of the *Devizes*, offered to swear against the Defendant who *resided at the same Place.*

Their Reason, and their only One, (for the Charge was exceedingly strong,) was Because the Exhibitant had not applied or endeavoured to apply to any Justice of Peace in his *own Neighbourhood*, but had chosen to come hither, at such a *Distance* from the Defendant's Residence: Which Method would put the Defendant to the unnecessary Inconvenience of being brought up hither, instead of finding Security in the Country.

For which Reason, They directed the Exhibitant to go before some Justice of Peace in the *Neighbourhood*; and there exhibit his Articles, and pray the Security of the Peace: Which the Defendant might then find in the Country, without coming up to *London* for that Purpose.

Monday 21st *May* 1759.

Rex *vers.* William Lewis, Capital Burgess and Alderman of *New Radnor*.

UPON shewing Cause against an Information in *Nature of a Quo Warranto*, to shew by what Authority the Defendant acted in the Characters abovementioned, it appeared to the Court, that the Charge was exceedingly groundless and frivolous, and could not but be known to the Prosecutor to be so.

Whereupon *Per Cur.*
The RULE was discharged, *with* COSTS.

Foster *verſ.* Snow.

Wedneſday 23d May 1759.

CAUSE was ſhewn on the Part of the Plaintiff, againſt *diſcharging an Order made by Mr. Juſt. Deniſon at his Chambers*; and againſt the Defendant's being at Liberty to *wave his Plea*, and plead the General Iſſue.

Mr. Juſtice *Deniſon*'s Order (made in the *Vacation*) was "That "the *Defendant ſhould* PLEAD SUCH PLEA AS HE WOULD STAND "BY." And it was objected to it "That *ſuch* an Order ought not "to have been made by a *Judge at his* CHAMBERS."

The whole Caſe was this. It was an Action on a Policy of Inſurance. The Declaration was delivered in *Hilary* Term laſt (on the 8th of *February*.) The Venue was laid in the County Palatine of *Lancaſter*. The Defendant's Attorney applied to Lord *Mansfield*, and obtained an Order from his Lordſhip, "for *ten Days* time to "plead; the Defendant pleading an *iſſuable* Plea, and conſenting to "take ſhort Notice of Trial (if neceſſary) for the next Aſſizes."

The Defendant had filed a Bill in Chancery: To which, No Anſwer was put in. The Defendant's Attorney, being deſirous to ſee what Anſwer would be made to this Bill in Chancery before he pleaded, endeavoured to ſtave off the Common-Law Trial till after the then approaching Aſſizes: In Order to obtain which End, He pleaded a *Sham Plea*, "of a Judgment recovered in another Court." On his pleading this Sham Plea, the Plaintiff's Attorney immediately applied (it being then *Vacation*-time) to Mr. Juſtice *Deniſon*, who made the above Order. Then the Plaintiff's Attorney put in a Replication "of *Nul tiel Record*;" and made up and delivered the Paper-Books, with the Common Rule indorſed thereon, "to re"turn them within Four Days; otherwiſe a Writ to iſſue." The Defendant's Attorney returned the Paper Books within the 4 Days: But at the ſame Time gave Notice that he would move the Court "That the Judge's Order might be diſcharged; and that the De"fendant might be at Liberty to wave his Plea." And he afterwards made Affidavit of all the above-ſtated Facts; and alſo "That he verily believed, from what Evidence he was at preſent "poſſeſſed of, together with ſuch further Evidence as he expected "to ariſe from the Plaintiff's Anſwer to the Bill in Chancery, that "the Defendant would be able to make a *good Defence* at the Trial "of this Common Law Cauſe." And he offered to *bring all the Money* demanded, *into Court*.

The Court All agreed in justifying the Order made by Mr. Justice *Denison*, not only as being rightly made upon the Circumstances appearing to Him; but also, as being such a One as might be properly made by a Judge at his *Chambers*.

Lord Mansfield said It was reasonable to indulge Defendants with some time to make their Defence, on Special Circumstances being made out; And that if the whole Matter had appeared to Him, when He gave the Defendant Ten Days, He might perhaps have granted an Imparlance.

Mr. Just. Denison observed that "Pleading issuably" meant Pleading SUCH *an Issue* as the Plaintiff *might go to Trial upon.*

Mr. Just. Foster observed that if the Ld. Ch. Justice had been acquainted with the whole Circumstances of the Case, when He made his Order for Ten Days; he would have granted so much Time as to have carried it over the Assizes.

This Matter ended at last in a Rule *by Consent*: And the Witnesses were to be examined before Commissioners &c.

Rex *vers.* Corporation of Wigan, or Rex *vers.* Curghey Esq; et al'.

UPON a Vacation in a Corporation, if a proper Application for a *Mandamus to go to Election*, be made and granted, It is NOT *of Course*, That any *other* like Motions may be made *by* OTHER *Parties*, for the same thing: But! if there be a *reasonable Cause to suspect* "That the Party who first moved for it does not *really mean* to "carry it into Execution," *this* must be particularly laid before the Court *by Affidavit*; and then a Rule shall be made "to shew "Cause." Which Method was taken in the present Case, where the other Party had made a Prior Application: For upon Affidavits of particular Circumstances, a Rule was made on Mr. *Aston*'s Motion, to shew Cause why a Cross-*Mandamus* should not issue to be directed to *William Curghey* Esquire, commanding Him to hold a Court Leet, in order to go to the Election of a Mayor.

Mr. *Morton* and Mr. *Winn* now shewed Cause against this Rule, and why the last Applier should *not* have a *concurrent Mandamus*, to command the Corporation of *Wigan* to go to the Election of a Mayor. They cited *Rex* v. *Corporation of Scarborough, M.* 1753. *Rex* v. *Corporation of Haslemere, M.* 1753.—Both which Cases turned upon this single Question, "Whether there was any reasonable Cause *to suspect* that the Party who first applied for the "*Mandamus*, did *not really mean* to carry it into Execution." Now here, They said, was no sort of Ground for any such Suspicion; Nor was there, in Fact, the least Intention of that kind.

And they added, that if the Application for a second Writ was at all proper, Yet it would be improper to *specify the Direction* of it to the *Particular Person named in* the *Rule*.

Mr. *Aston* Mr. *Yates*, and Mr. *Campbell*, *contra*, insisted that *They* were the *first Appliers* for a *Mandamus* "*to hold a Court Leet*," in Order to go to the Election of a Mayor.

The Case of *Scarborough* was *only quia timet*: And the Motion was, for *that* reason *only*, denied by the two Judges then in Court.

They relied on the *Act* of 11 *G.* 1. *c.* 4. Which, they said, was a very *plain Rule* to go by. In *Evesham*, *P.* 6 *G.* 2. *B. R.* on the Death of an Officer of the Corporation, *Cross Mandamusses* were moved for, on the same Day.

As to the particular Direction of the present concurrent Writ—The Court do very often *expressly* direct the *Mandamus* to *particular* Persons *by Name*. *M.* 9 *G.* 2. *Rex* v. *Burrough of Oreford B. R.* 1737. was so; and was a Cross *Mandamus*, *without* Affidavit.

And it is *rightly directed* to *Curghey*, *by Name*. *H.* 9 *G.* 2. *B.R. Rex* v. *Matthew Manning*, in *Thetford*, was directed to him *by Name:* And many other like Instances. There was another, which was expresly directed to Lord *Arundel* of *Wardour*, or to his Steward, to hold a Court Leet: This was in 1753 and 1754: *Rex* v. *Williams* was the Name of the Cause.

Their Mandamus is to the Corporation: *Ours* is under the third Clause of 11 *G.* 1. *c.* 4. and is to be directed to One particular Person, *viz.* the Person who ought to hold the Court Leet. They said, They only wanted to be *secure* of an Election *within the Year*.

Lord Mansfield—

The Question seems to be now taken up, (though not before disputed,) "Whether these *Cross* or *Concurrent* Writs of *Mandamus* "are to be granted *of Course*, without some *special* and *particular* "Reason." And therefore

I will

I will consider it, upon the *Precedents*; upon the Circumstances of *this* Case; and upon the *Reason* of the Thing.

The Priority of Application to the Court for the Writ of *Mandamus* to go to an Election, is generally casual and accidental. Where, (as in the present Case,) it depends upon the entering up the Judgment of *Ouster*, the prosecutor has some Advantage, by knowing the precise Time when the Judgment of Ouster was signed.

It has been now urged, as it seems to Me, from the two Precedents of *Oreford*, and of *Evesham*, " That Cross or Concurrent " Writs of *Mandamus* to go to Corporate Elections, are to be granted of *Course*." These two Instances passed without Argument or Opposition: Whereas the two *subsequent* precedents cited on the other Side, *viz.* those of *Scarborough* and of *Haslemere*, were debated and fully considered. And it is not the Course of the Court, (as the Master reports to Us,) to grant Cross or Concurrent Writs of *Mandamus*, *of Course*, without *special* Reasons.

If there is a *Ground of Suspicion* laid, " That the Party first applying for such a Writ does *not mean to execute* it," It is reasonable to grant the *Carriage* of another *like* Writ to the other Side. But here is *no* such Ground laid, nor is there any Reason at all to suspect it: On the contrary, they undertake peremptorily to execute the Writ which they have applied for. But there is *another Ground* laid in the present Case, and a very material One too; *viz.* a Doubt Whether they will execute it effectually and legally, by *directing their Writ* to the *proper* Person. The Court cannot take upon themselves, previously to issuing the Writ, to determine " *to whom* it shall " be directed." That may depend upon the very Question to be tried. The Court do not use to specify by Name, to *whom* the Writ of *Mandamus* shall be directed.

If We should grant Writs to *both* Parties, it would occasion not only *double Expence* and *double Trouble*, but *double Elections*: Which would be infinitely inconvenient to Corporations, and could not be prevented under such double Writs.

The very Words of 11 *G.* 1. *c.* 4. shew that it would be determining the Right before-hand, if We should Order *to whom* the Writ shall be directed.

As to the Cause of Suspicion *here* offered, The Affidavits are extremely loose, and built upon mere Imagination. Therefore there is no sufficient Ground for granting two Writs in this Case.

3 Mr.

Mr. Just. DENISON concurred in general: And He was particular in declaring Two things; *viz.* 1st. That the Granting two concurrent Writs of *Mandamus* "to go to Corporate Elections," is *not a Matter of Course* to be done without *Special* Reason; And 2dly. That the Court are not particularly to specify "*to whom* the Writ "shall be directed." And He mentioned a Case of *Rex* v. *Nants*.

Mr. Just. FOSTER also concurred. He said It was *at the Peril* of the Person who desires the Writ, to direct it to *a proper* presiding Officer: And He cited the Case of *Carmarthen*, where the Court would not specify in particular the Person to whom it should be directed.

Mr. Just. WILMOT likewise concurred clearly, "That it was "*neither right in itself*, nor the *Practice* of the Court, to issue Con-"current Writs without *special Reason*." And so, He said, were the Cases of *Scarborough* and *Haslemere*. And here, He saw *no Ground of Suspicion* "That the first Applier did not mean to exe-"cute it fairly."

And as to the Court's giving particular Instructions about the Person *to whom* the Writ should be directed; it was not usual, nor in this Case proper: For it might be in many Cases, and would be in this, a *Prejudging* the Right of the Electors, *before the proper Time*, and in an *improper Manner*.

Per Cur. unanimously,
RULE DISCHARGED.

Monday 28th *May* 1759.

Rex *vers.* Benjamin Cox Esq;

THE Court had granted a Rule for the Defendant, a Justice of Peace for the County of *Middlesex*, to shew Cause Why an Information should not be granted against him, for *refusing to receive* an Information regularly and duly laid before him against a *Baker* for exercising his *Trade on a Sunday*, contrary to the Statute of 29 *Car.* 2. *c.* 7. ("for the better Observation of the Lord's "Day;") Mr. *Cox* Giving it as a Reason for his Refusal "That "the Justices of *Middlesex* and of *Westminster* had come to such an "Agreement amongst themselves, not to receive such Informations."

They laid the Stress of the Case upon the Justices *Refusal to receive* the Information at all: Though

Mr. Just. FOSTER on the Original Motion, thought that there was no Need to *receive* it, if the Justice was of Opinion, upon it's being opened to him, "that the Case stated to Him was *not* an Offence "within the Act." And He intimated his *own* Opinion, pretty strongly, "that it was *not so*; and that it was better that *One* Baker and "his Men should stay at Home, than *many* Families and Servants." He said He was as much for the Observation of the Sabbath, as any One: But He did not think a Pharisaical or a Jewish Observation of it to be necessary.

Lord MANSFIELD likewise at the same Time, hinted His Opinion "that the Sabbath would be much more generally observed by "a Baker's staying at Home to bake the Dinners of a Number of "Families, than by his going to Church, and those Families or their "Servants staying at Home to dress Dinners for themselves."

However, They All agreed that it would be by no Means amiss, that the Justices at *Hicks's Hall* should have an Opportunity of knowing the *Opinion of this* Court upon this Subject: And (for that Purpose principally, as it seemed to Me,) they granted a Rule to shew Cause.

Mr. Serj. *Nares* and Mr. *Stowe* now shewed Cause; and observed that the Charge was not for baking *Bread*, but for baking Puddings, Pies, and other such Things for *Dinner*. And that the Act of 29 *C.* 2. *c.* 7. § 3. allows of *dressing Meat*, on a *Sunday*, for Dinner; And excepts Works of *Necessity* and Charity.

And all the Justices of Peace of *Middlesex* and *Westminster* have agreed that *this* is not an Offence which that Statute meant to punish. And this Gentleman, Mr. *Cox*, *heard* the whole Complaint; and then declared the Opinion of Himself and of his Brethren, "That it was *not* an Offence within the Meaning of the Act of "Parliament or any other Law: For that He and the other Justices considered it as a Cook's Shop, and as a Matter of *Necessity*, "and of Relief to poor People."

Mr. *Norton*, Mr. *Morton*, and Mr. *Ashurst contra*, for the Information, cited two Cases of *Rex* v. *Sergeson and Rex* v. *Dawson*.

This does not appear, they said, to have been a baking for the *Poor only*, or for the *Poor at all*; Which cannot be presumed: So that it does not appear to be a Work of Charity or Necessity. Nor is it to be ranked under the Appellation or Nature of a Cook's Shop; and consequently not within the Proviso in the third Section.

The Words of the Act are "That no Tradesman, Artificer, "Workman, Labourer, or other Person whatsoever, shall do "or exercise any wordly Labour, Business or Work of their "ordinary Callings upon the Lord's Day, or any part thereof; "(Works of Necessity and Charity only excepted.")

§ 3. "Provided, That nothing in this Act contained, shall extend to the prohibiting of dressing of Meat in Families, or "Dressing or Selling of Meat in Inns, Cooks Shops, or Victualling-Houses, for such as cannot otherwise be provided."

Lord MANSFIELD—The Complaint now appears to have been founded upon a Misrepresentation of the Fact: For the Affidavit charges this Justice of Peace to have refused *receiving* the Information; and that He told them the Justices had come to an Agreement "not to grant Warrants against Persons for *baking* on a *Sunday*." Whereas it now appears that He *did hear* the Charge; and that it was *not baking in general* on a *Sunday*; but baking *Pies Puddings* and *Meat for Dinner*; not saying a Word about *Bread*, which is the Business of a Baker's ordinary Calling. And He told them "That "THIS *Sort* of baking or *dressing Meat* on a *Sunday* was not, in his "Opinion and in the Opinion of the rest of the Justices, an Offence within the Act." I am not satisfied that their Opinion was wrong. And if he *really* judged it not to be within the Provision of any Law, and had consulted his Brethren who thought so too, the Court would never grant an Information against him; even though such Opinion had been erroneous.

Mr. Just. DENISON—This Court will never grant an Information against a Justice of Peace from a mere Error in Judgment. And He declared that He thought the Justices to be in the Right in their Opinion; and that this was *not* a Case within the Meaning of the Law: It seems to be within the *Equity*, though not within the Words of the Proviso of Section 3. Therefore the Rule ought to be discharged.

Mr. Just. FOSTER concurred that the Rule ought to be discharged. He was clear that this Case was not within the Provision of the Act: But it falls within the Exception of Works of Necessity and Charity, and also within the Proviso, as being a Cook's Shop. And it is reasonable that the Baker should *bake* for the Poor, as that a Cook should roast or boil for them: There is no Reason for any Distinction.

And as the Justice has acted rightly, and also upon right Motives, the Rule ought to be discharged *with Costs*.

A

A Justice of Peace has a Right to judge for Himself, Whether the Matter charged is an Offence within the Law: And if upon hearing the Charge opened, he thinks it *not* to be an Offence within the Law, he ought not to proceed upon it; which could be to no Purpose but merely to put Persons to unnecessary Trouble and Charge.

Mr. Just. WILMOT—It comes out now, that the Justice did *not* refuse to *hear* and *receive* the Complaint; though when it was opened to Him, he judged that He ought not to *proceed* upon it. And in this He judged *right*: For it is not an Offence within the Provision of the Act; It is particularly within the Equity of the Exception of *Cooks Shops*.

Therefore I think the Justice had no *Jurisdiction* to proceed upon the Complaint. I think that no Justice of Peace ought to be punished by an Information, for an Error in Judgment. But I think that the Justice was in the *right* in the present Case: And therefore that the Rule ought to be discharged *with Costs*.

Per Cur.
RULE DISCHARGED with COSTS.

Rex *vers.* Inhabitants of Nether Heyford.

TWO Justices removed *John Gare* and *Hannah* his Wife, from *Kislingbury* to *Nether Heyford*: And the Sessions confirmed their Order.

It appeared upon the Special State of the Case, That the Pauper's last Service for a Year, under a regular Hiring for a Year, was at a Farm-House called *Dirt-House*; which the Pauper sometimes said was in the Parish of *Nether Heyford*, and at other Times, that it was in *another* Parish (named in the Order of Sessions.) But they state that it lay in *One* OR *the Other* of the said two Parishes.

This Order was, by Consent, agreed to be too uncertain for the Court to judge upon: And it was ordered, by Consent, that the Matter should go back to the Sessions, for them to state, WHICH *Parish* the said Dirt-House stands in.

On *Thursday* the 10th *May* 1759, Sir *Richard Lloyd* moved to file the New Order of Sessions, made and returned pursuant to the last Rule, which was " To enlarge the former Rule for shewing Cause " why the Original Order made for the Removal of *John Gare* and

" *Hannah* his Wife from *Kislingbury* in the County of *Northampton* to *Nether Heyford* in the same County, should not be " quashed;" And also further Ordered, " That in the mean Time " it be referred back to the Justices of the Peace in and for the said " County, to settle the Fact particularly, and to state particularly " *in what Parish* the Dirt-House (mentioned in the said Order of " Sessions) lies; and afterwards to *return the same to this Court.*"

Which Motion was granted; And this Order of Return ordered to be filed.

It was as follows *viz.*

In Pursuance of and Obedience to the Rule hereunto annexed, This Court [the Sessions] doth hereby certify That upon hearing of the Appeal concerning the Settlement of *John Gare* and *Hannah* his Wife, at *Epiphany* Sessions, 31 *G.* 2. the Fact then appeared to be, That the said *John Gare* was *born in Farthingstone* in the County of *Northampton*. That before *Michaelmas* 1754, He was hired for one Year as a Servant to *Edward Judkins*, who then lived in a House called the Dirt-House adjoining to a High Road leading from *Towcester* to *Daventry*: Which Year's Service the said *John Gare performed at the said Dirt-House*. That it did not *then* appear Whether the said Dirt-House was in the Parish of *Stow Nine Churches*, or *Nether Heyford* in the County aforesaid. That he the said *Gare* before *Michaelmas* 1756, was *hired for One Year* to Widow *Bliss* of *Farthingstone* aforesaid; and continued in her Service until *Five Weeks* before *Michaelmas* 1757: When WITH *his Mistress's Leave*, he *parted with her* and went to work with one *Litchfield* a Farmer at *Kislingbury* in the County aforesaid, and stayed with Him, the said Five Weeks, at *Kislingbury*. That after *Michaelmas* 1757, the said *Gare* went to his said Mistress *Bliss* for his Year's Wages: The whole whereof she laid down to him, and He thereout *voluntarily deducted Ten Shillings for his Five Weeks Absence*; being the same Sum he had earned and received for his Five Weeks at *Kislingbury*. That the original Contract, nor any New One, with his Mistress *Bliss* was dissolved or made, save as aforesaid. And that *if* his said Mistress had, during the said five Weeks, *required him to return* to her, He *should* have so done. Therefore this Court [the Sessions] upon hearing the said Appeal, for the Reasons aforesaid, did confirm the Original Order of Removal.

And in further Pursuance of and Obedience to the said Rule, This Court [the Sessions] doth hereby further certify, That at this present Sessions, it fully appeared to the Justices of the Peace in the said Rule mentioned, who were then present, on the Examination of

 Witnesses,

Witnesses, that the said *Dirt-House* lies and is in the Parish of NETHER HEYFORD aforesaid, and not in any other Parish or Place.

Mr. *Caldecott*, who moved to quash these Orders, owning that it was now clear that the Dirt-House stood in *Nether Heyford*, urged that the Pauper had gained a Settlement by his Service with the Widow *Bliss* at *Farthingstone:* And He cited 1 *Strange* 423. *Rex* v. *Inhabitants of Islip.* 2 *Strange* 1232. *St. Peter in Sandwich* v. *Goodnestone.*

Sir *Richard Lloyd contra*, insisted that the Pauper's Contract with the Widow *Bliss* was totally and absolutely *dissolved*, by his parting from her Service * *Five Weeks* within the Year.

CURIA ADVISARE VULT.

* *V. ante, pa.* 592 to 596.

Lord MANSFIELD now delivered the Resolution of the Court.

The Question turns singly upon this, "Whether his *Absence* "*for Five Weeks* was a *Dissolution* of the Contract."

If he had his Mistress's Leave, it was *not: If* he had it not, it *was.* And We are All of Opinion, that it was only an Absence WITH *Leave.* For it appears that both Parties considered the Contract between them, as *subsisting* and *not dissolved.* He paid her the *Whole* that he had earned in the 5 Weeks that he was absent; that is He voluntarily deducted it from the Wages She laid down to him; considering himself as her Servant during that Time: For otherwise, the Deduction would not have been a Deduction of the particular *Sum earned* by him; but a Deduction in *Proportion* of his whole Year's Wages to the Time of his Absence. And he looked upon himself as liable to be called back within the 5 Weeks.

Therefore it was only a Leave to be absent for the *whole* Time, or for *part* of the Time, as She should call him back sooner or later. And as She did not call him back sooner, It was a *Leave for the whole* Five Weeks. It is stated that the Man was *willing to have returned* within the 5 Weeks, and *would have so done,* if his Mistress had required him to do it. And the Sum deducted was not *proportioned* to the *Time* of his Absence: Which would have been the Measure of Deduction if the Contract had been considered by them as totally dissolved and at an End, when he went away from her. But the paying her the *exact Sum that he had earned,* shews that these 5 Weeks Service was treated by them as a Part of the Service done *to Her.*

And it is stated, "That the Original Contract was not dissolved, "save as aforesaid."

Therefore, upon the whole Circumstances specially stated, We are All of Opinion "That the Contract was *not* dissolved."

Consequently, The RULE must be made ABSOLUTE, and The ORDERS QUASHED.

The End of *Easter* Term 1759.

Trinity

Trinity Term

32 & 33 Geo. 2. B.R. 1759.

Saturday 16th *June* 1759.

Rex *verſ.* Beardmore, (Under-Sheriff of *Middleſex.*)

MR. Attorney General had moved (on *Monday* the 29th of *January* laſt) for an *Attachment* againſt *Arthur Beardmore*, the Under-Sheriff, for a *Contempt* of the Court, in taking upon himſelf, without any Pretence of Authority, *to* REMIT *Part of the Sentence* pronounced upon *John Shebbeare* in *Michaelmas* Term laſt: One Part of this Sentence was, " That the Defendant *John Shebbeare* be ſet IN *and upon* the Pillory."

And ſeveral Affidavits were then produced by Mr. Attorney General which were very full in aſſerting " that the Defendant only " ſtood *upon* the Platform of the Pillory, unconfined and at his Eaſe, " attended by a *Servant* in *Livery*, (which Servant and Livery were " hired for this Occaſion only,) holding an Umbrella over his Head, " all the Time: But his *Head*, *Hands*, *Neck*, and *Arms* were NOT " *at all confined* or put *into* the Holes of the Pillory; only that he " ſometimes put his Hands *upon* the Holes of the Pillory, in order " to reſt himſelf." And it was proved " that Mr. *Beardmore* at- " tended as Under-Sheriff; with his Wand; and that He treated " the Criminal with great Complaiſance, in taking him to and from " the Pillory."

A Rule was thereupon to ſhew Cauſe why an Attachment ſhould not iſſue againſt Mr. *Beardmore*, the Under-Sheriff.

On *Thurſday* 8th *February* 1759, Mr. *Morton*, Mr. Serj. *Davy*, and M. *Howard* ſhewed Cauſe.

Mr. *Beardmore*'s Affidavit ſhewed that his officiating at all in this Affair was quite *caſual* and *unexpected*, on a ſudden Meſſage from his Brother Under Sheriff. It was as full and explicit as poſſible, " That he had no Sort of *Deſign* or *Intention* either directly or indi-

" rectly

" rectly to favour *Shebbeare*; that he gave no particular Direction to " his Under-Officers about it, but *meant* and *intended* that this Sentence should be executed in the *usual* and *ordinary* Manner, as other " Sentences of the like Kind were and *used* to be executed; and that " He stood at a Shop opposite the Pillory, during the whole Time, " without almost ever taking his Eyes off from it during the whole " Time, in order to see the Sentence *properly* executed; and that " He *would have obliged* him to stand in what He, (Mr. *Beardmore*,) " *took to be the proper* Manner, if *Shebbeare* had offered to withdraw himself from such Position." And He positively swore " That according to the best Information he could get, *He looked* " *upon* the Manner in which *Shebbeare* stood, *to be the* USUAL *and* " PROPER Manner of Standing, *pursuant to* Rules worded as this " Rule is: And that he did according to the *best of his Judgment*, " fully and duly execute the Judgment of the Court in the *usual* " and *common* Manner."

And He produced 14 or 15 Affidavits, proving that the manner in which *Shebbeare* actually stood, was with his *Hands in and* THROUGH *the small Holes*, and his *Head and Face* FULLY EXPOSED *through* (some of them said *in* and through) the LARGE *Hole*: And that he stood so *during* the WHOLE Time that the Rule required him to stand.

And several of the Deponents, (Sheriff's Officers and Others,) swore positively that the Standing *without confining the Head*, was the *usual ordinary* Manner and had been so for 30 or 40 Years in *Middlesex*, of Criminals standing pursuant to Rules of this Kind; and that it had been usual in that County, *not* to fasten or confine the Head in the Pillory, for a great *many Years backwards*, and ever since One or Two Persons who were locked down in the Pillory had been killed: And several of them particularized how much Inconvenience might follow from *fastening* it down upon the Head. And two of the Sheriff's Officers swore " That they always deemed and conceived it to be a full Execution of the Words of the Rule to stand as this Man stood, with the Hands in, and the Head and Face *exposed through* the Holes of the Pillory.

But Mr. *Beardmore* and his Counsel admitted (or at least did not pretend to contradict) that his *Arms* were not put through the small Holes, and that the Pillory was NOT *shut down* upon *Shebbeare*, nor his HEAD *absolutely* THRUST THROUGH *it*: Which the Sheriff's Officers swore they did not apprehend to be necessary or usual, unless the Person was *refractory*. Neither indeed was it pretended that the *upper* Board of this Pillory was at all *let down* over his Neck.

Mr. *Howard* obſerved, (amongſt other Things), that the Sentence of *quartering* and *burning the* BOWELS of Traitors is *never ſtrictly executed*, nor the Puniſhment of *burning in the Hand*, which is conſtantly and notoriouſly done in the *Face* and with the *Knowledge* of the *Judges themſelves*, with a *cold* Iron.

Lord MANSFIELD—If the Charge be true, it is admitted that ſuch a Diſobedience to the Rule of the Court, by their own Officer, is puniſhable in this *ſummary* Way.

The Fact charged is " That by the Permiſſion and under the In-" ſpection of the Under-Sheriff, the Criminal ſtood upright and erect " upon the Platform of the Pillory; and that his Head, Neck, " Arms or Hands were *not* put THROUGH the Holes of the Pillory; " nor his Head even inclined to it."

As to the Defence which Mr. *Beardmore* has ſet up,—It would have been more judicious to have made no Defence at all, than ſuch a One as this. The Attempt to juſtify, upon Oath, the Offender's Standing *Upright*, as a *Legal* Execution of the Sentence, is an Aggravation: It is contrary to every Man's Conviction; And the Form of a Pillory alone demonſtrates what is meant by being ſet *in*, as well as *upon* it. The Offender was no more *in* the Pillory, than the Footman who ſtood by Him.

Then as to the other Part of the Defence, the *Uſage*—There is *not a ſingle Inſtance* particularized or ſhewn of this kind; or to prove that there has been ſuch a Uſage.

None of his Affidavits ſwear that the Method now taken was the *uſual* and *ordinary* Method; though Two of them ſay they conceive it to be a full Execution of the Rule. They only ſay " that it was " not uſual or cuſtomary for many Years backward, in *Middleſex*, " to *faſten or confine* the Neck in the Pillory:" And they give the Reaſon of it too, and mention ſome Inconveniences of *that* Method.

One of them ſays that this Man ſtood as he had *uſually* ſeen others do: But he *ſpecifies no Inſtances. Revie*, One of the Perſons who makes Affidavit, ſays he has known this Practice about ſetting in the Pillory 40 Years, having lived ſo long near *Charing Croſs:* And he *never ſaw* a Criminal *ſo publickly expoſed* in and upon the Pillory before, as this Man was. To be ſure, The Face of a Man who ſtands upright, is more expoſed to View, than his whoſe Head is bent down and put *in* the Pillory. And therefore, though the *Words* of the Affidavit are artfully drawn, to convey another Meaning, the Mental Reſervation of the Swearer guards Him from Perjury, ſup-

poſing

posing the Fact to be that He never saw a Man stand upon the Pillory before, in the manner that *Shebbeare* did.

So many Affidavits, so studiously and artfully penned, to be safely sworn in One Sense and read in Another, are an Aggravation.

And therefore the Rule ought, in my Opinion, to be made absolute.

Mr. Just. DENISON concurred.

Nothing imports Us more, than to see that the Judgments of the Court be *duly* executed.

Now no Ministerial Officer, or any One that has seen a Pillory, can doubt about the Meaning of setting a Criminal IN the Pillory. The very Form of the Pillory shews what it must mean. And it cannot be pretended that Standing *erect* UPON the Pillory, is being set IN it.

If there had been such a Usage in *Middlesex*, it was high Time to put a Stop to it. But here is no such Usage *proved*.

Therefore the Under-Sheriff ought to answer upon Interrogatories.

Mr. Just. FOSTER concurred: And He considered this Affair, as highly concerning the Honour and Dignity of the Court, and the effectual Execution of Justice. Mr. *Beardmore* cannot think, nor will he venture to say, upon his Examination on Interrogatories, "that this is the usual Method of putting Offenders *in* the Pillory."

Mr. Just. WILMOT also concurred that this Inquiry was a Matter of the highest Importance to the Honour of the Court, and the due Execution of the Sentence on Offenders; and that this Offence is of the most pernicious Tendency; Nothing being of worse Consequence, than that an Officer of the Court should combine with a Criminal to frustrate the Sentence of the Court.

He mentioned a Passage that occurred to him upon this Occasion, which He remembered to have met with in the Year-Books, and which is quoted in the Mayor of *Oxford*'s Case in *Palmer* 454: Where the Reason given in the Record, for the Plaintiff's recovering a large Sum in a Special Action against the Defendant for beating him, being his Adversary's Attorney, was "Quia the Defendant, "*quantum in se fuit*, non permisit Regem regnare." And it may be be at least said, with as much Propriety, of this Under-Sheriff in the present Instance, "that quantum in se fuit, non permisit Regem regnare."

And He expressly declared "that in Order to execute the true Intent and Meaning of this Rule, the Head and Hands ought to be "*in* AND THROUGH the Pillory, and remain so *during the whole Time.*"

Mr. *Beardmore* does not swear that he ever *saw* a Sentence executed in *this* Manner: Nor do his Affidavits specify any Instance of it. He inquired into the Manner of executing the Sentence, only in order to elude it: No Man *could* doubt how it *ought* to be executed.

I think his Defence makes his Case worse, rather than mends it.

Therefore He was clearly of Opinion with His Lordship and the Rest of his Brethren, "that the Attachment should issue against "Mr. *Beardmore.*"

And the WHOLE COURT, Each respectively, commended Mr. Attorney General for bringing this Complaint before them; as the Honour and Dignity of the Court, and the End and very Essence of Justice were so materially concerned in the due and regular Execution of their Sentences.

Per Cur. unanimously, Rule for the Attachment made absolute.

On the *Monday* following, (*viz.* 12th *February* 1759,) the Defendant appeared and gave Bail to answer Interrogatories; and was sworn to make true Answer thereto.

N. B. He HAD *given Notice* "that he would come in and *con*-"*fess* the Contempt, and *submit* directly to the Judgment of "the Court." But this Notice was withdrawn; his Counsel being satisfied that this could not be done within the Course of the Court; especially as this was not a mere single Fact, but a complicated Charge, arising from several Circumstances."

Lord MANSFIELD said they were certainly right in withdrawing their intended Motion.

And Mr. *Morton*, of Counsel for the Defendant, said that this same thing was formerly attempted in Dr. *Colebatche*'s Case (who would immediately have come in and submitted to the Judgment of the Court:) But he was obliged to be examined upon Interrogatories.

The Defendant accordingly gave Bail, (Himſelf in 200*l.* and Each of his two Sureties in 100*l.*) to appear and anſwer to Interrogatories: And then was ſworn to make true Anſwer to ſuch Interrogatories as ſhould be exhibited againſt him.

And after having been examined, the Interrogatories and Examination were referred to me, as uſual: And I made my Report. The Examination was much to the ſame Effect as his Defence upon his Affidavits. And the Rule was as follows—

Saturday next after the Morrow of the *Aſcenſion &c.* 32 *G.* 2. (26th *May* 1755.)

Upon hearing the Report of *James Burrow* Eſq; Coroner and Attorney of this Court, It is adjudged by this Court, "That the "Defendant is *in Contempt*:" It is thereupon Ordered "That he be "*committed* to the Cuſtody of the Marſhal of the *Marſhalſea* of this "Court." *But by Conſent* of his Majeſty's Attorney General, It is Ordered that the ſaid Defendant be *continued upon his Recognizance*; And that he the ſaid Defendant do perſonally appear in this Court on the ſecond Day of next Term, to receive the Judgment of this Court. It is thereupon further Ordered that he the ſaid Defendant be now diſcharged out of the Cuſtody of the ſaid Marſhal.

The Defendant now perſonally appearing in Court purſuant to the laſt Rule—

Mr. Juſt. Denison pronounced the Sentence.

He firſt expatiated upon the Offence. In doing which, He declared, that it was at the Sheriff's Peril, to execute the Rule of the Court in a *proper* Manner; And that no One could poſſibly doubt that the Suffering a groſs Offender, an infamous Libeller of the King and Government, to ſtand *in Triumph*, erect upon the Pillory, with a Servant holding an Umbrella over his Head, inſtead of Standing with his Head *in* the Pillory, by way of Diſgrace and *Ludibrium* (which is the Intent of this kind of Puniſhment,) was a highly *improper* and *inſufficient* Manner of executing this Rule of the Court.

After which, He gave the Sentence upon the Defendant *Beardmore*, for this his Contempt; *viz.*

To pay a *Fine of* 50 *l.* and to be * *committed* to the Cuſtody of the Marſhal, for 2 Months, and till the Fine ſhall be paid.

* He was ſtill Under Sheriff at this Time.

Tuesday 19th *June* 1759.

Rex *verſ.* Mayor and Jurates of Rye.

SIR *Richard Lloyd* ſhewed Cauſe why an *Attachment* ſhould not iſſue againſt the *Mayor* AND *Jurates*, for not returning a *Mandamus* directed to them; commanding them "to admit and ſwear "*Edwin Wardroper* into the Office of One of the Jurates of that "Corporation; or to ſhew Cauſe *why they refuſe* to admit him."

His Cauſe was, "that it was not poſſible for them *jointly* to make "*any* Return at all." For the Mayor claims a ſole and excluſive Right to nominate this Jurate; And the Jurates deny that the Mayor has any ſuch ſole and excluſive Right: So that it is impoſſible for the Mayor and Jurates to *join* in any Return; unleſs either the One or the Other ſhould *give up* the Right which they inſiſt upon. The Jurates would return "*Non fuit electus*:" But the Mayor refuſes to join in this Return; becauſe He ſays that the Jurate *is* duly choſen; And the Jurates can *not force* him to *join* in *their* Return. Therefore it would be hard to puniſh the *innocent* promiſcuoſly with the guilty.

Sir *Richard* was for the *Jurates*; and he offered to put the Right into any Method of Trial: But He ſaid they could not give up their Franchize. It may be tried, either upon a Return of "*Non fuit* "*electus*," or upon a feigned Iſſue. We are not perverſe and obſtinate; but lie under a real honeſt Difficulty: We cannot pay Obedience to the Writ, conſiſtently with our Oaths.

And an Attachment will anſwer no End or Purpoſe: For if an Attachment ſhould go, and the Defendants ſhould be examined upon Interrogatories, it would come out to be a *mere Queſtion of* RIGHT.

Note—The Right claimed by the Mayor was "to fill up the Va-"cancy of Jurates happening during his Year, *generally*:" But the Jurates deny that the Mayor has ſuch a Right, *generally*; though they admit that he has it upon the *ſingle Day* of his Election, but not afterwards, (as they alledge.)

It ended in a Rule by Conſent, to try the Right in a feigned Iſſue, at the Sittings after this Term, for *Middleſex*; on the Queſtion— "Whether *Edwin Wardroper* was duly elected, or not:" And further, that the Books ſhall be inſpected, and Copies taken *&c*; and the Books themſelves produced at the Trial, on proper Notice *&c*; and that the Party who ſhall prevail, may be at Liberty to enter up his Judgment as of this Term.

V. 6 *Mod.*

V. 6 *Mod.* 152. *Domina Regina* v. *Chapman*, late Mayor of *Bath*: (7th Point.) *Comberb.* 373. Case of *New Sarum*. *Rex* v. *Church-Wardens and Overseers* of *St. Chad's*, *H.* 8 *G.* 2. *B. R.* reported in *Lucas* 56.

Prisoner's Case.

Wednesday 20th June 1759.

LORD MANSFIELD declared it was the Opinion of *All* the Judges, upon a Consultation had amongst them, "That the "late Act of 2 *G.* 2. *c.* 22. (for the Relief of Insolvent Debtors with "respect to the Imprisonment of their Persons) being *expired*, No-"thing further can be done upon *that* Act: But that they are with-"in the Provision of the *new* Act."

And the COURT declared to those now present in Court, That they must *immediately* give Notice pursuant to the * *new* Act: For that this new Act requires 14 Days Notice; And there are only 14 Days of the Term now remaining.

* 32 *G.* 2. *c.* 28. § 13.

Mr. Just. DENISON observed that the Judges came to a like Resolution upon the Expiration of the former Act, as they are come to now. [*V. ante* 747, 748.]

Note—That Act of 2 *G.* 2. *c.* 22. was a temporary Act: Which was explained and amended by an Act of 3 *G.* 2. *c.* 27. and continued by 8 *G.* 2. *c.* 24. and 14 *G.* 2. *c.* 34. (which perpetuates the Clause of setting † mutual Debts One against the Other;) and again amended and continued by 21 *G.* 2. *c.* 33. and finally revived and continued by 29 *G.* 2. *c.* 28. until the *first* Day of *June* 1759. So that *this* Act *expired on the 1st of June*. But the *late* Act, of ‖ last Session, does not COMMENCE till the 15th of the same *June*. Consequently, there is a CHASM of 14 *Days*.

† See this Point of setting off *mutual Debts*, and these Acts of 2 & 8 *G.* 2. and also that of 8, 9 *W.* 3. *c.* 11. § 8. most fully clearly and satisfactorily explained by Lord *Mansfield*, *Post* 28th *November* 1759. *Young* v. *Diego Arines*.

‖ 32 *G.* 2. *c.* 28.

Rex *vers.* Robert Robinson, Clerk.

Friday 22d June 1759.

THIS was a Motion in *Arrest of Judgment*, upon an INDICTMENT against the Defendant for *refusing to obey an Order of the General Quarter Sessions* for the County of *Stafford* made upon him for his keeping and maintaining *James* and *Peter Robinson* his two Infant Grand Children: In which, the Breach was laid according to 43 *Eliz.* *c.* 2. § 7.

It came on no less than four Times before the Court.

The Indictment recites an Order of Sessions made on the 11th of *January* 1757, 30 *G.* 2. * directing "That the Defendant *Robert* " *Robinson* should, from the Date thereof, Weekly and every Week " pay or cause to be paid unto the Overseer of the Poor of the Pa- " rish of *Waterfal* for the Time being, the Sum of 2*s.* for the Re- " lief and Maintenance of his said Grand-child *James Robinson*; " and the like Sum of 2*s.* for the Relief and Maintenance of his " said Grand-child *Peter Robinson*; and to continue such respective " Payments until further Order." With which Order the Defendant was duly and legally served, on 21st of the same *January*.

* *N. B.* The Order recites the Death of the Father of these Children; their being destitute of Subsistence; the Complaint of the Parish; the Ability of the Grandfather, to maintain them; and other proper Foundations for such an Order; And that the Facts were, by proper Evidence, made to appear to the Justices at Sessions.

And the Charge is, " That the Defendant not regarding the *said* " *Order nor the Laws and Statutes of this Realm relating to the Re-* " *lief of the Poor* of this Kingdom, did not on 21st *January*, 30 *G.* " 2. nor hath since the Date of the said Order, Weekly and every " Week or otherwise howsoever, paid or caused to be paid unto the " Overseer of the Poor of the said Parish of *Waterfal* for the Time " being, either the said Sum of 2*s.* for the Relief and Maintenance " of the said *James Robinson*, or the like Sum of 2*s.* for the Relief " and Maintenance of the said *Peter Robinson*, or any Part of either " of the said Sums; nor hath he the said *Robert Robinson*, at any " Time or Times from or since the Date of the said Order, relieved " maintained or provided for them the said *J. R.* or *P. R.* or either " of them, according to Law; But he the said *R. R.* upon the said " 21st Day of *January* 30 *G.* 2. and continually afterwards, until " the Day of the taking the Inquisition, unlawfully wilfully obsti- " nately and contemptuously did and yet doth *neglect and refuse* " to pay or cause to be paid unto the Overseer of the Poor of the " said Parish of *Waterfal* for the Time being, Weekly and every Week " from the Date of the said Order, the said several and respective " Sums abovementioned contrary to the Purport and Direction of the " said Order, and in manifest Breach and Contempt of the same; " To the great Damage of the Inhabitants of the said Parish of *Wa-* " *terfal*, To the evil and pernicious Example of all Others in the " like Case offending; and also against the Peace of our said Lord " the King his Crown and Dignity."

The Indictment was found at a Quarter Sessions holden the 12th of *July* 31 *G.* 2.

On *Monday* 5th *February* 1759, Mr. *Morton* moved in Arrest of Judgment—

This

Objection.

This is a * NEW *Offence*, with a *particular Penalty*: And Section 11th of 43 *Eliz. c.* 2. prescribes a very *summary* Method of recovering the Penalty. Therefore 'tis *not indictable*. 6 *Mod.* 86. *Watson*'s Case, and *Castle*'s Case; and *Cro. Jac.* 643. *Castle*'s Case: Both which Cases are express, "that where a Statute *creates a* NEW *Offence*, and gives a *particular Penalty*, the Party shall *not* be punished by *Indictment*." Now here, the 7th Section gives a particular Penalty, *viz.* "Upon Pain that Every One of them shall forfeit 20*s.* for every Month which they shall fail therein:" And the 11th Section directs how that Forfeiture shall be levied and emlpoyed.

* *V. ante Pa.* 543. *Rex* v. *Wright*, Clerk, *P.* 1758. 31 G. 2. 1st Obj. S. P.

But it being litigated by the Other Side, previously to their shewing Cause, "Whether the Motion in *Arrest of Judgment* was made WITHIN *Time*;"

The Secondary certified, (on *Thursday* the 3d of *May* last,) And

The COURT then held, (notwithstanding the Case in 1 *Salk.* 78. *The Queen* v. *Darby*, which seems contrary,) "That a Motion in Arrest of Judgment may be made (on the *Crown* Side) at ANY *Time* BEFORE SENTENCE *pronounced*." For that the Judgment signed in the Office is only an *interlocutory* Judgment; And the Award "quod capiatur" is only to bring the Defendant in, to receive the final Judgment or Sentence of the Court; but is *not* the final Judgment itself.

They observed that the Judgment in *Darby*'s Case, in *Salkeld* 78. is there said to be a "Capiatur *pro fine*;" and the Capias there issued might possibly be for the Fine, *after* a final Judgment.

As to the Objection in Arrest of Judgment, It was, for the present, Adjourned.

On the *Monday* following, Mr. *Aston*, supported by Mr. *Gilbert*, shewed Cause why the Judgment against the Defendant should not be arrested.

They did not dispute the Rule laid down in *Castle*'s Case; But denied that here *was* a particular Penalty prescribed by this Act of 43 *Eliz. c.* 2. § 7. And cited 2 *Hawk. P. C. c.* 25. § 4. *pa.* 211. from whence they endeavoured to prove that An Indictment is not excluded unless it be so *particularly expressed* in the Act of Parliament.

They urged That an Indictment is the *proper* Remedy for disobeying an Order of Sessions. And, in the present Instance, they said, the Remedy given by the Act of 43 *Eliz.* is *inadequate*: For

 the

the Child may die *within* the Month; And the Forfeiture is only 20 s. for *every Month* that they shall fail. Another Reason why an Indictment is not excluded, is because if the Party liable should *remove out of the County*, the Remedy given by the Statute would be of *no Effect*. And here, the Defendant in Fact did remove out of the County. They remarked that the Case in 5 *Mod.* 329. and 2 *Salk.* 474. S. C. *Rex* v. *Turnock* or *Turner* was exactly such an Indictment as this: And no such Objection was there made; but it was quashed upon One of quite another kind, (namely, the Omission of the Word "Quarteriali.")

* V. Post 803. S. C. cited at large.

† V. Post 805. S. C. cited at large.

The Case of * *Rex* v. *Davis*, *M.* 28 *G.* 2. *B. R.* proves "that an "Indictment will lie, where the Remedy is *not adequate*." (That was an Indictment against a Parish Officer, for refusing to receive a Pauper regularly sent to his Parish.) *Rex* v. *Boys*, † *P.* 26 *G.* 2. 1753. *B. R.* proves the same Thing.

‖ V. § 11th, which directs it to be "levied by Distress and Sale; or in defect thereof, the Offender to be committed without Bail or Mainprize, till the Forfeitures shall be satisfied and paid."

And here is *no particular Mode* prescribed *how* the Penalty is to be ‖ levied. And the Forfeiture is not given by way of *Execution*; but in the Nature of a *new* Judgment. Here is no Remedy at all given, in Case the Disobedience be in the Payment for *three Weeks*; being only so much *per Month*.

* But see the next Clause in the same Book— "That if the Act be *not* prohibitory, the particular Remedy only can be pursued."

2 *Hale's H. P. C.* 171. says "That if there *be a prohibitory* "Clause, an Indictment will lie, Upon the *prohibitory* Clause." *

An Indictment, (it must be agreed,) would not lie UPON *the Statute*; because it gives a *particular Remedy*. But yet the Statute does NOT TAKE AWAY the *Common Law* Remedy: And the rather, as this Remedy, prescribed by the Act, is *not an effectual and adequate* One.

This is an Indictment at *Common* Law, *for disobeying an Order of Sessions*; *not* an Indictment *upon the Statute*, for this PARTICULAR *Offence*.

Mr. *Morton contra*, in Reply, cited 7 *Co.* 36. *a.* where it is said "That an Act of Parliament which gives a Penalty, ought only to "be followed, in the Prosecution and levying of it."

And this Act specifies the Remedy, as well as makes the Offence. This is a *summary* Law; and is directory, "to pay such a "Sum as the Justices shall assess." And the Remedy *is* adequate. The Defendant does *not appear* to be removed out of the County: This is only asserted, not proved. As to the small Space of Time

within

within the Month, no Penalty at all is incurred, *till* there is a Month's Neglect: It was not the Intention of the Statute to inflict any, till *after* a Month's Failure of Compliance with the Order.

CUR. ADVIS'.

The Court having taken some Time to consider it,

Lord MANSFIELD now delivered their Opinion.

The Objection to this Indictment is, "That the Offence is NOT "*indictable*; because the Act of Parliament has * pointed out a "*particular Punishment* and a *specific Method* of recovering the "Penalty which it inflicts."

* V. § 7. & 11.

The Rule is certain, "That where a Statute CREATES *a new* "*Offence*, by prohibiting and making *unlawful* any Thing which "*was lawful before*; and appoints a *specific Remedy* against such "new Offence, (*not* antecedently unlawful,) by a *particular Sanc*"*tion* and *particular Method* of Proceeding, *that particular Me*"*thod* of Proceeding must be pursued, and no other." And this is the Resolution, in *Castle*'s Case, *Cro. Jac.* 643.

But where the Offence was antecedently punishable by a Common-Law Proceeding, and a Statute prescribes a particular Remedy by a Summary Proceeding, there *Either* Method may be pursued, and the Prosecutor is at Liberty to proceed either at Common Law, or in the Method prescribed by the Statute; because there the Sanction is CUMULATIVE, and does *not exclude* the Common Law Punishment. 1 *Salk.* 45. *Stephens* v. *Watson*, was a Resolution upon these Principles: In that Case, † Keeping an Alehouse without Licence was held to be *not* indictable, because it was *no* Offence at Common Law; and the Statute which *makes* it an Offence, has made it punishable in *another Manner*.

† The 3d Point of it.

There was a Case in this Court in *M.* 28 *G.* 2. *Rex* v. *Davis*, In Arrest of Judgment upon an Indictment against the Defendant, Overseer of the Poor of the Parish of *St. Peter ad Vincula* within the Liberty of the Tower of *London*, for refusing to receive and provide for *Hannah Gotbridge*, a Pauper removed to that Parish by an Order of two Justices made by Virtue of 13, 14 *C.* 2. *c.* 12. by which Act the Justices are impowered to *remove* a Pauper to the Place of his last legal Settlement. But there is no Provision by *that* Act, to punish the Officer, in Case he *refuses to* RECEIVE the Pauper: So that the *only* Remedy was at *Common* Law, to *indict* him. Afterwards, by 3, 4 *W.* & *M. c.* 11. It is enacted, that if an Officer *refuse to receive* a Person removed by an Order of two Justices, he shall forfeit 5*l.* to be recovered in a *summary* Way.—

It

It was objected, "that this was a Matter *not indictable*, because it "was a *New* Offence created, and a *particular Method appointed* "by this last-mentioned Act." On the other hand it was said "that notwithstanding the Remedy given by the last-mentioned "Act, the Common Law Remedy, by Indictment, *remains*; and "the Officer of the Poor may be proceeded against *either* way." The Court held the Offence to be INDICTABLE, and discharged the Rule to shew Cause why the Judgment should not be arrested: For they held the Offence to have been indictable *after* the Act of 13, 14 *C.* 2. *c.* 12. and consequently *not a new* Offence originally created by the 3, 4 *W.* & *M. c.* 11. *

* V. Rex v. Boyall, Tr. 1759. 32, 33 G. 2. B.R. 2d July 1759. Post, pa. a like Determination to Rex v. Davis.

So, in the present Case, a Remedy existed *before* the Statute of 43 *Eliz*: For *Disobedience to an Order of Sessions* is an Offence *indictable* at *Common* Law. Here, the Relief is to be assessed and directed *by Order of Sessions*: And a particular Proceeding, in a summary way, is prescribed by the Act, as a particular Sanction and Method of Punishment, in case of Failure. But it is to be presumed that the Legislature then *knew* and *considered* "that *Disobedience to an Order of Sessions* was an *Offence indictable at Common* "Law." So that they must have intended that there should be, and there actually are TWO Remedies in the present Case: One, To proceed by way of *Indictment for disobeying the Order*, where the Weekly Payment is neglected or refused to be made; The Other, to *distrain* for the 20*s*. Penalty, after the Expiration of the Month.

The *former* Method has been taken, in the present Case: And there is no Doubt but that an *Indictment* WILL LIE for *disobeying an Order of Sessions*.

† V. Post accord'.

But † notwithstanding that here are *two* Remedies *given*; Yet, it would be extremely OPPRESSIVE to take the *Remedy by Indictment*, if there are *no* Circumstances which *obstruct* the Proceeding in the shorter way of *summary* Remedy: This would indeed be very wrong and unreasonable, where the summary Remedy can be put in Practice.

But in *some* Cases it may be *impracticable* to proceed in the summary Method, by way of Distress: As if the Party upon whom the Order is made, be gone out of the County, (which is said to be the Case here;) In which Case, the Penalty cannot be levied by *Distress and Sale*, nor the Offender *committed* by the Justices.

And there may also be a Disobedience to the Order even *before* the Month is out: And the Forfeiture is only 20*s*. *for every Month* which they shall fail. However, that would be *too severe*, To indict

dict for Disobedience to the Order, with such *very great haste* as not to wait till the Month should be expired.

By 43 *Eliz.* c. 2. § 2. It is enacted "that the old Church-Wardens and Overseers shall account for the Money in their Hands, "and shall pay over the Balance to the Church-Wardens and Overseers, *upon pain of* * *forfeiting* 20 s. *for each Default*." Yet there was a Case in *P.* 20 *G.* 2. *B. R. Rex* v. *Bill*, where Two Overseers were *indicted* for not obeying an Order of Sessions whereby they were ordered to pay over the Balance of their Accounts to the new Church-Wardens and Overseers.

* *V.* § 4. which directs the Method of enforcing them to account and to pay over the Balance.

In the Case that has been † mentioned of *Rex* v. *Boys*, *Trin.* 27, 28 *G.* 2. *B. R.* there was no other Remedy but by way of Indictment. It was an Indictment before the Justices of the Liberty of *St. Albans* for not obeying an Order of Sessions whereby the Defendant was ordered to pay the Costs of an Appeal against a Poor Rate which by 17 *G.* 2. *c.* 38. ‖ is to be recovered in the same Manner as Costs upon an Appeal against an Order of Removal; which by 8, 9 *W.* 3. *c.* 30. * are recoverable by *Distress and Sale* (or Commitment where no Distress is to be had,) where the Party lives *out of* the Jurisdiction, (by Warrant of some Justice of Peace for the Place where the Party inhabits:) But *if* the Party lives WITHIN the Jurisdiction, (which *Boys* did,) there is *no other Remedy* but by way of *Indictment*. And on Demurrer, Judgment was given for the King.

† *V. ante* 802.

‖ *V.* § 4th.

* *V.* § 3d.

So that the Case seems to be exactly parallel and in Point with the present Case. For that was a Case where the summary Method could *not* be used: Because the Defendant inhabited *within* the Jurisdiction; and the Summary Remedy is given only against such as live *out* of the Jurisdiction: So that the *particular* Remedy *failed*; and an Indictment consequently lay.

The true Rule of *Distinction* seems to be, That where the Offence intended to be guarded against by a Statute, was *punishable* BEFORE the making of such Statute prescribing a particular Method of punishing it, There such particular Remedy is CUMULATIVE, and does *not* take away the former Remedy: But where the Statute only enacts "that the Doing any Act NOT PUNISHABLE BEFORE, shall *for the* "*future* be punishable in such and such a *particular* Manner," *There* it is necessary that such *particular* Method, by such Act prescribed, *must be specifically pursued*; And *not* the Common Law Method of an *Indictment*.

We are All of Opinion,

* V. Post, pa. — Rex v. Boyall, (3d Objection in that Case,) S. P. accord.

That the Judgment ought * NOT to be Arrested: And therefore the Rule must be *discharged*.

Saturday 23d June 1759.

Rex *vers.* Robert Parnell.

THE Defendant stood convicted of a very gross, malicious, corrupt and wilful PERJURY, in certain Articles of the Peace exhibited by him upon Oath, against Sir *Thomas Allen* and his Servants; for which Perjury he had, some time ago, been committed in Court, upon his voluntarily appearing there, to complain of Difficulties which he pretended to meet with, in obtaining Process upon his Articles: Which *Articles* were *very express and positive*; and, by the Course of the Court, must have been looked upon by the Court, to be *true*; according to the declared Opinion of the Court in * Lord and Lady *Vane*'s Case.

† Rex v. Ld. Viscount Vane, Hil. 17 G. 2. 1743. B. R.

But, upon this Man's subsequent Application as above, and upon reading the Affidavits offered by Sir *Thomas* and his Servants and Others, in Answer to that Complaint, it appeared manifestly to the Court to be a *malicious* voluntary and gross Perjury.

Whereupon the Court not only rejected his Complaint, and *stayed Process* against the Defendants, but also *committed* the Complainant for *Perjury*; taking a Recognizance from the Defendant's Clerk in Court "to prosecute him for the Perjury."

Which Perjury being afterwards fully proved upon the Trial, the Sentence now pronounced upon him was—

To be set in and upon the *Pillory* at Charing-Cross (on 16th *July* next,) for One Hour; and to be TRANSPORTED for *Seven* Years.

Note—He appeared, throughout the whole of this Transaction, to be a very malicious dangerous Fellow.

Aſtley Bart. *verſ.* Younge Eſq;

Tueſday 26th *June* 1759.

Tr. 32, 33 *G.* 2. *Rot'lo* 25.

THIS was an Action upon the Caſe, for ſpeaking and publiſhing defamatory, falſe, malitious and libellous Words, of and concerning the Plaintiff Sir *John Aſtley.*

The Plaintiff, after premiſing (as uſual) the Innocence and Integrity of his Character, good Manners, *&c,* ſets out in his Declaration, That the Defendant being One of the Juſtices of Peace for the County of *Wilts,* and having refuſed to grant a Licence to One *Henry Day* for the keeping of a public Inn and Ale-houſe in *Everly* in the County of *Wilts* aforeſaid; * Application was made to this Court concerning the ſaid Refuſal: And on that Application, Sir *John Aſtley,* the Plaintiff, made an Affidavit in Writing and upon Oath, which was produced and read before the ſaid Court, of certain Matters and Things relating to the ſaid Refuſal; and alledges that He had ſworn the ſame with great Truth and Veracity. That the Defendant, maliciouſly intending to ſcandalize Sir *John &c,* on the 1ſt of *September* 1757, at the City of *London,* in a certain Diſcourſe with diverſe Subjects of this Realm concerning the ſaid Sir *John* and his Affidavit aforeſaid, falſely and maliciouſly SPOKE *and* PUBLISHED to thoſe Subjects the following falſe defamatory and malicious Words, *viz.* "Sir *John Aſtley,* in his Affidavit, hath SWORN "FALSELY; and I have proved to the Court the contrary of what "Sir *John* hath ſworn. Sir *John* hath a great Eſtate: but I would "not, for his whole Eſtate, have ſworn as he did." And in another Diſcourſe on the ſame Day *&c* with diverſe other Subjects, the Defendant maliciouſly intending as aforeſaid, maliciouſly and falſely *&c* publiſhed the following Words, *viz.* "Sir *John is* FORSWORN;" (meaning that the ſaid Sir *John Aſtley* had been guilty of Perjury.) † Whereas in Truth and in Fact he the ſaid Sir *John* had not in his ſaid Affidavit nor in any Part thereof ſworn falſely, nor ever was guilty of any Perjury whatſoever. By reaſon of which ſaid malicious falſe and ſcandalous *Words &c,* He the ſaid Sir *J. A.* hath been grievouſly injured *&c.*

* *V. ante, pa.* 556, 561.

† Here, the Words are laid, in ſeveral different Manners, as to the *Phraſe* and *Expreſſions;* but without any material Difference of Import: As, "Sir *J. A.* hath ſworn falſely: Sir *John* hath a "great Eſtate, but, for his whole Eſtate, I would not have ſworn as He hath done." Again, "Sir *J. A.* "in his Affidavit, hath ſworn falſely; And I have proved to the Court the Contrary. Sir *John* hath a "great Eſtate; but, for his whole Eſtate, I would not have ſworn as He did." Again, "Sir *J. A.* hath "ſworn falſely; And I have proved the Contrary." Laſtly, Sir *John Aſtley* is forſworn."

Then the Declaration proceeds, to this Effect, *viz.*

And whereas, whilſt the aforeſaid Application to the Court of our ſaid Lord the King before the King Himſelf, concerning the ſaid Refuſal of the ſaid *Edward Younge* to grant a Licence, was depending in the ſaid Court, and before the Publication of the Libel hereinafter mentioned, to wit &c, the ſaid Sir *John* had made and exhibited his Affidavit as aforeſaid, and been ſworn to it &c, Nevertheleſs the Defendant, well knowing the Premiſſes, but again contriving and maliciouſly intending to vilify and aſperſe the Reputation and Character of the ſaid Sir *John* and to bring him into very great Infamy and Diſgrace, afterwards *viz.* on 24th *January* 1758, did wickedly and maliciouſly *make exhibit and publiſh to the ſame Court* of our Lord the King before the King Himſelf, a certain *malicious falſe and ſcandalous* LIBEL, contained in *a certain* AFFIDAVIT *in Writing* of Him the ſaid *Edward*, concerning (amongſt other Things) the ſaid Sir *John Aſtley* and his Affidavit aforeſaid; *In which Affidavit of the ſaid Edward Younge* there were and are contained (amongſt other Things) certain *falſe malicious* and *ſcandalous* Matters concerning the ſaid Sir *John* and his aforeſaid Affidavit, according to the Tenor following, *viz.* "And moreover he" (meaning the ſaid *Edward Younge*) "ſhould have thought himſelf deſerving of all which Sir *John Aſtley* "hath so FALSELY SWORN againſt him, if the Fear of any Power "upon Earth could have moved him to act judicially againſt his Judgment;" as by the ſaid Affidavit of the ſaid *Edward*, remaining affiled of Record in the ſaid Court &c, more fully appears. Whereas in Truth and in Fact, He the ſaid Sir *John Aſtley* did not in or by his ſaid Affidavit ſwear any Thing falſely againſt the ſaid *Edward*, nor ever was guilty of any Perjury or falſe Swearing whatſoever. By reaſon of which making exhibiting and publiſhing of the ſaid malicious falſe and ſcandalous *Libel* ſo publiſhed by the ſaid *Edward Younge* as aforeſaid, the ſaid Sir *John* is very much injured in his Character &c; To the Damage of the ſaid Sir *John* of 5000*l.* And thereupon he brings his Suit &c.

Plea. The Defendant (having obtained Leave to plead double,) firſt pleads "Not Guilty," to the whole Declaration: And Iſſue is joined thereupon.

Then for further Plea to the Second Count, The Defendant, ſetting forth the Complaint made againſt Him, as above, juſtifies That He made ſuch AFFIDAVIT as in the ſaid 2d Count is mentioned, in his OWN DEFENCE againſt the ſaid Complaint made to this Court againſt Him for his Refuſal to grant ſuch Licence, and in Anſwer thereto and to the ſaid Affidavit of the ſaid Sir *John* ſo made to ſupport corroborate and ſtrengthen the ſame Complaint as aforeſaid.

The

The Plaintiff demurred generally to the Defendant's Plea to the laſt Count: And the Defendant joined in Demurrer.

Mr. Serj. *Davy* argued this Demurrer, for the Plaintiff—The Plea, He ſaid, was inſufficient: For it admits the Charge of making the Affidavit *maliciouſly* and with *Intent to aſperſe* the Character of Sir *John Aſtley*. And the Defendant juſtifies it, not as being *true*, but only as being made *in Anſwer* to a Complaint ſupported by Sir *John*'s Affidavit; But does not alledge it to be a NECESSARY *Part* of his Defence. And every Thing muſt be taken moſt ſtrongly *againſt* the Party pleading. Therefore it muſt here be taken "that it was "NOT *a neceſſary* Part of his Defence."

And this is a *Libel* undoubtedly.

Lord MANSFIELD—Shew that a Matter given IN EVIDENCE *in a* COURT OF JUSTICE, may be proſecuted in a *Civil* Action, as a LIBEL. The Court, indeed, *before which* ſuch Evidence is given, may *cenſure* it.

Serj. *Davy*—I will prove it; (1ſt) from *Authorities*, (2dly) from the *Reaſon* of the Thing.

Firſt—He cited, as Authorities, that (as He ſaid,) would * *prove* it, 4 *Co.* 14. *b. Pl.* 3. *Buckley* v. *Wood*; and 1 *Hawk. P.C.* 194, 195. (where *Hawkins* offers his own private Opinion, and a very juſt and reaſonable One.) * Sed V. Poſt 810.

Secondly—It would be moſt highly *inconvenient*, if it was otherwiſe. For any Man's *Character* might be cruelly injured by ſuch an Artifice as this: And if he could not be protected by *legal* Methods, He might (as in a State of Nature) be driven to *revenge* HIMSELF. It is very ſeldom that the Court before whom ſuch an Affidavit is wantonly and maliciouſly exhibited, interfere by *their* Cenſure.

This is an abſolute direct and unprovoked *Charge of* PERJURY: 'Tis a LIBEL, in the *Form* of an Affidavit. *Recrimination* does not at all ſerve to ſhew Innocence. This was not done to *defend* himſelf, but to ASPERSE *Sir John*.

And the Plea is *no Anſwer* to the Matter Charged in the Declaration. He is charged with *meaning* and *intending* to accuſe Sir *John* of Perjury: And he does *not deny* it. This is a Mater of *Fact*; which He *ought* to have anſwered.

The Plea admits "that this *was a* LIBEL:" And the *Truth* of a Libel can *not* be *justified*.

Mr. *Winn*, *contra*, was beginning to argue the Case, on behalf of the Defendant.

But Lord MANSFIELD told Him it was unnecessary for Him to speak to it; as the Matter was so plain.

Here was a *Charge against the Defendant* in a *Court of Justice*, made *upon Oath*, and supported by an Affidavit of Sir *J. A:* And in the Affidavit of the Defendant *in Answer* to this Complaint, He mentions the Charge upon him, and denies it, with this Conclusion of calling it "what Sir *John Astley* has *so* FALSELY *sworn* against Him."

Now in *every* Dispute in a Court of Justice, *upon Oath*; where *One by Affidavit charges* a Thing, and the *Other by Affidavit*, *denies* it; the Case is ordinarily *much the same* (in Effect) with the present; And Each Party might bring a Civil Action against the Other: For it too often happens, that the Affidavits and Evidence *are*, in Terms, DIRECTLY OPPOSITE to Each Other.

As to the *Authorities* cited, the former is not applicable to this Case; And the latter even lessens the Authority of the former: And though there may be a good deal of Sense perhaps, in the Opinion of *Hawkins*, Yet neither of these two Authorities relate to *giving Evidence*, nor to a Court that *has* Jurisdiction.

And as to the *Reason of the Thing*—There can be *no* SCANDAL, if the Allegation is *material:* And if it is not, the Court *before whom* the Indignity is committed by *immaterial* Scandal, may *order Satisfaction*, and *expunge* it out of the Record, if it be upon Record.

This that is now under our Consideration, arose upon the very *Point in Question:* It is *not* a *collateral* Recrimination. And Nothing is more common than to use the Word "UNTRULY" upon these Occasions; *viz.* "As the adverse Party has *untruly* sworn: Which is much the same Thing as the Expression here used, "Which Sir *J. A.* hath so *falsely* sworn against Him."

In the Case of *Lake* v. *King*, 1 *Saund.* 131. The Matter charged as the Foundation of that Action, (which was an Action upon the Case for printing and publishing a scandalous Libel upon the Plaintiff,) was contained in a Petition to a Committee of Parliament for Grievances, exhibited in a Course of Justice. It was agreed "That "no Action lay for *exhibiting* the Petition, (which was lawful,) *al-*

" *though* the Matter contained in it was *false and scandalous*; BE- " CAUSE it was in a summary *Court of Justice*, and before Those " who had Power to examine Whether it was true or false:" And Judgment was given for the Defendant, upon this Point, " That it " was the *Order and Course of Proceeding* in Parliament, to *print* " *and deliver Copies &c*; Of which the Court ought to take judicial " Notice."

There is another Case, which is vastly stronger; *viz.* 1 *Ro. Abr.* 87. Title " *Action sur Case*," Letter *M. Pl.* 4. In an Action upon the Case by *A.* against *B.* the Plaintiff declares that he took his Oath in this Court of *B. R.* against *B.* of certain Matters, to bind him (*B.*) to his good Behaviour: And thereupon *B.* then said, falsely and maliciously, intending to scandalize the Plaintiff, in the Hearing of the Justices and Officers of the Court, and Others there being, " THERE IS NOT A WORD TRUE IN THAT AFFIDAVIT; *And I* " *will prove it by* 40 *Witnesses*." It was holden " That the Action " was NOT *maintainable*: For the Answer which *B.* made to the " said Affidavit was a *Justification in Law*, and spoken *only* IN DE- " FENCE *of Himself*; and that *in a* LEGAL *and* JUDICIAL *Way*, " (in as much as he said He would *prove* it by 40 Witnesses.")

As to the *Words*, that Case is quite parallel to the present: And they were only spoken *in his own Defence*, and by Way of *Justification in Law*, and *in a legal and judicial Way*, in Answer to a Complaint made against him to the Court. So here the Defendant's Affidavit is in Defence to a Complaint against Him; which Complaint was supported by the Affidavit of the present Plaintiff Sir *John Astley*: In Answer to which Affidavit of Sir *John*'s, the Defendant made the Affidavit containing the Words upon which the present Action is grounded.

This ought not to be made a Matter of Question: And We are All of Us clear in the same Opinion.

And if the Matter of *Fact* be justified, the *Epithets* that the Plaintiff has thrown into this Declaration fall to the Ground.

As to the Words *spoken* by the Defendant OUT *of Court*—There is a Plea of Not Guilty to that Count. So that *that Point* is not now before Us.

This Expression was taken Notice of by the Court, at the *Time* when the Affidavit was read; and *disapproved* indeed as to using the Word " falsely;" which was thought too *rough* and *coarse* an Expression, but yet was not judged to require a formal CENSURE from the Court.

Mr.

Mr. Just. DENISON concurred with his Lordship; and thought the Matter to be extremely plain.

As to the Epithets and Innuendoes thrown into the Declaration, They are *immaterial*; since the *Substantial Fact* itself is *justified*: For if the *Matter* is not actionable, the Manner is of no Consequence.

Mr. Just. FOSTER concurred.

Mr. Just. WILMOT also concurred; and added, That the Case in * 1 *Ro. Abr.* 87. *Pl.* 4. is in † Sir *William Jones* 431. and in ‖ *March* 20. *Pl.* 45: And, in Sir *William Jones* the very Word "*false*" is made Use of; *Le Defendant malitiose dit*, "que ceo fuit "FALSE *Affidavit*; et que 40. voilent jure al contrarie."

* There called *Moulton* and *Clapham*.
† There called *Boulton* v. *Clapham*.
‖ There called *Molton* v. *Clapham*.

Per Cur. unanimously and clearly,
JUDGMENT for the DEFENDANT.

Friday 29th *June* 1759.

Maud *vers.* Barnard.

THE Question, upon the *Regularity of* SERVING A WRIT, was "Whether a Writ returnable on such a Day, can be "served AFTER *the Court is risen* upon that Day."

This Service was at *Rochester*, in *Kent*; about 8 o'Clock in the Evening.

To prove it *irregular*, were cited *Cro. Eliz.* 761. *Wolley* v. *Mosely*, (*sub finem*:) "A Writ may be executed on the *Day* of the Return: "because the Sheriff *may* have it in Court, to return." 2 *Salk.* 626. *Harvey* v. *Broad*—"A Writ may be executed *the* DAY it is return- "able; but *not after*." 6 *Mod.* 130. *Parkins* v. *Woollaston*: "The "Execution of a *Capias* on the *Day* of the Return, SEDENTE CU- "RIA, is good: *Secùs*, NOT."

But *Per Cur'*—It must, at least, be *proved* by the Person who objects to the Service, "That the Court WAS up:" For, otherwise, We will *intend* it to be regular.

Lord MANSFIELD—And in the Reason of the Thing, it is as impossible for the Sheriff to bring the Defendant *into Court before it's Rising*, as before the End of the *Day* of it's Rising; in all Cases where the Distance is too great to bring him up *within* EITHER Time: As in the present Case, from *Rochester*, after 7 or 8 in the Evening; which was the Time when the Process was served.

2 But

But, however, there was a Case in Point in this Court, in the 11 *G.* 2. * *Powell* v. *Pugh*, or *Pugh* v. *Powell*; Where Process was holden to be well served on the Day of the Return, AFTER *the Rising* of the Court.

* It was *Moss* v. *Powell*, *Tr.* See the Note below.

Note—There have been more Determinations, of the *same* kind: *viz.* In the Case of *Weyburn* v. *Neale M.* 19 *G.* 2. 1745. *B. R.* Mr. *Miller* moved to stay Proceedings; For that the Defendant was served with the Writ, on the Day of the Return, at *Eleven* at Night. And it was sworn "that the Court was "*not sitting* upon that Day at *Five* in the Afternoon." (In fact, it rose at *two*, that Day.) And upon shewing Cause, The Rule "to shew Cause why the Proceedings should not "be set aside" was discharged.

In the Case of *Hall* v. *Gatton*, *H.* 2 *G.* 2. *B. R.* The Defendant was served on the 27th of *November* at *Seven* in the Evening: And the Court rose that Day at *Three.* It was denied "to "stay Proceedings."

In the Case of *Moss* v. *Powell Tr.* 11, 12 *G.* 2. *B. R.* The Defendant was served with a Copy of the Process, between 7 *and* 8 in the Evening of the Day when the Writ was returnable; *after* the Court was up. The Court held the Writ to be *well served*; and that the Plaintiff had the *whole* Day: And they would *not* take Notice at *what Hour* the Court rose.

Per Cur'—The Rule "to shew Cause why the Proceedings in "the present Case should not be set aside," was DISCHARGED.

[So that the Point is now settled.]

Symes *vers.* Symes.

A Motion for a Prohibition to the Ecclesiastical Court, was denied by the Whole Court; For that where the Ecclesiastical Court *have Jurisdiction* (as in the present Case they had,) And they have pronounced Sentence, the Remedy must be *by Appeal*, and *not* by Way of Prohibition: But if they proceed where they have *no Jurisdiction* at all; there a Prohibition may be applied for, *after* Sentence in the Ecclesiastical Court.

They were clear that the present Case *was within the Jurisdiction* of the Ecclesiastical Court: And they had already *given Sentence* of Excommunication.

Therefore They refused even to make a Rule to shew Cause: though it was much pressed by Mr. *Popham*.

Coppendale *vers.* Bridgen and Another.

Saturday 30th *June* 1759.

THIS was an Action on the Case, against the Defendants as Sheriff of *Middlesex*, for a false return, in returning "*Nulla bona*" to a *Fieri facias* directing them to levy 2050*l.* Debt, and 6*l.* 10*s.* Damages, on the Goods of *John Debonaire*, recovered against him by the Plaintiff, in the Court of Common Pleas.

A Special Case was settled and agreed upon at the Trial, (after the General Issue pleaded;) And a Verdict was taken for the Plaintiff, for 292*l.* 7*s.* Damages, subject to the Opinion of the Court upon the said Case: which is as follows—

It was proved at the Trial, that the Plaintiff sued out a Bill of *Middlesex* against *Debonaire*, on the 2d *of May* 1757, returnable on *Wednesday* next after 3 Weeks from the Day of *Easter*. That a Precept was made out thereupon; and the Party *arrested the same Day*. That being so under Arrest, on the 4th of the same *May*, He was *charged* with Process out of the Court of Common Pleas, at the *Suit of One Joseph Solomons*: And was, the same Day, brought by *Habeas Corpus*, to Mr. Just. *Clive's* Chambers in *Serjeants Inn*; and committed to the *Fleet*, *charged* with *both* Actions.

That the Plaintiff in *Trinity* Term 30, 31 *G.* 2. according to the Course of the Court, obtained a Judgment against him in the Court of Common Pleas, for 2000*l.* Debt, and 6*l.* 10*s.* Damages.

That on 17th *June*, a *Fieri facias* thereupon issued, at the Plaintiff's Suit, to the Sheriff of *Middlesex*, RETURNABLE *from the Day of the Holy Trinity in* 3 *Weeks*, (which was the 26*th Day of June*:) And that on the 18th of the same Month, the Defendants, being Sheriff, *took divers Goods* of the said *Debonaire*, in Execution, and levied thereout the clear Sum of 292*l.* 7*s.* And that on the 5th *Day of November* the Defendants *returned* "NULLA BONA."

It was also stated, That the said *Debonaire* was a *Trader* within the Intent of the several Statutes concerning Bankrupts; And that he *remained in Custody*, at the *Plaintiff's* Suit from the Time of the FIRST *Arrest*, (which was on the said 2d of *May* 1757. as aforesaid,) UNTIL *and* UPON *the* 2*d of July* following: On *which* Day, he was discharged out of Custody, *as to the Plaintiff's Suit*, but *continued in Custody*, as to the said *Solomons's Suit*, *until the* 6*th* Day of the same

July

July. And that a *Commission of Bankruptcy*, on the 5th Day of the said *July*, was issued against the said *Debonaire*; and He was duly declared a Bankrupt, on the same Day: And on the 21*st Day* of the same Month, his Effects were in due Manner *assigned*.

And the Question submitted to the Court is, "Whether upon "the Whole of this Case, the Plaintiff is intitled to recover against "the Defendants in this Action."

Mr. *Ashurst* for the Plaintiff.

The Question is Whether *Debonaire*'s Lying in *Prison* 2 *Months* will have so far RELATION to the Time of the *first Arrest*, as to affect his Goods which were taken in Execution upon a Process *returnable before* the two Months were expired; but not *actually returned* till *after* he had lain in Prison 2 Months.

The Act of 21 *Jac.* 1. *c.* 19. § 2. ought to be taken favourably for particular Creditors.

As to the Cases of *Came* v. *Coleman*, *Tr.* 2 *W.* & *M. in Cam' Scac'*, 1 *Salk.* 109. and *Duncombe* v. *Walter*, *Hil.* 32, 33 *C.* 2. in *C. B.* 3 *Lev.* 57. and *Hill et al.* v. *Shish*, *Pasch.* 3 *Jac.* 2. in 2 *Shower* 512. and *Smith* v. *Stracy* *Tr.* 2 *Ann. coram Holt* at *Nisi prius*, in 1 *Salk.* 110, 111.—There was a later Case than any of * these, in *P.* 17 *G.* 2. *C. B.* of † *Tribe* v. *Webber*; which *denied* that of *Smith* v. *Stracy*, and is full in Point *against* it.

* *V. ante, pa.* 438. *Rose* v. *Green*; where 4 of these Cases are cited and discussed. † *Davis's Laws relating to Bankrupts, pa.* 376. gives a full Report of the Case of *Tribe* v. *Webber*: And the different Reports of the Case of *Duncomb* v. *Walter* are there compared and adjusted.

And He cited *Skinner* 270. *Hinton*'s Case, and 1 *Ld. Raym.* 724. *Cole* v. *Davies et al'*, Assignees of *Maul*, a Bankrupt; and argued from them, "that the Execution is *good*, to all Intents and Purpo-"ses: And He insisted that even the *Plaintiff himself* would *not* "have been obliged to *refund* the Money, if it had been paid to "him, upon a Return that it was levied."

But the *Sheriff* is undoubtedly *liable* to the Plaintiff's Demand; because the Truth of the Return must be taken to be what was true *at the Return*-DAY of the Writ; and it must be considered as if it had been actually returned UPON the Day whereon it was *made returnable*.

The Case of ‖ *Cowper et al'* v. *Chitty et al'*, *B. R. M.* 1756. 30 *G.* 2. proves that no Wrong would have been done by the Sheriff, nor could he have been hurt, by returning "That he had levied "the

‖ *V. ante, pa.* 20.

" the Money and had it ready:" For at the *Return-Day* the Man was *not* a Bankrupt.

And no *subsequent* Relation can exculpate the Sheriff for returning " Nulla bona."

Mr. *Yates*, for the Defendant.

The Question turns upon two Considerations;

1st. Whether the present Return shall be taken as a Return made UPON *the Return-Day*: And if so, then Whether it was a good Return, as supposed to be made *upon* the Return-Day.

2d. Whether it is to be taken as a Return made upon the *subsequent* Day, when it was *actually* made.

First—The *Relation* is to the Time of the *first* Arrest. Consequently, the Goods were not the Bankrupt's Goods, even at the Time when the Writ was *returnable*; but were then, by such Relation, the Property of the *Assignees*: The Defendant *Debonaire* Himself had then (by reason of such Relation,) no Interest in them; Nor consequently, could the Plaintiff have any Right to them vested in him by the Seizure of them.

If a Judgment is reversed, a Plea of " *Nul tiel Record*" is good.

And as to the *Plaintiff's refunding* the Money, if he had received it upon a Return of it's being levied; He answered, that If the Plaintiff had actually received the Money of the Sheriff, He *must* have refunded it: And He cited 2 *Strange* 996. *Rush et al'* v. *Baker*, as a Proof of his Assertion.

But Secondly—The Sheriff was *not called upon* to make a Return, TILL *the 5th of November* which was long after the Bankruptcy and the Assignment.

And no *Fiction of Law* shall make an Officer *guilty of a false Return*. But here the Supposing the Writ to have been actually returned AT and *upon* the Day, is a *mere Fiction*, and contrary to the Fact stated.

The Sheriff had no Right to take the Goods of the Assignees: And Trover would lie against him for it, if He should do so. * *Cooper* v. *Chitty M.* 1756. 30 *G.* 2. *B. R.* was so determined. And the Sheriff ought not to be liable to an Action *both* Ways.

* *V. ante pa.* 20.

Mr.

Mr. *Ashurst*, in Reply—

This is a *complex* Act of Bankruptcy: Therefore it differs from a Bankruptcy arising upon a *single* Act. Here, the Man is not a Bankrupt, *till* he has lain 2 Months in Prison.

The Right of Seizure of the Goods was VESTED in the Plaintiff UPON the Day of the Return: And therefore could *not* be devested by a *subsequent* Assignment of them. And *upon* the Day when the Writ was returnable, no Body could *then* say "That the Defen-" dant WOULD *lie* in Gaol 2 Months, and by so doing become a "Bankrupt."

This is not like the Reversal of a Judgment; for here, the *Right to seize* the Goods was actually *vested* in the Plaintiff: Therefore the Sheriff is guilty of a false Return in returning "*Nulla bona.*" It was the *Duty* of the Sheriff, to make his Return ON the *Day* when the Writ was *returnable*: And He shall *not profit* by the *not* returning it in Time.

As to 2 *Strange* 996. *Rush et al'*, *Assignees of Ryland*, v. *Baker*; Though the Action might lie in *that* Case, against the Defendant *Baker*, Yet this Plaintiff would *not*, in the *present* Case, have been liable to refund the Money, if he had received it upon a Return "that it had been levied." But if he would, the *Sheriff* can *not avail* himself of that.

Lord MANSFIELD—This Bankrupt was *first* arrested at the Suit of the Man who is the present Plaintiff against the Sheriff: He was *afterwards* charged in Custody, at the Suit of *Solomons*.

The 1st Question is—Whether the Return be *false*; *i. e.* Whether these were the Goods *of* the *Bankrupt*, or not. And that depends upon the Bankruptcy of the Defendant in the Original Action.

If this Man, *Debonaire*, was a Bankrupt on the 2*d* of *May*, when he was first arrested at the Plaintiff's Suit; or even upon the 4*th* of *May*, when he was charged in Custody at the Suit of *Solomons*; The Goods could not belong to *Him*, but must have belonged to the *Assignees*, by *Relation* backwards to that Time.

Now the Words of the * Act are as plain as possible: They are "That all and every Person &c, who shall &c; Or, *being arrested* "*for Debt*, shall after his or her Arrest, *lie in Prison 2 Months* or "more, upon *that* OR ANY OTHER *Arrest or Detention in Prison* "*for*

* 21 *Jac.* 1. c. 19. § 2.

"*for Debt*; shall be accounted and adjudged a *Bankrupt to all Intents and Purposes*, FROM THE TIME *of his or her said* FIRST *Arrest.*"

This Man was *arrested on the 2d* of *May*; and on the *4th* of *May*, was *charged in Custody, with that and another Action*: And it is admitted, "that he *did lie 2 Months in Prison*;" *viz.* till the 6th of *July*, at *Solomons*'s Suit; and till the 2d of *July*, before he was discharged as to the Plaintiff's Suit.

The Lying two Months in Prison is a strong Presumption that the Person was *insolvent at the Time* of the Arrest. And the Act says that "if he lies in Prison 2 Months upon *that*, or ANY OTHER Arrest, He shall be adjudged a Bankrupt from the Time of the "*first* Arrest." So that here is plainly an Act of Bankruptcy on the *4th* of *May*; whatever Dispute may be made about there being One upon the 2d.

Consequently, the Sheriff's Return is TRUE.

If the Sheriff had returned, "that he had levied &c;" and had actually paid the Money to the Plaintiff, *on the 26th of June*, (which was WITHIN the two Months,) the *Sheriff* would have been excused; because it was impossible for Him, at *that* Time, to know that the Defendant WOULD lie 2 Months in Prison; And therefore He was under an *invincible Ignorance* of this Event. But the PLAINTIFF, could have had no Advantage by this: For still *He* would have been liable to REFUND the Money; although the *Sheriff* might be excusable in Paying it to Him.

But at the Time when this Return was *in Fact* made, it was *then* certainly true, and known to the Plaintiff to be true, "That the "Man was become a Bankrupt:" And the Goods were *then* the Property of the *Assignees*.

* *V. ante, pa.* 31 to 38.

And in the Case of * *Cooper* v. *Chitty et al'*, It was determined "That in such Case the Sheriff might and ought to return "*Nulla bona.*" Therefore this is a plain Case.

Nothing could support the Plaintiff's Claim, but his shewing that the Bankruptcy was not incurred till after the 18*th of June*; which was the Time when the Goods were *taken in Execution*.

Mr. Just. DENISON concurred.

WHEN the Sheriff *made* the Return, it was *then* certainly true, "That the Defendant was a Bankrupt, before the Taking of the "Goods."

"Goods." Indeed *if* He had returned the Writ *upon the Day*, when it was made *returnable*, perhaps He might have been HIMSELF justified in returning "that he had levied and sold the Goods," and even in paying the Money over to the Plaintiff: But yet the PLAINTIFF must have *refunded* it, even in *that* Case.

However, it is here stated, "that the Return was made on the "*5th of November*:" Which was long after the Relation had taken Place.

Mr. Just. FOSTER—The *Relation*, in *this* Case, is in *Favour* of Equity and Justice; and is expressly directed by the Statute.

And this Return is TRUE: For the Man was a Bankrupt *at the Time* of the Sheriff's making it, by such *Relation backward*, prior to the Taking of the Goods. *If* He had made this Return *on the Day* of the Return of the Writ, I cannot say that even *that* would have been a *false* Return: Because the *Relation* is made to be to the *Time of the first Arrest*, by the express Words of the Statute.

Mr. Just. WILMOT was of the same Opinion.

The Act is *positive*, in making the Bankruptcy to commence from the *Time of the first Arrest*; wherever the Trader shall lie in Prison 2 Months, upon that or any other Arrest. And the Reason why it should be so, is very obvious; *viz.* Because it is a Presumption of his *Insolvency at the* TIME *of the Arrest*: For a Man in Trade must be very low, both in Point of *Fortune* and *Credit*, who lies 2 Months in Prison, without being able either to pay his Debt or to procure Bail.

As to a Return of this Sort made *on the 26th of June*, which was the *very Day* upon which the Writ was made *returnable*; I have some doubt about it, if that had been the Case. I am not so clear that He could *then* have returned "*Nulla bona*:" Because at *that* Time, there was *no* Act of Bankruptcy; And it was impossible for the Sheriff to *know*, that there WOULD BE One in future, by the Man's lying 2 Months in Prison, and thereby becoming a Bankrupt *relatively* to the Time of the first Arrest.

But there can be no Sort of Doubt but that at the *Time* when the Return was *actually made*, it was *true* "that the Defendant was "become a Bankrupt, by having lain 2 Months in Prison:" And consequently, the Goods were *then* the Property of the *Assignees*, by *Relation* to the Time of the first Arrest.

It

It appears to Us, upon the State of the Case, That the Return was *not actually* made, TILL *the 5th of November*. And indeed if the Sheriff had, at the very Day of the Return of the Writ, returned "that he had levied the Money," and had thereupon immediately *paid it over* to the Plaintiff; there could be no Sort of Doubt but that the Assignees might nevertheless have *recovered* it back from the PLAINTIFF. So that the PLAINTIFF could not, even in *that* Case, have profited by such Return.

Per Cur. Let the *Postea* be delivered to the DEFENDANTS; in Order to have a Judgment of NON-SUIT entered thereon.

Monday 2d *July* 1759.

Collins, sen. *vers.* Collins jun.

Pas. 32 *G.* 2. *Rot'lo* 405.

THIS was an Action of Debt upon Bond.

The Condition appeared, upon *Oyer*, to be "to pay the Plaintiff "an Annuity of 10*l.* a Year during his Life; and likewise to *main*-"*tain* him in Meat Drink Washing and Lodging, IN THE DWEL-"LING-HOUSE AT CRUNDALL END, for and during his *Life*."

To this Declaration, the Defendant pleaded (by Leave) several Pleas.

As to the Payment of the Annuity of 10*l.* *per Annum*—There was a Plea of a *Set-off*; (*viz.* that only 60*l.* is due to the Plaintiff on Account of the said Annuity; And that the Plaintiff owes him more than 60*l.* *viz.* 500*l.*)

* See this Plea, more at large, *Post* 821.

As to the *maintaining* the Plaintiff &c,—There was a Plea * That the PLAINTIFF LEFT THE HOUSE VOLUNTARILY, and did not board and lodge *in* the House: So that He (the Defendant) was *not obliged* to board wash and lodge him. But the Defendant avers that he was always ready to maintain him &c, AT *the House*.

The Plaintiff demurs: And the Defendant joins in Demurrer.

The latter Plea depended upon the Words of the Condition; which was,—"That if *Joseph Collins* the Younger, his Heirs Executors "or Administrators, do and shall well and truly pay or cause to be "paid unto *Joseph Collins* the Elder and his Assigns, Yearly and every "Year during his Life, One ANNUITY of 10*l.* of lawful Money of "*Great Britain*, clear of All Taxes &c, on the 25th of *March* and

4 29th

" 29th of *September* Yearly; And if the said *Joseph Collins* the
" Younger shall find provide and allow to and for the said *Joseph*
" *Collins* the Elder, good and sufficient Meat Drink Washing and
" Lodging, IN *the Dwelling-house at Crundall-End* aforesaid; Then
" this Obligation to be void: But if Default shall be made in the
" Payment of the said ANNUITY of 10*l.* or any Part thereof, at or
" upon any or either of the Days abovementioned for the Payment
" thereof; *Or if* he the said *Joseph Collins* the Younger shall *neglect*
" *or refuse to* MAINTAIN AND KEEP the said *Joseph Collins* the
" Elder, during his natural Life, AS AFORESAID; Then, and in
" *Either* of the said Cases, to be and remain in full Force and
" Virtue."

The Defendant (having Leave to plead several Pleas &c,) pleaded a SET-OFF, (as is beforementioned) to the former Part of the Condition, which was for Payment of the *Annuity*. And, as to the latter, He pleaded That the *House at Crundall-End* was the House where the said *Joseph Collins the Younger dwelt*, and ever since has dwelt, with his Family; And that he did admit the said *Joseph Collins* the Elder, and receive him into the said House; and did, *until his Departure* aftermentioned, find provide and allow to the said *Joseph* the Elder Meat Drink &c [in the Words of the Condition;] But that he the said *Joseph* the Elder, *of his own Accord* DEPARTED FROM THE SAID HOUSE at *Crundall-End*, and has *never yet returned*, to be THERE provided with Meat Drink &c (*ut supra*); Nor hath *ever required* to be provided with any, or to have any allowed, THERE; And the said *Joseph* the Younger has *always been ready* to have provided the said *Joseph* the Elder with Meat Drink &c (*ut supra*) AT *and* IN *the said Dwelling-house*, if He had *not departed*, or would have *returned* THITHER; But that He always has refused and still does *refuse to return*; but has continued *absent from* THENCE: *Therefore* he could not provide him with Meat Drink &c (*ut supra*) AT *or* IN *the said Dwelling-house.*

To this Plea, the Plaintiff demurred; And the Defendant joined in Demurrer.

Mr. Serj. *Poole*, on Behalf of the Plaintiff, argued That this Case of an *Annuity* or *Yearly Payment* does not fall within the * Statute of 8 *G.* 2. *c.* 24. § 5. concerning Set-offs; because the Action is not brought for a Sum *complete* and *certain*, but for a Part of a growing Sum payable *for Life*; whereof *future* Payments will be continually becoming due.

* *V. ante*, pa. 799. *Prisoner's* Case.

Now if the Judgment be here entered for the Remainder (as that Act directs,) it passes *in rem judicatam*; and the Plaintiff cannot recover any more, on any *future* Default of Payment, upon the same Bond.

By § 4. of this Act, The Provision for setting mutual Debts one against the Other, was looked upon as highly just and reasonable at *all* Times: It is therefore provided that the Clause in 2 *G*. 2. *c*. 22. "for setting mutual Debts One against the Other" shall be and remain in full Force *for ever*.

Section 5. of this Act of 8 *G*. 2. *c*. 24. provides "That by Virtue of the said Clause in 2 *G*. 2. *c*. 22. (which is thereby made perpetual,) Mutual Debts may be set against each other, either by being pleaded in Bar, or given in Evidence on the General Issue, in the Manner therein mentioned, *notwithstanding* that such Debts are deemed in Law to be of a *different Nature*; Unless in Cases where either of the said Debts shall accrue by reason of a Penalty contained in any Bond or Specialty; and in all Cases where either the Debt for which the Action hath been or shall be brought, or the Debt intended to be set against the same hath accrued or shall accrue by reason of any such Penalty, the Debt intended to be set off shall be pleaded in Bar, in which Plea shall be shewn how much is truly and justly due on either Side: and in Case the Plaintiff shall recover in any such Action or Suit, *Judgment* shall be entered for NO MORE than shall appear to be *truly and justly due* to the Plaintiff, after one Debt being set against the other as aforesaid."

This is not a Bond conditioned for Performance of Covenants or Agreements contained in any Deed or Writing: It contains a quite different and distinct Condition. The present Action is an Action of Debt upon a Bond conditioned to *pay an Annuity* and *maintain a Parent*.

Mr. Serj. *Hewitt contra*—This is a new Case.

The Setting off of mutual Debts arises on 2 *G*. 2. *c*. 22. § 13. (which was a temporary Act,) and on 8 *G*. 2. *c*. 24. § 4, 5. (which makes the former perpetual.)

This last Section (§ 5.) provides, generally "That *wherever* the Debt arises upon a *Bond or Specialty with a Penalty*, and accrues by reason of such Penalty, a Set-off may be pleaded." My Brother *Poole* says, "It extends *only* to Cases where the Debt is a *Sum certain*." But the Words of the Act are *general*; and are not at all confined to Sums certain. And the Plaintiff *may* afterwards recover, for *subsequent* Defaults; notwithstanding the prior Judgment: For the *Penalty* will *always* remain a Duty.

Our Plea covers the whole Demand.

3 Mr.

Mr. Serj. *Poole* was beginning to reply—But

Mr. Serj. *Hewitt* desired it might stand over till next Paper-Day; (intending to make a Motion, in the Interim, for Leave to amend.) To which Request the Court agreed.

Ulterius Concilium.

On the next Paper-Day, (26th *June*,) Mr. Serjeant *Poole* now proceeded in his Reply; (Serjeant *Hewitt not* having moved to amend.) He argued that it could not be pleaded, under *this* Act: For this Act is general, and has no such Provision as there is in the Act of 8, 9 *W.* 3. *c.* 11. § *ult. viz.* "That the Judgment shall "*stand as a Security.*" And therefore if the Plaintiff should now recover Judgment, there would be an *End* of the Bond; And there would remain *no* Security at all for *future* Payment of the Annuity.

And He agreed with Mr. Serjeant *Hewitt*, That this is a *new* Case.

But Mr. Serjeant *Hewitt* insisted that this Act of 8 *G.* 2. *c.* 24. differs materially from 8, 9 *W.* 3. and from 4, 5 *Ann. c.* 16. § 13. for bringing in the Money, and having the Bond discharged. The present Act says "That the Plaintiff shall recover the Sum truly "and justly due, and *no more*." And my Brother *Poole* says, "That after the Matter is passed *in rem judicatam*, the Plaintiff "*cannot afterwards* recover any more upon the *same* Bond." But I answer that the Plaintiff *would be* at Liberty to bring an *Action for any future Breach*: For the present Judgment (upon the Set-off) would not be for the *Penalty*, but only for the *Sum truly and justly* due, and no more.

Lord Mansfield—These Clauses in 8, 9 *W.* 3. *c.* 11. and 8 *G.* 2. *c.* 24. are extremely *beneficial to the Subject.*

Therefore His Lordship chose, He said, to consider of it; and did not mean to give his Opinion at present. However, by way of breaking Case, He entered into an Explication of the Acts; which He thought ought to be considered *All together*, as being made *in pari materia*. So that *Stoppage* or *Setting-off* must have the same Effect, under the 8 *G.* 2. as *Payment* had under 8, 9 *W.* 3.

Therefore He thought, (at present,) that it was most beneficial to the Subject, that in the Case now before the Court, the Set-off *should* be allowed. But He assured Serjeant *Poole*, that if They should be of that Opinion on Deliberation, He should not, as it was a new Case, be caught by his Demurrer: For that They would give him Leave to withdraw it, and reply.

Cur. Advis'.

Lord

Lord MANSFIELD now delivered the Resolution of the Court; *viz.* That they were All (upon deliberate Consideration) unanimously and clearly of Opinion (as it struck him before) That this is a Case WITHIN 8 *G.* 2. *c.* 24. § 4, 5. Where mutual *Debts* may be set off, just as much as actual *Payment* of the Money might have been *before*.

He said He would consider how the Law stood, before the Acts of 2 *G.* 2. *c.* 22. and 8 *G.* 2. *c.* 24. and under the Act of 8, 9 *W.* 3. *c.* 11.

* § 8. The Act of 8, 9 *W.* 3. *c.* 11. is intitled "An Act for the better "preventing frivolous and vexatious Suits." The * last Clause of it is a Provision intended to meet the Case of Non-performance of Covenants and Agreements secured by Bonds or Indentures; and which Covenants or Agreements are to be performed at *different* Times, or the Monies paid by *Installments &c.*

Before that Act, a Plaintiff could only assign *One* Breach, upon such Bond or Indenture: And if the Defendant could prove that the *whole* Debt was *paid*, there was an End of the Matter. But if the Defendant had only paid *Part* of the Debt, and *not the Whole*, then the Judgment was taken for the *whole Penalty*: And this Judgment for the *whole Penalty* stood as a Security for the *Residue* of the Demand which remained unpaid. So that the Judgment stood for the *whole* Penalty, though only *Part* remained due; And the Plaintiff was justly intitled only to *that*, and *no more*: Which often forced the Defendant, in such a Case, into expensive Suits in Equity, for Relief.

* § 8. To prevent which, the * last Clause of this Act of 8, 9 *W.* 3. *c.* 11. provides "That in all Actions, in any of His Majesty's "Courts of Record, upon any Bond or Bonds, or on any penal "Sum, for Non-performance of any Covenants or Agreements in "any Indenture Deed or Writing contained, the Plaintiff or Plaintiffs may assign as many Breaches as he or they shall think fit; "And the Jury shall assess Damages and Costs on so many of them "as the Plaintiff shall prove to have been broken; And the like "Judgment shall be entered on such Verdict, as had been usually "done in such like Actions." Then there is a suitable Provision for suggesting several Breaches, where the Judgment passes by Default, Confession or on Demurrer. Then the Act provides, "That "if after Judgment and before Execution executed, the Defendant "shall *pay* into Court all the Damages and Costs on the several "Breaches assigned and found, a *Stay of Execution* on the Judgment shall be entered upon Record: Or if, by Reason of any

" *Execution executed*, the Plaintiff ſhall be *fully paid and ſatisfied* " all ſuch Damages and Coſts, and the Charges of ſuch Execution, " then the Body, Lands or Goods of the Defendant ſhall be diſ-" charged of ſuch Execution; which ſhall likewiſe be entered " upon Record. But yet, in each Caſe, the JUDGMENT ſhall *re-" main as a further Security* to anſwer Damages to the Plaintiff for " *future* Breaches: Upon which, the Plaintiff may have a *Scire " facias* on the Judgment, ſuggeſting *other Breaches*; whereupon " there ſhall be the like Proceeding as was in the Action of Debt " upon the Bond, for aſſeſſing Damages on *ſuch* Breaches; And " on Payment or Satisfaction, as before, of ſuch *future* Damages " Coſts and Charges as aforeſaid, All further Proceedings ſhall be " AGAIN *ſtayed*; And ſo, *toties quoties*; and the Defendant his " Body Lands or Goods ſhall be diſcharged out of Execution, as " aforeſaid."

A very beneficial Remedy, and a very juſt One to the Subject, this is. The JUDGMENT is to be for the *whole Penalty*, and is to *remain* as a *further Security*; though EXECUTION is to be ſtayed on Payment of the Sum due *&c.*: So that the *Penalty* is a *Security* for the Debt Intereſt and Coſts, upon any *future* Breach.

Before this Statute, the ACTUAL PAYMENT of Money in Diſ-charge of the Demand, was exactly upon the ſame foot, as the SET-OFF *of a Debt* is *now* put upon: And a *Plea of* PAYMENT of a Sum of Money ſufficient to diſcharge the *whole* Demand was juſt the ſame *then*, as a SET-OFF *of a Debt* large enough to balance the *whole* Demand, is *now*: That is to ſay, It was a *full Anſwer* to the Plaintiff's Demand; And he could have *no Judgment at all* againſt the Defendant.

But if it had come out, that there had been a Failure of *Payment* of *any Part* of the Plaintiff's juſt Demand, the Plaintiff would have been intitled to take his JUDGMENT for the *whole Penalty*; (though EXECUTION was to be ſtayed on Payment of the *Damages already incurred*, and *Coſts*:) And this Judgment for the *whole* Penalty was to ſtand as a *Security* to anſwer *future* Breaches.

But the Payment here intended was to be an ACTUAL Payment: For *Stoppage*, or *Setting off* Debt againſt Debt, was not *then* equivalent to actual Payment: But Croſs Actions muſt, at *that* Time have been brought, for the reſpective mutual Debts.

Since theſe two very beneficial Acts of 2 *G.* 2. *c.* 22. and 8 *G.* 2. *c.* 24. *Stoppage*, or *Setting-off* of mutual Debts, is *become equivalent to actual Payment*: And a *Balance ſhall be ſtruck*, as in Equity and Juſtice it ought to be.

At *Common Law*, before these Acts, If the Plaintiff was as much, or even more indebted to the Defendant than the Defendant was indebted to Him, Yet the Defendant had no Method to strike a Balance: He could only go into a Court of *Equity*, for doing what is most clearly *just* and *right* to be done.

* *V.* § 13. The 2 *G.* 2. *c.* 22. was made to answer this just and reasonable End; and enacts * generally, "That where there are mutual "Debts between the Parties, One Debt may be set against the Other." Upon which Act of 2 *G.* 2. Doubts about the *different Natures* of Debts having arisen, the 8 *G.* 2. *c.* 24. was thereupon made: The 5th Section whereof is a † *General* Provision † *without Exception*. So that the Objections which have been here made, on the Part of the Plaintiff, are made by *Construction* only.

† See it, at large, *ante* *pa.* 822.

Objection. It is objected, first, "That this is *not* an Action brought upon "a Penalty for Non-Performance of an Agreement or Covenant "*contained* in any *Indenture Deed* or *Writing*."

Answer. This is an *Agreement* between the Parties, and an Agreement *in Writing*: The *Condition of the Bond* is an *Agreement in Writing*; And People have frequently gone into Courts of Equity upon Conditions of Bonds, *as* being Agreements in Writing, to have a *specific Performance* of them.

Objection. It is said that if the Plaintiff should take his Judgment upon this Act of Parliament, it would *not* be a *Judgment* for the PENALTY, but a Judgment *only* for the *Sum due*, and NO MORE; and that after the Matter has once passed *in rem judicatam*, the Plaintiff *cannot afterwards recover any more* upon this Bond, whatever may become due by future Non-Payments; For that here is *no Provision* "that "the Judgment shall *stand as a Security for future Payments*," as there was in the Act of 8, 9 *W.* 3. *c.* 11. made for the better preventing frivolous and vexatious Suits.

Answer. The Judgment is indeed by this Act of 8 *G.* 2. directed to be entered "for no more than shall appear to be justly and truly due "to the Plaintiff:" But it is clearly *within the Words and Meaning* of the Act, That the *Penalty* is to *remain* as a Security against future Breaches, in this Case of a *Set-off* pleaded, as much as it would have done upon the Act of 8, 9 *W.* 3. *c.* 11. if *Payment* had been made agreeably to the Directions therein contained.

But as this has not been before settled, "That a Set-off may be "pleaded in such a Case as this, where the Condition is for the "Payment of an *Annuity* or *growing Sum*," It would be hard to bind the Plaintiff down strictly to his Demurrer. Therefore my Brother

Brother *Poole* may move to *withdraw the Demurrer*, and to reply in a proper Manner: Which will give the Plaintiff an Opportunity of disputing the Debt pleaded by Way of Set-off, if He thinks proper.

Which Mr. Serj. *Poole* moved accordingly: And the Court granted it; but added that it should be *upon Payment of Costs*.

Wilson *vers.* Day.

THIS was an Action of Trespass for breaking and entering the Plaintiff's House, and taking away his Goods. Not Guilty pleaded; And also (by Leave) a Justification under a Commission of Bankruptcy, awarded against one *Lawson*.

At the Trial, the Matter was referred to the Opinion of the Court.

N.B. John Day (the Defendant) was Messenger under the said Commission of Bankruptcy; and in this his Justification, made Title to the Possession of the House under an Assignment from the Commissioners.

The General Question reserved for the Opinion of the Court was "Whether an Assignment made by *Lawson* was, in itself, an *Act* "*of Bankruptcy*:" And it was directed to come on, by Way of Motion.

Lord MANSFIELD stated the material Facts of the Case to be to the following Effect.

One *Lawson*, a Trader, who was concerned with One *Titley* in circulating Notes, and was really indebted to the Plaintiff *Wilson*, being in a Fright on *Titley*'s Going off, sent for *Wilson* on the *Thursday* (the 16th of *November*,) and told him "that *Titley* was gone off, "and that many Notes were standing out against Him, and that he "could not stand his Ground;" and therefore proposed to secure *Wilson*: And on the *Saturday* following (the 18th of *November*) sent for an Attorney and pressed him to draw an Assignment immediately from Him the said *Lawson* to *Wilson*. The Attorney could not do it till the *Monday*, and it was privately executed on that Day, though it bore Date on the preceding *Saturday*. It was executed to *Wilson*, *to secure Money* REALLY DUE *to him*, and which He was *liable to pay* on *Lawson*'s Account: And it purports to be *only* a Security for such Money, but does *not liquidate* the Sum due. A Day or two after, a Defeasance was executed; which was a *Separate* Deed, making the former void upon Payment of all the Money due to *Wilson:* But this Defeazance did not specify how much it was, any more than the Assignment did. After Payment of *Wilson*'s Debt; as to the Residue, it was to be in Trust for *Lawson* Himself. The Assignment was a general Assignment of EVERY THING *that Lawson had in the World*; and imported that it was made to secure a large Sum (1800*l.* or upwards.) It begun with a Recital "*Whereas I am* "*obliged,* upon urgent and necessary Business to *leave London*;" It recited also "That *Lawson* had not then Money enough by Him, nor "could raise it soon enough to answer all the Demands that *Wil-*"*son* had upon Him." There was no Counterpart: And the Original *remained in the* CUSTODY AND KEEPING OF THE ASSIGNOR. No other Possession was delivered, but only that a Letter of Attorney was given to One *Betham* (who was Clerk to *Lawson* and privy to the Whole, and who was concerned in the bad Part of circulating the Notes,) "to collect, receive, dispose, &c &c:" But the Goods *continued in Lawson's House. No Notice* was given to the *Debtors* of *Lawson,* who owed Him money, till *Lawson* went off; which was in a few Days after. At the Trial it appeared that the Debt really due to *Wilson* from this *Lawson,* was about 1840*l:* although the Deed, which recited *Lawson*'s Circumstances to be bad, and their Manner of dealing, recited also that there might be about 3000*l.* that *Wilson* might be *liable* to pay, but mentions *only* 30*l.* as *actually due*; And then assigns every Thing in the World to *Wilson*; Debts &c &c, without any Exception whatsoever.

Mr. Serj. *Whitaker,* Mr. *Morton,* and Mr. *Yates* were of Counsel for the Defendant.

* § 2. They argued that the Deed itself is FRAUDULENT, and an ACT of *Bankruptcy* within * 21 *J.* 1. *c.* 19. For it was *in Trust for Lawson himself,* after *Wilson* should be paid; and was *executed privately,* at a Tavern, on the *Monday* at Night.

It was done *in Contemplation* of *Lawson*'s Running away: And with *Intent* to give *Wilson* the PREFERENCE *to other Creditors*; And was therefore a FRAUD upon the *Other* Creditors. It appears upon the Face of the Deed, "that *Lawson* was then become *insolvent*."

It assigns ALL his Effects whatsoever, and neither *values* the Effects assigned, nor *liquidates Wilson's Demand* upon *Lawson.*

The *visible Possession* was *not altered: Betham remained* the acting Agent, *as before.*

* V. ante, 467. This is like the Case of * Sir *Edward Worseley* v. *De Mattos et al'*, *H.* 1758. 31 *G.* 2. *B. R.*

Mr.

Mr. *Norton* and Mr. *Aston contra*, for *Wilson* the Plaintiff.

This Case *differs* from that of *De Mattos*. This is only in the *Nature of a* MORTGAGE, to secure Mr. *Wilson*'s Debt *only*, and indemnify Him against the other Demands to which he was liable, and what he was likely to suffer on *Lawson*'s Account. The Sum of 1840 *l.* was then actually due from *Lawson* to *Wilson*: And the principal Operation of this Deed was to secure that Debt.

And a Trader who is likely to become a Bankrupt *may* give the *Preference* to one Creditor, rather than to another, at any Time *before* his Bankruptcy.

But it will be objected, that this Assignment was *under a Contemplation* of his becoming Bankrupt; And therefore is itself an Act of Bankruptcy.

Answer. This is only, or chiefly at least, a Security for the 1840 *l.* by way of Mortgage; and was therefore made for a *valuable Consideration.*

The Deed does not import that he was *absolutely* unable to answer the Demands upon him; but only "that he had not *then* "Money enough by him to answer them."

And the Occasion and Necessity of his *Absence* from *London* is expressly recited to be "*upon urgent and necessary Business*:" Which is very different from his *Running away*, or *absconding*.

The Intent of this Deed is, expressly, to retain *only so much* as will *satisfy Wilson's Demands* (though those Demands are not indeed particularly liquidated.)

Lord MANSFIELD thought it a plain Case both upon the Deed, and upon the Collateral Circumstances.

The System of the Bankrupt Laws is, that the Bankrupt's Effects shall be taken *out of* his *own* Possession, and be divided *equally* amongst ALL his Creditors.

In * *Gainor*'s Case, (of the black Ginger,) the Deed was holden to be *void*, and to be itself an *Act of Bankruptcy*: And yet, in that Case, *only One* Creditor was virtually excluded.

* See this Case cited at large, in that of Sir *Edward Worsely et al'* v. *De Mattos and Slader*, ante 477.

It is not necessary that the Deed should be fraudulent, *as between* the *Parties*: Nor is this Deed at all so; for it is a very *fair* Deed, as to the *Parties*. But it is made to PREFER this *Samuel Wilson* to the Bankrupt's *other* Creditors.

Then he recited the Deed, and particularly the following Expressions in it, *viz.* "And whereas, by reason of &c, I cannot at present raise &c, so soon as the Money due to the said *S. W.* will become payable; And whereas I am obliged, on Account of necessary Business &c, to be absent &c." And He observed, that the Assignment is of *Every Thing that he had in the World*; not excepting even Apparel, &c.

Now though a Trader, *before* he becomes a Bankrupt may *prefer* One Creditor to Another, and may *pay* him his Debt; or may make a *Mortgage*, with *Possession delivered*; Or (as was the Case of * *Small* v. *Oudley*,) may assign *Part* of his Effects to One particular Creditor; Yet an Assignment of his WHOLE Estate is of a very *different* Consideration: THAT tends to *defeat the whole System* of the Bankrupt Laws.

* In *December* 1727. *in Canc'*, best reported in 2 *Peere Wms.* 427. But see it stated from the *Register-Book*, in *De Mattos*'s Case, *ante* 480, 481.

Here he assigns *All*, and invests his *own Clerk* with the Management of his Effects, *instead* of the *Commissioners*.

This Deed is an *Act of Bankruptcy, itself.* It defeats the whole Bankrupt-Law: *Nothing* remains for the Creditors in any Shape; But his WHOLE Estate is put into the Hands of his *own Trustees*, immediately. Therefore he is of Course a Bankrupt, the *Moment he has executed* this Deed: For there is Nothing at all left for his Creditors. And this is for an *unliquidated* Demand, too: Which makes it stronger.

Thus it stands upon the DEED.

But the CIRCUMSTANCES confirm it. For here is *no visible Change of Possession*: And the Letter of Attorney "to receive the "Debts" is a *secret Transaction*, unknown to every body else; Whereas, according to the Case of † *Ryal* v. *Rowles*, there ought to be *Notice* to the Creditors.

† 27th *January* 1749. *in Canc'*. See this Case also cited and discussed in that of *De Mattos*.

Therefore I think this Deed is *in itself an Act of Bankruptcy*.

Mr. Just. DENISON concurred, for the same Reasons.

And He also observed, that such a Deed as this ought not to be established; because the whole Power that ought to be in the *Assignees*,

4

ſignees, is put into the Hands of *Betham* the *Bankrupt's own Clerk*: Which is directly contrary to the very End and Intention of the Bankrupt-Laws.

It is apparent that where a Trader conveys his WHOLE Eſtate and Effects, it muſt be with an *Intent to defeat his Creditors in general.* And here, it is to ſatisfy an *unliquidated* Demand, too: Which is a Circumſtance that ſerves to confirm it's being the Intention of the preſent Deed.

All theſe Caſes muſt depend upon their *Circumſtances*: And here they are as ſtrong as I ever met with. It is a Caſe *within* the LETTER of the Act.

Mr. Juſt. FOSTER—A Trader, *before* Bankruptcy, may *pay* a particular Creditor; Or He may mortgage his Effects to a particular Creditor, *with Poſſeſſion delivered*; And here it is a Mortgage, 'tis true, with a reſulting Truſt to *Lawſon*: But here is NO ALTERATION OF POSSESSION, *no* DELIVERY, (which is the Badge of Ownerſhip.) * *Twyne*'s Caſe. * 3 Co. 81. a.

This, if it were to be permitted, would *defeat the whole Syſtem* of the Bankrupt-Laws.

Mr. Juſt. WILMOT was of the ſame Opinion.

If this ſhould be allowed, it would *defeat all the Bankrupt-Laws*.

The Deed is a Conveyance of his WHOLE Eſtate and Effects: And it appears to be made, when the Trader was *inſolvent* and *Running away*.

A MORTGAGE by a Trader, of his Effects, is good, if he PARTS WITH *the Poſſeſſion*: And the Reaſon is, becauſe he *might* have abſolutely *ſold* it, and paid the Creditor the Money.

But here is a Conveyance of his WHOLE Eſtate and Effects; And NO POSSESSION DELIVERED; *no* ALTERATION *of Poſſeſſion*: But the ſame Perſon, *Betham*, continued to act, juſt as he was uſed to do before.

Therefore THIS DEED ALONE is an *Act of Bankruptcy*, without meddling with any other Circumſtances collateral to it.

This Conveyance of the WHOLE, without leaving *any Thing at all* remaining towards ſatisfying the reſt of his Creditors, is a very different Caſe from an Aſſignment of a particular PART of his Effects, to a particular Creditor.

Lord

Lord MANSFIELD added that a *Colourable Exception* of a *small Part* of his Estate or Effects would not help the Matter: For the Court would never suffer that *an Evasion* should prevail, to take such a Case out of the General Rule, which is so essentially necessary to be observed, in Order to a due Execution of this System of Laws.

The COURT was therefore unanimous, (and clearly so,) That there ought in this Case to be a JUDGMENT of NONSUIT entered for the DEFENDANT.

Rex *vers.* Boyall.

MR. *Winn* shewed Cause against *quashing an Indictment* against the Defendant, a Parishioner of *Market-Deeping* in *Lincolnshire*, for not sending out his Carts *&c*, to the Six Days Highway Labour, pursuant to an Order from the Overseers *&c*.

The Indictment sets forth—That *John Mawly* and *J. Thornton*, on the 23d of *June &c*, at the Parish of *M.* BEING *then* and continually from thenceforth until after the 29th Day of the said *June*, the *Surveyors of the High-ways* in the said Parish, did appoint the said 29th Day of *June* for the providing Stones *&c*, for the Amendment of the High-ways; the same being One of the Six Days appointed for providing Stones *&c*, for Amendment *&c*, in the Year for which they were Surveyors, Then it sets forth that they gave public Notice in the Parish Church, of their having appointed the said 29th of *June* for providing Stones *&c*. But that nevertheless, the Defendant, who on the said 23d of *June*, and until and after the said 29th of *June*, at the Parish aforesaid, kept a Draught, well knowing the Premisses, did not find and send, on the said 29th of *June*, One Wain or Cart furnished after the Custom of the County with Oxen or other proper Cattle and other Necessaries meet to carry Things convenient for that Purpose, and also two able Men with the same, for the providing Stones *&c*, for Amendment of and working in the said High-way in the Parish aforesaid; but therein wholly neglected and made Default; In Contempt *&c*, and against the Form of the Statute *&c*.

V. 22 *G.* 2. *c.* 12. § 9: (which is the Statute here intended.)

Three Objections were taken to this Indictment: *viz.*

1st Objection—That *John Mawly* and *J. Thornton* are *not sufficiently alledged to be Surveyors* of the said High-Ways: It is only

3 "that

" that they BEING Surveyors &c;" And is not said *by whom* they were appointed.

2d Objection—It is not said, *on what Day* they were so *appointed*: Whereas a *particular Time is prescribed* by the Act of Parliament, for their Appointment. *V.* § 12. which limits it so *some* Day in *Christmas Week*.

3d Objection—That a * PARTICULAR REMEDY is appointed by this Statute of 22 *C.* 2. *c.* 12. namely, in § 9 and 12: And therefore, this being a NEW OFFENCE created by this Statute, and the Statute *prescribing a* PARTICULAR REMEDY, that particular Remedy must be *pursued*; And an INDICTMENT *will* NOT *lie*.

* *V. ante*, 802 to 807. *Rex v. Robinson*; particularly *pa.* 804.

Mr. *Winn*'s Answers to the Objections, were as follows.

To the 1st Objection, He answered, that 2 *Mod.* 128. *Rex* v. *Moor*, is in Point That the Words " BEING *above such an Age*," are good in an Indictment. And these Words are " BEING *then* " *Surveyors*."

To the 2d Objection,—He answered, That the Allegation " That " they *being* then Surveyors," is sufficient; *without* specifying when they were so appointed.

To the 3d Objection—That this is *in itself* an *indictable* Offence; and was so, AT *the Making* of 22 *C.* 2. *c.* 12.

The Act of 2 & 3 *Ph.* & *M. c.* 8. is the first Statute that gives a Forfeiture for Default in this respect. The 5 *Eliz. c.* 13. § 8. gives Power to the Sessions, to proceed to inquire of Defaults, and to assess Fines for them: (Which must be by way of *Indictment.*) In *West's Precedents*, 2d *part*, § 218. *Anno* 34 *Eliz.* There is an *Indictment* for this same Offence.

Or, perhaps, they might be out of the Jurisdiction of the Justices: And if so, the Justices could not proceed as the Act directs.

And this is a mandatory Statute.

Mr. *Vivian*, *contra*.

In Support of the 1st and 2d Objections—It ought to have been mentioned *by whom*, and *when* the Surveyors were appointed.

* V. ante 805. the true Rule of Distinction declared by Lord *Mansfield*.

In Support of the 3d Objection, He cited 2 *Hawk. P. C.* 211. § 4. Where the * Rule is particularly and expressly laid down. And 22 *C.* 2. *c.* 12. § 9. prescribes a particular Method: So also does § 12. of the same Statute. In 7 *Rep.* 36. (On penal Statutes,) It was resolved "that the Act which gives the Penalty, ought to be "pursued." *Brownl.* 106. *Rex* v. *Marriot*, 1 *Show.* 398. *Stephens* v. *Watson*, 1 *Salk.* 45. *Palm.* 388. S.P. 2 *Ro. Rep.* 299. *Cro. Jac.* 643. *Castle*'s Case. *Queen* v. *Watson*, cited in 6 *Mod.* 86. *Rex* v. *Davyes*, 3 *Keb.* 34. *Rex* v. *Sparks*, 3 *Mod.* 79.

Lord MANSFIELD—

† See it cited at large, *ante* 803, 804. ‖ V. *ante* 805. *accord'.*

As to the 3d Objection—It was an *Offence indictable*, BEFORE the Appointment of the Summary Remedy prescribed by the Statute of 22 *C.* 2. The Case of † *Rex* v. *Davis*, *M.* 28 *G.* 2. *B. R.* was of the same kind. Therefore the Summary Jurisdiction is ‖ CUMULATIVE, (although there is another Remedy given,) and *does* NOT *exclude* the Common-Law Remedy.

‡ V. *ante* 804. *accord'.*

I do not approve of *indicting*, where there is another Remedy: It carries the Appearance of ‡ Oppression. Yet it is not to be understood that We are OBLIGED to quash Indictments upon *Motion*, in *every* Case, where they are not to be supported upon a *Demurrer*.

As to the 1st Objection—" *Being*" is a sufficient Averment.

And the 2d Objection has Nothing in it.

Mr. Just. DENISON concurred.

The RULE was therefore DISCHARGED.

Tuesday 3d *July* 1759.

Rex. *vers.* Cowle.

* See both Rules (*verbatim*) at the End of this Case, *pa.*

ON shewing Cause (upon *Tuesday* 23d *January* last) why a SUPERSEDEAS should not issue, to a CERTIORARI directed to the Mayor and Corporation-Justices of BERWICK, " to remove an " *Indictment* for an Assault;" and also on the Adverse Party's shewing Cause (at the same Time) against other * Cross-Rules for ATTACHMENTS against the Justices to whom the said *Certiorari* was directed, " for refusing to receive or return the said *Certiorari*; and " for committing the Defendant to Prison on his Refusal to plead " in their Court of Sessions and Gaol-Delivery, *after* he had offered " his *Certiorari* to them, and tendered sufficient and proper Secu- " rity thereupon;—"

It was insisted by Sir *Richard Lloyd*, Mr. *Clayton*, and Mr. *Selwyn*, who were Counsel for the Corporation-Justices (and consequently, argued for the *Supersedeas*, and against the Attachments,) That *this* Court have *no Jurisdiction* over BERWICK, where the Proceedings are *not according* to the Laws of *England*, but according to a quite *different Law*.

BERWICK, they said, was formerly *Part of* SCOTLAND, and was our's only by *Conquest*, and *remains* un-incorporated with *England*, and is governed by it's *own* former Laws.

It is in the very same Situation as *Ireland* was, immediately after it's being conquered. (*V.* 8th *Vol.* of *State Trials*, *Pa.* 346. *Pryme's Argument in Lord Macquire's Case*.)

A *conquered Country* retains it's *own* Laws, *till Others* are given by the Conquerors.

No Certiorari therefore lies, to BERWICK.

The proper Method would be, to issue a Commission, to judge according to their own Laws. So, as to *Jamaica*, *Guernsey*, *Jersey*, *Sarke &c.* * 2 *Salk.* 411. *Blanckard* v. *Galdy*. *Hale's History of the Common Law* 183, 186, 187, 188, 189. *Calvin's* Case, 7 *Rep.* 21, 23. * *V.* 4 *Inst.* 286.

But suppose the *King* Himself to be a *Party*, It may be said "that "He *may choose his Court*." Yet still it ought to be tried according to the *Laws* of the *Place* where the Cause arises. And *Hale* 186. does not contradict this: For he does not say *where* it shall be tried.

In 11 *E.* 3. (amongst the Records of the *Tower*) as is asserted in *Calvin's* Case, 7 *Rep.* 23. *a. b.* there is a Commission to the King's Justice of *Berwick upon Tweed* and *Scotland*, to try according to the Laws of the *Place*, "*Secundùm legem et consuetudinem Regni Scotiæ.*" And as *Berwick* is in *no County*, *How* or *where* could this Matter be tried, if a *Certiorari* should go?

A *Certiorari* is a *mandatory* Writ *remedial*. Therefore it can *not extend beyond the Realm of England*. *Calvin's* Case 20. *a.* is expressly so. And *no Certiorari* ever *did go*; so as that there has been any Proceeding upon it: Perhaps they may have been sent out *ex improviso*; And Nothing further done upon them.

To prove that *Berwick* is no Part of *England*, they cited 1 *Sid.* 381, 462. *Jackson and Crispe* v. *Mayor &c of Barwick*, and *Godbolt*

bolt 387. *Cremer and Tookley*'s Case; where a Case is cited, of "Debt "on an Obligation, and the *Venue* laid at *Barwick*; which was "adjudged against the Plaintiff; *because the Court had* NOT *Juris-* "*diction.*"

Informations indeed were lately granted, for Bribery in the Election for *Berwick*; though they never came to any Effect. (*Rex* v. *Watson*, *Hil.* & *Pasch.* 1755.)

The Act of 8, 9 *W.* 3. *c.* 33. (which perpetuates 5, 6 *W.* & *M.* *c.* 11.) requires the Recognizance to be conditioned "to try at the "next Assizes *for the County*, where the Indictment was found." But *Berwick* is no County of *England*, 2 *Show.* 365. Mayor of *Berwick*'s Case declares so, And that the King's Writ does not run into *Berwick*.

Therefore if this *Certiorari*, should be granted, it would occasion a Failure of Justice.

Lord MANSFIELD said it was necessary for the Court to know the *Constitution* of *Berwick* perfectly, and search it to the Bottom, before they could give any Opinion. And for that Purpose,

Both THE COURT themselves and likewise the Defendant's Counsel desired an Opportunity of seeing the *Charters* of that Town.

The whole Matter was therefore ADJOURNED, that the Charters of the Corporation of *Berwick* might be inspected and produced: Which was accordingly afterwards done. And

The Substance of their several Charters is, as follows—

From the Year 1296, (when this Town was conquered by *Edward* the First,) this Corporation hath had several Charters granted to it by different Kings and Queens of *England*; particularly One in the Reign of *Edward* 4th: In the Introduction to which, it appears "that several Charters had been granted to the Town of *Berwick*, "by his Ancestors, *before* his Reign." It is to this Effect—

* *Edw.* 4th. * *Edward* by the Grace of God King of *England* and of *France* and Lord of *Ireland*, To all Arch-bishops Bishops Abbots Priors Dukes Earls Barons Justices Sheriffs Ministers and to all Bailiffs and

† *Edw.* 3d. his faithful People Greeting—We have seen the Charter of † *Edward* late King of *England* our Progenitor, made in these Words,—*Edward* by the Grace of God King of *England* and of *France* and Lord of *Ireland*, To all Arch-Bishops &c. &c. We have seen the Charter which We lately caused to be made, in these Words *Edward*

 by

by the Grace of God King of *England* and Lord of *Ireland*, To all Arch-Bishops &c. It appears to Us by Inspection of the Rolls of the Chancery of * *Edward* late King of *England* our Grandfather, that our said Grandfather caused his Charter to be made in these Words, "*Edward* by the Grace of God King of *England* Lord of *Ireland* "and Duke of *Aquitain*, To all Arch-Bishops Bishops Abbots Priors "Earls Barons Justices Sheriffs Mayors Ministers and to all Bailiffs and "others his faithful People, Greeting: Know Ye &c." It makes this Town of *Berwick* a Free Burrough, and the Men of it Free Burgesses: And after granting to them all the Liberties and free Customs of a free Burrough for ever, and impowering them to hold Guilds and choose a Mayor (to be sworn in before the King, or before the Chancellor or Treasurer and Barons of *Scotland*, if the King be not present,) and 4 Bailiffs, this Charter goes on as follows (*viz.*)—" We further grant, that the aforesaid Burgesses and their Heirs their Tenements which they have within the said Burrough and shall have hereafter, in their last Will and Testament may freely bequeath to whom they will, without Lett of Us or our Heirs or Ministers whatsoever; And that they shall *not implead nor be impleaded* ELSEWHERE THAN WITHIN *the same Town or Burrough before the Mayor and Bailiffs aforesaid, de aliquibus Tenuris intrinsecis Transgressionibus aut Contractibus intra eundem Burgum factis.* We grant furthermore (to the aforesaid Burgesses) that they have the *Return of all our Writs* touching that Burrough; So that no Sheriff nor other Bailiff or Minister of ours enter that Burrough, to do any Office there for any thing to that Burrough belonging, but in Default of the Mayor and Bailiffs of the same Burrough; And that the said Burgesses and their Heirs, *per brevia nostra de cancellaria Scotiæ*, may choose a Coroner *de seipsis* &c." Then it grants a Prison, and several Privileges.

* Edw. 1st.

Furthermore We will and grant that the said Burgesses shall not be put upon any Assizes Juries or Recognitions, by reason of their Intrinsic Tenure, against their Wills, out of the aforesaid Burrough.

This Charter of *Edward* 1st grants two Markets, a Fair, and sundry other Privileges to this Corporation; and bears Date on the 4th of *August Anno Regni* 30.mo

The Charter of *Edward* 3d recites " That the former Charter " (of *Edward* 1st) afterwards fell into the Hands of *Robert A Brus*, " when He took the Town of *Berwick*; and was carried away by " Him:" But *Edward* 3d by his first Charter (dated 4th *June Anno regni* 10.°) exemplifies and confirms it; And by his second Charter (dated 28th *March Anno regni* 30.°) which is an Inspeximus of his own former Charter, he furthermore grants and confirms as follows —" And because We are so much the more affectioned to our Realm "of *Scotland*, for that the said Realm, by our well beloved and trusty Cousin *Edward Balliol* late King of the said Realm of *Scotland*, was to Us given and granted; And therefore We affect with a more earnest Desire, the Honours and Advantages as well of the same Realm, as of the Town of BERWICK *upon Tweed*, which, from the Hands of the *Scots* our Enemies (who, at the Time that We were employed in the parts of *France* about the Expedition of our Wars there, had invaded and taken it,) is *by Us newly conquered*; We have granted and by this our Charter confirmed, for Us and our Heirs, that our Burgesses of the said Town of *Berwick* their Heirs and Successors in the same Town abiding and resident, Have and Hold all and singular the Liberties above specified, and the same Liberties and every of them from henceforth fully enjoy and use; And likewise that the same Burgesses their Heirs and Successors be *ruled by* THE SAME LAWS CUSTOMS AND USAGES that the Burgesses of the same Town had and used *in the Time of* ALEXANDER of famous Memory *late King of Scotland*; without Impeachment of Us or our Heirs Justices Escheators Sheriffs or other our Balliffs or Ministers whatsoever; And that the Customers Weighers and all other Officers whatsoever that in the same Town shall happen to be assigned by Us or our Heirs, be resident and abiding upon their Offices continually, So that by their Absence or Default Merchants upon Delivery of their Merchandise be not lett nor hindered; And the said Customers Weighers and Officers, *or Burgesses of the same Town, to give an Account for any Thing touching the said Town, or their Offices in the said Town, or to answer for any Trespasses, Debts Covenants or any Contracts made or to be made in the same Town, for the which they shall be bound to answer to Us or our Heirs*, SHALL NOT BE COMPELLED TO COME ELSEWHERE *than before our Chamberlain of the same Town of Berwick or our Justices thereunto assigned* WITHIN *the said Town of* BERWICK: So that the Chamberlain always of the aforesaid Town for the Time being, for all Things touching *his* Office, shall make his Account *before our Treasurer and Barons of our Exchequer of* ENGLAND, *as before this Time hath been accustomed.*"

The Charter of *Edw.* 4th concludes with approving and confirming *Cartam prædictam* (the 2d Charter of *Edw.* 3d) and bears Date on the 18th of *February Anno regni* 22mo.

QUEEN ELIZABETH by Letters Patent granted to the Town of *Berwick*, dated 4th *May Anno regni* 1mo. after mentioning the Letters Patent of Queen *Mary* and of King *Henry* the 8th, and the above Charter of *Edward* the 4th ratifies and confirms every Thing contained in *Edward* the 4th's Charter, *H.* 8th's and Queen *Mary's*: Which Charter of Queen *Mary* is dated on the 25th of *April Anno*

 regni

regni primo, and is an Inspeximus and Confirmation of that of King *H.* 8th. which Charter of *H.* 8th bears Date on the 6th *November* 2 *H.* 8. and is an Inspeximus and Confirmation of the Charter of *Edward* the 4th.

But the Charter under which the Corporation of *Berwick* now claim All their Privileges, and which is confirmed to them by * Act of Parliament, is that which was granted them by King *James* the 1st, dated 30th *April Anno regni secundo*. The Preamble to which, is as follows—

* 1 & 2 *Jac.* 1. c. 28.

James &c. Whereas our Burrough of *Berwick upon Tweed* is an ancient and populous Burrough; and the Burgesses of the said Burrough, sometimes by the Name of Mayor Bailiffs and Burgesses of the same Burrough, and sometimes by other Names, have had, used and enjoyed divers Liberties Franchizes Immunities Customs Pre-eminences and other Hereditaments, as well by divers Charters and Letters Patent of divers our Progenitors and Predecessors Kings and Queens of *England*, as also by reason of divers Prescriptions and Customs used and had within the said Burrough; And whereas our well-beloved Subjects the now Mayor Bailiffs and Burgesses of the Burrough of *Berwick upon Tweed* aforesaid, have humbly beseeched Us "that We would exhibit and extend our Royal Grace and "Bounty to the said Mayor Bailiffs and Burgesses on this Behalf, "and that We will vouchsafe (for the better governing ruling and "bettering of the said Burrough) by our Letters Patent to make "reduce constitute and create anew the said Mayor Bailiffs and "Burgesses into One Corporate and Politic Body, by the Name of "Mayor Bailiffs and Burgesses of the Burrough of *Berwick upon* "*Tweed*, with Augmentation and Additions of certain Liberties "Privileges Immunities and Franchizes as to Us shall seem most "expedient;" We therefore, willing that from henceforth for ever hereafter there be continually had and used one certain and undoubted Manner in our said Burrough, of in and about the *keeping of our Peace*, and for the ruling of the said Burrough and of our People there inhabiting and of others thither resorting, And that the said Burrough may be and remain in all future Times a Burrough of Peace and Quiet, to the Fear and Terror of evil and the Reward and Nourishing of good Men, And also *that our Peace and other Facts of Justice and good Government may the better there be kept and done*, and hoping that if the Mayor Bailiffs and Burgesses of the said Burrough and their Successors may by our Royal Grant enjoy greater and larger Dignities Privileges Jurisdictions Liberties and Franchizes, then they will think themselves more especially and strongly obliged unto the Performance and Execution of their best Service to Us our Heirs and Successors; And also at the humble Petition *&c &c* We have willed ordained *&c* And by the Presents *&c* Do will and ordain *&c*.

In

In this Charter, amongst many other Privileges, are the following: *viz.* A Power to make By-Laws, and to fine or imprison such as break them; and also these ensuing Clauses—

Power to hold a Court.

And We will, and for Us our Heirs and Successors Do grant to the said Mayor Bailiffs and Burgesses and their Successors, that they and their Successors, from henceforth for ever hereafter, may have and hold, and may be able to have and hold within the said Burrough, a *Court of Pleas*, every *Tuesday* in every second Week throughout the Year, to be holden *before the Mayor Bailiffs and Recorder* of the said Burrough for the Time being, or before any three of them (whereof We will that the *Mayor* of the said Burrough for the Time being shall be *One*,) in the Guild-Hall or Toll-Booth of the said Burrough; And that they may hold, in that Court, by Plaints in the same Court to be levied, or otherwise according to the laudable and reasonable Customs before used and accustomed in the said Burrough, *All* and *all Manner of* Pleas Actions Suits Complaints and Demands, as well real as personal and mixed, of all personal Transgressions whatsoever with Force and Arms, and of whatsoever other Transgressions done moved arising had or committed or hereafter to be done moved had or committed within the said Burrough Suburbs Liberties and Precincts thereof, And of all and all Manner of Intrusials Tenures Burgages Lands Tenements Goods Chattels Debts Pleas upon the Case Deceits Accounts Covenants Detinues of Charters Escripts Muniments and Chattels, the taking and detaining of Beasts and Cattle, and other Contracts whatsoever of whatsoever Cause or Thing arising or in Time to come happening to arise within the said Burrough Suburbs Liberties and Precincts thereof, to whatsover Sum or Value the said Transgressions Debts Accounts Covenants Deceits Detinues or other Contracts shall amount: And that such like Pleas Plaints Quarrels Suits and Accounts may be there heard and determined before the said Mayor Bailiffs and Recorder of the said Burrough for the Time being or any 3 of them (whereof We will that the Mayor of the said Burrough for the Time being shall be One) by such and such like Proceedings Ways and Means *according to the Laws and Customs of our Kingdom of England, or according to the ancient reasonable and laudable Customs of the said Burrough heretofore used and allowed in the said Burrough*, and in as large Manner and Form as in any Court of Pleas in any City Burrough or Town Corporate within this our Kingdom of *England* or in our said Burrough of *Berwick upon Tweed* heretofore hath been used and accustomed or may or ought to be done. And further We will, and by these Presents for Us our Heirs and Successors Do Grant to the said Mayor Bailiffs and Burgesses of the said Burrough and their Successors, that they and their Successors from Time to Time in all issuing Times may

Cognizance of Pleas, as anciently accustomed.

may have and may be of Force to have the Cognizance of all and all Manner of Pleas Quarrels Plaints Actions and Demands whatsoever as well real as personal and mixed, in what Courts soever of Us our Heirs and Successors moved and begun or to be moved and begun, of whatsoever Things Causes and Matters happening arising or growing within the said Burrough Suburbs Liberties and Precincts thereof, as they have been anciently accustomed within the said Burrough.

Furthermore We will, and by these Presents for Us our Heirs and Successors Do Grant to the said Mayor Bailiffs and Burgesses of the said Burrough and their Successors, that the said Mayor Bailiffs and Burgesses of the said Burrough for the Time being be not put in Assise Juries Attaints or other Recognizances, by reason of any Intrusials Tenures or against their Wills, without the said Burrough; And that the said Burgesses of the said Burrough and their Successors be not constrained or compelled by Us our Heirs or Successors or our Officers or Servants of Us our Heirs or Successors, to go or to be sent to *War* without the said Burrough and Suburbs Liberties and Precincts thereof, but by the Special Commandment of Us our Heirs and Successors, as before in the said Burrough hath been lawfully used and accustomed. And that no Man may take Lodging within the said Burrough by Force or by Livery of our Marshals of Us our Heirs or Successors, We have granted moreover, and by these Presents for Us our Heirs and Successors of our special Grace and of our certain Knowledge and mere Motion Do Grant to the said Mayor Bailiffs and Burgesses of the said Burrough and their Successors, that they may have the Return of all our Writs Precepts and Process of Us our Heirs and Successors, of whatsoever Courts of Us our Heirs or Successors coming and arising within the said Burrough, and the Execution of them; So that no Sheriff Minister or Bailiff for us our Heirs or Successors shall enter into the said Burrough Suburbs Liberties or Precincts thereof, to do any Office there for any belonging to the said Burrough, but in Default of the Mayor and Bailiffs of the said Burrough. And further of our Special Grace and of our certain Knowledge and mere Motion We have given and granted and by these Presents for Us our Heirs and Successors Do give and grant to the said Mayor Bailiffs and Burgesses of the said Burrough and their Successors, that the said Mayor Bailiffs and Burgesses of the said Burrough or any of them, or the Custom-house Officers or Weighters of Us our Heirs and Successors within the said Burrough for the Time being or any of them, shall not be employed nor shall be compelled to answer for any Intrusials Tenures or Transgressions Debts Contracts Accounts or any other Causes or Things within the said Burrough Suburbs Liberties Limits or Precincts thereof done or to be done, elsewhere than within the said Burrough before the Mayor and Bailiffs of the said Burrough and

Not to be put in Assise &c, *extra Burgum.*

Nor to be sent to War &c unless &c.

Return and Execution of Writs, within the Burrough.

Not to be compellable, to answer &c, *extra Burgum.*

their Successors, or before the Justices of Us our Heirs and Successors assigned unto it within the said Burrough and not elsewhere.

Mayor &c. to be Justices of the Peace &c, intra Burgum.

And further We will, and by these Presents for Us our Heirs and Successors Do Grant to the said Mayor Bailiffs and Burgesses of the said Burrough and their Successors, that the Mayor of the said Burrough for the Time being, and the Recorder of the said Burrough for the Time being, and such Burgesses and Aldermen of the said Burrough who have sustained the Office of Mayor of the said Burrough or hereafter shall sustain it, after they have executed the said Office of Mayoralty, as long as they shall be Burgesses and Aldermen of the Burrough, and every one of them, may and shall be for ever hereafter from henceforth, within the said Burrough and within the Suburbs Liberties and Precincts thereof, our Justices for Us our Heirs and Successors to keep and preserve and cause to be kept and preserved the Peace of Us our Heirs and Successors within the said Burrough Liberties and Precincts thereof, And also to keep and cause to be kept all Ordinances and Statutes for the Good of our Peace and for the Preservation of the same and for the quiet Ruling and Governing our People published within the said Burrough Suburbs Liberties and Precincts thereof in all their Articles according to the Force Form and Effect of such Ordinances and Statutes, And to chastise correct and punish all and all Manner of Persons whatsoever of what Estate Degree or Condition soever they shall be, offending against the Form of those Ordinances and Statutes or any of them within the said Burrough Suburbs Liberties and Precincts thereof, and to do that all those within the said Burrough Suburbs Liberties and Precincts thereof who shall threaten any of our People to hurt their Bodies or burn their Houses to find sufficient Security before them or any of them for the Peace and good Behaviour towards Us and our liege People, And if they shall refuse to find such Security then to cause them to be safely kept in the Gaol and Prison of the said Burrough until they find such Security ; And that the Mayor Recorder and such of the Aldermen or Burgesses of the said Burrough who have at any Time borne the Office of Mayor or hereafter shall bear it, after they have borne the said Office of Mayor of the said Burrough and as long as they shall be Burgesses or Aldermen of that Burrough, or any three or more of them (whereof We will that the Mayor and Recorder of the said Burrough for the Time being be Two) may have from henceforth for ever hereafter full Power and Authority from Time to Time to inquire and determine within the said Burrough Suburbs Liberties and Precincts thereof of all and all Manner of Felonies Murders Homicides Robberies Assaults Riots Routs Forces [forcible] Entries into Lands and Tenements Trespasses against the Peace of Us our Heirs and Successors unlawful Conventicles Ambidexters Conspiracies Contempts Concealments, And also of all Misprisons

Justices of Oyer and Terminer, intra Burgum.

prisions Offences Misdeeds Defaults Negligences Causes and Articles which do belong or hereafter may be able to belong to the Authority or Power of Justices or Keepers of the Peace of Us our Heirs or Successors, in as ample Manner and Form as any Justices or Keepers of the Peace of Us our Heirs or Successors in any of our Counties within this our Kingdom of *England*, *by the Laws and Statutes of the* SAME *Kingdom*, for the Offence so done and committed in the said County, as Justices of the Peace, may be and may be able to hear and determine. And also We will, and by these Presents for Us our Heirs and Successors Do grant to the said Mayor Bailiffs and Burgesses of the said Burrough and their Successors, That the Mayor and Recorder of the said Burrough for the Time being, and such like Burgesses and Aldermen of the said Burrough who at any Time have borne or hereafter shall bear the Office of Mayor of the said Burrough, after that they have borne the said Office, as long as they shall be Burgesses and Aldermen of the said Burrough, or any three or more of them (whereof We will that the Mayor and Recorder of the said Burrough shall be Two,) from Time to Time hereafter may be our Justices, And every One of them from Time to Time may be Justices of Us our Heirs and Successors, from Time to Time to deliver the Gaol of the said Burrough of the Prisoners being therein; And that the Coroner for the Time being shall make Return from Time to Time of all Juries Inquisitions Pannels Attachments and Indentures by him taken or hereafter to be taken before the said Mayor Recorder and the said Burgesses or Aldermen of the said Burrough for the Time being or any three or more of them (whereof We will that the Mayor and Recorder of the said Burrough for the Time being shall be Two,) when and as often as they will deliver the said Gaol of the Prisoners being in that Gaol; and be attending them in all Things touching the said Gaol-Delivery, and the Commandments of the said Mayor Recorder and Burgesses or Aldermen aforesaid for the Time being or any three or more of them (whereof We will that the Mayor and Recorder of the said Burrough be Two) shall execute from Time to Time, *in the same Manner and Form* as any Sheriff of our Kingdom of *England* have accustomed and ought to do return intend and execute (any Manner of way) *by the Laws and Statutes of this our Kingdom of* ENGLAND, before the Justices of Gaol-Delivery in any the Counties of the *said Kingdom*; And that the same Mayor Recorder and Aldermen of the said Burrough for the Time being or any three or more of them (whereof We will that the Mayor and Recorder of the said Burrough for the Time being be Two) may have and shall have, and may erect from henceforth hereafter, a Gallows within the said Burrough Suburbs Liberties or Precincts thereof, to hang and execute Felons Murderers and other Malefactors within the said Burrough adjudged to Death *according to the*

And of Gaol-Delivery, *infra Burgum.*

The Coroner, to return Juries &c, to attend the said Justices of Gaol Delivery, and execute their Commands as Justices of Gaol Delivery.

Power to erect a Gallows, *intra &c.*

Laws

And to arrest and commit Felons &c.

Laws of England; And that the ſaid Mayor, Recorder, and ſuch like Burgeſſes or Aldermen of the ſaid Burrough who at any Time have borne the Office of Mayor of the ſame Burrough or hereafter ſhall bear it, after that they have borne the ſaid Office, as long as they ſhall be Burgeſſes or Aldermen of the ſaid Burrough or any three or more of them (whereof We will that the Mayor and Recorder of the ſaid Burrough for the Time being ſhall be Two,) may take and arreſt whatſoever Felons Thieves or other Malefactors within the ſaid Burrough Suburbs Liberties and Precincts thereof found or to be found, by themſelves or by their Miniſters or Deputies conſtituted in the ſaid Burrough: And that they may carry them to the Gaol within the ſaid Burrough, there to be kept in ſafe Cuſtody until by due Proceſs of Law they ſhall be delivered, Any other Ordinance Decree or Cuſtom to the contrary notwithſtanding. Moreover We have granted and by theſe Preſents for Us our Heirs and Succeſſors of our ſpecial Grace certain Knowledge and mere Motion Do grant to the ſaid Mayor Bailiffs and Burgeſſes of the ſaid Burrough and their Succeſſors, That they and their Succeſſors from henceforth for ever hereafter may have enjoy and receive and may be able and of Power to have enjoy levy and receive, to the proper Uſe and Behalf of the ſaid Mayor Bailiffs and Burgeſſes of the ſaid Burrough and their Succeſſors, All and all Manner of Fines Ranſoms and Amerciaments whatſoever or for whatſoever Treſpaſs or other Offence or other Matters and Cauſes committed and to be committed within the ſaid Burrough Suburbs Liberties and Precincts thereof, And all and all Manner of Fines Iſſues Amerciaments Forfeitures Profits and Perquiſites of the ſaid Court, ſo to be impoſed or forfeited before the ſaid Mayor Recorder and Bailiffs in the Court of the ſaid Burrough, And before the ſaid Mayor Recorder and the ſaid Aldermen of the ſaid Burrough or any 3 or more of them as aforeſaid as Juſtices of the Peace or of our Gaol-Delivery within the ſaid Burrough Liberties or Precinct thereof, for whatſoever Cauſe or Cauſes coming happening ariſing or growing, as before hath been uſed and accuſtomed in the ſaid Burrough; And alſo all and all Manner of Goods and Chattels whatſoever waived, Deodands, Chattels of Felons and Fugitives outlawed and to be outlawed waived and to be waived condemned and to be condemned adjudged and to be adjudged attainted convicted and to be convicted, of Fugitives and Men put in Exigents, of all and ſingular Tenants Inhabitants and Men Reſident in the ſaid Burrough Suburbs Liberties and Precincts thereof, from Time to Time ariſing happening and coming: And that it ſhall be lawful to the ſaid Mayor Bailiffs and Burgeſſes of the ſaid Burrough and their Succeſſors, the ſame Fines Iſſues Amerciaments Forfeitures and Profits from Time to Time to levy and collect, by the proper Miniſters of the ſaid Mayor Bailiffs and Burgeſſes of the ſaid Burrough, according to the Laws and Cuſtoms of *England*, or according to the ancient Cuſtoms of the ſaid Burrough.

The Corporation to have all Fines, &c.

and Deodands, Goods of Felons and Fugitives &c, &c.

And

And farther, of our abounding ſpecial Grace and of our certain Knowledge and mere Motion, We grant and confirm, for Us our Heirs and Succeſſors, to the ſaid Mayor Bailiffs and Burgeſſes of the ſaid Burrough and their Succeſſors, All and all manner of lawful Liberties Grants Franchizes Immunities Privileges Exemptions Quittances Juriſdictions Cuſtoms and free Uſages, as well by Land as by Water, as well within as without the ſaid Burrough Suburbs Liberties Limits and Precincts thereof, through our whole Land and Power, in theſe our preſent Charters or in any other Charters of our Progenitors or Predeceſſors Kings and Queens of *England* expreſſed or not expreſſed; And alſo all and ſingular ſuch Lands Tenements Hereditaments Cuſtoms Liberties Privileges Franchizes Immunities Quittances Exemptions and Juriſdictions, which the Mayor Bailiffs and Burgeſſes of the ſaid Burrough or any of them, by what Means or Names ſoever, or by what Incorporation ſoever or Pretence of any Incorporation, heretofore have had uſed or enjoyed or ought to have hold uſe or enjoy, to them or their Succeſſors for ever, of State of Inheritance, by Reaſon or Pretext of any Charters or Letters Patent or of any Uſe Preſcription or Cuſtom or by any other Manner Right or Title heretofore had uſed or accuſtomed; Notwithſtanding that any Charters aforeſaid were carried away and removed from thence, by *Robert Bruce* King of *Scotland*, our Progenitor; And notwithſtanding that the ſaid Burrough of *Berwick* hath come into the Hands of our Progenitors Kings of *Scotland*, after the ſaid Grants of our ſaid Progenitors Kings of *England*; And although the ſaid Mayor Bailiffs and Burgeſſes of the ſaid Burrough or their Predeceſſors or Burgeſſes of the ſaid Burrough or any of them, by whatſoever Name or Names or by whatſoever Incorporation or Pretext of any Incorporation heretofore known or incorporated or not incorporated, have uſed or enjoyed or not uſed or enjoyed the ſaid Liberties Grants Franchizes Immunities Privileges Uſages and free Cuſtoms: And We, of our ſpecial Grace, All and ſingular the Things above before granted and recited, for Us our Heirs and Succeſſors, to the ſame Mayor Bailiffs and Burgeſſes of the ſaid Burrough and their Succeſſors, Do grant and confirm, and for ever ſtrengthen, by theſe Preſents. Wherefore We will and firmly command, for Us our Heirs and Succeſſors, that the ſaid Mayor Bailiffs and Burgeſſes and their Succeſſors may have hold uſe and enjoy for ever all Liberties Authorities Juriſdictions Franchizes and Quittances aforeſaid, according to the Tenor and Effect of theſe our Letters Patent, without Lett or Hindrance of Us our Heirs and Succeſſors, or Juſtices Sheriffs or other Bailiffs or Miniſters whatſoever, or of any other of them; Nulling and forbidding that the ſame Mayor Bailiffs and Burgeſſes and the Men of the ſaid Burrough, or any of them, or any of the Burgeſſes of the ſaid Bur-

Confirmation of Liberties, Grants, &c.

rough, by reaſon of the Premiſſes or any of them, by Us or by our Heirs Juſtices Sheriffs Eſcheators or other Bailiffs or Miniſters of Us our Heirs or Succeſſors whatſoever, be letted moleſted or grieved, or in any Thing diſturbed thereof.

Some other Clauſes of the Charter, (and which were produced by thoſe who ſupported the Rule for the *Certiorari*,) were as follows—

Power to make By-Laws.

And further, of our abundant Grace, We will, and by theſe Preſents for Us our Heirs and Succeſſors Do Grant to the ſaid Mayor Bailiffs and Burgeſſes of the ſaid Burrough and their Succeſſors, That the Mayor Bailiffs and Burgeſſes of the Burrough aforeſaid or the greater Part of them (whereof We will that the Mayor of the ſaid Burrough for the Time being ſhall be One) ſhall have and by theſe Preſents may have full Authority Power and Faculty of framing conſtituting appointing ordaining making and eſtabliſhing, from Time to Time, ſuch like Laws Statutes Ordinances and Conſtitutions which to them or the greater Part of them (whereof We will that the Mayor for the Time being of the ſaid Burrough ſhall be One,) in their beſt Diſcretion ſhall be thought to be good profitable wholeſome honeſt and neceſſary for the good Rule and Government of the Mayor and Bailiffs and Burgeſſes aforeſaid and all and ſingular other Burgeſſes Officers Miniſters Artificers Inhabitants and Reſidents whatſoever within the ſaid Burrough for the Time being.

Power to fine impriſon or amerce ſuch as break them; and to levy ſuch Fines &c, to the Uſe of the Corporation.

And that the Mayor Bailiffs and Burgeſſes of the Burrough aforeſaid for the Time being, or the greater Part of them (whereof We will that the Mayor of the ſaid Burrough for the Time being be One,) as often as they ſhall frame eſtabliſh or ordain ſuch like Laws Inſtitutions Orders Ordinances and Conſtitutions in Form aforeſaid, may and may have Power to make ordain limit and provide ſuch like Pains Puniſhments and Penalties, by bodily Impriſonment or by Fines and Amerciaments or by either of them, upon and againſt all Offenders againſt ſuch the Laws Inſtitutions Decrees Conſtitutions and Ordinances or any of them, as to the ſaid Mayor Bailiffs and Burgeſſes for the Time being or the greater Part of them (whereof We will that the Mayor of the ſaid Burrough for the Time being be One) ſhall be thought fit neceſſary and requiſite to be done for the Obſervation of the ſame Laws Ordinances and Conſtitutions; And to levy and have the ſame Fines and Amerciaments, To the Uſe and Behoof of the aforeſaid Mayor Bailiffs and Burgeſſes of the ſaid Burrough and their Succeſſors, without Hindrance of Us our Heirs or Succeſſors or any other Officers or Miniſters of Us our Heirs or Succeſſors, and without any Account therefore to be made to Us our Heirs or Succeſſors or Miniſters of Us our Heirs or Succeſſors: All and Singular which

which Laws Ordinances and Conſtitutions, to be made as aforeſaid, We Will ſhall be obſerved, under the Pains therein to be contained; ſo always that the ſaid Laws Ordinances Inſtitutions Conſtitutions Impriſonments Fines and Amerciaments may be reaſonable, and not repugnant or contrary to the Laws Statutes Cuſtoms or Rights of our Kingdom of *England* or reaſonable and laudable Preſcriptions and Cuſtoms in the ſaid Burrough anciently uſed and accuſtomed.

There are alſo ſeveral other Clauſes contained in King *James*'s Charter, not pertinent to the preſent Queſtion.

On *Friday* 25th *May* laſt, Sir *Richard Lloyd*, Mr. *Gould*, Mr. *Yates*, and Mr. *Selwyn*, who were of Counſel for ſuperſeding the *Certiorari*, argued upon the three following Queſtions.

1ſt Queſtion—Whether *Berwick* is *Part of the Realm* of *England*.

2d Queſtion—Whether it is *governed by the Laws of England*.

3d Queſtion—Whether, ſuppoſing that it is, it would *follow*, "that a *Certiorari* lies."

Firſt—To prove that *Berwick* is *not* part of the *Territorial* Realm of *England*, they cited *Calvin*'s Caſe, (6 *Jac.* 1.) 7 *Rep.* 23. expreſs, and *Craw* v. *Ramſey*, *Vaughan* 278, 300. 2 *Vent*. 4. S. C. and *Carre*'s Caſe, cited in 3 *Leon*. 20. and the Statute of 21 *H.* 8. *c.* 6. concerning Mortuaries, (5 or 6 Years before the Incorporating *Wales* with *England*) § 7. which ſhews the Senſe of the *Legiſlature*, "That *Berwick and Calais* were *not* comprehended within the Term "*Realm* of *England*." So alſo is 1 *Mod*. 37. *Criſp's Caſe* v. *Mayor of Berwick*; and *Vaughan* 414. concerning Proceſs into *Wales*.

And *not being Part of the Realm of England*, it is * *not bound by Act of Parliament*, *unleſs named*: For which Reaſon in 1 *W.* & *M.* (the Act for encouraging the Exportation of Corn,) *Berwick* not being mentioned, a new Act was made, which named it expreſſly.

* *Sed V.* 20 *G.* 2. *c.* 42. § 3. which declares and enacts, "that in all Caſes where *England hath been* or ſhall be mentioned in any Act of Parliament, the ſame *has been* and ſhall be deemed to comprehend and include *Wales* and *Berwick*."

Second Queſtion—The Charters could not make the Inhabitants of this *conquered* Place to be *Subjects* of *England*. And the Charter of *Ed.* 4. directs that they ſhall be governed by Laws received from *Alexander* King of *Scotland*. The Charter of 1 *Jac.* 1. (which was *confirmed by Act of Parliament*) eſtabliſhes their *old* Uſages; and gives them a Court of *Oyer and Terminer*, and a Court of Gaol-Delivery, with an *expreſs Excluſion* of all other Juriſdictions *out of* the Town of *Berwick*. But neither this Charter nor this Act of Parliament give them Title to the *Laws of England*.

21 *Ed.* 1. Parliament Roll—*Boyd* v. *Barnaby*, proves that they were governed by the Laws of *Scotland*. And it appears from 2 *Peere Wms.* 75, 76. * that the Laws of a conquered Country ſhall hold Place, till new Ones are given to them by the Conqueror. So alſo is 1 *Salk.* 411. *Blankard* v. *Galdy*. And if they are governed by their own Laws, it would be nugatory and fruitleſs, for this Court to iſſue a *Certiorari* to them.

* It is the 3d Reſolution of the Privy Council.

Third Queſtion—There is no Difference between *Berwick* and *Ireland*, as to *this* Point: And according to 2 *Ventr.* 7. A *Certiorari* will not lie to remove an Indictment from *Ireland.*

In *Vaughan* 403, 404. it appears that He was of Opinion "That "the Alteration of the Juriſdiction in *Wales* might moſt probably "be wrought by an *Act of Parliament* not now extant."

A *Certiorari* would not only create Delay; but would occaſion an inſuperable Difficulty of *Trial:* And it would be nugatory to grant One, where the Court cannot proceed upon it; as in Dr. *Sands*'s Caſe, 1 *Salk.* 145. where it was, for that very Reaſon denied.

Now all indictable Offences are *local:* Therefore, they muſt be *tried* † *there.* And yet no Proceſs of this Court would *lie there*; nor could the Trial be in the *adjoining Engliſh* County, becauſe *Berwick* is no County in *England.* 2 *Shower* 365. Mayor of *Berwick*'s Caſe. The Caſe of *County-Bridges* is the only *criminal* Caſe, where the Trial may be in the adjoining County, upon Suggeſtion: For all the Precedents are of *civil* Caſes, and thoſe *tranſitory* too. *Salk.* 651. Title *Trial, pl.* 31. *Way* v. *Yally*. And there is *no Precedent* of any Cauſe removed from *Berwick* and finally determined here.

† *V.* 5, 6 *W.* & *M.* c. 11. 8, 9 *W.* 3. c. 33. (but they only relate to Quarter Seſſions.)

Mr. *Norton contra*—The General Queſtion is, "Whether a *Certiorari* will lie to *Berwick*, to remove an Indictment found at a "General Gaol-Delivery there, for a Miſdemeanour."

The Caſe *now* under Conſideration requires it, *if any can*; ſince the Judge who is to try the Cauſe is both Party and Witneſs.

The Anſwer that has been inſiſted upon, is "that *Berwick* is an "*exempt Juriſdiction*; and no *Certiorari* lies thither."

Three Objections have been made to this *Certiorari:* (1ſt.) That *Berwick* is *not part of the Realm* of *England*; (2d.) If it is, yet 'tis *not governed by Engliſh Laws*; (3d.) That if the Court *ſhould* grant the *Certiorari*, yet they can *not proceed* upon it.

I premise that this Court hath a *General Supervision* of all inferior Jurisdictions in *England*: And, they may also grant *Certioraries*, *before* it appears whether they can proceed upon them or not.

Answer to 1st Objection—The Clause in 20 *G.* 2. *c.* 42. § 3. proves clearly "that *Berwick is* part of the Realm of *England*."

The Argument also from their *sending Members* to represent them in Parliament, is *irrefragable*. And *Prynne's Parliamentary Writs* prove that *Berwick* sent Members before the Time of *Ed.* 4.

This Court constantly sends *Certioraries* to the *Cinque Ports*.

Answer to 2d Objection—Their Charter of 1 *Jac.* 1. *ties them down* to proceed by the *Laws of England*, in *criminal* Matters. Consequently, this Court will superintend their Proceedings under their Charters. And their Acceptance of a Charter which subjects them to the Laws of *England*, renders them *liable* to this Superintendency.

The 3d Objection would come *more properly*, upon the *Return* of the *Certiorari*: The Writ ought to be obeyed, and a Return made.

Answer to 3d Objection—But however, from the *Necessity* of the Case, this Matter must be tried in the *adjoining County*; Like the Case of *Wales*, or of County-Bridges: Both of which are done by the Court's *General* Power, and to prevent Failure of Justice.

An Indictment is no more local than a *Real Action* is: And yet *these* are tried in *Northumberland*. And the Militia-Act considers *Berwick* as being in *Northumberland*.

Precedents too are not wanting. In 3 *Jac. B. R.* An *Information qui tam &c*, on the Statute of Uniformity, was brought up by *Certiorari*; And Process issued. In *M.* 8 *Ann.* An *Information* in this Court was granted for an Offence in *Berwick*; and the Rule made absolute. In 9 *G.* 1. *B. R.* there was a *Mandamus* to swear *Wilson* and 3 Other Churchwardens of *Berwick*. And *Berwick* is put under the Ecclesiastical Jurisdiction of the * Diocese of *Durham*, by their Charter. In 1754, an Indictment against *Moscroft* and two Others, for an Assault, was removd hither, from thence, by *Certiorari*: And they appeared and pleaded. In *H.* and *P.* 1755, in the Contest between Mr. *Wilkes* and Mr. *Watson*, *Informations* for Bribery were granted: the Rules were made absolute.

* *V. Post* (about 7 Pages.)

 The

The Affidavits of the Facts being read, It appeared that the Indictment was for an Assault upon the *then Mayor*, who still *continues a Justice of Peace* for the Burrough of *Berwick*.

Lord MANSFIELD said, that it would be proper to look into the Precedents that had been cited; and they would give their Opinion, next Term.

CURIA ADVISARE VULT.

Lord MANSFIELD now delivered the Opinion of the Court, to the following Effect.

The Objections and Arguments that have been urged against this *Certiorari* may be reduced to the following Heads—

1st. That this Court has *no Jurisdiction* over the Town and Burrough of *Berwick*, or any *local* Matters arising there; Because it is not to be deemed part of the *Realm* of *England*, and the King's Writ does *not run* there: Consequently, this Court has no Authority to remove a Record from thence, by Writ of *Certiorari*, for any Purpose whatsoever.

2dly. That supposing the Court may, for *some* Purposes have Jurisdiction there, Yet the *End*, for which the *Certiorari* is desired, upon the *present* Occasion, can *not be attained*.

3dly. That though the Court should have Authority, and the End be attainable; Yet the *Ground*, upon which the *Certiorari* is applied for, is *not sufficient*.

1st Head. 1st. As to being Part of the Realm.

As to the first—The best Way of considering it, may be, concisely to deduce the Condition and Constitution of *Berwick*, contrasted with *Wales*; to shew that Arguments from the Case of *Wales* hold to *Berwick*, equally at least, in all Respects; in many, *à fortiori*.

Edward the 1st conceived the great Design of *annexing* all other Parts of the Island of *Great Britain* to the Realm of *England*. The better to effectuate his Idea, as Time should offer Occasion; He maintained "that All the Parts thereof, not in his own Hands or "Possession, were HOLDEN OF HIS CROWN."

The Consequence of this Doctrine was, that, by the Feudal Law, supreme Jurisdiction resulted to *Him*, in Right of his Crown, as Sovereign Lord, in many Cases which He might lay hold of; And when the said Territories should come into his Hands and Possession, they would come back *as Parcel* of the Realm of *England*, from which, (by Fiction of Law at least,) they had been originally severed.

This Doctrine was literally true, as to the Counties Palatine of *Chester* and *Durham*.

But, (no Matter upon what Foundation,) He maintained that the *Principality of* WALES was holden of the Imperial Crown of *England:* He treated the Prince of *Wales* as a rebellious Vassal; subdued Him; and took Possession of the Principality. Whereupon, on the 4th of *December* in the 9th Year of his Reign, He issued a * Commission to inquire "Per quas Leges et per quas Consuetudines "Antecessores nostri Reges regere *consueverant* Principem Walliæ "et Barones Walenses Walliæ et Pares suos et alios inferiores et "eorum Pares &c"

* *Rotul' Walliæ*, 9 *Ed.* 1. *M.* 5. *Leges Walliæ, Hoeli Boni*, 518. (published by *Wotton*.)

If the Principality was *feudatory*, the Conclusion necessarily followed, "That it was under the Government of the *King's Laws*, "and the *King's Courts*, in Cases proper for them to interpose;" though (like Counties Palatine,) they had peculiar Laws and Customs, *Jura Regalia*, and complete Jurisdiction, at Home.

There was a *Writ* at the same Time issued to all his Officers in in *Wales*, "to give Information to the Commissioners:" And there were 14 Interrogatories specifying the Points to be inquired into. The * Statute of *Rutland* refers to this Inquiry. By * that Statute, He does *not annex Wales* to *England*, but recites it as a *Consequence* of it's coming into his Hands—"Divina Providentia Terram Walliæ, "PRIUS *nobis Jure feodali subjectam*, jam in Proprietatis nostræ Do- "minium convertit, et Coronæ Regni Angliæ, *tanquam partem* "*Corporis ejusdem*, annexuit et univit."

* 12 *Ed.* 1. See it in the 2d Vol. of the Book of Old Statutes, intitled "*Statuta Walliæ*." See also in *Hale's Hist. of the Common Law*, *pa.* 183, 184. this Preamble to it; and likewise in *Vaughan* 400.

The 27 *H.* 8. *c.* 26. adheres to the same Plan, and recites "that "WALES *ever hath been incorporated, annexed, united, and subject* "*to, and under the Imperial Crown of this Realm*, as a very *Member*, "and *Joint* of the same."

Edward the 1st having succeeded as to *Wales*, maintained likewise "that *Scotland* was holden of the Crown of *England*."

That Jurisdiction which resulted to Him as superior Lord, He often *exercised* as sitting in *this* Court.— * Upon a Complaint of a Burgess of *Berwick*, against his own Commissioners, whom He would not suffer to be tried in the Courts of the King of *Scotland*.— † Upon Complaint of a Merchant.— ‖ Upon a Complaint of M^c *Duff*.— ‡ Upon a Complaint of *Austria* claiming the *Isle of Man*.

* *Rymer*, 2 Vol. 596.
† *Rymer* 605.
‖ 21 *Ed.* 1. *Rymer* 606.
‡ *Rymer* 608.

* Rymer, 2 Vol 615. † 22 Ed. 1. Rymer 632. *Man.*— * Upon a Complaint of the Abbot of *Reading.*— † Upon a Complaint of the Bishop of *Durham* claiming the Town of *Berwick*, as belonging to his See. In the 24th Year of his Reign, he treated the King of *Scotland*, as a rebellious Vassal; and took *Berwick*, and the rest of *Scotland*, into his own Hands and Possession. And as this Court exercised that Jurisdiction which resulted to the King, in the Capacity of *Superior Lord* of *Scotland*; *à fortiori*, it did so, when the Country came into the King's *Hands* and ‡ Hale's Hist. Common Law, fo. 201. *Possession.* Therefore the Court of King's Bench ‡ *actually* sat at *Roxburgh in Scotland.*

* 30 Ed. 1. * While He continued in Possession of *Scotland*, He granted a *Charter* to the Town and Burrough of *Berwick*, under the *Great Seal of* ENGLAND, (though He then had a Great Seal of *Scotland.*) The Charter requires the Mayor to be sworn before His Chancellor or Treasurer and Barons of His Exchequer in *Scotland*: And the Writ to chuse a Coroner is to issue out of His Chancery in *Scotland*. He seems to consider the whole Country as *united* into *one Realm*: for the Privileges are given "Per totum Regnum et Potestatem "nostram-in Terra et Potestate nostra."

In a few Years, *Berwick* with the rest of *Scotland* was lost; and continued so, many Years.

† 2 Ed. 3. Rymer, 4th Vol. 337. † *Edward the 3d* renounced all Pretension to the Kingdom of *Scotland*, in Property, or Superiority, *divisum à Regno Angliæ.*

‖ 6, 7, 8 Ed. 3. Rymer, Vol. 4. pa. 536. 590 to 595. 614. ‖ *Edward* the 3d procured from K. *Ed. Baliol*, and the Parliament of *Scotland*, a *Grant* and *Cession* of BERWICK, *separate from* Scotland, "for ever, "et regali Dignitati et *Coronæ ac Regno* "*Angliæ* perpetuis temporibus *annexa, unita, et incorporata.*" In the 10th Year of his Reign, He granted to *Berwick* an Exemplification and Confirmation of the Charter of *Ed.* 1st.

BERWICK was *again lost*, when *Edward* the 3d was in *France*; and retaken after His Return: And, in the 30th Year of his Reign, He gave a *new Charter* confirming the former, with some *Additions*; particularly, that they should be governed by the Laws and Usages, which they enjoyed in the Time of *Alexander* late King of *Scotland*; (who reigned before the Competition about that Crown.)

Berwick was lost again; and again recovered by *Edward the 4th* who *confirmed* the former Charters, by a * Charter and † Act of Parliament.

* 22 Ed. 4. † 22 Ed. 4. c. 8.

Between this Time and the 33d of *Hen.* 8th. (the particular Time does not appear, because the Returns are lost,) *Berwick* was

2 summoned,

ſummoned, as a Burrough of *England*, to ſend *Members* to *Parliament:* And they did ſo, till the Union; and they ſtill continue to ſend Members to the Parliament of *Great Britain*, by Summons, as being Parcel of the Realm, not under any of their Charters, none of which give them ſuch a Right. That of *E.* 4. is an Inſpeximus of the preceding Ones: And the Charters of 19 *April*, 1 *H.* 8. 25 *April*, 1 Qu. *Mary*, 4 *May*, 1 Qu. *Eliz.* are Confirmatory Charters only. None of them give them a Right to ſend Members to Parliament: and yet they have ſent them, ever ſince King *Henry* the 8th's Time.

Their preſent Conſtitution is under Letters Patent granted in * 2 *Jac.* 1. Which are expreſſly confirmed by † Act of Parliament. Under *theſe*, they act: And they have had no Charter ſince.

* 20th *April*, 2 *J.* 1.
† 2 *J.* 1. *c.* 28. (called, in *Hawkins*'s Edition, 1 *J.* 1. *c.* 28.)

Before the Union, *Berwick* was *bound* by every *Engliſh general Act of Parliament*, in like Manner as *Wales* was bound: And that was as being *Part of the Realm* of *England*. Where it is particularly named in Acts of Parliament, that is *ſuperfluous:* And ſo alſo is the Naming of *Wales*. *If* it was not part of *England* before the Union, it is now no part of *Great Britain*; for only *England* and *Scotland* are united. It is *bound* by all *General* Laws ſince the Union.

In *General* Acts, not applicable to *Scotland*, and where *Scotland* is not intended to be included, the Method is, by Proviſo, To declare "it does *not extend to Scotland*." Where Proviſions are made for that part of *Great Britain* called England, *Wales* and *Berwick upon Tweed* are *comprehended* under that Deſcription.

Wales, from the Time it came into the Hands of *Ed.* the 1ſt. was deemed to be within the Realm, upon the Doctrine of having been *holden before of his Crown:* And in Conſequence of ſuch Tenure, by Deductions from the Principles of the Common Law, this Court exerciſes *Juriſdiction* over Matters in *Wales* given *by* no *Act of Parliament:* (For the ‖ Notion of "ſome Old Statute that "has been loſt," depends only upon a looſe ‡ imperfect Note of Ld. Ch. J. *Vaughan*'s.)

‖ *V. Vaughan* 403, 404.
‡ *V. Vaughan* 395. the Memorandum in the Margin.

Scotland was conſidered upon the *ſame* Foot.—*This* Court exerciſed the ſovereign Juriſdiction over it, *before* it came into the King's Hands; and *afterwards*, at the Time when the firſt Charter was granted to *Berwick*. The Chance of War refuted the Claim of the *Reſt* of *Scotland*, as belonging to *England*; and confirmed it, as to *Berwick*.

But, if *Berwick* was to be deemed a *Dominion of the Crown*, and *no* part of the Realm of *England*; It may be under the *Control* and *Superintendence* of the King in this Court.

The *Constitution* given to *Berwick*, by the Crown of *England*, approved by Parliament, shews it necessarily is so; much stronger than in the Case of *Counties Palatine*, or *Wales*. The People of *Berwick* have not *Jura Regalia*, or a *complete Jurisdiction* within themselves, like a *County Palatine*: They have no *Sovereign Courts* of the King within themselves, like *Wales*. They are made a *free Burrough*, to hold in *Burgage*, by *Rent*. Such a Creature of Law must necessarily be connected, as *part* of a Kingdom, and *subordinate*.

In the Time of King *Alexander*, they were subject to the Supreme Courts of *Scotland*. They could have no Laws or Customs but such as were suitable to the *subordinate* Condition of a *Burrough*.

The Metamorphosis from a *Scotch* to an *English* Burrough did *not* make them *independant*; but *only changed* the Sovereign Jurisdiction. They are made a *Corporation in England*; to sue or be sued, in that Capacity, *in England*; to take Lands, in that Capacity, in *England*. The Burgesses, in *that* Capacity, are to enjoy many Privileges in *England*: They send *Representatives to Parliament*, by Summons, *as a Burrough in England*.

This Court alone can judge of their Franchises, as a *Corporation*; and *Who* are intitled as *Members* of it; and what are their Privileges; and whether they continue to exist, or not: As, if you suppose a Question to arise "Whether they are *dissolved*;" or, "*Who* is *Mayor* "*&c*," Who can judge, but this Court? The Charter of *James* the 1st *supposes* it: Because He commands the Attorney and Solicitor General to bring *no Writ of Quo Warranto* for Things *past*. In *Hilary* Term 14, 15 *Car.* 2. A *Quo Warranto* was brought in this Court, against the Mayor Bailiffs and Burgesses of *Berwick*; but not proceeded in.

Another part of their Constitution, more immediately applicable to the present Question, is What relates to *Pleas of the Crown*.

The Charter grants them a Court Leet *agreeable to the Laws and Statutes of England*; A Commission of Peace and *Oyer and Terminer*, with the *same* Authority *which belongs, or hereafter may belong to Justices of the Peace in England*; and to hear and determine in *like* Manner *as Justices of Peace, by the Laws and Statutes of England*. It grants them a Commission of Gaol-Delivery, under which they must proceed by *Indictment*, according to the Course of the *Law of England*; as in Fact, they always do, and have done in the preſent Caſe. It grants a Gallows, to execute thoſe adjudged to Death, *according to the Law of England.*

The Charter gives them Power to make Ordinances with Penalties of Fine and Impriſonment; *ſo as they be reaſonable, and not repugnant to the Laws, Statutes, and Cuſtoms of England.* In ſhort, They have no CRIMINAL *Law, but* the Law of ENGLAND; and *no* CRIMINAL *Juriſdiction, but* with ſuch a *Reference* to the Law of ENGLAND, as *neceſſarily includes this Court.*

Suppoſe They ſhould adjudge a Man to *Death,* for a Crime *not Capital* by the Law of *England*;—Suppoſe they *indict* a Man for *diſobeying* an Ordinance *repugnant* to the Law of *England*;—Suppoſe they ſhould indict a Man *for Treaſon,* though the Fact would not amount to Treaſon within *our* Laws;—Suppoſe as Juſtices of the Peace, they make *illegal Orders,* without any Authority, in a ſummary Way; There can be *no Redreſs* BUT HERE: And if this Court could not interpoſe, they would, under the Grant of a *limited ſubordinate* Authority, be *abſolute.*

Another Objection is, "The King's Writ does *not run* there." 2d Diviſion of the 1ſt Head.

That is applicable only to the Writ of *Venire,* and other *Jury-Proceſs*; or perhaps, to *Original* Writs which are the Commencement of Suits between *Party* and *Party.*

When this Court removes, by Writ of *Certiorari,* an *Indictment* for a Miſdemeanour from WALES; the *Welch* Sheriff is commanded to cauſe the Defendant to appear: And When He has appeared, and Iſſue is joined, there is a Suggeſtion "That the King's Writ "does *not* run into *Wales.*" So, the *very Record* which ſays "the King's Writ does not run," ſhews many that *do.*

The Reaſon why a *Venire* does not run to *Berwick,* is, becauſe they are exempted from being ſummoned *out* of the Burrough, to ſerve upon Juries.

But the Charter ſuppoſes That *other* Writs, miniſterially directed, *may* run: Becauſe the *Return of* ALL *Writs Precepts and Proceſs iſſuing out of the King's Courts, and the Execution thereof, is granted to the Mayor Bailiffs and Burgeſſes, excluſive of any Sheriff, Miniſter, or Bailiffs.*

Writs, *not miniſterially* directed, (ſometimes called *Prerogative* Writs, becauſe they are ſuppoſed to iſſue on the part of the King,) ſuch as Writs of *Mandamus, Prohibition, Habeas Corpus, Certiorari,* are reſtrained by no Clauſe in the Conſtitution given to *Berwick*:

Upon

Upon a proper Case, *they* may issue to *every Dominion of the Crown of England*.

There is no Doubt as to the POWER of this Court, where the Place is under the Subjection of the Crown of *England*: The only Question is, As to the PROPRIETY.

To FOREIGN Dominions, which belong to a Prince who succeeds to the Throne of *England*, this Court has *no Power* to send *any* Writ of *any* Kind. We cannot send a *Habeas Corpus* to *Scotland*, or to the *Electorate*: But to *Ireland*, the *Isle of Man*, the *Plantations*, and, (as since the Loss of the Duchy of *Normandy*, they have been considered as annexed to the Crown, * in some Respects,) to *Guernsey* and *Jersey*, We *may*; And Formerly, it lay to *Calais*; which was a Conquest, and yielded to the Crown of *England* by the Treaty of *Bretigny*.

* *V. Hale's Hist. Com. Law* 184 to 189.

But, *notwithstanding the* POWER which the Court have, Yet where they cannot *judge* of the Cause, or give *Relief* upon it, they would not think PROPER to interpose. Therefore upon Imprisonments in *Guernsey* and *Jersey*, in *Minorca*, and in the *Plantations*, I have known Complaints to the *King* in *Council*, and *Orders* to bail or discharge: But I do *not* remember an Application for a Writ of *Habeas Corpus*. Yet Cases have formerly happened of Persons illegally sent from hence and detained there, where a Writ of *Habeas Corpus* out of this Court would be the *properest* and *most effectual* Remedy.

In *Cro. Jac.* 543. a Precedent is cited, in 43 *Eliz.* of a * *Habeas Corpus* to *Berwick*. I have caused the Records to be searched for that Case: And the Orders of the Court, and Return to the Writ of *Habeas Corpus* are found. The Court had fined the Mayor and Bailiffs of *Berwick* 2000*l.* for not returning the † Writ: They had also issued an *alias Habeas Corpus*. ‖ Then, the *Alias Habeas Corpus* not being returned, they ordered the Fine to be estreated; and that a *Pluries Habeas Corpus* should issue, *Sub pœna* 500 *Merc'*, returnable immediately, before the Chief Justice at his Chambers in *Serjeants Inn*. At the same Time They issued an *alias* Attachment against the Mayor and Bailiffs; and ordered Ld. *Willoughby*, then Governour of the Town of *Berwick*, to execute it, returnable *Octabis Hilarii*. The ‡ next Day, the Estreat of the Fine was suspended, upon *Henry Brearly*'s being discharged out of Prison, and bailed to appear in this Court, at the Octave of S. *Hilary*, (the Return of the Attachment against the Mayor and Bailiffs.)

* For one *Browley*, as He is there called.

† *M.* 43 *Eliz. Hab. Cor.* for *Henry Brearly*, *V. H.* 43 *Eliz. Rot'lo* 88.

‖ *Die Jovis prox' post* 15. *Sancti Martini.*

‡ The former was *die Jovis*; the latter, *die Veneris prox' post quinden' Sancti Martini* Aº 43 *Eliz.*

In

In *Hilary* Term, they are * ordered to return the *Pluries Habeas Corpus:* And afterwards, the Mayor and Two of the Bailiffs were committed, and examined upon Interrogatories, as in Contempt; and Two of them were † Ordered to find Bail at the Suit of *Henry Brearly*, before they were discharged.

* *Die Ven' prox' post Octab' Sancti Hil. anno supradicto.*
† *Die Sab'ti prox' post Oct. Sancti Hil. A° 43 supradicto.*

The Return states the Charter of *Ed.* 3d. and that by their Laws and Customs, the Guild had Authority to punish for colouring Foreigners Goods, or being in Partnership with a Foreigner, by Fine, Imprisonment and Disfranchising. They state that *Henry Brearly* was found guilty of being in Partnership with a Foreigner, and fined 100*l.* which He not only refused to pay, but treated them with scandalous and contumelious Reproaches. That they duly committed him to Prison, till the Fine should be paid; and disfranchised him.

There is an Order, the || same *Hilary* Term, stated to be upon the Recommendation of the Court, (therefore I suppose, by *Consent,*) " That the Fine of 100*l.* set upon *Brearly* by the Guild, should be " reduced to 50*l*; and that upon his Submission, He should be restored to his Freedom:" (But He was to remain disfranchised till he should make his Submission.)

|| *Die Jovis prox' post Octab' Pur'.*

As TO the *other* Prerogative Writ, of *Probibition*—It was *taken for granted*, in 2 *Ro. Abr.* 292. " That a Prohibition *lay*, out of " this Court to the Consistory Court of *Durham*, in a Matter ari- " sing in *Berwick*:" Though the Suggestion " that the Land out " of which the Tithes were claimed lay in *Scotland* and not in *Ber-* " *wick*," was holden insufficient. (How *Berwick* * *came* to be part of the Diocese of *Durham*, I have not learned.)

Tit. *Probibition*, Letter L. *pl.* 6. *Tr.* 11 *C.* 2. between *Morton* and *Rosden*.

* *V. ante*, 849.

• Then, as to Writs of *Mandamus*—In *Trin.* 9 *G.* 1. A *Mandamus* issued, directed to Sir *Geo. Wheeler*, to admit and swear Four Persons elected to be Church-Wardens of *Berwick*.

The Act of 11 *G.* 1. *c.* 4. proceeds upon the Ground " That a " Writ of *Mandamus*, out of this Court, lies to *Berwick*."

The last Sort of Writ not ministerially directed, is a *Certiorari*.

A *Certiorari*, for a proper Purpose, lies to ANY *Dominion of the Crown of England*. Mr. Justice *Dodderidge*, in † Sir *John Carew*'s Case, says " the Register makes mention of a *Certiorari* to remove " a Record taken at *Calais*."

† *V. Cro. Jac.* 484.

And there are Precedents of *Certioraries* to *Berwick*, directly.

In *Pasch.* 3 *Jac.* 2. An Indictment against *Scott*, *Howlettson* and *Watson*, for a Riot &c, was removed from *Berwick*, by *Certiorari*: Process issued upon it, out of this Court, against the Defendants, to appear. In *Michaelmas* Term following, the Indictment was quashed; and the Town-Clerk of *Berwick* amerced 5*l.* for not returning the Caption.

In *Trinity* Vacation 1754, Two Indictments were removed from *Berwick*, by *Certiorari*: The Defendants appeared in this Court, and pleaded Not Guilty.

There is *no Instance* of a *Doubt* ever having been made, before the present Case, concerning the AUTHORITY *of this Court*, to send a Writ of *Certiorari* to *Berwick*. And We are All clearly of Opinion, " That the Court, by Law, *has* such POWER."

Two great Authorities are indeed urged, in *Opposition* to this: They are no less than those of Ld. Ch. Justice *Coke* and Ld. Ch. Justice *Hale*.

* 7 *Co.* 23. *b.*

† *Hale's Hist. Common Law of England, pa.* 184. *V. Rot. Parl.* 16 *R.* 2. *n.* 41, 42.

Lord *Coke*, in * *Calvin's* Case, says " That *Berwick* is *no Part* of " *England*, nor governed by the *Laws* of *England*." And Ld. Ch. Justice *Hale* follows Him, and † says " *Berwick* was sometimes " Parcel of *Scotland*; but was won by Conquest by King *Edward* " the 1st. And after that, lost by King *Edward* the 2d, and afterwards regained by *Edward* the 3d. It was governed by the *Laws* " of *Scotland*, and their *own particular Customs*; and *not* according " to the Rules of the Law of *England*, further than as by Custom " it is there admitted." " Yet *now*," says He, *by* CHARTER, they " send Burgesses to the Parliament of *England*."

In *Calvin*'s Case, there was *no Question* concerning the *Constitution* of BERWICK. And We plainly see, by what has passed in the present Case, *how little was known*, even *at Berwick* itself, concerning it's own Constitution. What was dropped about it, in *Calvin*'s Case, was a mere *Obiter* Opinion, thrown out by way of Argument and Example. My Lord *Coke* was very fond of multiplying Precedents and Authorities; and, in order to illustrate his Subject, was apt, besides such Authorities as were strictly applicable, to cite other Cases which were *not* applicable to the particular Question under his judicial Consideration. In the Case then under judicial Consideration, the Question was ‖ " Whether *Robert Calvin* the " Plaintiff, born *in Scotland* after the Descent of the Crown of *England* to King *James* the first, was an *Alien born*, and consequently disabled to bring any Real or Personal Action for any " Lands within the Realm of *England*." But it never was a Doubt, " Whether

‖ *Calvin's* Case, *fo.* 2. *a.*

" Whether a Person born in the *conquered Dominions* of a Country " is subject to the King of the *Conquering* Country." And therefore the Argument did not hold, from the Case of *Berwick* to the Point then in Question: Neither was the Case of * *Calais* in any sort apposite to it. * V. Calvin's Case 22. a.

As to the *Laws* by which *Berwick* is governed—

Whatever may be the Case (when more particularly inquired into) with regard to their † *Civil* Constitution, It appears very sufficiently, That in *Pleas of the* CROWN, *Berwick* has *no other* Laws by which it is governed, *but* the Laws of ENGLAND. The Statute of 11 *G.* 2. *c.* 19. for the more effectual securing the Payment of Rents and preventing Frauds by Tenants, supposes this. All the Provisions of that Act are extended to *Berwick*, ‖ by Name. Some of these Provisions relate to ‡ *Ejectments*, which concern *civil* Matters: And they *do* proceed there, by *Ejectment*. But it is manifest, that Lord *Coke* is mistaken in saying, generally, " That *Berwick* was *not go-* " *verned by the Laws of England*." For, in *Criminal* Matters, the Fact is clearly otherwise.

† V. Fitz-Herbert's Abridgment, Title Obligation, pl. 15.

‖ § 1, 11.

‡ § 12, 13.

And Ld. Ch. J. *Hale* is as clearly mistaken, in saying " that *Ber-* " *wick* sends Members to the Parliament of *England*, *by* CHARTER." For 'tis by *Writ* of Summons that they send them thither, in *Consequence* of their being a Burrough. *Chester*, both County and City, first sent Members to Parliament, by virtue of an Act of Parliament § made in *H.* the 8th's Time. § 34 H. 8. c. 13.

Second Head.

BUT though the Court has *Power*, by Law, to send a Writ of *Certiorari* to *Berwick*, yet it ought not to issue *in vain*. And therefore We should be satisfied, that the *End* for which it is prayed be *attainable*; and the *Ground sufficient* for removing the Record, in Order to attain that End. The *End* here avowed is, that the Matter may be *tried in this Court*. And it is Objected that there can be no such Trial, because the Trial must be *local*, and *no Jury* can come from *Berwick*.

Objection.

Answer.

BUT the Law is clear and uniform, as far back as it can be traced. Where the Court has Jurisdiction of the Matter; if, from any Cause, it cannot be tried *in* the Place, it shall be tried as *near* as may be. All local Matters arising *in Wales*, triable in this Court, are by the * *Common* Law, tried by a Jury of the *next* County in *England*. So, as to the † *Cinque Ports*, the *Venire facias* shall be awarded *de vicineto* of the next Vill, either in the County of *Kent* or the County of *Sussex*. So ‖ it is also as to the Isle of *Ely*: So, ‡ likewise as to *Ireland*; A *Venire* was directed to the Sheriff of *Salop*, as the next *English* County. So, in Parts of *England* itself where an impartial Trial cannot be had in the proper County, it shall

* 19 H. 6. fo. 12. b. pl. 31.

† 2 Ro. Abr. Tit. Trial, Letter I. pl. 6, 7. pa. 596, 597.

‖ Howse v. Bishop of Ely. —Moore 88.

‡ 2 Ro. Abr. 597. pl. 8.

ſhall be tried in the next: As 5 *G.* 1. *Rex* v. *Inhabitants of the County of the City of Norwich*, about a County Bridge, the Trial was in *Suffolk*.

This is the ancient and general Rule, wherever the Court has Juriſdiction: And this General Rule has *often* been *applied to* BERWICK.

21 *Ed.* 1. *Ryley's Placita Parl.* 159.

Edward the Firſt, by an Ordinance in Parliament, extended theſe Rules as to Complaints againſt the King of *Scotland*, that they might be tried in this Court by a Jury of *Northumberland*, or *any other* County, or before *Commiſſioners* appointed by the King. There was a Precedent applying this Rule to *Berwick*, in 42 *Eliz.* affirmed upon a Writ of Error: And the like in 44 *Eliz.* The like, the * 20 *Car.* 2. *Criſpe and Jackſon* v. *Mayor and Burgeſſes of Berwick*. And the Mayor of *Berwick*'s Caſe, † 36 *C.* 2. lays down as a certain Principle, That where a *local* Matter ariſing at *Berwick* is tried here, there is to be a Suggeſtion made on the Roll, that "Breve Domini Regis ibi non currit," as it is in *Wales*. A Tip-ſtaff was in that Caſe ſent, to take the Mayor up.

* 1 *Lev.* 252. 1 *Mod.* 36, 37. 1 *Sid.* 381, 462. 1 *Ventr.* 58, 90. *Raym.* 173. 1 *Keb.* 414, 676.

† 2 *Shower* 365.

There are two Precedents in the Reign of *Ja.* 2. of *Informations in this Court, for Miſdemeanours* in *Berwick*: And in *Michaelmas* 8 *Ann.* the ‖ Attorney General filed an *Information here, for Miſdemeanours* in *Berwick*. In *Hilary* and *Eaſter* 1755, This Court, after much Litigation, granted *Informations for* ‡ *Bribery* in *Berwick*, at the Election of their Members to Parliament, as being an Offence and Miſdemeanour at the *Common* Law: Which ſhews *Berwick*, in reſpect of the Juriſdiction of this Court "to proceed "originally by Information for *Miſdemeanours* committed there," to be upon the *ſame* Foot, as any *other* part of *England*. And the Court never would have granted thoſe Informations, without being ſatisfied "that they might be *tried*:" Becauſe a Defect of Power to try, neceſſarily infers a Want of Juriſdiction.

‖ Sir *James Montagu*. It was againſt *Robert Mills* and *George Lindſay*.

‡ *V. ante* 849.

There is not One *Authority* to the contrary. And in *Reaſon* it would be moſt abſurd: Becauſe it would really be putting the Place out of the Protection of the Law; And there muſt, in many important Caſes, be a total Failure of Trial, and conſequently, of Juſtice.

Suppoſe the *Office of Mayor* ſhould be *uſurped*: The Uſurpation is a *Crime*; and cannot be tried before the Man *Himſelf* who is accuſed, or any Juriſdiction in the *Town*. Much leſs could a Queſtion, "Whether the *Corporation* was *diſſolved*," be tried before *themſelves*. Such Queſtions could not be tried originally before *Commiſſioners* ſent thither by the King: They could ONLY be judged in in this Court. To try Franchises of this kind in any *other* shape, would not only be contrary to the Common Law, but to the * Act abolishing the Star-Chamber, and all the Statutes there recited. * 16. 17 C. 1. c. 10.

Suppose an Action between the Corporation and their own Lessee to be depending at *Berwick*, or any Suit instituted there between the Corporation and any other Person, on a Point of Property; They could not judge in their *own* Cause: And *if* it could not be tried elsewhere, there must be a Failure of Justice.

Every Rule of the Common Law, which holds in the Case of *Wales*, concludes *à fortiori* to *Berwick*; both as to the Jurisdiction of this Court, and the Method of Trial. *Berwick* is only a Burrough; It has neither *Jura Regalia* nor *Superior Courts*: *Wales* had *Both*. A Small Part of the County of *Durham* is nearer to *Berwick* than *Northumberland* is: But at the Time of first sending Process to the latter, the King's Writ did not run to the former, being a County Palatine. So that *Northumberland* was the nearest *English* County, for the Purpose of Trial; as the King's Writ did not run to *Durham*.

† The Objection made when this Matter first came on, appears now to be groundless: "That they proceeded by Laws and Usages, "of which this Court *cannot judge*." Whereas, their Trials, as to *Criminal* Matters at least, are in the Course of the *Common* Law, and entirely governed by the Laws of *England*. † V. ante, pa. 835, 836.

Therefore We are All of Opinion That these *Indictments* may be tried in *this* Court, by a Jury of the County of *Northumberland*.

The 3d Objection urged against the *Certiorari*, was, That though it should be admitted that the Court have Authority to issue it, and that the End is attainable, yet there is *not* Ground *sufficient* to take the Trial from the ordinary local Jurisdiction of *Berwick*. Third Head.

Most certainly, The Court ought to be *satisfied of the Ground*, before they send a *Certiorari* for that Purpose. The *King* has a Right to choose his Court: But upon the Application of the *Defendant*, there should be always a Reason. The higher the inferior Jurisdiction is, and the greater the Inconveniences are of removing the Cause, the stronger the Reason should be: But a *Doubt*, "Whe-"ther a fair, impartial, or satisfactory Trial or Judgment can be "had there," is *a Reason* to remove from the *highest*.

In the Case of ‖ *Rex* v. *Lewis*, *Tr.* 12 G. 1. after considering the Matter at different Times, and looking into Precedents; and there being an Affidavit produced, inducing a *Suspicion* "that a fair ‖ 1 Strange 704.

"Trial could not be had in *Wales*;"—A *Certiorari* was granted to remove the Indictment from the Grand Sessions of *Anglesea*. This *Suspicion* only, being properly verified by Affidavit, was in that Case holden to be a sufficient Reason for Removing that Indictment from a very high Court.

Let Us inquire into the Reason alledged in the Case now before Us, "Why there can't be a fair Trial *in Berwick*."

The Defendant in *this* Case swears to his Innocence: And He and Five more swear "That he *cannot have a fair Trial*, owing to "Party Differences, and great Contentions that have lately hap-"pened in the Burrough." That the *Justices, before whom He is* "*to be tried*, warmly supported a Motion to disfranchise Him *for* "*the Offence* laid in this Indictment: Which was rejected by a "great Majority of the Burgesses. That the *Matter of the Indict-*"*ment* arose at an Assembly of the Corporation, in Consequence of "a *violent Division* which engaged the *whole Body*."

I suppose the Magistrates of *Berwick* may be in the Right, and Men of the greatest Integrity: But they *admit* a great Contention in the Burrough; That the Matter laid in the Indictment *arose* from a warm Dispute at the Guild, upon a Point of Business, which produced a Riot and Tumult, that broke up the Guild in great Confusion; That the *Justices are All of one Side*, upon this Point.

It is not denied that the *Justices vehemently pressed a Motion to disfranchise* the Defendant *for the Offence charged in this Indictment*; which was rejected by a great Majority of Burgesses. Whether the *Motive* for rejecting it, was because they thought the Defendant innocent, or because they thought the Motion premature and too violent, is immaterial.

Robert Selly's Affidavit against the *Certiorari*, shews it is considered as a Cause *against the Magistrates*, and that his Brother —— who made an Affidavit for the Defendant, listed as a Soldier on *that* Account, and declared he had rather go to the farthest Part of the World, than *fly in the Face of a Magistrate*.

Upon *this* Occasion, *All the Justices oppose the Certiorari*, and have produced Affidavits to prove the Defendants *Guilty*.—They *may* be so: And *if* they are, they ought to be severally punished. But it is impossible, that *under all these Circumstances*, the Trial or Judgment at *Berwick* should be *satisfactory*.

Every Body in the Town has already *pre-engaged his Opinion*. The *Burgesses* have all taken Sides: The *Justices* have already *de-*

clared him so *heinously guilty*, that he ought to be immediately disfranchised, without waiting for a Trial of the Indictment. I dare say they were of that Opinion, without Prejudice to the Man, but from Indignation at his Guilt: And perhaps, very justly; For a Man *may* judge impartially even in his own Cause. However, *We* must go upon *general* Principles. If a *Witness* in a Cause has an *Interest*, though it be small, He must be rejected: Or if a *Juryman* has declared his Opinion by a former Verdict, He may have done it very justly, but yet is liable to be challenged for this Cause, on a subsequent Trial. In the present Case, it is impossible but that All the Persons who would be concerned in trying this Matter at *Berwick*, must be *biassed* by their *preconceived Opinions*. I don't speak this, with the least *Imputation* upon the Magistrates of *Berwick*: But it is not fit that they should be Judges in their *own* Cause, and after having *already gone so far* as they have done.

Therefore We are, All of Us, of Opinion That the Rule to shew Cause "Why Writs of SUPERSEDEAS to these Writs of *Certi-*" *orari* should not issue," ought to be discharged.

But *unless* the Matter could have been *tried here*, A *Certiorari ought not to have gone*: Nor shall it now be used for *Delay*. To prevent which, the Prosecutors of the *Certiorari* shall engage to appear, and take short Notice of Trial, and try it at the next Assizes for the County of *Northumberland*.

I have settled the Form of a SUGGESTION to be entered upon the Roll: Which I will give to the Master of the Crown-Office, for that Purpose.

HIS LORDSHIP accordingly did so: And

It was as follows—" And because the Burrough of *Berwick* is a
" Place where the King's Writ of *Venire facias*, to summon a
" Jury to try the said Issue, doth not run; And because the Bur-
" gesses of the said Burrough, by reason of their Privileges, ought not
" to be put upon any Jury to try the said Issue out of the said Bur-
" rough; but the said Issue ought to be tried by a Jury of the County
" of *Northumberland*, which is the next adjacent County to the
" said Burrough of *Berwick*; which Allegations of the said *Henry*
" *Cowle* are not denied by the said *James Burrow* Esq; There-
" fore it is commanded the Sheriff of *Northumberland*, that He
" * cause to come &c."

* The Entry upon the Record has a Clause of *Non omittas*, (which is always inserted on the Crown-Side;) *viz.* " that He do not " forbear, by reason of any Liberty in his Bailiwick, but that he cause to come &c."

The

The RULE now made by the Court (in Consequence of their present Resolution) was afterwards drawn up and entered in these Words, *viz.*

Upon mature Deliberation had here in Court, *It is Ordered* by this Court, That the Rule made "that the Defendants should "shew Cause why a Writ of SUPERSEDEAS should not issue "to the two Writs of *Certiorari* lately issued out of this "Court, to remove all and singular Indictments against the "Defendants," be DISCHARGED.

And the said two Writs of *Certiorari*, and the Returns thereto, being now *returned* and *filed* in this Court, *It is further Ordered* that the said Defendants do *immediately appear and plead* to the said Indictments; and *proceed to the Trial* of the said Indictments, at the *next* Assizes to be holden in and for the County of *Northumberland*. *And it is further Ordered* that in Case the *Defendants* shall make Default or neglect to make up the Records and proceed to the Trial of the said Indictments, at the now next Assizes to be holden in and for the County of *Northumberland*, in such Case, the *Prosecutors* shall be at Liberty to make up the said Records, and proceed to the Trial of the same, at the said next Assizes in and for the County of *Northumberland*.

And as to the Application for an ATTACHMENT, for *not returning* the said two Writs of *Certiorari*,

It was *Ordered* That the Rule made, "that *Henry Hodgson*, "*William Compton*, *Fenwick Stow*, *William Temple*, and *Samuel Burn* Esquires should shew Cause why a Writ of ATTACHMENT should not issue against them, for their *Contempt*," be DISCHARGED.

The Indictment was afterwards tried at *Newcastle*.

Wednesday 4th *July* 1759.

Rex *vers.* Bootie.

ON *Tuesday* 19th *June* last, Mr. *Ashurst* moved in Arrest of Judgment, after Verdict for the King, upon an Indictment against a Constable, for a Misdemeanor.

The Charge in the Indictment was, That He, being One of the Constables of *St. Martins in the Fields*, and being in the Execution of of his ſaid Office, as Head of the Nightly Watch of the ſaid Pariſh, did wilfully and unlawfully ſuffer *Margaret Prince*, *being* a loose idle lewd and diſorderly Perſon, taken up by *Robert Miller*, One of the Nightly Watch of the ſame Pariſh, between 1 and 2 o'Clock in the Morning, as a Common Street Walker &c, *to eſcape* out of his Cuſtody, before She could be carried before a Juſtice of the Peace, to be dealt with by the Juſtice according to Law.

The whole Indictment was (in Subſtance) thus—That One *Robert Miller*, being lawfully appointed One of the Nightly Watchmen of and for the ſaid Pariſh, and being in his Office and Place as ſuch, performing his Duty of a Watchman there, at an unſeaſonable Time *i. e.* between One and Two in the Morning, did apprehend and take into his Cuſtody One *Margaret Prince* then and there BEING a looſe idle lewd and diſorderly Perſon and a Common Street-Walker, and *being* then and there behaving herſelf riotouſly, and walking the Streets there to pick up Men, in Breach of His Majeſty's Peace; And did then and there take lead and convey the ſaid *Margaret Prince* in his Cuſtody to a certain Priſon called the Watch-houſe in the ſaid Pariſh, and did there *deliver her* in Cuſtody unto One *John Bootie*, who then and there was One of the Conſtables of the ſaid Pariſh, and then and there being in the Execution of his ſaid Office of ſuch Conſtable, as the Head of the Nightly Watch of the ſaid Pariſh; and did then and there *leave and deliver up* Her the ſaid *Margaret Prince in Charge with the ſaid John Bootie*, ſo being ſuch Conſtable as aforeſaid, and in the Execution of his ſaid Office as aforeſaid; and did then and there CHARGE *and* REQUEST *the ſaid John Bootie* ſo being ſuch Conſtable as aforeſaid *to keep and detain* the ſaid *Margaret Prince* SO BEING ſuch looſe idle lewd and diſorderly Perſon and a Common Street-Walker walking the Streets there to pick up Men as aforeſaid, IN HIS CUSTODY, UNTIL the ſaid *Margaret Prince* could be carried and conveyed in Cuſtody before ſome One of His Majeſty's Juſtices aſſigned to keep the Peace in and for the ſaid City and Liberty, there to be dealt with by ſuch Juſtice according to Law for her ſaid Offence and Breach of the King's Peace: Neverthelefs the Defendant, ſo being &c, not regarding the Duty of his Office &c, *unlawfully and wilfully diſcharged* Her out of his Cuſtody, before that She had been carried before any Juſtice &c, and *would not keep or detain* Her in his Cuſtody for the Purpoſe aforeſaid, but *wilfully ſuffered and permitted Her to eſcape and go at large* &c.

Upon which Indictment, the Defendant having been tried; And a Verdict found againſt him;

Mr. *Aſhurſt* prayed a Rule to ſhew Cauſe why the Judgment ſhould not be arreſted; upon the following

Objection—That it is not charged that the Defendant KNEW that She was a Street-Walker &c, as this Indictment describes her to be: Nor indeed is it positively charged "that She *was* One." And if She was *not liable* to be detained by him, He would have subjected himself to an Action for false Imprisonment, *if he had detained Her*. It ought to have *expressly* charged "that She *was* so; and that "She was delivered to him *as* such."

Mr. *Norton* and Mr. *Stow* now shewed Cause against arresting the Judgment.

They insisted that the Expressions "BEING" and "So BEING" are sufficient Allegations "that She WAS so; And that She was de-"livered to the Defendant *as such*." And as this is *after Verdict*, it must be taken to have been proved at the Trial. It is almost impossible that He could be ignorant of it: And if He really was so, He might have pleaded it.

Mr. *Ashurst* and Mr. *Morton*, *contra*—The being *after Verdict*, is no Answer, in a *Criminal* Case; whatever it may be in a *Civil* One.

Indictments must be positive and certain, on the Face of them, But this Indictment does not sufficiently shew that She was lawfully in the Custody of the Constable. 1 *Hale's Hist. P. C.* defines what is lawful Custody.

This is *no positive* Allegation, "that She was delivered to Him *as* a loose idle and disorderly Person." She might, in Fact, be a loose idle and disorderly Woman &c; And yet not delivered to him, AS SUCH. It was at *his Peril* to detain Her, unless He was well satisfied that She was *liable* to be detained. * 1 *Salk*. 272. *Dominus Rex* v. *Fell*, is in Point, that the Defendant is not liable for the Escape of a Person not committed to his Custody *as charged* with a Crime.

* *V.* 4 *Mod.* 414. S. C. 12 *Mod.* 226. S. C.

Mr. *Norton*, in Reply to the Cases cited, insisted that the Term "BEING" is a sufficient *Averment* of the Fact.

Lord *Mansfield* and Mr. Just. *Denison* did not come into Court, till towards the End of the Motion: They therefore remained silent.

Mr. Just. FOSTER—*Fell*'s Case was † *Treason*: It was an Indictment against him, as Keeper of *Newgate*, for negligently suffering the Escape of a Person being in his Custody, charged with High Treason. But would not that have been sufficient Ground to have

† *V. Hale's H. P. C.* V. 1. pa. 234. and *Hawk. P. C.* V. 2. c. 19. § 22.

indicted him for a *Misdemeanour?* And the present Case is a Misdemeanour, and sufficiently charged upon the Defendant.

The Peace of this City can never be preserved, unless Watchmen are supported in Doing their Duty.

Mr. Just. WILMOT—I think it is a Misdemeanour in the Constable, to discharge an Offender brought to the Watch-house by a Watchman in the Night; though *without* any positive Charge. But, in the present Case, I think that this *is* a *sufficient Allegation* of the *Fact* of her being such a Person, and of her being delivered to the Defendant *as* such a Person as she is described to be.

Per Cur. The RULE "To shew Cause why the Judgment "should not be Arrested," was DISCHARGED.

Case of the Poor Prisoners on the Common Side.

THE Prisoners on the *Common* Side of the Prison of this Court conceived themselves to be intitled to the HIGH-BAR-MONEY paid to the Box, upon *certain Motions* made in Court, (*viz.* for Judgments, for Writs of *Mandamus*, *Certiorari*, *Habeas Corpus*, and other Original Writs, *every* Day in Term; and upon *all* Motions whatsoever, on the *last* Day of a Term;) and upon All *Affidavits* sworn *in Court:* Which *Box-Money* or *High-Bar-Money* (as they termed it) amounts to a large Sum in the whole Term; and has been always paid to the Youngest Judge's Clerk, at the End of every Term, by the Secondary of the Chief Clerk's Office, to be disposed of by the Judges *in Charity*, as they shall think proper.

This Money the Prisoners in the King's Bench, confined on the Common Side, fancied to belong to *them*; and accordingly applied for it, by Petition to the Court, as their Predecessors had done about 48 Years ago: But they were totally unable to make out their Claim now; And it appeared, upon Examination, that they had been equally unable to support it, at *that* Time.

Mr. Just. FOSTER happened to remember that former Application; and that the Matter was referred to Mr. *Harcourt:* And He said that He was present in Court, (in 1711. 10 *Ann.*) when Mr. *Harcourt* reported the "Claim of the Prisoners to be *without Foundation*;" and He had Himself taken a Note of Mr. *Harcourt*'s Report; Which Note He now produced and read publicly in Court.

Upon

Upon the Whole, The COURT (after having referred the Matter to Mr. *Athorpe*, the present Secondary of the Crown-Office,) made the following Rule, worded (by special Direction) thus—

King's Bench Poor Prisoners. } This COURT took into Consideration the Petition of the Poor Prisoners confined on the Common Side of the Prison of this Court, touching the Money usually paid into the Box of this Court, upon *Motions* and *Affidavits made in Court*; which the Petitioners claim, as due to *Them*.

And *Mr. Athorpe* (to Whom it had been referred, to examine into the Matters alledged in the said Petition,) having this Day *reported* to this Court "That He hath made diligent Inquiry into the "Premisses; And that no Living Witness was upon such Inquiry "produced on the Part of the Petitioners, who could give Evidence "touching the same; And that He had carefully inspected All the "Books Papers and Writings which could be found relative to the "Premisses; And that upon such Inspection and Inquiry, it *doth* "NOT *appear* that the said Money was *ever* paid to the said Poor "Prisoners or for their Use;" And *Mr. Clarke*, Secondary on the Plea-Side, having this Day informed the Court, "That during the "Time He hath been in the said Office, and also during the Time "his late Father Mr. *Giles Clarke* (long since deceased) was in the "same Office, the said Money hath been constantly paid by the "Secondary on the Plea-Side, into the Hands of the Clerk of the "Junior Judge of this Court for the Time being, in order to be "by Him paid over to the JUDGES of this Court, in equal Shares, "to be disposed of by THEM, for *such* CHARITABLE *Purposes* as "THEY in *their* Discretion should think proper;" *It is Ordered* that the said *Petition* be REJECTED.

The End of *Trinity* Term 1759, 32 & 33 *Geo.* 2.

Michaelmas

Michaelmas Term

33 Geo. 2. B.R. 1759.

Rex *verſ.* Corporation of Carmarthen.

Wedneſday 7th *November* 1759.

MR. Serj. *Nares* moved (very faintly, and without pretending to hope for much Succeſs in it) for an Information in Nature of a *Quo Warranto againſt* the *whole* Corporation (*as a* BODY,) To ſhew by what Authority they claimed to act *as a* CORPORATION.

But even He himſelf intimated a Doubt " Whether ſuch a Species of Information, (*viz.* filed by the Clerk of the Crown, under Leave of the Court, at the Relation of a *private* Proſecutor,) could be within the Act of Queen *Anne*." [*V.* 9 *Ann. c.* 20. § 4.]

The COURT gave no direct Opinion.

However, Lord MANSFIELD and Mr. Juſtice DENISON ſeemed to be pretty clear, That this Act was calculated only againſt INDIVIDUALS uſurping Offices or Franchiſes IN Corporations, and *not* againſt any *Corporation itſelf*, as a BODY: And the Words of the Act manifeſtly carry this Meaning.

It was obſerved by Them, and acknowledged by the Serjeant and Mr. *Aſton*, his Colleague in this Motion, " That there was no Inſtance of any Information in Nature of a *Quo Warranto* being brought againſt any Corporation *as a Corporation* for an Uſurpation upon the Crown, *but* by and in the Name of the ATTORNEY GENERAL, on Behalf of the *Crown*."

Whereupon, The Counſel made their Motions againſt the ſeveral *Individuals*, " To ſhew by what Authority they *reſpectively* claimed to exerciſe their particular Franchiſes;" and obtained the ordinary Rules againſt them, in the uſual Form.

Saturday 17th November 1759.

Rex verf. Inhabitants of St. Matthew Bethnal Green.

* This Name "Elizabeth" is a manifeft Miftake: It fhould be "Mary." But the Original Order is fo. See the Note below.

TWO Juftices removed * *Elizabeth Coiffeau*, Widow, and her 3 Children, (*John*, aged 6 Years, *Abraham*, aged upwards of 4 Years, and *Mary*, near 3 Years,) from the Parifh of *St. Matthew Bethnal Green* to the Precinct of *St. Katharine*. The Seffions, upon an Appeal, difcharged this Order of the two Juftices; Stating the Cafe fpecially, upon their own Order.

Special Cafe ftated upon the Order of Seffions.—*Elizabeth Taylor* was *born* in the faid Precinct of *St. Katherine*. She intermarried with *Edward Brazier*, whofe Settlement is *not known*. *Edward Brazier* died, many Years ago. *Elizabeth* afterwards *intermarried with Ifaac Coiffeau*, who was a *Frenchman* and *never gained any* Settlement in *England*. The faid *Ifaac Coiffeau* and *Elizabeth* lived, (Both of them,) many Years together in *Bethnal Green* Parifh: And *Abraham Coiffeau*, Son of the faid *Ifaac Coiffeau* and of *Elizabeth Coiffeau* (heretofore the Widow *Brazier*,) was *born in Bethnal Green* Parifh; And *fo was* his *Wife Mary*, (*the Pauper*,) the Daughter of *Peter Dormer*. *Abraham Coiffeau* and *Mary* his Wife *Both lived in Bethnal Green* Parifh: But *Neither of them gained any Settlement* in their own Right, fubfequent to what they might gain by being *Both born in Bethnal Green* Parifh. *Peter Dormer*, the Father of *Mary Coiffeau* the Pauper, was *born in, and ferved his Apprenticefhip in* the Parifh of *St. Leonard Shoreditch*.

The Seffions, upon Confideration of the Premiffes, allow of the Appeal, and difcharge the Order of the two Juftices.

Note—

The Original Order of two Juftices is "to remove *Eliz. Coiffeau*, Widow: But the *Certiorari* calls them "Orders "concerning the Settlement of *Mary Coiffeau*, Widow of "*Abraham Coiffeau deceafed*;" And the Order of Seffions defcribes the Order of two Juftices in the *fame* Manner. And it fhould be "*Mary*."

The Short of the Cafe is, That *Mary Coiffeau* the Pauper, who was *born in St. Matthew's Bethnal Green*, of a *Father fettled in St. Leonard's Shoreditch*, became the Wife of *Abraham Coiffeau*, born in *St. Matthew's Bethnal Green*; but Son of a Father who had *no Settlement* at all, and of a Mother ftated to have been *born* in *St. Katharine's*: And the Children are the Children of the faid *Abraham Coiffeau* by this *Mary Coiffeau*. The Queftion was "Whether *Mary* and her Children are fettled in *St. Katharine's*, or not."

4 The

The Objection which had been taken to the Order of Sessions, by Mr. *Stowe*, upon moving to quash it, was, "That the Settle-"ment of the *Anceſtor* ſhall here take Place of the Settlement by "*Birth*: And He treated this as a *Derivative* Settlement.

Mr. Serj. *Hayward* and Mr. *Gould* (for the Precinct of *St. Katharine*) ſhewed Cauſe againſt quaſhing the Order of Seſſions.

They argued that the *accidental* Settlement (that is, the Settlement *by Birth*) of the *Child itſelf* ought clearly to take Place of the *accidental* Settlement of the *Grandmother* or any other *Anceſtor*.

Settlements were never yet carried higher, they ſaid, than to the *immediate* Parent. And *till* the Caſe of *Everſley Blackwater* v. *St. Giles's Reading*, (2 *Ld. Raym.* 1332. and 1 *Strange* 580. S. C. *H.* 10 *G.* 2. *B. R.*) a Child could not be removed even to his *own Father*'s Settlement, AFTER *the Death* of the Father. But if it be carried *higher* than the immediate Parent, where ſhall the Line be drawn? The Confuſion would be infinite.

The Place of * *Birth* is not the Settlement of any *legitimate* Child; but only of an *illegitimate* One. And here, the Settlement of this *Grandmother* is ONLY *preſumed*, from it's being the Place of her *Birth*, to be the Place of her *Settlement*.

* *V.* 2 *Salk.* 528. *Inhab. of Cumner* v. *Milton, Tr.* 1 *An. B. R.*

Whereas *Mary Coiffeau* had an *acquired* Settlement in *St. Leonard Shoreditch*, by her Father Serving his *Apprenticeſhip* there.

Here is no Settlement in *St. Katharine's*, either *acquired* or *derivative*.

Mr. *Norton* and Mr. *Stowe contra*.

ALL Settlements are *equal*; whether by Birth, or acquired.

There is *no Limitation*, as to Settlements.

BIRTH, though *primâ facie* a Settlement, is *not* a Settlement for a legitimate Child, where the Settlement of the Parent can be ſhewn: It is only ſo, *till* a better appears; as the Caſe of *Everſley Blackwater* proves.

The Child's Settlement ſhall relate to what was the Father's at the *Time* when the Son *left* his Father's Family; And ſhall *not* follow the Settlement of it's *Mother*, if the Settlement of it's *Father* can be *found*.

But

But *Abraham Coiſſeau*, the Father, had *no* Settlement at all; nor *his Father*, *Iſaac Coiſſeau*. It was neceſſary therefore to have Recourſe to *Abraham Coiſſeau*'s *Mother*'s Settlement; which is ſufficiently ſtated to be in *St. Katharine's* where She was born; *As Nothing to the contrary appears:* For Birth is a Settlement, *primâ facie*.

The Settlement of *Mary Coiſſeau*, Daughter of *Peter Dormer*, is *loſt* in her *Huſband*'s Settlement: and *his* Settlement, *as* Son of his *Mother*, is found to be in the Precinct of *St. Katharine's*. So that *her Father*'s Settlement is out of the Caſe.

Lord MANSFIELD—There is *no Difference* between an *acquired* and a *derivative* Settlement.

The *Father's* Settlement is the Settlement of the Children.

The Father was, here, the Son of a Foreigner who *never* gained *any* Settlement, and of *Elizabeth Taylor*, who was *born* in *St. Katharine's*.

Upon this Order, as ſtated, it muſt be taken that *St. Katharine's*, where *Eliz. Taylor* was *born*, was the Place of her Settlement. Conſequently, *Abraham Coiſſeau* her Son was legally ſettled there.

Mr. Juſt. DENISON was clear in this laſt Point,—That it muſt be taken upon this Order ſtating *Eliz. Taylor* "to have been *born* in "*St. Katharine's*," that She was ſettled there.

And He ſaw no Reaſon for any Diſtinction between deriving a Settlement from an *immediate Father*, or from a *Grandfather*.

Mr. Juſt. FOSTER concurred—It is a common Caſe, that if the *Father*'s Settlement cannot be found, You go back to the *Grandfather*'s.

Mary Coiſſeau's Settlement is out of the Caſe; For *her* Settlement was that of her *Huſband*.

There is *no Diſtinction* between an *acquired* Settlement and a *derivative* One: All Paupers muſt be ſent to *ſome* Place or other, to accompliſh the End of the Acts relating to the Settlements of poor Perſons.

Mr. Juſt. WILMOT was clear in this Caſe, *if* it muſt be taken for granted "That *Eliz. Taylor* muſt be conſidered upon this Order,

as

as *settled* where She was *born*: Of which He said He had some Doubt at first; but was now clear "that it *ought* to be so taken."

The Children are always to follow the Settlement of their *Father*, if it can be *known*: And if it can be known, *then* the *Mother*'s Settlement is quite out of the Case.

Birth gives even a *legitimate* Child a Settlement, *if* the Parents of it had none.

Abraham Coisseau's Settlement must follow the Settlement of his Father, *if* his Father had any: But it could not follow his *Father*'s Settlement in the present Case; because his Father had *none*. But his *Mother* had One, (in *St. Katharine's.*) Therefore, as his *Father* had none at all, (being a *French-man* who had never gained any,) *his* Settlement was in *St. Katharine's*, where his *Mother* was settled.

There is *no Merit* in a Settlement: It depends upon *positive* Law. Therefore there is no Difference between an *acquired*, and a *derivative* Settlement.

And the positive Law in these Cases of Settlements, is "That the "Child's Settlement follows that of it's *Father*, if the Father's can "be *found*; and that no Recourse shall be had to the *Mother*'s Set-"tlement, *till* that of the Father can be *traced no further*."

But in the present Case, *Abraham's Father* had none; And therefore his *Mother's* was to be inquired into. And accordingly, the Settlement of *Abraham Coisseau* is traced up to his Mother *Eliz. Taylor*'s Settlement in *St. Katharine's*: Which is therefore the Settlement of *Abraham*'s Wife and Children.

Per Cur. unanimously,
ORDER of SESSIONS QUASHED:
Original ORDER AFFIRMED.

Goodman et al' *vers.* Goodright, Lessee of Richard Williams and Annabella his Wife.

Tuesday 20th *November* 1759.

ERROR from the Grand Sessions in *Wales*, upon a Judgment there given for the Plaintiff, in an Ejectment brought by *Richard Williams* and *Annabella* his Wife, for Lands in *Denbighshire*; In which, the Jury had, upon the Trial of it there, found a Special Verdict, to the following Effect.

That on the 4th of *August* 1714, *Susannah Mostyn* was seised in Fee, of the Lands in Question.

That on the same Day and Year, *Articles of Agreement* were made, by Deed indented, (which they find *in hæc verba,*) between *Edward Wynn* Dr. of Laws, on the first Part; *Margaret Wynn*, Mother of the said *Edward*, on the second Part; the said *Susannah Mostyn*, on the third Part; and *Elizabeth Lloyd*, on the fourth Part; Reciting an intended Marriage between the said *Edward Wynn* and *Anne Lloyd* (then 18 Years of Age,) Niece of the said *Susannah Mostyn* and *Elizabeth Lloyd:* Whereby (amongst many other Covenants not at present material) The said *Susannah Mostyn*, in Consideration of the said Marriage, COVENANTED for Herself her Heirs &c with the said *Edward Wynn* and his Heirs, *That She would*, on the Solemnization of the said Marriage, *at the Request* of the said *Edward Wynn* and *Anne Lloyd* or either of them or either of their Heirs, AT OR AFTER SUCH TIME as the said *Edward Wynn* should settle *his* Estate to the Uses therein mentioned, *settle and convey* (to Trustees therein named) All her Capital Messuage &c &c (the Lands in Question,) and all other the Messuages Lands &c of Her the said *Susannah Mostyn*, or whereof or wherein She had any Estate, in the said County of *Denbigh*, To hold to them and their Heirs, To the Use of the said *Susannah Mostyn*, for Life; then to the said Trustees, for 200 Years, upon Trusts therein afternamed; And from and after the Determination of that Estate, then to the Use of the said *Edward Wynn*, for Life; Remainder to Trustees (to be nominated by Her) to preserve contingent Remainders &c; Remainder to the said *Anne Lloyd*, *for Life*; And after the Decease of the said *Edward Wynn* and *Ann Lloyd*, To such Uses as are therein after named; Which Uses are afterwards declared to be To the Use of the first and every *other Son* of the Body of the said *Edward* on the Body of the said *Anne* to be begotten, and the *Heirs of the Body* of such first and other Son lawfully issuing, according to Seniority of Age; And for Default of such Issue, To the Use of the first and every other *Daughter* of the said *Edward* on the Body of the said *Anne* to be begotten, and the *Heirs of the Body* of such first and every other *Daughter* lawfully issuing, according to Seniority of Age; And for Default of such Issue, To the Use of the said *Susannah Mostyn* her *Heirs* and Assigns for *ever*.

The Trust of the Term of 200 Years was declared to be For the raising 500*l.* out of the Rents or by Mortgage &c; to be paid to such Person or Persons, and in such Manner, as the said *Susannah Mostyn*, by *Deed or Will*, should direct or appoint.

That the Marriage was accordingly solemnized between the said *Edward Wynn* and *Anne Lloyd*.

That *Susannah Mostyn*, after Making the said Articles, *viz.* on 1*st March* 1727, duly made and published her *last Will &c:* Wherein, *reciting the said Articles* and the *Provisions therein* made, as to her said Estate in the County of *Denbigh*, and appointing the 500*l.* to be raised, and paid to her Executrix, She goes on thus—" And " Whereas the Premisses so *agreed to be settled by me* as aforesaid, " from and after the Death of me the said *Susannah Mostyn* and of " the said *Edward Wynn* and his Wife and in Default of Issue of " their two Bodies, *are limited or agreed to be limited to Me and* " *my Heirs* as aforesaid, Now I do hereby give and devise the said " Messuages Lands Tenements and Hereditaments and the *absolute* " *Inheritance* thereof, to the Use and Behoof of the HEIRS OF THE " BODY OF THE SAID ANNE, *by any* OTHER *Husband lawfully to* " *be begotten*; And for Want of such Issue, to the Use and Behoof " of my Nephew CHARLES LLOYD of *Drenewith* in the County " of *Salop* Esq; and of *the Heirs of his Body lawfully issuing*; And for " Want of such Issue, to the Use and Behoof of my Niece *Catharine Longford* Widow, and the Heirs of her Body lawfully issuing; And for Want of such Issue, To the Use and Behoof of " *Elizabeth* now the Wife of *George Ball*, and the Heirs of her " Body lawfully issuing; And for Want of such Issue, To the Use " and Behoof of *Catharine Longford* Spinster, Youngest Daughter " of the said *Catharine Longford* Widow, and the Heirs of her " Body lawfully issuing; And for Want of such Issue, to the Use " and Behoof of the right Heirs of Me the said *Susannah Mostyn*, " for ever."

Susannah Mostyn, after Making her said Will, died seised, on 12*th March* 1728; leaving the said *Anne Wynn her Heir at Law.*

Edward Wynn and *Anne* his Wife entered; and by Deeds of Lease and Release, 1st and 2d of *March* 1730, *convey* the Premisses to make a *Tenant to the Præcipe*, in Order to suffer a *Common Recovery:* The Uses of which Common Recovery were to be such as should be declared by an Indenture to be made by the said *Edward Wynn* and *Anne* his Wife.

A COMMON RECOVERY was accordingly suffered, at the Great Sessions at *Wrexham* for the County of *Denbigh:* Wherein the said *Edward Wynn* and *Anne* his Wife were vouched &c.

And on the 29th of *May* 1731, by an Indenture of that Date, the Uses of the said Recovery were declared to be, as follows, *viz.* To the Use of the said *Edward Wynn* and his Assigns, for Life, without Impeachment of Waste; And after his Decease, to the said *Ann Wynn* and her Assigns, for Life, without Impeachment of Waste;

Waste; Then to Trustees, to preserve &c; Remainder to the first and every other Son of the said *Edward Wynn* on the Body of the said *Anne* to be begotten, and the Heirs of their Bodies respectively, according to Seniority of Age; And in Default of such Issue, To the first and every other Daughter, in like Manner; And after the Determination of the several Uses before limited, To such Uses as they the said *Edward Wynn* and *Anne* his Wife should, by any joint Deed or Writing, limit and appoint; And for want of such Appointment To the *right Heirs of the said* ANNE, *for ever*.

The said *Anne* afterwards died, *viz.* on 12th *July* 1739, without Issue of her Body, leaving ——— her Heir at Law.

The said *Edward Wynn* continued in the Receipt of the Rents and Profits till his Death: Which happened on the 9th of *June* 1755.

After the Death of *Susannah Mostyn, Charles Lloyd* died: He left Issue, ANNABELLA, his *only Daughter and Heir*, then and still the *Wife* of *Richard Williams*.

Richard Williams and *Annabella* intermarried in the Life-time of the said *Charles Lloyd*.

Richard Williams and *Annabella* his Wife, after the several Deceases of the said *Edward Wynn* and *Anne* his Wife, *viz.* on the 15th of *June* 1755, made an Entry &c, and demised &c to *Goodright*, who entered &c: And the Defendants below (claiming under the *Heir at Law of Anne Wynn*) entered upon *Goodright*, and ejected him.

But whether upon the Whole &c, They pray Advice of the Court: And if &c, then they find the Defendants below, guilty &c; But if &c, then they find them not guilty &c.

This Case was twice argued; first, in *Trinity* Term last; and again, in this Term: And the Court gave their Opinion, upon the next Paper-Day after the last Argument.

Both the Arguments were very diffused (especially the former,) and would be too tedious to repeat; though several Nice Points were discussed in them, and the Reasonings of the Counsel supported by a great Variety of Cases.

It was disputed, Whether *Ann Wynn* took an Estate-Tail by *Implication* by her Aunt's *Will*; (there being no Person *in Esse* named in it, to support the Remainder to the Heirs of *Ann*'s Body by a ſecond Huſband:) For it was urged on the Behalf of the Defendant in Error, "That this was a Deviſe *in verbis de præſenti*; and that "the Law will not ſuffer a *preſent* Deviſe to a Perſon not in being;" and "that *Charles Lloyd* conſequently took an *immediate* Eſtate *in* "*Poſſeſſion*, as much as if there had been *no* precedent Deviſe, as "this precedent One was totally and abſolutely void."

Alſo, "Whether the Will is to be taken as an *Execution* of the "Articles by Mrs. *Moſtyn*; and as a *Diſpoſition* of her Eſtate *ac-* "*cording* to her Covenant."

Alſo, "Whether *Ann's Iſſue by a ſecond Huſband* was a Matter "that ought to be *laid quite out of the Caſe*, in the ſame Manner as "if there had been no ſuch Deviſe;" Since the EVENT NEVER *happened*.

Alſo, "Whether *Charles Lloyd* could *take at all*, by this Will:" And, if He could, then "in *what Manner*." For the Counſel who argued on Behalf of the Plaintiffs in Error inſiſted That He could not take either as a *preſent* or as an *Executory* Deviſe; and that there was *no other* Way by which He could take: But the Counſel for the Defendants in Error endeavoured to ſhew that he might take *either* Way.

CUR. ADVIS'.

Lord MANSFIELD now delivered the Reſolution of the Court.

This Caſe, when ſtript of a great deal of Learning which may very well be laid out of it, as not being at all eſſential to the Determination of the preſent Queſtion, comes within a very narrow Compaſs.

The whole of the Caſe comes ſingly to this Queſtion—"Whether Mrs. *Moſtyn*, the Teſtatrix, INTENDED to give her Nephew "*Charles Lloyd* and the Heirs of his Body the Remainder or Reverſion AFTER *the Death* of Herſelf and of Dr. *Edward Wynn*, "and *Anne* his Wife, and of the Heirs of their two Bodies, and alſo "of the Heirs of *Anne*'s Body by any *ſecond* Huſband;" Or "Whether She *meant* to give him an Eſtate in POSSESSION." For it was admitted, that IF *She did not* INTEND to give Him an Eſtate *in Poſſeſſion*, the Leſſors of the Plaintiff can have no Title.

IF this Deviſe is to take Effect *after the Death* of the Teſtatrix Mrs. *Moſtyn*, and of Dr. *Edward Wynn*, and of *Anne* his Wife, and of the Heirs of their two Bodies, and of the Heirs of her Body by any Second Huſband; then it can be made good, *only* by One of theſe two Ways; *viz. Either* by Way of a *Contingent Remainder*, Or by Way of an *Executory Deviſe*.

 Now,

Now, to make it a *contingent Remainder*, All the *former* Eſtates ſpecified in the Articles muſt be conſidered as being *intended* to be given and deviſed BY *this Will:* And then it would follow, that the Eſtates would be of *One and the ſame Nature and Quality*, and limited in *One and the ſame Conveyance*; and not by ſeveral diſtinct Deeds or Conveyances.

And if the *ſame Kind of Eſtate* be, in the *ſame Will*, limited to *Anne Wynn* for Life, and to her Iſſue by her firſt Huſband, it would be an Eſtate-Tail executed in *Anne Wynn*; and She might ſuffer, and has in fact ſuffered a Common Recovery, which will bar the Remainders.

But it is not neceſſary for Us to go into the Queſtion " Whether " the Articles and the Will can be *tacked together*:" Becauſe, if a Deviſe of the particular Eſtates expreſſed in the Articles cannot be implied by Conſtruction; And ſuppoſing the Deviſe " to the Iſſue " of *Anne Wynn* by any ſecond Huſband" to be void; the Limitation " to CHARLES LLOYD *and the Heirs of* HIS *Body*," can *not* be coſidered as a *Contingent Remainder*.

And if it were to be conſidered as an *Executory Deviſe*, then, not being to take place till after an *indefinite* Failure of Iſſue of the Body of *Anne Wynn*, it is TOO REMOTE. And if it was too remote in it's *Creation*, the EVENT cannot vary the Conſtruction: So that her *actually* dying without Iſſue can make *no Difference*.

Therefore, *either* Way, 'tis clear that the Leſſor of the Plaintiff below had no Title, *unleſs* it is a PRESENT Deviſe " to *Charles Lloyd* " and the Heirs of his Body."

And therefore the Counſel for the Defendant in Error very judiciouſly laboured to prove that Mrs. *Moſtyn* meant, in this Deviſe " to " Him and the Heirs of his Body," to deviſe the Eſtate to him IMMEDIATELY. This, they found themſelves *obliged* to inſiſt upon, and to endeavour to maintain.

But neither the *Words*, nor the *Nature of the Proviſion* Mrs. *Moſtyn* was making, will admit of *this* Conſtruction. For the Words do by no Means import any ſuch Thing, or any Thing like it; but quite the reverſe. And it can never be imagined to be her Intention to exclude all the Iſſue of her favourite Niece *Anne Wynn*, in order to prefer *Charles Lloyd* and his Iſſue: Indeed, the direct contrary plainly appears.

It

It is a FUTURE Devise, to take Place after an *indefinite* Failure of Issue of the Body of a former Devisee: Which *far exceeds* the *allowed Compass* of a Life or Lives in being, and 21 Years after; (Which is the Line now drawn, and very sensibly and rightly drawn.)

The *Articles* can *not* be considered as EXECUTED: They are only a *Covenant* "That She *will*, on the Solemnization of the Marriage, "*at* the *Request* of *Edward Wynn* and *Anne*, AT OR AFTER *such* "*Time* as *Edward Wynn* should settle *his* Estate &c, settle and con- "vey hers." The *Will* does not profess to be an Execution of them; Nor does it mention any Trustees to preserve Contingent Remainders agreeable to the Articles.

But IF the *Will* was an *Execution of the Articles*, then *Anne Wynn* was *Tenant in Tail*, and might suffer the Recovery. If She took Nothing under the Will, She is *Heir at Law* to Mrs. *Mostyn*. And the Lessor of the Plaintiff has *no* Title.

Therefore this JUDGMENT must be REVERSED.

Hurst and Another *vers.* Earl of Winchelsea et al'.

A Special Case, out of the Court of Chancery.

Case—*Thomas Herbert* Esq; being seised *in Fee* of the Premisses in Question, made his last Will and Testament in Writing &c, bearing Date the 17th of *October* 1734, in these Words—"I give and "bequeath to my dear and beloved Wife *Elizabeth Herbert* (after "Payment of my just Debts) All my Money, Plate, Jewels, Hous- "hold-Goods and Furniture wheresoever, and all my Goods, Chat- "tels and personal Estate, REAL OR personal, whatsoever and where- "soever, that shall be in my Possession, or I shall be any ways in- "titled to at the Time of my Decease."

"And I further give devise and bequeath to my said dear Wife and "her Heirs SUCH PART of all my *real* Estate, that I have *any* POW- "ER *to dispose of* by this my Will. And I further give devise and "bequeath to my said Wife, out of the REMAINING Part of my "said *Real* Estate, for her better Support and Maintainance TILL *my* "*Son Thomas attain the Age of* 21 *Years*, the Sum of 400*l.* a Year. "And my Will is that the several Bequests and Devises to my said "Wife as aforesaid, shall *not* nor are intended to *prejudice* my said "Wife in her *Thirds* or *Dower* out of my said Real Estate."

 And

And He appointed Her Sole Executrix of his Will.

On the 15th Day of *March* 1736, the Teſtator died ſo ſeiſed; and left the ſaid *Elizabeth* his Widow; and *Thomas Herbert* (his only Child by Her) his Heir at Law.

Elizabeth Herbert entered upon, and enjoyed the Real Eſtates; and on 29th *April* 1739, intermarried with *John Powell* Eſq; (her ſecond Huſband.) And previous thereto, by * Indentures dated, reſpectively, on 24th and 25th *April* 1739, She, by Leaſe and Releaſe, conveyed the Premiſſes in Queſtion to Truſtees &c, to the following Uſes; *viz.* of Herſelf and her Aſſigns for Life, without Impeachment of Waſte; then to the Uſe of the Earls of *Hertford* and *Winchelſea* and their Heirs &c, for 200 Years upon Truſts ſince determined, and ſubject to the Truſts aforeſaid; Remainder to the ſaid *Thomas Herbert* her Son and his Aſſigns for Life, without Impeachment of Waſte; then to Truſtees to preſerve contingent Remainders; Remainder in † Tail, to the ſaid *Thomas Herbert* the Son, (*viz.* Remainder to the † firſt and every other Son and Sons of the Body of the ſaid *Thomas Herbert* in Tail Male; and in Default &c, to the Uſe and Behoof of the Heirs of his Body generally;) And in Default of ſuch Iſſue, to *ſuch* Uſes and to the Uſe and Behoof of ſuch *Perſon or Perſons*, and for ſuch *Eſtates* Intents and Purpoſes, as She the ſaid *Elizabeth Herbert*, by any *Deed or Deeds* to be by Her duly executed in the Preſence of two or more Witneſſes; or by her *laſt Will* in Writing, or any *Writing purporting to be her Will*, ſigned and publiſhed in the Preſence of three or more credible Witneſſes, whether Covert or Sole, and notwithſtanding her Coverture, ſhould limit or appoint; And for Want of ſuch Limitation or Appointment, to the Uſe and Behoof of the ſaid *Elizabeth Herbert* her Heirs and Aſſigns for ever.

* These Deeds are ſet out at large, in the Caſe ſtated: But this is the Subſtance of them.

† This is alſo ſet out at large and in proper Form, in the ſtated Caſe.

She died on the 8th of *July* 1739, in the Life-time of her Huſband *John Powell*; Leaving the ſaid *Thomas Herbert*, the Son, her only Child and Heir at Law, being alſo only Child and Heir at Law of the ſaid *Thomas Herbert* deceaſed, her firſt Huſband.

Before her Death, *viz.* on 8th *May* 1739, She, in the Preſence of 3 credible Witneſſes, and as the Law requires for the Diſpoſition of Real Eſtates, duly made and executed her laſt Will, or a Writing *purporting to be her Will*, which was ſigned ſealed publiſhed and declared by Her as and for her laſt Will; Whereby She gave ſeveral Legacies to the ſaid *John Powell* her Huſband, and Others: And She * alſo gave and deviſed thereby as follows, *viz.* "I give "to my dearly beloved Son *Thomas Herbert* and his Heirs and Aſ-"ſigns for ever *All* my REAL and perſonal Eſtate, Plate, Jewels, "&c &c, and all my Writings &c; but firſt *ſubject* to the Pay-"ment

* The whole Will is ſet out *verbatim*, in the Caſe.

"ment of my *Debts*, Funeral Expences, and Legacies, and Servants Wages, and *All other Debts*," (which She thereby *charges upon it.*) And She made her said Son *Thomas Herbert*, and the Earl of *Hertford*, her Executors, and gave the Earl of *Hertford* full Power to act as Guardian for her said Son. On her Death, The Earl, as Guardian to her Son, and for his Use and Benefit, entered, and received the Rents and Profits to the Time of the Death of the said *Thomas Herbert* the Son.

On the 25th of *February* 1739, *Thomas Herbert* the Son died, an Infant, Intestate, without Issue, and unmarried; leaving *Roger Powell* Esq; his *Heir ex parte* PATRIS; and *Lucy Allen*, Widow, his *Heir ex parte* MATRIS.

On the Death of the said *Thomas Herbert* the Son, *Roger Powell* entered, and received the Rents and Profits during his Life. But on 9th *June* 1741, *Lucy Allen* filed her Bill against the said *Roger Powell* and Others, praying to be let into Possession: And, She afterwards dying, *Edward Hurst* (the Father of the present Plaintiffs) as her Representative, exhibited his Bill of Revivor and Supplement. Several Abatements of the Suit having since happened, Bills of Revivor and Supplement were duly filed. And the *present Plaintiffs*, *William H.* and *Edward H.* now claim the said Estates *under* the said *Lucy Allen*, as She was Heir to the said *T. H.* the Son *ex parte* maternâ: And the *present Defendants Thomas Morgan*, *Capel Hanbury* and *William Powell* now claim the same *under* the said *Roger Powell* now deceased, as He was Heir to the said *T. H.* the Son *ex parte* paternâ.

The Original Cause was heard on the 10th of *May* 1755, before Ld. *Hardwicke*; who directed a Case to be made, and these Two Questions to be stated for the Opinion of this Court: *viz.*

1st Question—"Whether by the Will of *Thomas Herbert*, the "Father, (Husband of *Elizabeth Herbert*, afterwards *Powell*,) the "Estate in question, (the *Real* Estate of the said *Thomas Herbert*,) "passed to the said *Elizabeth in* FEE."

2d Question—"Whether it descended, upon the Death of *Thomas Herbert*, the Son, to his Heirs *ex parte* PATERNA; or to "his Heirs *ex parte* MATERNA."

The Suit afterwards abating by the Death of *E. H.* Father to the present Plaintiffs, they revived it. On 27*th January* 1758, The Cause came on to be heard before the Lord Keeper: Who ordered "That the said former Order on Hearing should be carried into "Execution in like Manner as if *Edward Hurst* had been Living.

 This

This Case was twice argued in this Court. It was first argued (very learnedly and elaborately) by Mr. *Sewell* for the Plaintiffs (claiming under *Lucy Allen* the Maternal Heir,) and Mr. *Yorke*, Solicitor General, for the Defendants (claiming under *Roger Powell* the Paternal Heir; on *Tuesday* 6th *February* 1759. The second Argument was by Mr. *Norton* for the Plaintiffs, and Mr. *Perrott* for the Defendants, on the 13th and 20th of *November* 1759.

On 27th *November* 1759, The JUDGES of this COURT certified their Opinion, as follows—

Having heard Counsel on both Sides, and considered of this Case, *We are of Opinion* That the Estate in question in this Cause *passed* by the Will of *Thomas Herbert* the Father, to the said *Elizabeth* in FEE. We are also of *Opinion* That *Thomas Herbert* the Son did *not* take the said Estate, from his Mother, by *Purchase*, but *by* DESCENT: Consequently, upon his Death, it descended to his Heir *ex parte* MATERNA.

Mansfield. *T. Denison.* *M. Foster.* *E. Wilmot.*

Lord Keeper HENLEY having afterwards decreed accordingly, The Defendants *appealed* to the House of Lords. But before Hearing, it was *compromised*, by a Composition as to the retrospective Account of the Profits of the Estate; but that the Decree should *stand*, with regard to the *Estate itself*.

Luke et al' *vers.* Lyde.

A Special Case from the last *Devonshire* Assizes; reserved by Ld. *Mansfield*, who went that Circuit, last Summer.

The Defendant *Lyde* shipped a Cargo of 1501 Quintals of Fish, at the Port of *St. John's* in *Newfoundland*, on Board the Ship *Sarah* belonging to the Plaintiffs, to be carried to *Lisbon*. The Plaintiffs were to be paid FREIGHT, at the Rate of Two Shillings *per* Quintal. The Original Price of the said Cargo was, at *Newfoundland*, Ten Shillings and Six pence Sterling *per* Quintal.

The Plaintiffs had also, on Board the said *Sarah*, a Cargo of 945 Quintals of Fish, which was their *own* Property.

The Ship failed from the Port of *St. John's*, on 27th *November* 1756; and had proceeded 17 *Days* on her Voyage; and was TA-

KEN on the 14th of *December* following, within 4 *Days* Sail of *Lisbon*, by a *French* Ship. And the Captain, the other Officers, and all the Crew (Except One Man and a Boy) were taken out of the *Sarah*, and put on Board the *French* Ship. The Ship *Sarah* was *retaken* on the 17th of the same *December* 1756, by an *English* Privateer; and on the 29th of *December* 1756, brought into the Port of *Biddeford* in *Devonshire*.

The Plaintiffs, having insured the Ship and their Part of the Cargo, *abandoned* the same *to the Insurers*. But the *Freight*, which the Owners were intitled to, was *not insured*.

The Defendant had his Goods, of the Recaptors, and paid them 5*s*. *per* Quintal Salvage, at the Rate of 10*s*. *per* Quintal Value.

The Fish could not be sold at all, at *Biddeford*, nor at any other Port in *England*, for more than 10*s*. *per* Quintal, clear of all Charges and Expences in bringing them to such Port. And the most beneficial Market (in the Apprehension of every Person) for dispo-sing of the said Cargo of Fish, was at *Bilboa* in *Spain*; to which Place the Defendant *sent it* in the *March* following: And there was no Delay in the Defendant in sending the said Cargo thither. And it was sold there for 5*s*. 6*d*. *per* Quintal; clear of the Freight thither, and of all Expences attending the Sale there.

The Freight from *Biddeford* to *Lisbon*, is higher than from *Newfoundland* to *Lisbon*.

From the Time of the Capture, the whole Way that the Ship was afterwards carried, was out of the Course of her Voyage to *Lisbon*.

The Question was "Whether the Plaintiffs are intitled to *Any* "and *what* FREIGHT; And at *what Rate*, and subject to *what* "*Deduction*."

Mr. *Hussey*, for the Plaintiffs, observed (by Way of Preface) That the Right of the Owners of the Ship was not so devested by the Capture, as to preclude them from bringing their Action for the Freight.

If the Capture made any Alteration, the *Recapture* put every Thing *in statu quo*.

When the Ship came into *Biddeford*, there was a total Incapacity and Inability in the Ship to proceed on the Voyage. And there was an Abandoning by the Owners, and Acceptance by the Insurers.

This

This Inability to proceed was *involuntary*, and *accidental*; without any *Fault* of the Owners, Master, or Mariners.

There was no Intention to carry the Goods to *Lisbon*: The Defendant the Owner of the Fish, considered *Bilboa* as the better Market for it; and accordingly sent them thither, and sold them there.

After premising this, He made two Questions:

1st Question—Whether ANY *Freight* at all, is due to the Plaintiffs.

2d Question—If any, then WHAT *Freight* is due.

First—He alledged it to be the Rule of the Maritime Law, " That Freight is due, *unless there be some Fault* in the Owners or " Master." If there be *no* Fault in the Owners or Master, the Freight must be paid, either *in toto*, or *pro rata*.

Molloy 263, lays down the Rule, that where the Disability of the Ship is inevitable, or accidental, without Fault of the Owners or Master, Freight is due; if the Master will either mend his Ship, or freight another. But if the Merchant will not agree to that, then Freight is due for so much as the Ship hath earned. *Lib.* 2. *c.* 4. § 4.

The *Shipwreck* of the Ship does *not dissolve* the Contract, where any Goods are saved: The Owners are intitled to their Freight. It is so far from dissolving the Contract, that it gives the Master his *Election*, whether to provide another Ship, or not.

In the present Case, there is nothing to prevent Freight being due. Freight became due from and upon the Freighters taking the Goods into their Possession; and continued due, by the Defendants not totally abandoning them.

Second Question—*What* Freight is due to the Plaintiffs.

He insisted on the *Whole*. *All* the Goods were *delivered*. The Money paid for Salvage will not lessen it: For they must have paid that, otherwise. The Deviation will not lessen it: For that was not voluntary.

The Privateer who retook this Ship, was intitled only to $\frac{1}{8}$ Part for Salvage: For it was not 96 Hours under Detention. Therefore, if more was paid, it was too much.

2 Lord

Lord MANSFIELD—It was compounded *at half*: And upon this Case, We *must* take that Proportion to be *right*.

Mr. *Hussey* cited, as a Foundation of his Argument, the Case of *Lutwidge and How* v. *Grey et al*, heard on the 22d of *February* 1733, in the House of Lords.

Lord MANSFIELD—The House of Lords determined upon these Reasons (delivered by the Lord Chancellor *Talbot*,) "That the "WHOLE *Freight* was due upon the Goods sent to *Bristol*; because "the *Master* OFFERED *a Ship* to carry the Goods to *Glasgow*, which "was the Port of Delivery: But as the *Master declined* carrying "the *other* Goods to *Glasgow* (the Port of their Delivery;) They "determined that as to *them*, he ought to be paid only *pro ratâ*, "*viz.* as much as was proportionable to his Carrying them to "*Youghall*, the Place where the Accident happened." And this was all agreeable to the Maritime Law.

Mr. *Hussey*—It appears by that Case, that the Contract is *not* dissolved by the *involuntary* Accident; that the Master had his *Election* to carry them to the Port of Delivery in another Ship; and that *if he did not*, he shall yet be paid *pro rata itineris* to the Place where the Accident happened.

But, at least, *Something* is due; Especially, as the Goods were carried to a beneficial Market.

Mr. *Gould*, for the Defendant, Mr. *Lyde*.

Upon computing the Account of the Prime Cost and Produce of these Goods, as stated in this Case, it appears that Mr. *Lyde* has *not saved a Farthing*.

As to the *Property* not being *devested*—The *Plaintiffs have abandoned the Ship*, and given it up absolutely, to their Insurers; and never provided any other to carry the Fish to *Lisbon*. He mentioned the Case of * *Goss* v. *Withers M.* 1758, 32 *G.* 2. *B. R.* to shew that they were not obliged to abandon the Ship.

* *V. ante* 683 to 698.

The Plaintiffs have no Pretence of Satisfaction. Though the Mariners of this Ship were taken out by the Enemy, Yet other Mariners might have been procured. Therefore there was *not* a *total* Inability to proceed.

The Plaintiffs received their *whole* Insurance upon the Ship, and upon *their* Part of the Goods. And they *never offered* nor meant to furnish *another* Ship, *to carry the Fish to Lisbon:* They had even given up their own Cargo.

The *Value* of the Fish depended upon its being carried to *Lisbon*, to be there against the Lent Season.

* 'Tis § 5. and *pa.* 254, 255. in the 6th Edition.

Malines Lex Mercatoria, fo. 98 & 21. *par.* 5. (transcribed by *Molloy, V. lib.* 2. *c.* 4. § 4. *) says, " If the Master of the Ship, " after his Ship is become disabled (without his Fault) will *either* " mend it, *or* freight another, to carry the Goods to the destined " Port." And in this Case, he will be intitled to freight *in toto.* " But if the *Freighter disagrees* to the Master's Carrying them in " another Ship, the Master shall receive his Freight, in Proportion " to what he has already carried." This relates to *Accidents inevitable*, and *without any Fault* of the Master.

† 7th Edit. 1722.

Molloy 259 † puts the same Case, of a Ship *taken by the Enemy*, and retaken, and not otherwise incapacitated; and says that after Restitution, She may proceed; And the *entire* Freight will become due. ||

|| *V. Lib.* 2. *c.* 4. § 13. *pa.* 259. of 6th Edit.

And the Case of *Lutwidge and How* v. *Gray et al'* falls in with this Rule, and goes upon the same Principles.

It may perhaps be said That the *Freighter* has *not* an absolute Right to demand his Goods, and carry them *Himself* to the destined Port of Delivery, and abate a rateable Proportion of Freight: But the Master has his *Option*, to provide another Ship, and carry the Goods in it, and receive the *whole* Freight, if he chooses to do so.

But *here*, it is the same Thing as if the Goods had been sunk in the Bottom of the Sea: The Freighter has *totally lost* his *whole* Risque. It would be hard, therefore, if he were liable to pay Freight for it.

Mr. *Hussey* in Reply—*Lyde* was *not a third* Person; but the *Contractor to pay the Freight.*

The Plaintiff's Abandoning the Ship to their Insurers could not destroy their Right to the *Freight:* For the *Freight* was neither insured nor abandoned.

Mr. *Gould* says " The Freight *must* be paid, and the *Agreement* " *performed, if* the Master provides another Ship to carry the Goods " to the destined Port; but *not* if he does not do so, but the *Freighter agrees* to carry them Himself."

2. But

But the Maſter, though he *may* provide another Ship, is not, at all Events, abſolutely obliged to it: He has his *Option*. And the Caſe of *Lutwidge et al'* v. *Gray et al'* ſhews that the Maſter is intitled *pro rata itineris, though* he does *not* proceed on his Voyage: And there he had an Allowance *pro rata*; though he refuſed to carry the Goods any further.

Lord MANSFIELD ſaid That though He was of the ſame Opinion at the Aſſizes, as He was now; Yet He was deſirous to have a Caſe made of it, in order to ſettle the Point more deliberately, ſolemnly, and notoriouſly; as it was of ſo extenſive a Nature; And eſpecially, as the Maritime Law is not the Law of a particular Country, but the general Law of Nations: " Non erit alia Lex " Romæ, alia Athenis; alia nunc, alia poſthac; ſed et apud om-" nes gentes et omni tempore, una eademque Lex obtinebit."

He ſaid, He always leaned, (even where He had Himſelf no Doubt,) to making *Caſes* for the Opinion of the Court; Not only for the greater Satisfaction of the Parties in the particular Cauſe, but to prevent other Diſputes, by making the Rules of Law and the Ground upon which they are eſtabliſhed *certain* and *notorious:* But He took particular Care that this ſhould not create *Delay* or *Expence* to the Parties; And therefore He always dictated the Caſe in Court, and ſaw it ſigned by Counſel, before another Cauſe was called; and always made it a Condition in the Rule, " that it ſhould be ſet down " to be argued within the firſt 4 Days of the Term." Upon the *ſame* Principle, the Motion " *to put off* the Argument of this Caſe to " the next Term," was refuſed: And the Plaintiff will now have his Judgment within a few Days as ſoon as he could have entered it up if *no* Caſe had been reſerved; at the Expence of a ſingle Argument only; And ſome Rules of the Maritime Law, applicable to a Variety of Caſes, will be better known. He ſaid, before He entered into it particularly, He would lay down a few *Principles*; *viz.*

If a freighted Ship becomes *accidentally* diſabled on it's Voyage (*without* the Fault of the Maſter,) The Maſter has his *Option* of *two* Things; either to *refit* it, (if that can be done within convenient Time;) or to hire *another* Ship to carry the Goods to the Port of Delivery. If the Merchant diſagrees to this, and will not let him do ſo, the Maſter will be intitled to the WHOLE Freight of the *full* Voyage. And ſo it was determined in the Houſe of Lords, in that Caſe of *Lutwidge and How* v. *Gray et al'*.

As to the *Value* of the Goods—It is Nothing to the Maſter of the Ship, " whether the Goods are ſpoiled or not," Provided the Freighter takes them: It is enough if the Maſter has *carried* them; For *by doing*

doing so, he has *earned* his Freight. And the Merchant shall be obliged to take *All* that are saved, or *None*: He shall not take *some*, and abandon the *rest*; and so pick and choose what he likes, taking that which is not damaged, and leaving that which is spoiled or damaged. If he abandons *All*, he is excused Freight: And he may abandon *all*, though they are not All lost. (I call the Freighter, the Merchant; And the Other, the Master, for the clearer Distinction.)

Now here is a Capture *without any Fault of the Master*; And then a *Re-Capture*. The Merchant does not abandon, but takes the Goods; and does *not require* the Master to carry them to *Lisbon*, the Port of Delivery. Indeed, the Master *could not* carry them in the same Ship; for it was disabled, and was itself abandoned to the Insurers of it: And he would not desire to find Another; because the Freight was higher from *Biddeford* to *Lisbon* than from *Newfoundland* to *Lisbon*.

There can be no Doubt but that SOME Freight is due: For the *Goods* were *not abandoned* by the Freighter; but *received* by him of the Recaptor.

The Question will be "WHAT Freight?"

The Answer is "A RATEABLE Freight:" *i. e. pro rata itineris.*

If the Master has his *Election* to provide another Ship, to carry the Goods to the Port of Delivery; and the Merchant does not even desire him to do so; The Master is still intitled to a Proportion, *pro rata of the former* Part of the Voyage.

I take the Proportion of the *Salvage* here, to be HALF of the whole Cargo; upon the State of the Case as here agreed upon. And it is reasonable That the Half here paid to the Recaptor, should be considered as *lost*. For the Recaptor was *not obliged to agree to a Valuation*; But he might have had the Goods *actually sold*, if he had so pleased, and taken *half the Produce*: And therefore the Half of them are as much *lost*, as if they remained in the *Enemy's Hands*. So that *Half* the Goods must be considered as *lost*; and *Half* as *saved*.

Here, the Master had come 17 Days of his *Voyage*, and was within 4 Days of the destined Port, when the Accident happened. Therefore he ought to be paid his Freight for 17/21 Parts of the full Voyage, for *that Half* of the Cargo which was *saved*.

I find by the ancientest Laws in the World (the *Rhodian* Laws,) that the Master shall have a *rateable* Proportion, where he is in *no Fault* *. And *Consolato del Mere*, a *Spanish* Book, is also agreeable thereto. Ever since the Laws of *Oleron*, it has been settled thus. In the Usages and Customs of the Sea, (a *French* Book,) with Observations thereon, The 4th Article of the Laws of *Oleron* is, "That if a Vessel be rendered unfit to proceed in her Voyage, and "the Mariners save as much of the Lading, as possibly they can; "If the Merchants require their Goods of the Master, He *may* deliver them, IF *he pleases*, They *paying the Freight* in *Proportion* "to the Part of the Voyage that IS PERFORMED, and the Costs of "the Salvage: But if the Master can readily *repair* his Ship, He "may do it; Or if he pleases, He may freight *another* Ship to "perform his Voyage." Amongst the Observations thereon, The first is "that this Law does not relate to a total and entire loss, but only to *Salvage*; Or rather, not to the Shipwreck, but to the *Disabling* of a Ship, so that She can not proceed in her Voyage without refitting: In which Case, the Merchants may have their "Goods again, *paying* the Freight, *in Proportion* to the Way the "Ship made." †

* *V.* Artic. 27, 32, 42.

† *Wisbuy*, Artic. 33. The Emperor *Charles* 5. Ord. Art. 40.

The Observation adds further—"That if the Master can, in a "little Time, *refit* his Vessel and render her fit to continue her "Voyage; (that is, if he can do it in 3 Days Time at the most, according to the Hanse-Town Laws;) Or if he will Himself take "Freight for the Merchandize, aboard *another* Ship bound for the "*same* Port to which He was bound, He may do it: And, if the "Accident did not happen him by any *Fault* of his, then the "*Freight shall be* PAID HIM." The 37th Article of the Laws of *Wisbuy* is to the very same Purport.

Roccius de Navibus et Naulo, in Note 81st. says—"Declara hoc "Dictum. Ubi Nauta munere vehendi *in parte* sit functus, quia "tunc *pro parte itineris* quo merces inventæ sint, vecturam deberi "Æquitas suadet; et pro eâ rata mercedis solutio fieri debet. Ita "Paul de Castro &c." (Then a String of Authorities follows:) "Et probat Joannes de Evia &c; Qui hoc extendit in casu quo "merces fuerint *deperditæ* (*totally lost*) unà cum Navi, et certa Pars "ipsarum mercium postea fuerit salvata et recuperata; tunc naulum "deberi pro rata mercium recuperatarum, *et pro rata Itineris usque "ad locum in quo Casus adversus acciderat*, fundat &c." (And then He goes on with Authorities.) "Item declara, quòd si Dominus "seu magister navis solverit mercatori pretium mercium deperditarum, tunc tenetur mercator ad solutionem nauli; quia merces "habentur ac si salvatæ fuissent."

In another Book intitled *The Ordinance of Lewis the 14th*, eſtabliſhed in 1681, (collected and compiled under the Authority of *M. Colbert*,) the ſame Rules are laid down; particularly in the 18th, 19th, 21ſt and 22d Articles.—Art. 18th directs That *no* Freight ſhall be due, for Goods *loſt* by Shipwreck, or *taken* by Pirates or Enemies. Art. 19th is, That if the Ship and Goods be ranſomed, the Maſter ſhall be paid his Freight *to the Place* where they were taken: And he ſhall be paid his *whole* Freight, if he conduct them to the Place agreed on; He contributing towards the Ranſom. (Art. 20th ſettles the Rate of Contribution.) Art. 21ſt. The Maſter ſhall likewiſe be paid the Freight of Goods ſaved from Shipwreck; *He conducting* them to the Place appoitned. Art. 22d. If he can not find a Ship to carry thither the Goods preſerved, He ſhall *only* be paid his Freight IN PROPORTION *to what he has* PERFORMED of the Voyage.

And the Caſe in the Houſe of Lords between *Lutwidge and How* and *Gray et al'* is alſo in Point; and was well conſidered there: And Ld. *Talbot* gave the Reaſons of the Judgment of the Houſe, at length.

Therefore in the preſent Caſe, a *Rateable Proportion* of Freight ought to be paid for *Half* the Goods.

It is quite immaterial What the Merchant made of the Goods afterwards; for the Maſter has Nothing at all to do with the Goodneſs or Badneſs of the Market: Nor indeed can that be properly known, till after the Freight is paid; For the Maſter is *not bound to deliver* the Goods, *till after* he is paid his Freight. No Sort of Notice was taken of *that* Matter, in the Caſe of *Lutwidge and How* v. *Gray in the Houſe of Lords:* And yet there the Tobacco was damaged very greatly; even ſo much that a great Part of it was burnt at the Scales, at *Glaſgow*.

Therefore the Verdict muſt be for 60 *l.* 14 *s.* which, upon Computation, amounts to the rateable Proportion of the Freight; being ½ of 75 *l.* the half of 150 *l.*

Conſequently, the Verdict which was for 70 *l.* muſt be ſet right, and made 60 *l.* 14 *s.*

Per Cur.
Let the *Poſtea* be delivered to the PLAINTIFF.

Moriſſet

Moriſſet verſ. King.

Friday 23d November 1759.

THIS was an Action of Debt on Bond, in the Penalty of 200*l.* conditioned for the due Performance of certain Articles: Which Articles recited that *Mary Moriſſet* had lent *Daniel King* the Sum of 100*l.* to be repaid to Her at the End of 4 Years, *without Intereſt*; but in Conſideration that the ſaid *Daniel King* his Executors and Adminiſtrators ſhould find and provide for *Mary Dubois*, *Daughter* of the ſaid *Mary Moriſſet* (the Obligee,) *Meat and Drink in the Houſe* where he dwelt or ſhould dwell, *for four Years*, if the ſaid *Mary Dubois* ſhould ſo long live; And that She ſhould, during the ſaid Term, *board with him*; And that ſhe ſhould be *Co-partner with Mary King, Wife of the ſaid Daniel King*, in the Buſineſs of a *Millener*; And ſhould, all that Time, *bear one Moiety* of the Loſſes, Charges (except Houſe-keeping) Shop-Rent, and Materials neceſſary for carrying on the Trade, (which the ſaid *Daniel King* did agree to provide;) And they ſhould be Partners, and Each do their utmoſt to carry on the Trade; and ſhould *equally divide the Profits*; And alſo that the ſaid *Daniel King* ſhould *lodge the ſaid Mary Moriſſet*, She paying Him 10*l.* a Year. And at the End of the four Years, *Daniel King* was to repay the 100*l.* And in Caſe of the Death of the ſaid *Mary Dubois*, to pay the Principal together with *lawful* Intereſt for the 100*l.* to the ſaid *Mary Moriſſet*.

The Defendant, after having demanded and had Oyer of the Condition of this Bond and of the Articles therein recited, pleads "That "this was a *Corrupt Agreement*;" with an Averment "That the "Board of *Mary Moriſſet* (the Mother) was worth 20*l.* a Year; "And the Board of *Mary Dubois* (the Daughter) was worth 10*l.* "a Year."

To this Plea, the Plaintiff demurs.

The only Queſtion was Whether this was an *Uſurious Contract*, within the Statute of 12 *Ann. Stat.* 2. *c.* 16. Which makes void All Bonds, Contracts and Aſſurances, where more than 5*l. per Cent. per Annum* is directly or indirectly taken for any Loan.

Mr. *Aſpinall* argued, as Counſel for the Plaintiff; and Mr. *Wedderburn*, for the Defendant.

The Court were extremely clear that This Caſe cannot be within the Statute of Uſury.

2

Lord

Lord MANSFIELD obſerved, That it is impoſſible to ſay that *King might not* receive ſo much Advantage by this Partnerſhip, as to be *worth* the Conſideration. It *might* be a very advantageous Bargain to *King:* Here might be Recommendation, Skill, Labour or other Benefits ariſing to Him from it.

He mentioned the Caſe of Mr. *Hubert*, who entered into a private ſecret Partnerſhip with *Nelſon*, who drew him into a Bankruptcy thereby. So here, the Plaintiff's Daughter might have been drawn into a Bankruptcy, by Means of this Agreement: Which would have been more ſevere to Her, perhaps, than the Penalty of this Statute of Uſury would be.

* Mr. Juſt. *Deniſon* was abſent.

* Mr. Juſt. FOSTER and Mr. Juſt. WILMOT concurred with the Chief Juſtice. They ſaid, It did not explicitly appear whether this was a prudent Agreement or not: But it *might* be beneficial to *King* upon the *Whole*; at leaſt, it was not *ſuch* a Contract as could be adjudged by the Court to be *uſurious* within the Statute.

JUDGMENT for the PLAINTIFF.

Saturday 24th *November* 1759.

Rex *verſ.* Maſter and Warden of the Company of Surgeons in London.

THIS was a Cauſe that ſtood in the Crown-Paper, upon a Return to a *Mandamus* directed to the Maſter and Wardens of the Company of SURGEONS of *London*; Reciting a Cuſtom in the ſaid City, "That every Freeman of the ſaid City, uſing and exer-" ciſing the Art Science or Myſtery of *Surgery* within the ſaid City, " hath *a Right*, in reſpect thereof, *to have and take* APPRENTICES, " of the Age of 14 Years or upwards, to be educated and inſtructed " in the ſaid Art Science or Myſtery, for the Space of 7 Years; " Which ſaid *Apprentices* have been uſed and accuſtomed to be " ADMITTED *and* BOUND *in the Preſence or with the Conſent of the* " *Maſter and Wardens or ſome of them*;" And reciting that *Richard Guy*, a Freeman of the ſaid City, and alſo One of the Freemen of the ſaid Company of Surgeons of the ſaid City, being deſirous of taking *Melmoth Guy*, his Son, aged 15 Years, to be his Apprentice for the Term of 7 Years, to be educated and inſtructed in the ſaid Art Science or Myſtery of Surgery, had often offered the ſaid *Melmoth Guy* to be admitted and bound, before the ſaid Maſter and Wardens or ſome of them, his ſaid Apprentice for the Term of 7 Years, in the ſaid Art Science or Myſtery, according to the ſaid Cuſtom; And that the ſaid *Melmoth Guy* had alſo often offered Himſelf to them or ſome of them, to be admitted and bound before them or ſome of them, an Apprentice to the ſaid *Richard Guy* for the ſaid Term, in the ſaid Art Science or Myſtery; And that the ſaid Maſter and Wardens had *not permitted* the ſaid *Melmoth Guy* to be bound Apprentice to the ſaid *Richard Guy*, for the Term of 7 Years, before them or any of them, but have altogether refuſed and ſtill refuſe ſo to do; And Commanding them, immediately and without delay, in due Manner to *permit* the ſaid *Melmoth Guy* to be ADMITTED *and* BOUND, before them or ſome of them, *an Apprentice* to the ſaid *Richard Guy*, for the Term aforeſaid, in the ſaid Art Science or Myſtery according to the ſaid Cuſtom, Or ſignify Cauſe to the Contrary.

The Return of the Maſter and Wardens admits the Whole of the Cuſtom and Facts, to be as they are alledged in the Writ. But they further certify and return, That long before the ſaid *Richard Guy* offered his ſaid Son *Melmoth*, or the ſaid *Melmoth* offered Himſelf to them or any of them, to be admitted and bound before them or any of them, an Apprentice for the ſaid Term of 7 Years, in the ſaid Art Science or Myſtery of Surgery, according to the Cuſtom aforeſaid; and after the Making of a certain Act of Parliament intitled "An Act for making the Surgeons of *London*, and the Barbers of "*London*, two ſeparate and diſtinct Corporations;" to wit, on the 7th Day of *April* in the Year of our Lord 1748, at *Stationers-Hall* in *London* aforeſaid; *John Freke*, then and there being Maſter of the ſaid Company of *Surgeons*, and *William Pyle* and *Legard Sparham*, then being two of the Governors of the ſaid Company of Surgeons, before that Time duly elected choſen appointed and ſworn into their ſaid reſpective Offices; And alſo *John Ranby* Eſq; *Cæſar Hawkins* Eſq; *William Petty* Eſq; *Joſeph Sandford*, *William Cheſelden* Eſq; *James Hickes*, *Peter Sainthill*, *Noah Roul*, *John Weſtbrook*, *William Singleton*, *James Phillips*, *Joſeph Webb*, *Mark Hawkins*, *Chriſtopher Fullagar*, *Edward Nourſe*, *John Girle* Eſq; and *John Townſend*, being then and there Nine and more of the Members of the Court of Aſſiſtants of the ſaid Company of Surgeons, before that Time duly elected choſen appointed and ſworn to be of the ſaid Court of Aſſiſtants, did hold a Court and Aſſembly, at *Stationers-Hall London* aforeſaid, in order to treat and conſult about and concerning the Rule Order State and Government of the ſaid Company of Surgeons; And that the ſaid *John Freke*, ſo being then and there Maſter of the ſaid Company of Surgeons, and the ſaid *William Pyle* and *Legard Sparham*, ſo being then and there Two of the ſaid Governors of the ſaid Company of Surgeons, and the ſaid *John Ranby* Eſq; *Cæſar Hawkins* Eſq; *&c. &c. &c*, ſo being then and there Nine and more of the Members of the ſaid Court of Aſſiſtants of that Company, being All then and there duly aſſembled as aforeſaid, did then and there, according to the Form of the Statute in that Caſe made and provided, make ordain conſtitute and eſtabliſh a certain BY-LAW *and* ORDINANCE, for the Regulation Government and Advantage of the said Company of Surgeons, in the Words following, To wit, *Item*, It is *Ordained* " That *no Member* of the said Company *shall* " *take* any Person into his Service, *As his Apprentice*, to be instruct-" ed in the Art or Science of Surgery, for any shorter Time than 7 " Years; *Which Person* SHALL UNDERSTAND *the* LATIN *Tongue*; " His ABILITY *wherein* shall, BEFORE *his being bound*, be *tried by* " *the Governors or One of them*. And every Freeman of this Com-" pany or Foreign Brother shall, within One Month next after his " Entertainment of any Person in Order to being his Apprentice, " *Present* such Person before the Governors or Two of them, *at* " *a Court to be by them held*; and *there bind* such Person to Him, " *before the said Governors*, by Indenture; Upon pain of forfeiting " 20*l*. of lawful Money: And the Clerk of the said Company " SHALL NOT BIND any Person who has *not* been so presented and " examined; upon pain of forfeiting the Sum of 10 *l*. of lawful " Money and being liable to be amoved from his said Office. And " no Apprentice shall be turned over from One Master to Another, " but at a Court in the Presence of the Master and Wardens or " One of them: And One Guinea, and no more, shall be paid for " the same."

Which said *Ordinance* or *By-Law*, so made as aforesaid, after the Making thereof as aforesaid, and long before the said *Richard Guy* had offered the said *Melmoth*, or the said *Melmoth* had offered Himself to be admitted and bound before them or any of them, an Apprentice to the said *Richard Guy*, for the Term of 7 Years, in the said Art Science or Mystery of Surgery, according to the Custom aforesaid, to wit, on the 9th Day of the same *April* in the said Year of our Lord 1748, was examined approved and allowed by the Right Honourable *Philip* Lord *Hardwicke* the then Lord Chancellor of *Great Britain*, and by Sir *William Lee* Knt. the then Lord Chief Justice of His Majesty's Court of King's Bench, and Sir *John Willes* Knt. the then Lord Chief Justice of His Majesty's Court of Common Bench, according to the Form of the Statute in that Case made and provided.

They further return That the said Ordinance or By-Law, so made examined approved and allowed as aforesaid, hath ever since the Making Examination Approbation and Allowance thereof as aforesaid, been, and now is in full Force and Effect, and in no wise annulled revoked or vacated.

They then return That after the Making Examination Approbation and Allowance of the said Ordinance or By-Law as aforesaid, and before the Issuing of this Writ, to wit, on the 3d of *May* in the Year of our Lord 1759, at a certain Court then holden at *Sur-*

geons Hall in the *Old Bailey London*, by *Mark Hawkins* then Maſter, and *Chriſtopher Fullagar* and *Edward Nourſe* then Governors of the ſaid Company of Surgeons, (They the ſaid *Mark Hawkins Chriſtopher Fullagar* and *Edward Nourſe*, having before that Time been duly elected choſen appointed and ſworn into their ſaid reſpective Offices, according to the Form of the Statute in that Caſe made and provided,) came the ſaid *Richard Guy* before the ſaid Court, and offered and preſented his ſaid Son *Melmoth*; And the ſaid *Melmoth* did then and there offer Himſelf to the ſaid Maſter and Governors then being at that Court, to be admitted and bound, before them, an Apprentice to the ſaid *Richard Guy*, for the Term of 7 Years, in the ſaid Art Science or Myſtery of Surgery; And that the ſaid *Melmoth Guy*, being ſo offered and preſented as aforeſaid, was then and there *examined* touching his Knowledge in the *Latin* Tongue; And his Ability therein, *in Purſuance* of the Ordinance or By-Law aforeſaid, was then and there *fairly*, *candidly*, and *impartially* TRIED by the ſaid *Edward Nourſe*, He the ſaid *Edward* being then and there One of the Governors of the ſaid Company of Surgeons: And that the ſaid *Melmoth Guy*, UPON *ſuch his Examination*, and *upon his Ability* in the *Latin Tongue* being ſo as aforeſaid *tried* by the ſaid *Edward Nourſe* (ſo being One of the Governors or Wardens of the ſaid Company as aforeſaid,) *was found*, NOT *to underſtand* the *Latin* Tongue, but to be WHOLLY IGNORANT *thereof*; and was then and there SO ADJUDGED *and declared* to be, by the ſaid *Edward Nourſe*, on ſuch Trial.—Wherefore the ſaid Court could not conſent, but did then and there refuſe to permit the ſaid *Melmoth Guy* to be admitted and bound an Apprentice to the ſaid *Richard Guy*, for the Term of 7 Years, in the ſaid Art Science or Myſtery of Surgery, according to the Cuſtom aforeſaid, UNTIL ſuch Time as the ſaid *Melmoth ſhould underſtand* the *Latin* Tongue, as by the aforeſaid Ordinance or By-Law is in that Behalf required.

They further return expreſſly and poſitively, That the ſaid *Melmoth Guy*, when he was ſo preſented and offered as aforeſaid, before the aforeſaid Maſter and Governors or Wardens of the ſaid Company of Surgeons, at the ſaid Court, by them held for the Purpoſe herein before in that Behalf mentioned, DID NOT underſtand the *Latin* Tongue; but WAS UTTERLY IGNORANT of the ſame: And that the ſaid *Melmoth Guy* hath NOT, at any Time before or ſince his being ſo examined and tried as to his Ability in the *Latin* Tongue as aforeſaid, *offered himſelf or been preſented* to the ſaid Company or Governors thereof, or any One of them for the Time being, *to be tried* as to his Ability in the *Latin* Tongue.

And therefore they cannot permit the ſaid *Melmoth Guy* to be admitted and bound before them an Apprentice to the ſaid *Richard Guy* for the ſaid Term of 7 Years, in the ſaid Art Science or Myſtery ftery of Surgery, according to the Cuftom aforefaid, as by the Writ they are commanded.

Mr. *Field pro Rege* objected and argued " That this was an *in-* " *fufficient* Return :" For that the *By-Law* is a *bad* One, being made in *Reftraint of a natural general and common Right.*

The *firft* Reftriction of the common Right that every Perfon has of learning and exercifing any Art in any Place, except where it happens to be reftrained by Cuftom, is the Act of 5 *Eliz. c.* 4.

The City of *London* have indeed, *by Cuftom*, a Power over the Youth of their City, and a Power of excluding Foreigners from exercifing Trades within their City.

1 *Rep.* 53. *Taylors of Ipfwich Cafe* fhews the *general* Law to be, that a Perfon ought not to be reftrained in his lawful Myftery.

Private Companies can not make Laws contrary to the *General* Law or to the *Cuftoms* of great Cities: Though great Cities and Towns may do fo. This Diftinction is mentioned in 6 *Mod.* 123. * *Cuddon* v. *Eftwick*. And He cited the Cafe of *the City of London* v. *Vanacker*, in 1 *Ld. Raym.* 496. where *Holt* Ch. J. faid that " if " the By-Law was for the *Benefit of the City*, it would be good."

* *V.* 1 *Salk.* 193. S. C.

This By-Law, therefore, is not good, without a particular Cuftom to fupport it: For it *reftrains a Common-Law Right.*

The Return does not aver that the underftanding the *Latin* Tongue *is* a *neceffary Qualification* of a Surgeon: And their Art may certainly be performed *without* it. At leaft, 'tis no Objection to a young Perfon's being put out to *learn* the Art; Whatever it might be to the Admiffion of a Man to *practife* it.

Befides, " Underftanding the *Latin* Tongue," is a very *indefinite* and *vague* Expreffion: And a very different Idea of it would be conceived by different Perfons; as by Dr. *Bentley* (for Inftance) and by a † Warden of the Surgeons Company.

† *N. B.* Mr. *Nourfe* was, in Fact, a very good Scholar.

Bad Confequences too, may arife from this By-Law: And if fo, it fhall not prevail. *Godbolt* 254. S. C. with that of *the Taylors of Ipfwich*, (there called *The Cloth-workers of Ipfwich Cafe.*)

If the *By-Law is bad*, this Young Man's not Underftanding *Latin* will *not cure or help* it. However, the By-Law does *not expreffly forbid* fuch a Perfon to be admitted: It is *not mandatory*, but only *directory*.

Mr.

Mr. Serjeant *Hewitt contra*, was rising up, to speak in Support of the Return.

But Lord MANSFIELD said It was too plain to argue.

Whereupon, *Per Cur.*
RETURN ALLOWED.

Rex *verf.* Inhabitants of Preston near Faversham.

Monday 26th *November* 1759.

TWO Justices removed *Edward Young* the Younger, and *Rebecca* his Wife, and *Mary* their Child, from *Chilham* to *Preston* near *Faversham* (Both in *Kent*:) And the Sessions confirmed (in *all Points*) the Order of the two Justices.

The Case, as stated to appear to the Sessions, was, That the said *Edward Young* the Younger, being legally settled in *Preston*, and not being then a Widower was on the 25th of *January* 1758, WITHOUT *the Consent of his Father*, who was then living, *married by Licence* in the Parish Church of *Tenham*, to *Rebecca Drury*, (who was settled in the said Parish of *Tenham*, and who is removed to *Preston* by the said Order, AS *the* WIFE of the said Pauper,) The said *Edward Young* being *then an* INFANT of 20 Years: And that afterwards, the said *Rebecca* was brought to Bed, in the Parish of *Chilham*, of the said *Mary*, removed by the Order. Whereupon They adjudged and ordered That the said Order so made by the 2 Justices be, in *all* Points, confirmed.

Mr. *Lee*, who had moved to quash these Orders, objected to that *Part* of them which relates to the *Woman* and *Child*: For that the *Marriage* was ABSOLUTELY *null* and *void*, by the express Words of the Marriage-Act 26 *G.* 2. *c.* 33. § 11. As the Pauper not being a Widower, and being *under Age*, was married by Licence, WITHOUT *the Consent of his Father* (who was then living.)

Mr. *Knowler* was to have shewn Cause now, against quashing these Orders: But He owned that the Words of the Act were so strong that He could not get over them; (being "That it shall be "*absolutely* null and void to all Intents and Purposes *whatsoever*:") UNLESS, (He said,) the Court shall think a *Declaratory Sentence* to be necessary.

But Mr. *Robinson*, who was on the ſame Side, entered into the Defence of theſe Orders, and cited 2 *Strange* 1066. *between the Pariſhes of St. Peter* and *St. Nicholas in Ipſwich*; To ſhew that the Word "void" may be conſtrued "*voidable*." He alſo cited the Caſe of *Barber* v. *Dennis*, in 1 *Mod.* 69. and in 1 *Salk.* 68. where it was holden to be immaterial Whether the Apprentice *de facto* was *legally* ſo, or not. (And he obſerved that in 2 *Strange* 1067. The Caſe of *Cuerden* v. *Leyland* is taken Notice of, and diſtinguiſhed from the Caſe *then* before the Court.) So, on 23 *H.* 6. *c.* 10, and 21 *H.* 8. mentioned in *Hob.* 166. in the Caſe of *Winchcombe* v. *Biſhop of Winchester and Pulleſton*. So, on *Weſtm.* 2. So, on 8 *H.* 6. *c.* 10. concerning Sheriffs Bonds, (inſtanced in the ſame Caſe in *Hobart*.) So, on 1 *Eliz.* *c.* 19. concerning College Leaſes, (there alſo mentioned.)

He urged, that it is highly *unreaſonable*, that a virtuous young Woman and her innocent Children ſhould be turned adrift, and be conſidered as a Whore and Baſtards, without having any *Opportunity to conteſt* ſo ſevere a Judgment againſt them.

Therefore this Marriage ought to be avoided *by a Sentence* in the Eccleſiaſtical Court; and not in a *Collateral* Method, by an *ex parte* Order of Juſtices made WITHOUT *hearing them or any Perſon on their Behalf*.

Mr. *Norton*, *contra*, was beginning to ſpeak. But

Lord MANSFIELD (conceiving the Point to be clear, and commending Mr. *Knowler* for his Candour in giving it up,) ſtopt Him; and took the Diſtinction between Acts of Parliament made againſt *One* of the Parties, and for the *Benefit of Another* of the Parties, (and where ſuch Other Party has an *Election* either to take Benefit of it, or not;) and Acts of Parliament made *againſt* BOTH.

* *V.* § 11.

This is an Act made *againſt* BOTH: And the Marriage is * thereby expreſſly declared "abſolutely null and void to ALL Intents and "Purpoſes *whatſoever*."

So that it is not like the Caſes cited, nor like the Caſes on the Statute of Bigamy 1 *Jac.* 1. *c.* 11. Which was made only againſt *One* of the Parties.

The other Judges concurred with his Lordſhip: and *They* alſo obſerved that this Act was made againſt *Both*; And

(Mr. Juſtice FOSTER added—) " Againſt the *innocent* CHILDREN " of Both." And He ſaid it would be againſt the Spirit of the Act to underſtand it *otherwiſe* than that the Marriage ſhall be ABSOLUTELY *void*.

Wherefore, *Per Cur.*

The ORDERS muſt be confirmed as to the Man; but quaſhed as to the *Woman* and *Child*.

RULE accordingly.

Collins *verſ.* Gibbs.

Tueſday 27th *November* 1759.

MR. *Burland* had moved, on *Thurſday* laſt, in Arreſt of Judgment, after a Judgment *by* DEFAULT, and a Writ of Inquiry executed, in an Action upon the Caſe on *Aſſumpſit*.

His Objection was The *Want* of an *Averment* of Performance of what He inſiſted to be a CONDITION PRECEDENT.

The Queſtion was, Whether it was a CONDITION PRECEDENT, or not.

It was an Action upon the Caſe wherein the Plaintiff, having firſt recited the Dependency of a former Action brought by the Defendant againſt him, and a Compromiſe thereof, upon an Agreement for the Payment of the Coſts of it by the preſent Defendant to the preſent Plaintiff, on the now Plaintiff's giving him a General Releaſe; lays the Defendant's Promiſe to pay him his Demand in the preſent Action to have been made, " *In Conſideration* that the " ſaid *William* (the now Plaintiff) at the *Special Inſtance and Re-* " *queſt* of the ſaid *John* (the now Defendant) *would* execute to the " ſaid *John* a *General Releaſe*, to bear Date on the 27th Day of *July* " in the Year aforeſaid," (which was the Day *before* the Agreement,) " And to be filled up in the common and uſual Form of Ge- " neral Releaſes; He the ſaid *John* (the preſent Defendant) under- " took and faithfully promiſed the ſaid *William* (the preſent Plain- " tiff,) to pay him All the Coſts and Expences that He the ſaid *Wil-* " *liam* had been at in defending the ſaid Suit, feeing Counſel, ſub- " pœnaing Witneſſes, Journies, and all other Charges and Demands " in the ſaid Suit whatſoever; As ſoon as a Bill of ſuch Coſts could " be prepared and produced to Him the ſaid *John*."

Then the Plaintiff avers his Coſts and Expences in the ſaid Suit to have been 21*l.* 3*s.* 7*d.* And that a Bill of ſuch Coſts and Expences was prepared, and produced to the Defendant; whereof He had Notice. But the ſaid Defendant &c, &c.

Mr.

Mr. *Burland* urged, that the Plaintiff ought to have *averred* "That He had *given or tendered* to the Defendant a *General Release* "*executed*:" For that his giving such a Release appeared to be a *Condition precedent*; the Defendant's Promise being made *in Consideration that He would do so*. In Proof of which He cited *Hobart* 106. *Ro. Rep.* 1 *Ld. Raym.* 662. *Thorp* v. *Thorp*.

Mr. *Dunning*, *contra*, cited 1 *Salk.* 29. *Roe* v. *Haugh in Cam' Scac'*: Where the Judges held that they ought to do what they could to help the Declaration. (Which Case he acknowledged to be *after a Verdict*.)

Mr. *Burland* replied that *that* was after a *Verdict*: This is only after a Judgment by *Default*.

The Release would be *no Bar* to the Demand, in the present Case; because it is agreed that it should bear Date the Day *before* the Agreement: So that the Cause of Action was *subsequent* to it, and therefore could *not be barred by it*.

The Plaintiff made no *Promise* "*to execute the Release*." Therefore We have *no other Method to oblige* him to it. The Payment of the Money is to be "*On* his executing it."

Lord MANSFIELD—The Release is to be given "at the *Special* "*Instance and Request* of *John*" (the now Defendant:) But perhaps he may *never request* it. We will see if it can be made good by Construction.

CUR. ADVIS'.

Lord MANSFIELD now delivered the Resolution of the Court.

This is a Motion made by the *Defendant* in Arrest of a Judgment, by Default: So that it comes before the Court, exactly as if it had been upon *Demurrer*; And is not like the Cases of Objections to Judgments *after Verdict*.

The Plaintiff has *not averred Performance* of what was to be done on *his* Part; nor shewn that he was *ready* to perform it.

Therefore We are All of Opinion, That it can *not* be made good, as laid in the Declaration: And the true *Distinction*, as to Supplying such Defects, is, whether the Objection be made *after* a Verdict, or *not*.

Therefore the JUDGMENT must be ARRESTED.

Where-

Whereupon Mr. *Dunning* moved to *amend*, upon Payment of Costs; by inserting such an Averment, as (he said) the Fact really was. Which was opposed by Mr. *Burland*; as being *too late*, after Judgment was *arrested*; and as having never been done.

Lord MANSFIELD—As it is doubtful Whether this *can* be done or not; and as it is certain that the Difference between paying Costs to amend, and beginning a fresh, is very trifling in this Case, it is better to let the Rule be as it was pronounced: And accordingly—Let the Judgment be arrested.

Per Cur.
JUDGMENT ARRESTED.

The * Insolvent Debtors Case: or Young *vers.* Diego Aimes.

Wednesday 28th *November* 1759.
* *V. ante* 799.

THE Court declared that as the † Act of 32 *G.* 2. *c.* 28. for Relief of Debtors with respect to the Imprisonment of their Persons, &c, which did not † commence till the 15th of *June* 1759, (being the first Day of *Trinity* Term 1759) could *not*, undoubtedly, *mean* to leave, between the Expiration of the former Act and the Commencement of this, a *Chasm of* 14 *Days*, to the *Prejudice* and *Disadvantage* of insolvent Debtors, (for whose *Relief* it was calculated,) They thought they ought to construe this Act EQUITABLY, for the Benefit and Relief of such insolvent Debtors and Prisoners; Especially as the Words of it are "That the Prisoner may exhibit "his Petition before the End of the first Term which *shall be* next "after he shall be charged in Execution." And therefore They thought themselves at Liberty to construe it, and did accordingly declare their Construction of it to be, "That TRINITY Term 1759, "ought to be considered as the *Term in which* such Prisoners were "*charged* in Execution;" And consequently, "that they or such "of them as were precluded by the Expiration of that Act, from "completing their Discharge under it, had the *present Michaelmas* "*Term*, for the first Term next after their being charged in Execution; At any Time before the End of *which*, they might *petition*." By which Construction, The Court took Care That these Debtors should not suffer any Inconvenience, merely by such undesigned Expiration of an Act made for their Relief, and undoubtedly *meant* (they said) to be continued on *without* any intermediate Chasm.

† *V. Sect.* 13.

Rex *verſ.* Inhabitants of Fulham.

TWO Juſtices removed *Alice Brooks*, Widow of *John Brooks*, and her 4 Children by him, (naming and deſcribing them,) from *St. Margaret's Weſtminſter* to *Fulham*: And the Seſſions confirmed their Order, Stating the Caſe ſpecially.

Caſe—*John Brooks* deceaſed, late Huſband of *Alice*, being ſettled at *Fulham* 14 Years ago, afterwards took a Meſſuage or Tenement in *St. Margaret's Weſtminſter*, at 6*l.* 10*s.* a Year. He entered into and continued in Poſſeſſion thereof ſeveral Years; And during his Reſidence in the ſaid Meſſuage or Tenement, He the ſaid *John Brooks* was *aſſeſſed* and *taxed*, *by the Aſſeſſors of the Land-Tax there*, in Proportion to his ſaid Rent, for the LAND-*Tax* due in reſpect of his occupying the ſaid Premiſſes; *and* PAID the ſaid Tax or Aſſeſſment, during ſuch his Occupying and Reſidence in the ſaid Meſſuage or Tenement, *to the Collector* of the Land-tax in the ſaid Pariſh of *St. Margaret*. Afterwards He was ALLOWED the ſaid Tax or Aſſeſſment *by his Landlord*, on his ſettling his Account with him for the Rent of the ſaid Houſe. The ſaid *John Brooks* never gained any Settlement in any Pariſh ſince. *Alice Brooks*, his Widow, and her 4 Children by Him (naming them) are become poor: And neither the ſaid *Alice* or either of the ſaid Children have gained any Settlement in their own Right. The Seſſions therefore ratify and confirm the Original Order, and diſmiſs the Appeal.

Mr. *Norton* (who had moved to quaſh theſe Orders) ſaid the Juſtices had determined wrong, from imagining that *John Brooks* had gained no Settlement in *St. Margaret's*, becauſe He was *allowed* the *Land-tax* again by his Land-lord. To prove which, He cited the following Caſes—(all determined in this Court,) *Rex* v. *Inhabitants of Oakehampton*, *M.* 7. & *Paſch.* 7 *G.* 2; the Caſe of the Tide-waiter, who was rated and paid to the Land-tax for his Salary; but was repaid by the Collector of the Cuſtoms. * *Rex* v. *Inhabitants of* † *Chidingfold*, in *H.* 30 *G.* 2. *Rex* v. *Inhabitants of* ‡ *Uffculme*, in *Tr.* 1757, 30 & 31 *G.* 2. and *Rex* v. *Inhabitants of* ‖ *Painſwick*, in *Tr.* 1758, 31 *G.* 2.

* *V. ante* 247.
† *V. ante* 368.
‖ *V. ante* 621.

Mr. *Burton* now ſhewed Cauſe againſt quaſhing the Orders; and Mr. *Morton* ſupported Him. They Both argued from the Inconvenience; and would have had it ſuppoſed that it was the Collector of the Land-tax, and not the Pariſh Officer, who made the Aſſeſſment.

2

Mr.

Mr. *Norton* and Mr. *Stowe*, *contra*, cited the Case of * *Armley v. Bramley*; Where it was determined, That the being affessed and paying two quarterly Payments to the Land-tax gained a Settlement: And insisted that this was a Point long since, and very often, fully and formally settled.

* Rex v. Inhabitants of Bramley, H. 9 G. 2.

And upon that Foot, of it's being a *settled Point*,
The COURT made the RULE ABSOLUTE.
Both ORDERS QUASHED

The End of *Michaelmas* Term 1759.

Hilary

Hilary Term

33 Geo. 2. B.R. 1760.

Friday 25th *January* 1760.

Gardiner *verſ.* Croaſdale.

THIS Caſe came before the Court, upon a Queſtion reſerved by Lord *Mansfield* at *Niſi prius* at *Guildhall*, upon an Action upon the Caſe, on a *Policy of Inſurance.*

The Inſurance was made upon One fourth Part of the Ship *Encouragement*, and of it's Cargo, from *Greenland* to *London*, free from Average under a certain Value, from the Ice.

The Plaintiff declared upon a *total* Loſs of the Ship: The Declaration *expreſſly ſtated a* TOTAL Loſs of it; And the *Damages* were laid for a *total* Loſs.

But the *Evidence* only proved an AVERAGE *or* PARTIAL Loſs: It was not attempted to prove a *total* One; And it was only ſhewn that the Ship had received *ſome Damage*, (ſcarce more than 50*l.* would have repaired.)

The Defendant's Counſel objected, at the Trial, "That this "Evidence did *not maintain* the Plaintiff's *Declaration* :" And they repreſented the *Practice* to have been on their Side; *viz.* "That "Proof of a partial Loſs was not ſufficient to ſupport a Declaration "for a total Loſs."

A Verdict was taken for 20*l.* as for an *Average* Loſs: But it was agreed on both Sides, that this Verdict ſhould be ſubject to the Opinion of this Court, "Whether it was maintainable in Point of Law." If the Court ſhould be of Opinion "That it was," then the Plaintiff was to have Judgment: But if the Court ſhould be of Opinion "That it was not" Then the Plaintiff was to be Non-ſuited.

It was now urged by the Defendant's Counsel, That this Action is in the Nature of a *special* Action upon the Case; and the Plaintiff rests his Case upon a TOTAL Loss of the Ship: It is not laid as a Consequence of the Events set forth in the Declaration; But He has made this the *Gist* of his Action. The *Damages*, they said, must be taken, upon this Record, to have arisen from a *total* Loss: And the Jury are obliged to give Damages *agreeably* to the Plaintiff's *own express Allegation*; and can *not* take into their Consideration any Damages that are *not alledged*. And here is no Allegation at all of any Average-Damage. They denied that any thing was *put in Issue*, upon the *Non Assumpsit* pleaded, but the *total* Loss, which the Plaintiff has alledged and the Defendant has denied: And they said that the *Defence* upon an Average Loss was, or at least might be, quite *different* from the Defence upon a total Loss. They added, That if the Defendant had chosen to suffer Judgment to go *by Default*, it must have been taken, upon this Record, that he had acknowledged it to be a *total* Loss: And the Damages must have been assessed against him accordingly.

They said this was not like a Case of *Walker* v. *the Royal Exchange Assurance Company*, in 1746 at *Nisi prius*, before Ld. Ch. J. *Lee*: Which was an Action of Covenant upon a Policy of Insurance, for 800*l.* on the Ship *Argyle* from to *Viana*. The Breach assigned was, "That before the Ship's Arrival at *Viana*, "She was *taken by Enemies*, and *thereby totally* lost." The Defendant alledged "That She left her Convoy improperly; That She "was *retaken* by an *English* Man of War; That She was thereupon "sold; That ⅛ of the Value was paid to the Re-taker; That the "Rest of the Purchase-Money was left at *Oporto*, in the Hands of "the *English* Consul." And the Defendant's Counsel objected "That upon these Circumstances, the Ship was *not totally lost*." It was answered on the Plaintiff's Part, "That the Objection "would not hold: For that notwithstanding the *Recapture*, it was "a *total* Loss by the Capture." Whereas in the present Case, *here* is only a *partial* Loss: So that the two Cases do not resemble Each other.

They cited the Case of *Hambleton* v. *Veere* 2 *Saund.* 169. as being more apposite to the present Case. They also cited 1 *Strange* 1250, *Dean* v. *Dicker*, to prove that a Recapture does *not hinder* it's being a total Loss; when it had once become so by the Capture.

The COURT were clearly of Opinion with the Plaintiff, even without hearing his Counsel.

Lord MANSFIELD—At the Trial, it appeared to me, and ſo the Jury thought, That the preſent Caſe could *not* be conſidered as a *total* Loſs. The Defendant's Counſel objected (as they do now,) " That the Jury could not take a *partial* Loſs into their Conſidera-" tion, upon an *expreſs Declaration* for a TOTAL Loſs:" And I underſtood from them, " that the *Practice* ſupported their Objec-" tion."

Mr. *Norton*, who was Counſel for the Plaintiff at the Trial, then argued to the contrary, upon *Principles:* And He alſo cited the Caſe of *Walker* v. *the Royal Exchange Aſſurance Company.* (But that Caſe does not prove much; becauſe that was a *total* Loſs.) I was ſatisfied upon the *Principles*; provided the *Practice* did not interfere with them: Which I was then told it did.

I choſe to put it in ſuch a Shape that the Opinion of the Court might be had, without Delay or Expence.

No Hardſhip was done to the Defendant, upon the *Quantum* of the Damages found: For the Plaintiff took a great deal *leſs* than it clearly appeared upon the Evidence that the Loſs amounted to.

I cannot hear of any ſuch *Determination* as can ſupport the Objection that has been made by the Defendant's Counſel.

Therefore it ſtands ſingly upon *Principles.* And upon *Principles*, it is extremely clear That the Plaintiff may, upon *this Declaration*, recover Damages as for a *partial* Loſs.

This is an *Action upon the Caſe:* Which is a *liberal* Action. And a Plaintiff may recover *leſs* than the Grounds of his Declaration ſupport; though *not more.* This is agreeable to Juſtice, and conſiſtent with his Demand.

Here are two Grounds of the Plaintiff's Declaration; *viz.* The *Policy*, and the *Damage to the Ship.*

As to it's being a *total* Loſs, or a *partial* Loſs, *That* is a Queſtion more applicable to the QUANTITY *of the Damages*, than to the *Ground* of the Action. The *Ground* of the Action is the ſame, whether the Loſs be *partial*, or total: *Both* are Perils *within* the Policy.

As to the Defendant's not coming *prepared* to defend a *partial* Loſs—This indeed would be an Objection, *if* it was *true.* But the Defendant does, in Truth, come prepared to ſhew " that *either* no

" Damage

" Damages had happened *at all*; Or, at leaſt, that Damages have " not happened to *ſuch a Degree* as the Plaintiff has alledged in his " Declaration;" Or " That he did not ſign the Policy."

As to the Effects of a *Judgment by Default*—The Defendant could *not* have been hurt by a Judgment by Default. For the Plaintiff could not have recovered, even upon a Writ of Inquiry, any *greater* Damages than the Plaintiff could *prove*, to the Jury ſworn to aſſeſs them, " That he had *actually ſuffered*."

If the preſent Objection was to prevail, it would introduce the Addition of unneceſſary Counts in Declarations, and an enormous Swelling of the Records of the Court. It is more convenient to lay the Caſe ſhort, than prolix.

There is *no Proof* of any PRACTICE contrary to the Principles. It was the *Apprehenſion* of ſuch a contrary Practice, that was the *only Occaſion* of my having any Doubt at the Trial. I am now fully ſatisfied that the Plaintiff may recover either the whole, *or* LESS, than he has laid. And therefore this Verdict ought, in my Opinion, *to ſtand*. In an *Ejectment* for more, the Plaintiff may recover leſs: 'Tis every Day's Practice.

Mr. Juſt. DENISON concurred; and thought it a very plain Caſe. It is an Action *for Damages* for the Loſs of the Ship. Now, in an Action *for Damages*, the Plaintiff is to recover his Damages, according to his Proof, *pro tanto:* But He is not, in an Action *for Damages*, obliged to prove *All* that he has alledged. If it had been an Action of Covenant for pulling down a Houſe, would not the Plaintiff be intitled to recover Damages for pulling down *half* the Houſe, provided he had proved that the Defendant did it? This is *no Variance* of the Evidence from the Declaration: The Evidence tends, in a *certain Degree*, to the Proof of what is alledged in the Declaration. It is not neceſſary to lay two Counts in ſuch a Declaration as this.

Mr. Juſt. FOSTER concurred in the Opinion " That the Verdict " ought to ſtand."

Mr. Juſt. WILMOT alſo concurred. He ſaid that in Actions *for Damages*, the Plaintiff may recover for All, or for any *Part:* The Damages are ſeverable, and may be given *pro tanto*. Here, Damages are laid for a *total* Loſs; which is only the *Meaſure* of the Damages: And the Plaintiff *proves a partial* Loſs; which only affects the *Meaſure* of the Damages, but is *no Variance* from the Allegations contained in the Declaration.

And

And if this had been a Judgment *by Default*, yet the Plaintiff *could not*, even in *that* Case, have recovered Damages for *any more* Loss than he was able to *prove* under the Writ of Inquiry of Damages.

And as to the Defendant's not having sufficient *Notice* that he should come *prepared* to defend against a *partial* Loss—I think He *has* sufficient Notice to come thus prepared: For He ought to come prepared to prove "That *No* Damage at all happened." *If any* at all happened, he will be liable *pro tanto*, if it be proved.

Per Cur. unanimously,
Let the *Postea* be delivered to the PLAINTIFF.

Saturday 26th *January* 1760.

Rex *vers.* Benjamin Burgess.

A Trial at Bar.

INDICTMENT for a *Nusance*, in obstructing an ancient and common *Highway* leading from *Richmond*, through and over *Richmond-Hill* and from thence *through and over Richmond New Park*, to *Coomb-Neville*, for all the King's Subjects, with their HORSES, to go return pass and RIDE at their free Will and Pleasure.

Note—

* On 13th *November* 1754.

The * former Trial at Bar was for obstructing an ancient and common Highway for *Carriages Horsmen* AND *Foot-Passengers*: Which was laid JOINTLY, *viz.* as a common Highway for *all* these.

† On 28th *May* 1756.

An Indictment was afterwards found for obstructing a FOOT-Way: Which was not defended; (being † given up by the then Attorney General, now Ld. *Mansfield*.)

These two last-mentioned Indictments (as well as the present One) related to *Richmond-Hill* Gate.

Another Indictment was afterwards found against *Marthay Gray*, Keeper of the *East-Sheen* Gate; and was tried.

‖ At Lent Assizes 1758.

That Second Trial (which was at *Kingston* Assizes before ‖ Mr. Just. FOSTER) was for a FOOT-Way only, through the Park at *East-Sheen* Gate: And the Gate-Keeper was convicted.

This was for a HORSE-Way only; and the Way was described to lead through *Richmond* Gate.

Upon the firſt Trial, it ſeemed clear beyond all Poſſibility of Doubt, (and ſo the Attorney General now acknowledged,) "That there "was an indiſputable Right for Foot-Paſſengers, and that there had always been *Ladders* at certain Gates:" But the Right of paſſing and repaſſing with Carriages or on Horse-*back* was very weakly ſupported at *that* Time, and moſt ſtrongly contradicted by a great Over-balance of more credible Evidence.

Upon the preſent Trial, the Pretence of Claim to the Horse-Way was ſo ill ſupported by Evidence on the Part of the Proſecutors; and ſo clearly ſhewn to be ill-founded and imaginary, by the ſtrongeſt Evidence on the other Side, (which fully proved "That 50, "60, 70 Years ago, there were *Locks* upon all the Gates; that no "Perſons could paſs on Horſe-back or with Wheeled Carriages, "*without Keys or Permiſſion* of the Ranger or his Subſtitutes; and "that there had always been a *Fence-Month*, during which Seaſon "No One at all could even make Uſe of the Keys which the Ran-"ger had given them, to be uſed at all other Times but that "Month;") that the Court and Jury and Audience and alſo the Proſecutors own Counſel were convinced that the Proſecutors had *failed in their Evidence:* And accordingly, the Jury themſelves declared voluntarily and without being aſked their Sentiments, "That they were quite ſatisfied with the Evidence which had been "already given on the part of the Defendant."

Whereupon the Defendant's Counſel reſted the Matter here; although they had 45 more Witneſſes ſtill remaining un-examined: And it was thought needleſs for them to ſum up their Evidence, or to ſay any thing more upon the Subject.

The Jury therefore, without hearing any Remarks or Reply or Summing up the Evidence at all, and without going from the Bar, or having the leaſt Doubt or Heſitation,

Acquitted the Defendant.

N.B. Soon after the Trial at *Surrey* Aſſizes for a Nuſance in obſtructing the *Foot*-Way, whereof the then Defendant *Martha Gray*, Gate-Keeper at *Eaſt-Sheen*-Gate was *convicted* as aforeſaid, very convenient Ladders were erected, at *thoſe* Gates to which the two former convictions extended, and where there had anciently been Ladders, till Sir *Robert Walpole* (then Ranger) took them away; *viz.* at *Richmond*-Gate, and at *Eaſt-Sheen*-Gate.

Thursday 31st *January* 1760.

Rex *verſ.* Inhabitants of Hitcham.

TWO Juſtices made an Order for the Removal of *Thomas Death* and *Anne* his Wife and ſeveral of their Children (naming and deſcribing them) from *Hitcham* to *Ringſhall* (both in *Suffolk.*) Upon Appeal to the Seſſions, they ſet aſide the Juſtice's Order, ſtating the Caſe ſpecially.

Caſe—The ſaid *Thomas Death*, the Father, AND *Anne his* WIFE, having a legal Settlement in *Ringſhall*, afterwards, about 18 Years ago, before the *Michaelmas* in that Year, LET *himſelf for One Year*, to *William Death* his Brother, who was a legal Inhabitant of *Hitcham*, and exerciſed the Trade of a *Carpenter* in the ſaid Pariſh; and entered his ſaid Service at *Hitcham* aforeſaid, and continued his ſaid Service for a Year according to his ſaid Contract: But was, by his Agreement with his Brother, to receive NO *Money by Way of Wages*; but his Brother was to *teach* him as much as he could, during the ſaid Year, of the *Trade* of a Carpenter; And his Brother was to provide him Meat Drink Waſhing and Lodging during the ſaid Time; And the ſaid *Thomas Death* was to do all his ſaid Brother's lawful Buſineſs in his *Farming Way*, (the ſaid *William*, his Brother, occupying a ſmall Farm at *Hitcham* aforeſaid;) and was employed by his ſaid Brother in his ſaid Buſineſs of a *Carpenter* and his *farming* Way, and in *doing any other Work* that his ſaid Brother ordered him; And particularly, in the *Harveſt-time*, the ſaid *William Death* having taken ſome Corn to cut, of a neighbouring Farmer, the ſaid *William Death* ordered the ſaid *Thomas Death* to cut it, which the ſaid *Thomas Death* did; And the ſaid *William* his Maſter, took the Money for cutting it. And it further appeared (to the Seſſions) that the ſaid ſeveral Children had not gained any Settlement, ſeparate or diſtinct from their ſaid Parents. Whereupon, the Seſſions were of Opinion, that the ſaid *Thomas Death* gained a legal Settlement for himſelf and for his ſaid Wife and for their ſaid ſeveral Children, in the ſaid Pariſh of *Hitcham*, by reaſon of the Facts above ſtated; And therefore allow the Appeal, and ſet aſide the Order of two Juſtices for removing them from *Hitcham* to *Ringſhall*.

In *Michaelmas* Term laſt, Mr. *Norton* moved to quaſh this Order of Seſſions: Becauſe, as the Pauper was a *married* Man with a Family, He could not gain a Settlement by a Hiring and Service; And this *Letting* Himſelf is Nothing more than a HIRING *for a Year and Service for a Year*.

Afterwards, Mr. *Morton* (who was for the Parish of *Ringshall*) moved That the Order of Sessions might be sent down to be *amended* in the *State of the Facts*. He produced an Affidavit "that the "Pauper was *not*, in Fact, a *married* Man at the Time of his let-"ting himself to his Brother for a Year; nor was his being a *sin-"gle Man* at that Time, at all contested: But that the Recital of "his having a Wife at that Time was inserted by a *Mistake*; And "that it then *appeared* to the Sessions, upon the Evidence, that he "was then a *single* Man."

Lord MANSFIELD—Otherwise, there is no Question about the Settlement: And I wondered at it's being made One.

A Rule was made to shew Cause why the Order of Sessions should not be sent back in Order to be amended. Which Rule was now made absolute, though very strenuously defended: For the Court thought it likely to be a Mistake, for two Reasons. One of them was an Observation of Mr. Just. *Denison*'s "That *if* He was *not* a *Single* Man at the Time of his Hiring himself, no Question at all "could have arisen at the Sessions, about the Rest of the Case." The other Reason to suspect that it was a mere Mistake, was added by Mr. Just. *Foster*; Namely, "That the Counsel concerned for "the Parish of *Hitcham* were so vehement in their Opposition to it's "being stated agreeably to the real Truth of the Fact."

The Sessions thereupon re-examined the Matter, and heard *new* Evidence, which proved the said *Thomas Death* to have been a *single* Man at the Time of the Hiring: And They amended their Order accordingly. This amended Order was afterwards AFFIRMED.

But as it was made upon *new* Evidence, The COURT ordered the Recognizance to be DISCHARGED.

Strong,

Friday 1st February 1760.

Strong, Clerk, *verſ.* Teatt, Leſſee of * Mervyn et al'.

* The ſix Leſſors of the Plaintiff, in *Ireland*, were *Mervyn Fanning*, *Arthur Mervyn*, *Henry Carey*, *Weſley Harman*, *Eleanor Irvine*, or *Irvin*, and *Anne Mervyn*: But *only three* of the ſix Demiſes, *viz.* Thoſe of *Weſley Harman*, of *Eleanor Irvine*, and of *Ann Mervyn*, (who All claim by virtue of the Deviſes to the Teſtator's Daughters,) were material.

THIS was a Writ of Error, brought upon a Judgment given by the Court of King's Bench in *Ireland*, for the Plaintiff in Ejectment.

The Ejectment was brought for Lands in the County of *Tyrone*: And upon the Trial, a Special Verdict was found.

The Special Verdict firſt ſtates a long Pedigree of the Family of the *Mervyns*; and alſo ſeveral Deeds, not neceſſary to be here taken Notice of, (as no Queſtion at all ariſes upon them.)

Then it finds That *Audley Mervyn* Eſq; and *Henry* his Son, on the Marriage of the ſaid *Henry* with Mrs. *Mary Titchburn*, executed Deeds of Leaſe and Releaſe dated the 21ſt and 22d of *December* 1711; And that, in Purſuance thereof, a Fine was levied, and a Recovery ſuffered, whereby the Manor of *Arleſtown* in *Tyrone*, (of which the Premiſſes in queſtion are Part,) was ſettled, in ſtrict Settlement, on the ſaid *Audley* (the Father) for Life; then on the ſaid *Henry* (his Son) for Life; Then on the firſt and other Sons of *Henry &c*, and the Iſſue of that Marriage (in common Form,) with ſeveral Terms, Powers, and Proviſoes; with the REVERSION IN FEE to the ſaid *Audley*, the Father. (Which Marriage took Effect: But there was no Iſſue of it.)

That *Audley Mervyn* had Iſſue, beſides the ſaid *Henry* (his Eldeſt Son,) three other Sons, *viz. Audley*, *James*, and *Theophilus*; and four Daughters, *viz. Lucy*, (who, in her Father's Life-time, married with *Wentworth Harman*,) *Eleanor*, (One of the Leſſors of the Plaintiff, and who afterwards married with *Chriſtopher Irwin*, who has been many Years dead,) *Anne*, (One of the Leſſors of the Plaintiff, who married *James Mervyn* otherwiſe *Richardſon*, long ſince dead,) and *Jane*.

That the ſaid *Audley the Elder*, being ſeiſed as the Law requires, of the ſaid Lands and Tenements, on the 15th of *June* 1717, duly made

made and published his last *Will and Testament*, in Writing; whereby, after reciting "that He was desirous to make the best Provision "in his Power, for the Support of his Children and the Peace and "Settlement of his Family;" He devised as follows; *viz.* "And as to the WORLDLY ESTATE wherewith it hath pleased God to bless me, I give and bequeath the SAME, in Manner following. I give and bequeath to my dearly beloved Wife *Olivia*, to her proper Use and Benefit, All my Plate and Houshold Goods and Furniture of what kind soever, and also my Coach and Horses and their Harnesses, and three Saddle-Horses. I also constitute and appoint my said dear Wife sole Executrix of this my last Will and Testament; and do give and bequeath unto Her All the Rest and Residue of my personal Estate, of what kind soever. And I do hereby will and require my said Executrix, assoon as She conveniently can, after my Death, to sell all the Rest of my Horses and all my Stock of Cattle; and to apply the Money arising by such Sale, and all such Debts as are or shall at the Time of my Death be due to me, (particularly, the Sum of 1100*l.* due to me by Judgment affecting the Estate of *Richard* late Earl of *Bellamont*; the Sum of 1000*l.* due to me by my Son *Henry Mervyn*; and a Debt of 1000*l.* or 1200*l.* due to me by *Hugh Mervyn*;) and also All Arrear of Rents which are or shall become due unto me, to the Payment and Discharge of such Sums of Money as shall be due by me, to any Person or Persons, at the Time of my Death; and to the Intent that all my Debts may be honestly and truly paid and discharged.

I do hereby give and devise to my said dear Wife OLIVIA *and her* HEIRS, All that and those the Towns Lands and Tenements &c &c (Specifying them by their particular Denominations;) All which Lands and Tenements are situate lying and being in the County of *Tyrone*; As also the Town and Lands of &c; All which last mentioned Lands are situate lying and being in the Barony of *Duleek* and County of *Meath*; And *also all* OTHER *the Lands Tenements and* HEREDITAMENTS *in the said Counties of Tyrone and Meath or either of them, whereof I am seised in Fee Simple, or of which any other Person is seised in Trust for me*; Together with their and every of their Appurtenances; *To the Use Intent and Purpose* that my said dear Wife shall take and receive out of the said *Lands*, as an Addition to her Jointure, One Annuity or Yearly Rent-Charge of 100*l.* *per Annum*, during her natural Life, to her own proper Use and Benefit: And to this *further Use and Purpose*, that *my said* WIFE may, by SALE of such of the said *Lands* hereby to her devised, raise so much Money as may be sufficient to pay off and discharge such of the said DEBTS, as shall not be paid off and discharged out of my personal Estate. And as to so much part of the said Lands and Tenements as shall remain *unsold*, To the Use following, (*subject nevertheless* to the Payment of the said Sum of 100*l.* *per Annum* to my said dear

 Wife

Wife during her natural Life,) *viz.* To the Use of my Son *Audley Mervyn*, for and during his natural Life; And from and after his Death, To the Use of his first and every other Son and Sons severally and successively, and to the Heirs Male of their several and respective Bodies; And for want of such Issue, To the Use of my Son *James*, for and during his natural Life; and from and after his Death, To the Use of his first and every other Son and Sons severally and successively, and to the Heirs Male of their several and respective Bodies; And for want of such Issue, To the Use of my Son *Theophilus*, for and during his natural Life; and from and after his Death, To the Use of his first and every other Son and Sons severally and successively, and the Heirs Male of their several and respective Bodies; And for Want of such Issue, To the Use of my Son HENRY, for and during his NATURAL LIFE; and from and after his Death, To the Use of his first and every other Son and Sons severally and successively, and the Heirs Male of their several and respective Bodies; And *for Want of such Issue*, To the Use of Each and Every of my *Daughters* and the Heirs of their several Bodies, as Tenants in Common, and not as Jointenants; And for want of such Issue, To *Mervyn Archdall* and *Henry Carey*, my Nephews, and their Heirs.

And it is my further Will and Intention, and I do hereby devise, That *if* it shall so happen, that my Sons *Henry* and *Audley* shall Both of them die without Issue MALE, in the *Life-time of my Son James*, Whereby the Estate settled upon my Son *Henry*, upon his Marriage, shall descend come or remain unto my said Son *James*, That then and in such Case, my said Son *James* shall *not* take any Interest or Estate in the *Lands and Tenements herein before devised unto him*; but that the same shall *remain and go over* to my Son *Theophilus*, according to such Interest and Estate as is herein before to him devised for want of Issue Male of my said Son *James*.

And I will and devise that my Executrix shall have full Power and Authority, by her last Will and Testament in Writing, to charge or incumber All or any of my Lands and Tenements herein mentioned, with such Portions and Provisions for All or any of my Daughters, as She shall think reasonable.

And it is my further Will and Intention, That Whoever of my Sons shall be seised of an Estate or Use for Life in the said Lands, shall have Power to commit Waste; as also to settle a Jointure on any Woman he shall marry, in Proportion to her Fortune; and likewise to make Leases for One two or three Lives or 21 Years, at the highest Rent that can be had from a solvent Tenant.

And

And whereas, by the Settlement made upon the Marriage of my Son *Henry*, I have Power to charge the Eſtate ſettled on my ſaid Son with the Sum of 2500 *l.* for the Portions of my Younger Children, I do hereby will and direct my Executrix, immediately after my Death to receive the ſaid Sum of 2500 *l*, for the Uſe of my Younger Children, and to apply the Intereſt thereof to their Education and Maintenance, in ſuch Manner as She ſhall think fit, and to diſpoſe of the Surplus thereof in Manner following, that is to ſay, To my Sons *James* and *Theophilus* and my Daughters *Eleanor Anne* and *Jane*, the Sum of 500 *l.* Each, at ſuch Time as He or She ſhall marry or attain the Age of 21 Years, (which ſhall firſt happen:) And in Caſe any of my ſaid Sons or Daughters ſhall die unmarried and before the Age of 21 Years, I will that my ſaid Executrix ſhall divide among the Survivors of my ſaid Sons *James* and *Theophilus* and my ſaid Daughters *Eleanor Anne* and *Jane*, the Sum of 500 *l*, deſigned for Him or Her ſo dying, in ſuch Manner as She ſhall think fitting.

And I alſo will and deviſe, That in Caſe my ſeveral *Lands* herein mentioned or any of them ſhall by virtue of this my laſt Will remain and come to my ſaid Son HENRY, that my ſaid Executrix ſhall have Power and Authority to charge and incumber the *ſame* with any Sum not exceeding the Sum of 5000 *l.* Sterling, for the Uſe and Advantage of ſuch of my Daughters as ſhall be then alive and unmarried, as an Addition to their Portions.

The Jury find That the ſaid *Audley* the Elder, at the Time of making the ſaid Will, and at his Death, was ſeiſed in Fee, in Poſſeſſion, of the Lands deviſed by expreſs Denominations in his ſaid Will, as in his ſaid Will; and likewiſe ſeiſed in Fee, in Poſſeſſion, at the ſame Time, of the Lands of *Gortmore* in the County of *Tyrone*, of about 200 Acres; And that the Lands in *Tyrone* expreſſly deviſed by the ſaid Will, (including the Value of *Gortmore*,) were of the yearly Value of 500 *l*; And that the Eſtate ſettled by the Deed of the 22d of *December* 1711, was in the Year 1720 or 1721, of the yearly Value of 1800 *l.*

That the ſaid *Audley Mervyn* died on the 17th of *June* 1717, ſeiſed as the Law requires, of the Lands and Premiſſes compriſed in the ſaid Settlement of the 22d of *December* 1711; of which, the Lands and Premiſſes in queſtion are part. And upon his the ſaid *Audley* the Elder's Death, his Eldeſt Son and Heir at Law, HENRY, became ſeiſed thereof as the Law requires; And being ſo ſeiſed, He the ſaid *Henry*, by Leaſe and Releaſe of 29th and 30th of *September* 1729, in Conſideration of 1500 *l.* paid, *granted and releaſed the Premiſſes in queſtion, to* JOHN STRONG, Clerk, his Heirs and Aſſigns;

signs; Which said *John Strong* entered, and continued the Possession during his Life. On the 9th of *March* 1744, *John Strong* died seised: And on his Death, JAMES STRONG, his Eldest Son and Heir, entered, and continued the quiet Possession till the 11th of *June* 1756.

Olivia Mervyn, who was Wife and Widow to *Audley* the Father, died in the Year 1720.

James Mervyn, Son of *Audley* the Elder, died in 1726, unmarried, and without Issue.

Jane Mervyn died in 1725, unmarried, and without Issue.

Theophilus Mervyn died in 1736, unmarried, and without Issue.

Lucy Harman died in 1737; leaving *Wesley Harman*, one of the Lessors of the Plaintiff, her Eldest Son and Heir.

Mary, the Wife of *Henry Mervyn*, died in 1735, having never had Issue by the said *Henry*.

Audley, the Younger, died in 1746, unmarried, and without Issue.

HENRY, *the Eldest Son*, (there called *Henry* the Younger,) died on the 1st of *February* 1747, having NEVER *had Issue*.

Mervyn Archdall, in the Will mentioned, died in 1727.

Henry Carey, survived him; and died in *September* 1756.

Hugh Mervyn, Son of Sir *Audley Mervyn*, died in 1727; leaving the said *Arthur Mervyn*, One of the Lessors of the Plaintiff, his Eldest Son and Heir.

Then the Special Verdict finds That the Lessors of the Plaintiff, before making the Leases in the Declaration mentioned, entered and were seised, and then made the several Demises in the Declaration *&c*, *&c*.

But whether, upon the whole Matter aforesaid, the Defendant *James Strong* be guilty of the Trespass *&c*, the Jurors know not, *&c*, *&c*.

The Court of King's Bench in *Ireland* gave Judgment for the Plaintiff in the Ejectment.

The whole Estate which depended upon the Title set up by the Lessors of the Plaintiff, was of very great Value. The Cause had depended a great many Years, and had been argued a great many Times, in *Ireland.*

The Court there held " That the *Reversion in Fee* of the Lands " comprized in the Settlement of 1711, *passed by the Will*;" And " that the *Uses* were *legal* Estates *executed*, subject to a Charge for " the Payment of the Testator's Debts (if any there were,) and to a " Power in *Olivia* to sell for that Purpose; and were *good at Law*, " though devised after an indefinite Payment of such of the Testa-" tor's Debts as should not be discharged by his Personal Estate."

This Case was first argued in *Michaelmas* Term last, by Mr. *Perrot* for the Plaintiff in Error, and Mr. *Winn* for the Defendant in Error; But more fully, a second Time, on *Tuesday* last, the 29th of *January* 1760, by Mr. *Knowler* for the Plaintiff in Error, and Mr. *Norton* for the Defendants in Error; The Court having refused repeated Applications to put off the Argument till the next Term. It was argued very elaborately upon the Question " Whether the " Lessors of the Plaintiff in the Ejectment had any *Legal* Estate;" The Counsel for the Defendant in the Ejectment insisting " that *Oli-* " *via* took the *legal Fee*;" which descended (they said) to *Henry* her Eldest Son and Heir, and was by Him conveyed to the Father of the Defendant in Ejectment: *Or if* She did not, " that the De-" vises thereof after Payment of Debts GENERALLY, were *executory* " and *too remote.*"

This Point concluded to a *Nonsuit* at *Law* only; and to turn the Plaintiffs round to try *another* Kind of Remedy.

The *final Merits* and Question of *Right* depended upon the CONSTRUCTION of the WILL.

It was adjourned, upon the last Argument, (for want of Time to go through with it,) to the *Friday* next following. On which Day, Mr. *Knowler* was beginning to make his Reply: But

Lord MANSFIELD said, They need not give Him the Trouble of a Reply.

The Questions are Two; *viz.* (1st.) Whether the *Reversion* be *within* the Devise; And if it be, (2dly.) Whether it is a good Devise to the Lessors of the Plaintiff.

If the first be against the Lessors of the Plaintiff, the second is immaterial. Upon the first, We are quite clear, that the Judgment is wrong: And therefore it is not necessary to give any Opinion upon the other.

The Points of Law have been argued with a great deal of Skill and Learning; and much has been said upon the Subject of them, very well worth Attention: But as the Case stands, it is not necessary for Us to enter into them; And I give no Sort of Opinion upon them. However, thus much I will mention, for the Sake of those who heard the Argument; *viz.* That this Case is *not like* the Cases that have been cited; and particularly *not like* to that of *Bagshaw* v. *Spencer*. That was not to the Trustees and their Heirs "*to the Use* of them and their Heirs" (as Mr. *Norton* cited it:) But to them and their Heirs and Assigns, "*upon Trust* that they and "the Survivors and Survivor of them should, out of the Rents and "Profits, or by Sale or Mortgage, raise enough to pay all the "Testator's Debts *&c*: And after those Debts *&c* should be paid, "then to Trustees for a Term of 500 Years; then to Trustees to "the Use of his Nephew *Thomas Bagshaw* (as to One Moiety) for "Life without Impeachment of Waste; Remainder to Trustees (by "Name) to preserve contingent Remainders; Remainder to the "Heirs of the Body of *Thomas*, in strict Settlement; Remainder to "*Benjamin Bagshaw* for Life; then to Trustees to preserve contingent Remainders; and after the Decease of *Benjamin*, then to "the Heirs of his Body lawfully begotten." Great Debts were due from the Testator: And Money was raised to pay them.

Thomas Bagshaw died without Issue: And *Benjamin* entered, and supposed Himself Tenant in Tail in Possession; And being so in Possession, the said *Benjamin Bagshaw* suffered a Common Recovery; and then devised to his Wife.

A Bill was brought by the Wife (claiming under the Recovery,) to carry the Trusts into Execution; and for a Conveyance in Fee: And there was a Decree at the Rolls "to carry them into Execution "accordingly."

The Litigation was between the Remainder Man, and the Devisee of *Benjamin*: And the Question was "Whether *Benjamin* "*Bagshaw* was Tenant for *Life*, or in *Tail*." And the Master of the Rolls took it to be an Estate Tail in *Benjamin Bagshaw*. The Plaintiff claimed under the Common Recovery suffered by *Benjamin*: The Defendants, under the Will of *Benjamin Ashton*, the original Devisor. Neither *Party* doubted of its being a *Trust*: The

 Dispute

Dispute was about the Estate devised to *Benjamin Bagshaw*; "Whe- "ther it was for Life, or in Tail."

But my Lord Chancellor started a Doubt, "Whether the De- "vise to *Benjamin Bagshaw* was a *Trust*; or whether it was a *Use* "*executed*." And *if* it had come out to have been a *Use executed*, then the Authority in the Case of *Coulson* v. *Coulson*, and the Certificate given by this Court in that Case, would have stood in the Way; and He would have sent it back to be reconsidered by this Court. But if it was a *Trust*, then it fell under different Considerations.

There, the Trustees and their Heirs and the Survivor of them, were directed to do *three* Things: And what they were to do, was of such a Nature, that they *must necessarily* have a *descendible* Estate in them, to answer the *Ends* of the Trust. But there arose a decisive Dilemma; Which put an End to it's being a Question. The Plaintiff claimed under the Common Recovery. But the Testator's Debts were *not paid* at the Time of suffering it. It was argued on Behalf of the Plaintiff, "That *Benjamin Bagshaw* took by Execu- "tory Devise *after* the Debts should be paid; and that there was "no Danger of a Perpetuity." But it was allowed that there was a *legal* Estate in the Trustees, *till* the Debts were paid.

Now, IF the legal Estate had not taken Effect in *Possession* in *Benjamin Bagshaw*, then there was *no* good Tenant to the *Præcipe*. But *if* it was an *Equitable* Estate, then an *Equitable* Tenant to the *Præcipe would have done*. Therefore they were *obliged* to maintain it to be a *Trust*: For if they had insisted on the Authority of *Coulson* v. *Coulson*; there the Common Recovery was a bad One.

So that that Case of *Bagshaw* and *Spencer* was not applicable to the present Case now before Us.

I thought it not improper to say thus much, as to the Cases that have been cited: But I give no Sort of Opinion upon the *present* Case, as to this Point. It might be worth considering too, "Whe- "ther this be not a *double* Contingency;" *viz.* "*If there should be* "*Debts*, then my Wife to have the Estate for Payment of them: "*If no Debts*, then, those in Remainder to take." However, here it does *not appear* that there *were* any Debts.

As to the nice Points of Law, and the Form of the Remedy—It is not necessary to give any Opinion, if the Plaintiff has NO *fundamental Right* to recover.

Now, as to the *fundamental Right* of the Plaintiff, the Case is shortly this—

His

His Lordſhip then ſummarily ſtated the Facts found by the Special Verdict, and particularly the Settlement in *December* 1711; the Circumſtances of the Family; the Will; and the General Clauſe on which the Queſtion ariſes: and then proceeded, to the Effect following.

The Queſtion is "Whether, by this Sweeping Reſiduary Clauſe, " the Teſtator *intended* to deviſe the REVERSION of the Eſtate ſettled " on the Marriage of his Eldeſt Son *Henry*, with *Mary Tichburn*, " by the Settlement of *December* 1711."

The *Generality of the Expreſſion*, " And alſo ALL *other the Lands* " *Tenements and* HEREDITAMENTS in the ſaid Counties of *Tyrone* " and *Meath* or either of them, whereof I am ſeiſed in Fee Simple, " or of which any other Perſon is ſeiſed in Truſt for Me; together " with their and every of their Appurtenances;" *if unreſtrained* and unqualified by other Words, would carry ALL the Teſtator's Eſtate *in Poſſeſſion, Reverſion* or *Remainder*.

But theſe General Words *may*, by other Words and Expreſſions in the Will, be *reſtrained* to any or either of theſe: And it is the ſame Thing, Whether it be directly *expreſſed*, or clearly and plainly to be *collected* from the Will.

Now here are *plain Expreſſions* in this Will, which are fully ſufficient to ſhew, that the Teſtator *did* NOT *intend* to deviſe the *Reverſion* of this ſettled Eſtate. One Inſtance is, the Clauſe " That if " *Henry* and *Audley* ſhould both of them die without Iſſue Male " in the Life-time of *James*, then *James* ſhould not take any In- " tereſt or Eſtate in the Lands and Tenements therein before deviſed " to Him; But that the ſame ſhould remain and go over to *Theophilus*."

Every part of this Clauſe is inconſiſtent with any Suppoſition that He meant to deviſe the REVERSION of the Lands in Settlement. And there is another Clauſe which manifeſts the ſame Intention: *viz.* " That if all or any of his Lands ſhould *by Virtue of his Will* " remain and come to his Son *Henry*, that then his Executrix ſhould " have Power and Authority to charge and incumber the *ſame* with " any Sum not exceeding the Sum of 5000*l.*" So that He ſuppoſed *Every Thing* mentioned in and deviſed by his Will *might* come to *Henry*. But the *Reverſion* of the ſettled Eſtate *after the Death* of *Henry*, *never could* come to *Henry*. From whence it follows, that the Teſtator did *not* intend this Reverſion to be included in his Will.

And

And there are Powers given by this Will, " to which ever of his " Sons ſhould be ſeiſed of an Eſtate or Uſe for Life in the *ſaid Lands*, " to commit *Waſte*, to ſettle *Jointures*, and to make *Leaſes*:" Which Powers are, in their Nature, applicable to *Poſſeſſions* and not to *Reverſions*; and are referred, by the expreſs Words of the Will, (*viz.* " in the ſaid Lands,") to *Lands only*, as what he meant to deviſe. And they could never take Effect at all in *Henry* (who was One of the Sons:) For he had them before, and did not want any further Authority to exerciſe them.

If Henry had had no Iſſue Male by his firſt Wife *Mary Tichburn*; and had had Iſſue Male by a ſecond Wife; the *Son* by the *ſecond Wife* could never have taken *any Thing*; though he would have been Grandſon of the Teſtator by his Eldeſt Son, and Heir of the Family: So that the Heir of the Family would have ſtood totally diſinherited. And yet the Reaſon why *Henry* and his Iſſue were, by this Will poſtponed to the Younger Brothers, appears plainly to be, " becauſe " they were much *better* provided for:" And the Teſtator underſtood and ſuppoſed that the Lands were ſo ſettled, that ALL the Iſſue Male of *Henry* ſhould have the Eſtate, in their Turns.

Suppoſe *Henry* and *Audley* the Younger Both dead without Iſſue Male; then *James* muſt, upon the Conſtruction of the *Reverſion's paſſing* by the Will, forfeit *every* Thing; not only the Lands *ſettled*, but alſo the Lands *deviſed*; and ſo would not have a Farthing; But the *whole* Eſtate muſt go over, and paſs by Him. For the *Reverſion* of the ſettled Lands being in ſuch Caſe *fallen in*, by the Death of *Henry* without Iſſue of his firſt Marriage, the *whole ſettled Eſtate* muſt go over to *Theophilus* under ſuch a *Conſtruction* of the Will, And by the *expreſs Words* of it, He could take no Intereſt in any of the *Reſt*.

IF the Queſtion had ariſen between the Iſſue Male of *Henry*, which he might have happened to have by a *ſecond* Wife; could it poſſibly be imagined to have been intended by the Teſtator, that in *ſuch* a Caſe, *Henry*'s Sons by a ſecond Wife ſhould be *totally diſinherited?* And yet they *muſt* have been ſo, if the Reverſion of the ſettled Eſtate paſſed by this Deviſe.

If *Audley* had died without Iſſue Male, whilſt there were Sons or Male Deſcendants of *Henry* by a *ſecond* Marriage, in being; Can it be imagined that the Teſtator ever intended that *James* and his Iſſue Male ſhould take the ſettled Eſtate, in *Excluſion of the Eldeſt Branch* of the Family? And yet He *would* have done ſo, after *Henry*'s Death without Iſſue of his firſt Marriage, *if the* REVERSION *of it paſſed* by the Will.

Or if there had been no Iſſue at all of either *Henry* or *Audley*; Can it be imagined that he intended to *diſinherit James?*

The Conſequence is too manifeſt to bear an Argument, if it be but attended to, what *Abſurdities* muſt follow from conſtruing the Reverſion to paſs. The Teſtator manifeſtly puts the *deviſed* Eſtate in *Oppoſition* to the *ſettled* Eſtate. He plainly means to deviſe only his *Lands in Poſſeſſion:* And He directs that if ever *James* ſhall come to the Poſſeſſion of the *ſettled* Eſtate, the *deviſed Lands* ſhall then go over to *Theophilus.* And the Conſtruction cannot be varied by the *Event:* We muſt conſtrue it juſt in the *ſame* Manner, as if *Henry had* left Children by a *ſecond* Marriage; or the ſettled Eſtate *had* fallen in to *James.*

It is plain that the Teſtator did NOT *intend* to deviſe the REVERSION of the Lands compriſed in the Settlement made upon the Marriage of *Henry.* Probably, He himſelf, or the Perſon who drew his Will, did not imagine that he had any *Intereſt in* or *Power over* thoſe SETTLED Lands. But it is plain, at leaſt, that He *meant* and had then in *Contemplation,* ONLY the *Lands* whereof he was ſeiſed in Fee in POSSESSION.

He deſcribed ſeveral Lands *nominatim*; and others, *as well as He then could:* But as He could not be minute and *particular* in ſuch Deſcription, it was thought proper to add *General Words.* The Lands He meant to deviſe, were either in the County of *Tyrone,* or of *Meath*; but, it being then uncertain to Him, in *which* County they lay, He ſays "in them *or either* of them:" But ſtill, the whole Deſcription is *Local*; And *Locality* has been conſtrued to mean *Lands* only. Here, the Deſcription is tied up to *Lands:* The former part of the Deviſe ſpecifies them particularly by Name; And the General Sweeping Words are only deſcriptive of *Lands*; "All "other the Lands Tenements and Hereditaments in the ſaid Coun- "ties &c." If it had been intended to have carried *Eſtates,* the Drawer of the Will would have added, "And all his *Eſtates* "whereof He or any Perſon in Truſt for him, were ſeiſed in Fee, "in Poſſeſſion, Remainder, or Reverſion;" that is, He would have thrown in a ſweeping Clauſe to carry *Eſtates in* the Lands, as well as the *Lands themſelves.*

An *Annuity* is given to *Olivia,* payable out of the *ſaid Lands* deviſed: And there are Powers given to whichever of his Sons ſhou'd be ſeiſed of an Eſtate or Uſe for Life in the *ſaid Lands,* to commit Waſte, ſettle Jointures, and make Leaſes; which Powers (as I before obſerved) are applicable to *Poſſeſſions* only.

4

But

But theſe minute and critical Obſervations ſerve only to weaken the Argument: Since there are, in this Will, *ſufficient* GENERAL *Words*, which expreſſly and clearly ſhew that the Teſtator had *no* Intention to include the Reverſion of the ſettled Eſtate in his Will, as much as if He had uſed *particular* Words and Expreſſions to declare it directly and explicitly.

In the Caſe of *Coryton* v. *Hellier*, the Teſtator omitted to add the Words "if he ſhall ſo long live," to the Eſtate which He gave to his Son for 99 Years: And yet Lord *Hardwicke* conſtrued it, that it muſt mean not an abſolute Term of Ninety-nine Years, but an Eſtate for 99 Years *qualified by that Reſtriction*, "*if* he ſhould ſo "long live;" Becauſe it ſo appeared upon the Face of the Will conſidered in *all it's Parts* and *taken all together*.

But *this* Caſe is ſtronger; Becauſe it appears clearly upon the very *Words* of the whole Will taken together, that there can be no Doubt of the Teſtator's Intention "That the *Reverſion* of the Settled Eſtate ſhould NOT be included in it; But only the Lands which He had in *Poſſeſſion*." And this makes an End of the Queſtion, upon the FUNDAMENTAL MERITS of the Caſe.

Mr. Juſt. DENISON, having been abſent during the Argument, declined giving any Opinion; But ſeemed ſatisfied with what Lord *Mansfield* had ſaid.

Mr. Juſt. FOSTER ſaid He had made ſome Obſervations upon the Will; But Lord *Mansfield* had gone through it ſo fully, that He needed only to declare his entire Concurrence in the ſame Opinion.

Mr. Juſt. WILMOT alſo entirely concurred; and wondered how any One could entertain any Doubt about it, It being as clear, He ſaid, upon the *whole Tenor and Complexion of the Will*, as the ſtrongeſt *expreſs negative* Clauſe could have made it.

Per Cur.

JUDGMENT REVERSED.

A Writ of Error was brought in the Houſe of Lords: And their Lordſhips confined the Counſel, to ſpeak to the Conſtruction of the Will, *firſt*.

After hearing *that* Queſtion argued, Their Lordſhips aſked the Opinion of the Judges; who were All unanimous "That the *Re-* "*verſion* was NOT INTENDED *to paſs*:" And thereupon, their Lordſhips

Lordſhips, on the 7th of *May* 1760, unanimouſly *affirmed* the *Judgment of Reverſal.*

As neither the Court of King's Bench, nor the Houſe of Lords took into Conſideration the *Points of Law* upon which the Leſſors of the Plaintiff "having or not having a good Legal Eſtate" depended, It would have been to no Purpoſe to report the Reaſonings uſed at the *Bar*, upon thoſe Points.

Note. By the Court's having *refuſed to adjourn* the Argument of this Verdict, the final Judgment of the Houſe of Lords was obtained ſo ſoon: And a Cauſe which held a great many Years in *Ireland*, went through the Court of King's Bench and the Houſe of Lords here, within the Space of about ſix Months.

Stoteſbury *verſ.* Smith.

THIS was a Writ of Error upon a Judgment given in *White-Chapel* Court, for the Plaintiff there.

The Declaration ſtates That One *Joſhua Redſhaw* had ſued out a *Capias* from the Court of Common Pleas, againſt One *Cooper Stanton*; and that a Writ iſſued accordingly againſt the ſaid *Cooper Stanton*, directed to the Sheriff of *Middleſex &c*, returnable *&c*; And that before the Return of the ſaid Writ, a Warrant was iſſued by the Sheriff, directed to *Miles Smith* One of his Bailiffs, (the Plaintiff below) to arreſt the ſaid *Cooper Stanton*; By Virtue whereof, the ſaid *Miles Smith* did arreſt the ſaid *Cooper Stanton.*

That the ſaid *Cooper Stanton* being ſo in Cuſtody of the ſaid *Miles Smith*, the ſaid *Stoteſbury* (the now Plaintiff in Error) undertook and promiſed to *Smith*, IN CONSIDERATION that the ſaid *Miles Smith* would *accept* of the ſaid *Stoteſbury* and of One *Antony Rippon* to be and *become Bail* for the ſaid *Cooper Stanton*, "that he "the ſaid *Stoteſbury* would well and faithfully pay to the ſaid *Miles* "*Smith* the Sum of 6 Guineas and a half, when and aſſoon as the "ſaid *Cooper Stanton* ſhould pay the Sum of 15 Guineas to him the "ſaid *Stoteſbury*."

Then *Smith*, in his Declaration, avers That He took the ſaid Bail accordingly, for *Stanton*; *viz.* the ſaid *Antony Rippon* and *Stoteſbury*; and that *Cooper Stanton* had paid to the ſaid *Stoteſbury* the Sum of 15 Guineas; but that *Stoteſbury* had not paid the 6 Guineas and a half to him the ſaid *Miles Smith*, according to his ſaid Promiſe and Undertaking.

There

There was another Count in the Declaration for 99 *s.* had and received by the Defendant *Stotesbury* for the Use of the Plaintiff *Smith.*

Upon *Non Assumpsit* pleaded, A General Verdict was given for the Plaintiff below; and *entire* Damages for 99 *s.* and a Judgment thereupon: And upon that Judgment, this Writ of Error was brought.

Mr. *Gould*, who was Counsel for the Plaintiff in Error, Objected " That the Contract is founded upon an *illegal Consideration:* And " consequently, as the Damages are *entire*, if One of the Counts " be bad, it is bad for the *Whole.*"

Now this Contract is in the Nature of an EXTORTION: It was a Consideration required by *Smith* for doing what the Duty of his Office *obliged* Him to do. He was *obliged* to accept Bail without any Reward or Gratuity: And any Promise " to give either," is an illegal Consideration, and *quasi* Extortion. The Cases of *Bridge* v. *Cage Cro. Jac.* 103. and *Badow* v. *Salter*, Sir *William Jones* 65. are both of them in Point, to prove this.

Wherefore He prayed that the Judgment might be reversed.

Mr. *Aspinall contra*, for the Defendant in Error—It is objected that this Contract was unlawful, " Because the Officer was to have " this Money for doing what it was his *Duty* to have done without " it."

But at *Common Law*, the Officer was *not* obliged to admit him to Bail. And the *Stat.* of 23 *H.* 6. *c.* 10. which obliges him to do it upon reasonable Sureties, is a PRIVATE Act of Parliament, and cannot be taken Advantage of it, without being *particularly pleaded.* In Proof of which, He cited a Case which is expressly so in Point; namely, *Benson* v. *Welby*, 2 *Sand.* 154: Where the Court unanimously agreed it to be a settled Point, " that this is a private Statute, and that they could not take Notice of it, unless specially " pleaded."

If the Officer was *not* obliged to admit *Stanton* to Bail, *then* there might be a sufficient Reason why *Stotesbury* might have an Interest in having the Custody of the Prisoner. In the Case of *Barkly and Gibbs* v. *Kempstow*, *Cro. Eliz.* 123, the Consideration of the Defendant's Promise to keep the Prisoner safely, was holden a good One; though it was the Gaoler's Duty.

It does not appear that *Stotesbury* was a *proper* Person to be Bail: And *if not*, then the Officer was liable to suffer for accepting him; and consequently, had *Reason* to require an Indemnification.

But on *this Plea*, the Consideration must be taken to be legal, *after* Verdict. *Battersey*'s Case in *Winch* 48. proves this. For as the Defendant might there have given the unlawful Imprisonment in *Evidence*, if in Fact, it had been unlawful; so here, *if* the Contract *had been illegal*, they might have *proved* it upon the Trial, to have been so.

Mr. *Gould*'s Cases were plain *Extortion*; because there the Officer took Money for doing what was his *Duty*: Whereas here, it was *not* his Duty to take Bail; At least, the Court can *not take* it to be so, unless the Statute had been *pleaded*.

Mr. *Gould* in Reply—It's being *after Verdict* will not help it: Because it is Extortion upon the *Face* of the Declaration.

The 23 *H.* 6. *c.* 10. can not be considered as a *private* Act which the Court cannot take Notice of, unless *pleaded*: It is a *General* Law; And the Officer *was* obliged to let *Stanton* to Bail. That Act was *declaratory* of the *Common* Law.

Mr. *Aspinall*'s Cases are only Promises "to *indemnify*:" This is a *Reward*; Which is *Extortion*.

Lord MANSFIELD—The Man who was arrested, and gave the 15 Guineas to procure the Bail, is injured by Both these contending Parties: They have Both acted wrong towards Him.

But though both Parties are equally faulty, *in pari delicto potior est Conditio Defendentis*. A Court of Justice ought not to relieve a Plaintiff, upon a Ground of Action *immoral* or *illegal*.

Where a Person is arrested for Debt; Either the Officer is not obliged to admit him to Bail, *at all*; Or he is obliged to admit him to Bail, as of *Duty*; Or he may use his *Discretion*. Now, in *any* of these Cases, it is *Oppression* to take *Money*, for doing what he *ought* to do; even though it be the mere using his Discretion, "whether "he should admit him to Bail, or not."

Therefore, it is not necessary to meddle with any Questions about the *Stat.* of 23 *H.* 6.

There is no Pretence for our presuming the Consideration to be legal, because it is after a Verdict; Whatever We might do, in a Matter that stood indifferent. For here it does *not* stand indifferent: It is fully stated upon the *Face* of the Declaration; and manifestly appears to Us to be *illegal*.

Mr. Just. DENISON was of the same Opinion, " That this was an " *illegal Consideration*;" and said, He never saw such a Demand stated in a Court of Justice. The Officer would have been liable to an *Attachment* for this Fact, if he had been complained of for it.

As to the *Verdict*, That can never be a Reason for presuming the Consideration to be legal; when it is fully stated in the Declaration, and appears manifestly to be *illegal*.

As to the *Statute* of 23 *H*. 6. *c*. 10. It was made to prevent the Oppressions of Sheriffs and Bailiffs; and obliges them to let Persons arrested by them, out of Prison, upon reasonable Sureties of sufficient Persons. But at *Common* Law, the Defendant was to be let to Bail in such an Action as *this*.

However, be the Bailiff's Duty as it may, yet it is certainly oppressive to take *Money* for doing it. If this was to be permitted, it would introduce such a Scene of Oppression and Injustice, as would be insufferable.

Mr. *Gould's* Cases cited from *Cro. Jac.* and Sir *William Jones*, shew the Caution of Courts of Justice, not to endure the Oppression of Officers of Justice: And this Case is ten Times worse than the Case of the Promise made to the Special Bailiff, in Sir *William Jones* 65.

Mr. Just. FOSTER concurred in thinking that it would be a great Inlet to Oppression, if such a Consideration as this, should be established as legal.

The Case is not oppressive merely with respect to the *Friends* of the Person in Custody, or others indifferent to him: But, even an *Enemy* to the Defendant may, by these Means, get him into his Hands, merely in Order to surrender him when he is become Bail for him.

We should have *punished* this Officer for such a Piece of Behaviour, if a Complaint had been made to Us against him for it: And shall We help and assist him to obtain the End of it, and carry it into complete Execution in a Court of Justice? Surely, not.

Mr.

Mr. Just. WILMOT said He thought this to be a most shameful and scandalous Action.

It would be a strange thing, if We should assist him in establishing a Contract grounded upon a Consideration, for which he would have been *punished* by this Court, if he had been indicted for Extortion, or complained of by Way of Motion for an Attachment.

As to his not being *obliged* to admit the Man to Bail—The 23 *H.* 6. *c.* 10. is so far indeed a *private* Law that it must be PLEADED in Cases arising immediately and directly upon it: But I will take Notice *judicially*, That an Officer *is obliged* to admit a Man to Bail, in such an Action as this, if good and sufficient and unexceptionable Bail be offered him. It is his *Duty* to do it. And it is the Principle of the *Common* Law, that an Officer ought not to take *Money* for doing his *Duty*. It is his Duty to take *good* and *sufficient* Bail; though he is not obliged to accept *insufficient*.

But such a Contract as this is, upon a Promise made to the Officer, by One of the Bail, "that if the Officer would accept of Him-"self and One *Antony Rippon* as Bail for the Man, He, in Con-"sideration of this, would pay him Six Guineas and a half when "the Man should pay him Fifteen;" (whereby it manifestly appears to be agreed amongst them, that *Stanton* was to give *Stotesbury* 15 Guineas, to become Bail for him; And *Stotesbury*, when he should receive the 15 Guineas, was to give the Officer 6 Guineas and a half out of it;) is grounded upon a Consideration, which is *manifestly illegal*. Therefore the Judgment ought to be reversed.

Per Cur.
JUDGMENT REVERSED.

Wednesday 6th *February* 1760.

Rex *vers.* Inhabitants of Weyhill.

TWO Justices removed *John Pollard West*, from *Corfe Castle* in *Dorsetshire* to *Weyhill* in *Hants*: And the Sessions, upon an Appeal, confirmed their Order.

The Facts were stated by the Sessions, to appear to them, on the Evidence of the said Pauper, (the only Witness produced on either Side,) to be as follows; *viz.* That *Thomas West* deceased, residing and being legally settled in *Corfe Castle*, about the Year 1711, had Issue the Pauper; who continued *there* with his Father, till he was about 8 Years of Age: At which Time, his Father being under Mis-

Misfortunes, *Robert Pyke* Esq; (since deceased) who then lived in the Parish of *Worth Matraverse* in the said County of *Dorset*, and to whom a small Estate that belonged to the said *Thomas West* the Father was then in Mortgage, took the said Pauper into his Family, FROM CHARITY, and gave him his Meat Drink Lodging and Clothes, while he continued with Him; which was about Two Years in the Parish of *Worth Matraverse* aforesaid, and afterwards Four Years more in the said Parish of *Weyhill*, (to which Parish the said Mr. *Pyke* and his Family removed.)

That neither at or before the Time of the said *Pyke's* taking the Pauper into his Family, nor at any Time after, was there *any* CONTRACT between the said Parties, in relation to the Pauper's *Service* of the said Mr. *Pyke* or his *Continuance* with Him, or to any *Wages* or *other Gratuity* to be paid him therefore.

That during the Pauper's Continuance with the said Mr. *Pyke*, He was employed in running of Errands and doing whatsoever the said Mr. *Pyke* or his Servants thought fit to bid him. That *no Wages* were ever paid or given him. And that, in the *Pauper's Apprehension*; He was, during all the Time aforesaid, *at* LIBERTY TO QUIT the said Mr. *Pyke*; Or the said *Mr. Pyke to turn him off*; as either Party should think fit.

That the Pauper quitted the said Mr. *Pyke* and the said Parish of *Weyhill*, after *Four Years* Residence there as aforesaid; and hath done no Act, to gain a Settlement, except as aforesaid.

The Sessions were of Opinion, "That, at this *Distance of Time*, " a *Hiring for a Year*, agreeable to the Statute, between the said " Mr. *Pyke* and the Pauper or his Father, ought to be PRESUMED;" and DO PRESUME the same accordingly: For which Reason *only*, they are of Opinion and do adjudge that the Settlement of the said *John Pollard West*, the Pauper, is in the said Parish of *Weyhill*; and therefore confirm the Order of the two Justices.

Mr. *Glynn*, who moved to quash these Orders, said That the Sessions were mistaken in their Opinion; and had no Right to make this *Presumption*, contrary to the Evidence.

Mr. *Gould*, on Behalf of *Corfe Castle* Parish, now shewed Cause against quashing them.

Upon a regular Service for above a Year, a *Hiring* shall be *presumed*: It was so, in the Case *between the Parishes of* * *Crediton* and *Wincanton*. In the present Case, the Lad continued *Six* Years in the Service.

* *Rex v. Inhabitants of Wincaunton*, M. & H. 1750. 24 G. 2. B. R.

Wages are not neceſſary: So the Caſe juſt now cited proves. The *Pauper's Apprehenſion* does not vary the Caſe: And ſo the ſame cited Caſe proves. The only Witneſs ſpeaks to a Tranſaction when he was *but* 8 *Years old.* And He *might* have been hired out *by his Father*, though not by Himſelf.

Mr. *Norton contra*, for *Weyhill* Pariſh, and for quaſhing the Orders.

A *Hiring* is as eſſential as a Service. And if the Juſtices have drawn a *wrong Judgment* upon the Facts ſtated, the Court will quaſh their Order. It is manifeſt, there was no Hiring at all: Mr. *Pyke* took the Pauper into his Family, FROM CHARITY.

The COURT were clear that this was *no Hiring* at all, *no Contract*: But he was taken OUT OF CHARITY, a Child 8 Years old, to run on Errands and do whatever he was bid; and left Mr. *Pyke*, when he came to be 14 and capable of doing more Service. And it is expreſſly ſtated "That there was * NO *Contract*."

* *V. Rex v. Inhabitants of Berwick St. John*, P. 1760. *B. R. poſt.* holden to be a Hiring for a Year; though the Contract was *not quite explicit*.

Indeed where there is a *Hiring ſtated*, the Court will preſume it to have been a regular One; (unleſs the contrary appears:) And *that* was the Caſe of *Wincaunton*. A *General Hiring* was there *ſtated*: But here was *no Hiring at all.*

Per Cur. unanimouſly,
RULE MADE ABSOLUTE, to quaſh Both Orders.

Saturday 9th *February* 1760.

Rex *verſ.* Spragg and Another.

THE Defendants had been CONVICTED of a *Conſpiracy* to charge a Perſon with a *Capital* Felony: And the *Record* of Conviction had been removed up hither by *Certiorari*; but *not* the PERSONS of the Defendants. And Mr. Serj. *Davy* being ready on behalf of the Defendants, to move *in Arreſt of Judgment*;

Mr. *Gould*, *pro Rege*, objected to his going on with the Motion; For that the Defendants ought to be PERSONALLY PRESENT. And He cited the Caſe of *Rex* v. *Elizabeth Nicholls*, (2 *Strange* 1227.) which was exactly the ſame Offence as this; and it was agreed "That *after Conviction*, the perſonal Preſence of the Defendant is "neceſſary upon ſuch a Motion as this."

Serj. *Davy*, for the Defendants, attempted to explain away this Rule; and urged that the Defendants were ſafe in Cuſtody already, and

and therefore amenable to the Juſtice of the Court; and offered that the Defendants Clerk in Court ſhould undertake to bring the Defendants up, at the Defendants own Expence, in Caſe the Objection ſhould not prevail.

But the Secondary of the Crown-Office, being appealed to, alledged "That the Rule was as Mr. *Gould* had aſſerted."

The COURT held this to be a fixed and invariable Rule of Practice in this Court, "That the Defendants muſt, *after Conviction* of "ſuch an Offence as this, be *preſent in Court*, if they would move "in Arreſt of Judgment."

Serj. *Davy* finding the Opinion of the Court and the Allegation of the Secondary of the Crown-Office to be ſo directly againſt him, as to the abſolute Neceſſity of the *perſonal Preſence* of the Defendants, prayed a *Habeas Corpus* to bring up their Bodies; which was granted: And He * aſterwards renewed his Motion, and had the Defendants in Court. * V. poſt pa.

Note—This Caſe of a CONVICTION differs from that of a SPECIAL VERDICT; where the Preſumption of Innocence may be ſuppoſed to *continue*, and therefore the perſonal Preſence of the Defendant is *not* neceſſary at the Argument of it.

Foxcroft et al' Aſſignees of William Satterthwaite, a Bankrupt, *verſ.* Devonſhire & al'.

Monday 11th February 1760.

THIS Matter came before the Court upon a Motion for a *New Trial*, on the Ground of a *Miſdirection* by the Judge who tried the Cauſe.

It was an Action upon the Caſe, upon an *Indebitatus Aſſumpſit*, brought by the Plaintiffs againſt the Defendants, for Monies had and received by the Defendants, to the Uſe of the Plaintiffs as Aſſignees of the Bankrupt. To which, the Defendants pleaded the General Iſſue "That they did not undertake &c: And Iſſue was "joined thereon.

The Cauſe was tried at the *Lancaſter* Aſſizes, before Mr. Juſtice *Noel*. A Verdict was found for the Plaintiffs: And the Judge declared Himſelf *ſatisfied* with the Verdict.

It was admitted at the Trial, on the Part of the Defendants, "That *Satterthwaite* was a *Trader*:" The *Debt* of the petitioning Creditor

Creditor was alſo admitted; And ſo were the *Commiſſion*, and the *Aſſignment*. But they diſputed the *Act of Bankruptcy* ſuppoſed to have been committed by *Satterthwaite*.

The Action was brought for Money ariſing from the Sale of Goods conſigned by *Satterthwaite* to the Defendants *as* FACTORS for Him, (which they had long been,) and ſold by them as ſuch; Which Money was admitted to be in the Hands of the Defendants, and amounted to 5314 *l.* 17 *s.* 9 *d.* ½.

The Defendants, on the other Hand, had paid ſeveral Sums of Money upon *Satterthwaite*'s Draughts, and otherwiſe, to his Uſe and upon his Account.

The Plaintiffs, at the Trial, proved ſome *ſecret* Acts of Bankruptcy, by his being denied to his Creditors about *Chriſtmas* 1751: After which, He appeared again publickly as uſual, till about the Month of *Auguſt* following; (as was proved on the Part of the Defendants.) In *Auguſt* 1752, He totally ſtopt Payment: And thereupon, the Commiſſion was taken out. Theſe *ſecret Acts of Bankruptcy*, at *Chriſtmas* 1751, *over-reached the Conſignment* to the Defendants, the *Sale*, and the *Time when the Money was advanced* by them to the Uſe and Order of the Bankrupt. And the Counſel for the Plaintiffs produced a Series of * Letters from the Defendants to *Satterthwaite*, which fully proved, as they alledged, "That the "Defendants were *privy to his Inſolvency* at the *Time* when they "advanced the Money to his Uſe and Order."

* See theſe Letters *verbatim*, *poſt*

The Counſel for the Defendants would, at the Trial, have entered into the two following Points; *viz.* 1ſt. Whether the Defendants were not intitled, *as* FACTORS for *Satterthwaite*, to *retain* for the *general Balance* of their Account: 2dly. Whether they were not within the *Protection of the Statute* of 19 *G.* 2. *c.* 31. § 1. Which, after reciting "that Bankrupts frequently commit *ſecret* Acts of Bank-"ruptcy *unknown* to their Creditors and other Perſons with whom, "in the Courſe of Trade, they have Dealings and Tranſactions; and "after the Committing thereof, *continue* to appear publickly and "carry on their Trade and Dealings &c;" And after reciting "that "the permitting ſuch *ſecret* Acts of Bankruptcy to avoid and defeat "Payments *really and bonâ fide* made in the Caſes and under the "Circumſtances before mentioned, where the Perſons receiving the "ſame *had* NOT *Notice of or were privy to* ſuch Perſon's having "committed any Act of Bankruptcy, would be a great Diſcourage-"ment to Trade and Commerce, and a Prejudice to Credit in ge-"neral;" enacts that No Perſon who ſhall be *really and bonâ fide a Creditor* of any Bankrupt, for or in reſpect of any *Bill or Bills of Exchange really and bonâ fide* drawn, negotiated, or accepted by ſuch

4 Bankrupt

Bankrupt, in the *usual and ordinary Course of Trade and Dealing*, ſhall be liable to *refund or repay* to the Aſſignees of ſuch Bankrupt's Eſtate, any *Money* which before the *ſuing forth* of ſuch Commiſſion was *really and bonâ fide* and in the *uſual and ordinary* Courſe of Trade and Dealing, *received by ſuch Perſon of any ſuch Bankrupt*, before ſuch Time as the Perſon receiving the ſame ſhall *know underſtand* or *have Notice* " that He is *become* a Bankrupt or that He is in *inſolvent* " *Circumſtances.*"

But the Counſel for the Plaintiffs objected " That this Tranſaction " of the Defendants was FRAUDULENT; For that they plainly *knew* " and were *apprized* that *Satterthwaite was inſolvent* at the *Time* " when the Effects came to their Hands."

The Jury were of this Opinion; and gave a Verdict for the Plaintiffs, for the *whole* Money, except *Commiſſion* and *Charges of Sale*.

This *previous* Point concerning the FRAUD having been ſtrongly inſiſted upon by the Counſel for the Plaintiffs, at the Trial, the Counſel for the Defendants were thereby precluded from entering into *other* Points which they thought to be material for their Clients, and which They ſaid they were otherwiſe ready to have entered into at that Time. Upon this Precluſion they grounded their preſent Motion for a new Trial: For they alledged that the Jury had founded their Verdict upon *wrong Concluſions* drawn from the Evidence, and upon a *Miſtake of the Law*; and that the Defendants had been unjuſtly precluded from entering into the two preceding Points, or any Thing elſe that might have been material to their Defence.

And they now inſiſted, 1ſt. That the Defendants had a GENERAL *Lien*, as *Factors*, upon the Bankrupt's Goods conſigned to them; 2dly. That they were *Purchaſers* of them for a *valuable Conſideration, without Notice* that *Satterthwaite* was become a Bankrupt or in inſolvent Circumſtances; 3dly. That in *this* Action (upon an *Indebitatus Aſſumpſit,*) it is not in the Power of the Aſſignees, to affirm the Contract *in part*, and deny it *in part*; But if they *affirm it in part*, they affirm it *in toto*. Now here, they *do affirm it in part*; They affirm part of their Conduct, *as Factors:* Therefore they *can not diſaffirm* the Reſt of their Conduct *as Factors.*

They ſaid that the preſent Verdict would not ſtand in their Way; Becauſe FRAUD is a *Concluſion* of LAW, from Facts: And therefore the *Court*, and *not the Jury*, are the *proper Judges* " *What* Facts " do import Fraud," and " *What* Facts do not import Fraud." And they denied that the Letters or any part of the Facts given in Evidence were at all *unfair:* At leaſt, it could never be ſaid, " that " they ſupported a Concluſion of FRAUD."

 This

This Case was argued on *Thursday* 24th of *January* last, by Mr. *Norton* for the Plaintiffs, who shewed Cause against setting aside the Verdict and granting a New Trial upon Payment of Costs; and by Mr. *Winn*, *è contrà*, for the Defendants, who had moved for a New Trial.

The COURT having taken Time to consider it—

Lord MANSFIELD now delivered their Resolution.

This Matter came before the Court, upon a Motion for a *New Trial*, on the Ground of a *Misdirection* by the Judge who tried the Cause.

It was an Action upon the Case upon an *Indebitatus Assumpsit*, for Monies had and received by the Defendants, to the Use of the Plaintiffs as Assignees of the Bankrupt. The Defendants pleaded the General Issue. And the Cause was tried at *Lancaster* Assizes, before Mr. Justice *Noel*.

It was admitted at the Trial, That *Satterthwaite* the Bankrupt was a Trader: And the Debt of the petitioning Creditor, the Commission and the Assignment were likewise all admitted.

The Action was brought for Monies arising from the Sale of Goods which had been consigned by the Bankrupt, to the Defendants as Factors for Him, and sold by them as such; which Money was admitted to be in the Defendants Hands, and amounted to 5314 *l.* 17 *s.* 9 *d.* ½.

It appeared that the Defendants had paid several Sums of Money, to *Satterthwaite*'s Use, upon Bills drawn upon them by Him, and otherwise.

The Plaintiffs (the Assignees under the Commission) *proved some* SECRET *Acts of Bankruptcy* to have been committed by *Satterthwaite* about *Christmas* 1751; namely, his being denied to his Creditors. On the other Side, it was proved that He soon *appeared again publickly as usual*; and continued to do so, till about the Month of *August* following, (1752.) But in *August* 1752, He stopt Payment: And thereupon, the Commission was taken out.

These secret Acts of Bankruptcy committed at *Christmas* 1751, *over-reached the Consignment* of the Goods, the *Sale* of them, the *Receipt* of the Monies for which they were sold, and likewise the *Time when the Defendants advanced the Monies* to the Use and Order of the Bankrupt.

It

It was insisted by the Counsel for the Defendants, That from the Nature of the present Action, an *Indebitatus Assumpsit*, the Defendants, being FACTORS, ought to be allowed not only for their Commission and all Charges and Expences, but also *whatever Money they had paid on Account* of BILLS *drawn upon them by Satterthwaite*; And that the Plaintiffs in this Action could only recover the BALANCE of the *general* Account.

The Counsel for the Plaintiffs admitted that the Defendants were intitled to be allowed their *Commission* and all *Charges* and *Expences*, as Factors; but *not the Bills of Exchange* drawn by *Satterthwaite*, which they had paid *subsequent to the Act of Bankruptcy*.

THIS *Question* was agreed to be *reserved*, (if it should be necessary to have Recourse to it,) as a Point for the future Consideration and Determination of the Judge who tried the Cause.

But the Counsel for the Plaintiffs insisted on a *Preliminary* Point; *viz.* "That the Defendants were guilty of a FRAUD, in paying "these Bills of Exchange drawn upon them by the Bankrupt:" Which *Preliminary* Point of FRAUD was sufficient to *destroy* any Right that the Defendants might *otherwise claim* (supposing the Transaction had *not* been fraudulent,) *to an Allowance of the Money paid in discharge of them*; and, consequently, to *preclude* them *from entering at all* into the *Question abovementioned*. For if it should be admitted on the Part of the Plaintiffs, "that this Action of *Indebitatus Assumpsit* affirmed the Contract," Yet if their Payment of the Bills was *fraudulent*, it would at once put an End to their Claim of an Allowance of the Money as *fraudulently* paid. They granted that in Case the Defendants should appear *not* to have been guilty of any Fraud, but to have paid the Bills fairly and honestly, they would then have a Right to enter into the Point reserved (as above) for future Consideration: But they insisted that upon Supposition that in a *Common* Case, this Sort of Action *would confirm the Contract*, so as to make the Consignment, Sale, and Payment of the Bills to be considered as *before* any Act of Bankruptcy committed; and consequently, that the Defendants would be *intitled to retain what they had paid upon the Bills*; (For every thing that could be alledged by the Defendants, must, *pro hac vice*, be *admitted*, upon a previous Bar to their going into the Question;) Yet the Bar of FRAUD would *destroy* any Demand they could have upon that Account.

And the FRAUD which they *charged* upon the Defendants was this, "That they were PRIVY to *Satterthwaite*'s Insolvency, at the "*Time* when they advanced the Monies to discharge his Bills."

Upon this *preliminary* Point *only*, of FRAUD, It was left to the Jury: And upon *this* Point *only*, they found their Verdict. Upon hearing all the Evidence, They were of Opinion " That the Transaction *was fraudulent* on the Part of the Defendants;" And they gave a Verdict for the Plaintiffs, for the whole Money; deducting only the Commission due to the Defendants, and the Expences of the Sale of the Goods.

THOUGH the *Ground* of the Verdict should be wrong, Yet if it clearly appeared to Us *now*, " That, upon the whole, *no Injustice* " had been done to the Defendants;" or if it clearly appeared to " Us *now*, " That the Plaintiffs, by *another Form of Action*, could " recover all they have got by this Verdict;" We think the Court ought not to grant a new Trial. But if *Injustice* be done to the Defendants by the present Verdict; and if it be *not* certain and clear " that the Plaintiffs might have equal Redress, and recover as " much, by *another Form of Action*; then We ought to grant a new Trial.

Two Points have been argued, and urged on the Part of the Plaintiffs.

1st Collateral Point.

1st. That clearly the Defendants were not to be allowed to retain for the Bills: Because (1st.) They were not paid till *after* an Act of Bankruptcy; (2dly.) *This* Action (of *Indebitatus Assumpsit*) only admits the Sale of the Goods, and Nothing else but the Agency of the Defendants in *that* single respect; and (3dly.) *If* it admitted *every* Thing, so as to put the Assignees in the very Condition the Bankrupt would have been, had *He* brought this Action, Yet a *Factor* has *no Lien* for Items of a * *general* Account, (his Lien being confined to his *Commission* and *Expences* about the particular Goods.)

* V. ante 494.

These Points have not been at all considered in this Action: And therefore it is enough if they are *doubtful*. They went off, upon the preliminary Question of the *Fraud* being taken up and pursued; and were never afterwards taken into any further Consideration, at the Trial.

We are not clear that this Action of *Indebitatus Assumpsit* does not affirm the Power of the Bankrupt and the Contract, throughout the *whole* Transaction. Where such an Action is brought by Assignees of a Bankrupt's Effects against a *Vendee* of Goods, It affirms the Sale, and also the *Payment to the Bankrupt* of any Part of the Price. It is agreed here, that it admits the *Consequence* of the Defendants being Factors; and allows a Lien for *Commission* and *Expences*.

" That a *Factor* has also a *Lien* upon Goods consigned, (*whilst* " they *remain in his Possession*,) for Items of a *general* Account with his

" his Principal," has been * solemnly determined. However, The present Case differs from the Case of *Krutzer* v. *Wilcocks*, where it was so determined. For there, the Fact *remained in Possession of the Goods:* But here the Goods have been *sold*, and turned into *Money*. In *such* a Case, there never was a Doubt but that *mutual Items* of Account *might be set off:* The Demand and Recovery can only be for the Balance. Therefore it is impossible to say, that the Question the Defendants would have made upon this Point, had they been permitted, *may* not be very material. And if it *might* have been material to their Defence, they have a Right to have it tried and considered.

* In the Case of *Krutzer* v. *Wilcocks*.

2dly. Another Matter gone into at the Trial, and urged by the Counsel for the Plaintiffs, was, " That in an *Action of* Trover, the " Plaintiffs might certainly recover the Value of the Goods, *without* " making *any Allowance*."

2d Collateral Point.

Mr. *Winn* convinced me, That it would depend upon a Variety of Circumstances, (some of which He offered to lay before Us by Affidavit,) which were not gone into at the Trial, because the Counsel for the Defendants were stopped and cut short, by the Preliminary Bar of the Fraud, which was alone sufficient to invalidate their Claims as upon a fair Transaction.

I do not choose to say more particularly what may possibly assist the Defendants in an Action of Trover; because I would not prejudice the Matter: It is enough to say, " It does not sufficiently " appear to Us, that they could make *no* Defence to an Action of " Trover."

This makes it necessary to examine the Ground *of the Verdict*, which proceeded from the Direction given.

Principal Point.

I will admit " that the Evidence proved the Fact and every Con- " clusion deducible from it:" But I cannot think that the Fact so proved, or Conclusion so drawn, amounts to that Offence which the Law calls Fraud, to avoid the Debt. And in examining this Matter, We must remember, that, *pro hac vice*, the whole Transaction is admitted to be *before* any Act of Bankruptcy.

Mr. *Norton* rightly said, " That *Fraud* is *sometimes* mere Matter " of Fact; and *sometimes*, the Conclusion of Law from Facts."

So is High Treason. Levying War is mere Matter of Fact: Compassing the Death of the King is a legal Conclusion from Facts. So it is, almost, as to every other Offence.

Fraud often is a *mere Fact*; as when it depends (as on a Policy of Insurance, for Instance,) upon What the Party said or did: Or It may be, and often is a Question of *Law*.

Suppose a Creditor, *knowing* a Trader likely to break, *conceals* it from the Knowledge of other Creditors, till He gets, even by Threats of legal Process, Payment of his Debt *before* any direct Act of Bankruptcy; And the Assignees should insist this was a Fraud, and that he should refund: This is a Matter of *Law*; And the *Law* would say "that this was *not* fraudulent."

Suppose a Man *bonâ fide*, lends Money to a Trader upon a *Mortgage*, after an Act of Bankruptcy *without* Notice; and *then knowing* of the Commission of Bankrupt and Assignment, gets in an old Term, even for little or no Consideration; And the Assignees bring an Ejectment; And it becomes a Question "Whether this be a "Fraud, or not;" This is a Matter of *Law*: And the Law will say "It is *no* Fraud;' For the Mortgagee had a Right to do this.

The Evidence of Fraud in *this* Case, as stated by the Report, are the following Letters—The first is dated, *Bristol*, *5th May* 1752, Signed "*Devonshire* and *Reeves*," and directed to *William Satterthwaite*. "We wish You had been *open*, and *told us in Time* how "Your Affairs stood—It appears to us very evidently, you have "risqued your Reputation and Credit on the Faith of those S. Do "but consider where You must have been in point of Reputation, "had We done otherwise than we did—It is now over; and we "will not do any Thing that should lessen your Credit—Therefore "ship not an Ounce of Goods more, till your Affairs are settled."

The next Letter is dated *Bristol*, *15th May* 1752, Signed "*De*-"*vonshire* and *Reeve*," and directed to *William Satterthwaite* Merchant in *Bristol*; and contains the following Passage—"We can not "help being *uneasy* to think you have drawn on Us again for 120*l*. "Really You will make Us let your Bills *go back protested*, in spight "of our Inclinations. We will pay this; but take Notice—*don't* "*draw another*: We friendly hint it."

The next Letter is dated *25th June* 1752, signed and directed as above; and is thus—"*William Satterthwaite*, * Esteemed "Friend—We really *fear* these Proceedings will *greatly hurt your* "*Credit* in the Eyes of every judicious Person: It is very natural to "think, that will be the Consequence. For our part, we would "make a thousand Shifts, rather than trifle with our Reputation, as "You do with Yours—It's a Matter well worth your serious Con-"sideration."

* They were Quakers.

" *P.S.* Inclosed We return You *Liebenrood*'s Draft 150 *l.* which, " with one Shilling Postage, place to our Credit. This is such a " Thing we never did before, nor ever will again."

The next Letter is dated 27th *June* 1752, signed as before, and directed to *William Satterthwaite.* After referring to the last, it goes on thus—" In this last Letter, * Thee mentionest nothing of " remitting for *Liebenrood*'s Bill, which Thee ordered us to send " for from *London* 4 Days before due, (which we did, and re- " turned thee in our last;) tho' Thee promised us faithfully to re- " mit for the same, last 6th Day was a Week: And having had " sundry Letters that take no Notice thereabout, We can not help " thinking and saying that thee *trifles with thy Creditors and Us.* " We are so much in Want of Money *as Thee canst possibly be*; and " had we thought, Thee wouldst have treated us in this Manner, " We would not have advanced one Quarter of the Sum, to be " allowed 10 *l. per Cent.* The Disappointment to Us gives more " Uneasiness than all the Profits of a Year's Trade will do Us."

* *V.* the Note on last Page.

The next Letter is dated 14th *July* the same Year, and signed as before; And is as follows—" *William Satterthwaite*, Esteemed " Friend, So much for your Affairs in and under our Care; which " shall be managed with all Care and Frugality.

" But what next We say, *appears to Us in a very odd light*—For " *Edward Wilcox* has been with us, and says you have *made over* " *our Goods* on the *Sarah* and *Martha.* If true, gives us *such Ideas* " *that we dare not put Pen to Paper to say our Sentiments.* If you " send Us any more Bills—If ever We do return a Bill, We *will* " *return your's.*"

The next Letter is the 28th *July* the same Year, signed as before, and is as follows—" *William Satterthwaite*,—The *Sarah* and " *Martha*, your ¼ths. The *Carolina*, how much? Tell Us: For " *you must secure Us, by a Bill of Sale of Each*,—that is your Parts—, " unless you send here some *Security.*—Say, your Father *Moss*— " join in a Bond, or some good Man. Claimants will be made " upon Us, for their Proportions of Cargoes We have sold; as " *Touchetts* did of the Rice. We are willing to stand by You as " far as We can with Prudence: but *an undoubted Counter-Security* " *We must have*—We *dread the Consequences* of these repeated " Strokes—We *very much suspect, You have not the Money*—We " *must have your Affairs cleared up.* Whatever *you* are, *We are* " *almost broken-hearted, to see how you are going on*, and *have of* " *late.* And what will be the Consequence, if you are worth " 3000 *l*? We know, and have seen the Consequence elsewhere."

Some

Some vague Suspicions beside, have been mentioned at the Bar, by the Counsel for the Plaintiffs: as, that they were All of them Quakers, and endeavouring to play into Each other's Hands, to the Prejudice of *Satterthwaite*'s other Creditors; That *Sattherthwaite* had broke before; That all the Bills were after *May*; (which the Other Side denies.)

But as I proceed upon *allowing* the Evidence to *prove* the Conclusions contended for, It is only necessary to examine what those *Conclusions* are. The Report says, that " a false Credit was given " the Bankrupt:" *i. e.* He would have broke openly, unless they had lent him Money. The Counsel for the Plaintiffs say, the Defendants lent him Money, to keep him from failing, *till* his Ships and Goods might come Home, consigned to Themselves, or even to the Bankrupt's own Hands: Whereas if a Commission had issued *before* that Time, the *Assignees* would have had them.

It was left to the Jury, That if they believed, from the Evidence, that the Defendants *knew* or *understood* the Bankrupt's Circumstances to be *insolvent* at the *Time* they paid his Bills; they might find against them, *upon the Ground of* FRAUD. And they found in the Affirmative.

* V. § 1. Had the Question turned upon the Validity of a Payment made *after* an Act of Bankruptcy committed, within the * Act of 19 G. 2. *c.* 32. (which was One of the Points made at the Trial,) the Direction would have been quite agreeable to the Terms of that Act. But, as the Question was, " Whether, supposing the whole " Transaction *before* any Act of Bankruptcy committed, the Defen- " dants were to be excluded from claiming Satisfaction for the " Money they had advanced upon *Satterthwaite*'s Bills, by Reason " of their Fraud in advancing it;"—We are all of Opinion " that " the *Direction was a* MISTAKE."

It is NO *Fraud*, for a Factor, *knowing* the Circumstances of his Principal to be desperate, and *believing* that he must break unless he can procure Credit, to *advance Money* upon his Bills, *to save him from an immediate Failure.* On the Contrary, it is an honourable, friendly, and generous Act. *No Prejudice* can arise but to the *Lender* Himself. *He* may lose the Whole, or the greatest Part of the Money so advanced: But the *Principal*'s Estate, if he breaks, is by so much a *Gainer*; or *some particular Creditors*, to whom this Money has been *paid*, are *Gainers*. *If*, by this Assistance, the Principal has the good Luck to *stand his Ground*, He and *all* his Creditors are *benefited*: But *none* of his Creditors can *suffer* by the Advancement of Money to their Debtor. Many beneficial Instances of this kind have saved the most considerable Houses from Ruin.

If

If the Factor trusts that Effects of his Principal will come over from abroad consigned to him, by which Means he may *acquire a Lien* upon them for his Reimbursment, the Factor's Conduct is a little more prudent: But still it is free from all Colour of *Fraud*. It is the *usual Method* of Dealing between Principals and Factors in *good* Credit; the latter advance Money upon the Faith of Consignments: But when a Factor, knowing his Principal to be in *great Distress*, and in *immediate danger of failing*, advances Money upon the *Faith* "that Effects beyond Sea *will* come over consigned to him," He acts *meritoriously*.

The richest Man in Trade may be ruined, while his Effects are abroad, and not in his own Power, to answer immediate Demands upon Him, (which was the Case of the *Woodwards*, who could not save themselves from failing; though they had sufficient to pay 30*s*. in the Pound.) But the Factor may actually save him by this Assistance, till they come Home: and yet the Factor himself runs a great Risque, and trusts to a *precarious* Security. For the Goods may in Fact be consigned originally to *Another*; Or The Consignment to Him may be *countermanded*; They may be *sold*; They may be *mortgaged*, or *burnt*, or *lost*, and never come into his Possession so as to give him any Lien: And it appears by the Letters that have been read, that in this very Case, *Satterthwaite* unworthily made over to other Persons part of the Goods to which the Defendants had trusted for their Security.

A *Mortgage* of Ships abroad, or of Cargoes upon the high Seas, by a Trader, to any Body, is *good*, notwithstanding the Clause in * 21 *Jac.* 1. *c.* 19. though Possession has not been actually delivered: For a Bill of Sale is all the Possession that can be delivered, till the Ship comes Home. * Sect. 11th.

There scarce happens a Bankruptcy in which it does not appear that a fictitious Credit has been acquired by drawing and redrawing Bills of Exchange, and by Accepting and Indorsing Promissory Notes: Yet there never was a Doubt, but that the Persons lending their Names, by which they render themselves at last liable, may come in as Creditors. The Case of a Man who has *actually paid his Money* to support the Credit of another, is infinitely stronger than that of lending a Name only, without advancing any Money at all.

There cannot be a greater Paradox, than that a Man should be guilty of a *Fraud*, in lending his Money with *no other Prospect* but the *Chance* of being repaid it.

A Notion "that Lending Money to Traders, knowing them to "be in dubious, tottering, or diſtreſſed Circumſtances, upon Mort-"gages or Liens, is fraudulent; and conſequently the Contract void "in Caſe a Bankruptcy enſues;" would throw all mercantile Dealing into inextricable Confuſion. Men lend their Money to Traders upon Mortgages or Conſignments of Goods; *becauſe* they ſuſpect their Circumſtances, and will not run the Riſque of their general Credit.

Though We have All been clearly of Opinion, that no Concluſion attempted to be drawn from the Evidence in this Caſe, allowing it to be true, amounted in Point of Law to the Offence of *Fraud*, and a Forfeiture of the Debt on *that* Account; Yet I have ſo great a Regard for the Authority of my Brother *Noel*, (whoſe Knowledge and Experience is as great, and his Opinion of as much Weight, as any Man's, both in Courts of Law and Equity,) that I was deſirous to talk the Matter fully over with Him; which I have done.

He ſays, the Point upon which the Defendant's Caſe is now put, and which was reſerved for his Opinion if it ſhould be neceſſary, was not explained, or underſtood at the Trial, as it is now: And the Queſtion of Fraud was intangled, by not diſtinguiſhing this Caſe from that of a Factor having Goods in his Poſſeſſion conſigned to him before an Act of Bankruptcy; and *after Knowledge* of an Act of Bankruptcy, advancing Money to the Bankrupt, with a View of covering the Effects and playing them into his own Hands, in Oppoſition to the Bankrupt's Aſſignees.

But in this Caſe, where the Factors did not know of the Act of Bankruptcy, He is now fully convinced that the Facts did *not* amount to *Fraud*, and that the Jury ſhould have been ſo told; And concurs in Opinion, that there ſhould be a *new Trial*.

* In Chancery, *M.* 1749.

If We did not grant it, the Precedent of * *Villain* v. *Hyde* muſt be followed; where a Bill in Chancery was brought by the Defendant at Law in an Action upon an *Indebitatus Aſſumpſit*, becauſe Allowances, which ought in Juſtice to have been made to Him at the Trial, were not made. Lord *Hardwicke* was, in that Caſe, under great Difficulties how to proceed, upon ſuch a Ground, to give Relief in Equity: But the ſtrong Juſtice of the Caſe prevailed upon Him to ſhew ſuch a Diſpoſition, as induced the Aſſignees to conſent to the Allowance, and make a Satisfaction agreeable to the real Juſtice of the Caſe.

We are all of Opinion that the Rule be made absolute for a NEW TRIAL: But the new Trial must be upon *Payment of* COSTS.

RULE made ABSOLUTE, for a *New Trial*, Upon Payment of Costs.

N. B. The Assignees acquiesced; and never tried the Matter again, in this Action, nor brought any Other.

Rex *vers.* Turkey Company.

MR. *Norton* moved, on *Wednesday* last, for a *Mandamus* to admit Mr. *Isaac Rogers* into their Company; He having tendered 20 *l.* as the Act directs, and to make his *Affirmation* pursuant to the Directions of the late Act of Parliament made relating to that Company, 26 *G.* 2. *c.* 18.

The only Reason of his being refused, was, That he declined to take the *Oath* prescribed by that Act. Whereas Mr. *Norton* alledged, that as Mr. *Rogers* was a *Quaker*, his *Affirmation* was sufficient: For which, He cited the Statute of 22 *G.* 2. *c.* 46. * "for allowing "Quakers to make an Affirmation, in Cases where an Oath is *or* "*shall* be required."

* *V.* § *penult.* & *ult.*

Mr. *Harvey* offering now to shew Cause—

It was agreed by the COURT and Counsel on both Sides, That this was a proper Matter to come before the Court by way of *Return* to a *Mandamus*, rather than upon *Motion*. Wherefore the

RULE for a MANDAMUS was made absolute. *V. post, pa.*

The End of *Hilary* Term 1760.

Easter

Easter Term

33 Geo. 2. B.R. 1760.

Friday 2d May 1760.

Fletcher *verſ.* Hennington.

THIS was an Action of Debt, on a Bond conditioned for Payment of Money *on* OR *before* ſuch a Day. The Defendant (having prayed Oyer of the Condition) pleaded Payment at a Day *before* the particular Day ſpecified for Payment of it. The Plaintiff demurred to this Plea, as offering an *immaterial Iſſue*. The Defendant joined in Demurrer.

Mr. *Haward* (who was Counſel for the Plaintiff) prayed Judgment for the Plaintiff; as this Iſſue might be quite immaterial, if found for the *Plaintiff*; ſo that the Plaintiff could not have Judgment upon ſuch a Finding: (though indeed it would be a material One, if found for the Defendant; as Payment before the Day, would be Payment *at* the Day.) The Defendant ought to have pleaded it as Payment *at* the Day: For Payment before the Day is, in point of Law, Payment at the Day.

Mr. *Aſpinall contra*, for the Defendant, admitted that this Reaſoning would hold in Caſes of Money made payable, by the Condition, at and upon a *fixed* certain Day: But the Caſe, He ſaid, was quite different, where the Money is made payable at *or before* ſuch a Day; which is the *preſent* Caſe. To prove which, He cited the Caſe of * *Tryon* v. *Carter*, *M.* 8 *G. B. R.* where Lord *Hardwicke* laid down the Rule of pleading to an Action of Debt upon Bond with a Special Condition to be, " That wherever the Defendant pleads a *Performance* of the Condition, the Plaintiff muſt " aſſign an abſolute Breach; though this be not neceſſary where he " pleads a *collateral* Matter (as a Releaſe.")

* There is an imperfect Note of this Caſe in 2 *Strange* 994.

And The COURT agreed to this Diſtinction; and ſaid that the proper Method, in Caſes where the Money is made payable " at *or*

" before such a Day," was to plead, as is done here, (if the Fact was so,) " that it was paid at such *precedent* Day." And then, if the Plaintiff disputes the Reality of any Payment at all, he may reply " That it was not paid at the particular Day mentioned in the " Plea, *nor at any Time before or after that Day*:" And this will bring the Point to the material and proper Issue, " Whether it has " been ever paid at all, or not."

They held, consequently, That the Plaintiff, in the present Case, ought to have *replied*, and *not* to have *demurred*.

Whereupon, Mr. *Howard* prayed a Day or Two's Time, to move to withdraw his Demurrer, and reply to the Defendant's Plea.

Which was granted.

Rex *verf.* Inhabitants of Christchurch.

Saturday 3d May 1760.

TWO Justices made an Order for the Removal of *Elizabeth Maxey* Spinster, from *Christchurch* to *St. Matthew's Bethnall Green*, (both in the County of *Middlesex*:) And the Sessions, upon an Appeal, discharged the said Order; Stating the Case specially.

The Special Case stated—On the 24th of *August* 1757, the said *Elizabeth Maxey* was hired into the Service of *Robert Gilman* of *Christchurch*, for a Year; and *continued* in such Service there, from that Day TILL THE 7TH OF AUGUST *then next following*; When She was *frightened into Fits*, and *thereby rendered incapable of doing* ANY *Service*. That her Master being taken very ill, and being disturbed by the said *Elizabeth Maxey*'s Fits, her Mistress desired the Sister of the said *Elizabeth Maxey* to go with the said *Elizabeth Maxey* to One Mr. *Lemonier*'s in the said Parish of *St. Matthew Bethnall Green* (where the said *Elizabeth Maxey*'s said Sister then lived as a Servant,) and to *request Mrs. Lemonier to receive* her into their House, that She might be there under the Care of her Sister: But if the said Mr. *Lemonier* refused to admit Her, She was then to bring the said *Elizabeth Maxey back* to her said Master's House again. That Mr. *Lemonier* accordingly *received Her*; and She resided there *about Five Days*; and then She was taken into the *Hospital*. That the Day after the said *Elizabeth Maxey* had been received into Mr. *Lemonier*'s House, She *returned* to her said Master's House, *to fetch away her Cloaths*: And her *Mistress gave her two Shillings*; which, with what She had before received, made up the *full Year's Wages*. That NO WORDS *of Discharge* passed between the said Pauper and her Mistress: But the said *Elizabeth Maxey* LOOKED UPON Herself as then *discharged* from her said Service; *but believed* that had She recovered her Health, her Master *would have received her again* into his Service. That She *continued under the same Indisposition, till after the Year* from the said Time of Hiring was expired; and *never returned again* into her said Master's Service. And that on the 17th of *August* 1758, her Master *hired another Servant in her Place.*

And it is admitted, on behalf of the Appellants, That the said *Elizabeth Maxey* was legally *settled* in the said Parish of *St. Matthew Bethnall Green*; *Unless* a subsequent One was gained by Her in the said Parish of *Christchurch, under* the abovementioned Circumstances.

The Sessions, upon Consideration of the Premisses, allowed of the Appeal, and vacated the Order of the two Justices: And they further Ordered the Pauper to be removed from *St. Matthew's Bethnal Green* to *Christchurch*, and require the Parish of *Christchurch* to *receive and provide* for Her, until they can free themselves from the Charge thereof by due Course of Law.

Mr. *Norton*'s Objection to this Order of Sessions, (upon his Motion to quash it,) was, " That this SERVICE in *Christchurch* was *not* " sufficient to gain a Settlement; being 17 *Days* SHORT *of the Year* " for which She had been hired."

Mr. *Aston* and Mr. *Stowe* now shewed Cause Why the Order of Sessions should not be quashed; and argued this to be a GOOD *Service*, within 8, 9. *W.* 3. *c.* 30. § 4.

This was either an *Inability by* SICKNESS, or *an Absence with* LEAVE of her Master. In *either* Case, it is a good Settlement.

In 1 *Strange* 423, 424. *Rex* v. *Inhabitants of Islip*, Sickness during 6 Days in the Middle of the Year, was no Objection to the Service; Nor Absence 3 Days, at the End of the Service, upon a reasonable Cause; Nor an Absence of 4 Days, without Leave, in the Middle of the Year. So, in the Case of * *Rex* v. *Inhabitants of Goodneston*, *Tr.* 18, 19 *G.* 2. *B. R.*—Leave to go to the Herring-Fishery, though the Servant was absent about 3 Weeks at the End of the Year, and did not return till 3 Weeks after the Expiration of it, was held a good Settlement.

* 2 *Strange* 1232.

In the Case of † *Rex* v. *Beccles*, (cited in 2 *Strange* 1207,) Absence, by his Master's Leave to work for other Persons 3 Weeks and 3 Days (in all) was holden " not to prevent the Gaining a Settlement."

† *P.* 1744. 17 *G.* 2. *B. R.*

And

And here are *no Words of Discharge*; nor any *Consent* of the Master to her being discharged.

Besides, the Master was *bound to provide for and take Care* of Her, whilst She was sick: And therefore it must be taken that She *continued in the Service.* The Failure arose only from the *Act of God.*

Mr. *Norton*, Mr. *Morton*, and Mr. *Lane*, *contra*—argued that this Service was *insufficient* to gain Her a Settlement in *Christchurch*: For She did not "*continue and abide* in the Service, one *whole* Year," as the Act of Parliament expressly requires.

In the *Islip* Case, The Servant's Absence (to visit his Mother) and his Sickness too, were in the *Middle* of the Year: And the Absence was *purged*, by the Master's *receiving him again.* And the 3 Days Absence at the *End* of the Year, (to go to the Statute-Fair,) was holden to have been unreasonably opposed and denied by the Master, and with a fraudulent Declaration "that the Servant should gain no "Settlement with him."

In the *Goodneston* Case, where the Servant went to the Herring-Fishery—It was holden that the Servant was to be considered as all the While *in* the Service of the Master; It being by Leave, and another Person hired by the Servant to do the Business: And the Servant returned again to his Master after the Expiration of the Year, and received from Him his whole Year's Wages.

But here, the Absence was 17 Days at the *End* of the Year; and She *looked upon Herself* as *discharged*; and the Master *hired another Servant* in her Place. If this be allowed at the *End* of the Year, where can the Court stop? It may as well be a Want of 3 Weeks, or a Month, or 2 Months.

In 2 *Strange* 1022. *Seaford* v. *Castlechurch*, "Going away (with-"out Leave) 12 Days before the End of the Year, prevented a "Settlement; though the Master paid him the whole Year's "Wages."

The *Master's Generosity*, in paying the whole Wages, makes no Difference in the Case. To gain a Settlement, there must be a *complete* Hiring for a Year, AND SERVICE for a Year: So it was determined in 1 *Strange* 143. *Coombe* v. *Westwoodbay*; Where a Week being wanting at the *Beginning* of the Year, it was holden to be no Settlement.

The

The Acquiring a Settlement in a Pariſh, by Service, is *no Benefit* to the *Servant:* For a Servant has *no more Benefit* (in general) by having a Settlement in *One* Pariſh, than in *Another*.

Lord MANSFIELD—This Caſe is an additional Proof, amongſt many others, upon how inconvenient a Foot the Law of Settlements ſtands.

This muſt appear a very clear Caſe to any Perſon of common plain Senſe and Underſtanding. It is certainly a fair *bonâ fide Service for a Year*, without any Fraud on either Side, either of the Maſter or of the Servant.

If a Maſter gives his Servant *Leave* to go upon any other Service, or to be abſent for a ſhort Time, and pays him his *whole* Wages, This is a fair *bonâ fide* Service.

If the Servant is taken *ill*, by the Viſitation of God, It is a Condition incident to Humanity, and is *implied* in all Contracts. Therefore the Maſter is *bound* to provide for and take Care of the Servant ſo taken ill in his Service; and *can not deduct* Wages in Proportion to the Continuance of the Servant's Sickneſs.

Here, the Maſter requeſted Mrs. *Lemonier* to take in his Servant; the Maſter himſelf being, at the ſame Time, ſick at Home. Then She was afterwards ſent to the Hoſpital by her *Maſter's Conſent*. And the Maſter and Miſtreſs paid Her her *whole* Wages, and were *ſatisfied* with what was done. Can any One doubt of this being a Service, *bonâ fide*, for a Year? Being ſent to an Hoſpital by a kind Maſter ought not to hurt the Settlement of a Servant viſited by Sickneſs.

And I ſee no Difference between ſuch an Accident of *Sickneſs* happening in the *Middle*, or happening at the *End* of the Year: It is equally the Act of God, and without any Fault of the Servant.

Mr. Juſt. DENISON ſaid He thought this the weakeſt Ground of Objection to a Settlement that he had ever met with. He concurred with His Lordſhip, That the Illneſs of the Servant happening at *One* part of the Year, or at *Another*, (being always the Act of God,) could make no Sort of Difference. And He was extremely clear that this *Act of God* ought not to prevent the Servant from gaining a Settlement. And if, by the Conſent of the Maſter, She be ſent to an *Hoſpital*; ſhall that alter the Caſe, and make it different from her being kept at Home in the Maſter's own Houſe? Surely, not. She certainly does " *continue and abide in the Service*"

 of

of her Master. For, "*Continuing and abiding* in the Service" means "*Not deserting it:*" And she can not be considered as having *deserted* her Service.

There was no Need of any Cases being cited upon this Occasion: That of *Islip* comes *nearest* to the present Case.

Mr. Justice FOSTER concurred with His Lordship and Mr. Just. DENISON. He said that the Relation between the Master and Servant certainly *continues:* It is not put an End to, by this *Visitation of God.* And He observed that the Sending her out of the Master's House to Mr. *Lemonier*'s, and afterwards to the Hospital, was for the *Ease* of the Master, and for his *own* Convenience.

Mr. Just. WILMOT said It was the clearest Case that could be.

The Distinction between the Servant's Absence in the *Middle* and at the *End* of the Year, turns upon the Absence in the Middle of the Year being *purged* by the Master's *receiving the Servant again*; which is not the Case of an Absence at the *End* of his Year, when He does not return.

But with regard to the Act of God, *Illness*; It is just the same Thing, whether *that* happens at the Beginning, Middle or End of Year: The *Time* makes *no Difference*, in the Reason of the Thing. And in the present Case, the Servant's being at Mr. *Lemonier*'s, or in the Hospital, is just the same Thing as her being kept in the Master's House, under his own Roof.

I do not agree to the Position "That the Servant has *no Benefit* "by gaining a Settlement in a Parish." It is *not* indifferent to a Servant (very often) in *what Parish* he gains a Settlement: It is, in many Cases, an Advantage, in Fact; and has always been, and ought to be looked upon as such. It is a *Reward* for their Labour and Service: And in *that* Light, it is but reasonable to consider it.

Mr. Just. FOSTER agreed with Mr. Just. WILMOT, in this. Is it indifferent to a FOREIGNER who has *no* Settlement of his own? It is certainly a Benefit to *such* a Person: For He *obtains* a Settlement by the Hiring and Service, instead of being (as he was before) without *any* Settlement at all.

Per Cur. unanimously,
ORDER of SESSIONS confirmed:
ORDER of two Justices quashed.

Tuesday 6th *May* 1760.

Johnson and Another, Assignees of Hargreaves a Bankrupt, *vers.* Smith, Widow, Executrix of Thomas Smith, her late Husband.

Hil. 33 *G.* 2. *Rot'lo* 24.

THIS was an Action upon the Case upon *Assumpsit*, brought by the Assignees of the Bankrupt's Estate and Effects, for 200*l.* for Goods sold and delivered by the Bankrupt (before his becoming so) to the Defendant's Testator, in his Life-time.

It came before the Court, upon a Demurrer to the Defendant's Rejoinder: And it is necessary to state the Pleadings particularly; because a great Part of the Argument turned upon them.

Declaration.

The Action was laid in *Lancashire:* And there was Nothing extraordinary in the Declaration. It was a Common and Usual Declaration, containing several Counts. The first Count was—For that Whereas the Defendant's Testator *Thomas Smith*, in his Life-time, before the said *Richard Hargreaves* became a Bankrupt, to wit, on the *first Day of January in the Year of our Lord* 1753, at *Preston* in the said County, was indebted to the said *Richard Hargreaves* in 200*l.* of lawful Money of *Great Britain*, for divers Goods Wares and Merchandizes by the said *Richard Hargreaves* before that Time sold and delivered to the said *Thomas* at his Special Instance and Request; And being so indebted, He the said *Thomas* in Consideration thereof, afterwards in his Life-time, to wit, On the *same Day* and Year aforesaid, at *Preston* aforesaid, undertook and to the said *Richard Hargreaves* before He became a Bankrupt *then* and there faithfully promised to pay to Him the said 200*l.* when He the said *Thomas* should be afterwards thereunto requested; And whereas &c. (This is upon a Promise to pay what they were reasonably worth, and an Averment of their being worth 200*l.*) Nevertheless the said *Thomas*, in his Life-time, and the said *Mary* (the Defendant) since his Decease, hath not nor hath Either of them paid &c. There were two Other like Counts, differing only in this, that they laid the Promise to be on 1*st March* 1756; and charged the Debt to be due, and the Promises made *to the Assignees*, (not to *Hargreaves.*)

1st Plea.

The Defendant, having Leave to plead several Pleas, first pleads "that her Testator did not, in his Life-time, undertake and promise, in Manner and Form &c." And upon this, Issue is joined.

And

And for further Plea, She says " That the said *Thomas Smith did* 2d Plea. " *not promise or undertake*, in Manner and Form as the said *William* " *Johnson* and *Richard Leigh* have above complained against Her, " at *any Time within Six Years next before the Day of exhibiting the* " AFORESAID BILL *of the said William Johnson and Richard Leigh*."

And for further Plea, as to the two first Promises mentioned in 3d Plea. the Declaration, She pleads a Sett-off.

The Plaintiffs reply, as to the Defendant's second Plea in Bar, Replication to 2d Plea. " That after the making of the said several Promises and Undertakings in the said Bill mentioned, and after the said *Richard Hargreaves* became a Bankrupt, and also after the Decease of the said " *Thomas Smith*, and WITHIN *six Years* next after the making of " the said several Promises in the said Bill mentioned, to wit, *on the* " *28th Day of November in the 32d* Year of the Reign of our Lord " the now King, They the said *William Johnson* and *Richard Leigh*, " for the Obtaining and Recovery of their Damages by reason of " the Non-Performance of the Promises and Undertakings in the " said Bill mentioned, *sued out* of the Court of our said Lord the " King before the King Himself, (the said Court then being at " *Westminster* in the County of *Middlesex*,) *against the said Mary*, " a certain Writ of our said Lord the King called a LATITAT, directed to the then Sheriffs of the City of *York*; By which said " Writ, our said Lord the King commanded the said Sheriffs that " they should take the said *Mary*, in the said Writ called *Mary* " *Smith* Widow and Executrix of *Thomas Smith* her late Husband " deceased, and *John Doe*, if they might be found in their Bailiwick, and safely keep them, So that the said Sheriffs might have " their Bodies before our said Lord the King at *Westminster* on *Tuesday* next after the Octave of *St. Hilary* then next following, to " answer the said *William Johnson* and *Richard Leigh* Assignees of " the Debts Goods and Effects which were of the said *Richard Hargreaves* a Bankrupt, in a Plea of Trespass; And that the said " Sheriffs should have then there that Writ: Which said Writ they " the said *W. J.* and *R. L.* as Assignees in Form aforesaid sued " out against the said *Mary* as Executrix as aforesaid, WITH INTENT *that the said Mary might be personally served with a Copy* " *thereof* according to the Form of the Statute in such Case made " and provided, *and that the said Mary might appear at the Return* " of the said Writ in the said Court here, at the Suit of the said " *Wm. J.* and *R. L.* and that the said *Wm. J.* and *R. L.* as Assignees in Form aforesaid *might thereupon exhibit their Bill* in the " said Court here, against the said *Mary* as being Executrix as aforesaid, for the Obtaining and Recovery of their Damages by Occasion of the Non-Performance of the several Promises and Under-

" takings in the said Bill mentioned, according to the Custom of " the said Court here. At which said *Tuesday* next after the Oc- " taves of *St. Hilary*, the said *W. J.* and *R. L.* as Assignees in " Form aforesaid, came by their Attorney aforesaid; And the said " *Mary* likewise came by the said *T. H.* her Attorney, and ap- " peared in the same Court here at the Suit of the said *W. J.* and " *R. L.* acording to the Exigency of the said Writ and the Custom " of the said Court here; And thereupon the said *Wm. J.* and " *Rd. L.* as Assignees in Form aforesaid, *according to their afore-* " *said Intention*, in the Term of *St. Hilary* in the 32d Year of the " Reign of our said Lord the now King, *exhibited their aforesaid* " *Bill* in the said Court of our said Lord the King before the King " Himself, against the said *Mary* as being Executrix in Form afore- " said, for the Obtaining and Recovery of their Damages by oc- " casion of the Non-Performance of the several Promises and Un- " dertakings in the said Bill mentioned." And the said *Wm. J.* and *Rd. L.* further say, " That the said *Thomas Smith* in his Life- " time, WITHIN *six Years next before the suing out of the said Writ* " *called* a LATITAT, *did undertake and promise*, in Manner and " Form as the said *Wm. J.* and *Rd. L.* have above complained " against the said *Mary*." And *this* the said *W. J.* and *R. L.* are ready to verify: Whereof they pray Judgment, and their Damages by reason of the Non-Performance of the aforesaid Promises and Undertakings to be adjudged to them &c.

Replication to 3d Plea.

And as to the last Plea in Bar to the two first Counts, They reply " that *Hargreaves* was not indebted in Manner and Form as the " Defendant has in that Plea alledged:" Upon which, Issue is joined.

Rejoinder.

And the said *Mary*, as to the aforesaid Replication of the said *Wm. J.* and *Rd. L.* to the Plea of the said *Mary* secondly above pleaded in Bar, says, " *That* BY THE COURSE AND CUSTOM OF " THE COURT *of our Lord the King here, a Writ of* LATITAT " *sued out* AFTER THE END OF ANY TERM *is* SUPPOSED *to have* " *issued out of the said Court here* WITHIN *the Term then* PRE- " CEDING." But the said *Mary* further says " That the *said* " *Writ of Latitat* in the aforesaid Replication *mentioned was* " REALLY AND TRULY *sued out of the said Court here, by them* " *the said William and Richard,* AFTER *the said 28th Day of No-* " *vember in the same Replication mentioned, (being the* LAST DAY " OF MICHAELMAS TERM *in the said 32d Year of the Reign of* " *our said Lord the King,) that is to say, on the* EIGHTH *Day of* " DECEMBER *in that Year; and on the* SAME *Day and Year, was* " SIGNED *according to the Form of the Statute in such Case made* " *and provided; And that the said Thomas Smith did* NOT *promise* " *or undertake, in Manner and Form as the said William* and *Richard*

" *have above complained, at any Time* WITHIN SIX YEARS NEXT " BEFORE THE SAID EIGHTH DAY OF DECEMBER, *on which* " *Day, the said Writ of Latitat was so* REALLY *and* IN TRUTH " *sued out as aforesaid:" And* THIS *the said Mary is ready to verify.* Wherefore She prays Judgment Whether the said *William* and *Richard* ought to have or maintain their aforesaid Action against Her.

To this Rejoinder the Plaintiffs demur, generally: And the Defendant joins in Demurrer. Demurrer.

This Demurrer was argued, on *Tuesday* 5th *February* 1760, by the two Counsel who had signed the Pleadings; *viz.* by Mr. Serj. *Poole* for the Plaintiffs, and Mr. *Yates* for the Defendant.

The only Question was, " Whether the Truth of the Fact " could, in this Case, be averred *contrary* to the Fiction of Law."

Mr. Serj. *Poole*, for the Plaintiffs, argued that the Rejoinder was a *bad* One, for two Reasons:

1st. It is *averring against the Record*:

2dly. It is contrary to, and destructive of the *Practice* of this Court; and tends to *destroy* the Writ of *Latitat* itself; For the Writ would be a *Nullity*, if tested in Vacation.

First—It is an Averment *against the Record*. For the *Teste* of the Writ *is a Matter of Record*. 1 *Siderf.* 271. *Baily* v. *Bunning*. 1 *Mod.* 188. *Farrer* v. *Brooks*, *Administrator of Jo. Brooks*. *Cro. Car.* 264. *Watts* v. *Baker*. 1 *Ro. Abr.* 538. Title *Court*, Letter *M. pl.* 4. S. C. 1 *Sid.* 53. *Dacy* v. *Clinch*. *Style* 156. *Coles* v. *Sibsye*. *Carthew* 233. *Culliford* v. *Blandford*. *Sir T. Jones* 150. *Walburgh* v. *Saltonstall*. 1 *Lutw.* 333. *Aldworth* v. *Hutchinson*. 1st Objection.

In *Pas.* 5 *G.* 2. *C. B.* The Case of *Jones* v. *Burnet* was an *Assumpsit* against the Defendant, brought by the Plaintiff as Indorsee of a Promissory Note, by an Attachment of Privilege. The Defendant pleaded " that the Attachment issued on the 12th of *February*, and that the Note was not indorsed till after that Day." The Replication was " That *reverâ* the Writ was sued out in the " Vacation *&c*, on such a Day, though tested on the 12th of " *February*; and that the Note was indorsed before that Day." And on Demurrer, the Replication was held bad. This is a Case in Point: For it was " That *reverâ* it *was sued out in Vacation-time*, " *viz.* on such a Day *&c*."

The only Cases where this has been attempted in *this* Court, are the two following; *viz. Hoare* v. *Yates*, *P.* 5 *G.* 2. *B. R.* *usq*; *Tr.* 7, 8.

7, 8. and *M.* 8 *G.* 2. But no Judgment was given in that Case; it having been, at last, ended between the Parties. It was upon a *Bill of Middlesex*, which has *no* Teste: But *this* is on a *Latitat*, which *has a Teste*. The other Case was that of *Medcalfe* v. *Burroughs*, *M.* 14 *G.* 2. *B. R.* S. P. But this Case, though solemnly argued, was never determined: It was to have been argued a second Time; but never came on any more.

2d Objection. * *V. Fitz-Gibbon* 66. In Proof of the Second Position, He cited the Case of * *Eastwick* v. *Cook*, *P.* 2 *G.* 2. *B. R.* 1 *Saund.* 298. *Greene* v. *Jones.* 1 *Siderf.* 304. *Mandamus, pur Sterling, al Moniers.* 2 *Salk.* 700. *Shirley* v. *Wright*.

These Cases are in Point, to prove "that a *Latitat really* tested "in Vacation would be void." And if the Plaintiff should have a Verdict and Judgment upon such an Issue as this, it would be a Nullity and erroneous. And yet if the Rejoinder be proper, the Plaintiff must be obliged to surrejoin accordingly: Which would be nugatory.

Suppose upon a Fine, (where the Writ of Covenant always bears Teste before the *Dedimus*,) It should be averred "that *in Fact* the "Writ of Covenant did not issue till *after* the *Dedimus*," This would, if it were to be permitted, set aside all the Land Securities in the Kingdom. So, in the Case of Recoveries, any such Averment of the Process issuing, *in Fact*, in Vacation-time, would be bad. *By Law*, no Process *can* issue, but in *Term*-time, in *any* Case whatever. This Method of Pleading might be extended to *all* Cases, if it were to be allowed in *any*.

3d Objection. (Estoppel.) And the Defendant is *Estopped* from averring this Fact: For the Objection arises from One who is *Party and Privy to the Suit*; Which differs from Cases of Averments by *Strangers*, who are intitled to many Privileges which *Privies* can *not* claim.

Mr. *Yates*, *contra*, for the Defendant.

This is an Action on several Promises made by the Defendant's Testator; To which, She pleads *Non assumpsit infra sex Annos* of the Time of *exhibiting the Bill*. The Plaintiffs reply "That the "Plaintiff sued out a *Latitat* tested on the 28th of *November*." The Defendant rejoins "That *in Fact* the *Latitat* was issued out on the 8th of *December*; And that the Defendant's Testator did not promise within 6 Years of *that* Day. To which Rejoinder, the Plaintiffs have demurred.

4

This

This Point depends upon the Construction of the *Statute of Limitations:* And the Question is *What is* a COMMENCEMENT or SUING of the Action *within that Statute*; And Whether the Defendant be *at Liberty* to aver the *real* and *true* Day, on which the *Latitat* in Fact issued.

Mr. Serj. objects "That this is Averring *against the Record*; That "it would be *destructive* of the *Practice of the Court*, and even of "*the very Writ itself*;" and "that the Defendant being *Party* and "*Privy* to the Suit, is *estopped* from averring this Fact."

It may be observed, in the first Place, that *No* TESTE *of this Writ is expressly* SHEWN; nor is there even a *Reference* "*prout patet* "*per Recordum:*" The Plaintiff *only alledges* "That he *sued out* a "*Latitat tested* on the 28th of *November*."

However, what We deny is the Fact "that the Writ ISSUED *on* "*the 28th of November*." The very *Issuing* of the Writ *at all*, may be denied: Much more, the *Time* of issuing it, or the *Day* upon which it issued. We say "That *in Fact* it did *not issue*, *till* "the 8th of *December*." This Fact We aver, and rely upon.

And the *true* Time of taking out the *Latitat may* be averred, *contrary* to the nominal Teste: The Plaintiff may *declare* so; And the Jury may *find* so. This was determined in the Case of *Walburgh* v. *Saltonstall*, 1 *Vent*. 362, 363.

The *Suing out* the Writ is a Matter of *Fact*; an Act done by the Plaintiff: And the Court will *not intend* "That this *Latitat* was "really *sued out and issued* in Term," *merely* because it is *tested* in Term-time; Especially, when the Fact *appears upon the Record* to be otherwise. And the Fact *does* so appear upon the Record: For the *Demurrer admits* "That the Writ was, *in Fact*, sued out and "issued OUT of Term."

And there is nothing to preclude the Defendant from shewing and averring this Fact: Here is *no Estoppel* at all; because the Truth is *apparent upon the same Record. Co. Litt.* 352. *a. b.* lays down the Rules of Estoppels; and the 8th Rule is expressly so. The Case of *Kemp* v. *Goodal* in 1 *Salk.* 277. settles the Difference about Estoppels; and lays it down "That where the Estoppel *appears upon the Record*, "the other Side may demur." 1 *Lutw.* 329, 333, 334. *Aldworth* v. *Hutchinson* was the same Point: And it is there observed "That if that Judgment was given upon the Reason of an "Estoppel, a Covenant might be in Judgment of Law broken, "where, in Fact, it was *not broken*."

But

But even supposing the Teste to have been formally and expressly shewn, yet the *Time* when a *Latitat* ISSUED, is *traversable*, and *may* be averred different from the Teste. The Case of *Bilton* v. *Johnson and Long*, in 2 *Keb.* 173, 198. and *Raymond* 161. is a Resolution in Point, most express and strong. The Case of *Chancy* v. *Rutter*, 3 *Keb.* 213. was a subsequent Determination of the same Point, accordingly; and upon the Authority of the former Case, and of *Bennet* and *Pilkin*'s Case. The Case of *Lazall* v. *Dyer*, 2 *Salk.* 650. is strong in Point: Where the Court held a Writ tested of a preceding Term, though *legally* a Proceeding of that Term, yet not to be so in *Fact*. And 1 *Ro. Abr.* 552. Letter *F. Pl.* 4, 5. is to the same Effect, and distinguishes between the *Purchase* of the Writ, and the *Date* of it.

The Case of *Man* v. *Adams*, in 1 *Siderf.* 432. was an Action of Debt against an Executor; who pleaded *plene administravit*: And there was a Replication of "Assets *die exhibitionis billæ*, *scilicet* the "23d of *October*." The Court saved to the Defendant, upon Evidence, the *Time of the Coming in* of the Bill.

The *Stamp-Act* requires the Officer who signs the *Latitat* to set down the Day and Year of *Signing* the Writ. Now the Officer could never be *convicted* of a Neglect of his Duty, if no Averment could be made contrary to the Teste. Therefore there *are* Cases where this *may* be done.

The next Consideration is, "Whether *this* be a Case, where it "*may* or *ought* to be done."

As to the Case of *Watts* v. *Baker*, in *Cro. Car.* 264. It concludes Nothing to the present Case. The Time of *suing out* the Writ could not be in question in that Case: For the very *Arrest* itself was prior to the Tender of Amends.

The Cases of *Dacy* v. *Clinch*, 1 *Sid.* 53. and *Coles* v. *Sibsye*, in *Style* 156. and *Culliford* v. *Blandford*, in *Carthew* 233. are only, "That Suing out a *Latitat* within 6 Years will save the Statute:" They prove Nothing more.

In the Case of *Metcalfe* v. *Burroughs*, the Return was set forth; and the Record referred to. As to the Case of *Aldworth* v. *Hutchinson*, in 1 *Lutw.* 333. there was no final Judgment nor any Cause shewn: And the Reporter's own Note upon the Judgment *nisi*, is *against* it.

The Case of *Jones* v. *Burnet* differs from this Case: And there, the Plaintiff contradicted his *own* Writ. He might have brought his Action sooner too. And that was an Attachment of Privilege: This is a *Latitat*.

In the Case of *Walburgh* v. *Saltingstall*, *Holt* only argued as Counsel: He did not speak as a Judge. Therefore what He there said, was no Authority at all: Especially, as the Court determined *against* him.

The Cases of *Baily* v. *Bunning*, and *Farrer* v. *Brooks*, were Questions on *Common-Law* Points: This is on the Construction of an *Act of Parliament*. And the *fictitious* Relation of the Teste ought not to clash with the *Intention of the Legislature*, in the Construction of an Act of Parliament. Much less shall the *fictitious* Relations of Law *overturn* the Intention of the Legislature in a Statute made for the *Security* of the Subject, and to *prevent* stale Demands from being set up.

The Case of *Green* v. *Rivett*, in *Salk*. 421. and 422. particularly mentions *this* Statute as being to be *favoured*; "because the Security of all Men depends upon it."

The Words of the Statute are "*commenced and sued* WITHIN 6 *Years, and* NOT AFTER:" Therefore the Plaintiff *can not* enlarge the Time to 6 Years *and* 4 *Months*. The Word "*sued*," is as strong as if it had been "*actually sued*:" And it is confined to "*not after*" the Six Years. So that the Plaintiff was *actually barred* by the Statute, *before* he sued this Writ. And *Fiction* shall not elude the Statute, when the Plaintiff was *already barred* by it. These Fictions do *not always* prevail: And they shall never prevail so as to work a *Wrong*. The Cases of *Bilton* v. *Johnson and Long*; and *Chancy* v. *Rutter*; and 1 *Ro. Abr*. 552; and *Man* v. *Adams*, all prove this.

It has been urged, "That this Rejoinder would *destroy the Latitat* itself, by *making* it a *Nullity* and erroneous." But this Writ was, *in Fact*, *originally a Nullity*, within the Meaning of this Statute; as being sued in Vacation, *after the* 6 *Years were expired*. However, here the *Averment* is *essential* to the Merits of the Case, and the Provision of the Statute. *If* the Writ was *in Fact* sued out, *after* the Six Years expired; it is *immaterial*, Whether it be a Nullity or not, in Point of *Legal Form*: For the *Time of Suing out*, must here be taken in the true *substantial* Sense of the Words.

He alledged that the Justice of the present Case was on his Client's Side; And relied upon his Observation abovementioned, that this Rejoinder pursues the very *Words* of the Statute, which is a *beneficial* Law, and ought to be *favoured.*

Mr. Serj. *Poole*, in Reply. It appears upon the *Face* of the *Record*, "That the Teste and Suing out of this Writ was in *Term-time*:" For it is *necessarily to be presumed* that the Writ *must have actually issued* on the Day when it was tested, which must be in Term-time. And it is here, in this Replication, alledged in the *Common* Way of setting it out in Pleading.

And the *Estoppel* here appears *upon* the *Record* itself; And therefore it *need not be pleaded* by a *Party* to the Record.

As to the Case of *Bilton* v. *Johnson* and others, in 2 *Keble* 173, and 198, and in *Raymond* 161. That may safely be admitted to be Law: For that is the Case of a *Stranger*; (for the Defendant, the * Sheriffs Bailiff, was a *Stranger* to the Original Action;) and it was for the *Furtherance of Justice*, and to prevent Frauds. But that Case does not prove "That it may be done by *Parties* and *Privies*. *Harrison*'s Case cited in 3 *Keb.* 213, 214. in the Case of *Chancy* v. *Rutter*, expressly takes the Distinction between *Strangers*, and *Parties* or *Privies*; and says "That a Stranger is not concluded; but "the Party is." The Case of *Pigot* v. *Rogers*, *Cro. Jac.* 561. was also the Case of a *Stranger*; not of a Party or Privy.

* *V.* 2 *Keble* 173.

As to the *Stamp-Act*, and the *Statute of Frauds*—The *former* only relates to the *Officer*; It does not affect the present Doctrine. The *latter* relates only to *Purchasers:* The Judgment is the same as it was *before*, with regard to *all other* Persons.

As to Construing the *Statute of Limitations* according to the *Intention*—The "*Commencing a Suit*," and "*Suing out Process*," (the two Expressions used in the Statute,) must mean the very *same Thing*: and this must be determined by the TESTE of the Process sued out, as a *Commencement* of the Suit.

Lord MANSFIELD—This is the seventh or eighth Time that this Question has been argued at the Bar: Therefore there needs no further Argument. We will consider of it.

CUR. ADVIS'.

Lord MANSFIELD now delivered the solemn Resolution of the Court; (having first stated the Pleadings very particularly; in which, he said a great Part of the Argument consisted.)

This

This Demurrer can only be supported upon one of these two Grounds; either (1st.) That the *Fact averred is not relevant*; Or (2dly.) Supposing it relevant, That *Proof cannot be received*, to *shew* the Truth.

The first depends upon the Construction of the Statute of Limitations * 21 *Jac.* 1. *c.* 16. * Sect. 3.

Now there never was a plainer Proposition, conceived in plainer *English* Words, than the Rule laid down by this Act of Parliament: It enacts "That all Actions upon the Case (other than such Accounts " as concern the Trade of Merchandize between Merchant and Mer- " chant their Factors and Servants) shall be COMMENCED AND SUED " within Six Years next after the Cause of such Actions or Suit, *and* " NOT *after*."

The Statute is *Negative*, and prohibits that which must be the Act of the Party. Be the *Form* as it may, The SUING, COMMENCING or BRINGING an Action, must be by some *Act* of the Party: And THAT is the *Thing prohibited*, after the Expiration of the limited Time.

The preceding Act of Limitations 32 *H.* 8. *c.* 2. computes the Prescription, from the Time run before the † TESTE of the Writs † *V.* § 1, 2, 3. therein mentioned: But, because *that* would not be a *true* Criterion of the Time of commencing Suits within the Provisions of this Statute of 21 *Jac.* 1. *c.* 16; The Legislature has, in the latter, (which professes to be made for quieting of Mens Estates and avoiding of Suits,) *purposely avoided* mentioning the Teste of Writs, the Exhibiting Bills, the Arresting, the Holding to Bail, Summoning, Serving or any other Form of Process; but leaves to every Court, to say " *What Act of the Party* COMMENCES *the Suit*;" and, after the limited Time, forbids *that* being done. The Moment the Six Years expire, the Prohibition *attaches*: The Legislature says " he shall *not sue* " AFTER that Time." If the Time expired in *June*, and He *takes out* his first Process in *October*; That *Act* done by him in *October* is prohibited, and against the Law: For the Statute says he shall NOT *sue* AFTER. If by *Antedating* the Writ, He does sue after; then this *Effect* of the *Antedate* is directly *contrary* to both the Words and Meaning of the Act of Parliament.

No Answer has ever been given to this, but by supposing that the Statute *meant* to prolong the Time, as to Suits in the *King's Bench*, as far as the *Course* of that Court, of Ante-dating Writs, would carry it.

This

This begs the Question, against Demonstration. The *Words* are *general:* The *Reason* of the Law is *general*, and *incompatible* with this Exception.

Why bar the bringing Suits by *Original*, and not by every *other* Writ? *Why* shut the Door of every *concurrent* Jurisdiction throughout the Kingdom, while the Court of *King's Bench* was left open? What *should be* the Period, was at first arbitrary and indifferent; but when it is once fixed, It must *equally* bar, in *every* Court: Otherwise, it is *no* Limitation of Actions, nor Avoidance of Suits.

The Course " of Ante-dating Writs sued out in the Vacation, and " supposing them to be of the precedent Term," affords no Colour for implying such an Exception. The Legislature *might* have said, " that after Six Years a Writ should not be sued out in the Vacation, *though* bearing Teste before the End of the Six Years." *If Taking out* the Writ be that *first Step* by which the Party *brings* or *commences* his Suit, The Legislature *has* said, " That after Six " Years He shall *not take out* the Writ. The Statute considers the Time when the Suit is *really* brought; and can by no Possibility be implied to refer to the retrospective Teste of the Writ, *by the Course of this Court*.

If so plain a Thing can be made plainer, there happens to be a Clause in the Act, which is decisive *—" Sufficient Amends may " be tendered for an involuntary Trespass, *before the Action brought*." Apply the Argument to this Clause, and the Provision will be thus;—" To prevent frivolous and vexatious Suits, there may be " a Tender of sufficient Amends, BEFORE *the Action brought*; but, " by an *implied Reference to the Course of the Court of King's Bench*, " the Party may, AFTER *the Tender*, bring his Action with an " *Ante-date*, which shall *over-reach and defeat* the Tender:" and so the *implied Reference* repeals the *express Text*.

* The 5th Clause.

It happens most unfortunately too, for this Hypothesis " of an " *implied Reference* to the *artificial* Commencement of an Action " by the *Course of this Court*," that *if* it was *admitted*, the Suing out a LATITAT would *not* save the Running of the Statute. The BILL here is *as* an Original Writ; and the Want of it *equally cured*, after a Verdict: It is the first Process upon Record; and, by the Course of this Court, the Commencement of the Action. The Form of pleading the Statute of Limitations shews *that:* It is " *Ante Impetrationem Brevis*," in the one Case; " *Ante Exhibitionem Billæ*," in the other.

It was not settled till many Years after the Statute, "that the "Plaintiff *might* reply a LATITAT sued out within the Six Years." In the Case of * *Coles* v. *Sibsye*, in 1649, it came before the Court; And the Point was adjourned. But in *Mich.* 13 *C.* 2. in the Case of *Dacy* v. *Clinch* †; and lately, in *M.* 21 *G.* 2. *Henderson* v. *Whitaker et al'*: It was determined "that the Plaintiff *may* reply a *Latitat*." There could be no Doubt but that *Exhibiting the Bill* was bringing the Action; and therefore the Plea that Six Years had run before *Exhibiting the* BILL," was *certainly* good: But the LATITAT was held (and rightly held) to save the Bar, within the *Reason* and *Equity* of the Case. The Statute did not intend to bar, unless the Party had *acquiesced* Six Years. But he who sued out a *Latitat*, to bring the Defendant into Custody that He might declare against him, *did not acquiesce*, within the *true Meaning* of the Act; though, *artificially*, the BILL is, upon the Record, the *first* Step. The Day He sued out the *Latitat*, He *might* have taken out an ORIGINAL: And any Construction of the Statute, to make it bar *One* Form of Suing, while *Others* were open, was nugatory and contrary to it's true Intent. But to bring it within the *Equity* of the Law, the *Latitat* must be taken out *with Intent to declare in that Action*, and must be *continued* to Filing the Bill.

* Style 156. M. 1649. Banc. Sup.

† 1 Siderfin 53.

When the Replication of a *Latitat* came to be allowed to save the Bar and prevent the Running of the Statute, *because* Suing out a *Latitat* was, *in real Truth*, an Act of Diligence in the Party, and the *first* Step towards recovering his Demand by the Action depending, (though in a *strict legal* Sense, by the Course of this Court, such Action is not deemed to be brought till the Bill is filed;) It would be most extraordinary and most unequitable, *not to allow this Equity to be rebutted* by the Defendant, by shewing "that *in real* "*Truth* the Time *was run* before the Plaintiff took *any* Step." He was *actually barred*, before He sued out the *Latitat*; though, in *Form*, by the Course of this Court, As the *Action* is supposed to be brought *later*, the *Latitat* is supposed to be taken out *earlier*, than the *real Truth*.

Very unequal would that Interpretation be, which should construe the same Words, *for* the Plaintiff, *according* to the real substantial *Truth* of the Thing, in *Opposition* to legal Forms; and *against* the Defendant, *according* to legal Notions and Forms, *contrary to real Truth*: More especially when the Law, from the Nature of it, ought to be taken liberally in *Favour of Defendants*.

The Limitation of Suits is founded in public Convenience; and attended with so much Utility, that Courts of Equity adopt this Statute as a positive Rule, and apply it, by Parity of Reason, to Cases not within it.

This very Caufe, between Parties who (on both Sides) are *Strangers* to the whole Tranfaction, fhews the Wifdom of *fome Limitation*.

Therefore We are All clearly of Opinion, That, within the true Meaning of the Act of Parliament, *Six Years having expired* BEFORE *the Latitat was* IN FACT TAKEN OUT, is fufficient to rebutt the Matter of the Plaintiff's Replication; which alledges "that although the Suit was not brought within the Six Years, *according to the Courfe and legal Notions of this Court*, Yet, *in Fact*, It was brought within the Time, *by fuing out the Latitat*." Which brings Me to the

Second Point—Whether the Party may be *permitted to* SHEW that the *Latitat* was taken out after the Six Years expired.

If the TESTE of a *Latitat* was *conclufive*, Wrong muft neceffarily be done, in many other Cafes as well as the prefent; And great Inconvenience and Abfurdity would follow. No Man, whofe Caufe of Action arofe in the Vacation, could fue out this Procefs till the next Term: Which would be an Injury to *Plaintiffs*, and defeat the very End for which this Practice was introduced. The Defendant might be arrefted long before the Writ; He might be fued after he had made a legal Tender: which would be a manifeft Injury to *Defendants*.

But the Court would not endure that a *mere Form* or *Fiction of Law*, introduced for the Sake of Juftice, fhould work a *Wrong*, contrary to the real Truth and Subftance of the Thing: and they have (for 150 Years) uniformly held, "That where it became *material* to diftinguifh, They would confider the Day when the Writ was *taken out*, as the *Subftance*; and the *Tefte*, as the *Form*."

* H. 17 J. 1. Cro. Jac. 561. In the Cafe of * *Pigot* v. *Rogers*, it was held That a *Latitat* bearing *Date before* the Bond upon which the Action was brought, but *returnable after*, was right; becaufe, fays the Court, "the Procefs always bears Tefte the laft Day of the Term before." So, in 3 *Keb.* 213. An Obligation "not to profecute before a limited Time," was holden not to be broken by a *Latitat taken out* AFTER the Time, though it was *tefted* BEFORE: The Reafon given is, "becaufe the *Latitat* is not fuable with any other Tefte than of the preceding Term."

Where the *Arreft* is before the *Actual* Suing out of the Writ, It has been often determined "that it cannot be juftified; and that the *Day when it iffued* may be averred, notwithftanding the *Tefte* is before the Arreft."

The

The Case of * *Bilton* v. *Johnson and others*, was Trespass and falsé Imprisonment in *London*. The Defendant pleads that *J. S.* sued forth a Writ of *Latitat*, the last Day of *Trinity* Term, directed to the Sheriff of *R*; and by Virtue of that, the Sheriff of the said County made a Warrant to the Defendant, whereupon he took the Plaintiff; (Which is the same Imprisonment;) *absque hoc* that He is Guilty in *London*, *vel aliter*, *vel alio modo*. The Plaintiff replies "That the said Writ was *in Truth* prosecuted *after* the Imprison-"ment, to wit on the 9th of *August*." Upon this, the Defendant demurs. And it was Adjudged for the Plaintiff; "Because "although the Teste of the Writ is upon Record, And the Plain-"tiff can't aver against it, Yet here will be great Inconveniences if "the Plaintiff cannot set forth the *very Time* when it was *pur-*"*chased:* And the Relation of the Date to the last Day of the pre-"ceding Term is only calculated to *prevent* Fraud, but NOT to "*justify* a *Tort*." And in the same Case, Ld. Ch. J. *Kelynge* is † reported to have said, "That the *Time when a Latitat issued forth* "*is traversable*, and *may be averred otherwise than according to the* "*Teste:*" Which was Agreed by the Whole Court; "For a *Rela-*"*tion shall not work a* WRONG." "If a Man be taken in the Va-"cation by Warrant *without Writ*, and a *Latitat* be procured *tested* "*in the preceding Term*, it shall not discharge the Wrong done *after* "*the Teste*, and *before the actual Taking out* of the Writ; but the "Plaintiff may take Issue, *when* it was prosecuted *in Truth*."

* P. 19 C. 2. Raym. 161. and 2 Keble 198.

† 2 Keble 198.

In the Case of || *Hanway* v. *Merrey*, It was holden, "that though "a *Latitat* may be *taken out before* the Cause of Action, yet the "Party can not be *arrested* upon it till *after:*" And in that Case, the Court discharged the Arrest.

|| P. 21 C. 2. 1 Ventr. 28.

In the Case of * *Chauncy* v. *Rutter*, In Trespass and false Imprisonment, the Defendant justified by Arrest on a *Latitat*; The Plaintiff replied, "that the Writ was *taken out after the Arrest*;" To which Replication, the Defendant demurred: *Et per Curiam*, "The *Ante-date* of the Writ will *not* suffice, if the *Proceeding* be "*after*."

* M. 25 C. 2. 3 Keble 213.

So, as to *Tenders*—In the Case of † *Watts* v. *Baker*, It was holden "That a Tender came too late *after an Arrest* upon a *Latitat*." But the *Ground* of that Case *implies*, that if a Tender was made before the *Latitat* taken out in Fact; the *retrospective Teste* of the Writ, (which might be even before the Cause of Action,) could not deprive the Defendant of the Benefit of that Tender.

† Tr. 8 Car. 1. Cro. Car. 264.

In an Action upon the Case, where it is necessary to state the Taking out a *Latitat*, the Party may *declare* "that it was *sued out* "such

" such a Day in the *Vacation*, bearing Teste the last Day of the " preceding Term:" Or, if the *Teste only* be stated in the Declaration, and the Question should turn upon the *precise Day* when it was *taken out*, the Jury may *find* it. And this was * Adjudged so long ago as the Reign of *Charles* the Second. The Declaration alledged the *Latitat* to be sued out of the Court on the 21st of *January*: The Jury found that the Teste of it was on the 28th of *November*, being the last Day of the preceding Term; but that it was *indeed sued out* of the Court on the 21st of *January* as the Plaintiff had declared. The Declaration was held to be good, *because it was according to the Truth of the Fact*, though the *Teste* of a *Latitat* must be of the *preceding Term*.

[* *H.* 33, 34 *C.* 2. *Walburgh* v. *Saltonstal*, Sir *T. Jones* 149. and 1 *Ventris* 362.]

In the † same Case, reported in † 1 *Ventr*. 362. It is stated that a Special Verdict was found, " that the *Latitat* bore Teste the 28th " of *November* 32 *Car*. 2. but was *really taken out* the 21st of *January* following." *Holt*, who was Counsel for the Defendant, argued that *by Law* it must be deemed to be taken out the 28th of *November*, when the *Teste* is. Ld. Ch. J. *Pemberton* is reported to have given the Rule in the following Words—" We know the " *Course of this Court* is, to Teste *Latitats* taken out in the Vacation, as of the Term preceding: and the *Course* of a Court is " the *Law* of a Court. The Plaintiff might have *declared*, That " he sued out a *Latitat* the 21st of *January*, tested the 28th of " *November* preceding: And if he be not estopped to *declare* so, " Surely the Jury may *find* the whole Matter." And so Judgment was given for the Plaintiff.

[† This is another Argument of it, three Terms later than that in Sir *T. Jones*.]

Numberless are the Acts of Parliament in the Statute-Book, which give Actions " *so as* the Suit be *brought* or *commenced* within One, " Two, Three, or Four Months, or some longer Time, *and not* " *afterwards*:" And many give Actions to the Party aggrieved, to be brought within 2, 3, or 4 Months; And *if* the Party aggrieved do not sue *within* that Time, then to a common Informer.

Notwithstanding the Doubt in the Case of || *Culliford* v. *Blandford*, It is now settled " that a *Latitat* is a good Commencement of " a penal Action;" and was so holden in this Court, in *H.* 22 *G.* 2. in the Case of ‡ *Bridges qui tam*, v. *Knapton*.

[|| 4 *Mod.* 129. *Tr.* 4 *W.* & *M.* 1692. in *B. R.*]

[‡ I find the *same Point* solemnly determined in *another* Case in the very Term next preceding, *viz. Hardman, qui tam* &c. v. *Whitaker* & 8. *al'*. *M.* 1748. 22 *G.* 2. *B. R.*]

If the *Teste* of a *Latitat* was to be *conclusive* as to the Time of Suing, the Time given by the Legislature might be *enlarged* to double or triple the Number of Months. After Expiration of the Time given to the Party aggrieved, the common Informer might take out a Writ: and then the Party aggrieved might *defeat* his Right, *after* it had attached, by taking out a *Latitat* with an Ante-date. By this meer Form, or Fiction of Law, (which for good Purposes gives

gives the *Latitat* an Ante-date, merely as a Matter of Form,) Penal Statutes would be rendered *more* Penal; and Men would be subject to Penalties, to which, by Law, according to the Truth of the Case, they are *not liable*.

The Plaintiff who sues upon any of these Acts, (which are very numerous,) must take out the Writ, in *Fact*, within the Time: The *Teste* of the Writ will not be sufficient. The *Act* done by him, in commencing the Suit within the limited Time, is in the Nature of a *Condition precedent*, to intitle him to maintain that Action.

If the Legislature had not taken for granted, "That the true "Time of suing out a Writ might be shewn, in Opposition to the "Teste," It would have been absurd to have limited the Time to One, Two, or Three Months, followed by the Negative Words "*and not afterwards*;" Or, in Default of the Party aggrieved Suing within such Time, to give an *immediate* Right to a common Informer: And yet this is the Form in which such Acts are Penned, from the Beginning to the End of the Statute Book.

The Act of 23 *H.* 6. * gives a Penalty of 40 *l.* to the Burgess chosen and not returned, *so as* He sue for the same *within* 3 Months; or to any other Person, who, in Default of him so chosen, shall sue for the same. * C. 15.

Suppose *Latitats* were taken out, upon this Act, by the Party aggrieved, and *also* by many *other* Persons, in the *Long Vacation*; all bearing Date the last Day of *Trinity* Term; How could it be determined "*Who* had a Right to sue," but by shewing the *true* Times when the Writs were respectively prosecuted?

The 9 *Ann.* *c.* 14. gives an Action to the Person losing 10 *l.* at Play, to be brought within 3 Months; and if he do not sue *within* that Time, then to any Body else. There are a Multitude of Modern Acts, down to the present Session of Parliament, penned exactly in the same Way.

I have been told, That at *Nisi prius* it has often been ruled, in Suits upon such Statutes, "That the *true* Time of taking out the "Writ may be shewn, notwithstanding the *Teste*."

The very Penning of 8 *G.* 1. *c.* 19. is absolutely inconsistent with the Notion of the *Teste being conclusive*; because it says, "the Suit "shall be brought *before* the End of the next Term:" Which this Doctrine would construe to mean "*after* the End of the next Term."

 But

But there is One Act in the Statute-Book, which *alone* would be decisive, "that the true Time of Suing out the Writ *may* be "shewn:" And that is the 5 *W.* & *M. c.* 21. § 4. * where, (for preventing Abuses by arresting Persons without legal Process,) the Officer is required to enter the *very* DAY *when* the Writ is signed. But if the very Day could never be shewn in Pleading, or Evidence, it would have been most absurd to have provided a Record from which it might appear. The Statute does *not* ENACT that the Teste *shall* not be conclusive; but takes it *for granted*, that it *is* not.

* 'Tis *Sect.* 46. in the original printed Statute. And it is repealed in the 9, 10 *W.* 3. *c.* 25. § 42.

It was due to the great and long Litigation which this Question has born in *Westminster-Hall*, to consider carefully every Thing that has been said, and to look into every Case or Authority that has been quoted on the other Side.—I have done so: And, upon the most minute Examination, am not able to find any Principle of Law, Determination, or Authority, which contradicts the Proposition I have endeavoured to prove, *viz.* "That where the *true* Time "of Suing out a *Latitat* is *material*, It may be *shewn*, notwith- "standing the *Teste*."

The Arguments against allowing such an Averment, are drawn from Rules and Cases, the *Reason* of which is not the same, though they bear a seeming Similitude in *Sound*.

No Conclusion can be drawn from Rules established in the Case of a Writ which OUGHT *to bear Date the Day it is sued out*, and which may be quashed upon Motion, for Irregularity, if it be antedated.

I allow the Maxim laid down in † *Plowden*, and many other Books, "That no Man shall be allowed to plead or prove that "*such* a Writ was sued out on a different Day from that on which it bears Date." *Plowden* gives the *Reason*;" "Because contradict- "ing the Teste tends to discredit some judicial or other Officer of "Record."

† *Plowd.* 491. *b.* 492. *a.*

But this only goes to the *Mode* of Redress: The false Date does not *finally* conclude the Party. His Redress is in a *Summary Way*, by Application to the Court out of which the Writ issues. And therefore in the Court of Exchequer, in the Case of the || *King* v. *Mann*, upon an Extent, The Court inclined to disallow the Plea; and set aside the Writ *upon Motion*, because it was ante-dated.

|| 2 *Strange* 749.

But an Averment "that a LATITAT tested the last Day of the "precedent Term, issued in the Vacation," does NOT tend to "discredit the Officer:" For, by Law, it *may* so issue, and *ought* to be so ante-dated. It can not be set aside upon Motion for Irregularity; because it is right. The Averment does NOT *contradict* the Record; because, taking the *Course of this Court* together with the Teste of the Writ, it stands *indifferent* whether the Writ was sued out the last Day of the Term, or in the Vacation. And *there* is the Difference between such a Writ as *this*, and those that are intended by *Plowden*.

The Reason why No body shall be permitted to aver "that a "*Judgment* was signed *after* the first Day of the Term," or "that "a *Fieri facias* was taken out in the *Vacation*," is, because the FACT is *not relevant*: The legal Consequences do *not* depend upon the Truth of the *Fact*, on what Day the Judgment was completed, or the Writ of *Fieri facias* actually taken out; but upon the *Rule of Law*, "that they shall be deemed complete, and bind to all Intents and Purposes, *by Relation*."

The Moment the *Law* said, "Judgments should bind Purchasers *only from the Signing*," it followed, that, in the Case of Purchasers, the *Time* of Signing might be *shewn*.

If, to invalidate the Writ, there was an Averment "that it "ISSUED *on a Day in the* VACATION;" There the Inference would hold from the Case of a Judgment, or *Fieri facias*: And, to be sure, *such* an Averment could not be allowed; because, to *that* Purpose, the *Fact* is *not relevant*; For, by Law, a *Latitat may* issue in the Vacation, tested the last Day of the precedent Term.

Authorities, "that a *Latitat* is *void*, if it *bears Teste out of Term*," (which is the Case of * *Buckeridge* v. *Wright*,) prove Nothing to the present Purpose; because it is equally certain that it may be *purchased* out of Term, provided the *Teste* be formal. * *H.* 12 *G.* 1. in *B. R.*

The Case of † *Jones, an Attorney*, v. *Burnet*, upon a *Writ of Privilege*, is not applicable. The Court there held the Replication to be insufficient, but abated the Writ: And the Ground they went upon, was, That it appeared on the Plaintiff's own Shewing, "that "his Writ *bore Date* BEFORE his Cause of Action, though in Fact taken out after." But they considered that Writ as *in the Nature of an* ORIGINAL, and *therefore* abateable, if it bear Date before the Cause of Action. † *P.* 5 *G.* 2. in *C. B.*

Now the direct contrary is the established Law in the Case of a LATITAT; for it *may* bear Date *before*, if really prosecuted *after* the Cause of Action.

The

* 1 *Lutw.* 329. 333.

The Case of * *Aldworth* v. *Hutchinson* has been much relied upon, though it was never argued again: Judgment *Nisi* is said to have been given for the Plaintiff; and no Cause shewn. But no Judgment is entered upon the Roll. And there might be a very good Reason to give Judgment for the Plaintiff, upon the true Construction of the Covenant. The † *Words* might very fairly take in *all* Process *as of that Term*; especially a *Judicial* Writ, which must proceed upon a Ground *prior* to the End of the Term. The Reporter, Supposing the Time of suing out the *Scire facias* to be material, passes a strong Censure upon the Judgment, *if* it stop the Party from shewing the Truth. For He says, "*If* such be the "Ground, then, in Judgment of Law a Covenant may be broken, "when in Reality and Truth it never was broken: *Quod nota.*" And it would be well worth Noting indeed: for no Proposition could be more unjust.

† *V.* 1 *Lutw.* 331. "Ita quòd tal' Secta, Actio, Processus, Querela, Perturbatio, Clameum, vel Demand', contingerent incipi &c, per vel ante finem termini Sci' Mich' tunc prox' sequen'."

Upon the Argument in this Cause, It was said "that Ld. *Hardwicke*, in the Case of *Hoare* v. *Yates*, was of Opinion against the "Averment; and that Mr. J. *Lee came over* to that Opinion; and "that His Lordship was *ready* to have given Judgment, when He "was told the Parties had agreed."

I cannot form an Opinion upon a Point of Law, which would not be shaken by so great an Authority. But His Lordship has been so good as to let me have his Notes of the two Arguments, in that Case, before Him. There is no Notice taken in his Lordship's own Notes, of what might fall from Himself: And it does not appear from His Lordship's Notes of what Mr. Just. *Lee* said, that He changed his Opinion. His Lordship says, He believes He had not formed a conclusive Judgment in his own Mind; and that He certainly had made no Preparation towards delivering it in Court. And He has been pleased to tell me, that He inclined to the Opinions of Mr. Justice *Page* and Mr. Justice *Lee*, (who were for *admitting* the Averment in the Defendant's Rejoinder,) against the Opinion of Mr. J. *Probyn*, who thought it could not be admitted, by Law.

And We are All most clearly of Opinion, "That the *Averment* "in the Defendant's Rejoinder ought, by Law, to be *admitted.*" Consequently the Demurrer must be over-ruled; and

Judgment for the Defendant.

Martin,

Martin, ex dimiss. Henry Weston, *vers.* Mowlin.

Thursday 8th *May* 1760.

THIS was a Special Case from *Dorsetshire* Assizes, Upon an Ejectment brought for the Recovery of a Close of Pasture, of 12 Acres, called *New Close*, Parcel of the Manor of *Wyke Regis* and *Ellwell* in the County of *Dorset*. On "Not guilty" pleaded, and Issue thereon, the Cause came on to be tried: And a Verdict was found for the Plaintiff, Subject to the Opinion of the Court, on the following Case.

It appeared That the Premisses are Copyhold of Inheritance, holden of the said Manor; And that on 29th *April* 1691, One *Andrew Buckler* and *Rachel* his Wife did duly make a Surrender of the Premisses, to *Henry Weston*, in the Words following.

Then the Case sets forth this Surrender, *in hæc Verba:* Which is to the Use of the said *Henry Weston* in Fee; Who was, at the same Court admitted accordingly; *Under a* PROVISO *and* AGREEMENT "That if the aforesaid *Andrew Buckler* and *Rachel* his Wife or Either of them, or the Heirs Executors and Assigns of Either of them should *pay or cause to be paid* to the said *Henry Weston* his Heirs Executors or Assigns, the Sum of 5*l.* 10*s.* upon the 29th Day of *October* then next, and the full Sum of 225*l.* 10*s.* at or upon the 29th of *April* 1692, Then the said *Henry Weston* his Heirs or Assigns, should, upon the Request and at the Costs of the said *Andrew* and *Rachel* or One of them, SURRENDER into the Hands of the Lord and Farmers of the said Manor, the Premisses aforesaid with the Appurtenances, To the Use and Behoof of the said *Andrew*, for the Term of his Life; And after his Decease, to the Use and Behoof of the said *Rachel* for Term of her Life; And after the Decease of them and Both of them, to the Use and Behoof of the *Heirs of the Bodies* of Them, begotten or to be begotten; And for Default of such Issue, then to the Use and Behoof of the Right Heirs of the said *Andrew* for ever, according to the Custom of the said Manor. But if the said *Andrew* and *Rachel* their Heirs or Assigns should make Default in Payment of the several Sums aforesaid, or any of them, according to the Tenor and true Intention of this Condition, that then this present Surrender shall remain to the said *Henry Weston* his Heirs and Assigns for ever, in Force and Effect as aforesaid."

That by Virtue thereof, the said *Henry Weston* did enter into Possession thereof, and was in Possession at the Time of his Death, which happened on the 6th of *April* 1705.

That the ſaid Sum was *not paid* according to the Condition of the ſaid Surrender: And it appeared that the *Equity of Redemption* of the Premiſſes was *not foreclosed or releaſed* during the Life of the ſaid *Henry Weſton.*

It further appeared that the ſaid *Henry Weſton*, on the 22d of *July* 1699, ſurrendered the Premiſſes and divers other Copyhold Eſtates in the ſame Manor, in the Words following, " Ad hanc " Curiam venit *Johannes Gray* Unus Cuſtomar' Tenen' iſtius Ma- " nerij, et hic in plenâ Curia, virtute cujuſdam Scripti vocat' a " Letter of Attorney ei direct', et Authoritate per idem Scriptum " conceſſ' ſub Manu et Sigillo Henrici Weſton al' Cuſtomar' Tenen' " Manerij prædict' geren' Dat die et anno ſupradict', et in no- " mine et ex parte ipſius Henrici Weſton, ſurſum reddidit in manus " Dominorum et Firmar' Manerij prædict', Un' le Gentleman's " Land vocat' Lane Houſe &c &c &c (deſcribing ſeveral Parcels " lying within the ſaid Manor,) *Aceciam Un' Clauſ' Paſturæ de* " *novo incluſum* continen' per eſtimationem *duodecim Acras* &c &c " (deſcribing the Premiſſes in queſtion,) Necnon totum Statum " Jus Titulum Intereſſe Clam' et Demand' quæcunque prædict' " Henrici Weſton *tam in Lege* QUAM *in* ÆQUITATE de et in " Præmiſſis prædict' et qualibet inde Parte et Parcella; Ad Opus et " Uſum prædicti Henrici Weſton pro termino Vitæ ſuæ; Et poſt " Ejus deceſſum, Ad Opus et Uſum talis Perſonæ ſive Perſonarum " cui vel quibus, et pro tali Statu ſive Statibus qual' ipſe prædictus " Henricus Weſton, *per Ultimam Voluntatem ſuam* aut per aliquod " aliud Scriptum ſub Manu et Sigillo prædicti Henrici Weſton, da- " bit deviſabit limitabit declarabit ſive appunctuabit; Et pro de- " fectu talis Donationis Deviſamenti Limitationis Declarationis ſive " Appunctuationis, Ad Opus et Uſum rectorum Hæredum ipſius " Henrici Weſton in perpetuum, Secundùm Conſuetudinem Ma- " nerij prædict. Super quo, ad iſtam eandem Curiam venit præ- " dictus Henricus Weſton, et cepit de Dominis et Firmar' prædictis " Præmiſſa prædicta ſuperius ſurſum reddita cum omnibus et ſingu- " lis eorum pertin', Habend' et Tenend' omnia et ſingula Præ- " miſſa prædicta cum ſuis pertin', præfato Henrico Weſton pro " termino Vitæ ſuæ; et poſt Ejus Deceſſum, tali Perſonæ ſive " Perſonis cui vel quibus, et pro tali ſtatu ſive ſtatibus qual' " ipſe prædictus Henricus Weſton, *per ultimam Voluntatem ſuam* " aut per aliquod aliud Scriptum ſub manu et ſigillo ſuis, da- " bit deviſabit limitabit declarabit ſive appunctuabit, prout ſupe- " riùs limitatur; Et pro defectu inde, rectis Hæredibus ipſius Hen- " rici Weſton in perpetuum, ſecundùm Conſuetudinem Manerij " prædicti; SUBJECT' *tamen ſeparalibus* CONDITIONIBUS *in qui-* " *buſdam Copijs Rotulorum Cur' Manerij præd' mentionat'*, quarum " ſeparal' Dat' ſunt prout ſequen', viz. Un' geren' Dat. 24to. die " Januarij

" Januarij 1682; Alter' geren' Dat' 17 die Octobris 1689; et un' " al' geren' Dat' 29 *die Aprilis* 1691; per antiq' Redd' inde per " annum, ac per omnia al' Onera Opera Consᶠ Sectas et Servitia " inde prius debita et de jure consueta. Et pro tali statu et In- " gressu &c, prædictus Henricus Weston dat' &c: Et sic admissus " est inde Tenens, fecitque &c."

That the Premisses in the lastmentioned Surrender called by the Name of " One Close of Pasture newly inclosed, containing by Esti- " mation 12 Acres," are the Premisses in Question, and the same as were contained in the said first mentioned Surrender.

On the 30th of *September* 1701, (the said *Andrew Buckler* being then dead, and the said *Rachel* his Widow living,) the said *Henry Weston* made and published his *last Will*, in Writing; and thereby devised in the Words following—" As to my Worldly Estate, I dis- " pose thereof as followeth. And first I give to my Son *William* " *Weston* the Sum of 200*l.* of lawful *English* Money, to be paid to " Him, within One Year next after my Decease: And as to the " *Security* for the Payment thereof, I do hereby CHARGE *All those* " my Lands Tenements and Hereditaments *within and Parcel of* " *the Manor of Wyke Regis aforesaid* which were heretofore *surren-* " *dered to Me by John Gray* deceased; And also All that my Close of " Meadow called *Orchard Meadow*, lying and being in the Town " of *Weymouth* in the said County. *Item*, I do hereby strictly charge " and command my Son *Henry Weston* to take great Care of my " Wife his Mother; and to find and provide for Her, during her " Life, sufficient and convenient Necessaries of all Sorts. *Item*, I " give and devise unto my Daughter *Mary Wallis* Widow, One " Yearly Annuity or Yearly Rent-Charge of 15*l.* to be paid to Her " Yearly and every Year from my Death, for and during the Term " of her Natural Life, clear of all Deductions, and to be issuing due " and payable to Her out of those my Lands called *Marsh* and " *Bowneham*, within and Parcel of the said Manor of *Wyke Regis*: " Which said Yearly Annuity or Rent-Charge I do hereby direct " to be paid to my said Daughter Yearly and every Year by 4 equal " quarterly Payments to be made on *&c*; the first Payment to be " made *&c*. And if Default shall be made at any Time or Times " in Payment of the said Annuity or Yearly Rent-Charge of 15*l.* " on any or either of the Feasts aforesaid, then I do hereby devise " unto my said Daughter the said Lands called *Bowneham* and *March*, " for and during the Term of her natural Life. *And whereas Ra-* " *chel Buckler Widow stands indebted to Me, in a Considerable Sum of* " *Money, I do hereby appoint and give Her twelve Months Time after* " *my Death, to pay the same: And I do give Her 50l. to be allowed* " *out of the said Debt*. *Item*, I give to the Poor of the Parish of " *Wyke Regis* aforesaid, the Sum of 4*l.* to be distributed amongst

 them,

" them, by my Executor herein after named, at my Funeral. *Item,* " ALL *my Lands Tenements and Hereditaments* WITHIN AND PARCEL OF THE SAID MANOR OF WYKE REGIS, And also all other " my Lands Tenements and Hereditaments in the County of *Dorset,* " (*Such Parts thereof as are above charged* for the Payment of the " said 200*l.* to my said Son *William,* and for my said Daughter's " Annuity, *subject thereto,*) I do give and devise unto my said Son " *Henry Weston,* and unto *Ann* his now Wife, and to the *Heirs of* " *the Body* of my said Son *Henry on the Body of the said Ann* law-" fully begotten and to be begotten; and for Default of such Issue, " to my Right Heirs for ever. *Item,* I give and bequeath to my " said Son *Henry Weston* All my Goods and Chattels and Personal " Estate whatsoever; He paying my Debts Legacies and Funeral " Expences: And I do hereby make and appoint Him my said Son " *Henry Weston* my Executor.

That the said Testator was seised in Fee of the said Close called *Orchard Meadow,* in the said Will mentioned.

That the Testator died on the 6th of *April* 1705, without revoking or altering his said Will; which was proved by the said *Henry Weston* the Son, in the Month of *May* following.

That it did *not appear* Whether the said *Rachel Buckler* was or was not *indebted to the said Testator otherwise than on Account of the Mortgage aforesaid.*

That the said *Money* NOT *having been paid,* and the said *Rachel* being also dead, JOHN BUCKLER *Son and Heir of the said Andrew and Rachel,* was on the 24th Day of *July* 1705, at a Court of the said Manor, *admitted Tenant of the Premisses;* and did, at the same Court, make the following *Surrender* of the Premisses in question, to the said *Henry Weston the Son:* Which Admittance and Surrender are set forth *in hæc Verba.* The Admittance is in Common Form: And the Surrender is " Of the Premisses, necnon totum Statum Jus " Titulum Interesse Clam' et Demand' sua quæcunque *tam in lege* " *quam in æquitate* de et in Præmissis prædict' et qualibet inde parte " et parcella; Ad opus et usum Henrici Weston Hæred' et Assign' " su' in perpetuum, secundum Cons' *&c.*" Upon which Surrender the said Henry *Weston* was admitted.

That the said *Henry Weston* (the Son) having Issue, amongst Others, the Lessor of the Plaintiff (his Eldest Son) and a Daughter *Sarah Weston,* did on the 27th Day of *April* 1738, at a Court of the said Manor, make the following Surrender: Which Surrender is set out *in hæc Verba,* and appears to be a Surrender of the Pre-" misses, in common Form, by the said *H. W.* To the Use and

" Behoof of Him the said *Henry Weston*, for and during the Term " of his Life; and from and after his Decease, To the Use and " Behoof of SARAH WESTON Daughter of Him the said *Henry* " *Weston*, her Heirs and Assigns for ever." And the said *Henry* was, at the same Court, admitted according to his said Surrender.

That the Premisses in the last mentioned Surrender called " New " Close," are the Premisses in question.

That the beforementioned ANN, the *Wife* of *Henry Weston* the Son, was *then living*, and *did* NOT *join* in the said Surrender.

That the said *Sarah Weston* afterwards intermarried with *John Mowlin*: Both of whom are *dead*, leaving the *Defendant* their *Eldest Son and Heir*.

That the said *Henry Weston* the Son died on the 18th of *December* 1749; having survived his said Daughter *Sarah*.

The said *Ann* his Wife died on the 28th Day of *November* 1756.

On the Death of the said *Henry Weston* the Son, The Defendant, by his Guardian, entered; and hath been hitherto in Possession of the Premisses in question.

It appeared that, by the Custom of the Manor, Copyhold Estates *may be intailed*, and *barred by Surrender*.

The Question submitted to the Judgment of the Court was— " Whether the Plaintiff, upon this Case, is intitled to recover."

This Case was argued, on *Tuesday* the 6th of *May* 1760, by Mr. *Glynn* for the Plaintiff, and Serjeant *Stanniford* for the Defendant.

Mr. *Glynn* (for the Plaintiff) divided it into two Questions; *viz.*

1st. Whether *Any Estate Tail* was CREATED by the Will of Old *Henry Weston* the Grandfather, to *Henry Weston* the Son and *Ann* his Wife and the Heirs of their two Bodies:

2dly. If any such Estate Tail was thereby created, Then Whether it was BARRED *by the Surrender of Henry Weston the Son*, WITHOUT *his Wife Ann*, on 27th of *April* 1738.

First—He insisted that an *Estate Tail* WAS *created* by Old *Henry Weston*'s Will. 1st Point.

He argued that the Testator clearly considered this as a *Real* Estate, and meant to *devise it as such*, and not as personal Estate. He was in *Possession* of it; He had advanced near the full Value upon it; and He saw *no Prospect of it's being redeemed*; and He *had surrendered it to the Use of his Will.*

The Estate *passed* by the *Surrender:* The Will is no more than a Declaration of the Uses of the Surrender.

And as to the Clause in the Will relating to *Rachel Buckler's* "*standing indebted* to the Testator in a considerable Sum of Money," It does not at all appear, *what* Pecuniary Connexions subsisted between the Testator and Her: This might be some *other* distinct Debt, that had no Relation to this Mortgage of her Husband's.

The *Surrender* made by *John Buckler*, the Son and Heir of *Andrew* and *Rachel*, to *Henry Weston* the Son, is by no Means a conclusive Circumstance. For *John Buckler* did not mean to assert any Right *to Himself*, in the Estate: He only meant to *confirm Henry Weston's* Title to it.

If the Money should be paid in, A Court of Equity would direct it to be *laid out in Land.*

2d Point. Secondly—The Estate Tail could NOT *be barred* by the single Surrender of *Henry Weston* alone, WITHOUT *his Wife*. For He and his Wife took a *Joint-Estate* for their Lives, by ENTIERTY, under the Will of old *Henry Weston*. 1 *Inst.* 183. Marquis of *Winchester's* Case. 3 *Co.* 1. *Owen* v. *Morgan*, there cited, and reported in 3 *Co.* 5. *a*.

And if this be the Construction as to *Freeholds*, it must be the same as to *Copyholds:* For the same Rule holds in Both. *Coke's Complete Copyholder* 69.

No *Bar* could arise from this Surrender, Whether it be considered as analogous to a *Fine*, or as a *Recovery*.

1st. Considering it as analogous to a *Fine*, It only makes a *Discontinuance*. A Surrender can't have the Effect of an *Estoppel*. 2 *Ro. Rep.* 256. *Southcott* v. *Adams*, (2d Point of that Case.) It is a Deed-Poll. No Conclusion arises, as to the Reversion in Fee to Himself.

2dly. Considering it as a *Recovery*, It would *not be good*, by the Case of *Owen* v. *Morgan*, just now cited: For He has assumed to Himself a *different* Tenancy, from what He was intitled to.

But

But Fines and Recoveries are not to be applied to *Copyholds*, or compared to *Surrenders of Copyholds*.

A *Surrender* is in the Nature of a *Conveyance*, and operates as an *Extinguishment*. A Surrenderor can't make a Discontinuance, unless He has a Capacity of surrendering *both the Inheritance and Estate*. *Co. Litt.* 325. *a.* But *this* Surrenderor had no Power to convey it as a Remainder: He had no Power over the Tenancy; which He took by *Entierty*. This Surrender is totally *void*: Nothing could be conveyed by it. Surrenders are upon the Foot of *Grants* or *Releases*: A Person can neither grant release nor surrender *more than He has in him*. A *Lease* by the Husband would have been void after his Decease: The Tenancy is in the Wife. And thus it is, in Cases of Waste: So also of a Copyhold Manor. *Cro. Jac.* 99. Therefore this Act of the Husband alone, *without* his Wife, is not voidable, but *void*: He could only convey an Estate of Freehold for his *own Life*.

Consequently, There is a good Estate in the Lessor of the Plaintiff; And it is not affected by this Surrender.

Serjeant *Stanniford*, who argued on behalf of the Defendant, previously observed, that whether this Estate is to be considerad as *Copyhold*, or as *Personal* Estate, it still comes to the *same Person*, *viz.* *Henry Weston* the Son, who is both *Devisee* and also *Executor*: And Copyhold Lands are liable to pay Debts; And it does not appear that there was sufficient, without it, to pay the Testator's Debts. And He also took Notice of the Clause in old *Henry Weston*'s Surrender to the Use of his Will, " That the Limitations in his Will " were to be SUBJECT TO THE CONDITIONS *mentioned in certain* " *Copies of Court-Rolls* of the said Manor;" And this very Court-Roll of *Andrew Buckler*'s Surrender to Him is *particularly specified* as One of them; By which Court-Roll and the Copy of it, the said *Henry Weston* the Testator was admitted to this Estate, *not absolutely*, but as *subject to Redemption* by *Andrew* and *Rachel Buckler*: And, *Andrew* being dead when the Will was made; the Testator gives *Rachel* Time to redeem it, and also 50*l.* out of the Debt. This, He said, amounted to a clear and full Proof " that the Testator did " *not* consider Himself as absolute Owner of this Estate." Besides, The Devise to his Son *Henry* is only in *general* Terms: And there are *other* Estates mentioned in the Will, which are sufficient to satisfy a Devise in such general Terms, *without* having Recourse to this Mortgage of Copphold Lands.

Then He proceeded to answer Mr. *Glynn*, upon the two Points which He had made.

As

1st Point. As to the former, He denied that any Estate-Tail was created by Old *Henry Weston*'s Will; or that the Testator had any such Intention. He knew He was *but a Mortgagee:* And He has *not* devised this particular Land by *particular Words.* And He manifestly considers *Rachel Buckler* as having the *Right of Redemption.* Therefore He could not mean to intail it. And though He lived till 1705, He never foreclosed the Equity of Redemption.

Neither did the Persons who claimed under his Will, claim under the *Intail*, but as *Executor* and *Residuary Devisees.* In *July* 1705, *John Buckler*, who was Heir both to his Father and Mother, surrendered to the Use of *Henry Weston* the Son, in Fee; Who was admitted accordingly; and who accepted it as *Executor* of his Father's Will; and who lived till *December* 1749. *Ann* his Wife, who survived Him near seven Years, did *not enter:* But the present Defendant entered on the Death of his Father, and hath been in Possession ever since.

2d Point. As to the latter, He insisted That although it should be admitted that this Land did pass by the Devise as *Real* Estate, and that *Henry Weston* the Son and *Anne* his Wife were *seised of it as Devisees*, Yet they were seised of it in such a Manner, that the Surrender of it by *Henry Weston alone, without his Wife*, was a *sufficient* BAR.

Copyholds are not intailable, He said, under the *Statute de Donis*; but by *Custom:* And the Intail of them can be barred *only by Custom.* And they are barrable, in 3 Methods only; *viz.* by *Surrender* in the Lord's Court, by *Recovery*, by *Forfeiture.*

Here, The *Wife*'s Estate was *no Impediment* to the Surrender. The Husband and Wife were seised to them and to the Heirs of his Body by Her: And the Husband and Wife took by *Moieties.* Therefore the Recovery is good as to a *Moiety.* And it is not like the Case of * *Owen* and *Morgan:* For there the Husband and Wife took by *Entierty.* And † *Cuppeldike*'s Case fully proves "that if "the Husband alone had been vouched, it had been a good Bar." And He cited Lord *Sheffield's Case* v. *Ratcliffe*, in *Hob.* 334. and several other Books, (*Godb.* 300. *Palmer* 352. 2 *Ro. Rep.* 312, 333, 374, 496, 501. *Sir Wm. Jones* 69. and *Jenkins* 286.) and also 2 *Ro. Abr.* 394. Tit. *Recovery Common*, Let. *A. pl.* 4. to the same Effect. From whence He argued, that the Case of *Owen* v. *Morgan* was not founded upon the Wife's Interest in the Estate; but upon the Husband's not being a good Tenant to the *Præcipe.*

* 3 *Co.* 5. *a.* *Moore* 210. 4 *Leon.* 26, 93, 222.
† 3 *Co.* 5. *b.* 6. *a.* 2 *Ro. Abr.* 395. Let. D. *pl.* 5.

He said, it must be taken that there is, in this Manor, a Custom "to suffer a Recovery." And this is an effectual Bar to the Estate Tail.

Therefore He prayed Judgment for the Defendant, as in Case of a Nonsuit.

Mr. *Glynn* replied,

That the Estate is particularly described in the *Surrender to the Use of Old H. W.'s. Will,* though not in the said Will itself: And *Nothing appears,* to shew that the Testator meant to consider this as Part of his *Personal* Estate. 1st Point.

A *Surrender* is *not analogous to a Recovery;* It is not to have the Effect of a Recovery with double Voucher; which stands upon a peculiar technical Reason, (*viz.* the Recovery in Value, which would go to the Heir in Tail;) which Reason don't hold in the present Case. The Husband can only make an Estate for his *own Life:* He can't affect his *Wife*'s Estate. And her Estate, remaining unaffected, will *protect the subsequent Remainders.* Therefore this Surrender cannot operate as a Bar. 2d Point.

The Court took two Days Time, to advise:

And on *Thursday* the 8th of *May* 1760,

Lord Mansfield delivered their Resolution: Which was for the Defendant, on both Points; *viz.* That the Estate did *not pass* by the Devise; and that it was *well barred,* if it had.

After having particularly stated the Case, his Lordship observed That at the Time of Old *Henry Weston's* making the Surrender to the Use of his Will, He manifestly considered this as a Mortgage *subject to Redemption,* though forfeited: For in this Surrender He has inserted the Words " totum Statum Jus Titulum Interesse &c " prædicti Henrici Weston, *tam in Lege quam in Æquitate,* de et " in Præmissis." Then, by his Will, He charges these Lands, together with his Orchard-Meadow in *Weymouth,* for Security of the Payment of a Legacy of 200*l.* to his Son *William.* Then He mentions *Rachel Buckler*'s standing indebted to Him; and gives Her Time for Payment of the Debt, and 50*l.* out of it. And afterwards, by a *general* Description, He gives and devises " All his Lands Tenements and Hereditaments within and Parcel of the said Manor " of *Wyke Regis,* and also All other his Lands Tenements and " Hereditaments in the County of *Dorset,* (Such Parts thereof as " are above charged for the Payment of the said 200*l.* to his said " Son *William,* and for his Daughter's Annuity, subject thereto,) " to his Son *Henry Weston* and *Ann* his Wife and to the Heirs of the " Body of the said Son *Henry* on the Body of said *Ann* lawfully begotten;

" gotten and to be begotten." And He bequeaths all his Perſonal Eſtate whatſoever, to his ſaid Son *Henry*; and makes Him his Executor.

The Plaintiff is the only Son and Heir of *Henry Weſton* (this Son of the Teſtator) by the ſaid *Anne* his Wife: And He claims this Parcel of Land called *New Cloſe*, as Heir of their two Bodies, in ſpecial Tail, Under the Will of his Grandfather, as being deviſed thereby under this general Deſcription.

To this Claim, thus founded on a Special Intail, Two Anſwers are given, on the Part of the Defendant. The firſt is, That it was not deviſed *as Land*, but *as Money*; it being only a Security for Money, and redeemable at that Time, by *Rachel Buckler*. (And if this be ſo, it makes an End of the Caſe.) The ſecond Anſwer is, That ſuppoſing it to be deviſed *as Land*, and ſuppoſing it to be *intailed* too, Yet an Eſtate Tail may, by the *Cuſtom* of this Manor, be *barred by a Surrender* in the Lord's Court; And that here has actually been ſuch a Surrender made by *Henry Weſton*, *ſufficient to bar the Intail*, though made by Him *alone* without his Wife, and though his Wife Herſelf might not have been prejudiced by it.

1ſt Point. As to the Conſtruction of the Will of Old *Henry Weſton*—If it appeared that the Teſtator really *meant and intended* to deviſe this Cloſe *as Land*, it would then be a Deviſe of *Land*; the Mortgage being forfeited by Law, and the Eſtate in the Land become abſolute. But if it appears that the Teſtator meant and intended it as a Bequeſt of *Money* only, Then it would be conſidered, in a Court of Equity, as a ſpecific Bequeſt of the *Money*: And a Court of Equity would not direct the Money to be laid out in Land, without expreſs Words in the Will to ground ſuch Direction upon.

It ſeems to Me, That the Teſtator all along underſtood this to be Part of his Personal Eſtate; and that He meant to diſpoſe of it *as ſuch*, by this Will. He ſurrendered it as charged with a *Condition of Redemption and Re-Surrender*: And in his Will, He manifeſtly conſidered it as a Debt due from *Rachel Buckler*; and that Debt, as Part of his *Perſonal* Eſtate.

It will be neceſſary to conſider *What Species* of Property the Teſtator had in this Eſtate.

A Mortgage is a *Charge* upon the Land: And whatever would give the *Money*, will carry the Eſtate in the Land *along with it*, to every Purpoſe. The Eſtate in the Land is the *ſame Thing* as the Money due upon it. It will be *liable to Debts*; It will *go to Executors*; It will paſs by a Will *not* made and executed with the So-

2 lemnities

lemnities required by the *Statute of Frauds.* The *Assignment of the Debt*, or *forgiving it*, will draw the *Land* after it, as a *Consequence*: Nay, it would do it, though the Debt were forgiven only by *Parol*; For the Right to the Land would follow, notwithstanding the Statute of Frauds.

The Rule of Law *attaches* at the Time of the *Testator's Death*: No *subsequent* Act of the Mortgagor can alter the Nature of the Property. It is the Rule of Law, that governs the Property, and leaves no Election to any Body to vary it after the Death of the Testator.

Though the Testator has not in his *Will* expressly mentioned this Estate to be redeemable, Yet he has done so in the *Surrender to the Use of his Will*: He surrenders it *as* liable to a Condition *in Equity*; (For at *Law*, it was become absolute;) And there had not run above 8 or 9 Years upon this Mortgage, when he made this Surrender. So that He appears to have made the Surrender of it, only to substantiate his Claim upon the Estate; and upon the Face of the Surrender, plainly considered it as *redeemable*.

And so He did in his *Will* too. We must take it, upon the *Will*, that the Widow *Buckler* owed Him *no other* Debt but this: For de *non existentibus* et de *non apparentibus* eadem est Ratio. He gives her Time to pay it; He gives her a specific Legacy, out of it; He gives it *as a Debt*, towards Payment of his Debts and Legacies, "I give and bequeath to my Son *Henry Weston* All my Goods "Chattels and *Personal Estate whatsoever*, He *paying my Debts, Le*-"*gacies* and Funeral Expences." And there is Nothing to control this, but the *general* Words "All my Lands Tenements and Here-"ditaments within and Parcel of the said Manor *&c.*" But his *Creditors* and *Legatees* had a *Right* to have it considered as *Personal* Estate.

Therefore We All agree in Opinion, "That He *meant* to pass it *as a* DEBT." And there is no Colour to imagine that it could be considered in a Court of Equity as a specific Bequest of Money which they would direct to be laid out in Land.

AS TO the Estate's being BARRED, in case it had passed by the Devise; There is no Doubt but that it would have been *well barred by this Surrender*. 2d Point.

By the Custom of this Manor, intailed Copyhold Estates are barrable by Surrender in the Lord's Court: And *Henry Weston* the Son has here actually made such a Surrender. Though He could not bar it in *One* Form, He might do it in *another*. Wherever the Tenant

Tenant in Tail of a *Freehold* Estate could by *any* Means bar the Estate, there this Tenant in Tail of this Copyhold might do it by Surrender; And his Surrender shall *operate as a good Recovery*.

Consequently, Upon *this* Point, the Lessor of the Plaintiff can have no Title.

Therefore, *quâcunque* via datâ, the Plaintiff appears to have *no Title*: And the Defendant must have Judgment as in case of a Nonsuit.

RULE accordingly, That the *Postea* be delivered to the Defendant; and that Judgment be entered for Him, as in case of a Nonsuit.

Rex *verſ.* Benfield and Saunders.

MR. Serj. *Nares*, Mr. *Aston* and Mr. *Stowe* shewed Cause Why the *Judgment* against these two Defendants should *not be arrested*.

An Information had been filed against these two Persons, together with Three others, for a Misdemeanour: Which Information consisted of 4 Counts; One, for a Riot; Another, for publishing a Libel; A third, for a Riot and Libel; And the 4th and last, as hereafter follows.

The other Three Defendants were acquitted of the whole Information.

Benfield and *Saunders* were acquitted of all the Rest of the Information, excepting this 4th Count: But they were found Guilty of this Count, which is as follows, *viz.*

That they the said *Thomas Benfield*, *Thomas Wills*, *Thomas Kyte*, *John Saunders*, and *Thomas Jones*, being such Persons as aforesaid, and most unlawfully wickedly maliciously and unjustly devising designing contriving and intending (as much as in them lay) further to *disturb molest and disquiet* Him the said *Daniel Cooke*, and to *destroy his domestic Peace and Happiness in his Family, and the Comfort He had in his said two Children John and Jane Cooke, and to hurt and injure* HIM THE SAID DANIEL COOKE *in his Trade and Business* of a Grocer, which He the said *Daniel Cooke* then and there, to wit, at *Cheltenham* aforesaid, in the County of *Gloucester* aforesaid, exercised, and for a long Time before there had exercised and followed with great Credit and Reputation, and thereby to reduce him the said *Daniel Cooke* to Want and Poverty; and also most unlawfully wickedly maliciously and unjustly devising designing contriving and intending to *traduce scandalize and vilify* THEM *the said* JOHN COOKE *and* JANE COOKE, Son and Daughter of the said *Daniel Cooke*, being Persons of good Name Fame Credit Character and Reputation, and being Persons of honest chaste and virtuous Lives and Conversation, and being then in great Credit and Esteem with all the honest Liege Subjects of our said present Sovereign Lord the King with whom they the said *John Cooke* and *Jane Cooke* were acquainted; And also most unlawfully unjustly wickedly and maliciously devising designing contriving and intending *to represent suggest and make it be believed and thought that the said* JOHN COOKE *was a dishonest immoral and ill disposed Person, and that the said* JANE COOKE *was a lewd wanton dissolute disorderly and ill-disposed Person and had been guilty of Incontinency Lewdness Debauchery and Fornication, and also to make it be believed and thought that She the said Jane Cooke had been got with Child of a Bastard and had been delivered of a Bastard Child at London in order to conceal the Birth thereof*; and also devising and contriving most unlawfully and unjustly to *hurt* and *injure* THEM *the said* JOHN COOKE *and* JANE COOKE *in* THEIR *good Name Fame Credit Character and Reputation, and to expose the said* JOHN COOKE AND JANE COOKE *to Shame Infamy Scandal and Dishonour, and to bring* THEM *into Disgrace Hatred and Contempt with all the Liege Subjects of our said present Sovereign Lord the King knowing* THEM *the said* JOHN *Cooke and* JANE *Cooke*; *and the sooner to complete perfect and bring to Effect their said most unlawful wicked and unjust Purposes aforesaid*; THEY the said *Thomas Benfield* the Younger, *Thomas Wills*, *Thomas Kyte*, *John Saunders*, and *Thomas Jones*, afterwards, *viz.* upon the 26th Day of *May* in the said 32d Year of the Reign of our said present Sovereign Lord the King, in the Evening of the same Day, with Force and Arms, at *Cheltenham* aforesaid, in the County of *Gloucester* aforesaid, to wit *in the public Street and King's Common Highway there, before and near unto the Dwelling-house of him the said* DANIEL COOKE there situate, with *loud Voices* and in a *public open and ludicrous Manner*, in the Presence and Hearing of divers Liege Subjects of our said present Sovereign Lord the King, did unlawfully wickedly and maliciously SING say speak utter *publish* and pronounce, and did cause to be SUNG said spoken uttered *published* and pronounced divers other *false scandalous malicious obscene* and *libellous* SONGS Verses and Matters, *of and concerning the said* JOHN *Cooke and* JANE *Cooke*, greatly reflecting upon the *Characters and Reputations* of THEM the said JOHN *Cooke and* JANE *Cooke:* In One of which said *libellous Songs*, of and concerning the said *Jane Cooke*, were contained divers false scandalous infamous and malicious Words, Matters and Expressions, according to the Tenor following, that is to say, "There are two People in *Cheltenham*

" Town; The One, a Lusty Spark: They Both do take Delight " in *Game*; Each One doth keep a Park. In One, there is a *Buck*; " In the other, there's a *Doe*;" (meaning the said *Jane Cooke*:) " And if you can but Favour get, *A Hunting you may go.* But if " that She" (meaning the said *Jane Cooke*) " is going proud, and " like to be at Rut; They turn Her," (again meaning the said *Jane Cooke*,) " into a Neighbour's Park; And there to take the Buck. " And when that He has done his Best, And this fine *Doe*," (again meaning the said *Jane Cooke*,) " is cloy'd; Then up She goes to " *London* Town, her Young One for to hide;" (meaning to hide a Bastard Child of Her the said *Jane Cooke*) And when She" (again meaning the said *Jane Cooke*) " had been there a While, If " that You will but mind, Then out She" (again meaning the said *Jane Cooke*) " cometh from that Park, and leaves her *Fawn*," (meaning a Bastard Child of the said *Jane Cooke*) " behind. But " yet a while in Town must stay; till all Things safe and sound: " Then, Home She," (again meaning the said *Jane Cooke*,) " comes, to her own Park, to take the other Round." And in *One other* of the said *libellous Songs*, of and concerning the said John *Cooke*, were contained divers other false scandalous infamous and malicious Words Matters and Expressions, according to the Tenor following, that is to say, " Come all you jolly Wonters " bold; and take a Turn with me: Such Sport I'll shew, each " Night, (though cold,) before you ne'er did see. And a Wont-" ing We will go, We'll go, We'll go; And a Wonting We will " go. My Master *Johnny Moll*" (meaning the said John Cooke) " has got such Tricks enough in Store; His Fame" (meaning the Fame of Him the said John Cooke) " is spread from East to " West, on Shutters, Posts and Doors &c. When Night has spread " her sable Veil, and all Things safe and sure, He'll" (meaning that the said John Cooke will) " shew You Tricks; He'll" (again meaning the said John Cooke will) " never fail; if you'll " but nick the Hour, &c. We hire Men to catch our Wonts; " who *steal* them" (meaning the Wonts or Moles,) " when 'tis " done. We love our Puggs; We dearly hugg: And is not this " good Fun? &c. For every Trap has got a Trick, to make the " Game his own: The like was never known before, in Country, " City or Town, &c. No begging Dish-Clout e'er shall wipe " away so great a Blot: For all their Talk, and all their Balk, it " will not be so soon forgot, &c. And the Fame of *Johnny*'s " Moll" (meaning the said John Cooke) " is seen on every Door: " Each Yard, each Gate, each Stile, each Post, shall spread it " more and more. And a Wonting We will go, We'll go, We'll " go; And a Wonting We will go." To the great Damage Scandal, Infamy and Disgrace of the said Daniel Cooke, John Cooke, and Jane Cooke; In Contempt of our said present Sovereign Lord the King and his Laws; To the evil and pernicious Example &c; and against the Peace &c.

Upon this Count only, and the Matters therein charged, the Two present Defendants were found Guilty.

The Motion in Arrest of Judgment, made by Mr. *Ashurst*, on *Friday* 26th of *April* last, and now supported by Mr. *Morton*, as well as Himself, was grounded upon three Objections.

1st. That an Information or Indictment will not lie, for publishing Two *distinct* Libels, *upon* Two *distinct Persons*; any more than an Indictment will lie, for an *Assault* UPON Two: And that such an Indictment is not good, was determined in this Court in *Tr.* 1730, 3, 4 *G.* 2. in the Case of *Rex* v. *Clendon*, reported in 2 *Strange* 870, and 2 *Ld. Raym.* 1572. The Reason is, because these are *distinct Offences*, and require different and distinct Judgments, and may require different and distinct Fines: And therefore they can *not* be *joined* in One and the same Indictment; but there ought to be a *several* Indictment for *Each*. The Libel upon *John Cooke* was an absolutely distinct and quite different Libel from that on *Jane*.

In *Carthew* 226, 227. *The King* v. *Roberts*, *P.* 4 *W.* & *M. B. R.* The whole Court were of Opinion, after great Deliberation, That an Information against a Ferryman, "for taking more than the "usual Rate from *divers* Persons, for the Passage of themselves and "their Cattle," was too general and uncertain: And *per Holt*, Ch. J. "In every such Information. a *single Offence* ought to be "laid and ascertained; because *every Extortion from every particular* "*Person* is a *separate* and *distinct* Offence; And therefore they ought "NOT *to be accumulated under a* GENERAL *Charge:* because Each "Offence requires a *separate and distinct Punishment*, according to "the Quantity of the Offence; and 'tis not possible for the Court "to proportion the Fine or other Punishment to it, unless it is sin-"gly and certainly laid." And that Judgment was arrested.

The Answer given to this first Objection, by the Counsel for the Prosecutors, was, "That the Cases cited are *distinct Offences:* Where-"as the Whole of *this* is but *One single* Offence." And as to the Case of *Rex* v. *Clendon*, there is in *West's Symboleography*, a Precedent of an Indictment against One for assaulting and beating *Two*, in the Highway, to the Intent to have killed or robbed them. *Part* 2d. Title *Indictments*, § 191.

The COURT thought that this 1st Objection had received a sufficient Answer, *in both respects*. For they looked upon this to be ONE Offence: The Gist of the Charge is *Singing* these Songs, in the Manner and with the Intent charged in the Information; And singing them

them at the Father's Door, with Intent to discredit Him and his Children, and disturb his domestic Peace and Comfort.

And as to the Case of * *The King* and *Clendon*, They treated it as a Case that was not well considered; and held it *not to be Law*. Can not the King call a Man to Account for a Breach of the Peace; because he broke *two* Heads instead of One? How many Informations have been for Libels upon the King *and His Ministers*? This is a Prosecution in the *King's Name*, for the Offence charged: It is *not* an Application at the Suit of each particular *Party* injured. It is not like an *Action*; where each Person injured is respectively to recover *separate Damages*.

* 2 *Strange* 870. 2 *Ld. Raym.* 1572.

Therefore this 1st Objection was *over-ruled*.

The 2d Objection upon which this Motion was founded, and which was now further enforced, was "That *several distinct Defendants*, charged with *several and distinct Offences*, can *not* be *joined together* in the same Indictment or Information; because the "Offence of *One* is *not* the Offence of the *Other*: And the *present* "Charge is made up of *separate and distinct Offences*; for which the "several Defendants can no more be joined, than several Defendants "can be charged with † *Perjury*, or being ‡ *Scolds*, or keeping ‖ *open* "*Shop* on Fast-days, or exercising a § *Trade* without having served "an Apprenticeship; in all which Cases, the Offence of the *One* "cannot be considered as the Act of the *Other*." So here, the Publication by *Benfield* was not a Publication by *Saunders*; nor *è converso*.

† 2 *Strange* 921. *Rex* v. *Philips et al'*: Where 6 Persons were jointly indicted for *Perjury*; and the Judgment was arrested. *Palmer* 535. there cited, and many other Cases; And the Point was settled. ‡ 2 *Strange* 921. S. C. where the Case of Perjury was compared to the Case of *Scolds*; for which an Indictment will not lie against Two; *Regina* v. *Hodson et al'*, *Tr.* 6 *Ann.* ‖ 6 *Mod.* 210. *Anonymous.* § 1 *Strange* 623. *Dominus Rex* v. *Weston et al'*.

The Answer given to this 2d Objection was, "That several Defendants *may* be *joined* in One and the same Indictment or Information; if the Offence WHOLLY arises from such a *joint Act* as is "criminal in itself, without any regard to any particular personal "Default of the Defendant which is peculiar to Himself: As, for "Instance, it may be joint for keeping a Gaming House &c; but "not for exercising a Trade without having served an Apprentice- "ship, because Each Trader's Guilt must arise from a Defect peculiar to Himself."

2 *Hawk. P. C.* 240. is clear and express in this Distinction.

Style 244. *Paul Williams and his Wife*, against *the Custodes*, was a joint Indictment for *Words spoken by Both*: And the Court held the *Joint*-INDICTMENT good; though a joint *Action* on the Case could not have been brought against them.

Style 312. *Custodes* v. *Tawny and Norwood, jointly* indicted for blasphemous Words severally spoken by them: *Roll* Ch. J. held the Indictment *good* enough, though joint.

Can not *several* Persons join in *singing* One and the *same Song*? Forty People may join in the *same Chorus*. And if such Song or Chorus be libellous, the Doing so is *one joint Act*, criminal *in itself*, without regard to any peculiar personal Default.

The Court thought this 2d Objection to have likewise received a satisfactory Answer. They held this to be an *entire Offence*; One *joint Act*, done by both; They both joined in the Act of Singing this libellous and scandalous Matter, in the public Street, at the Father's Door, with Intent to discredit Him and his Children. And Whether it be two Songs, or One; or a first and second part of the same Song; or separate Stanzas, One on *John*, another on *Jane*; Yet it is one entire Offence: And the more there are that join in it, the greater is the Offence.

It is *not* like the Case of *Perjury*. Where the Perjury of One is not the Perjury of another; but the Perjury is a *separate* Act in Each: Whereas this is a *joint Act*.

The 3d Objection on which the Motion in Arrest of Judgment was grounded, was "That this is an entire *general* Judgment upon the "*whole* 4th Count: And yet, the *latter Song* contained in it, (name- "ly, the Song upon *John Cooke*,) contains *no libellous Matter*, at all. "Consequently, no Judgment can be entered up for the Prosecutors."

The Answer given to this 3d Objection was, First "That the "latter Song *is libellous*; and exposes this *John Cooke* to *Ridicule*." However, Secondly, If *either* of the two Songs be libellous, the Judgment is good and well warranted: For upon *Indictments* or *Informations*, the Court will give Judgment on *that Part* which is indictable. And it is *not* like the Case of an Action, where *general Damages* are given, and One of the Counts appears to be bad; in which Case, the Plaintiff in the Action can not indeed have Judgment: But the Reason why it is so in *Actions*, don't hold in Indictments or Informations.

The Court over-ruled this 3d Objection also; Holding this latter Song to be libellous and defamatory; and likewise, that if this Part of the Charge had not been so, it would, in an *Information* or *Indictment*, only go towards lessening the Punishment; but would not be a sufficient Reason for arresting the Judgment.

Wherefore, upon the Whole,
Per Cur. unanimously,
The Rule (to shew Cause Why the Judgment should not be arrested) was discharged.

Friday 9th *May* 1760.

Rex *verſ.* Inhabitants of Kniveton.

TWO Juſtices removed *Iſaac Wibberley* and *Mary* his Wife, and *Iſaac* his Son, and *Mary* and *Elizabeth* his two Daughters, from *Kniveton* to *Tiſſington*, both in the County of *Derby*.

On Appeal, the Seſſions ſtate this Caſe—That *Iſaac Wibberley*, being *ſettled at Tiſſington*, did upon *Lady-day* 1749, take *and enter* upon a *Farm at Kniveton*, of the Yearly Value of *Eight* Pounds, of Mr. *Hanſon* Vicar of *Kniveton*, To hold from *Lady-day* 1749 to *Lady-day* 1750. And that alſo, at the ſame Time, He *with* One *Thomas Hill*, JOINTLY *took and entered upon another Farm* in the ſame Liberty, of *Thomas Daniel*, To hold from *Lady-day* 1749, *to Lady-day* 1750, of the Yearly Value of 3*l.* 15*s.* And at the ſame Time of taking the ſaid Farm of 3*l.* 15*s.* it was agreed between the ſaid *Iſaac Wibberley* and *Thomas Hill*, "That *Thomas Hill* ſhould "have and take *One Half of the Corn and Hay* to be cut from the "ſaid Farm of 3*l.* 15*s.* Rent; And that the ſaid *Iſaac Wibberley*, "*after* that the ſaid *Thomas Hill* had taken and carried away his "Half Part of the ſaid Corn and Hay, ſhould be poſſeſſed of and "occupy the *Whole* Farm of 3*l.* 15*s.* Rent, till *Lady-day* follow-"ing; paying to the ſaid *Thomas Hill* 4*s.* for the ſaid *Hill*'s Share, "of the ſaid Farm." And that the ſaid *Thomas Hill* did on or *before the* 1*ſt Day of October* 1749, take and carry away One Half of the ſaid Hay and Corn; And that the ſaid *Iſaac Wibberley* did *thereupon* immediately take and continue the Poſſeſſion of the *whole* Farm, till *Lady-day* 1750; and paid the ſaid 4*s.* to the ſaid *Thomas Hill* for the ſame.

All which Facts being ſtated ſpecially to the Court of Seſſions, by the Counſel on the Behalf of the Appellants, and conſented unto by the Counſel on the Behalf of the Defendants; And the Court [of Seſſions] being EQUALLY DIVIDED in Opinion; They allowed the Caſe to be found as ſtated; in Order that the Appellants might take the Opinion of the Court of King's Bench at *Weſtminſter*, and the Matter be finally determined there.

Mr. *Edward Wilmot* moved, (on *Saturday* 23d *June* laſt,) to quaſh theſe * Orders; And a Rule was taken "to ſhew Cauſe Why "the *Orders* ſhould not be quaſhed."

* But, in Fact, this Act of the Seſſions is *no Order* at all: For it neither confirms nor diſcharges the Original Order; but, in effect, adjourns the Appeal *hither*. Yet no Notice was taken of this, at the Time of making the Motion.

4

Note—

Note—After the foregoing Motion and the Rule thereupon made "To ſhew Cauſe why the Orders ſhould not be quaſhed;" A *ſubſequent Rule of this Court* was made (on *Wedneſday* next after 15 Days from *St. Martin*, 33 *G.* 2.) whereby it was Ordered "That the Orders returned with the *Certiorari* in this "Cauſe be ſent back to the Seſſions."

In Conſequence whereof, at the *Epiphany* Seſſions holden on the 15th of *January* laſt, That Court made an Order, whereby (after reciting the former Tranſactions, and alſo that the Counſel had alledged "that the Court of King's Bench *could not proceed* "to give Judgment, for want of the Court of Seſſions having "either confirmed *or* diſcharged the former Order,") They "therefore Order That the ſaid Order of Removal be *diſ-* "*charged.*"

This ſecond Order of Seſſions being returned up, in Obedience to the above mentioned Rule of this Court—

Mr. *Ley* (on Behalf of the Pariſh of *Kniveton*) moved, upon *Tueſday* the 12th of *February* laſt, to quaſh it; and obtained a Rule to ſhew Cauſe Why it ſhould not be quaſhed.

(Note—This Caſe had now *changed it's Name*: For, upon the Order of Removal from *Kniveton* to *Tiſſington* being diſcharged by the Seſſions, the Pariſh of *Kniveton* became chargeable with the Paupers; and, according to the Rule in *Pa.* 1. were to be named Defendants here: Whereas, *before* this laſt Order of Seſſions, the Pariſh of *Tiſſington* ſtood charged with them, and conſequently were at *that* Time to be named Defendants here.)

To this Order of Seſſions (diſcharging the Original Order of the two Juſtices, who had holden the Settlement to be at *Tiſſington*,) Three Exceptions were taken on behalf of the Pariſh of *Kniveton*, who *now* ſtood charged under the preſent Order of Seſſions.

Two of them were not very important: And the Court laid no Sort of Streſs upon either of them in reverſing the Order of Seſſions.

One of them was "That it did not appear that the Pauper *reſi-* "*ded* in *Kniveton*:" (though it is ſtated "That he *entered upon* the "Farm there and *continued the Poſſeſſion &c.*")

The Other was, "That the Juſtices at Seſſions had *no Juriſdiction* "to make this preſent Order of Diſcharge; becauſe the former "Seſſions had not, upon the Original Appeal, adjourned ſuch Ap- "peal to a *ſubſequent Seſſions*, but to the Court of *King's Bench*."

But

But the material and principal Objection was, " That this Case " as stated upon the Orders, appeared to be a Tenement UNDER *the* " YEARLY VALUE *of Ten Pounds*, within the Intent and Meaning " of the Statute of 13, 14 *Car.* 2. *c.* 12."

The Counsel for the Parish of *Tissington* denied this, and alledged " That it was ABOVE the Yearly Value of 10*l.*" Which they thus endeavoured to prove.

First—They argued that *Wibberley*, the Pauper, was *liable* (as being *Joint-tenant* with *Hill*,) to *answer for* and pay the *Whole* 3*l.* 15*s.* And, moreover, that He was *Sole* Tenant of that Farm, for and during the *last* Half Year.

Secondly—But taking it at the strictest, It is really and properly a Payment of 10*l.* 1*s.* 6*d.* *per Annum*, by *Wibberley* the Pauper. For He is to * pay 8*l.* *per Annum*; *plus*, Half 3*l.* 15*s.* which is 1*l.* 17*s.* 6*d.*) *plus* 4*s.* for the last Half Year: Which is, in all 10*l.* 1*s.* 6*d.*

* 8*l.* + $\frac{3l.\ 15s.\ 0d.}{2}$ + 4*s.* = 10*l.* 1*s.* 6*d.*

But The COURT unanimously held " That this Tenement thus " rented by the Pauper, in *Kniveton*, was UNDER the Yearly *Value* " of 10*l.*"

The Act of Parliament fixes the Yearly *Value* at *Ten Pounds*: And the VALUE must be estimated by the *Rent*; and always is taken to be *according to the Rent*. And here, the Rent is 8*l.* *per Annum* and the half of 3*l.* 15*s.* Which two Rents taken together, do *not* amount to 10*l.*

Indeed, He was to pay *Hill* 4*s.* for the Advantage he was to have, after the Crop was off. But an Agreement of this Sort, between the two Joint-tenants can not be considered as a *Rent*.

Wherefore, *Per Cur.* unanimously,
ORDER of SESSIONS quashed:
ORDER of two Justices affirmed.

Monday 12th *May* 1760.

Rex *vers.* Inhabitants of Berwick St. John.

TWO Justices made an Order for the Removal of *Benjamin Beach* and *Mary* his Wife and *Elizabeth* and *William* their Children, from *Handley* in *Dorsetshire*, to *Berwick St. John's* in *Wiltshire*: And the Sessions, upon an Appeal, confirmed this Order; Stating the Case specially.

Special

Special Case stated—Sometime in *September* 1756, The Pauper, *Benjamin Beach*, being then an unmarried Man and legally settled in *Handley*, happening to meet Mr. *Stephen Jones* then Head-Keeper of *Rushmore-Lodge* (One of the Lodges of *Cranborne Chace*,) Who resided at *Rushmore-Lodge* aforesaid, which lies within the Parish of *Berwick St. John* aforesaid, and had then *lately parted* with One *Edward Hill*, who had been for many Years One of his Servants or Under-keepers at the Wages of 3*l. a Year* and a Keeper's Livery besides Meat Drink and Lodging; The said Mr. *Jones* addressed the Pauper in these Words, "*Do You like the Life of a Keeper?*". Which being answered in the Affirmative, He said further, "*Then go into Ned Hill's Place; And You shall want no Encouragement: I'll give You a Suit of Clothes directly.*" That the Pauper readily *consented*; and, *without further Conversation, went immediately into the said Service*, and *continued therein for the Space of three Years*, residing all that Time with his said Master at *Rushmore-Lodge* aforesaid within the Parish of *Berwick St. John* aforesaid. That upon or soon after his entering into the said Service, He was furnished with a *Keeper's Livery*; was, during the said 3 Years, provided with *Meat Drink and Lodging*; and at the End thereof, was paid 9*l.* for his Service. That at the Time of the Conversation before mentioned, the said Pauper did *not know* upon *what Terms* the said *Hill* had served the said Mr. *Jones*. That the Pauper's Service being agreeable, the Question "Whether or no he was at Liberty to *quit* it," never occurred to him: But that, in *his Apprehension*, if it had been *disagreeable*, he *should* have thought himself at Liberty to have quitted it; *since Nothing to the Contrary* had been stipulated between them, in the Conversation beforementioned. And that the said Pauper *thought* he *ought* to be paid the *same Wages Hill* had; but did *not consider himself* as having a *legal Title to Wages*, since there had been NO *mention of any*, in the Conversation before mentioned. That the said Pauper, after quitting the said Service, married the said *Mary* now his Wife, and had Issue by her the Children mentioned in the Order; and has done no Act to gain a Settlement, except as aforesaid. Therefore the Sessions are of Opinion "That the Settlement is in the Parish of *Berwick St. John*;" and therefore *confirm* the Order of the two Justices.

Mr. *Glynn*, who had moved to quash these Orders, on *Wednesday* the 6th of *February* last, had then objected "that this was NO HIRING in the Parish of *Berwick St. John*;" and had cited a * Case *between the Parishes of Gregory Stoke* and *Pitminster, in M.* 13 *G.* 1. *B. R.*

* *V. Sess. Cases*, Edit. 1750. 2d Vol. 132. Case 120.

Mr. *Norton*, Mr. *Grove*, and Mr. *Dunning* now shewed Cause Why the Orders should not be quashed; And argued this to be a *Hiring for a Year*: For the Law knows *no other* Servant but One *for*

for a Year. *Co.* 1 *Inst.* 42. *b.* A *General* Hiring is a Hiring *for a Year*. So, on 5 *Eliz. c.* 4. § 7. Besides, this has an express *Reference* to HILL's Service; Which was for a Year.

This Point was fully discussed and settled in the Case of *Rex v. Inhabitants of Wincanton*, 31st *January* 1750. (*Crediton* was the other Parish.) *

* *V. ante* 929. S. C. cited.

The Case cited, *between the Parishes of Gregory Stoke* and *Pitminster*, is not like this: *That* was a Living with a Grand-mother.

Mr. *Gould*, and Mr. *Glynn*, *contra*—Here is *no actual Hiring at all*: And None can arise by *Implication*, from the bare *Service alone*. *Pitminster* Case was holden to be no Hiring for a Year.

The *Reference* to *Ned Hill's Service* relates to *Hill's Work* only; not to his *Contract*: For the Pauper did *not know* upon what TERMS *Hill* had served Mr. *Jones*.

They mentioned a * Case of a Boy who lived from 8 Years of Age till he was 14, with his Master; and yet was holden to have gained no Settlement.

* *V. ante*, pa. 928. *Rex v. Inhabitants of Weyhill*. *N. B.* There, it was expresly stated "*That there was no Contract.*"

The Statute of 5 *Eliz. c.* 4. § 7. enacts "that every Boy, above "12 Years of Age, shall be compellable to be hired in Husbandry." And in *Wincanton*-Case, the Boy was 17, and was hired in Husbandry.

Lord MANSFIELD—This Man served 3 Years; and received 3 Years Wages: But it is objected "that he was *never* HIRED *at* "*all*."

It is admitted "That *if* He was hired at all, it would, by Law, "be a Hiring *for a Year*." And upon this Dialogue stated in the Order of Sessions, it is a *clear Hiring*: For *Hill* was a *hired* Servant.

Therefore the Justices have done right.

The Three Other JUDGES were clear of the same Opinion.

Both ORDERS AFFIRMED.

Rex

Rex *verſ.* Vandewall Eſq.

Tueſday 13th *May* 1760.

THE only Queſtion in this Caſe was, " Whether the *Lord of* " *a Manor* is *aſſeſſable to the* POOR-*Rates*, under 43 *Eliz.* " *c.* 2. § 1. for the QUIT-RENTS, HERIOTS, *and* CASUAL PRO- " FITS *of his Manor*."

It firſt came before the Court, on *Thurſday* 21ſt *June* 1759, upon a Motion to quaſh an Order of Seſſions which had confirmed ſuch a Rate made upon Mr. *Vandewall*, Lord of the Manor of *Aldenham*; from which Rate, He had appealed to them. But the Caſe not being ſtated with ſufficient Particularity, upon this firſt Order of Seſſions, It was ordered (on *Wedneſday* 4th *July* 1759,) " That the " Order, together with the *Certiorari*, ſhould be ſent back to the " Seſſions, to be ſtated more fully, as to the Matters of Fact, and " afterwards to be returned again to this Court."

This was accordingly done: And the new State of the Caſe was as follows, *viz.*

That *Samuel Vandewall* Eſq; was charged to the Poors Rate of the Pariſh of *Aldenham*, bearing Date the 28th of *March* 1759, in the Manner following, that is to ſay, " For the Tithe, 3 *l.* 15 *s.* " *For the* MANOR, 2 *l.* 5 *s.* *More, for the* QUIT-RENTS, 10 *s.* 6 *d.* " More, For the Wood-lands, 10 *s.*"

That it appeared that the ſaid *Samuel Vandewall* did *not*, at the Time of making this Rate, hold or occupy *any* Lands Houſes Tithes Coal-mines or ſaleable Underwoods within the ſaid Pariſh, Parcel of or belonging to the Demeſnes of the ſaid Manor or otherwiſe, within the ſaid Pariſh; Except the Tithes for which the ſaid *Samuel Vandewall* is aſſeſſed and charged in the ſaid Rate at 150 *l.* *per Annum*, and the Wood-lands for which the ſaid *S. V.* is aſſeſſed and charged at 20 *l.* *per Annum.*

That the LANDS *from which the Quit-Rents ariſe*, for which the ſaid *Samuel Vandewall* is aſſeſſed and charged in the ſaid Rate, are *Free and Copyhold Lands* HOLDEN *of the ſaid Manor*, and in the *Occupation* of divers Perſons *Tenants of the ſaid Manor*, or their Leſſees or Under-tenants, WHO ARE RESPECTIVELY CHARGED AND ASSESSED FOR THE SAID LANDS, in the ſaid Rate, *as Occupiers thereof*, according to the RACK-*Rent* of the ſaid Lands: But that the ſaid QUIT-RENTS are NOT *otherwiſe charged* in the ſaid Rate, than by the Charge on the ſaid Mr. *Vandewall* under the Article of Quit-Rent.

That

That the PROFITS *of the said Manor*, exclusive of the said Quit-Rents, arise by and consist of *Escheats*, *Heriots*, *Reliefs*, and *Fines* on the Admission of Copyhold Tenants on Deaths and Purchases, and other *Casualties* arising within the said Manor: Which, *together with the said Quit-Rents*, are by Computation *communibus annis* 111 *l. per Annum*; *viz.* the Quit-Rents 21 *l.* and the *other Profits* of the Manor 90 *l. per Annum.*

That it does *not* appear that the said *Quit-Rents* and the said Manor of *Aldenham*, or Either of them, HAVE EVER BEEN RATED to the Poors Rate of the said Parish of *Aldenham*, *till within two Years* last, and since the said *Samuel Vandewall* purchased the same, (which was in or about the Year 1754.)

Mr. *Norton* moved (on *Friday* 1st *February* 1760,) to quash this Order, *confirming* the Rate (as the former had done;) and obtained a Rule to shew Cause.

On *Thursday* 24th *April* 1760, Mr. *Gould* and Mr. *Knowler* shewed Cause against it's being quashed: And they cited some loose Scraps of Cases, relating to the Subject; *viz. Comberb.* 62. and again 264. both Anonymous, and *Hull's* Case in *Carthew* 14. and likewise 2 *Ld. Raym.* 1280. *Dalton* 165. (in the large Folio Edition.) 3 *Keble* 540. S. C. *The Corporation of Wickham* against *the Mayor*. 2 *Bulstr.* 354. Sir *Antony Earby's* Case; 2 *Inst.* 703. and *Jeffrey's* Case, 5 *Co.* 67. *b.*

Mr. *Norton* and Mr. *Field*, on the Other Side, argued that the Quit-Rents and Casual Profits of a Manor were not rateable to the Poors Tax, within either the Words or Meaning of 43 *Eliz. c.* 2. no more than *Ground-Rents* are. *Quit-Rents* have been *already* rated to the full, in the Hands of the respective Occupiers: So that this is Rating the same thing *doubly*. And the *Casual* Profis are quite *uncertain*; and can never be considered as that Sort of Fund, out of which the Poor of a Parish are to be supported.

The COURT took some Days to consider of the Point; as it was a very general and extensive Question; but not from any great Doubt that they had about it.

On *Tuesday* 13th *May* 1760—

Lord MANSFIELD very shortly declared their Opinion "That "these Quit-Rents and Casual Profits of the Manor are *not* rate-"able to the Poors Tax." Which, he said, was so clear, that there was no Need to enter into Reasonings about it. They were *never rated before*, in *this* Parish; and, *as far as appears to Us*, the Rating such Quit-Rents and Casual Profits has never been *at all* attempted before: And there is no Colour for this Attempt now, after more than a Century and an Half since the making of the Act of Parliament upon which it is grounded.

RULE made absolute, for quashing the Rate and the Order of SESSIONS confirming it.

Rex *vers.* John Spragg and Mary Elizabetha Spragg.

Wednesday 14th May 1760.

V. ante 930. (the first Attempt towards this Motion.)

THE Defendants (who were Father and Daughter) had been convicted of a CONSPIRACY, upon the following Indictment—That *John Spragg* of &c, Mill-Wright, and *Mary Elizabetha Spragg* of &c, Single-Woman, being Persons of an evil Mind and wicked Disposition, and devising and intending to deprive One *Walter Gilmore* of his good Name Credit and Reputation, and also to subject the said *Walter Gilmore*, without any just Cause, to the *Loss of his* LIFE and Forfeiture of his Goods and Chattels Lands and Tenements, upon the 31st Day of *July* in the 30th Year of the Reign of our Lord *George* the Second King of *Great Britain*, and so forth, and at divers other Times and Days thentofore, at *New Sarum* in the County of *Wilts*, and at divers other Places within the County aforesaid, *wickedly* and *maliciously* did CONSPIRE combine and agree among themselves, *to indict and cause to be indicted* the said *Walter Gilmore*, for a Crime or Offence liable by the Laws of this Kingdom to be punished *capitally*, and to prosecute the said *Walter Gilmore* upon such Indictment. And the Jurors aforesaid, upon their Oath aforesaid, *also present*, That the said *John Spragg* and *Mary Elizabetha Spragg*, ACCORDING TO *the* CONSPIRACY *Combination and Agreement* AFORESAID *between them as aforesaid* BEFORE HAD, afterwards, to wit on the said 31st Day of *July* in the said 30th Year of the Reign of our said now Lord the King, at the Session of *Oyer* and *Terminer* of our said Lord the King then holden at *New Sarum* aforesaid in and for the said County of *Wilts*, before the Honourable Sir *Richard Adams* Knt. One of the Barons of His Majesty's Court of Exchequer, *Edward Willes* One of His said Majesty's Serjeants at Law, and Others their Fellows, Justices of our said Lord the King assigned by Letters Patent of our said Lord the King under the Great Seal of *Great Britain* [*prout* in the said Letters Patent commissioning them to hear and determine,] by the Oath of [naming the Grand Jury,] good and lawful Men of the County aforesaid, then and there sworn and charged to inquire for our said Lord the King for the Body of the said County, FALSELY *wickedly* and *maliciously*, and without any reasonable or probable Cause, *did indict* and cause to be indicted the aforesaid *Walter Gil-*

more, by the Name of *Walter Gilmore* late of the Burrough and Town of *Marlborough* in the County of *Wilts* Bookseller and Stationer, for that he, unlawfully and unjustly devising and fraudulently intending to get and obtain to Himself unjust Lucre, and to defraud our present Sovereign Lord King *George* of certain Duties granted by certain Statutes lately made and provided and payable to our said Lord the King, and to diminish the public Revenue in this Behalf, after the making the Statutes in such Case lately made and provided, and after the second Day of *August* in the Year of our Lord 1726, that is to say, on the 3d Day of *May* in the 29th Year of the Reign of our Sovereign Lord *George* the Second by the Grace of God of *Great Britain France* and *Ireland* King Defender of the Faith, at the Burrough and Town aforesaid in the County aforesaid, by Force and Arms, unlawfully knowingly fraudulently and FELONIOUSLY did COUNTERFEIT AND FORGE A STAMP to resemble a certain Stamp which had before been there duly provided made and published in Pursuance of the Statutes in such Case made and provided, and which was then and there used in Pursuance of the said Statutes, to stamp Vellum Parchment and Paper charged, by Virtue of the said Statutes in such Case made and provided, with the Payment to our said now Lord the King, of the Duties of 6*d. and* 6*d.* thereby then and there to defraud our now said Lord the King of the Duties of 6*d.* and 6*d.* granted by the Statutes in that Behalf lately made and provided, and then payable to our said now Lord the King; against the Form of the Statutes in such Case made and provided, and against the Peace of our said now Lord the King his Crown and Dignity. And also—[laying, by another Count, the Counterfeiting the two Stamps, by the said *Gilmore*, another Way:] And also that—[It then goes on, and charges that they indicted *Gilmore* with *knowingly* UTTERING two such Counterfeit Sixpenny Stamps.] And that the said *Gilmore*—[laying the *uttering* them another Way.] And that the said *Gilmore*—[Then follow other Counts laid by them against him, for counterfeiting and knowingly uttering *treble Sixpenny* Stamps.]

The *present Defendants*, *Spragg* and his Daughter, were *convicted* at the Assizes, upon this *Indictment for the Conspiracy*, laid in the Manner just mentioned. However, no Judgment was *there* given; but it was *adjourned*, at the first and also at the subsequent Assizes, "quia Curia nondum advisatur." The *Record* of this Conviction

* *V. ante* 930. was at first removed, WITHOUT *their Persons:* For which Reason, the * former Motion could not proceed. *

† *V. ante* 931. But this Omission was afterwards rectified: The Record was now † removed by *Certiorari*; and the Defendants were also *brought up by Habeas Corpus*. Whereupon, on *Saturday* 26th of *April* 1760, Mr. Serj. *Davy* moved for the Opinion of *this* Court; or (in Effect) in *Arrest of Judgment*, (the Defendants being *present* in Court.)

4 He

He made two Objections: *Viz.*

(1st.) It is not alledged *in the Charge itself*, "That the Defendants conspired FALSELY to indict *Gilmore*;"

(2dly.) Nor does it appear, *in the said Charge, of what particular Crime or Offence* they conspired to indict him. 'Tis only charged in *general*, "That they did wickedly and maliciously "(without adding *falsely*,) conspire to indict and prosecute him for "A Crime or Offence liable to be capitally punished by the Laws "of this Kingdom."

BOTH these Matters are *essentially necessary*; and *can not be supplied* by any thing that goes before or comes after.

First Point. CONSPIRATORS are those only who confederate Themselves FALSELY and maliciously to indict or cause to indict. The Statute of 33 *E.* 1. (intitled "A Definition of Conspirators."—) defines Conspirators in these very Terms. 1 *Hawk. P. C.* 189. 2 *Inst.* 562. *Register* 134. *a. b.* 135. accordingly. *F. N. B.* Title *Writ of Conspiracy*, *folio* 114. in Old Edit. (260. in *Hale*'s Edit.) accordingly. So, *Rastal's Entries* 123 to 127. Title *Conspiracy*. So, *Co. Entries* 109. Title *Conspiracy*. And *Pulton* 232. *a.* 233. *b.* but particularly 232. *b.* Title *Writ of Conspiracy*. So likewise it is said by Justice *Richardson*, in *Tailor* and *Towlin*'s Case, *Godbolt* 444. All these Authorities prove that the Words "FALSELY *and maliciously*" are necessary, even in a *Count*. 1st Point.

Hale's Hist. P. C. 2d Vol. *pa.* 183. says "That the same Certainty is required in an *Indictment* for Goods, as in Trespass for "Goods; And that Certainty is much more necessary in an *Indictment* than in Trespass." 2 *Hawk. P. C.* 225. *c.* 25. § 59. proves also that Indictments must be certain. *West's Precedents 2d Part*, Title *Indictments and Offences pa.* 102. *b.* § 97. is an Indictment for a Conspiracy *falsely* &c. to indict.

The present Indictment is only "That they *wickedly and maliciously* conspired to indict this Man:" Which may be true; And yet it might not be FALSELY. It must be *both* malicious *and* false; to make it indictable as a Conspiracy.

The Offence consists in the *unlawful Agreement* to indict *falsely* and maliciously: And such an unlawful *Agreement* "maliciously to "indict FALSELY," would be indictable, though never carried into Execution. But Nothing more than the malicious Agreement "*to indict* this Man" appears in the *Charge* itself of this Indictment.

Second

2d Point.

Second Point. As the *Charge* itself is only *general*, The Setting forth the Indictment *verbatim*, *afterwards*, can not help this *Defect in the Charge*.

* *Vr.* 24 *E.* 3. *pl.* 34 to 34. *b.* accordingly. And see this villainous Judgment at large, in 3 *Inst.* 143.

There are two Instances of * *villainous* Judgment being awarded: 27 *Assize*, *pl.* 59. *fo.* 141. *b.* (by Inquest;) 46 *Assize*, 11. *fo.* 307. *a.* (by Indictment.) But in neither of them does it appear that the Conspiracy was for a *Capital* Offence: It is only said "That "they were *attainted of Conspiracy*."

Hawk. P. C. Lib. 1. *c.* 72. § 9. under the Title *Conspiracy*, says "That he who is convicted at the Suit of the *King*, of a Con-"spiracy to accuse Another of a Matter which may touch his Life, "shall have the *villainous* Judgment, which is given by the Com-"mon Law and not by any Statute." And the *villainous* Judgment is certainly the proper Judgment, where the Conspiracy is "to indict for a *Capital* Crime." But then the Capital Offence ought to be EXPLICITLY set forth: "A Crime liable to be punish-"ed Capitally, is not enough, without specifying WHAT Capital Crime. For this is a *Matter of Law*: And therefore the *Jury* are not the proper Judges of *this*. And the Want of this Allegation, if it be omitted in the *Charge* of the Conspiracy itself, can not be *supplied* by any Thing that precedes or comes after.

The CONSPIRACY *itself* is the Offence indictable, *though no Indictment* be drawn up or found, or any Thing done in Pursuance of such Conspiracy. And *if* there was *no such* Conspiracy, then there could be no Indictment *according* to it. So that the *Charge* itself is here *insufficient*. But if these subsequent Words *could* be connected with it, yet at most, it is a Charge by way of IMPLICATION only; *not* a clear *direct positive* Charge.

He therefore insisted upon these two Things:

1st. This is a Charge of a mere *Conspiracy* "to indict" *only*; not of a Conspiracy to indict FALSELY: And if it be not good, no Judgment can be given upon this insufficient Indictment.

2dly. It cannot be made good by any IMPLICATION, if not *positively* and *directly* alledged at first. 2 *Hawk. P. C. pa.* 227. *c.* 25. § 60. is express to this Purport. *Hale H. P. C.* 2d *Vol.* 182, 183. 4 *Co.* 44. *b. Vaux*'s Case, (for poisoning *Nicholas Ridley*.) *Staundford P. C. Lib.* 2. Title *Enditement*, *c.* 31. *pa.* 96. *b.* is express "that an "Indictment *is not good*, which must have an Argument or Impli-"cation to *make* it good." *Certainty* in Indictments is the Subject's Security.

3 The

The Precedents in *Tremaine* 82 *and* 85. are not such Precedents as that any Thing can be collected from them.

Mr. *Gould*, *contra*, *pro Rege*. The Term " *Conspiracy*" is always taken in *malâ parte*. So it appears by the Register. 1st Point.

There is but One Count in this Indictment; And the *Whole* of it must be TAKEN TOGETHER, as *One Charge:* It is not to be separated and divided, One part of it from another. It consists of the Inducement, the Charge itself, and the recited Indictment, (which is set forth *verbatim.*)

This is an Indictment at *Common* Law. 2 *Inst.* 562. says " The " Statute of 33 (or as he says it really was, the 21) *Ed.* 1. intitled " A Definition of Conspirators, is in *Affirmance* of the *Common* " Law."

In 6 *Mod.* 186. *Rex et Regina* v. *Best*, *per Holt*—" A Conspira- " cy, *latè loquendo*," or a Confederacy *to charge One falsely* (with- " out more) *is a Crime:* though it be not an Indictment for a for- " med Conspiracy, *strictly* speaking; which requires an Infamous " Judgment and Loss of *liberam Legem.*"

No *Villainous* Judgment has been given, since the Time of *E.* 3.

In *F. N. B. fo.* 253. 8vo. *Edit.* of 1704. (and also of 1718.) The Form of the Writ is " *Ostensur' Quare* Conspiratione inter Eos " præhabitâ, præfat' A de &c *indictari*, et ipsum eâ occasione capi " &c, *falsò* et malitiosè procuraverunt; ad &c, et contra &c provis." So that there, the " *falsely and maliciously*" is applied to the *Indictment not* to the *Conspiring*. 2 *Inst.* 562. The Case of *Welbye* (for citing in the Spiritual Court,) does *not* charge the Conspiracy to be false; but *only* malicious.

1 *Hawk. P. C. c.* 72. *pa.* 189 to 191, shews that if there be a *Conspiracy*, it is punishable in an exemplary Manner. *Conspiracy ex vi Termini* only, is indictable.

Tremaine's Entries, 85. *Rex* v. *Freeman*, only charges " That " illicitè diabolicè nequiter et malitiose conspiraverunt (to charge " with an Attempt to bugger,) *without the Word* FALSO." It is *not necessary* to apply the " falsò et malitiosè" to the *Conspiring*. So that the " falsely wickedly and maliciously" does here come in, in its *proper* Place. * *V. ante*

Consequently, here *is sufficient Certainty*. It appears, and is found, " That they did wickedly and maliciously conspire falsely to indict " this Man." And this is an Indictment at Common Law.

3 *Inst.* 143. in making the lawful Acquittal of the Party grieved, a Requisite to constitute the Guilt of the Offender, lays down a Proposition, which is not true. And this appears clearly by *Hawk. P.C. Lib.* 1. *c.* 72. *Pa.* 189, 190. and is confirmed by the Poulters Case in 9 *Co.* 56. And 9 *Rep.* 56. *b. Les Poulters* Case, mentions the Commission; Which does not speak of Conspiracies *executed*, but only of "*Conspiracies*" in general.

2d Point. As to the 2d Objection—It is an Offence, undoubtedly, "to conspire to indict a Person, falsely and maliciously, of SOME Capital Crime, in *general*; And then ACCORDING *to* such Conspiracy, afterwards *actually* to indict him, falsely and maliciously, for a PARTICULAR Capital Crime.

The Indictment concludes "contra form' Statut':" And therefore the Court may pronounce the Villainous Judgment, if they think proper.

Mr. Serj. *Davy*, in Reply—There is a Distinction between a *Writ* of Conspiracy, and an *Indictment* for a Conspiracy. In an *Action*, the *Damage* is the Gist of the Action; And therefore the Writ and Declaration must charge "That he was indicted and *sustained* "*Damage*:" But that is not necessary, in an *Indictment*; which is an Offence against the Public. And this Distinction explains Ld. *Coke*'s Meaning in 3 *Inst.* 143.

It's being *after Verdict* or *before* Verdict, makes no Difference. *Hale's* 2 *H. P. C.* 193. is express "That a defective Indictment is "*not aided by Verdict*. For an Indictment is not within any of the "Statutes of Jeofails: None of them extend to an Indictment."

It is not denied "That this is an Indictment for a mere *Conspiracy* "ONLY;" and nothing more: And there is no Allegation of it's being a *false* One.

Therefore the Indictment is bad: And no Judgment can be given upon it.

Lord MANSFIELD—We'll think of it. The Argument turns upon it's being an Indictment for a *Conspiracy only*.

Mr. Just. DENISON—In the Case of *Moor* v. *Kinnersley*, It was holden "that an Indictment would lie for a *Conspiracy only*."

CURIA ADVISARE VULT.

N.B. The Defendants (who had been brought into Court by Virtue of the *Habeas Corpus*,) were now committed to the *Marshal*, while the Court took Time to consider.

On

On *Wednesday* 14th *May* 1760,
Lord MANSFIELD delivered the Opinion of the Court.

He stated the Case, and the Objections: (Which, He said, had been very ingeniously argued.)

But, That they All agreed that in Reality there was no Colour for the Objections.

IF this had been a bare *unexecuted* Conspiracy, which had *never taken Effect*, (as that in *Kinnersley*'s Case was,) the Objections might have had *more* Weight (though He gave *no Opinion*, He said, *what Degree* of Weight they might have had even in *that* Case.)

But here is much *more* than a BARE *Conspiracy without Effect*. Here is an *Overt Act* laid, as I may call it; And it is found "That "the Defendants, ACCORDING TO *the Conspiracy Combination and* "*Agreement between them before had*, actually DID, *falsely* wickedly "and maliciously and without any reasonable or probable Cause, "*indict* this Man;" And the *very Indictment itself* is particularly *specified* in the present One.

So that *this* was a *complete* formed Conspiracy, *actually* CARRIED *into Execution*. *

We are All very clear, that there is no Colour for the Objections, in the present Case; And that the Rule ought to be discharged.

Per Cur. The RULE to shew Cause Why the Judgment should not be arrested, was DISCHARGED. *V. post.*

* The Fact was, That though *Gilmore* was indeed discharged, *for want of Prosecution*; yet he had been actually *indicted*, and long kept in *Prison* upon such Indictment.

Rex *vers.* Turkey-Company; Or (rather now) Rex *vers.* March, Deputy Governor of the Turkey-Company. (*V. ante* .)

Saturday 17th *May* 1760.

THIS Case, (pursuant to what had been before settled) came on in the *Crown-Paper*, upon the Return to a MANDAMUS which had issued since the † last Motion: Which *Mandamus* and Return were as follow—

† *V. ante*

The Writ was directed to *John March*, Deputy Governor of the Company of Merchants of *London* trading into the *Levant* Seas, commonly called the *Turkey*-Company.

4 It

It recited that Whereas since the 24th Day of *June* 1754, that is to say, upon the 13th Day of *November* now last past, (and the Writ bore Teste on the *12th February*, 33 *G.* 2.) ISAAC ROGERS (being then a Subject of this Realm of *Great Britain*, and also One of the People commonly called QUAKERS,) desiring Admission into the said Company, did in due Manner make and subscribe his *solemn Affirmation and Declaration* in that behalf requisite, before *William Alexander* Esq; and Sir *William Stephenson* Knt. two of His Majesty's Justices assigned to keep the Peace in and for the City of *London*, and also to hear and determine divers Felonies Trespasses and other Misdemeanours committed within the said City; And Whereas the said *Isaac Rogers*, after the making the said Affirmation and Declaration as aforesaid, *offered Himself* and did make Request to him the said *John March to be* ADMITTED *into the said Company*; and did then *tender to Him*, for such his Admission, for the Use of the said Company, the Sum of 20 *l.* and at the same Time did also produce to Him a *Certificate* under the Hands and Seals of the said *William Alexander* and Sir *William Stephenson*, the Justices aforesaid Certifying "that on the 13th Day of *November* in the Year of "our Lord 1759, the abovenamed *Isaac Rogers One of the People* "*called* QUAKERS, appeared before them (the said Justices,) and "had to Him administered, by them, the above AFFIRMATION;" Yet he the said *John March*, well knowing the Premisses, but not regarding his Duty in this Behalf, hath absolutely *refused*, and yet doth *refuse to admit* the said *Isaac Rogers* into the said Company; In Contempt &c, and to the great Damage and Grievance of the said *Isaac Rogers*, and in manifest Injury of his Estate &c: We therefore, being willing &c, Do Command &c, That immediately after the Receipt of this our Writ, You *admit* or cause to be admitted the said *Isaac Rogers* into the *said Company* of Merchants trading into the *Levant* Seas, commonly called the *Turkey*-Company; or shew to Us Cause to the Contrary thereof; Lest &c. And how &c. Witness &c.

The RETURN—The Answer of *John March*, Deputy Governor of the Company of Merchants of *England* trading into the *Levant* Seas, commonly called the *Turkey*-Company, to the within Writ.

I *John March*, Deputy Governor of the Company of Merchants of *England* trading into the *Levant* Seas, commonly called The *Turkey*-Company, in the within Writ called "The Deputy Gover-"nor of the Company of Merchants of *London* trading into the "*Levant* Seas, commonly called The *Turkey*-Company," (to whom the said Writ hath been delivered,) Do most humbly Certify and Return to &c; That long before *Isaac Rogers*, in the said within

within Writ named, offered himself to me to be admitted into the said Company, to wit, in the 26th Year of His present Majesty's Reign, *by a certain Act of Parliament*, made at a Session of Parliament of our Lord the present King held at *Westminster* in the County of *Middlesex* on the 11th Day of *January* in the Year of our Lord 1753, in the 26th Year of the Reign of his present Majesty, intitled "An Act for enlarging and regulating the Trade "into the *Levant* Seas," It was and is (amongst other Things) *enacted* "That from and after the 24th Day of *June* 1754, a cer-"tain OATH (the Form of which is set forth in the said Act) in "lieu of the *Oath* theretofore taken by Persons upon their Admis-"sions to their Freedom in the said Company, *should be taken by* "EVERY *Person, upon his Admission to his Freedom*; either before "the Governor or Deputy Governor of the said Company, or be-"fore two of His Majesty's Justices of the Peace (who were and "are thereby respectively impowered and required to administer "the said Oath:") Which Justices are thereby required to certify under their Hands and Seals, "That the said OATH *was taken* "*before them*."

And I do further humbly certify and return to our said present most serene Sovereign Lord the King, That the said *Isaac Rogers*, in the said Writ named, hath NOT *taken*, but hath REFUSED *to take* the said OATH by the said last mentioned Act of Parliament required; either before the Governor or Deputy Governor of the said Company, or before two of His Majesty's Justices of the Peace: AND THEREFORE I cannot admit or cause to be admitted Him the said *Isaac Rogers* into the said Company of Merchants trading into the *Levant* Seas, commonly called the *Turkey*-Company, as by the said Writ I am commanded.

John March, Deputy Governor.

Mr. *Norton* argued, (on *Wednesday* last) for the *Mandamus*.

The only Question is, Whether a QUAKER, who has in due Manner made and subscribed his SOLEMN AFFIRMATION AND DECLARATION to the Effect of the Oath, can be admitted to the *Freedom of this Company* without actually taking the OATH appointed by the Act of 26 G. 2. *c.* 18. § 2. enabling every Subject of *Great Britain*, desiring Admission into that Company, to be admitted into it, upon paying or tendering 20 *l.*

He argued that he *ought* to be admitted to this Freedom. The Act of 22 G. 2. *c.* 46. § 36. (& *penult.*) *po.* 945. (for allowing Quakers to make Affirmation in Cases where an Oath is or shall be required) extends to *all* Cases of Oaths of *all* Kinds, required by *any* Act of Parliament to be taken by Quakers: And the three

 Excep-

* § ult. Exceptions in the * Proviso, excluding them from "being thereby "qualified or permitted to give Evidence in any *Criminal* Cases, "or to serve on *Juries*, or to bear any Office or Place of *Profit in* "*the Government*," still more strongly shew the Sense of the Legislature. And this Case is *not* within *any* of these 3 Exceptions: It is only a Claim of an Admission into a *trading* Corporation; not of any Emoluments from the public Offices of Government.

But this Question has been already determined in the Case of *Rex* v. *Morris*, *P.* 10 *W.* 3. *B. R.* in 1 *Ld. Raym.* 337. upon a *Mandamus* to admit *Morris* (who was a Quaker) to his Freedom of the City of *Lincoln*; He having served an Apprenticeship there, for 7 Years. *Carthew* 448. S. C. *Rex* v. *Maurice, Mayor of Lincoln.* 5 *Mod.* 402. S. C. *Rex* v. *Mayor of Lincoln*—It was holden "That the Quaker *might* take the solemn Affirmation (by the Act of 7, 8 *W.* 3. "*c.* 34.) *instead of the Oath*, And that such Freedom was *not* a "Place of *Profit in the Government* within the Meaning of the Exception in that Act."

Lord MANSFIELD—This Case explains the Proviso in this Act of 22 *G.* 2. and the Declaration "That it was made to explain "a Doubt, Whether the Solemn Affirmation prescribed by "8 *G.* 1. could be allowed and taken instead of an Oath, in "any Case wherein by any Act or Acts of Parliament an Oath "is required; unless the said Affirmation or Declaration be by "such Act or Acts of Parliament *particularly and expressly directed* to be allowed and taken instead of such Oath."

Mr. *Harvey*, for the *Turkey*-Company, argued (1st) That this Case was *not* within the *Purview of the Act*: (2dly.) That if it is, yet it *is* within the *Meaning of the Exception.*

First—The Act did not mean to give Quakers any Privilege of Affirming instead of Swearing, where they were under no Penalty or Forfeiture, or had some antecedent Right vested in them.

The Act of 13, 14 *C.* 2. *c.* 1. was *highly penal* upon Quakers. 1 *W.* & *M. c.* 18. § 13. (the Act of Toleration) gave them *some* Indulgencies. 7, 8 *W.* 3. *c.* 34. *permits* the solemn Affirmation or Declaration, instead of an Oath, under the 3 Exceptions which have been mentioned. 8 *G.* 1. *c.* 6. (which is the Act recited in this Act of 22 *G.* 2. *c.* 46.) alters the *Form* of the solemn Affirmation or Declaration.

The *enacting* Part of the Act of 22 *G.* 2. *c.* 46. § 36, 37. (a Hotchpot Act,) does indeed extend the solemn Affirmation or Declaration to *all* Cases wherein, by any Act or Acts of Parliament then

then in Force or thereafter to be made, an Oath is allowed or required; although no particular or express Provision be therein made for it. But this Act itself, in it's *Purview*, is a good deal *confined*, and extends *only* to their *giving Testimony*: The Words are—" By reason " of which Doubt, the *Testimony* of the said People called Quakers " is frequently refused, whereby the said People, and Others re- " quiring their Evidence, are subjected to great Inconveniences; " Therefore &c be it enacted &c."

Secondly—They are *within the third Exception* contained in the Proviso of this Act of 22 *G.* 2. § 36. For it is a *Place of Profit*.

In the Case cited, it was an Office in a *Corporation, without* Profit.

This is not a Place *under* the Crown, or under the Government: But it is * IN the Government, (which is the Expression used in the * Act;) as *Corporations for managing Trade*, are *Part* of the *Government*. And the very PRINCIPLES *of the Quakers* are *prejudicial* to trading Corporations carrying on great Trade in foreign Countries; as their Rights often require to be supported by *Force*, as well as (in the present Case) with Pomp and Shew (by their Ambassador at the Port.) * *V.* § 37.

This Case may be distinguished from the cited Case of *Rex* v. *Morris*: For that was a Right to the Freedom of a *particular Place*, acquired by serving an Apprenticeship there; And it appears from 5 *Mod.* 403. that the Man had there an *antecedent vested Right*; *viz.* by having served such Apprenticeship; Whereas here is *no* antecedent vested Right; but only a *general* Claim, common to all other Subjects.

Mr. *Norton* in Reply—The Acts relating to Quakers do All of them give Privileges and Indulgencies to the Species of Dissenters, called Quakers: So, particularly, it appears from the Preamble to 8 *G.* 2. *c.* 6. which speaks of them with high Regard and Commendation.

The Case cited shews that there was a *Profit* to the Freeman; (*viz.* a Vote for Members of Parliament, and also Pasture in a Common;) And that they had a *Government* in their Corporation: Whereas this is a *mere trading Company*.

Here is just as much an *antecedent* Right, as there was in *that* Case. Our Claim is *founded* upon such a Right.

Therefore He prayed a peremptory *Mandamus*, commanding the Company to admit him.

Lord MANSFIELD ſaid He could not even ſtart a Doubt; the Point was ſo clear.

This can never be conſidered as a Place of Profit in the Government. And the Caſe cited is ſtronger than this: There was a Right to *vote in Elections to Parliament*, as well as a Right to have *Common of Paſture*.

However, As Mr. Juſt. DENISON choſe to read the Act of Parliament at more Leiſure, before He gave a poſitive and direct Opinion upon the Queſtion;

The COURT therefore took a few Days to conſider of it. And

Lord MANSFIELD now delivered the Reſolution of the Court.

He ſaid, It was not poſſible to find any Colour of Doubt. It was very clear, He ſaid, on the Act of King *William*: * And the Caſe of the Mayor of *Lincoln* is a Determination in Point.

* V. 7, 8 W. 3. c. 34.

The Preamble of the 36th Section of 22 *G.* 2. *c.* 46. recites, as the Reaſon of the enacting Part, That a Doubt had ariſen "Whether "the ſolemn *Affirmation* of Quakers, preſcribed by 8 *G.* 1. could "be allowed in any Caſe where an Act of Parliament had required "an OATH; Unleſs the *Affirmation* be by ſuch Act *particularly* "and *expreſſly* directed to be allowed and taken inſtead of ſuch "Oath:" For Removing which Doubt, it enacts that "in ALL "ſuch Caſes, upon Acts of Parliament then in Force, *or thereafter* "*to be made*, which direct or require an Oath, it *ſhall* be allowed, "although *no* particular or expreſs Proviſion be made for that Pur-"poſe in ſuch Act or Acts."

As to its being "an Office or Place of Profit *in the Govern-*"*ment*."—It is impoſſible to ſupport *that* Notion: For it can never be conſidered in *that* Light, moſt certainly. Even the *Remittances* of public Money for the *Uſe* and *Account* of the Government, if given by the Miniſtry to Quakers, may be very profitable Appointments to the Remitters: But yet, they are *no Places or Offices in the Government*.

This Man's Claim is nothing more than to be admitted into a Company of MERCHANTS trading to a particular Part of the World. And ſurely, there can be no Pretence to call THIS a *Place or Office of Profit in the Government*.

Therefore this Return must be quashed; And there must be a peremptory *Mandamus*.

> RULE accordingly; *viz.* That the Return be quashed, for the Insufficiency thereof; and that a PEREMPTORY MANDAMUS do issue.

Moses *vers.* Macferlan.

Monday 19th *May* 1760.

LORD MANSFIELD delivered the Resolution of the Court in this Case; which stood for their Opinion, "Whether the "Plaintiff could recover against the Defendant, in the *present Form* "*of Action*; (an Action upon the Case for *Money had and received* "*to the Plaintiff's Use*;) Or whether He should be obliged to bring "a *Special Action upon the Contract and Agreement* between them."

It was an Action upon the Case, brought in *this* Court, by the now Plaintiff, *Moses*, against the now Defendant, *Macferlan*, (heretofore Plaintiff in the *Court of Conscience*, against the same *Moses* now Plaintiff here,) for *Money had and received to the Use of Moses* the now Plaintiff in this Court.

The Case, as it came out upon Evidence and without Dispute, at *Nisi Prius* before Lord *Mansfield* at *Guild-hall*, was as follows.

It was clearly proved, That the now Plaintiff, *Moses*, had *indorsed* to the now Defendant *Macferlan*, four several Promissory Notes made to *Moses* Himself by One *Chapman Jacob*, for 30*s*. each, for Value received, bearing Date 7th *November* 1758: And that this was done, *in Order* to enable the now Defendant *Macferlan* to recover the Money in his *Own* Name, against *Chapman Jacob*. But previous to the now Plaintiff's indorsing these Notes, *Macferlan* assured Him "that such his Indorsement should be of no Prejudice to Him:" And there was an AGREEMENT *signed by Macferlan*, whereby he (amongst other Things) *expressly agreed* "That *Moses* should "*not* be liable to the *Payment of the Money* or any Part of it; and "that He should *not be prejudiced*, or be *put to any Costs*, or *any way* "*suffer*, by reason of such his Indorsement." NOTWITHSTANDING *which express Condition and* AGREEMENT, and contrary thereto, the present Defendant *Macferlan summoned* the present Plaintiff *Moses* into the *Court of Conscience*, upon each of these 4 Notes, *as the Indorser* thereof respectively, by 4 separate Summonses. Whereupon *Moses*, (by One *Smith* who attended the Court of Conscience at their second Court, as Solicitor for him and on his behalf,) *tendered* the said *Indemnity to the Court of Conscience*, upon the first of the

the said four Causes; and *offered to give Evidence of it and of the said Agreement*, by Way of Defence for *Moses* in that Court. But the Court of Conscience *rejected* this Defence, and *refused* to receive any Evidence in Proof of this Agreement of *Indemnity*, thinking that they had no Power to judge of it; and gave Judgment against *Moses*, upon the *mere foot of his Indorsement*, (which He Himself did not at all dispute,) without hearing his Witnesses about the *Agreement* "that "he should not be liable:" For the Commissioners held this Agreement to be no sufficient Bar to the Suit in *their* Court; and consequently decreed for the Plaintiff in that Court, upon the undisputed *Indorsement made by Moses*. This Decree was *actually pronounced*, in only *One* of the 4 Causes there depending: But *Moses*'s Agent, (finding the Opinion of the Commissioners to be as above mentioned,) paid the Money into that Court, upon *all* the four Notes; and it was *taken out of Court by the now Defendant Macferlan*, (the then Plaintiff, in that Court,) by Order of the Commissioners.

All this Matter appearing upon Evidence before Lord *Mansfield* at *Nisi prius* at *Guildhall*, there was no Doubt but that, upon the *Merits*, the Plaintiff was intitled to the Money: And accordingly, a Verdict was there found for *Moses*, the Plaintiff in this Court, for 6*l.* (the whole Sum paid into the Court of Conscience;) but subject to the Opinion of the Court, upon this Question, "Whether "the Money could be recovered in the PRESENT FORM *of Action*, "Or whether it must be recovered by an *Action brought upon the* "SPECIAL AGREEMENT *only*."

On *Saturday* the 26th of *April* last,—

Mr. *Morton*, on behalf of the Defendant *Macferlan*, moved to set aside this Verdict found *for* the Plaintiff; and to have Leave to enter up Judgment *against* the Plaintiff, as for a Non-Suit.

And in Order to shew that the Action was *not maintainable* in it's *present Form*, He laid down a Position "That *Indebitatus Assumpsit* "will *not* lie, but where DEBT will lie." It lies not upon a *Wager*; nor upon a *mutual Assumpsit*; nor against the *Acceptor of a Bill of Exchange*; Neither will it lie for Money *won at Play*: For it will never lie, but where Debt will lie; And can never be, upon mutual Promises. 1 *Salk.* 23. *Hard*'s Case; and 6 *Mod.* 128. *Smith* v. *Aiery*, are expressly so, in Terms.

And, to maintain *Debt*, there must be either an *express* Contract broken; or an *implied* Contract broken. But there is *no* Contract, either express or implied, "That *Moses* would have this Cause of "Action against *Macferlan*:" *Chapman Jacob* was only to pay *Moses* the Money *when* it should be recovered by *Macferlan*. An Indorsement

dorsement of a Promissory Note is a just Cause of Action: And *Macferlan* recovered this Money, of *Moses* the Indorser, by Judgment of a Court of Justice.

But *this* Action, "for Money had and received to his Use," is not the proper Way of setting right the *Judgment of a Court of Justice*.

This *Agreement* could *not repel* the Action before the Court of Conscience: It was only the Subject of an Action to be brought *upon itself*. This appears from the Case of *Beston* v. *Robinson*, in *Cro. Jac.* 218: Where *Beston* was in Execution upon a Statute Merchant at the Suit of *Robinson*; and brought an *Auditâ Querela*, and produced Articles between Him and Robinson, as a *Discharge*: Which was holden *not* good, to discharge him of the Execution; But that his Remedy was to have an *Action of Covenant* upon them. So in 1 *Bulstr*. 152. *Anon'*: By *Williams* and the Rest of the Judges, "If "the Party be taken and imprisoned upon a Judgment Execution, "where he has paid the Money, He shall not have a *Supersedeas* "*quia erronicè*, nor no Remedy, but only an *Auditâ Querela*: And "upon *Promise of Enlargement*, and not performing it, an Action "on the Case only lieth for this, and *no other* Remedy."

Mr. *Norton contra* for the Plaintiff.

We have *not* misconceived our Action: We were *not confined* to bring an Action upon the Special Agreement; but were *at Liberty to bring this* Action, "for Money had and received to our Use," to recover this Money *unfairly received* by the Defendant.

I do *not agree* to the Position, "That *Assumpsit* will *not* lie, *but* "*where Debt* will lie."

In the Case of *Astley* v. *Reynolds*, * This Principle was settled, *viz.* "That *wherever* a Person has *wrongfully paid Money*, He may have "it back again, by *this Action* for Money had and received to his "Use." And yet in that very Case, there *was another Remedy*. And there was the *Consent* of the Payer too. * *M.* 5 *G.* 2. *B. R.* (*V.* 2 *Strange* 915.)

So likewise, for Money paid on a Contract which is never performed.

So, on a Wager (on a Horse-Race,) against the Stake-holder, after the Thing is completed and over.

And no Inconvenience can arise: Every Thing is done and finished, in the present Case; And no Writ of Error lies to the Court of Conscience; nor can it's Judgments be over-haled.

The

The COURT, having heard the Counsel on both Sides, took Time to advise.

Lord MANSFIELD now delivered their unanimous Opinion, in *Favour* of the *present* Action.

There was no Doubt at the Trial, but that upon the *Merits* the Plaintiff was intitled to the Money: And the Jury accordingly found a Verdict for the 6 *l.* subject to the Opinion of the Court upon this Question, "Whether the Money might be recovered by "*this* Form of Action," or "by an *Action upon the special Agree-* "*ment only.*"

Many other Objections, besides that which arose at the Trial, have *since* been made to the Propriety of this Action in the present Case.

1st Objection. The 1st Objection is, "That an Action of *Debt* would not lie "here; and no *Assumpsit* will lie, where an Action of Debt may "not be brought:" Some Sayings at *Nisi prius*, reported by Note-Takers who did not understand the Force of what was said, are quoted in Support of that Proposition. But there is *no Foundation* for it.

Answer. It is much more plausible to say, "That *where Debt lies*, an Ac- "tion *upon the Case* ought *not* to be brought." And that was the

* 4 Co. 92. the Point relied upon in * *Slade*'s Case: But the Rule then settled and followed ever since is, "That an Action of *Assumpsit* WILL *lie* in "many Cases where *Debt lies*, and in many where it does *not* lie."

A main Inducement, *originally*, for encouraging Actions of *Assumpsit* was, "*To take away the Wager of Law:*" And *that* might give Rise to loose Expressions, as if the Action was *confined* to Cases only where that Reason held.

2d Objection.—"That no *Assumpsit* lies, except upon an *express* "or *implied* Contract: But here it is impossible to presume ANY "*Contract* to *refund Money, which the Defendant recovered by an* "*adverse Suit.*"

Answer. IF the Defendant be under an *Obligation*, from the Ties of *natural Justice*, to *refund*; the LAW *implies a Debt*, and *gives this Action*, founded in the Equity of the Plaintiff's Case, *as it were upon a Contract* ("*quasi ex contractu,*" as the *Roman* Law expresses it.)

This Species of Assumpsit, ("for Money had and received to the "Plaintiff's Use,") lies in numberless Instances, for Money the

Defendant has received from a *third* Person; which he claims Title to, in Opposition to the Plaintiff's Right; and which he had, by Law, *Authority to receive* from such third Person.

3d Objection. Where Money has been *recovered by the* JUDGMENT *of a Court having competent Jurisdiction*, the Matter can never be brought over again by a new Action.

Answer. It is most clear, "that the *Merits of a Judgment* can "*never be over-haled* by an *original* Suit, either at Law or in "Equity." Till the Judgment is set aside, or reversed, it is *conclusive*, as to the *subject Matter* of it, to *all Intents and Purposes*.

But the Ground of this Action is CONSISTENT with the Judgment of the Court of Conscience: It *admits* the Commissioners did right. They decreed *upon the Indorsment of the Notes by the Plaintiff:* Which Indorsment is not now disputed. The Ground upon which this Action proceeds, was no Defence against that Sentence.

It is enough for Us, that the Commissioners adjudged "They "had *no Cognisance* of such *Collateral* Matter." We can not correct an Error in their Proceedings; and ought to suppose what is done by a final Jurisdiction, to be *right*. But We think, "the "Commissioners *did right*, in *refusing to go* into such *Collateral* "Matter." Otherwise, by Way of Defence against a Promissory Note for 30*s.* they might go into Agreements and Transactions of a great Value: And if they decreed Payment of the Note, their Judgment might *indirectly* conclude the Balance of a large Account.

The Ground of this Action is not, "that the Judgment was "wrong;" but, "that, (for a Reason which the now Plaintiff "could not avail himself of *against* that Judgment,) the Defen- "dant ought not in Justice to KEEP the Money." And at *Guildhall*, I declared very particularly, "that the Merits of a Question, "determined by the Commissioners, where they had Jurisdiction, "*never could be brought over again*, in any Shape whatsoever."

Money may be recovered by a right and legal Judgment; and yet the Iniquity of *keeping* that Money may be manifest, upon Grounds which could not be used by Way of *Defence against the Judgment*.

Suppose an Indorsee of a Promissory Note, having *received Payment* from the *Drawer* (or *Maker*) of it, sues and recovers the same Money from the *Indorsor* who knew nothing of such Payment.

Suppose a Man recovers upon a Policy for a Ship *presumed to be lost*, which afterwards comes Home;—Or upon the Life of a Man *presumed to be dead*, who afterwards appears;—Or upon a Representation of a Risque *deemed to be fair*, which comes out afterwards to be grossly fraudulent.

But there is no Occasion to go further: For the Admission "that, "*unquestionably, an Action might be brought upon the Agreement*," is a decisive Answer to any Objection from the *Judgment*. For it is the *same* Thing, as to the Force and Validity of the Judgment, and it is just *equally* affected by the Action, Whether the Plaintiff brings it upon the *Equity* of his Case arising *out* of the Agreement, that the Defendant may refund the *Money* he received; Or, upon the *Agreement itself*, that, *besides* refunding the Money, he may pay the *Costs and Expences* the Plaintiff was put to.

This brings the Whole to the Question saved at *Nisi prius*, *viz.* "Whether the Plaintiff may elect to sue by this Form of Action, "for the *Money only*; or must be turned round, to bring an Action upon the Agreement."

One great Benefit, which arises to Suitors from the Nature of *this* Action, is, that the *Plaintiff needs not state the Special Circumstances* from which he concludes "that, *ex æquo & bono*, the Money received by the Defendant, ought to be deemed as belonging to "him:" He may *declare generally*, "that the Money was received "to his Use;" and make out his Case, at the Trial.

This is equally beneficial to the *Defendant*. It is the most favourable Way in which he can be sued: He can be liable no further than the Money he has received; and against *that*, may go into every equitable Defence, upon the General Issue; He may claim every equitable Allowance; He may prove a Release without pleading it; In short, He may defend himself by every Thing which shews that the Plaintiff, *ex æquo & bono*, is *not intitled* to the *Whole* of his Demand, or to any *Part* of it.

If the Plaintiff elects to proceed in this favourable Way, it is a *Bar* to his bringing another Action *upon the Agreement*; though he might recover *more* upon the Agreement, than he can by *this* Form of Action. And therefore, *if* the Question was open to be argued upon Principles at large, there seems to be *no Reason or Utility* in confining the Plaintiff to an Action upon the special Agreement only.

But the Point has been long *settled*; and there have been many Precedents: I will mention to You One only; which was very solemnly considered. It was the Case of *Dutch* v. *Warren*, *M.* 7 *G.* 1. *C. B.* An Action upon the Case, for Money had and received to the Plaintiff's Use.

1 The

The Case was as follows—Upon the 18th of *August* 1720, on Payment of 262*l.* 10*s.* by the Plaintiff to the Defendant, the Defendant agreed to transfer him 5 Shares in the *Welch* Copper Mines, at the Opening of the Books; And for Security of his so doing, gave him this Note—" 18th of *August* 1720. I do hereby acknowledge " to have received of *Philip Dutch*, 262*l.* 10*s.* as a Consideration " for the Purchase of 5 Shares; which I do hereby promise to transfer to the said *Philip Dutch* assoon as the Books are open; being " 5 Shares in the *Welch* Copper Mines. Witness my Hand *Robert* " *Warren.*" The Books were opened on the 22d of the said Month of *August*; when *Dutch* requested *Warren* to transfer to him the said 5 Shares; which he refused to do; and told the Plaintiff, " he " might take his Remedy." Whereupon the Plaintiff brought this Action, for the Consideration Money paid by him. And an Objection was taken at the Trial, " that *this Action* upon the Case, " for Money had and received to the Plaintiff's Use, would *not lie*; " but that the Action should have been brought for the *Non-Performance of the Contract.*" This Objection was over-ruled by the * Chief Justice; who notwithstanding left it to the Consideration of the Jury, Whether they would not make the Price of the said Stock, as it was upon the 22d of *August*, when it should have been delivered, the *Measure* of the *Damages*: Which they did; and gave the Plaintiff but 175*l.* Damages.

* Sir *Peter King* was then Ld. Ch. J. of *C. B.*

And a Case being made for the Opinion of the Court of Common Pleas, the Action was resolved to be *well brought*; and that the *Recovery was right*, being not for the whole Money paid, but for the *Damages, in not transferring the Stock at the Time*; which was a Loss to the Plaintiff, and an Advantage to the Defendant, who was a Receiver of the *Difference-Money*, to the PLAINTIFF's *Use*.

The COURT said, that the *Extending* those Actions depends on the Notion of *Fraud*. If one Man takes another's Money to do a Thing, and refuses to do it; It is a Fraud: And it is at the *Election* of the Party injured, either to affirm the Agreement, by bringing an Action for the Non-performance of it; or to disaffirm the Agreement *ab initio*, by reason of the Fraud, and bring an Action for Money had and received to his Use.

The Damages recovered in that Case, shew the *Liberality* with which this kind of Action is considered: For though the Defendant received from the Plaintiff 262*l.* 10*s.* yet the *Difference-Money only*, of 175*l.* was *retained by him against Conscience*: And therefore the Plaintiff, *ex æquo et bono*, ought to recover *no more*; agreeable to the Rule of the *Roman* Law—" *Quod condictio indebiti* " *non datur ultra, quam locupletior factus est, qui accepit.*"

IF

If the five Shares had been of *much more Value*, yet the Plaintiff could only have recovered the 262 *l.* 10 *s.* by this Form of Action.

The Notion of FRAUD holds much more strongly in the *present* Case, than in *that*: For here it is *express*. The Indorsment, which enabled the Defendant to recover, was got *by Fraud and Falshood*, for *one* Purpose, and *abused* to *another*.

This kind of equitable Action, to recover back Money, which ought not in Justice to be kept, is *very beneficial*, and therefore *much encouraged*. It lies *only* for Money which, *ex æquo et bono*, the Defendant *ought* to refund: It does *not lie* for Money paid by the Plaintiff, which is claimed of Him as *payable in Point of Honour and Honesty*, although it *could not have been recovered* from him by any Course of *Law*; as in Payment of a *Debt barred by the Statute of Limitations*, or *contracted during his Infancy*, or to the Extent of Principal and *legal* Interest upon an *Usurious* Contract, or, for Money *fairly lost at Play*; Because in all these Cases, the Defendant may *retain it with a safe Conscience*, though by *positive* Law he was *barred* from recovering. But it *lies* for Money paid by *Mistake*; or upon a Consideration which happens to *fail*; or for Money got through *Imposition*, (express, or implied;) or *Extortion*; or *Oppression*; or an *undue Advantage* taken of the Plaintiff's Situation, contrary to Laws made for the Protection of Persons under those Circumstances.

In one Word, The Gist of this kind of Action is, that the Defendant, upon the Circumstances of the Case, is *obliged by the Ties of natural Justice and Equity* to *refund* the Money.

Therefore We are All of Us of Opinion That the Plaintiff *might* ELECT *to wave* any Demand *upon the Foot of the Indemnity*, for the *Costs* he had been put to; and *bring* THIS *Action*, to *recover the* 6 *l.* which the Defendant *got and kept* from him *iniquitously*.

RULE—That the *Postea* be delivered to the PLAINTIFF.

The End of *Easter* Term 1760.

Trinity

Trinity Term

33 & 34 Geo. 2. B.R. 1760.

Crawford *verſ.* Powell.

Friday 6th *June* 1760.

THIS was a Caſe reſerved at *Niſi prius* before Lord *Manſfield* at *Guildhall*, upon the Trial of an Action for a *falſe Return to a Mandamus*. The *Mandamus* was directed to *Griffith Powell*, commanding him to deliver to *Gibbs Crawford*, the Common Seal, Books, Papers and Records of the Corporation of *Harwich*; which the ſaid *Crawford* claimed to belong to his Cuſtody, as having been *duly elected* Town-Clerk of that Corporation; And his Election was ſet forth in the Writ. To this Writ of *Mandamus* (to deliver the *Inſignia &c, ut ſupra*) the Defendant *Griffith Powell* returned "That the ſaid *Gibbs Crawford* was NOT "DULY ELECTED Town-Clerk:" Upon which Return, alledged to be a falſe One, the preſent Action was brought.

The Declaration ſhewed That the Plaintiff *Crawford* was duly elected Town-Clerk *&c*, upon the 20th of *March* 1758; In virtue of which Election, it alledged, that the Common Seal, Books, Papers and Records belonged to Him *&c*: But that the Defendant *Powell* refuſed to deliver them to Him. The Declaration then ſhewed that the Plaintiff, upon ſuch his Refuſal, did, upon the 12th of *April* 1758, proſecute a Writ of *Mandamus returnable on Friday next after One Month from Eaſter* 1758, (being the ſame Writ upon which the Action is brought;) which was accordingly returned *upon the ſaid Return-Day*.

So that it appeared upon the Face of the Declaration, that this *Mandamus* was actually returned WITHIN SIX MONTHS after the Plaintiff's Election to the Office.

There was a Verdict for the Plaintiff; But it was objected on the Part of the Defendant, That the Plaintiff ought to PROVE *his having taken the Sacrament* according to the Rites of the Church of *England within a Year next before his Election.*

This Point was reserved at the Trial, for the Opinion of the Court, and was twice argued; once, by Sir *Richard Lloyd*, on *Wednesday 4th July* 1759; and a second Time, by Mr. *Gould*, on *Friday 6th June* 1760.

They urged that it was incumbent upon the Plaintiff to *shew* that He was *duly* elected: And they contended that He could not have been duly elected, unless He had taken the Sacrament within a Year; For by the Statute of 13 *Car.* 2. *Stat.* 2. *c.* 1. "No Person "*can be elected* into the Office of Town-Clerk of a Corporation, "that shall *not* have within One Year next before such Election ta-"ken the Sacraments of the Lord's Supper according to the Rites "of the Church of *England*; And in Default thereof, Every such "Election is thereby declared *void.*" Consequently, in order to make out his Title, He ought to prove his having taken the Sacrament within One Year next before his Election: And his not having done this, is without doubt a fatal Objection, upon *this* Statute of 13 *C.* 2. And it remains equally fatal, even *since* the Act for quieting and establishing Corporations, 5 G. 1. *c.* 6. as the Return to this *Mandamus* was made WITHIN six Months after the Plaintiff's Election.

By this Act of 5 *G.* 1. *c.* 6. § 3. "No Person thereafter to be "elected into such Office shall be removed by the Corporation or "otherwise prosecuted for or by reason of such Omission; Nor shall "any Incapacity Disability Forfeiture or Penalty be incurred by rea-"son of the same; UNLESS such Person be *so removed*, or such "*Prosecution be commenced*, WITHIN *six Months* after such Person's "being placed or elected into his respective Office *&c.*"

But this Act does not affect the *present* Case; where the Return was made within *two* Months after the Election of the Officer.

For although such Incapacity and Disability might be taken away by this Statute of 5 *G.* 1. in a Case where SIX *Months had elapsed* after the Election, without any Removal by the Corporation or Prosecution commenced and carried on without delay; and consequently, a Return of "*Non fuit electus*," founded only upon this Incapacity and Disability, but not made till AFTER *the Expiration* of the six Months, would indeed be a false Return, and the Plaintiff would have no Need (in *such* a Case) to prove his having taken the Sacrament within a Year; Yet in the *present* Case, (where the Return is made *within* the six Months) it is not a false, but a *true* Return, if the Fact was "that He really had not received the Sa-

"crament within a Year next before his Election:" For, as the Incapacity and Disability incurred by the 13 *C.* 2. stands in this Case *unremoved* by the 5 *G.* 1. the Plaintiff *remains still open and liable* to a Removal by the Corporation, or to a Prosecution to be commenced within the six Months. So that there is a vast Difference between a Return of this kind made *within* the six Months (as this is,) and a Return made AFTER THE EXPIRATION of the six Months: The former, if supported by the Fact, is a *true* Return; the latter, a *false* One.

In the *present* Case, therefore, As this Statute of 5 *G.* 1. *c.* 6. had *never taken Place*, it was incumbent upon the Plaintiff to *prove* "that He had taken the Sacrament within the Year next before "his Election;" as his Election would otherwise be *void*, by 13 *C.* 2.

In the Case of *Tufton Esq*; v. *Nevinson, Mayor of Appleby*, 2 *Ld. Raym.* 1354. (which was in *Easter* Term 10 *G.* 1.) upon an Issue taken on a "*Non fuit Electus*" returned by the Mayor to a *Mandamus* commanding Him to swear the Plaintiff Mr. *Tufton* into the Office of an Alderman of that Burrough, being (as the Writ suggested) duly chosen, Mr. Serj. *Pengelly*, who was for the Defendant, made this very Objection, "that Mr. *Tufton* ought to prove that He "had received the Sacrament within a Year before his Election;" (though six Months were, in that Case, elapsed since his Election.) And the whole Court were unanimous in Opinion, First, that the Case was not within the 5 *G.* 1. *c.* 6. because the Plaintiff *Tufton never was admitted* into the Office, and therefore could not be *removed out of it* nor *incur a Forfeiture*; Secondly, that it *was incumbent on the Plaintiff* to prove "that He had received the Sacrament "*&c* within a Year before his Election, by 13 *C.* 2. *c.* 1. Else, his "Election was *void*:" And so it was said to have been ruled in other Cases there mentioned.

Marten v. *Jenkin*, *M.* 14 *G.* 2. *B. R.* mentioned in 2 *Strange* 1145. was a *Mandamus* directed to *Jenkin* the late Mayor of *Winchelsea*, commanding him to swear *Marten* into that Office: Who returned "*Non fuit electus*;" and an Issue was joined thereon. A Special Verdict found, that the Mayor was to be chosen out of the Jurats; and that the Plaintiff *Marten* was on 1st *May* 1739, chosen a Jurat and sworn in, and continued so till 7th *April* 1740, when He was chosen Mayor; and that He had received the Sacrament within a Year before his Election to be Mayor, but had *not* done so within a Year next before his Election to be a *Jurat*. The Court held the Statute of 5 *G.* 1. *c.* 6. § 3. to operate so as to give Him the Benefit of Non-Prosecution within six Months, with regard to the previous Qualification, and remove his Incapacity and Dis-

Disability arising from such Neglect: And they held the Verdict to be sufficient for them to give Judgment upon, although it was not found negatively, "that there was *no* Prosecution within the six "Months;" as his Election did appear, and nothing appeared to avoid it, (which should have come on the *other* Side.) And they gave Judgment for the Plaintiff.

In both these Cases, the Officers (Mr. *Tufton* and Mr. *Marten*,) were *settled* in their respective Offices, by the six Months being expired without Prosecution. Here, the Plaintiff Mr. *Crawford* was *not* so: His Incapacity and Disability, if ever it existed at all, must *remain* the same, *till after* the Expiration of the 6 Months.

Therefore the Action for a false Return can't be maintained in the present Case, without the Proof insisted upon: Nor ought the Defendant *Powell*, who was the preceding Officer, to have delivered over the Books and Insignia of the Corporation, to a Man at that Time liable to Removal or Prosecution for not having taken the Sacrament within the Year next before his Election.

But The COURT (notwithstanding all this plausible Reasoning) over-ruled the Objection, and gave Judgment for the Plaintiff.

* *Vide* § 3.

Lord MANSFIELD said that *since* the Statute of 5 *G.* 1. *c.* 6. * the Election of a Person who had not taken the Sacrament within a Year next preceding it, is *not* VOID, but *only* VOIDABLE *in Case of a Removal or Prosecution within the Time thereby limited:* And consequently, as here was no such Removal or Prosecution within that limited Time, the Plaintiff's Election stood *confirmed* and became *absolute*. He therefore thought this a clear Case; and that there was no real Force in the Objection. He did not think it like to the Case of *Tufton* v. *Nevinson* that had been cited from *Ld. Raymond's Reports:* Because that arose upon the Officer's bringing a *Mandamus* to swear Him *into his Office*, being then *out of Possession*; whereas this Plaintiff is *in Possession* of the *Office*, and only brings his *Mandamus* for the *Insignia* and other Things belonging to it.

Per Cur. JUDGMENT for the PLAINTIFF.

Oldknow

Oldknow *verf.* Wainwright;
or
Rex *verf.* Foxcroft.

Tuefday 10th *June* 1760.

Tr. 31 *G.* 2. *Rot'lo* 159.

THIS Cafe of *Oldknow* v. *Wainwright* was a feigned Action, under a Rule by Confent, to try a RIGHT OF ELECTION to the Office of Town-Clerk of *Nottingham:* Which Rule was made in the other Caufe of *Rex* v. *Foxcroft*, againft whom an Information had been prayed by *Seagrave* his Competitor.

The *Confent-Rule* was to the Effect following—"*Rex* v. *Fox-* "*croft &c.*" The firft Part of the Confent is, "That the *Matters* "*in difference between the Parties* fhall be tried in a feigned Action:" Then the Rule goes on, "That *Oldknow* fhould be Plaintiff, "and *Wainwright* Defendant;" And particularly fpecifies and fettles the feveral Iffues that were to be tried. Then comes a Claufe of Confent "That the Judge who fhould try the Caufe fhould be "at Liberty to indorfe any Special Matter that might arife at the "Trial, upon the *Poftea.*" Then it concludes thus—"And by "the like Confent, it is laftly Ordered That THE COSTS fhall "abide the Event of the Iffue."

There were 4 Iffues to be tried: 1ft. "Whether the Mayor alone "had a Right to appoint the Town-Clerk." And it was found "That He had *not.*" 2d Iffue—*Suppofing* He had, then "Whe- "ther *J. Foxcroft* was duly appointed by Him." On this Iffue, a Verdict was given "*Againft* the Mayor's Appointment." 3d Iffue.— "Whether the Mayor Aldermen and Common Council have the "faid Right of Election." This was found in the *Affirmative.* (So that thefe 3 Iffues were All found for the Defendant.) 4th Iffue—Suppofing the Mayor Aldermen and Common Council *have* the Right, then "Whether *Thomas Seagrave* was DULY *elected* by "them." As to this 4th Iffue, there was a Special Verdict to the following Effect. It fets out the Conftitution of the Burrough, and that the Voices were All equal Votes. Then it fets out the Vacancy of the Office of Town-Clerk, and a regular Summons to elect Another. That the whole Number of Electors was Twenty-five; and that out of that Number, Twenty-one affembled on the 26th of *May*, purfuant to the faid Summons. That the Mayor put *Thomas Seagrave* in Nomination; And that No *other* Perfon was put in Nomination. That Nine of the Twenty-one voted for

 him:

him: But Twelve of them did *not vote at all*, but Eleven of them PROTESTED against *any* Election *at that Time*; because the Office was already full (as they alledged) of *Foxcroft*, whose Right was then under Litigation in this Court. That there was a *written Protest* against any Election at all, either of *Seagrave*, or any other Person, by Four Aldermen and Six Common-Council-Men; because a Suit was then depending in the Court of King's Bench concerning the Right of *Foxcroft*. These Ten signed the written Protest: Another (*Hollins*) did not sign, nor vote; but declared "that "He *suspended doing any Thing*."

However, at the same Court or Assembly, the Mayor declared the said *Thomas Seagrave* duly elected: And he took the Oaths of Office, and the other requisite Oaths, in due Manner and Form.

The Question now before the Court was Whether the said *Thomas Seagrave* was DULY ELECTED into the Office of Town-Clerk.

Mr. *Caldecott*, on Behalf of the Plaintiff, argued (on *Tuesday* 6th of *May* last) That *Seagrave* was *not* duly elected. For Twenty-five had a Right of voting; All had equal Voices; And of Twenty-one that met, Eleven PROTESTED *against* ANY *Election at that Time*: Therefore, these Eleven were all *negative* Voices, and AGAINST *Seagrave*; And *only Nine* were *for* him.

Besides, this was NO *Corporate* Act.

All the Twenty-five were summoned; And 21 appeared: The Voice of the Majority of these who were *present*, was the Voice of the *Whole* 25; And Mr. *Seagrave* had *not* a Majority of them.

Therefore the Issue is found for the Plaintiff: And We pray that the *Postea* may be delivered to him.

Mr. Serj. *Hewitt contra*, for the Defendant.

The substantial Matter in Question was "Whether the *Right* of "*appointing* the Town-Clerk was in the *Mayor*; or in the *Mayor*, "*Aldermen and Common-Council*." The Mayor Aldermen and Common-Council-men make the 25, who are the Corporate Body.

Here was a regular Summons of the whole Body; and a Corporate Meeting of 21 of them, for the Business of this Election; And they *entered upon* the Election: Therefore they could *not desert* it unfinished.

At this Meeting, the Mayor *nominated Mr. Seagrave*; Which No *One then opposed*: A Vote was taken; And Nine voted *for* Mr. *Seagrave*.

3

grave. After which, Ten, or (as it is said) Eleven *protested against* any Election at all, at that Time. But mere *Silence* is *not* a Negative, either expressed, or implied: And as *No other* Person was proposed, And Nine voted for him, and *None against* him, He was well elected.

The Protesters *then* thought the Office was full already, of *Foxcroft:* But it *now* is found "That *Foxcroft* was *not* duly elected." They thought that the Office being full (as they apprehended) of *Foxcroft*, precluded them from electing another Person. But if *Foxcroft*'s Nomination and Appointment were bad, they *were* at Liberty to elect another Person. The Case of *Aberystwith*, in 2 *Strange* 1157, and also that of *Tintagel* there cited, shew That the Protesters proceeded upon a Mistake, in fancying they could not elect Another whilst a former claimed upon a controverted Title.

Though the *Presence* of a Majority of the whole Number be necessary, yet the Concurrence and *Consent* of a *Majority of the whole Number* is *not* necessary: A Majority of the Number present is sufficient. This appears from the Case of Sir *Robert Salisbury Cotton* v. *Davies*, 1 *Strange* 53.

If these Protesters had *gone away*, and left the Assembly, it had made no Difference, after the Business was *once begun*. In such Case, the Rest had a Right to *proceed*. *M.* 4 *G.* 2. *Rex* v. *Norris*, *B. R.* 1 *Barnardiston*, 385, 386.

It does not appear that these Protesters would *not* have voted for Mr. *Seagrave*, *if* they had voted *at all*. And, at this very Assembly, He was declared by the Mayor to be duly elected; and was accordingly sworn in, in the Presence of the Protesters.

This is clearly a Corporate Act.

Mr. *Caldecott*, in Reply.

Though there *was* a Question, "*In whom* the Right of appointment or *Election* lay;" Yet this Right of the Person *elected* was *also* in Question.

Mr. *Foxcroft* had a Prior Nomination or Election, by the Mayor: And the Protesters thought, that whilst his Right was *sub lite*, they ought not to go on at all to the Election of another Person. Eleven of them formally protested against it: Which certainly is Voting *against Seagrave*'s Election.

The

The Case of *Aberystwith*, in 2 *Strange* 1157. is certainly true— "That where there is a *void* Election, the Court will grant a *Mandamus* to go to an Election." But that is Nothing to *this* Case.

In the Case of *Rex* v. *Norris*, The Presence of the Mayor was necessary.

Lord Mansfield saw no Doubt in this Case. Here was an Assembly *duly summoned*; One Candidate was named; *No other* was named; The *Poll* was *taken*; They had *no Right to stop*, in the Middle of the Election; The Mayor did not put any Question for Adjournment; nor was there any.

But, Mr. *Caldecott* prayed another Argument; Because Mr. Serj. *Poole* was retained to argue it on the same Side with Him, for the Plaintiff.

Whereupon, The Court gave Leave that it should be argued again; and ordered an

Ulterius Concilium.

On *Tuesday* 10th *June* 1760, This Cause stood in the Paper for further Argument. But

Mr. Serj. *Poole*, for the Plaintiff, said He but very lately received his Instructions; and therefore prayed further Time.

But the Court refused to grant it; Because it was his own Client's Fault, not to have instructed him sooner; as the further Argument was indulged to the Plaintiff, at his own Desire, in the last Term. However, They offered and even desired to hear what Mr. Serj. *Poole* might *now* have to say: For that they were quite open to Conviction.

But the Serjeant not urging any Thing further—

Lord Mansfield confirmed his former Opinion.

He said, The protesting Electors had no Way to stop the Election, when once entered upon, but by voting for *some other* Person than *Seagrave*, or at least against Him: Whereas here they had *only protested* against any Election at that Time.

Mr. Just. Wilmot—There was a Case of *Rex* v. *Withers*, *Pasch.* 8 *G.* 2. *B. R*; Where out of Eleven Voters, Five voted, and Six *

* It was an Election of a Burgess of *Westbury*, upon a single Vacancy. Six voted for *Withers* singly: Six others voted for *two* Persons *jointly*, (tho' it was upon a single Vacancy.) The Court held clearly, "that the double Votes were absolutely thrown away;" and refused to grant an Information against *Withers*.

" refused:

refuſed: And the Court there held "That the Six *virtually con-* "*ſented.*"

In the Caſe of *Regina* v. *Boſcawen*, *P.* 13 *Ann. B. R.* (in *Truro*,) where Ten voted for *Roberts*; and Ten for *Boſcawen*, a Non-Inhabitant: The Votes given for a Non-Inhabitant, where Inhabitancy was neceſſary, were holden to be *thrown away*. So, in the Caſe of *Taylor* v. *Mayor of Bath* * *Temp.* Ld. Ch. J. *Lee*, *B. R.*

* *M.* 15 *G.* 2. 21ſt *November* 1741.—It was holden "that Votes given for an unqualified Perſon, under Notice of his Incapacity, are thrown away."

Lord MANSFIELD—Whenever Electors are preſent, and don't vote at all, (as they have done here,) "They virtually acquieſce in "the Election made by Thoſe who *do*."

Therefore, *Per Cur.*
JUDGMENT for the DEFENDANT,
(on this * 4th Iſſue, upon the Special Verdict.)

* Note—The 3 Other Iſſues had been *found* for the Defendant, as is above mentioned.

Afterwards, on *Wedneſday* 25th of *June*, this Caſe then bearing the latter Name, *viz. Rex* v. *Foxcroft*;—Mr. *Caldecott*, on Behalf of the Defendant therein, ſhewed Cauſe Why the ſaid Defendant *Foxcroft* ſhould not pay to the Proſecutor in this Cauſe, his COSTS as well in *this* Cauſe of *Rex* v. *Foxcroft*, as in the *Information* in the Nature of a *Quo Warranto againſt Robert Seagrave*; and *likewiſe* the Coſts in the *Mandamus* moved for againſt *Cornelius Hutbwaite* Eſq; late Mayor of *Nottingham*.

He urged that No OTHER *Coſts* were payable but thoſe that aroſe upon the CIVIL Action, *viz.* the *feigned Iſſue* which had been tried by Conſent of the Parties, in order to determine the Right; and which feigned Iſſue had been found in Favour of *Seagrave*, and againſt *Foxcroft*.

And for this, He relied upon the Authority of the Caſe of the † Burrough of *Walſall*, (in the Diſpute between the Burrough and the Foreign of that Place,) *Tr.* 28 *G.* 2. *B. R.* as a Reſolution directly in Point: Where it was determined "That *no* Coſts were "payable upon theſe feigned Iſſues; but the Coſts in the CIVIL "*Suit* ONLY." ‖

† *Rex* v. *Nichols & al'* 12 *June* 1755.

‖ And ſo it was alſo determined in *Rex* v. *Griffiths*, *M.* 29 *G.* 2. *B. R.* and in *Thomas* v. *Powell*, *P.* 31 *G.* 2. *B. R.*

Mr. *Norton*, *contra*, on Behalf of Mr. *Seagrave* the Proſecutor, inſiſted upon Coſts of the WHOLE; *viz.* the Coſts in *this* Cauſe of *Rex* v. *Foxcroft*, the Coſts in the *Information againſt Seagrave*, and the Coſts of the *Mandamus directed to Hutbwaite*, as well as the Coſts of the Civil Suit upon the feigned Iſſue.

Lord MANSFIELD was of Opinion That the Court were *tied down* by the * *Consent-Rule*, to direct the Costs of the WHOLE to be paid by the Defendant *Foxcroft*. It was made in the Cause where an Information was prayed against him, in the Nature of a *Quo Warranto*, to shew by what Authority He claimed to be Town-Clerk of *Nottingham*; to which Office *Seagrave* also claimed a Right. *Foxcroft* thereupon consents "That the Matters in difference between the Parties shall be tried in a feigned Action;" And then he consents, in express Terms, "That THE *Costs* shall abide the Event of the Issue:" Which must mean the *Whole* Costs; or else it has no Meaning at all; For the Costs on the CIVIL Side (arising upon the feigned *Issue only*) would *of Course* abide its Event, *without needing* any Rule or any Consent for *that* Purpose; (that Point having been fully settled long before the Making of the present Consent-Rule.) Consequently, this Consent takes in the OTHER Costs, on the *Crown*-Side.

* V. the Consent-Rule before pa. 1017.

The Other Three JUDGES were of the same Opinion.

RULE made ABSOLUTE.

Trapaud *vers.* Mercer.

Hil. 32 *G.* 2. *Rot'lo* 984.

THIS was a Cause in the Paper, upon a Demurrer: And the whole Question turned upon the *Pleadings*. The Replication concluded to the *Country*: And the Defendant insisted that it ought to have concluded with an *Averment*.

The PRINCIPLE was agreed, by both Bar and Bench, "That where there was an Affirmative and a Negative, the Conclusion ought to be to the Country:" But the present Demurrer was grounded upon a Supposition "that as these Pleadings stood, here was *not* an Affirmative and a Negative."

The Pleadings were as follow—

It was an Action of Debt on Bond. On Oyer, It appeared to be conditioned thus—The Condition first recited that One *Robert Grier* had been appointed by the Plaintiff, who was Lieutenant-Colonel of the 2d Battalion of the Buffs, and by Mr. *Hughes*, the Major, to be Pay-master of the said Battalion; and then went on, That if the said *Grier* should within 30 Days after *any* Demand in Writing, render an Account of All Monies received by him &c; And in case there ſhould be any Deficiency &c, then if the Defendant ſhould make good any ſuch Deficiency, not exceeding 1000*l*; the Obligation to be void. And the Plaintiff aſſigned the Breach, in *Grier's* not rendering an Account within 30 Days after a Demand in Writing.

The Defendant (who ſtood thus bound as Security for *Grier*) pleaded (by Leave of the Court) two ſeveral Pleas; *viz.* 1ſt. That no Demand in Writing was made &c.; 2dly. (Proteſting that no Demand &c was made,) He for Plea ſays that *Grier* DID *render an Account* within 30 Days after *any* Demand in Writing, and paid the Monies due &c; and that no Deficiency at all was made to appear.

To this 2d Plea, (which 2d Plea alone was now before the Court,) the Plaintiff replied "That a large Sum of Money, that is to ſay, "the Sum of 2000*l.* was received by *Grier* &c; and that, *on ſuch* "*a Day* (particularizing it) a DEMAND *in Writing was made* &c; "And yet *no Account* was rendered by *Grier*, within 30 Days &c:" Which Replication *concluded* to the COUNTRY.

To this Replication, the Defendant demurred: And

Mr. *Yates*, for the Defendant, argued in Support of the Demurrer, That the Replication *ought* to have concluded with an AVERMENT: For that this was not a proper Affirmative and Negative, but a *Matter newly alledged* in the Replication; which *newly-alledged Matter* the Defendant ought to have an Opportunity of *Anſwering*. And as the Plea is *general*, it was neceſſary for the Plaintiff to aſſign a particular Breach, in his Replication.

Mr. Serj. *Hewitt*, for the Plaintiff, urged that it was NOT *new Matter*, but a *proper* Negation of the Matter pleaded, and made a *ſufficient Affirmative and Negative*; and therefore the Concluſion was as it ought to be. And

The COURT were of this Opinion.

Lord MANSFIELD—The material Queſtion between the Parties is—"Whether an Account has been *demanded* in Writing; ſuch an "Account *rendered* within due Time; And the *Money paid*." The Sum of the Defence is, "That NO DEMAND was made: But *ſuppoſing* that a *Demand* WAS *made*, yet an Account WAS RENDERED "within due Time after EVERY ſuch Demand; and the *Money paid*." The Replication alledges "that an Account *was demanded* in Wri-"ting, *on ſuch a particular Day*; but that *Robert Grier* DID NOT, "then or at any Time after, *render an Account*." This is undoubtedly, a *proper* FACT *to be tried*.

Mr.

Mr. Juſtice DENISON concurred that it was; and that this was a proper Affirmative and Negative.

The Plea, "that *Grier did* render an Account within 30 Days " after ANY Demand *&c*," muſt be underſtood as if it had been worded "after EVERY Demand;" and imports that He had done it after EVERY Demand. To which, the Plaintiff replies, "That a " *Demand was made upon ſuch a particular Day*; yet *Grier* did *not* " render an Account within 30 Days after it." It is objected " That as the Plea is *general*, the Replication ought to *aſſign a par-* " *ticular Breach*."

And it is ſo, in *ſome* Caſes; as, for Inſtance, in a Plea of a *general Performance of Covenants*: But it is *not* ſo, in the *preſent* Caſe. For the Queſtion here is *not* " Whether *Grier* rendered an Ac- " count;" but " Whether a DEMAND *was made upon Grier*, ſo as " to *intitle* the Plaintiff to an Account." It is as much an Affirmative and a Negative (to my Apprehenſion,) as if the Defendant had pleaded " That after Demand made upon ſuch a Day, He *had* " *rendered* an Account;" To which, the Plaintiff had replied, " That he had *not*."

Mr. Juſt. FOSTER alſo thought that the Whole Merits might have been tried upon this Iſſue, " Whether there was a *Demand*, " or not."

Mr. Juſt. WILMOT concurred, that the Replication does here meet the Plea; and is properly concluded to the Country. For the Plea ſays, " You made no Demand: But if you did, He rendered " an Account." The Replication ſays, " I *made* a Demand, on " ſuch a Day; Yet He rendered *no* Account." Which is a ſuffi- " cient Affirmative and Negative.

Per Cur. unanimouſly,
JUDGMENT for the PLAINTIFF.

Nedriffe *verſ.* Hogan.

THIS was an Action on ſeveral Promiſes; *viz. Indebitatus Aſſumpſit* for 40*l.* lent, 40*l.* had and received to the Plaintiff's Uſe, and 40*l.* laid out and expended for the Plaintiff's Uſe.

The Defendant (having had Leave to do ſo) pleaded ſeveral Pleas: One of which was a Plea of a Sett-off; namely, of a PENALTY of 200*l.*

200*l.* incurred by the Non-Performance of certain *Articles of Agreement*, relating to the Sale of a Ship.

The Plaintiff demurred, for Cause: And One of the Causes specified, was "that the PENALTY of Articles of Agreement (which "sounds in *Damages* only, and is *not* a liquidated certain Debt or "Demand) CAN NOT *be* SET OFF."

To this, there was a Joinder in Demurrer.

Mr. *Walker*, for the Plaintiff.—This Sett-off is not within the Act of 2 *G.* 2. *c.* 22. § 13. For *no* PENALTY *at all* can be set off, under *that* Act. Whereas this is not the Penalty of even a Bond conditioned for Payment of Money only, but a *Penalty of a Bond conditioned for Performance of Articles*; Which Penalty *sounds in Damages*: And *Damages* cannot be set off. It ought to be a *certain* Demand: A Penalty founded in Damages was never meant or intended by this Act of Parliament.

But the * second Act of 8 *G.* 2. *c.* 24. § 5. is clearer still: For this § 5. fixes it to the Sum *truly and justly due*; even on Bonds conditioned for Payment of *Money* only. Which fully proves "that "the *Penalty* of such a Bond as *this* is, can not be set off."

* *V. ante, pa.* 822 to 826. where these two Acts are discussed and explained.

A Second Objection (which was also the 2d Cause of Demurrer,) was mentioned: But no further Notice was taken of it, either by Court or Counsel.

Mr. *Field*, for the Defendant.—The former Act is *general*, "that "mutual Debts may be set One against the Other." Upon which, There was a Doubt, and a Difference of Opinion between this Court and the Court of Common Pleas, concerning Setting-off Debts of different Natures. The 8 *G.* 2. *c.* 24. § 5. allows it, notwithstanding the Debts are deemed in Law to be of a different Nature, And the Purpose of 8 *G.* 2. was to extend, and not to restrain the former Act. Indeed it restrains the Case of a Debt accrewing by reason of a Penalty *so far*, (*but no farther*,) "that it shall be † PLEA-"DED."

† But this Clause (§ 5) adds, "that "in such Plea shall be shewn how much is *truly and justly due* on either Side;" and that Judgment shall be entered for no more than what shall appear to be truly and justly due.

Lord MANSFIELD stopt Mr. *Field*; and declared it to be, most clearly, a Case *not* within these Acts; as it was for the WHOLE *Penalty*.

He said, He expected that it would have been put upon the Foot of Setting-off the Sum that the Defendant *imagined to be* REALLY *due*

due for the *Damages sustained:* But He now perceived that it was insisted that the WHOLE PENALTY might be set off. He said, It is clearly most *unjust*, and contrary to the *Intention* of the Acts of Parliament, "That the WHOLE *Penalty* should be admitted to be "pleaded by Way of Sett-off, when perhaps a very small Sum was "really due for such Damages as the Defendant had actually sus-"tained."

Therefore the COURT, without further Argument, gave JUDGMENT for the PLAINTIFF.

Maxwell *vers.* Mayer Esq;

MR. *Norton*, on Behalf of the Defendant, moved to stay the Plaintiff's Proceeding, until *Security* should be given for *answering the* COSTS of this Suit, in Case it should go against him.

It was an Action against the Defendant as a Justice of Peace, for illegally convicting the Plaintiff upon the Acts of Parliament relating to Hawkers and Pedlars; Which Acts give Costs to Magistrates, upon Actions brought against them for acting in Pursuance thereto, to be paid by Persons who fail in such Actions.

He moved this, upon an Affidavit "That the Plaintiff was a "*Scotchman resident in Scotland:*" Whom the Process of this Court could not therefore reach, in Case he should fail in his Action.

But The COURT answered, that it was, at the *utmost*, no more than the Case of a FOREIGNER who brings an Action here: In which Case, the Court will never oblige him to give Security for the Costs.

And Mr. *Norton* acknowledged that He did not expect to prevail in his Motion; and had told his Client so.

Per Cur.
Take Nothing by your Motion.

Rex

Rex *verſ.* John Spragg and Mary Elizabetha Spragg (his Daughter.)

Wednesday 11th *June* 1760.

V. ante 930, and 993.

MR. Juſtice FOSTER (in the Abſence of Mr. Juſt. DENISON) pronounced the * Sentence upon the Defendants: Whoſe Offence (of *maliciouſly conſpiring to indict* and actually *falſely indicting* a Perſon of a CAPITAL *Crime*, whereof He was innocent,) would have been in Point of real Guilt, an aggravated and atrocious Murder, He ſaid, if it had *ſucceeded* according to their Intention; and even now deſerved a very exemplary Puniſhment, notwithſtanding it had *not* ſucceeded according to their Wiſh.

* *V.* 2 *Inſt.* 384. Where it is ſaid "that the *Villainous* Judgment (there particularly ſpecified,) *remains* a conſtant Law, in ſuch Caſes as the preſent, *to this Day.*"
But Mr. *Gould* and Serj. *Davy* agreed that they could find *no Inſtance* or *Entry* of ſuch a Judgment ACTUALLY given. *V. ante* 996, 997.

John Spragg (the Father) was ſentenced to be remanded to the Priſon of this Court, for One Month; To be ſet twice, in and upon the Pillory, (for an Hour each Time,) Once at *Charing-Croſs*, and again at the *Royal Exchange*; To be impriſoned, in the Priſon of this Court, for two Years from the End of the ſaid Month; To pay a Fine of 50 *l.* to the King; To find Security for his good Behaviour for 3 Years, (Himſelf in 40 *l.* and Each Security in 20 *l.*) And to be committed *quouſque*.

Mary, the Daughter, (being conſidered by the Court as leſs Criminal, partly from her * Youth, and partly as She was under the Direction and Influence of her Father,) was only committed to the Cuſtody of the Marſhal, to be impriſoned for the Space of † 6 Months from this Time.

* She ſeemed to be under 20.

† Note—They had been, Both of them, *already in Cuſtody*, (in Town and Country) near a Year and a half.

Lancaſter *verſ.* Thornton.

Thurſday 12th *June* 1760.

THIS was a Caſe out of Chancery for the Opinion of this Court: The Subſtance whereof was as follows.

George Lancaſter being ſeiſed in Fee of ſome Lands (the Premiſes in queſtion) and poſſeſſed of other Lands for a Term of Years, made his laſt Will and Teſtament dated the 3d of *June* 1734; Which, after having given certain Legacies, goes on thus—"I do

" hereby *Charge and make Chargeable* All and every my Lands and " Inheritance and Leafehold with the Payment of my Debts Fune- " ral Expences and Legacies: And for more fpeedy raifing Money " for Payment of them, *I devife* to *George*, *Edmund*, and *Dorothy* " *Lancafter* (who were his two Sons and his Daughter) their Heirs " Executors and Adminiftrators, the *Leafehold*-Eftate (defcribing " it,) for all the Refidue of the Term therein to come &c; Upon " Truft to fell the fame &c, and to apply the Money &c to the Pay- " ment of my Debts Legacies and Funeral Expences." But *in cafe* the Money arifing from the Sale of the faid Leafehold Eftate fhall not be fufficient to pay and difcharge All his Debts Legacies and Funeral Expences, Then He *devifes* "*That his faid two Sons and Daugh-* " *ter* SHALL AND MAY ABSOLUTELY SELL *mortgage or other-* " *wife difpofe of his* FREEHOLD *Eftate*, for the Payment of fuch of " his faid Debts Legacies and Funeral Expences, as his faid Leafe- " hold Eftate fhould not be fufficient to pay and difcharge." And *from and immediately after Payment of All his Debts Legacies and Funeral Expences*, He devifes the faid Freehold Eftate or fo much of it as fhould remain after fuch Payment of his Debts Legacies and Funeral Expences as aforefaid, to *Thomas Dobfon* and *James Lancafter* and their Heirs and Affigns: Upon Truft that They and the Survivor of them and his Heirs fhould ftand feifed thereof (except a Parlour and Room over it, which He devifed to *Dorothy* fo long as She fhould remain unmarried,) To the Ufe of his Son *Edmund* for Life, without Impeachment of Wafte; and from and after the Determination of that Eftate, to the faid *Thomas Dobfon* and *James Lancafter* and their Heirs during his Life, to fupport &c; with Remainder to the Heirs Male of the Body of the faid *Edmund*; Remainder to the faid *Thomas Dobfon* and *James Lancafter*, for the Term of 1000 Years, to raife 120*l*. for his Grand-Daughters (the Daughters of faid *Edmund*.) Then He devifes the Remainder, fubject to the faid Term, to the Ufe of his Son *George*, in Tail Male; with Remainder to his Grandfon *George*. And He appoints his faid Sons *Edmund* and *George* and his Daughter *Dorothy*, his Executors.

The Teftator died, and left two Sons, *viz.* the faid *Edmund* his Eldeft Son and Heir, and *George*; and two Daughters, *viz.* the beforementioned *Dorothy*, and *Hannah*.

Edmund entered, and proved the Will.

The LEASEHOLD-*Eftate* was NOT *fufficient* to pay and difcharge the Teftator's Debts Legacies and Funeral Expences.

Edmund fuffered a *Recovery*, to the Ufe of Himfelf in Fee: And in 1740, He made a Mortgage to fecure a Bond-Debt to One *Machil*, upon a Bond made by the Teftator, whereby the Teftator had bound his Heirs.

Some

Some of the Teſtator's Debts are ſtill remaining due and unpaid.

Edmund died, leaving Iſſue two Daughters.

George filed his Bill in Chancery, to eſtabliſh the Will; and inſiſted "that the Deviſe to *Thomas Dobſon* and *James Lancaſter never* "*took Effect in Poſſeſſion*; as the Debts Legacies and Funeral Expen-"ces were *not paid*:" And He inſiſted "that the *Freehold Eſtate*, "ſubject to the ſaid Debts &c, does therefore belong to *Him*, in "Tail Male."

On the other hand, The Daughters of *Edmund* inſiſt "that the "Recovery was well ſuffered by their Father, *Edmund*; and that "*They* are intitled to the *Freehold Eſtate*, ſubject to the Mortgage "abovementioned."

The Lord Keeper directed the following Queſtion to be referred to this Court for their Opinion; *viz.*

Whether, by Virtue of theſe Words, *viz.* "In caſe the Money "ariſing from the Sale of the Leaſehold Eſtate ſhall not be "ſufficient to pay and diſcharge All the Teſtator's Debts Le-"gacies and Funeral Expences, That then He *deviſes* that "his two Sons and his Daughter SHALL AND MAY ABSO-"LUTELY SELL *mortgage or otherwiſe diſpoſe of* his Freehold "Eſtate, for the Payment of ſuch of his ſaid Debts Legacies "and Funeral Expences as his ſaid Leaſehold Eſtate ſhould "not be ſufficient to pay and diſcharge"—Any Estate paſſed to *Edmund*, *George*, and *Dorothy*; Or ONLY *a* Power *to ſell*.

It was argued on *Tueſday* 10th *June* 1760.

Mr. *Aſhurſt*, for the Plaintiff *George Lancaſter*, though He admitted that, *in general*, where the Deviſe was "That the Teſta-"tor's Executors *ſhould* ſell his Land for the Payment of Debts "&c," the *legal* Eſtate will *not* paſs, nevertheleſs argued that in the preſent Caſe, a *Conditional Fee paſſed to the Executors*, either by expreſs *Words*, or at leaſt by the *Intention* of the Teſtator.

1ſt. As to the *Words*. The Teſtator uſes the Word "*Deviſe*;" which alone is ſufficient to paſs an Eſtate. And *Litt.* § 383. proves "that a defeazible Eſtate will paſs to Executors by a Deviſe of Te-"nements, *to be ſold* by his Executors." And there is * no Difference between a Deviſe, "to be ſold by Executors; and a Deviſe "to them, *to ſell*."

* So is Co. *Litt.* 236. *a.* Yet ſee Co. *Litt.* 112. *b.*

2dly. But the *Intention* plainly is, to convey a *legal* Eſtate. The Teſtator's primary Intention was the certain and ſpeedy Payment of his Debts Legacies and Funeral Expences. And this Intention will be beſt anſwered, by conſtruing it to be a Deviſe of the *legal* Eſtate. The Caſe in 10 *H.* 7. cited in *Plowden* 414. *a.* is ſimilar to this: Where *Ceſtuy que Uſe* deviſed "That his Wife, being his Executrix, *ſhould ſell* his Land," and died; and She ſold it to her ſecond Huſband; And this was adjudged a good Sale. In 1 *Vern.* 45. *Newman* v. *Johnſon*, a Deviſe "of all his Eſtate, both Real "and Perſonal, to *J. S.* my Debts and Legacies being firſt de-"ducted," was holden to amount to a Deviſe "to ſell, for Pay-"ment of his Debts." The *Intention* is alſo apparent from *other* Parts of this Will. For *if* it was only a *bare Power* to ſell mortgage &c, the Eſtate muſt *deſcend* to the Heir at Law, in the mean Time; who would NOT be compellable to refund or to account for the Rents and Profits which he ſhould receive prior to the Sale; even though the whole Real and Perſonal Eſtate ſhould not ſuffice to anſwer the Charge of the Debts Legacies and Funeral Expences. A Deviſe "That they *ſhall and may* ABSOLUTELY SELL *mortgage* "*or otherwiſe diſpoſe* of his Eſtate," gives them an ESTATE in the Land; and includes giving them the Rents and Profits; Eſpecially, as the Heir would be *unaccountable* for them, if they were to deſcend to him, till Sale &c: And the rather ſtill, for that the Teſtator has taken *expreſs* Notice of his Heir at Law, by a *particular Bequeſt to him.*

Mr. *Clayton*, for the Defendant (the Heir at Law) and alſo (as he ſaid) for the Mortgagee, argued that NO LEGAL ESTATE paſſed to the Executors; but *only a* POWER to ſell mortgage or otherwiſe diſpoſe of this Eſtate, in Caſe the Leaſehold Eſtate ſhould prove deficient.

And He inſiſted that this Conſtruction was agreeable both to the *Words* of the Will and to the *Intention* of the Teſtator.

There are many Caſes where the Word "*Deviſe*" is uſed, and yet no Fee paſſes. Sir *William Jones* 327. *Dike* v. *Ricks*. *Cro. Car.* 335. S. C. and a Caſe in 1 *Leon.* 31. *Caſe* 38. *Tr.* 23 *Eliz.* in *C. B.*

1 *Inſt.* 113. *a.* is agreeable to *Windham*'s Opinion in 1 *Leon.* 31. "that the Vendee is in by the *Deviſe*, and *not* by the Conveyance "of the Executors;" And to *Plowd.* 414. *a.* (the cited Caſe in 10 *H.* 7.) 1 *Inſt.* 236. *a.* comments upon, explains and diſtinguiſhes the Text of *Littleton* § 383. (cited by Mr. *Aſhurſt*,) and ſhews the Diverſity between a Deviſe "that his Executors *ſhall*

" *sell*," and a Devise " *to* his Executors to be sold:" The former of which is a bare naked Power.

And here is Nothing at all *devised to* the Executors: They have *only a bare Power to sell &c.*

The Case of *Yates* and *Compton*, in 2 *Wms.* 308, 309. proves " that the legal Estate did *not* pass."

Though the Devise be *general*, " That they shall and may abso-" lutely sell mortgage or otherwise dispose of;" It is still *Nothing more* than a POWER.

And as to the intermediate Rents and Profits from the Death of the Testator till Sale or Mortgage or other Disposal, The Heir at Law will be *accountable* for them, if he receives them: And they may be come at, by Application in Equity, or otherwise.

Mr. *Ashurst*, in Reply, relied on the *Intention* of the Testator; who meant, he said, that No One should take Benefit, *till* after his Debts Legacies and Funeral Expences should be paid.

Lord MANSFIELD thought it a plain Case.

Here are *no* WORDS by which the Estate is devised *to* the Executors. Therefore, *if* it be construed, that there *is* a Devise to them, it must be raised by *Implication*. But, by the Frame of the Will, it is plain that the Testator did NOT *so intend*: For he shews, by the Expressions that he has used, that He *knew the Distinction* between a Devise of an *Estate* TO *them*, and giving them only a *Power to sell*. As to the Term " *Devise*;" The Expression " *I* " *devise*," is here synonimous to saying " *I will*," or " *my Mind is*."

The INTENTION of the Testator, Mr. *Ashurst* says, can not be complied with, in this Case, *without* an Implication of a Devise *to* the Executors; because it must otherwise descend to the Heir at Law in the mean Time; Who, he says, would NOT *be chargeable* with the intermediate Rents and Profits, but altogether *unaccountable* for them.

That, clearly, is *not* so. The Land could only descend to the Heir, subject to the Charges; and would be liable, in his hands, to the Payment of Debts Legacies and Funeral Expences. So that the Testator's Intention is equally answered, One Way, as the Other.

The Certificate was as follows—Having heard Counsel on both Sides, and considered this Case, (which the Parties delayed bringing

bringing on to be argued, until this Term,) We are of Opinion That NO ESTATE passed to the said *Edmund George* and *Dorothy Lancaster*; but *only* a POWER to sell demise mortgage or otherwise dispose of the Premisses.

Moultby *verſ.* Richardson.

MR. *Howard* moved that the Defendant might be discharged on *Common Bail*; the Affidavit to hold to Bail, being only "That the Defendant was indebted to the Plaintiff in such a Sum, "AS *He computes it*."

But Mr. Just. FOSTER and Mr. Just. WILMOT (the only Judges then in Court) thought it sufficient: And they added "That Cases "of * this Sort had gone a great Way;" (intimating that they had gone full far.)

* *V. ante* 652, 653.

MOTION DENIED.

Friday 13th *June* 1760.

Ferguson et Ux' *verſ.* Cornish.

THIS was upon a Demurrer by the Defendant, to a Declaration in an Action of Covenant upon an Indenture of Lease, assigning a Breach in Non-Payment of Rent.

The Declaration set forth that *Adam Harper* and *Phœbe* his Wife demised the Premisses to the Defendant *John Cornish*, from &c, for 7, 14, OR 21 Years, *as the Lessee* (*Cornish*) *should think proper*; at 60*l.* *per Annum* Rent; And the Defendant covenanted to pay to the said *Adam Harper* and *Phœbe* his Wife, THEIR Executors Administrators and Assigns, the said Rent, during the *said* TERM; And that *Cornish entered*, and was possessed, and *continues in Possession*. Then it shews the Death of *Adam Harper*, and the Intermarriage of *Phœbe* with the now Plaintiff *Ferguson*; and that so much Rent &c, became due and in Arrear; And assigns the Breach in this, that the Defendant has not paid &c (in the Words of the Covenant,) TO *the Plaintiff Ferguson and Phœbe his Wife*. *

* Note—The Arrear of Rent upon which the Breach is assigned, was alledged to have incurred *within the* FIRST *seven* Years.

To this Declaration, there was a General Demurrer by the Defendant; And a Joinder in Demurrer, by the Plaintiffs.

Mr. *Eyre*, for the Defendant, argued in Support of the Demurrer.

Question—

Queſtion—Whether the Plaintiffs have made a *good Aſſignment* of a Breach, in Non-Payment of Rent ſuppoſed to have become due upon *this* Leaſe.

1ſt Objection—This Covenant is a *relative* Covenant: 'Tis to pay *for and during* a TERM of 7, 14, or 21 Years. But *if* NO *Term* was ever granted, the Covenant fails.

Now NO *Term* was *created* by this Indenture: For it is VOID *for Uncertainty*. This appears from the two following Caſes.

Plowd. 273. *Say* v. *Smyth and Fuller*, proves "That every Con-"tract ſufficient to make a Leaſe for Years ought to have CER-"TAINTY in three Limitations; namely, the *Commencement*, *Con-"tinuance*, and *End* of the Term."

6 *Co. Rep.* 35. *The Biſhop of Bath's Caſe*, lays it down, "That "the *Certainty* of CONTINUANCE is to be intended, Either where "the Term is made certain by an *expreſs Enumeration of Years*: Or "by *Reference to Certainty*; or by *reducing* it to Certainty, by *Mat-"ter ex poſt Facto*, or by *Conſtruction in Law* by expreſs Limita-"tion."

Therefore, the *Habendum* in this Leaſe is *void* for UNCERTAIN-TY. It is a Demiſe, to hold from *Michaelmas &c*, for the Term of 7, 14, *or* 21 Years, *as the Leſſee ſhall think proper*. Now, *if* the Leſſee ſhould not elect, the Leaſe could *never* COMMENCE.

But, at leaſt, the CONTINUANCE of it is quite *uncertain*. It is *not* (as the uſual Way of making theſe Leaſes is,) a Leaſe *for* 21 *Years* certain, covenanted to be defeaſible at the Election of the Leſ-ſee; *nor* is it made certain by any *Reference* to a Thing which has Certainty at the Time of the Leaſe made; *Nor* is there any Thing *ex poſt facto* to be done, or averred to have been done; (And the Leſſee's Entry determines Nothing; It can be no more than *Evidence*, even *after* 7 Years Poſſeſſion;) *Nor* can here be any *Conſtruction of Law, by expreſs Limitation*.

2d Objection—But if the Court ſhould think it to be a *ſubſiſting* Covenant; then a 2d Queſtion will ariſe, "Whether it ſubſiſts *be-"tween the* PRESENT *Parties*."

The Covenant is, "to pay to the *deceaſed* Huſband *and* his Wife, "(*Adam Harper* and *Phœbe*,) and to THEIR Executors Admini-"ſtrators and Aſſigns." Therefore the *Executors of the deceaſed Huſband* ought to have joined in this Action.

3d Objection goes to the *Manner of assigning the Breach:* It ought to have been shewn "that the Rent was *not paid* to the EXECU-"TORS *of the Husband.*"

Lord MANSFIELD—The Lessee has certainly *entered*, and continues in *Possession:* And it is as certain, that he *must pay the Rent.*

It is undoubtedly a good Lease for 7 Years; (whatever may be the Validity of it as to the other two eventual Terms, of 14 and 21 Years:) And the Breach is assigned for Non-Payment of Rent incurred *within the first Seven* Years.

Mr. Serj. *Poole* was for the Plaintiff: But the Chief Justice was so clear in his Opinion, that there was no need for Him to interfere; nor did He.

Per Cur. JUDGMENT for the PLAINTIFFS.

Hewson *vers.* Brown.

MR. *Winn* moved, on behalf of the Plaintiff, for an ORDER upon the proper *Officer of the Court of* COMMON PLEAS, to ATTEND HERE with the *Record of that* Court (between *Watson* v. *Hewson*) in Order for it's being inspected by this Court.

The Defendant in *this* Court, who was sued *here* upon a Bond to indemnify the present Plaintiff, had pleaded "*Non damnificatus:*" To which Plea, the Plaintiff replied a *Recovery* in the Court of Common Pleas against him, by one *Thomas Watson*; whereby he was damnified. To this Replication, the Defendant here had rejoined "*Nul tiel Record:*" And the Plaintiff sur-rejoined, "That there *is* "such a Record."

Mr. *Winn* acknowledged that the *ordinary* Course and Method of Practice in these Cases, was to issue a CERTIORARI, and have it *certified*; And He also acknowledged that he could not find any Precedent that came up to the present Case: But he urged that it would save Time and Expence; and that this Court by their *General Jurisdiction*, had such a Power over all *inferior* Jurisdictions.

* Mr. Just. *Denison* was absent.

But Lord MANSFIELD and the * Two other Judges now in Court were very clear that as here was no Sort of Reason to go out of the common and ordinary Course, It would be wrong to break the established Rules and Methods of Proceeding: And therefore They

DENIED the MOTION.

Rex

Rex *verʃ.* Inhabitants of Hitcham. *V. ante, pa.* 910.

THE * amended Order was now Affirmed: * *V. ante, pa.* 911.

But, being made on *new Evidence* (proving him to have been a Single Man at the Time of the Hiring,)

The COURT thought it reaſonable, and accordingly Ordered that the

RECOGNIZANCE be DISCHARGED.

Rex *verʃ.* Pemberton. *Saturday* 14th *June* 1760.

ON ſhewing Cauſe againſt a Rule for quaſhing an Indictment on 5 *Eliz. c.* 4. § 31. for exerciſing the Occupation of a TANNER, not having ſerved an Apprenticeſhip therein for *Seven* Years.

Mr. *Sayer*, on the Part of the Defendant, objected,

1ſt. That though the Trade of a *Tanner* was undoubtedly a Trade uſed within the Realm of *England* at the Time of making this Act of 5 *Eliz.* yet it was *not meant and intended to be* INCLUDED *in this prohibitory Clauſe*; being at that very Time under Regulation by *other* Statutes (no leſs than 16 in Number) made for the Purpoſe of regulating it; and particularly, by 1 *Eliz. c.* 9. which allows the Uſe of it to Apprentices or Covenant-Servants brought up in that Trade *Four* Years: And Another Statute made in the very ſame Year with the preſent One, *viz.* 5 *Eliz. c.* 8. deſcribes who may be Tanners. So that it can not be imagined that *this* Occupation was ever meant to be included on the Prohibition of 5 *Eliz. c.* 4. § 31.

And though both theſe Statutes (of 1 *Eliz. c.* 9. and 5 *Eliz. c.* 8.) are *now* repealed, yet they are equally an Argument to ſhew the Conſtruction of the Clauſe in queſtion, as if they ſtood unrepealed: And ſo the Court conſidered a repealed Statute, in conſtruing the unrepealed One of 43 *Eliz. c.* 2. in the Caſe of *Rex* v. *Loxdale et al'*, *H.* 1757. 30 *G.* 2. *B. R.*

2d Objection.—IF the Trade of a *Tanner* was meant to be included in the prohibitory Clauſe of 5 *Eliz. c.* 4. § 31. yet that Statute was, *as to this particular Trade or Occupation*, REPEALED by

1 the

the 5 *Eliz. c.* 8. and 1 *J.* 1. *c.* 22. § 5. which are *repugnant* to, and consequently a *virtual Repeal* thereof, so far as concerns *this* Trade. The former is indeed now repealed: But the latter is not. They admit of 5 *or* 6 OTHER *Qualifications* besides having served an Apprenticeship for 7 Years; Namely, Such as *then had Tan-houses* and *used* the Trade; Also the *Wives* and *Sons* of *Tanners* having used the Mystery four Years; Also such Persons as should *marry* the Wives or Daughters, to whom Tan-houses and Fats should be left. So that there are now *many other Qualifications* that justify using the Trade, *besides* that of Serving a 7 Years Apprenticeship.

3d Objection.—An Indictment will not therefore now lie upon 5 *Eliz. c.* 4. § 31. *alone* and *generally*: But it ought to SPECIFY all these OTHER *Qualifications* allowed by the subsequent Statute; and to shew that the Party is *not within any of them*; as is done in Convictions upon the Game-Acts, and Convictions for Swearing, and upon the Act of 8, 9 *W.* 3. *c.* 26. "for the better preventing "Counterfeiting the current Coin of this Kingdom." And for this, He cited * *Rex* v. *Maurice Jarvis, H.* 1757. 30 *G.* 2. and *Rex* v. † *Sparrow*; (as He called it,) where a Conviction for prophane Cursing and Swearing was quashed, because it did not alledge "That the Defendant was *not* a Servant, Labourer, Common Sol-"dier or Sailor."

* *V. ante* 148 to 151.
† *Rex* v. *Sparling, H.* 8 *G.* 1. S.C.

This Indictment is upon a Statute not favoured: And the Case is the harder upon the Defendant, and the more oppressive, for that he is under another Indictment on 1 *J.* 1. *c.* 22.

Mr. *Norton*, for the Prosecutor, having been heard in Answer to the Objections; and having made the proper Distinctions between the Cases cited and the Case now in question;

The COURT were unanimously of Opinion—That *whatever Licence* might be given by any Statute *subsequent* to 5 *Eliz. c.* 4. to Persons who had not served a Seven Years Apprenticeship, to exercise the Trade of a Tanner under certain *other Qualifications* therein described; Yet, as the Trade of a Tanner was clearly a Trade *used* at the Time of making the 5 *Eliz. c.* 4. (and seems ackowledged even by 1 *J.* 1. *c.* 22. § 5. to be *included* in 5 *Eliz. c.* 4.) It is *not necessary*, in an Indictment *upon* 5 *Eliz. c.* 4. § 31. for having used this Trade without having served such an Apprenticeship, to *aver* the *Want of the* OTHER *Qualifications*, which by the *subsequent* Statute intitle a Person so qualified, to use the Trade: But such *other* Qualifications or Exceptions must be SHEWN BY THE DEFENDANT, by Way of Excuse, either by *Plea*, or in *Evidence*. It is enough for the Prosecutor, to bring the Case within the General Purview of the

the Statute *upon which* the Indictment is founded; if that Statute has *General prohibitory Words* in it. For where an Indictment is brought *upon* a Statute which has *general prohibitory Words* in it, it is sufficient to charge the Offence *generally*, in the Words of the Statute: And if a *subsequent Statute*, or (as Mr. Just. *Foster* and Mr. Just. *Wilmot*, who spoke after Lord *Mansfield* and Mr. Just. *Denison*, added,) even a Clause of *Exception* contained in the *same* Statute, excuses Persons under such and such Circumstances, or gives Licence to Persons so and so qualified, so as to *excuse* or *except* them out of the general prohibitory Words, *That* must come *by Way of Plea, or Evidence*, "That the Party is not within such general Prohibition, but *excepted* out of it."

Indeed, where the Words of a Statute are descriptive of the *Nature* of the Offence, or the *Purview* of the Statute, or necessary to give a *summary* Jurisdiction, *there* it is necessary to specify in the particular Words of such Statute. In the Statute to prevent Counterfeiting the Coin (8, 9 *W*. 3. *c*. 26.) it is the Purview of the Statute; not a general Prohibition: 'Tis Description—" Any Smith, " Engraver, Founder, or other Person or Persons whatsoever, other " than and except the Persons employed in or for his Majesty's " Mint &c."

N.B. Mr. Just. Foster said, He believed there were not less than a hundred Trades mentioned in other Clauses of 5 *Eliz. c.* 4. And that He had once taken the Pains to extract them and range them alphabetically.

Per Cur. unanimously,
The Rule to shew Cause Why the Indictment should not be quashed, was DISCHARGED.

King's Bench Prisoners *vers.* Marshalsea Prisoners: on Mr. Frederick Ashfield's Will.

Tuesday 17th *June* 1760.

THIS was a Claim of a Legacy, supposed by the Prisoners in the Prison of this Court to be left to *Them*: And the Matter came on, (by Order of the Court,) in the Paper, to be argued. The short and single Question was " Whether the following Bequest was " made to the *Prisoners* in the Prison of *this* Court, or to Those " who were in the Prison of the *Palace* Court."

Frederick Ashfield, of *Richmond* in *Surrey* Gentleman, devised his Copyhold Estate (already surrendered to the Use of his Will) and also all his personal Estate, (after *&c*,) to Trustees to be sold; and directed the Produce to be laid out in Freehold Lands. Then he further directs, that his Trustees shall, for ever, issue pay and dispose of the Rents and Profits, unto and amongst such Persons, who, for the Time being, shall be poor Prisoners and insolvent Debtors *in the* MARSHALSEA *Prison in the Burrough of Southwark in the County of Surrey*, and real and fit Objects of Charity; for and towards their Subsistance during their respective Imprisonments *there*; in such Manner, and in such Parts and Proportions, as his said Trustees and the Survivors of them and their Heirs should from Time to Time order direct and appoint.

Mr. *Gould*, for the Prisoners in the Prison of *this* Court, argued that this Devise belongs to the Prisoners of *this* Court.

The Jurisdiction of this Court, in the present Question, depends upon the Act of 32 *G.* 2. *c.* 28. § 9. which gives Power to the several Courts therein named, to examine into and order Payment of Bequests made to poor Prisoners in the several Gaols or Prisons within their respective Jurisdictions. By which Order, the Prisoners of *this* Court will be *bound*, if the Determination shall turn *against* them: But the Prisoners of the *Palace-Court Prison* will *not* be bound by *any* Determination of the Judges of *this* Court; in Favour of the Prisoners of *this* Court.

The Devise is "to the Prisoners in the MARSHALSEA-PRISON "*in the Burrough of Southwark*:" Which must mean *the Prison of this Court.*—In Support whereof, He cited *Co.* 10 *Rep.* 69, 71, 72. The Case of the *Marshalsea*; and *Spelman's Glossary*, Title *Marshal.* And He observed that the Defendant who is a Prisoner in the *King's Bench* Prison is, and is always supposed (in the Declaration against him) to be, *in Custod' Mareschalli* MARESCHALSIAE *Domini Regis:* The other, (the Defendant in the *Palace-Court*,) *in Custod' Mareschalli Mareschalsiæ* HOSPITII *Domini Regis.* He also cited 1 *Bulstr.* 207 to 212. *Cox* v. *Gray*, at large: And argued that therefore, *propter Excellentiam*, this Devise is to the Prisoners of the Prison of THIS Court.

Mr. *Field*, *contra*, for the Prisoners of the *Palace-Court*, argued and sufficiently shewed that this Devise *must* be understood to be to the Prisoners in the Prison of the *Marshal of the* HOUSE-HOLD.

Lord

Lord MANSFIELD was clearly of that Opinion. He observed, that not only in vulgar Speech, but likewise in many Acts of Parliament, the Prison of *this* Court is called the KING'S BENCH Prison; and the * *Other* is called the MARSHALSEA-Prison. Both of them indeed are in the Burrough of *Southwark*: But Each of them has it's respective Appellation. And this Testator used the Name that was always used by every Body else in *Common Parlance*; without searching *Spelman's Glossary* or my Lord *Coke*'s or *Bulstrode's Reports*, to find the *strict* and *legal* Name. This is a sufficient Reason for Us, *not* to make any *Order* at all in the present Case.

* *V. Cowel's Interpreter, sub verbo Marshalsee*, expressly *accord*: Also *Blount's Nomolexicon, Marshalsee.*

Note—This respective Appellation of each of these Prisons was agreed by the Marshal of this Court, (on Appeal to his own Candor, by Lord *Mansfield*,) to be the Name used in Common Parlance.

Therefore No RULE was taken.

Rex *vers.* Pearson.

Thursday 19th *June* 1760.

MR. *Baynham* moved, upon the usual Affidavit, that the Defendant might be admitted to defend *in Forma Pauperis.*

But, upon it's appearing that this was *upon an Attachment for a Contempt*, and NOT *a* CAUSE *in Court*; And Mr. *Baynham* not being able to produce any Precedent of such a Rule having ever been made where *no Cause* was depending in Court;

The MOTION was DENIED.

Margaret Hutt's Case: or Rex *vers.* Bowmaster and Epworth.

ON this Woman's offering to exhibit Articles of the Peace against these two Persons, It appeared that the Facts charged were done at *Portsmouth*.

Whereupon The COURT objected to Her, that She might as well have applied to a Justice of Peace in the Neighbourhood: And then the Defendants would not be under a Necessity of Coming up to *London*, to put in Bail.

It was answered, That if there should be any particular Inconvenience arising therefrom, there might be a *Mandamus* to a Justice of of Peace in the Country impowering Him to take the Security *there:* And of this, Mr. *Harvey* (as *Amicus Curiæ*) mentioned several Instances within his own Observation and Memory.

At length, Mr. *Athorpe* (Secondary of the Crown-Office) proposed, and The COURT came into this Expedient, *viz.* That on issuing the Attachment of the Peace, which is of Course made out upon the Court's receiving the Articles praying Security of the Peace, an *Indorsement* should be at the same Time made thereon, authorizing and directing any Justice or Justices of Peace in that County (*Southampton*) to take the Security of the Peace there; specifying the particular Sums wherein the Principals and also their Sureties should be bound.

Per Cur.
It was ORDERED accordingly.

Saturday 21st *June* 1760.

Rex *vers.* Moreley; Rex *vers.* Osborne; Rex *vers.* Reeve; and Rex *vers.* Norris.

MR. *Knowler* and Mr. *Filmer* shewed Cause against the *issuing* of a CERTIORARI to remove several Orders made by Mr. *Moneypenny*, a Justice of Peace in *Kent*, upon the CONVENTICLE-*Act*, 22 *Car.* 2. *c.* 1: By which Orders he had convicted a Methodist-Preacher, and the Master of the House wherein He preached, and Several of the Audience, in the respective Penalties following.

* *V.* Sect. 3. † *V.* Sect. 4. ‡ *V.* Sect. 1. ‖ *V.* Sect. 5.

The * Preacher (*Moreley*) was convicted in 20 *l.* The † Master of the House (*Osborne*) in 20 *l.* and Several of ‡ the Persons present, in 5 *s.* a-piece. Two of the Auditors (*Reeve* and *Norris*) had had 10 *l.* ‖ a-piece levied upon them; (by virtue of the 3d Section of this Act,) the Preacher Himself not being to be found. The Penalty had been levied upon *Osborne*, (the Master of the House,) as well as upon *Reeve* and *Norris*. They had All appealed (within the Week) to the Sessions: And Mr. *Moneypenny* had returned to the Sessions, the Monies levied, and certified the Evidence, with the Record of the Conviction, agreeable to the Directions of the 6th Section; And the Defendants had pleaded and been *tried by a Jury* at the Quarter-Sessions; And there had been both *Verdict* and *Judgment* given against them.

Mr. *Knowler* and Mr. *Filmer*, on behalf of the Prosecution, urged, that after All this had passed, a *Writ of Error* might lie; but *not* a CERTIORARI, which will only lie when there is *no other Remedy*.

And

And there is a Clause in the 6th Section, which is express, "That NO *other Court* WHATSOEVER *shall intermeddle* with any "Cause or Causes of Appeal upon this Act: But they shall be *finally* "determined in the Quarter-Sessions ONLY." Which *Negative* Words must include *All* the Courts of Judicature in the Kingdom, and this Court in particular, as being most likely to meddle with Matters of this kind.

And the 13th Section directs "that this Act, and *all Clauses* there- "in contained, shall be *construed most largely and beneficially* for the "*Suppressing* of Conventicles, and for the *Justification* and *Encou-* "*ragement* of all Persons to be employed in the Execution thereof; "And that no Record Warrant or Mittimus to be made by Virtue of "this Act, *or any Proceedings thereupon*, shall be reversed avoided "*or any Way impeached*, by reason of any *Default in Form*."

Therefore, to *what Purpose* should a *Certiorari* issue, when the Court can neither intermeddle with the *Fact or Form*?

The *Penalties* are (by the 2d Section) to be *distributed* into three Parts; ⅓ to the King, ⅓ to the Poor, ⅓ to the Informer: And these Penalties *have been* so distributed; And this Court can *not order Restitution*.

As to the Penalties *under* 10*s*. the Act gives *no Appeal*: If the Justices have done wrong in the Matter of *these*, 'tis in a Matter *coram non Judice*.

Mr. *Knowler* and Mr. *Filmer* had Affidavits of the Facts which they alledged.

Lord MANSFIELD, asked them Whether the Negative Words in the 6th Section would not conclude strongly against a *Writ of Error*.

Mr. *Knowler* and Mr. *Filmer* answered, That as to *Fact*, they might; but, perhaps, *not* as to *Law*. They cited a little printed Book, said to be written by Ld. Ch. J. *Saunders*, (a Comment on this Conventicle-Act) *Fo.* 69. § 6. & § 13: Which shewed *Him* to be of Opinion "That *no Certiorari* would lie upon it."

Mr. Just. DENISON observed, "That there have been many De- "terminations to the Contrary since."

Mr. *Norton*, Mr. *Stow*, and Mr. *Leigh*, who were for the *Certiorari*, insisted That the *General* Jurisdiction of *this* Court is *not* taken away by *mere negative Words* in an Act of Parliament: This

Court ſhall *never* be *ouſted of its Juriſdiction* without *Special* Words. Dr. *Foſter*'s Caſe, 11 *Co.* 64. *b.* 1 *Ro. Rep.* 92, 94. S. C. 1 *Ventr.* 66. *Smith*'s Caſe. 1 *Mod.* 45. S. C.

Beſides, Theſe Words "That no other Court whatſoever ſhall "intermeddle *with any Cauſe or Cauſes of Appeal*; but that *they* ſhall "be finally determined in the Quarter-Seſſions only;" mean no more than that the FACTS ſhall *not be re-examined*: But the *Legality* may; or a *Want of Juriſdiction* may be taken Advantage of. The Caſe *may* be ſuch as that the Juſtices have *no Juriſdiction* of the Matter. And where a Statute does not *expreſly* and *totidem verbis take away a Certiorari*, and direct "that *no Certiorari* ſhall iſſue," the Court will grant One. And *Peat*'s Caſe, in 6 *Mod.* 228. proves "That a *Certiorari does lie* upon *this* very Act." The Court there ſay, "That the Juſtices of Peace being Judges of the Matter, *if* "*they wrong* You, *You* HAVE *your* REMEDY *by* CERTIORARI, or "Appeal to the Seſſions." And it appears in that Caſe (at the End of it,) that a *Certiorari* had then *actually iſſued.*

As to Five of theſe Convictions, which were againſt Perſons *preſent* at this Aſſembly, and under 10*s.* (namely, only 5*s.* a-piece,) *No Appeal* is given: And conſequently, there can be no Doubt but that a *Certiorari does lie*, as to *them*.

Mr. *Norton*, being aſked "*What* was the Objection that he had to "theſe Convictions," anſwered, That it was *not alledged* "that the "Defendants *were* * *Subjects of this Realm*:" Which is an eſſential Requiſite.

* *V.* Sect. 1.

The COURT were unanimouſly of Opinion that a *Certiorari* OUGHT *to iſſue.* A *Certiorari* does not go, to try the *Merits* of the Queſtion; but to ſee whether the *limited* Juriſdiction have *exceeded their Bounds*. The *Juriſdiction* of *this* Court is *not taken away*, unleſs there be *expreſs Words* to take it away: This is a Point ſettled. Therefore a *Certiorari* ought to iſſue: And after a Return ſhall be made to it, You will be at Liberty, and it will ſtill be open to You, to move to ſuperſede it, if there ſhould appear Reaſon for the Court's ſo doing.

RULE made abſolute, for a CERTIORARI.

Rex

Rex *verſ.* Blooer.

Wednesday 25th June 1760.

MR. *Norton* and Mr. *Madocks* ſhewed Cauſe againſt the Iſſuing of a MANDAMUS which had been prayed to be directed to One *Samuel Blooer*, a Pariſhioner of *Matfield* in *Staffordſhire* and an Inhabitant of the Chapelry of *Calton* within that Pariſh, (Who had turned Mr. *William Langley* the Curate of that Chapel, out of it, after he had been *Eleven Weeks in Poſſeſſion*, and locked it up,) Commanding him to *reſtore* the ſaid *William Langley*, Clerk, to the Place and Office of CURATE *of the ſaid* CHAPEL.

This Chapel is a *Donative*, and is endowed with *Lands*: And the Inhabitants of 4 different Pariſhes *contribute to the Repair* of it. The Curate of it has a *Stipend*, Mr. *Evans*, the Vicar of *Matfield* ſwore in his Affidavit, "That he *believes* HE has the *Right of Nomination* to it; And that it has been executed; And that Mr. "*Langley* is appointed and nominated by Him." But there were contrary Affidavits; wherein the Deponents ſwear "That *they* believe the Right of Nomination to be in the Inhabitants." It appeared that Mr. *Langley* had a *Licence*.

The two Gentlemen beforementioned, Who were Counſel for the Pariſhioner and againſt the *Mandamus*, argued That this Chapel appeared to be a *Donative*; and as the particular Nature of it was not ſtated, it muſt be conſidered as only a *private* Chapel, and *not* as a *public* Office: And conſequently, no *Mandamus* will lie.

Beſides, the Right of Nomination is not eſtabliſhed. The Vicar only ſwears "That he *believes* He has Right of the Nomination:" Which is contradicted by the adverſe Affidavits. And if it were not, Yet a Vicar has Nothing to do with a *Donative*.

They mentioned *Preſcot*'s Caſe, the Chaplain of *Mancheſter* College, reported in 2 *Strange* 797. by the Name of *Dominus Rex v. Epiſcopum Cheſter*. But there, they ſaid, were Letters Patent: The College was of the Foundation of the Crown. The Ground of the Court's interpoſing in that Caſe, was becauſe there was no other Remedy.

This Man may have *another Remedy*: He may bring an *Ejectment* for the Farm which He ſays belongs to him as Curate of this Chapel; Or He may have his Action of Treſpaſs.

Every Vicar might as well come for a *Mandamus* to be reſtored, as this Man.

Mr.

Mr. *Morton* and Mr. *Aston* argued for the *Mandamus*; and urged that this was an *Office* or *Degree* that *concerned the public Weal*; and therefore a *Mandamus* would lie to restore to it, upon the Principle laid down by Chief Justice *Glyn*, in the Case of the Clerk of the City Works of *London*, 2 *Siderfin* 112, 113. Who says that a *Mandamus* shall be granted in these two Cases; first, to restore to an Office which concerns the Execution of Justice; Secondly, If the Office or Degree be for the Weal Public.

A *Mandamus* will lie to restore even a *Sexton*. *Raym*. 211. *Isle's* Case, Sexton of *Kingsclere*; and 2 *Lev*. 18. S.C. *Rex* v. *Church-Wardens of Kingsclere*. So it will, to restore a *Parish-Clerk*. 6 *Mod*. 253. *Parker* v. *Clerk*. And surely a Curate of a Chapel, with a *Stipend*, is more a *public Officer*, than a *Parish-Clerk* or *Sexton* is.

Non constat that this is a Donative. But if it be, yet no Licence is necessary in Case of a Donative; though in the Case of a perpetual Curacy, it is necessary.

And it is no Objection, to say "that We have *another* Remedy;" if We are intitled to *this*.

The Counsel on the other Side (against the *Mandamus*) observed that Parish-Clerks and Sextons are *temporal* Officers; whereas this was *Ecclesiastical*: And a *Vicar* or *Rector* may just as well apply for a *Mandamus*, as the *Chaplain of a Donative*.

The Court proposed to the Parties, to try the Merits in a feigned Issue: Which was declined, on the Part of *Bloer*; who insisted on taking the Opinion of the Court "Whether the Rule "ought not to be discharged."

Lord Mansfield—This is a mere *temporal* Question.

Three Objections have been offered against making the Rule absolute.

The 1st was, "That there is no sufficient *Ground* for asking a *Mandamus*.

Answer. But this Chaplain has shewn an *Appointment*, and a *Licence*; and was in quiet *Possession* for 11 Weeks.

2d Objection. That he has *not* the Right: For the Nomination was not in the Vicar, but in the Inhabitants.

4 Answer.

Anſwer. We can not try the Merits upon *Affidavit.* He *claims a Right,* though it is litigated: And that is ſufficient for the preſent Purpoſe,

3d Objection.—That, even ſuppoſing him to have a Title, and to have been in Poſſeſſion, and turned out of it; yet he ought not to be aſſiſted by Way of MANDAMUS, but be left to his ordinary legal Remedy, by Ejectment or an Action of Treſpaſs.

Anſwer. A *Mandamus to reſtore* is the true Specific Remedy, where a Perſon is wrongfully diſpoſſeſſed of any Office or Function which draws after it Temporal Rights; in all Caſes where the eſtabliſhed Courſe of Law has not provided a *Specific* Remedy by another Form of Proceeding: Which is the Caſe with regard to Rectories and Vicarages.

Here are Lands annexed to this Chapel, which belong to the Chaplain in reſpect of his Function. If the Biſhop had refuſed, without Cauſe, to licenſe Him, He might have had a *Mandamus* to compel the Ordinary to grant Him a Licence. He is now turned out of the Chapel and every Thing belonging thereto, by Force. Such Chapels were not Objects of Attention in the Days when the Regiſter was formed: And therefore there is no particular Remedy provided for *this* Caſe.

It is ſaid "He may bring an Ejectment or an Action of Treſ-"paſs." I am not ſure that he could. It don't appear that the *Legal* Property is in *Him:* On the contrary, it is certain that it is *not*. It might originally be in Feoffees. Thoſe Feoffees may not have been regularly continued. It may be impoſſible to find the Heir of the Survivor. If they have been continued, the preſent Feoffees may refuſe to let Mr. *Langley* make Uſe of their Names. *Neither* of theſe Actions, if he could bring them, would be a *Specific* Remedy. In the one, He might recover Damages; In the other, He might recover the Land: But by neither would He be reſtored to his Pulpit, and quieted in the Exerciſe of his Function and Office. We may very well take Notice too, that the Inhabitants refuſe to try the Merits, in an Iſſue. If a *Mandamus* goes, We ſhall ſee what Return they make to it. And this is what ought to be done in the preſent Caſe.

Mr. Juſt. DENISON concurred.

Where there is a *temporal* Right, the Court will aſſiſt by Way of *Mandamus*; becauſe it is a *Specific Remedy.*

* V. post, pa. Rex v. Barker et al' S. P. accord'.

RULE made abſolute (for * granting a *Mandamus*.)

No Return was made: But the Parties agreed to try the Merits in a feigned Iſſue; which was accordingly tried.

Note—Upon this Caſe being afterwards mentioned, The COURT took Occaſion to ſay "that they had reconſidered the Point, "and weighed all the Principles and Authorities applicable to "it; and were fully ſatisfied that the propereſt and moſt ef-"fectual Method of trying the Right to officiate in ſuch "Chapels, whether it depended upon Nomination or Election, "was by *Mandamus*."

Doe, ex dimiſſ. Ruſt, *verſ.* Roe.

In Ejectment—

MR. *Norton* ſhewed Cauſe why the Tenants in Poſſeſſion ſhould not have leave to plead "That the *Lands* ſpecified in the "Declaration are *holden in* ANCIENT DEMESNE."

* See *Alden*'s Caſe, 5 *Co.* 105. accord'.

He admitted, that ſuch a Plea might be received, in * this Action (of Ejectment,) with LEAVE of the Court and upon a proper AFFIDAVIT: But He objected to the *Sufficiency* of the preſent *Affidavit*; becauſe it only alledges "That the LANDS in Queſtion are holden "in Ancient Demeſne, and that they are holden of the Manor of "*Godmancheſter*;" but does not go on to alledge "that the MANOR "of *Godmancheſter* is (*itſelf*) *holden in Ancient Demeſne*," (as it ought to do.) In the Caſe of *Denn* v. *Fenn*, *Trin.* 24 *G.* 2. *B. R.* the Affidavit was "That the Lands were holden of ſuch a Manor, "*which* MANOR was holden in Ancient Demeſne."

Beſides, this may be *only a* TERM, in the Leſſor of the Plaintiff: And if ſo, he cannot ſue *there*; For the Writ of Right Cloſe will only lie, where the Demandant has a *Fee* or a *Freehold*.

See alſo *Alden*'s Caſe, 5 *Co.* 105. and *Smith* v. *Arden*, *Cro Eliz.* 826. and *Smith* v. *Arden*, 2 *Anderſon* 178. All S. C.

Mr. *Gould contra*, in Support of the Rule, cited the Caſe of *Ferrers* v. *Miller*, *P.* 4 *W. & M. B. R.* reported in 1 *Salkeld* 217. *Carthew* 220. 1 *Shower* 386. and *Caſes in B. R. temp. W.* 3. *Fo.* 21. Where Ancient Demeſne was pleaded in Ejectment: So, in *Lilly*'s *Practical Regiſter*, Title *Abatement*; and in the abovementioned Caſe of *Denn* v. *Fenn*.

Indeed, *Leave* muſt be aſked of the Court to plead it: And by 4, 5 *Ann. c.* 16. § 11. It is required, in Caſe of Pleading a Dilatory

tory Plea, "That the Party offering it do by Affidavit prove the "Truth of it, or ſhew ſome *probable Cauſe* to the Court to induce "them to believe that the Fact of it is true."

Now this Affidavit does ſhew *probable Cauſe* to induce ſuch Belief. It ſhews "That the *Lands are holden in Ancient Demeſne*; that "they are *holden of the Manor of Godmancheſter*; and that there is a "*Court of Ancient Demeſne* in the Burrough of *Godmancheſter*, where "they might have proceeded:" Inſtead of which, they have brought their Ejectment in *this* Court.

"Whether theſe Lands are PARCEL *of the ſuperior Manor*," is a Fact triable by a *Jury*: Though the Queſtion "Whether *that* "*ſuperior Manor* be or be not holden in Ancient Demeſne," muſt be tried by *Record*, (by *Dooms-day Book*.)

Mr. Juſtice FOSTER and Mr. Juſt. WILMOT, the only two Judges at this Time in Court, concurred in Opinion, that there was *not ſufficient Ground* laid for obtaining Leave to plead this Plea.

Mr. Juſt. FOSTER obſerved that as it was agreed to be neceſſary to *aſk the Leave* of the Court to plead this Plea to a Declaration in Ejectment, it follows of Courſe, that it muſt be in the *Diſcretion* of the Court, either to grant or to refuſe their Leave. And He thought that this Affidavit was *not ſufficient* to ouſt this Court of Juriſdiction. He ſpoke of theſe Courts of Ancient Demeſne, as putting People out of the Protection of the Law, and fitter to be totally * deſtroyed, than to be favoured and aſſiſted.

* *Sed V.* 5 *Co.* 105. *b.* where that Reporter is of a different Sentiment.

Mr. Juſt. WILMOT ſaid it was a ſtrange wild Juriſdiction; where the Jurors are Judges both of Law and of Fact, and ignorant Country Fellows are to determine the niceſt Points of Law: And therefore He was not for granting ſuch Leave, unleſs compelled by Authority. Indeed if the Caſe is brought *ſtrictly within the Rule*, then the Leave *muſt* be granted: We cannot help it.

The Authorities, down from *Alden*'s Caſe to this Time, it is true, are "That Ancient Demeſne is a good Plea in Ejectment."

But if You would ouſt this Court of Juriſdiction, You muſt ſhew "that *another* Court *has Juriſdiction*."

Now this Affidavit does not ſhew "*That there are Suitors*, in the "other Court;" nor "that theſe Lands are holden of a Manor "*which Manor* is holden in Ancient Demeſne:" Whereas, if the *Lands* only, and *not the Manor*, are Ancient Demeſne, the Matter can not be tried in the Court of *that Manor*.

The

The Affidavit ought to have ſhewn "That the Lands are holden "of a Manor, *which Manor* is Ancient Demeſne:" And ſo was the Affidavit in the Caſe of *Denn* v. *Fenn*; And ſo is the Plea, 1 *Show.* 386. and *Carthew* 220. in the Caſe of *Ferrers* v. *Miller*, S. C.

It can not be tried "Whether the LANDS *themſelves* are Ancient "Demeſne." *Doomſday* will not ſhew *this*: *Doomſday* will only ſhew Whether the *Manor* is ſo or not. The Form of the Plea makes this as clear as the Sun.

This Affidavit does not therefore purſue the proper Form.

And it ought to be ſhewn that the Leſſor of the Plaintiff has a *Freehold*. How can he ſue *there*, in Ejectment, as *Leſſee of a Term?*

Upon ſuch a ſtrange wild Juriſdiction as this, and upon ſuch an Affidavit, I am not for giving the Defendant Leave to plead this Plea.

RULE DISCHARGED.

Hutchins *verſ.* Kenrick: Hills et al' *verſ.* Kenrick.

ON ſhewing Cauſe, (upon *Saturday* 21ſt *June*,) in both theſe Cauſes, "Why the Defendant ſhould not be DISCHARGED "*out of the Cuſtody of the Marſhal*, as to each of theſe Actions, reſpectively," It appeared that the Circumſtances of the two Caſes were a good deal different: *Viz.*

In the Cauſe of *Hutchins* v. *Kenrick*, The Defendant was regularly INTITLED *to be ſuperſeded*; Yet was *not actually* ſuperſeded, but REMAINED *in Cuſtody of the Marſhal.* (For although the Order for his being ſuperſeded had become abſolute, two Days *before* the End of a preceding Term, Yet the Defendant had ſtill *continued* in the Cuſtody of the Marſhal, without ever carrying this Order into Execution by getting Himſelf *actually and in Fact* ſuperſeded: And upon the 5th Day of the then next following Term, whilſt the Defendant ſo *remained* actually in Cuſtody, although *intitled* to have been ſo long ago ſuperſeded, a Declaration was delivered to him, at the Suit of HUTCHINS.)

In the other Cauſe wherein HILLS *and Others* were Plaintiffs, the Declaration was delivered to him, whilſt He was regularly and indiſputably in the Cuſtody of the Marſhal, and NOT intitled to be ſuperſeded: But the Objection to this was, "that it was VACA-

" TION-*time*, when *this* Declaration was *delivered*, and likewise " when the *Bill* (whereupon it was grounded) was *filed*."

Note. The *ordinary* modern Practice and Method of charging Defendants in Custody in *Vacation*-time, is by previously issuing a *Habeas Corpus* (*ad respondendum*) tested the last Day of the preceding Term, and returnable in this Court the first Day of the next. This the present Practisers look upon to be a good Foundation for charging a Defendant in Custody, in *Vacation*-time.

And *Mr. Day* (who had been Clerk of the Declarations in the King's Bench Office about 30 Years) certified (*ore tenus*) " That from the Beginning of his Time, *some* Bills had, all " along, been filed with him in Vacation-time: But, that " (not being clear that this was quite regular,) He had always " used the Precaution of marking upon them the exact Time " WHEN *he received them*."

The Marshal also (upon being asked,) said that he had found, upon a Search for 5 or 6 Years backward, (but he had looked no further back,) " that *many* Declarations had been left in " *Vacation*-time, for Prisoners in Custody."

Note also, that there is a Book kept in the King's Bench Office, called the *Marshal's Book*; in which are entered the Names of Persons charged in Custody, previously to their being so charged. But this is a Book of *no Authority*; and only meant for the Marshal's Convenience, that he may readily see what Persons are charged in Custody: So that it is, (in Truth and Reality,) only a *Memorial* of the Defendant's being charged in Custody of the Marshal; and *not the Cause* or *Foundation* of such Charge and Detainer.

It was agreed, on all Sides, that a *Habeas Corpus to remove from One Court to Another*, was a plain and intelligible Proceeding: But it was very difficult to account either for the Reason or the Original or the Validity of this Practice of issuing an *Habeas Corpus returnable in the* SAME *Court*; or to discover how that Method could answer the Purpose intended by it.

Mr. *Gould*, who argued on Behalf of the Defendant in both Causes, urged, as to the former of them (in which *Hutchins* was Plaintiff,) That the Defendant being regularly INTITLED *to be superseded* was not in *legal* Custody of the Marshal; And that no Person could be charged as in Custody of the Marshal, who was *not* LAWFULLY SO. He cited the Case of *Unwin* v. *Kirchoffe*, 2 *Strange* 1215, Where (upon a Motion to supersede the Defendant as not

 being

being charged in Execution within two Terms,) it is holden, "That "the *Committitur* must be actually *entered on Record, before the* "*End* of the *second* Term; And that there is *no Extension* of the "Time, to the *Continuance-Day* after Term; Nor was it sufficient, "that there was an *Entry in the Marshal's Book*, in Time." And Mr. *Gould* laid it down as a Rule, "That a Defendant *once* super-"sedable is *always* supersedable."

As to the latter Cause (wherein *Hills* and Others were Plaintiffs,) He cited the Case of *Tilsden* v. *Palfriman, M.* 3 *Ann. B. R.* reported in 1 *Salk.* 213. and 345. and more largely in 6 *Mod.* 253, 254. Where it is said "That there is no Way to charge a Defendant in "*Custod' Mar'*, in *Vacation*, but to go to the *Marshal's Book* in the "[King's Bench] Office, and make an Entry therein, *quod* REMA-"NET *in Custod' Mar' ad Sectam &c:* And this is SUFFICIENT *to* "*charge him*, provided he be in *actual* Custody; (for if he be out "of Gaol, he may be arrested.") But this *Entry in the Marshal's Book*, Mr. *Gould* insisted, could be *no sufficient Foundation* for such a Charge: No more could the modern extraordinary Practice of issuing a *Habeas Corpus*. The *Old* Method of charging a Defendant in Custody, both in this Court, and (as appears by 8, 9 *W.* 3. *c.* 27. § 13.) in the Common Pleas too, was by bringing him *into Court*, and *there* charging him when *actually present in Court:* Which could not possibly be ever done, but *in* TERM-*time*, when the Court was *sitting*. And this clearly and fully shews that the Defendant can *not* be *at all* charged in Custody, *in* VACATION-*time*, when the Court is *not* sitting.

Mr. *Norton*, who shewed Cause on behalf of the Plaintiffs in both Causes, urged, as to the former (at the Suit of *Hutchins*,) That the *Entry* in the *Marshal's Book* is right and proper; provided there be (as here was) a *previous Affidavit*, sworn before the proper Officer, and filed: And so is the Practice in the Court of Common Pleas. The Defendant was *found* in the *actual* Custody of the Marshal; and consequently, *could not be arrested*, (as he might have, if he had been at large.) And his being INTITLED to be superseded makes no Difference: For if a Defendant still *continues* in Custody and is actually *found* in Prison, He is subject to be *charged in Custody*, at the Suit of a *third* Person. The Rule "that a Defendant *once* "supersedable is *always* supersedable," holds *only* with Regard to the SAME *Plaintiff*, at *whose Suit* he was supersedable: It does *not* extend to a *third Person*, to *another* Plaintiff.

As to the latter Cause, (at the Suit of *Hills* and Others,) Little needs to be said: For if the Defendant is properly in Custody at the Suit of *Hutchins*, these other Plaintiffs can soon charge him *regularly*; (whether their *present* Charge will hold, or not.) To be sure, fure, the *Habeas Corpus* feems an odd Method; efpecially, when the Cuftody is never altered.

The Statute of 8, 9 *W.* 3. *c.* 27. § 13. only regards the Method of charging Prifoners in Cuftody in the *Fleet* Prifon; and enacts "That the Delivering a Copy of the Declaration (after filing it, "and then giving a Rule to plead &c, and making Affidavit of the "Delivery of the Declaration,) fhall intitle the Plaintiff to fign "Judgment, as if the Defendant had been *actually charged at the "Common Pleas or Exchequer Bar.*"

And there is a *Rule* in the Court of Common Pleas in *H.* 1734. 8 *G.* 2. fimilar to the Rule of this Court, made in 1742.

The COURT were extremely clear, in the former Caufe, wherein *Hutchins* was Plaintiff, That the Defendant was REGULARLY *charged.* For the Plaintiff *found* the Defendant in ACTUAL *Cuftody*, and had a *Right to charge him in Cuftody*, without inquiring whether he was *intitled* to be fuperfeded, or not. IF He could not charge his Debtor *in Cuftody*, the Debtor would not be amenable to Juftice *at all:* For the Plaintiff could not *arreft* him, not being at large; nor could have any *other* Way of coming at him. The Rule of a Defendant's being "*always* fuperfedable, after he is once "fo," holds *only* between the *Parties themfelves*, the Plaintiff and Defendant in *that* Caufe: It does not extend to *Other* Perfons, to Plaintiffs in *other* Caufes.

And Mr. Juft. FOSTER added That He had known, (in Experience,) of Defendants remaining *many Terms* in Cuftody, *after* they were intitled to be fuperfeded.

As to the latter Caufe, wherein *Hills* and Others were Plaintiffs, and the Charge was in VACATION-*time*—

The COURT were All of Opinion that there ought to be *fome* Method of charging a Prifoner in Cuftody, *in Vacation-time:* Becaufe, not being at large, he can not be arrefted; and fo his being in Cuftody would be an *Afylum* during the whole Vacation.

But *what* this Method fhould be, was not fo clear, and deferved (they faid) a good deal of Confideration. The *Habeas Corpus* they All looked upon to be a *ftrange* Method: And they agreed that the cheapeft and eafieft Way would be the *beft*.

Mr. Juft. DENISON was explicit, "That, by the Practice of *this* "Court, No Declaration can be delivered to a Prifoner in Cuftody "in THIS *Court, but* in TERM-*time.*" In Proof of which, He cited

* Note— The whole Court there agreed, (and the Officers had certified,) "That the Delivery of the Declaration was IRREGULAR, as being delivered in *Vacation*-time:" But All the Court, except Mr. Justice *Wright*, thought "That the Defendant had, by craving Oyer of the Bond, WAVED *this Irregularity*;" And upon *that* foot discharged the Rule to shew Cause Why there should not issue a *Supersedeas*.

cited a Case in Point. *P.* 17 *G.* 2. *B. R.* * *Holloway* v. *Cross*: Where it was holden "That every Declaration against a Prisoner "in Custody of the Marshal must be delivered *in* TERM-*time*: For "Prisoners are considered in the same Light with Attornies (who "are supposed to be always present in Court;) against Whom, Bills "can not be filed, *but* in *Term*-time." And *this* was * agreed; though the Point was *determined* upon * another Question.

He added, That *formerly* the Defendant (when in Custody) was brought up *into Court*, *by* RULE, in Order to be charged: There was no Occasion for a *Habeas Corpus*, when it was in the *same* Court. And He cited *Lilly's Practical Register*, Title *Prison and Prisoner*, *per Roll* Ch. Just. accordingly.

And this Practice, of bringing up the Prisoner *into Court*, still remains in the *Counties Palatine*.

The *Modern* Practice of delivering Declarations to Defendants in Custody, takes its Rise from this *Old* One of *actually* bringing them *into Court*, in *Term*-time, and *there* charging them: Which must still, in Point of Law, be *supposed* to be done; and which can not be done but *in* TERM-*time*.

Per Cur. In *Hutchins* v. *Kenrick*, The Rule to shew "Cause why "the Defendant should not be discharged out of the Custody "of the Marshal, as to *this* Action," was discharged, (the Cause shewn being holden clearly to be sufficient.)

In *Hills et al'* v. *Kenrick*, The Matter was Ordered to stand over till the last Day of this Term, (in order to have the Practice settled.)

And accordingly,

Lord MANSFIELD now delivered the Resolution the Court had come to: Which was to the following Effect.

We have considered of the Practice of this Court, and of that of the Common Pleas: And We are of Opinion that the right Method is (like that which is taken in the Common Pleas) To *file a* BILL *as of the* PRECEDING *Term*; and then to deliver to or leave for the Defendant, being in Custody, a *Copy of the Declaration* as of the *preceding* Term; and to make an *Affidavit* thereof. We think this to be the right Method for the Purpose of charging such a Defendant with a *new* Suit; and that it ought to be used in this Court for the future: And We think there is *No* Occasion for a HABEAS CORPUS.

The End of *Trinity* Term 1760.

Michaelmas

Michaelmas Term

1 Geo. 3. B.R. 1760.

Rex *verf.* Occupiers of St. Luke's Hofpital.

Friday 7th November 1760.

ON *Monday* 29th of *January* 1759, Mr. *Williams* moved to quafh an Order made by the Juftices of Peace for the County of *Middlefex*, at their Quarter Seffions at *Hicks's Hall*, confirming an Affeffment or Rate for the Relief of the Poor, made upon One *Jofeph Mansfield*, and charging him as OCCUPIER *of St. Luke's Hofpital*; Being of Opinion, upon Confideration of the Circumftances therein fet forth, "That the faid "*Jofeph Mansfield* is the *Occupier* of the faid Hofpital:" Whereas in Fact, He was (as Mr. *Williams* alledged) *only a Servant* there. He cited 2 *Strange* 745. *Rex* v. *Inhabitants of St. Thomas's in Southwark*; where a *Preacher* at a Meeting-Houfe was holden *not* to be rateable as an Occupier.

A Rule was thereupon made, to fhew Caufe. And on *Tuefday* 8th *May* 1759, Mr. *Gould* moved to make that Rule abfolute; infifting upon two Objections to the Validity of the Rate; *viz.* 1ft. "That this Man is only a SERVANT;" and therefore could not be "rated as *Occupier*:"

2d. "That this HOSPITAL is *not rateable at all.*"

Mr. *Norton*, (who was for the Rate,) agreed that, ftrictly fpeaking, it could not well be fupported "that a *Servant* was rateable "AS OCCUPIER:" But He offered to defend it upon the *Merits*; *viz.* Whether this *new-erected charitable Hofpital for Lunatics*, be or be not *rateable.*

And if the other Side would not agree to that, He faid He muft object to the *Certiorari*, as having *irregularly iffued*; *viz. not till after* the Six Months were expired; (it being more than nine Months from the 2d of *February* to *Michaelmas* Term.)

And accordingly, a Rule was then made to ſhew Cauſe "Why "the *Certiorari* ſhould not be quaſhed." But afterwards,

On *Wedneſday* 16th *May* 1759, It was Ordered, by *Conſent* of Counſel on both Sides, "That the Orders returned with the *Cer-"tiorari* in the Cauſe of the *King* againſt *Joſeph Mansfield* (who "then ſtood charged as Occupier of this Hoſpital) ſhould be ſent "back to be RE-*ſtated*." In Conſequence of which Rule by Conſent, The following *re-ſtated* Order was afterwards ſent up, as the Return to the ſaid Writ: *viz.*

Note—The *Re-ſtated* Order was under the *like* Caption (*verbatim*) with the old One.

A *Complaint* and *Appeal* being made unto this Court, againſt a certain Article contained in the Rate or Aſſeſſment made on the 19th Day of *July* in the Year of our Lord 1757, for Relief of the Poor of the Pariſh of *St. Luke* in the ſaid County, which Article is as follows, *viz.*—"The OCCUPIERS of a Meſſuage or Tenement and Premiſſes called *Saint Luke's Hoſpital for Lunatics:* Rent 80 *l.* Rate 2 *l.* 13 *s.* 4 *d.*" By which Article, the ſaid Meſſuage called *St. Luke's Hoſpital for Lunatics* is valued after the Rate of 80 *l. by the Year*, and aſſeſſed (accordingly) to pay 2 *l.* 13 *s.* 4 *d. by the Quarter* of a Year; *And this* COURT having fully heard and examined the ſaid Complaint and Appeal, *It appears* in Evidence unto this Court, That by Indenture made the 21ſt Day of *November* in the Year of our Lord 1750, Between the Mayor Commonalty and Citizens of the City of *London* of the One Part, and *James Sperling* of *Mincing Lane* in the Pariſh of *St. Dunſtan in the Eaſt London* Merchant, *Henry Bankes* of the Pariſh of *St. Mary Hill* Citizen and Grocer of *London*, *Richard Speed* of *Old Fiſh Street* in the Pariſh of *St. Mary Magdalen London* Druggiſt, *Thomas Light* of *Mincing Lane* aforeſaid in the ſaid Pariſh of *St. Dunſtan in the Eaſt* Merchant, and *William Prowting* of *Tower Street* in the ſaid Pariſh of *St. Dunſtan in the Eaſt* Apothecary, of the other Part, The ſaid Mayor Commonalty and Citizens, as well for and in Conſideration of the Sum of 100 *l.* of lawful Money of *Great Britain* already paid to Sir *John Boſworth* Knt. Chamberlain of *London* to and for the public Uſes of the ſaid Mayor Commonalty and Citizens, as alſo for and in Conſideration that they the ſaid *James Sperling*, *Henry Bankes*, *Richard Speed*, *Thomas Light* and *William Prowting*, ſhould and would *build* or *convert* the Premiſſes in the ſaid Indenture mentioned or ſome Part thereof into an HOSPITAL *for* LUNATICS; And for and in Conſideration of the Rents and Covenants in the ſaid Indenture contained on the Part and Behalf of the ſaid *James Sperling*, *H. B. R. S. T. L.* and *W. P.* their Executors Adminiſtrators and Aſſigns to be paid and performed, and for divers other good Cauſes and Conſiderations them the ſaid Mayor and Commonalty and Citizens eſpecially moving, *Did*, purſuant to an Order

Order of the Court of Common Council made the 15th Day of *November* then next preceding, demise grant and to Farm let unto the said *J. S. H. B. R. S. T. L.* and *W. P.* their Executors Administrators and Assigns, All that Piece or Parcel of *Ground*, with the *Buildings thereupon erected*, situate and being on *Windmill-hill* in the Parish of *St. Luke* in the County of *Middlesex*, containing from West to East, on the South Side fronting the *Upper Moorfields*, 180 Feet of Assize (little more or less,) and from South to North on the East Side, 178 Feet of Assise (little more or less,) and from East to West on the North Side, 165 Feet of Assise (little more or less,) And from North to South on the West Side, 180 Feet 2 Inches of Assize (little more or less,) and abutting on the Way leading to *St. Agnes le Clair*; All which said Premisses were formerly demised, by two separate Leases, to *Philip Whiteman* and *John Davis*, and do more fully appear by a Scheme or Draft thereof, with a Scale made to the same, unto the said Indenture annexed: *To have and to hold* the said Piece or Parcel of *Ground* with the Appurtenances, unto the said *J. S. H. B. R. S. T. L.* and *W. P.* their Executors Administrators and Assigns, from the Feast Day of the Birth of our Lord Christ next ensuing the Date of the same Indenture, for and during and unto the full End and Term of 32 Years from thence next ensuing and fully to be complete and ended; *Yielding and paying* therefore yearly and every Year during the said Term, unto the said Mayor and Commonalty and Citizens, in the Office of Receipts and Payments of Money of the said Chamberlain of the said City for the Time being, the Rent or Sum of *Ten Pounds* of lawful Money of *Great Britain*, on the Four most usual Feasts or Terms in the Year, that is to say, the Feast of the Annunciation of the Blessed Virgin *Mary*, the Nativity of St. *John* the Baptist, St. *Michael* the Archangel, and the Birth of our Lord Christ, by even and equal Portions, without making any Deduction Defalcation or Abatement for or by reason of any Taxes Rates or Assessments imposed or to be imposed during the Term aforesaid upon the Premisses hereby demised or any Part thereof, by any Act or Acts of Parliament or otherwise howsoever; the first Payment thereof to begin and to be made on the Feast of the Annunciation of the Blessed Virgin *Mary* next ensuing the Date of the same Indenture; And that it was amongst other Things *covenanted and agreed* by the said Indenture and between the said Parties thereto, that they the said *J. S. H. B. R. S. T. L.* and *W. P.* their Executors Administrators or Assigns or some of them should and would *build* or *convert* the Premisses thereby demised or some Part thereof into an Hospital *for poor* Lunatics, and employ the same to no other Use Intent or Purpose whatsoever during the said Term; And that among other Things in the said Indenture, are contained two Clauses and Provisoes in the following Terms, "*Provided* " always that if the said yearly Rent of 10*l.* be behind and unpaid

3 " in

" in part or in all by the Space of fourteen Days next after any of " the said Days of Payment on which the same ought to be paid as " aforesaid, being lawfully demanded at the Place of Payment afore- " said, Or if the said *J. S. H. B. R. S. T. L.* and *W. P.* their " Executors Administrators and Assigns do not well and truly per- " form and keep all and singular the Covenants herein contained on " his and their Parts to be performed and kept, that then and at all " Times afterwards it shall and may be lawful to and for the said " Mayor and Commonalty and Citizens or their Assigns into all or " any Part of the said demised Premisses in the Name of the Whole " wholly to *re-enter*, and the same to have again retain and re-possess " in their former Estate, and the said *J. S. H. B. R. S. T. L.* and " *W. P.* their Executors Administrators and Assigns and all other " Occupiers of the Premisses thereout and from thence utterly to ex- " pel put out and amove, these Presents or any Thing therein con- " tained to the contrary notwithstanding: *Provided* also, And these " Presents are upon this *Condition*, that if the said *J. S. H. B. R. S.* " *T. L.* and *W. P.* their Executors Administrators or Assigns or any " of them do or shall at any Time or Times hereafter during the " said Term *convert the said Premisses to any* OTHER *Use than that* " *of the Charitable Design of poor Lunatics*, then these Presents and " every Thing herein contained shall cease determine and be utterly " *void*; any Thing herein contained to the Contrary thereof in any " wise notwithstanding."

It appears likewise in Evidence unto this Court, that BEFORE *the Erecting* the said Hospital, Divers, to wit, 29 HOUSES *were situate* UPON *the* LAND *and* PREMISSES in and by the said Indenture contained and demised; And that in the several Rates made by the Overseers of the Poor for the Relief of the Poor within the said Parish of *St. Luke*, for in and during the several Years between the Year of our Lord 1744 and the Date of the Indenture herein before mentioned, *the said* 29 HOUSES *were valued and estimated at the annual Value of* 196 *l. by the Year*: And that in the Year of our Lord 1745, the SAID 29 HOUSES being assessed in the Rate made in the *said Year* for the Relief of the Poor within the said Parish of *St. Luke*, after the Rate and Proportion of THREE SHILLINGS *in the Pound Sterling*, did yet *pay and yield* NO MORE to the said Overseers in Satisfaction of the said Rate and towards the Relief of the Poor, than *Ten Pounds and One Shilling*; And that in the Year of our Lord 1746, the said 29 HOUSES being assessed in the Rate made by the Overseers of the Poor of the said Parish of *St. Luke* in the said last mentioned Year for the Relief of the Poor within the said Parish after the Rate and Proportion of THREE *Shillings* in the Pound Sterling, did yet pay and yield *no more* to the said Overseers in Satisfaction of the said Rate and towards the Relief of the Poor, than 8 *l.* 11 *s.* And that in the Year of our Lord 1747, the said

29 Houses being aſſeſſed in the Rate made in the ſaid laſt mentioned Year for the Relief of the Poor within the ſaid Pariſh of *St. Luke* after the Rate and Proportion of 3 *s.* 3 *d. in the Pound Sterling*, did yet pay and yield *no more* to the ſaid Overſeers in Satisfaction of the ſaid Rate and towards the Relief of the Poor, than 8 *l.* 14 *s.* 9 *d.* And that in the Year of our Lord 1748, the ſaid 29 Houses being aſſeſſed [*ut ſupra*] after the Rate and Proportion of 3 *s.* in the Pound Sterling, did yet [*ut ſupra*] *no more* than 7 *l.* 1 *s.* And that in the Year of our Lord 1749, the ſaid 29 Houses being &c. after the Rate and Proportion of 3 *s.*&c. *no more* &c. than 6 *l.* 3 *s.* And that in &c 1750, the ſaid 29 Houses being aſſeſſed [*ut ſupra*] after &c of 2 *s.* 9 *d.* in the Pound Sterling, did yet &c no more &c than 2 *l.* 8 *s.* 9 *d.*

It appears alſo in Evidence to this Court That the Premiſſes demiſed *were accordingly built and converted into the* Hospital *mentioned in the ſaid Article of the Rate in queſtion*, called, "*St. Luke's* "*Hoſpital for Lunatics*," for the affording a *charitable* and *free* Suſtentation and Cure to poor and helpleſs Lunatics; And that every *Apartment and Parcel* of the ſaid Premiſſes ſo built and converted into ſuch Hoſpital as aforeſaid, is laid out and applied, either in Wards or Cells for the Lodging of ſuch Lunatics as aforeſaid, or in Offices neceſſary for their Suſtentation and Cure, or in Apartments neceſſary for Perſons who are *hired* from Time to Time to *attend on ſuch Lunatics* for their better Suſtentation and Cure, and in no other *Apartments or Buildings whatſoever*; And that the *ſaid Edifice* was *originally erected*, and *ſtill is ſupported*, and *very many poor and helpleſs Lunatics* continually have been and ſtill are *ſuſtained and taken Care of therein*, And the *menial Servants attending upon ſuch Lunatics* have been and ſtill are *hired and paid*, And *all other Expences* relating to and neceſſary for the maintaining the ſaid Hoſpital and Charity have been and ſtill are from Time to Time *defrayed and born*, by the free and voluntary Contribution of divers Perſons; Out of whom, a Committee annually is appointed, who meet Weekly, to order the Admiſſion and Diſcharge of Patients, the hiring and retaining Servants, the Payment of Bills, and the Regulation of all other Matters relative to the Maintenance and Upholding of this *Charity*; And that None but ſuch poor and helpleſs *Lunatics*, and the *Perſons neceſſarily attending upon them*, have *any kind of* Dwelling *or* Occupation in the ſaid Hoſpital; And that One *Joſeph Manſfield* (the Appellant) is the principal *Perſon hired* from Year to Year by the ſaid Committee of Contributors, and *receiving certain Wages*, and *living in the ſaid Hoſpital for the Purpoſes of attending on the ſaid Lunatics*, and having no other *Abode Occupation or Eſtabliſhment therein*; And that the ſaid *James Sperling*, *Henry Bankes*, *Richard Speed*, *Thomas Light* and *William Prowting* or any of them, their or any of their Executors Adminiſtrators or Aſſigns, *have not* nor *ever had* or *can have* any *Profit Benefit* or Advantage from the ſaid Premiſſes or any Part thereof, nor any *Poſſeſſion* or *Occupation* thereof otherwiſe than as aforeſaid.

This COURT [The General Seſſion at *Hicks Hall,*] upon Conſideration of the Circumſtances above ſet forth, is of Opinion, "That the ſaid Tenement called *St. Luke's Hoſpital* OUGHT *to be* "*aſſeſſed and rated* towards the Relief of the Poor, by the ſaid "Rate;" and doth accordingly DISMISS *the ſaid Appeal,* and CONFIRM *the ſaid Rate.*

By the Court.

WALLER.

Mr. *Gould,* Mr. *Thurlow,* and Mr. *Lane,* on Behalf of *St. Luke's Hoſpital,* moved (on *Monday* 23d *June* 1760,) to quaſh this *reſtated* Order of Seſſions, thus again *confirming* the ſaid Rates.

They argued, 1ſt. That this BUILDING itſelf, (an Hoſpital ſupported by voluntary charitable Contributions) was *not rateable* towards the Support of the Poor; And 2dly. That *no particular Perſon* whoſoever was chargeable as OCCUPIER of it.

Firſt—This is only a *mere* BUILDING, a Houſe ſupported by private free and voluntary charitable pecuniary Contributions; and *uſed only as an* HOSPITAL for the Suſtentation and Cure of poor and helpleſs Lunatics: It has *no Apartments* in it, nor any *Accommodations* for the *Reſidence* of any Perſons whatſoever, except the Patients and the hired Servants neceſſarily attending them. It is *not endowed* with any *Land*; nor has it any *Land about it,* being the mere *Site of the Houſe* itſelf. Therefore it can not poſſibly be included within the Intention of the Dictum of Ld. Ch. J. *Holt,* mentioned in a Scrap of an anonymous Caſe in 2 *Salk.* 527. "That "*Hoſpital*-LANDS are chargeable to the Poor, as well as other "*Lands:* For no Man, by appropriating his *Lands* to an Hoſpital, "can diſcharge or exempt them from Taxes to which they were "ſubject before, and throw a greater Burthen upon their Neigh-"bours." For He there plainly means Lands *leaſed out* to Tenants and bringing in an *annual Profit:* Which is, by no means, the preſent Caſe. This is *no beneficial* Leaſe: The Leſſees receive *no Profit* by it; Nor *can* they, by the * Proviſo in their Leaſe, put it to any *other Uſe* than that of the charitable Deſign of poor Lunatics.

* *V. ante, pa.* 1056.

The Statute of 43 *Eliz. c.* 2. § 14, 15. directs "That a *Propor-*"*tion of the Money* to be raiſed by virtue of that Act, ſhall be ſent "for the *Relief of Hoſpitals* in the reſpective Counties." And it would be abſurd to ſuppoſe, that that *ſame* Statute intended to *tax* Hoſpitals towards the *Relief* of Hoſpitals.

In 2 *Bulstr.* 354. the Judges (*Hutton* and *Croke*) put the Matter of taxing One or the Other of the Persons there in Question, upon the Foot of the *Profit* or *Advantage* received by them. But these Lessees receive no Sort of Profit or Advantage, nor can possibly receive any, under *this* Lease.

And Nothing is subject to be rated towards the Relief of the Poor, but a *beneficial* Interest. There is *no Instance* of an *Hospital* having ever been rated, as to *such Part* of it as is *only applied to charitable Uses:* Whatever may have been done, as to those large and fine Apartments in the great Hospitals, wherein the *Officers* (who are Gentlemen of Fortune and Fashion) reside with all their *Families*, and use them as their Dwelling-houses.

Secondly—No particular Person whosoever can be charged as OCCUPIER of this House of mere Charity.

By the 43 *Eliz. c.* 2. § 1. The Taxation is to be upon every *Occupier* of Lands, Houses, Tithes, Coal-mines, or Sale-Underwoods in the Parish.

But None of the Persons mentioned in this Order are OCCUPIERS of this House, *within the Meaning and Intention* of the Makers of this Act. They have no Possession or Enjoyment of any *lucrative* or *profitable* Tenement. Therefore there is no Rule or Medium or Proportion whereby to rate them: For if they were rateable at all, it must be in Proportion with Others. But these Persons receive *no* Profit or Emolument at all: And there can be no Proportion to *Nothing*. Therefore they are not rateable at all.

For the same Reason, No Person can be rated as an Occupier of a Church, a Meeting-house, or an Alms-house.

* In *H.* 13 *G.* 1. in this Court, One *Read* was charged to the Poors Rate in respect of his being an *Occupier* of a *Meeting-house* where he preached: and He was holden *not* to be liable; Because, as a Preacher, he is no more chargeable as an Occupier, than any of his Audience. And the Court there took Notice, that it was not stated "That he *let out* Pews;" so as to make him a Person that occupies, and receives a *Profit* from it. * V. 2 Strange 745.

So, in the present Case, No One can be charged as *Occupier*; because No One receives any lucrative *Profit*.

And this Circumstance makes it widely different from the Case of *Eyre* v. *Smallpace et al'*, *P.* 1750. 23 *G.* 2. *B. R.* Where the Question

Queſtion was "Whether the Plaintiff, being *Controller of Chelſea* "*College*, and reſiding in the Controller's Apartments there, was "aſſeſſable towards the Maintenance of the Poor of the Pariſh of "*Chelſea*, for the *Apartments* which He occupied there by virtue of "his ſaid Office:" And the Court held him to be *chargeable*, as *Occupier*; grounding their Opinion upon a then recent and unanimous Opinion of all the Judges, upon a like Queſtion, in the Caſe of *Greenwich*-Hoſpital, concerning the Payment of the Window-Tax; in which Caſe, All the Twelve Judges unanimouſly held, "That the Act of Parliament relating to the Window-Tax *did* "extend to the *Apartments of Officers* in *Greenwich*-Hoſpital;" which Caſe of *Greenwich*-Hoſpital They thought not diſtinguiſhable from that of *Chelſea*-Hoſpital then in Judgment before them.

But that was an Hoſpital of *Royal Foundation*, and the *King's own Houſe*. The Officers have *large noble Apartments* there, with *diſtinct Doors*: They reſide in them with their *Families*, and live diſtinctly in them, at their ſeparate Expences. Thoſe Apartments are ſubſtantially their Houſe, their Domicil. In *this* Hoſpital, there are only Cells for the Lunatics, and a bare Lodging for thoſe who neceſſarily attend them, and are always about their Perſons.

On 6th *November* 1760,
Mr. *Norton* and Mr. *Stowe* argued in Support of the Order.

They inſiſted, 1ſt. That this Building was *rateable*; and 2dly. That the Charge is *ſufficiently* laid upon it, although no *particular Occupier* be perſonally and ſpecifically named.

Firſt—*Hoſpital-Lands* are rateable to the Relief of the Poor of the Pariſh wherein they lie, as well as other Lands are: This appears from 2 *Salk.* 527. And this Charity is only a *voluntary* Act of *private* Perſons, Proprietors of this Building: Which private Perſons have it not in their *Power*, by applying it to the Uſe of a Charity, to *diſcharge* it of legal Rates and Payments duly charged upon it for the Relief of the Pariſh; and thereby to take away this Relief from the Pariſh. And it would be moſt unreaſonable that this Property which was always rateable before, ſhould, merely by the *voluntary Act of the Proprietor*, be rendered unrateable; when, by that very Act, the Proprietor introduces many Servants into this Building, who will gain Settlements in the Pariſh by their Service performed therein: So that theſe Gentlemen would *load the Pariſh* with Poor, and yet *exempt themſelves* from paying any Thing towards it's Relief. Therefore the Pariſh are *ſtill intitled to their Rates*; whether the Proprietors make a *beneficial* Intereſt of it, or chooſe to apply it to the Purpoſes of a *Charity*.

And

And there are many *Instances* of Hospitals and charitable Foundations being *in Fact rated* to the Relief of the Parishes wherein they are situated: Particularly, The *British* Lying-in Hospital, in *St. Giles's*; An Hospital in *St. Botolph's Aldersgate*; Another in *St. James's Clerkenwell*; (which last never, till now, refused to pay.) And this very Hospital pays the *Land*-tax, and also the *four Rates* (*viz.* Scavengers, Lights, *&c.*)

And the Cases of *Window-Lights* are not unlike to the present Case.

The *Foundling Hospital* pays the *Window-tax*; as appears by the Tax-Book (*Fo.* 48:) And all the Judges, (upon the Question being referred to them,) were of Opinion, "That they *ought* to do "so."

So, *St. Bartholomew's Hospital* was an Instance where the *Officers* were assessed for their Apartments: And on 7th *June* 1748, All the Judges held them rateable. So also in the Case of *Christ's* Hospital (at the same Time,) and of *St. Bride's*, and *St. Thomas's*, the general Point determined was "That the Officers are chargeable to the "*Window Lights.*"

In the Case of the *French Hospital* in *St. Luke's*, The Judges held it not to be assessable, as to the *Lunatics* maintained therein: But They gave no Opinion as to the Charge upon One *Romier* (who was personally assessed,) because it did not appear to them, Whether he did or did not *live* in it.

In the Case of *Sutton's* Hospital, where Some of the Officers have their Apartments intermixed with the Rooms of the Persons supported by that Charity, The Commissioners thought "That none of "the Inhabitants of those *intermixed* Rooms were chargeable, (nei- "ther the Officers, nor the poor Men;)" And the Judges confirmed that Opinion of the Commissioners.

In the present Case, the *five Lessees* may be considered as Occupiers by their Servants, who are under their Control; And they are properly chargeable, as such: The *Patients* indeed neither are nor ought to be rated.

And they concluded this Head, with observing "That the "43 *Eliz. c.* 2. is a beneficial Law made for the Benefit of the "Poor of the Parishes."

Secondly—As to the not charging any *particular* Person, as Occupier—

They insisted that it was *not necessary* that any particular Person should be *specifically* rated as Occupier.

They cited a Case, from 8 *Mod. Pa.* 38. *Rex* v. *Inhabitants of* * *Brickhill, P.* 7 *G.* 1. *B. R.* where a Man who had been rated by the Name of "*The Occupier of Roscoe's Tenement*," and not by his own proper Name, and had paid the said Rates under such Assessment, was holden to have gained a Settlement under this general Rate.

* This Case really was *Rex* v. *Inhabitants of Brightmen* (in *Lancashire*) *P.* 8 *G.* 1. 1722. The Point was indeed determined as is mentioned in 8 *Mod.* 38: (though the Names Persons and Places are there mistaken.) But the Man had actually *paid* the Rate no less than *eleven Years*, under this Assessment, which described Him without specifying his Name, *viz.* calling Him only "the Occupier of *Hoscoe's* Tenement."

They also urged the Case in 2 *Salk.* 527. *P.* 1 *Ann. Anonymous*: Which they said, was probably the same Case with a Case of *Rex* v. *Staines*, † relating to the Parishes of *Ilford* and *East-Ham*. And they said they had a Certificate "that the Parishes of *Ilford* and "*East-Ham do* now pay."

† *Rex* v. *Staines* was *H.* 13 *W.* 3. *William Staines* was taxed to those two Parishes, for the Concerns of an Hospital in them. The Sessions, upon Appeal, discharged the original Order as being founded upon Misinformation and Surprize.

Mr. *Gould* and Mr. *Lane*, who had made the Objections to the Order, replied—

1st. That the Cases and Instances cited by the Counsel on the other Side proved Nothing to the present Point: For they went no further than the Case of *Chelsea*-Hospital, *Eyre* v. *Smallpace et al'*, *P.* 1750. 23 *G.* 2. *B. R.* where it was settled "That all Apart-"ments of Officers, *used as Dwelling-Houses*, are liable to be taxed "to the Window-Lights, *as* Dwelling-Houses." And the Window-Light Acts are positive and affirmative, "That *all Dwelling-*"*Houses* shall pay to that Tax." The Officers have a *Benefit* from their *Apartments*. But *here* could arise *no* Benefit at all, to *any* Person whatsoever: Therefore *No One* could be taxable to the Relief of the Poor.

And as to their loading the Parish by introducing Servants who would gain Settlements by their Service in the Hospital, They denied that these Servants would gain a Settlement by such Service.

2dly. The Case of *Brickhill*, being cited from a Book of no Authority, deserves no Answer. Besides, in that Case, the Man had long acquiesced under the Order, and paid the Tax.

The

THE COURT did not give any Opinion Yesterday; But inclined "That the Occupier ought to be particularly specified;" And "also, that the Whole turns upon the *Person or Persons who* "ought to be rated."

Indeed, if a Person rated generally, by the Appellation of Occupier of such Tenement, acquiesces, and takes the Charge upon him, and pays it; It would be unreasonable that he should be excluded from gaining a Settlement, if He afterwards has Occasion to claim it. But *that* is not this Case.

The Instances of the several Hospitals, mentioned by the Counsel for supporting the Order, carry the Matter no further than the Case of *Chelsea*-Hospital has settled it: And the Judges have unanimously determined, "That all Apartments of Officers in Hospitals, which "are *used* AS *Dwelling-houses*, ought to be taxed to the Window-"Lights, as Dwelling-houses."

However, They said they would consider of it, and then declare their Opinion. CUR. ADVIS.

Lord MANSFIELD now delivered the Opinion of the Court; (having first stated the Order, and the Objections taken to it.)

Cases of this kind depend upon the particular Nature of the respective Hospitals: Each stands upon its own distinct Circumstances. Therefore no *General* Consequences will arise from the Determination of this particular Case.

The *Land*-Tax differs from the *Poors*-Tax. The *Land-lord* who receives the Rent, is to pay the Land-Tax: But the *Poors*-Tax is payable by the *Occupiers*. Therefore the Rating Hospital *Lands* to the *Land*-Tax is not applicable to the present Question.

The *Occupier* ought to be rated, regularly, by *Name*. But in the present Case, it is *more* than a mere Defect in *Form*: The Fault in Form here arises from the *Essence* of the thing. For if they can not fix upon some particular Person who may properly be rated as Occupier of this Building, It follows, as a necessary Consequence, "That *no* Rate can *at all* be made upon it."

As to the Argument that has been urged in Support of the Order, "That a Proprietor of Lands or Houses can not, by his own pri-"vate voluntary Act, discharge such his Property, from Payments "legally due to Other Persons upon and out of it"—It does *not* hold

hold true in *Fact*. For this Rate payable to the Parish, as well as several other Payments arising from Property and chargeable upon it, *do* and *must* depend upon the *Will of the Proprietor*. The Owner of a House may, if he pleases, pull it quite down, and convert it into a Toft. The Owner of Lands may, if he pleases, suffer them to lie barren and unoccupied. Tithes and the Right of them vary, according to the different Species of the Produce of the Land: Yet the Land-holder may sow it, or plant it, or use it in the Manner he likes best; or even not at all, if he so chooses.

The *material* Question in this Case is, "WHO can be named and charged as the *Occupier*.

There are only *three* Sorts of Persons that occur to Me. If they can find any *Others* who may be properly charged as Occupiers, Such other Persons will not be included in or affected by the Opinion which We now give.

The only Persons that I can think of, are 1st. The five *Lessees*; 2dly. The *Servants* attending this Charity; and 3dly. The *poor mad Persons*, who are the Objects of it.

First—As to the *Lessees*—*Mere* NOMINAL *Trustees* can not be esteemed Occupiers, or rated as such. Besides, these Lessees are expressly excluded, by a special * Proviso inserted in the Lease, from converting the Building to any other than this specifical Use: And the Lease is to determine and become void, if they do. They are so far therefore from being *Occupiers* of it, that they are *merely nominal*; mere *Instruments of Conveyance*; and have no more *Interest* in the Thing, than the Crier of the Court of Common Pleas has, when he is named as the last Vouchee in a Common Recovery.

* V. ante, pa. 1056.

Secondly.—As to the *Servants* attending this Charity—They are not in a like Situation with the Officers of *Chelsea*-Hospital, or of the other Charitable Foundations that have been mentioned at the Bar, where there are *large distinct Apartments* appropriated to the Use of the respective Officers, wherein they and their *Families* reside. Those Officers are *not* charged *as Servants* of such Hospitals, or as Inhabitants and Occupiers of the *ordinary* Rooms and Lodgings therein; but as having *separate* and *distinct Apartments*, which are considered as their *Dwelling-houses*. The Cases that have been determined by the Judges, relating to the *Window-Tax*, are uniform in rating *Officers* of Hospitals for their *distinct Apartments*: But in *this* Hospital, there are neither any such *Officers*, or any such *Apartments*, as were in those Cases determined to be rateable.

If the first of these Orders, which rated *Joseph Mansfield* as the Occupier of this Hospital, had stood as it was originally drawn up, without being afterwards altered; And *if Mansfield* had actually had a separate and distinct Apartment in it (which is not now pretended;) Yet certainly He could not have been rated for any Thing more than his OWN *particular and distinct Apartment*. However, that Matter ceases now to be any part of the Case; there being no Foundation, by the *new* Order, to ground such a Question upon.

Thirdly.—As to the poor miserable Wretches who are the unhappy *Objects* of this Charity—It would be too gross to conceive *them* to be proper Persons to be rated to the Relief of the Parish. Therefore it is unnecessary to say any Thing on this head; And the rather, as it appeared so very unreasonable to the Counsel themselves who argued in Support of the Order, that they gave it up.

And *if* NO *Person* can be found, who is rateable to this Tax, It follows, by necessary Consequence, "That there can be *no Rate* " at all."

Therefore the ORDER must be QUASHED.

Goodtitle, ex dimiss. Bridges et al', *vers.* Duke of Chandos.

Thursday 13th *November* 1760.

UPON a Motion for a new Trial, made on the Part of the Defendant, upon the Foot of a *Misdirection* given to the Jury by the Judge who tried the Cause; (upon which Direction of the Judge, the Jury had found a Verdict for the Plaintiff;) the Case appeared, upon the Report of Mr. Just. *Noel*, (the Judge who tried the Cause,) to be as follows; *viz.*

Sir *Thomas Bridges*, being seised in Fee, of the *Manor* and *Demesne* Lands of KEYNSHAM in *Somersetshire*, and of several *other* Lands in KEYNSHAM aforesaid, and also of several Estates in various other Places, made a Settlement of *all* these Estates, at the Time of the Marriage of his Eldest Son, Mr. *Harry Bridges*, with his first Wife the Lady *Diana Holles*; Sir *Thomas* having at that Time Five Sons living, *viz.* this Mr. *Harry Bridges*, *Edward Bridges*, *George Bridges*, and two younger Sons.

The Settlement was to the Use of Sir *Thomas* himself for Life, as to *Part*; with Remainder to his Eldest Son *Harry*, for Life; Remainder to the Heirs Male of *Harry*'s Body by that first Marriage; Remainder to the Heirs Male of his Body by any other Marriage;

Remainder to Sir *Thomas*'s second Son *Edward Bridges*, in strict Settlement; Remainder to *George Bridges*, for Life; Remainder to *George*, in *Tail Male*; with Remainder to the right Heirs of Sir *Thomas*. The *Rest* of the Estate was settled to the same Uses, with this Difference only, *viz.* That there was no Life-Estate to Sir *Thomas* Himself therein; but Mr. *Harry Bridges*'s Estate for Life took Place immediately. There was a Power given, by this Settlement, to Mr. *Harry Bridges*, to make a *Jointure upon a second Wife*.

Mr. *Harry B.* had no Issue by Lady *Diana*: But, during her Life, He had an illegitimate Son, named *James Bridges*, by another Woman. After the Death of Lady *Diana*, and after the Birth of *James*, Mr. *Harry Bridges* (in his old Age) married a young Woman, (of the Name of *Freeman*;) Upon whom, pursuant to the Power given him, He settled about 280 *l. per Annum* (being *Part of the Demesne Lands of Keynsham*,) for her *Life*: And She survived him, and lived till 1759.

Mr. *Harry Bridges* having no Issue by this last Wife nor by his former, and being Reversioner or Remainder-Man in Fee (as before mentioned) of the *whole* Family-Estate; and his Brother *Edward*, and his two youngest Brothers being all dead without Issue; and his Nephew *George Rodney Bridges*, (the only Son of his Brother *George*) having no Child by his Lady; the said Mr. *Harry Bridges* did, in his Life-time, by Bargain and Sale inrolled, grant this his Reversion of the *Whole* settled Estate, to his natural Son *James Bridges*, the Lessor of the Plaintiff.

But after the Death of *Harry*, and DURING THE LIFE of his Widow, (who was *Tenant for Life* of this 280 *l. per Ann. Part of the Demesne Lands of Keynsham*,) the said *George Rodney Bridges*, (the only Son of *George* then deceased,) being Tenant in Tail in *Possession* of *all the* REST of the Estate, except that Part which was settled upon the Widow, (who was *then living* and in *Possession* of *that* Part;) but being Tenant in Tail in REMAINDER *only*, of THAT Part whereof the said Widow was in Possession as *Tenant for Life*; suffered a *Recovery*, in the Year 1728, of the *Whole* settled Estate; Using (at least) such Descriptions as might be *sufficient* to include ALL *the Estate that lay in* KEYNSHAM, under the general Description of *that* Part of the Estate: After the suffering of which Recovery, He settled the Whole Estate *included in the Recovery*, upon the Duke of *Chandos*; and then died. The Duke, upon the Death of the said Mr. *George Rodney Bridges*, came into immediate Possession of all the *Rest* of the Estate, *Except that Part* which the Widow of *Harry* was in Possession of for her Life as aforesaid: And upon her Death, in 1759, He took Possession of *that Part* also.

Where-

Whereupon, Mr. *James Bridges*, the Bargainee of the Reversion in Fee, which was granted to him by his Father *Harry* as aforesaid, brought this Ejectment against the Duke, for *that Part* of the KEYNSHAM-Estate which *Harry*'s Widow died in Possession of; Supposing that Mr. *George Rodney Bridges* could have *no* Power to settle THAT *Part* upon the Duke, whatever Power he might have over the *Rest* of the Estate, (of which He was Tenant in Tail in *Possession*, when He suffered the Recovery.)

The Duke, at the Trial, would have defended his Title, by setting up this Common Recovery suffered by *G. R. B.* the Remainder-Man in Tail; which He produced and proved: But the Duke being unable to give any Sort of Evidence of an *actual* SURRENDER of the Widow's *Life-Estate*, (which the Plaintiff urged to be necessary, in order to enable the Tenant in Tail in *Remainder* to make a good Tenant to the *Præcipe*;) the Counsel for the Defendant (the Duke of *Chandos*) insisted at the Trial, "That a *Surrender* of the "Life-Estate ought, *after so long a Time*, to be PRESUMED; even "although they should give no Evidence whatsoever, relating to "any such Surrender."

But Mr. Justice *Noel* was of Opinion, "That a Surrender by "the Tenant for Life could NOT *be presumed*; when no Evidence "at all had been given to render it in the least probable; and when "the Possession had not gone along with the Recovery, but conti-"nued in the Tenant for Life till the Time of bringing the Eject-"ment." And accordingly, He directed the Jury to find for the Plaintiff: Which they did.

Upon this *Misdirection*, as the Duke's Counsel called it, they moved for a new Trial, and obtained a Rule to shew Cause: And Mr. Just. *Noel*'s Report was, by Mr. Just. *Wilmot*, stated to this Court as above.

Upon it's being argued in this Court,

The Defendant's Counsel (Mr. *Norton*, Mr. *Webb*, and Mr. *Thurlow*) relied upon the Case of *Warren, ex dimiss. Webb*, v. *Greenville, P.* 13 *G.* 2. *B.R.* reported in 2 *Strange* 1129: Where, upon a Trial at Bar, the Lessor of the Plaintiff claimed under an old Entail in a Family Settlement, by which, Part of the Estate appeared to be in Jointure to a Widow, at the Time her Son suffered a Common Recovery, (which was in 1699;) And the Defendant, who claimed Title under the Recovery, *not* being able to *shew a Surrender* of the Mother's *Estate for Life*, it was insisted "That "there was no Tenant to the *Præcipe* for *that Part*; and that the "Re-

Argument ex parte Def.

"Remainder, under which the Leſſor claimed, was *not barred*." To obviate this, it was inſiſted by the Defendant, "That at that "*Diſtance of Time*, a Surrender ſhould be PRESUMED; according "to 1 *Ventr.* 257. and what is * laid down in Mr. *Pigott*'s Book of "*Common Recoveries*." And to *fortify* this Preſumption, they offered to produce (in Evidence) the *Debt-Book* of Mr. *Edwards* an Attorney at *Briſtol*, then long ſince deceaſed, wherein He had charged 32 *l.* for ſuffering the Recovery; Two Articles of which Charge are—"For *drawing a Surrender of the Mother*, 20 *s.*"—and "For "*engroſſing two Parts thereof*, 20 *s.* more;" And that it appeared by the Book, "that the ſaid Bill was *paid*." And this being objected to, as improper Evidence; The Court was of Opinion to *allow it*: For it was a *Circumſtance material* upon the Inquiry into the Unreaſonableneſs of preſuming a Surrender, and could not be ſuſpected to be done *for this Purpoſe*; And if *Edwards* was living, He might undoubtedly be examined to it; And after his Death, this was the *next beſt* Evidence. And it was accordingly *read*. After which, The Court declared, "That *without* this Circumſtance, they would "have PRESUMED *a Surrender*;" and deſired it might be taken Notice of, "That they *did* NOT REQUIRE *any Evidence* to *fortify* "the Preſumption, AFTER SUCH A LENGTH OF TIME."

* V. Pigott 41.

The Caſe referred-to in 1 *Ventr.* 257. is there Anonymous: But it is S.C. with the Caſe of *Green* and *Froud*, in 3 *Keb.* 310, 311. and *Greene* v. *Proude*, in 1 *Mod.* 117. (though differently reported.) In *Ventris*, whoſe Report is much the beſt, it is ſaid, That in an Ejectment, upon a Trial at Bar, for Lands in Ancient Demeſne, there was ſhewn a Recovery in the Court of Ancient Demeſne, to cut off an Entail which had been *ſuffered a long Time ſince*, and the Poſſeſſion had gone accordingly: It appeared that Part of the Land was *leaſed for Life*; and the Recovery (with a ſingle Voucher) was ſuffered by him in Reverſion; and ſo *no Tenant to the Præcipe*, for *thoſe* Lands. But, in regard the Poſſeſſion had followed it for ſo long Time, The Court ſaid "They would PRESUME *a Sur-* "*render*:" As, in an Appropriation of great Antiquity, there has been preſumed a Licence, though none appeared.

The Paſſage in Mr. *Pigott*'s Book (referred to by Sir *J. Strange*) is in Page 41. "It is apparent there muſt be a Tenant to the *Præ-* "*cipe*, either by Right or Wrong. And therefore, in many Caſes, "it may ſeem wholly impracticable for thoſe who have the *Re-* "*mainder in Tail*, to ſuffer a Recovery. The moſt uſual Way is, "for Him in Remainder, to get the Tenant for Life to ſurrender to "him *conditionally*: And in this, *though the Tenant for Life* KEEPS "*the* POSSESSION, yet the Recovery will be GOOD."

In the Case of Dame *Griffin* v. *Stanhope*, *Cro. Jac.* 455, A Common Recovery being produced, the Counsel for the Defendant pressed the Lady's Counsel to *prove* who was Tenant to the *Præcipe*, at the Time of the Recovery. But the Court would not allow thereof: For it shall be INTENDED to be a *good* Recovery; And if it was otherwise, the Proof ought to be made by the *other* Party.

And in 2 *Lutw.* 1549, at the End of the Case of *Leigh* v. *Leigh*, this last-cited Case appears to have been confirmed by Mr. Just. *Powell*, at *York* Assizes: And Sir *Edward Lutwyche* there lays it down, " That in *every* Common Recovery, it shall be *intended* that " there was a good Tenant to the *Præcipe*, *till the contrary is shewn* " on the *other* Side."

Indeed it appears from *Lincoln*-College Case, 3 *Co.* 58. *b.* (there also cited,) " That where a Common Recovery was had against " the Remainder-Man in Tail, in the Life-time of his Mother " who was Tenant for Life; and She was *expresly alledged* to be " AD TUNC *Tenens* liberi Tenementi; It could *not* there be intend- " ed that She had surrendered her Estate, or that her Son had " entered for a Forfeiture." Yet even there, *rather* than the Common Recovery should be taken to be void for Want of a Tenant to the *Præcipe*, The Court *intended* " That He was in by " *Disseisin*."

There indeed She could not be intended to have surrendered; because it was alledged " that She was *ad tunc Tenens*." But in an *Ancient* Recovery, if Nothing appears to the Contrary, such a Surrender shall be *presumed*.

And it appears from *Pigott* 41. " That the Tenant for Life's " *continuing in Possession* makes no sort of Difference."

They observed, that all the Cases lay the whole Stress of the Reason of their Determination, singly upon the *Length* of Time from the *actual* SUFFERING *the Recovery*; without shewing any kind of Regard to the Time of the *subsequent Continuation* of the Life-Estate, or to any *other* Circumstances whatsoever. And, as those Cases were in Ejectment, the Question could not turn upon the Length of Time that the Tenant in Tail in Remainder had been come into *Possession*: For after 20 Years, He would have been barred from bringing an Ejectment.

Now the Time in the present Case is about 32 *Years*: Which is *alone* sufficient to create this Presumption; especially since the Act of 14 *G.* 2. *c.* 20: By the 5th Section whereof, it is enacted, " That

" That *after* 20 *Years from the* TIME OF SUFFERING, All Com-
" mon Recoveries ſhall be deemed good and valid to all Intents
" and Purpoſes; if it appears upon the Face of ſuch Recovery,
" that there was a Tenant to the Writ; And if the Perſons joining
" in ſuch Recovery had a ſufficient Eſtate and Power to ſuffer the
" ſame; *Notwithſtanding* the Deed or Deeds for *making* the Tenant
" to ſuch Writ ſhould be loſt or NOT APPEAR."

If it ſhould be objected, " That in the preſent Caſe Mr. *George* " *Rodney Bridges* had NOT *a ſufficient Eſtate and Power* to ſuffer " this Recovery," as being only Remainder-Man in Tail; The " Anſwer is, " That *if* there *was* a Conditional Surrender of the " Tenant for Life, then He *had* ſuch Power: And as nothing ap- " pears to the *contrary*, but that there might be ſuch a Surrender, " It muſt therefore be *preſumed*; And this Statute only limits the " Time *within which* the Preſumption ought to ariſe."

Argument *ex parte Quer'.*

The Plaintiff's Counſel, (Mr. *Gould*, Mr. *Huſſey*, Serj. *Davy*, and Mr. *Burland*,) who ſhewed Cauſe againſt granting a New Trial, argued in Support of Mr. Juſtice *Noel*'s Opinion; and aſſerted his Direction to be *right*.

They ſaid, there could be *no Preſumption* without ſome *Facts* to ground it upon. In Mr. *Greenville*'s Caſe, in 2 *Strange* 1129, there was a *very ſtrong* Preſumption, ariſing from the Articles in Mr. *Edwards* the Attorney's Bill; the Proof whereof, the Court allowed to be entered into, and received Satisfaction from.

And there is no Caſe where a Preſumption of a Surrender has been raiſed, without *Poſſeſſion* accompanying and following the Recovery. In 1 *Ventris* 257, (upon which Caſe, that in 2 *Strange* 1129 is ſaid to be founded,) there was a *Poſſeſſion* which had followed the Recovery for a long Time: And that is the *very Reaſon there given* for the Court's making the Preſumption that they then made. That Reporter was a very eminent Man; and much more to be credited than *Keble*, or the Author of 1 *Mod.* So that that Caſe was not ſimilar to *Greenville*'s Caſe, or at leaſt not enough ſo to ſupport the Poſition which is ſaid to have been founded upon it.

As to 2 *Lutw.* 1549—It is nothing more than the Reporter's *own* Speculations; not any Determination of the Court.

And in the Caſe of *Lady Griffin* v. *Stanhope*, *Cro. Jac.* 455, the Perſon who ſuffered the Recovery was Himſelf Tenant in Tail; and the *Poſſeſſion* had gone along with the Recovery.

The

The *latter* Part of Sir *J. Strange*'s Report of *Greenville*'s Cafe is *inconfiftent* with the former Part of it. For it fays, " That the " Court declared, and defired it might be taken Notice of, that " they did NOT *require any Evidence* to fortify the Prefumption after " fuch a Length of Time:" And yet it appears by the former Part of the Cafe, " That they had *entered into* fuch Evidence; after it " had been objected to as improper, and the Objection had been " confidered and over-ruled."

As to the Statute of 14 *G.* 2. *c.* 20. § 5. It never meant to alter the Law, fo as to *give* Power to a Perfon to fuffer a Recovery, who had *no Power before*; (which a Remainder-Man in Tail had not:) It is expreffly confined to " Perfons *having* a fufficient Eftate and " Power to fuffer the fame."

The Statute of Limitations 21 *J.* 1. *c.* 16. only takes place from the Time of the *Title's Accruing*.

And the Rule, in all the Cafes cited, and in all Cafes of this kind, muft, in Reafon and Common Senfe, neceffarily be underftood to relate to the Length of Time that has elapfed *fince the Tenant in Tail's Coming into* POSSESSION; and *not* to the Length of Time fince the *Suffering* of the Recovery. For where the Tenant in Tail has been a long Time in Poffeffion, and has done Nothing to complete and confirm his former Act; there indeed, it is *reafonable to prefume* that all was rightly tranfacted before; Becaufe if he knew his former Act to be defective, and his Title infufficient, He would not have neglected to fet it right affoon as it was in his Power to do fo: But no fuch Prefumption can arife from the mere Antiquity of the Recovery, *prior* to the Poffeffion of the Tenant in Tail.

The Outftanding Life-Eftate, even till 1759, is the ftrongeft Prefumption to the *Contrary*; *viz.* " That She did *not* furrender " her Eftate."

Befides, It does not at all appear from the Judge's Report, that Mr. *George Bridges*, the Tenant in Tail in Poffeffion of *all the Reft* of the Eftate, and of which he *had* Power to fuffer a Recovery, ever *meant or intended* to fuffer a Recovery of THESE *fettled Lands*, of which He had *no* Power to do fo. He had OTHER Lands in KEYNSHAM, *upon which* the Recovery *operated*: And there is no Reafon to imagine that He *meant* to include *thefe*, or ever *attempted to procure* a Surrender of the Life-Eftate in *them*.

Lord MANSFIELD—I was of Counfel in that Cafe of Mr. *Greenville*, reported in Sir *John Strange's Reports*: And I remember very well,

well, that the Point of Evidence was *strongly litigated*. The Attorney, who had been concerned in the Transaction of the Common Recovery, was One Mr. *Edwards* of *Bristol*, who had been then long dead. The *Entry* in his Bill-Book was made at the *Time* of the Transaction; and a *Receipt* had been given upon the Bill which contained the Articles for *drawing and engrossing the Surrender:* So that there was *positive Proof*, in that Case, of an *actual Surrender*. And there, the Jointress had been *dead a vast Number of Years*; And the Person who suffered the Recovery, and his Son after him, had Both of them (during their respective Lives) sufficient *Opportunity to have set it right*, after they came into Possession, *if* they had known or suspected it to have been defective: Which was certainly a *Presumption*, "That it was *regular*, and *not* defective." I am confident, that *All* that the Court did, or intended to do, in that Case, was only to take Care that it should be understood, "That they did not mean to *shake the Authority* of any one Case "that had been founded upon Presumption;" and "That they "would not require *positive Proof* of a Surrender, in any Case "where there was *sufficient* Presumption of it." This Report is incorrect, considered as a Foundation for a Principle or Rule of Property; though it might be enough to serve the Taker of such a Note, for a Memorandum, to refresh his own Recollection.

If that be so, then consider the present Case, upon *Principles*.

There are *two* Sorts of *Presumptions:* One, a Presumption of *Law*, not to be contradicted; The Other, a Species of *Evidence*; which (latter) must have a *Ground* to stand upon, something *from whence* it is to arise.

It is now fully settled and established, That a Tenant in Tail may, if he pleases, either turn his Estate Tail into a *Fee*, or *alienate* it for his own Benefit, by duly suffering a Common Recovery.

* *V. ante* 116 to 119. But He must have * a SUFFICIENT *Estate* and *Power*, to qualify him to suffer such Recovery.

He must either be the Tenant in Tail *in Possession*; or He must have the Concurrence of the Freeholder who claims under the same Settlements.

† *V. ante* 116. This Principle is † adhered to, by the Statute of 14 *G.* 2. *c.* 20.

The *Tenant for Life*, whose Consent is necessary to the Tenant in Tail in Remainder, to enable him to cut off the Entail, is *not* the Lessee of the Land under a beneficial Lease; but the *Original* Tenant for Life claiming under the Family-Settlement, and having

a

a Life-Estate settled upon him, *prior* (in order of Succession) to the Other's Remainder in Tail.

Where a Person has *Power* to suffer a Recovery and thereby bar the Estate Tail, *Omnia præsumuntur ritè et solemnitèr acta*, until the Contrary appears: And it is reasonable that it should be so. But if the *Contrary* shall *appear*, there is an End of the Presumption. This was the Case of the Earl of *Suffolk*'s Recovery, upon a Trial at Bar in this Court in *Easter* Term 1747. * There, the Contrary *did* appear: And the Presumption was thereby destroyed. There were blundering Deeds actually produced, which appeared clearly to be wrong; And it was manifest, upon the Evidence disclosed, that there was NO good Tenant to the *Præcipe*. It was therefore impossible for the Court, in *that* Case, to presume "that there "*was* One."

* *Keene, ex dimiss. Lady Portsmouth, Mr. Whitwell, and Lord Hervey, v. Earl of Effingham:* 20 *May* 1747.

But if a Man has *Power* to suffer a Recovery, That is a solid and reasonable Ground for presuming "that all was done rightly and "regularly;" *unless* something to the contrary shall appear.

So, where the Freeholder is a *Trustee* for the Tenant in Tail Himself, and *under his Power and Direction*, It is a reasonable and just Cause for presuming "that every thing was regularly transacted."

So, where the Person or Persons interested to *object* against the Validity of a Recovery, have had *Opportunity to make Objections* to it, but instead of doing so, have *acquiesced* under it, and not at all disputed it's Validity; This is a Presumption "That all was right "and regular," forasmuch as they never did object to it.

But there can be no Presumption of the Nature of Evidence, in *any* Case, without *Something from whence* to make it; *some Ground* to found the Presumption upon. Whereas here is *absolutely Nothing* from whence to presume; *no Sort of Ground* to build any Presumption upon. The single Pretence to any the least Ground of Presumption in the present Case, can be only this, "That no Tenant "in Tail in Remainder would suffer a Recovery, *without* first get-"ting a Surrender of the Life-Estate, in order to make it valid and "effectual."

But even that Ground (slight as it is) will not hold in the Case *now* before Us: For it does not at all appear, upon the Report of the Judge, that Mr. *George Bridges* (who suffered the Recovery in Question) had the *least Intention* whatsoever to include *those* PARTICULAR *Lands*, in the Recovery which He suffered, and had a *full Power in Himself alone*, to suffer, of *all the Rest* of the Estate, whereof He was at that Time Tenant in Tail in *Possession*. He was then

then in Poſſeſſion of the *Manor* of *Keynſham* and of OTHER *Lands in Keynſham* ſufficient to anſwer the general Deſcriptions uſed in the Recovery, relating to ſuch Part of the recovered Eſtate as lay in *Keynſham*. He muſt probably know or have been informed by his Counſel or Agents, that he could have no ſuch Power over the ſettled Part, without obtaining a Surrender of the Life-Eſtate. He might perhaps be ſatisfied that He *could not obtain a Surrender* of the Life-Eſtate in theſe ſettled Lands: Or, He might have attempted to obtain it, and *failed* in ſuch Attempt.

IF the *mere* ſingle Fact of the Remainder-Man in Tail ſuffering a Recovery, was *alone* ſufficient to ground a Preſumption of a Surrender of the Life-Eſtate, It would be in the Power of *every* Remainder-Man in Tail, to bar the Eſtate Tail, notwithſtanding that the Tenant for Life ſhould *abſolutely refuſe* to join with him in ſuffering a Recovery. Therefore it is neceſſary that there ſhould be Facts and Circumſtances to ground a Preſumption of ſuch a Surrender upon.

Whereas, in the preſent Caſe, it is ſo far from being reaſonable to preſume "That there *was* ſuch a Surrender from the Jointreſs, "in order to bar the Eſtate Tail in Remainder, and give the "Power of Diſpoſal to *George* in Prejudice to *James Bridges*;" that there are, on the contrary, many Reaſons to induce a Suſpicion, "that there was *not* ſuch a Surrender." She might have more Regard for *James*, than for *George*; She might have a Friendſhip for *James*, and a Diſlike to *George*: She might think it wrong or unkind, to hurt the Reverſioner; Or even Whim and Peeviſhneſs might prevent her from interfering: There is no Defining the various Reaſons ſhe might have, to hinder her from ſurrendering her Life-Eſtate for ſuch a Purpoſe.

Mr. *George Bridges* being only Tenant in Tail in Remainder, and the Life-Eſtate under the ſame Settlement ſtill ſubſiſting, at the Time of his ſuffering the Recovery; It is clear that He had NO POWER to alien or to bar: And there is *Nothing from whence to preſume a Surrender* of the Life-Eſtate, to enable him to do ſo.

IF He had had a *Power* to bar or alien, then indeed *no Preſumption* could have been *too large*; in order to prevent Slips in legal Forms and Methods of Conveyance, and effectuate the Intention of a Perſon who had a legal Right to do ſuch an Act.

The Act of 14 *G.* 2. *c.* 20. means to preſerve the ſame Negative to Perſons claiming under the Family-Settlement, as they had before.

And

And no Argument can be drawn, in the present Case, from *Length of Time*; Because the Jointress died but in 1759; and the Ejectment was instantly brought.

Upon the Whole, there is no Colour for objecting to the Judge's Direction.

Mr. Just. DENISON and Mr. Just. WILMOT concurred: And

Mr. Just. WILMOT added, That He had no Notion of a *Presumption*, without some *Facts or Circumstances* to found it upon. This would be inferring something seen, from something not seen.

Length of Time ALONE is Nothing: The Presumption must arise from some *Facts* or *Circumstances* arising within that Time.

The COURT were All clear and unanimous, That this Rule ought to be discharged.

AT the Sitting of the Court, the next Morning,

Lord MANSFIELD mentioned this Case again.

He said He had looked into his own Notes of the Case of *Warren, on the Demise of Webb*, against *Greenville*, where the Recovery was of 40 Years Standing: And the Court did lay it down, in that Case, "That *after* a Recovery of 40 *Years Standing*, they would, *without any other Circumstances*, presume a Conditional Surrender to have been made by the Tenant for Life;" And they relied upon 1 *Ventr.* 257. and Mr. *Pigott*'s Book, *Pa.* 41. But his Lordship observed, that there are *other Circumstances*, in the Case in *Ventris*: And there is *Nothing*, in *Pigott*, to justify this *general* Position. And He added, that in the Case then at the Bar, The Court did (as He had taken it down) *admit as Evidence* the Entry in the Attorney's Book, as has been mentioned.

He said, He was rather more strongly of Opinion than He was Yesterday, "That, in the present Case, there is *no Ground for a Presumption* that there was any Surrender by the Tenant for Life." Here are two particular Reasons *against* making any such Presumption. One is, That there does not appear to have been any *Intention* in the Remainder-Man in Tail, to suffer a Recovery of *these* particular Lands: The other is, That here was *no Possession* at all, under this Recovery; but, on the Contrary, the Ejectment was brought, and the Validity of the Recovery put into Litigation, *immediately* after the Death of the Tenant for Life.

If the Eldeſt Son, who has a Remainder in Tail under a Family-Settlement, ſhould privately ſuffer a Common Recovery, and his Father live many Years afterwards; It might as well be argued " that Length of Time from the Date of the Recovery ſhould induce " a Preſumption that the Father ſurrendered his Eſtate for Life."

And his Lordſhip declared himſelf as clear, that if there *had* been a long Poſſeſſion by the Tenant in Tail after the Death of the Tenant for Life; though ſuch a Poſſeſſion might be aſcribed to the Entail; the Preſumption *ought* to have been made, upon the Ground of *Acquieſcence* under it, and the Probability ariſing therefrom, " That " the Parties KNEW that the Recovery was *not* defective."

Rules of Property ought (His Lordſhip ſaid) to be *generally known*, and not to be left upon looſe Notes, which rather ſerve to *confound* Principles, than to *confirm* them. He therefore propoſed to have a *Conference* with all the Judges upon this Caſe: Which Propoſal did not ariſe, He ſaid, from any *Doubt* about the Matter; (for He was more confirmed in his Opinion, than He was Yeſterday;) but for the Sake of having ſo conſiderable a Rule of Property *ſettled*, and of rendering it *notorious* and *public*. For which Purpoſe, He (at firſt) ordered it to ſtand over till next Term: But afterwards, upon it's being agreed by all the Parties, that in Mr. *Greenville*'s Caſe, there was a great Number of Years during which the Tenant in Tail had been in *Poſſeſſion*, after the *Death* of the Tenant for Life; and upon the now Defendant's Counſel candidly declaring " That they " themſelves were *fully ſatisfied* with the preſent Opinion of the " Court;" He retracted his Propoſal, and ſaid He would not trouble the Judges with it, ſince the Counſel were ſo candid as to acquieſce entirely in the Opinion that the Court had already intimated.

His Lordſhip further added, That he would have it underſtood, That POSSESSION *of the Tenant in Tail*, *after* the *Death* of the Tenant for Life, *does* leave a *Ground* of Preſumption " That there was " a Surrender." But in the preſent Caſe, here is NO *Poſſeſſion* after the Death of the Tenant for Life: The Ejectment was brought *immediately*.

Therefore, Let the RULE of Yeſterday ſtand.

Palmer

Palmes Robinſon Eſq; *verſ.* Anne Bland, Spinſter, Adminiſtratrix de bonis non of Sir John Bland Bart. deceaſed. *Saturday* 15th *November* 1760.

THIS was a Caſe reſerved at *Niſi prius* at *Weſtminſter-Hall,* before Ld. *Mansfield,* 22d *May* 1760.

The Action was an Action upon the Caſe upon ſeveral Promiſes: And the Declaration contained 3 Counts. The 1ſt Count was upon a *Bill of Exchange;* drawn at *Paris,* by the Inteſtate Sir *John Bland,* on the 31ſt of *Auguſt* 1755, and bearing that ſame Date; *on Himſelf in* ENGLAND; for the Sum of 672*l.* Sterling, payable to the Order of the Plaintiff, TEN DAYS *after Sight,* Value received and accepted by the ſaid Sir *John Bland.* The 2d Count was for 700*l.* Monies *lent and advanced* by the ſaid Plaintiff to the ſaid Sir *John Bland,* at his Requeſt. The 3d Count was for 700*l.* Monies *had and received* by the ſaid Sir *John Bland,* to and for the Uſe of the Plaintiff. And the Plaintiff's Damage is laid at 800*l.*

The Defendant pleaded the General Iſſue, "That Sir *John Bland* "did not undertake and promiſe &c:" And Iſſue is joined thereon.

A Verdict was found for the Plaintiff, and 672*l.* given for Damages; ſubject to the following Caſe ſtated for the Opinion of the Court, on the following Facts proved and admitted: *Viz.*

That the Bill of Exchange was given at *Paris,* for 300*l.* there LENT by the Plaintiff to Sir *John Bland, at the* TIME *and* PLACE *of* PLAY; and for 372*l.* more, LOST at the *ſame Time and Place,* by Sir *John Bland,* to the Plaintiff, *at* PLAY.

That the Play was *very fair:* And there is not any Imputation whatſoever on the Plaintiff's Behaviour.

That there were ſeveral Gentlemen and Perſons of Faſhion then and there at Play, beſides the Plaintiff and Sir *John Bland.*

That in FRANCE, *Money* LOST AT PLAY, *between* GENTLEMEN, *may be* RECOVERED, *as a Debt of Honour,* before the *Marſhals of France,* who can enforce Obedience to their Sentences by *Impriſonment;* though ſuch Money is NOT *recoverable* in the ORDINARY *Courſe of Juſtice.*

That Money LENT *to play with*, or at the *Time* and *Place* of *Play*, *may be recovered there*, AS A DEBT, *in the* ORDINARY *Course of Justice*; there being NO *positive Law* against it.

That Sir *John Bland* was, and the Plaintiff is a *Gentleman*.

The Question was—Whether, under *these Circumstances*, the Plaintiff is intitled to recover ANY *Thing*, and WHAT, against the Defendant.

It was first argued on *Tuesday* 17th *June* last, by Mr. Serj. *Hewitt* for the Plaintiff, and Mr. *Blackstone* for the Defendant: And again, Yesterday and To-Day, by Mr. *Wedderburn* for the Plaintiff, and Mr. *Coxe* for the Defendant.

Upon the Conclusion of this second Argument,

Lord MANSFIELD said That in the present Case, the Facts stated scarce leave Room for any Question; because the Law of *France* and of *England* is the same.

The first Question is Whether the Plaintiff is intitled to recover *upon* this BILL OF EXCHANGE, by Force of the *Writing*.

The second Question is, Whether He is intitled to recover upon the original Consideration and CONTRACT, by the Justice and Equity of his Case, *exclusive* of any Assistance from the Bill of Exchange, and taking that to be a *void Security*.

1st Question. As to the 1st Question, the Defendant has objected "That the "Consideration of the Bill of Exchange is, wholly, Money won "and lent *at Play*: Therefore, *by force of the* WRITING, the "Plaintiff can not by the Law of *England* recover; such Security "being utterly void." And, no Doubt, the Law of *England* is so.

There are *three Reasons* why the Plaintiff cannot recover here, upon this *Bill of Exchange*.

1st. The Parties had a *View* to the Laws of *England*. The Law of the *Place* can never be the Rule, where the Transaction is entered into with an *express* View to the Law of *Another* Country, as the Rule by which it is to be governed. *Huberi Prælectiones, Lib.* 1. *Tit.* 3. *Pa.* 34. is clear and distinct: "*Veruntamen &c locus in* "*quo Contractus &c potius considerand' &c. se obligavit.*" *Voet* speaks to the same Effect.

Now

Now here, the *Payment* is to be in *England*: It is an *English Security*, and so intended by the Parties.

2d Reason—Mr. *Coxe* has argued very rightly, "That Sir *John* "*Bland* could never be called upon abroad for Payment of this Bill, "*till* there had been a wilful Default of Payment *in England*." The Bill was drawn by Sir *John Bland* on Himself, *in England*, payable ten Days after Sight.

In every Disposition or Contract where the Subject Matter relates *locally* to *England*, the Law of *England* must govern, and must have been intended to govern. Thus, a Conveyance or Will of *Land*, a *Mortgage*, a Contract concerning *Stocks*, must be all sued upon *in England*; and the *local Nature* of the Thing requires them to be carried into Execution according to the Law here.

3d Reason—The Case don't leave Room for a Question. For the Law of *both* Countries is the *same*. The *Consideration* of the Bill of Exchange might, in an Action upon it, be gone into *there*, as well as here. And as to the Money *won* at Play, It could not be recovered in any Court of Justice *there*, notwithstanding the Bill of Exchange.

This Writing is, *as a Security*, VOID, (being for a Gaming Debt,) both in FRANCE and in *England*. We may therefore lay the Bill of Exchange out of the Case: It is very clear, the Plaintiff can not recover upon *that* Count.

Second Question. Then as to the *other Counts*, for Money had and received to the Plaintiff's Use, and for Money lent and advanced to him.—Consider it distinctly, as to each Part; the Money WON, and the Money LENT. 2d Question.

1st. As to the Money *won*.—By the Rule of the Law of *England*, no Action can be maintained for it.

To this it has been objected, "That the Contract was made *in* "FRANCE: Therefore, *ex Comitate*, the Law of *France* must pre-"vail, and be the Rule of Determination."

I admit that there are many Cases where the Law of the Place of the Transaction shall be the Rule: And the Law of *England* is as liberal in this respect, as *other* Laws are. This is a large Field, and not necessary now to be gone into.

It has been laid down, at the Bar, "That a *Marriage* in a "foreign Country must be governed by the Law of *that* Country "where

" where the Marriage was had :" Which, in *general*, is true. But the Marriages in SCOTLAND, of Perſons going *from hence for that Purpoſe*, were inſtanced by way of Example. *They* may come under a very *different* Conſideration; according to the Opinion of *Huberus*, *pa*. 33. and other Writers.

No ſuch Caſe has yet been litigated in *England*, except One, of a Marriage at *Oſtend*; which came before Lord *Hardwicke*; who ordered it to be tried in the Eccleſiaſtical Court: But the Young Man came of Age, and the Parties were married over again; and ſo the Matter was never brought to a Trial.

The Point that the Defendant muſt reſt upon, in the preſent Caſe, is this—" The Money was *won in France*; Therefore it ought " to be governed by the *Law of France*; And it is recoverable " *there* before the Marſhals of *France*, who can inforce Obedience " to their Sentence."

The *Parliament of Paris* would pay no Regard to *their Judgment*, nor carry it into Execution. The Marſhals of *France* proceed PERSONALLY againſt *Gentlemen*, as to Points of Honour, with a View to prevent Duelling.

They could not have taken Cognizance of the preſent Matter. It was not within their Juriſdiction. It was no Breach of Honour *in France*: For the Money was payable *in England*; And Sir *John Bland* could not be ſaid to have *forfeited* his Honour, *till* the Ten Days were out, and *till* the Money had been demanded in *England*, and Payment refuſed there. Sir *John Bland* was actually *dead* in a very ſhort Time after he gave the Note. The Marſhals of *France* can only proceed *perſonally* againſt the Gentleman who loſes the Money; but have no Power over his *Eſtate* or *Repreſentatives*, after his *Death*.

Therefore, as to the Money WON, The Contract is to be conſidered as *void* by the Law of FRANCE, as well as by the Law of *England*: Which makes it unneceſſary to conſider " how far the " Law of *France* ought to be regarded."

Next, as to the Money LENT—The Senſe of the Legiſlature ſeems to Me to be agreeable to the * Caſes that have been cited.

* *V. Huſſey* v. *Jacob*, *Carthew* 356. 5 *Mod.* 175. 1 *Salk.* 344. 1 *Ld. Raym.* 87. *Bowyer* v. *Bampton*, 2 *Strange* 1155. *Barjeau* v *Walmſley*, 2 *Strange* 1249. and *Slater* v. *Emmerſon*, before *Eyre* Ld. Ch. J. C. B. at the Sittings at *Guildhall*, after *M.* Term 1 *G.* 2.

The Act of 16 *C.* 2. *c.* 7. § 3. does not meddle with Money LENT at Play. But, as to Money (exceeding 100 *l.*) *loſt*, and not paid down at the Time of loſing it, It ſays " That the Loſer ſhall

 " not

"not be compellable to make it good; but the CONTRACT AND "CONTRACTS *for the same and for every Part thereof*, and all "Securities shall be utterly void *&c*." The Words "*Contract and* "*Contracts for the same*" are not in 9 *Ann*. * and I dare say were *designedly* left out: It only says "That all Notes, Bills, Bonds, "Judgments, Mortgages or other *Securities &c* for Money WON *or* "LENT *at Play*, shall be utterly void *&c*." * C. 14

Here the Money was *fairly lent*, without any Imputation whatsoever. Sir *John Bland*, the Borrower of it, being in a foreign Country, might very naturally have been distressed, under his then Situation amongst Foreigners, for want of having ready Money or knowing how to procure it: And it might be even a kind and generous and commendable Act, to lend it to him at that Time, to extricate him from his Difficulties, as He was then circumstanced. The Jury have left it quite open to the Court to determine "Whether *any* Thing, and WHAT, is recoverable." As to the Money "WON, We think it can *not* be recovered: As to the Money LENT, The Plaintiff is *intitled* to it, both by the Law of *England* and by the Law of *France*.

INTEREST will be payable upon this Bill, after the Expiration of the Ten Days. The Question will be, "How FAR the Interest "ought to be *carried down*." It is generally said, To the Day of "the *Writ brought*;" i. e. of Commencing the Action. But I do not see why it should not be carried *further*: It is equally *reasonable*, it is the *Right* of the Party, to have it to the *last Act of the Court ascertaining* the Sum due.

I have long wished for an Opportunity to have this Point considered by the *Court*; Because I would not take upon Myself, at *Nisi prius*, to change what has commonly been the Practice.

But, as to this *last Point*, We will think of it for a Day or two.

Mr. Just. DENISON gave no Opinion now, on this last Point. As to the Rest, He said It is a plain clear short Case: It is determinable by the Rules of the *Common* Law, and *no other* Law.

The Money is made *payable in England*. As it is a *foreign* Bill of Exchange, it must of Course be *dated* abroad: But it is to be *paid* here at Home. And the Plaintiff has appealed to the Laws of *England*, by bringing his Action here; and ought to be determined by *them*.

But, by the Laws of *England*, the SECURITY is *void*: Which might have been *pleaded*, as well as it might be given in *Evidence*;

 And

And the Defendant needed not, in his Plea, to have ſaid WHERE it was won at Play. And being a tranſitory Action, it muſt then have been tried where the Action was *brought:* And ſo it muſt have been, if the Plea had been *local.* Indeed in many Caſes that *might* be put, the Determination muſt have been according to the Laws of the Place where the *Fact* aroſe. But the *preſent* Caſe is not ſo: *Here,* the Security is *void* by the Laws of the Country where he brings his Action upon it. And this Security is one *entire* Security *both* for the Money *won* at Play, and the Money *lent* at Play.

There is a *Diſtinction* between the *Contract,* and the SECURITY. If Part of the CONTRACT ariſes upon a *good* Conſideration, and Part of it upon a *bad* One; it is *diviſible.* But it is otherwiſe as to the SECURITY: That, being *entire,* is bad for the *Whole.*

Therefore the Plaintiff ought to be barred of this Action *upon* this *Bill of Exchange,* as being a void Security by the Laws of this Country, were he brings his Action. But ſtill the CONTRACT *remains:* And he has a Right to maintain his Action for *ſo much* of his Demand as is *legal;* which is the Money LENT.

As to the Time of Carrying down the *Intereſt,* it may be proper to conſider of it a little While.

Mr. Juſt. WILMOT—Here are two Sums demanded, which are blended together in one Bill of Exchange; but are *diviſible* in their Nature.

As to the Money LENT—The Caſes that have been cited are in Point "That it is *recoverable.*" But if there were None, yet I ſhould be clear that the Plaintiff may maintain an Action for *that.*

As to *Contracts* being good, and the *Security* void—The *Contract* may certainly be *good;* though the Security be void: And I think that this Contract is good; though the Security is void, by the Statute of 9 *Ann.* * This is not ſtated to be Money lent to *play with,* or for the *Purpoſe* of Play; but "lent at the *Time* and *Place* of "Play" only: Nothing appears upon this Caſe, to induce any Suſpicion that it was lent for any *bad* Purpoſe.

* 9 *Ann. c.* 14. § 1.

The Statutes meant to prevent exceſſive Gaming, and to vacate all *Securities* whatſoever for Money won at Play: And the genuine true and ſound Conſtruction of 9 *Ann.* is to underſtand it as intended to prevent any *Securities* being taken for Money *won* at Play, or lent *to play with,* when the Borrower had loſt all his *ready* Caſh; but *not* to make the *Contract* itſelf void, where the Money is *fairly* and *bonâ fide lent,* though at the Time and Place of Play.

2 As

As to the INTEREST that ſhall be given to the Plaintiff upon the *Sum lent*, in the Aſſeſſment of the Damages—This is an Action that ſounds in *Damages:* And the *true Meaſure* undoubtedly is the *Damage* which the Plaintiff ſuſtains by the Non-performance of the Contract; And that Damage is the *whole* Intereſt due upon the Sum lent; *viz.* from the Time of it's being payable, up to the Time of *ſigning the Judgment.* Nay, even then, He may *ſuffer*; He may *ſtill* be kept out of his Money, by Writ of Error, for a ſtill further Time. According to my Memory, Lord *Coke*'s Expoſition of the Statute is, that the "*Coſts of the* WRIT" ſhall extend to all the* legal Coſts of the *Suit*.

* *V.* 2 *Inſt.* 288. on *Stat. Glouc.* 6 *Edw.* 1. *accord'.*

The preſent Caſe, notwithſtanding the Queſtions that have been agitated in arguing it, comes out to be no Caſe at all; no Point at all; no Law at all.

Indeed, "Whether an Action can be ſupported in *England*, on "a Contract which is void by the Law of *England*, but *valid* by "the Law of the Country where the Matter was tranſacted," is a great Queſtion: (though I ſhould have no great Doubt about *that.*) But *that* Caſe does not exiſt here: For it is *not* here ſtated, "that "ſuch a Debt as this, for Money *won* at Play in *France*, *is recover-"able* in the *ordinary* Courts of Juſtice there;" but quite the *Contrary.* So that the Laws of *France* and of *England* are the SAME as to the Money WON: The Contract is void as to *that*, by the Laws of *both* Countries.

And as to this wild, illegal, fantaſtical Court of HONOUR, the Court of the Marſhals of *France*, acting only *in perſonam*, contrary to the univerſal and general Laws even of the Country where the Tranſaction happened, and contrary to the Genius and Spirit of our own Law too; It would be abſurd to ſuppoſe, that the bare poſſible accidental Chance of a Recovery in that Court ſhould be a Foundation for maintaining an Action here, upon a Matter prohibited by the Laws of *both* Countries.

Beſides, Sir *John Bland* Himſelf, as it ſeems, was not, and the *preſent Defendant*, the Perſon *now* before this Court, *could never have been* the Object of the Juriſdiction of *that* Court. The Remedy there, in it's utmoſt Extent, was only *in Perſonam*; And this Defendant is an *Adminiſtratrix*, only.

A ſtrong Reaſon for the Plaintiff's recovering in this Action the Money LENT, is, that the Bill of Exchange is payable *in England*; And therefore it ſhall be determined according to the *Laws* of *England*, where it is payable. As in the Caſe of Sir *John Champant* v. *Ld.*

Ld. Ranelagh, *Mich.* 1700. *in Chancery*, (reported in *Precedents in Chancery* 128.) A Bond was *made in England*, and *ſent over to Ireland*, and the Money to be *paid* there; But it was not mentioned *what Intereſt* ſhould be paid: My Lord Keeper was of Opinion, " That it ſhould carry *Iriſh* Intereſt." Therefore, as *this* Money was *payable in* ENGLAND, the Law of *England* muſt be the Rule of recovering it.

I give *no Opinion* as to the *other* Point: Yet I can not help thinking, that where a Perſon *appeals* to the Law of *England*, He muſt take his Remedy according to the Law of *England*, to which He has appealed.

There is no Difference, in this Caſe, between the *Statute Law*, and the *Common* Law of *England:* A Contract can not be *maintained* upon the One, that is *void* by the Other.

The *Law of the Place* where the Thing happens does not *always* prevail. In many Countries, a Contract may be maintained by a Courteſan for the Price of her Proſtitution; And One may ſuppoſe an Action to be brought here, upon ſuch a Contract which aroſe in ſuch a Country: But that would never be allowed in *this* Country. Therefore the *Lex loci* can not in *all* Caſes govern and direct.

The *Sentences* of foreign Courts have always *ſome* Degree of Regard paid to them, by the Courts of Juſtice here: And it is very right that an Attention ſhould be paid to them, as far as they ought to have Weight in the Caſe depending.

But if a Man *Originally* appeals to the Law of *England* for Redreſs, He muſt take his Redreſs according to that Law to which He has appealed for ſuch Redreſs. Therefore if this Rule of Determination was different, by the Law of *France*, from our Rule here, yet I ſhould *incline*, that the Law of *England* where the Action was brought, ſhould prevail againſt the Law of *France*, if they did really claſh with Each other; becauſe the Party ſeeking Redreſs has choſen to *apply here*. But I give *no Opinion* at all, on this Point.

As to the Money LENT—There can be no Doubt; becauſe there is no Law either in *England* or *France*, that hinders the Plaintiff from maintaining his Action for it.

As to the *Carrying down the* INTEREST to a fixed Time,

THE COURT took Time to conſider that *ſingle* Point.

And

And on *Saturday* the 22d of *November*,
Lord MANSFIELD delivered the Resolution of the Court, upon that Point, to the following Effect.

We have given our Opinion already upon all the Parts of this Case, except the single Point of CARRYING DOWN THE INTEREST: Which Opinion was, "That the Plaintiff could only re-" cover 300 *l.* the Principal Sum *really and bonâ fide* LENT by the "Plaintiff to Sir *John Bland* at *Paris*.

The remaining Questions are—" Whether it should CARRY *In-*" *terest*;" And, "*To* WHAT TIME such Interest ought to be" computed and allowed."

As to the former of these two Questions, The Case stated is, "That the Bill of Exchange was given *at Paris*, for 300 *l. there*" LENT *by the Plaintiff* to Sir *John Bland*; for which, He gave" the Plaintiff a Security, *void*, in Point of Law, AS a *Security*." But the GIVING *the Bill of Exchange, upon such Consideration*, is stated in the Case, as a *Fact admitted*; and shews that, upon the Loan, the *Intention and Agreement* of the Parties was, "that the" Money *should carry Interest*, if not repaid within the limited Time."

The CONTRACT remains *good*, though He gave a *void* SECURITY to perform it. So that it is a LIQUIDATED Sum which *carries Interest* from the Time at which it was *agreed to be paid*.

But the Question is, "Whether it is to STOP at the *Commencement of the Action*; or to be *carried on* to the Time of *liquidating*" the Debt by the *Verdict* or by the *Judgment*."

This Difference is very small, in the present Case, and scarce worth litigating between these Parties. But I am glad of the Opportunity which this Case offers, of *discussing the Question* and *settling the Point*, to be a Rule for all Cases of the same Nature that may hereafter arise.

The *general Practice* of Associates, in taking Damages in these Cases, is (I am informed) to stop at the *Commencement* of the Action, and to allow the Interest *no further down*. But this Practice, however general, is NOT *founded in Law*, but in *Mistake* and *Misapprehension*. And this will appear very plain, whether it be considered upon the Foot of natural *Justice*, or *Law*.

First, in Point of JUSTICE—Nothing can be more agreeable to *Justice*, than that the Interest should be carried down quite to the *actual Payment* of the Money. But as that cannot be, it should be carried on as far as to the Time when the Demand is * *completely liquidated.*

* *V. post Bedilly v. Bellamy*, 22d November 1760. S. P.

Although this be *nominally* an Action for *Damages*, and *Damages* be *nominally* recovered in it; yet it is really and effectually brought for a *specific Performance of the Contract.* For where Money is made payable by an Agreement between Parties, and a *Time given for the Payment* of it, This is a Contract to pay the Money *at* the given Time; and to *pay Interest* for it *from* the given Day, in Case of Failure of Payment at that Day. So that the Action is, in Effect, brought to obtain a *specific Performance* of this Contract. For *pecuniary Damages* upon a Contract *for Payment of Money*, are, from the nature of the Thing, a specific Performance; And the Relief is defective, so far as *all* the Money is not paid.

Then, to consider it upon the *Common* and *Statute* LAW.

There is *no Statute*, nor any Principle of the *Common* Law, against it. We have looked into all the *Statutes* that can be supposed to concern this Practice: And there is *no Statute* that has any Reference to the Matter.

The Damages given by *Statutes*, are Where the Action is against such as come in *under Wrong-Doers* only; or where a *specific thing* is to be recovered.

It is agreeable to the Principles of the *Common* Law, that wherever a Duty has incurred, *pending* the Writ, for which *no Satisfaction* can be had by a *new Suit*, such Duty shall be INCLUDED in the Judgment to be given upon the Action *already* depending.

Of this, there are many Instances. In a Writ of * *Account*, the first Judgment is, "*quod computet:*" And on such Account, all Articles of Account, though incurred since the Writ, shall be included, and the Whole brought *down to the Time* when the Auditors make an End of their Account. So in the ancient Writ of *Annuity*; Intermediate Sums grown due pending the Action, shall be *included* in the Judgment; because a new Action can not be brought for them.

* See *New Abridgment of the Law*, Vol. 1. pa. 21. (very short and clear.)

On the Statute of *Gloucester* 6 *Ed.* 1. (Whereby Damages are given in real Actions, on a Writ of Entry to recover the specific Lands;) That Statute gives Damages *generally*, without saying *till* what Time:

Yet the Construction upon it has been, "That they shall compute "*All* the Damages that have arisen, *pendentè Brevi*." * * V. 2 Inst. 288.

When a *new* Action *may* be *brought*, and a *Satisfaction obtained thereupon*, for any Duties or Demands which have arisen since the Commencement of the depending Suit; *that* Duty or Demand shall *not* be included in the Judgment upon the former Action. As in *Covenant* for Non-Payment of Rent, or of an Annuity payable at different Times, You may bring a *new* Action *toties quoties*, as often as the respective Sums become due and payable. So in *Trespass*, and in *Tort*; New Actions may be brought, as often as new Injuries and Wrongs are repeated: And therefore Damages shall be assessed only up to the Time of the Wrong complained of.

But where a Man brings an Action of *Assumpsit*, for Principal and Interest, upon a Contract obliging the Defendant to pay such Principal Money *with Interest* from such a Time; He complains of the Non-Payment of *Both*: The *Interest* is an *Accessary* to the Principal; And He can *not* bring a *new* Action for any Interest grown due *between* the Commencement of his Action, and the Judgment in it.

Here, the Plaintiff can *not* bring a *new* Action for the *Interest*: For, He has *already* had a Satisfaction upon the Defendant's PROMISE.

The Court of *Chancery* has, in Cases of this kind, often a *concurrent* Jurisdiction with the Courts of *Common* Law, on Account of Assets; (*not* an extraordinary, but an ordinary Jurisdiction, by reason of the Fund.) And it seems absurd, that two Courts of Justice who have concurrent Jurisdiction should go by *different Rules*; They ought to act *uniformly*, as far as may be: The Court of Chancery follows the Ecclesiastical Court, in Cases where they have concurrent Jurisdiction. Now in *Chancery*, Interest is computed even *up to the Day* when it is conjectured or agreed that the Master's Report will be *confirmed*, (though a *future* Day,) which they fix according to probable Conjecture. I don't know of *any* Court, in *any* Country, (And I have looked into the Matter,) which don't carry Interest down to the Time of the *last Act* by which the Sum is liquidated.

Why then may not *Juries* compute Interest to the Time of the Verdict, or even till the End of 4 Days within the next Term; (before which Time the Plaintiff cannot sign his Judgment?)

I think I can see how this Mistake has happened: I dare say that Associates have not distinguished between this Species of Action, (it

* See the Distinction between these, in the Case of *Haward* v. *Bankes*, in this Term, *post*

(it being called an Action of Trespass on the Case,) and * *common* Actions of *Trespass*; (such as Actions for Assaults, Batteries, false Imprisonments &c.)

Carrying down the Interest does a Plaintiff *complete Justice*. It is agreeable to the Principles of the Common Law, and interferes with no Statute. It takes from Defendants the Temptation to make Use of all the unjust Dilatories of Chicane. For if Interest is to stop at the *Commencement* of the Suit; where the Sum is large, the Defendant may gain by protracting the Cause in the most expensive and vexatious Manner; And the more the Plaintiff is injured, the less He will be relieved.

Here, the Jury having left the Matter quite open to Us, We can bring the Interest down to the Time of the Liquidation and Ascertainment of the Sum really due from the Defendant to the Plaintiff; which is the Time of *giving the Judgment*. And the Sum, (a Trifle indeed in this Case,) for which the Judgment is to be entered, will then be about 375*l.* (a little more or less.) Therefore let Judgment be entered for that Sum.

Rule—That "the *Postea* be forthwith delivered to the Plaintiff's "Attorney; and that the Plaintiff shall be at Liberty to "enter up Judgment on the Verdict obtained in this Cause: "But it is further Ordered That such Judgment shall only "stand Security to the Plaintiff for the Sum of 375*l.* Parcel of "the Sum of 672*l.* (the Damages assessed by the Jury;) And "the Plaintiff's Costs to be taxed by Mr. *Owen*."

Thursday 20th *November* 1760.

This being *Grand-Jury* Day, It was intended by the Sheriff, and pressed by the two Knights of the Shire for *Middlesex*, that *All* the Principal Gentlemen of the County (not fewer than *fourscore* in Number) should be *sworn* of this Grand Jury, in order to their being included in an Address to his Majesty, from and in the Name of the Grand Jury of *Middlesex*, upon his Accession to the Crown. But, upon the Sheriff's Mention of this to Me, it seemed to Me to be irregular and improper to swear more than 23: Because if a Number amounting to *two full Juries* or more should be sworn, it might happen that a *Complete Jury of Twelve* might find a Bill to be a *true* One, though *other Twelve* or even Many more than twelve of the very same Jury might reject it as an *untrue* One; which would be inconvenient as well as contradictory, and even somewhat absurd and ridiculous.

Lord Mansfield, upon being apprized of this, said It would be monstrous to swear Fourscore; And that the Officer could not properly swear more than *three and twenty*.

Goodtitle,

Goodtitle, ex dimiss. Paul Esq; *vers.* Paul, Spinster.

Friday 21st November 1760.

UPON the Trial of an Ejectment before Lord *Mansfield* at *Hertford* Assizes, a Case was reserved for the Opinion of the Court: And the single Question was, " Whether certain Woodlands *passed*, " by the *Will* of the late Dr. *Paul*, to his Widow; or *descended* to " his Son and Heir, as *undevised*."

The Ejectment was brought by the Son for the Recovery of them, by the Description of " twenty Acres of *Woodland* in the Parish of " *Bovington* in the County of *Hertford*."

The Substance of the Case stated was, that Dr. *Paul*, being seised of divers Freehold and Copyhold Estates, and (amongst others) of the Premisses in question, made his Will, dated 4th *October* 1752, in Manner following. As to my *Worldly Estate*, I dispose of it in Manner following—Then He leaves Fortunes to his two Daughters; and 20*l. to his Son George*, (the Lessor of the Plaintiff, who was his *only Son and Heir*,) for Mourning. He then gives all his Stocks Securities &c, &c, to his Wife. Then the Will proceeds thus—" Whereas I am intitled to a Lease-hold Estate, being a " House and Yard in *Ave-Mary Lane*, I give the same to my dear " Wife. I have purchased a Barn and Field, in Reversion expec- " tant on the Death of Lady *Williams*, of Mr. *Ralph Day*: I give " and devise the same to my dear Wife, subject to her sole Disposal. " I give devise and bequeath my two Farms purchased of the Trus- " tees of his late Grace of *Chandos*, in the Parish of *Little Stanmore*, " One in the Occupation of *Henry Grubb*, the other in the Occupa- " tion (lately) of Mr. *Jully*, to my dear Wife; subject to her Dispo- " sal by Will, or by Deed or Sale. I give devise and bequeath all " my Estate in *Fleet-Street*, consisting of Houses in *Johnson's Court*, " *Boars head Court*, the *Bolt and Tun Inn*, and *Bolt and Tun Pas-* " *sage*, to my dear Wife; with all the Right and Property of en- " joying them; And also my Estate in *Saint Mary Axe*, in the Oc- " cupation of Mr. *Jacob Castre*, in as full and ample a Manner as " I enjoy the same. I give devise and bequeath my Freehold and " Copyhold Estate in the Parish of *Aldenham*, in the Tenure of " *John Wrench*, and my Freehold House and Orchard in the Back " Lane of *Bushey*, to my dear Wife; subject to her sole Disposal, " by Will Deed or Sale; As also my Copyhold Lands in *Shedlington* " in *Bedfordshire*. I give devise and bequeath my Dwelling-house " and the Lands therewith held, in *Bushey*, and the Farm in the " Tenure of *John Staines*; together with my Blacksmith's Shop in " the

" the Tenure of *James Wilking*, and the little House adjoining, to " my dear Wife, in as full and ample Manner as I enjoy the same, " and subject to her Disposal as effectually as I have Power to give. " I also give my dear Wife my Estate at *Chain-Gate* in *Southwarke*, " conveyed from my Daughter *Valentina Snow*. I give and devise " to my *dear Wife my* FARM *at Bovington in the* TENURE *of* JOHN " SMITH, subject to her Disposal in as full and absolute a Manner as " I could dispose of the same if living. Lastly, I make my dear " Wife *Susannah Paul* my sole Executrix; And give devise and grant " to her and her Heirs All my Estate Real and Personal, Freehold " and Copyhold, mentioned in this my Will: And I give Her full " Power to sell give or grant the same in Fee Simple, in as ample " a Manner as I could do if living. I wrote this with my own " Hands; being in good Health."

That in the Year 1718, *Jonathan Hammond*, as Heir to his Father, was admitted to the *Farm at Bovington* in the above Will mentioned; for which, *One* Quit-Rent was reserved, and *One* Heriot: And his Admission is as follows; *viz.* " Ad Curiam Baron' " Henshaw Halsey Arm' Domini Manerij præd', ibidem tent' diebus Martis et Mercurij viz. decimo et undecimo diebus Junij " anno Regni Domini nostri Georgij D. G. M. Br. Fr. et Hiberniæ " Regis F. D. &c. quarto, Annoq; Domini 1718, coram Carolo " Pultney Armigero tunc Seneschallo ibidem. Ad hanc Cur' Præsentatum est per Homagium, quod Jonathan Hammond alias " Cooper, Senior, de Great Marlow in Com' Bucks, Generosus, " unus Customar' Tenent' hujus Manerij, Qui de Domino Maner' " præd' tenuit sibi et Hæredibus suis, per copiam Rutolorum hujus " Curiæ, Unum Messuagium sive Tenementum et *Firmam* tent. " per copiam Rotulorum, in Parochia de Bovendon, vocat' *Great* " *Shantocks*, per annualem Reddit' 3 *l.* 6 *s.* 2 *d.* ½ obiit inde seisitus: " Ratione inde accidit Domino pro Heriotto, Unus Equus, Valoris " 6 *l.* 5 *s.* Et quod Jonathan Hammond aliàs Cooper, de Great " Marlow præd' Generosus, est ejus Filius et Hæres, et plenæ Ætatis: Qui quidem Jonathan Hammond alias Cooper, præsens hic " in Curia, petiit à Domino Manerij præd' se admitti Tenent' ad " Præmiss. prædict' cum eorum pertinentiis. Cui Dominus prædictus, per Seneschallum suum, concessit inde Seisinam per Virgam; Habend' et Tenend' præmissa præd' cum eorum Pertinentiis præfato Jonathan' Hammond alias Cooper, Hæred' et Assign' " suis imperpetuum, per Virgam, ad Voluntatem Domini, secund' " Consuetudinem Manerij præd', per annualem Reddit' 3 *l.* 6 *s.* 2 *d.* ½ " et alia Servitia inde priùs debit' et de jure Consuet': Deditq; " Domino pro Fine pro tali Statu sic inde habend' 1 *l.* 13 *s.* 1 *d.* ½; " et admissus est inde Tenens, et fecit Domino fidelitatem."

That

That the said *Jonathan Hammond* kept the Whole of the Estate to which He was so admitted, in his *own Hands*, till the 19th of *March* 1719; and then by Lease of that Date, *demised* to *William Smith* and *John Smith* his Son, All that Messuage or Tenement and Farm, with all and every the Closes Fields Pieces and Parcels of Arable Land Lay Meadow and Pasture-Ground, with their Appurtenances thereto belonging or appertaining, situate lying and being in the Parish of *Bovingdon* in the County of *Herford*, and which said Messuage or Tenement and Farm is commonly called or known by the Name of *Great Shantocks Farm*, and is now in the Possession of *John Harding* his Under-Tenants or Assigns, or by whatsoever other Name or Names the same now is or hath been called or known; And also all Houses Out-houses Edifices Buildings Barns Stables Yards Orchards Gardens Backsides Ways Waters Commons Profits and Commodities Hereditaments and Appurtenances whatsoever to the said intended to be hereby demised Messuage or Tenement and Farm Lands and Premisses belonging or appertaining or therewith letten or enjoyed or accepted or taken as Part or Parcel thereof; Except and always reserved out of the said Demise, unto the said *Jonathan Hammond* his Heirs and Assigns, *all and all Manner of* Wood, Wood-Ground, Hedge-Rows, Timber, *and* Trees whatsoever, with the *Lops Tops* and *Shrowds* of the same, (other than the Lops of Pollard-Trees, and other than Fruit-Trees for their Fruit only,) now standing or growing or being, or which shall at any Time or Times hereafter stand grow or be in or upon the demised Premisses or any Part thereof; with free Liberty of *Ingress Egress* and *Regress* to and for the said *Jonathan Hammond* his Heirs and Assigns, with Workmen Servants Horses Carts and Carriages, at all seasonable Times, to fell sell cut down hew out have take carry away and dispose of the said Wood Under-Wood Hedge-Rows Timber and Trees at their Pleasure, doing no wilful Spoil or Damage to the said *William Smith* and *John Smith* their Executors Administrators or Assigns, their standing Corn or mowing Grass: To hold the said Messuage or Tenement and Farm Arable Lands Lay Meadow and Pasture Grounds, except *before excepted*, unto the said *William Smith* and *John Smith* their Executors Administrators and Assigns from the Feast-Day of St. *Michael* the Archangel then next ensuing, for 3 Years at 85 *l. per Annum*.

That in the Year 1721, Dr. *Paul* purchased from the said *Jonathan Hammond* All the Premisses to which the said *Jonathan Hammond* had been admitted as aforesaid: of which Premisses a *Plan* had been made in the Year 1719; Which, after the Purchase, was hung up by Dr. *Paul* in his Hall. That this Plan was intitled " An exact Draught of the *Estate or Farm* of Dr. *George Paul*, " *called Shantacks*, lying in the Parish of *Bovingdon* in the County " of

" of *Hertford*, about 3 Miles East from *Chesham*, 4 South from " *Berkhampstead*, 4 South-West from *Hempstead*, and about 22 " North-West from *London*; containing

	A	R	P
Arable	171	2	12
Wood	20	0	30".
	191	3	2".

That *William Smith*, the Father, and *John Smith*, the Son, without any new Lease, enjoyed what had been so demised by the said *Jonathan Hammond*: And *Dr. Paul* kept in his OWN HANDS, *till the Time of his Death*, the *Premisses* EXCEPTED; Which consist of *Hedge-Rows*, which in some Places are 3 Poles thick, and in Others less and only two; and of *Chalk-Dells* where Wood has grown up after the Chalk has been taken away, entirely surrounded by the Lands in the Tenure of the Tenant; and also of ONE ENTIRE WOOD of *Six* Acres, entirely inclosed by the Lands in the Tenure of the Tenant or by the Lands of other Persons.

The Question is, " Whether the *Premisses so* EXCEPTED in the " Lease to *Smith*, and so *occupied by* Dr. PAUL HIMSELF at the " Time of making his Will, were by such Will DEVISED *to his* " *Widow*."

Mr. *Eliab Harvey* was of Counsel for the Plaintiff, the Heir at Law; And argued that the WOODS which were EXCEPTED *out of the Lease* from Mr. *Jonathan Hammond* to *William Smith* and *John Smith*, and were *occupied by Dr. Paul Himself*, did NOT *pass* to the Widow, by this Will; but DESCENDED to the Plaintiff, his Son and Heir, as being *un*-devised at all.

He urged that the Plaintiff's Case was intitled to a *favourable* Construction; as he appears to be an only Son and *Heir at Law*, disinherited by his Father, without any apparent Reason, (perhaps from Caprice only:) And therefore mere *presumptive* Arguments ought not to hurt Him.

He observed, that the Words of this Devise are " I give to my " Wife my Farm at *Bovingdon* in the Tenure of *John Smith*:" But the Testator does not say " ALL my Farm at *Bovingdon*;" nor does he express it—" AND in the Tenure of *John Smith*." 'Tis only " *my* Farm at *Bovingdon in the Tenure of J. S.*" The Court will not, in Prejudice to the Heir at Law, *reject* those Words " *in the* " *Tenure of J. S.*" which make the *Description* of what the Testator meant to devise to his Wife: For the Expression in the first Part of the Will is not certain, but doubtful.

4 He

He cited *Bacon's* * *Maxims of the Law*; *Cro. Jac.* 21. *Tutteſham* v. *Roberts*. *Cro. Car.* 129. *Chamberlaine* v. *Turner*. *Plowd.* 191. *b. Wroteſley* v. *Adams*; and *Shaw* v. *Bull*, *Caſes in B. R. temp. W.* 3. *Pa.* 592. and prayed to have the *Poſtea* delivered to his Plaintiff. * Pa. 102, 107.

Mr. *Thomas Clerk* (of *Lincolns Inn*) was for the Defendant: But the Court ſaved him the Trouble of ſpeaking.

Lord Mansfield—This is too plain a Caſe, to need any Thing to be ſaid on the Defendant's Side.

I never deny making a Caſe for the Opinion of the Court, whenever it is aſked of me, by the Counſel for either Party, at *Niſi prius*; provided that the Caſe be ſet down to be argued within Four Days. But I did and ſtill do think the preſent Caſe to be a very plain One.

I am ſorry that Dr. *Paul* has not thought fit to make a better Proviſion for his only Son: But He certainly meant and intended to give ALL his Eſtate to his *Wife*. He not only expreſſes this Intention as to all his Eſtates Freehold and Copyhold, *generally*; but He likewiſe enumerates the *Particulars*: He gives them All to Her, *abſolutely*; And He likewiſe gives Her a Power to diſpoſe of them in as full and ample a Manner as He himſelf could do, if living. He puts into his Will, All poſſible Words that can give *Every Thing* to Her.

The Queſtion turns only upon the DESCRIPTION of the Thing meant to be here given. The Words "*In the Tenure of John Smith*" cannot be underſtood as a *Reſtriction*: They are an *additional* Deſcription; which will † *not vitiate* any Thing that is ſufficiently deſcribed before. He had before given Her "*his Farm at Bovingdon*"; (Which had gone at *One Rent*, and had been uſed and paſſed as *One entire Thing*; and for which, *One entire Quit-Rent* had been paid:) And He adds, as a *further* Deſcription, That it was "in the Tenure "of *John Smith*."

† V. Plowden 191. b. Wroteſley v. Adams accord'.

What was *not in Leaſe to Smith*, is to be conſidered in two Lights; *viz. Hedge-Row Trees and Chalk-Dell Trees*; and alſo *Six Acres of Wood*.

But the *Hedge-Rows* and *Chalk Dells* themſelves *are actually in the Tenure of John Smith*; though the *Trees* are excepted.

As to the Six Acres of *Wood-land*—Indeed the *Soil* is excepted out of *Smith*'s Leaſe, as well as the *Trees*. But Dr. *Paul* gives his Wife a Power to diſpoſe of the *Farm* in as full and abſolute a Manner *as He himſelf* could diſpoſe of the ſame, if living: And He himſelf might certainly diſpoſe of the Soil of theſe Six Acres.

It is manifeſtly intended, that the *whole* Farm ſhould paſs by this Will: And the Teſtator never thought of any *Reſtriction* of his Deviſe, but meant theſe Words "in the Tenure of *J. S*"—only as an *additional* and fuller Deſcription of a Thing ſufficiently aſcertained before.

Mr. Juſt, Denison concurred, that the Teſtator's Intention certainly was, to deviſe the *Whole* Farm to his Wife; And that He never thought of the Exception of the *Wood-Lands*, nor intended to *reſtrain* the Deviſe; And that the Words "*in the* Tenure *of J. S*" are only an *additional* Deſcription.

Mr. Juſt. Wilmot was of the ſame Opinion: And He likewiſe thought it a clear Caſe. The Teſtator meant this as an *Additional* Deſcription, and *not* as a *Reſtriction*. He certainly did not intend to die *inteſtate*, as to *any* Part of his Eſtate. The Words—"in the "*Tenure of J. S.*" are *not* to be conſidered as Words of *Limitation* or *Reſtraint*. "My Farm at *Bovingdon*," is, "*All* my Farm at *B*." If the Teſtator had meant otherwiſe, He would have *ſpecified* that Part of it which He meant to *exclude* and *except* out of this Deviſe: But this Deviſe of the Farm is tantamount to his deviſing it by the ſpecific Name of *Shantacks Farm*. The *Nature* of the Property ſhews it. The very Exceptions in the Leaſe indicate that it was intended to keep theſe excepted Parts *connected* with the Farm, and *not ſevered* from it. And the Teſtator could never mean to give Mrs. *Paul* the Lops and Maſt of the Pollards, and the Fruit of the Fruit-Trees, and not the Trees themſelves. And yet She would, upon this Will, be intitled to *theſe*; as appears fully in *Richard Liford*'s Caſe, 11 *Co*. 48.

Per Cur. unanimouſly,
Let there be Judgment for the Defendant.

Saturday 22d *November* 1760.

Bodily *verſ.* Bellamy.

Mr. *Norton*, on Behalf of the Plaintiff, ſhewed Cauſe againſt a Rule which had been obtained by Mr. *Morton*, (of Counſel for the Defendant,) "For the Plaintiff to ſhew Cauſe why, upon "Payment of the whole Penalty of the Bond, together with "all the *Coſts in this Court*, and alſo the *Coſts of the Writ of Error* "brought upon the Judgment given by this Court, The Execution "ſhould not be *ſtayed*, and *Satisfaction entered* upon the Record."

The Caſe was very *particular*.

It was an Action brought here, in this Court, upon a *Bond* given at *Calcutta* (in *Bengal*) in the East Indies, where both Parties then reſided, and where the Plaintiff ſtill reſides; but the Defendant is in *England*: At which Place (*Calcutta*) the allowed Intereſt is 9*l*. *per Cent*; Which is the Rate payable by the Condition of the Bond on which the preſent Action was brought.

The *Declaration* was in Debt; for 1546*l*. 14*s*. 6*d*. It contained *two* Counts. One was upon the *Bond*, for the *Penalty* of 9165 Rupees of *Calcutta*, of the Value of 1031*l*. 3*s*. of lawful Money of *Great Britain*: The Other was upon a *Mutuatus*, for 4582 Rupees, of the Value of 515*l*. 11*s*. 6*d*. (Reſidue of the ſaid Sum of 1546*l*. 14*s*. 6*d*.) The Plaintiff laid his Damage at 10*l*.

The Plea was, "*Non eſt factum*," as to the 1ſt Count; And "*Nil debet*," as to the 2d. The Action was brought in 1756: And the Cauſe was tried before Ld. *Mansfield*, in *Michaelmas* Term 1759.

Upon the Trial, the Bond was *proved*: But *no Evidence* at all was given upon the 2d Count, of any Money *lent* to the Defendant; Nor had he, in Fact, borrowed any *other* Money of the Plaintiff, than the very Sum for which He gave the Bond. Notwithſtanding which, the Verdict was taken (through Miſtake, or Inadvertency) for the Plaintiff *generally*, upon BOTH Counts; And the Judgment was entered accordingly, and remained unimpeached.

At the *Time* of the Judgment, the *Penalty* of the Bond was *ſufficient* to have anſwered the *Whole* of the Debt, Intereſt, and Coſts *then* incurred.

But the Defendant had affected very great *Delay*, in various Methods. He had brought a Bill in Equity for an Injunction; and had taken Exceptions to the Anſwer; and hindered the getting the Injunction diſſolved, till *Hilary* Term 1759; When (after arguing the Exceptions) it was diſſolved on the Merits. He then immediately brought a Writ of Error in the Exchequer Chamber, merely for Delay; and aſſigned the Common Errors. Then He pleaded "*Nul tiel Record*" to the *Scire facias* upon the Judgment. So that he prevented the Plaintiff from ſigning his final Judgment, till the 13th Day of this very Month (9 Days ago.)

Theſe Delays having coſt much Time and Money too (as the Coſts taxed always fall ſhort of the Coſts out of Pocket,) and the Intereſt running on; The Caſe was ſo altered, that at *this* Time, the

Penalty

PENALTY of the Bond *alone* was become *insufficient* (by about 150*l.*) to answer the Total of the Debt Interest and Costs *now* incurred.

It was therefore insisted by Mr. *Norton*, on behalf of the Plaintiff, That the Court would not interfere to give their Assistance to the Defendant *contrary* to the plain clear obvious JUSTICE of the Case. He admitted that if no Evidence was given at the Trial, on the second Count, of any Money borrowed by the Defendant of the Plaintiff, there should indeed have been a Verdict taken for the *Defendant*, upon *that* Count; and it was a Mistake, to neglect it: But he is *too late* to complain of that Mistake *now*. If he had complained in *proper* Time, the Penalty of the Bond would *then* have answered the Plaintiff's whole Demand at *that* Time due to him: But as the Defendant had *wilfully and obstinately delayed* the Plaintiff, till the Case is much otherwise, He has no Pretence to apply to the Court to stop the Plaintiff's taking out his Execution upon the Judgment as it now stands.

Lord MANSFIELD—It is admitted that there is a Mistake in the Taking this Verdict; and, consequently, in the Judgment. It may be proper then, first to consider "What is the fair honest Justice "of the Case;" and "whether the Plaintiff cannot come at it, "*although* this Mistake should be rectified." *If* he can, it is to no Purpose, for the Defendant to desire it to be *rectified:* His wisest way will be, to make Satisfaction immediately, without more Expence.

The Plaintiff don't insist to avail Himself of the Mistake in the Verdict and Judgment, *beyond* his *just* Demand.

The Plaintiff is *in Justice* intitled to recover the Sum *really lent* to the Defendant, together with INDIAN *Interest* till the Signing of the *Judgment*; but with only the legal Interest of *this* Country (which is no more than Five *per Cent.*) from the Time of the *Liquidation* of the Debt by the Judgment.

The Plaintiff, having been kept out of his Money by a Writ of Error brought after a Verdict, is intitled to a Satisfaction for this Damage, *under the Statute* of * *Car.* 2; which obliges the Plaintiff in Error to give Security as well for Damages as Costs: Or He may bring an Action of *Debt on the Judgment*, and have Damages *pro detentione Debiti*.

* *V.* 13 *Car.* 2. *Stat.* 2. *c.* 2. § 8, 9, 10.

There are four Courts, (all included under the same Act of Parliament,) to which Writs of Error may be made returnable; namely, The House of Lords; The Court holden before the Lord Chancel-

lor

lor and Treasurer and Judges (under 31 *Ed.* 3.) for examining erroneous Judgments in the Exchequer; The Court of Exchequer-Chamber, holden before the Judges of the Common Pleas and Barons of the Exchequer (under 27 *Eliz. c.* 8.) for examining into Errors in the Judgments of * this Court; And this Court itself, for correcting the Errors of the King's Bench in *Ireland*, Common Pleas here, and other Courts.

* N. B. This is confined to Causes *not commencing here by Original*: For where the Action commences in this Court *by Original*, the Writ of Error is returnable in *Parliament*.

In the first of these, (the House of Lords,) they give sometimes very large, sometimes very small Costs, in their *Discretion*, according to the Nature of the Case and the Reasonableness or Unseasonableness of litigating the Judgment of the Court below.

In the second, It is done by the Lord Chancellor or Lord Keeper personally: And the Practice is, To give Interest from the Day of signing the Judgment to the Day of affirming it there; computed according to the *current*, *not* according to the strictly *legal* Rate of Interest.

In the third, (the Exchequer-Chamber,) the Course is, for the *Officer* to settle it, unless any particular Direction be given by the Court: And He, in taxing the Costs, allows double the Money out of Pocket or thereabouts, but adds no Interest.

In *this* Court, upon Writs of Error from *C. B. &c*, the *Officer* taxes the Costs of Affirmance; and taxes them in the same Manner as he taxes other Costs, though somewhat more liberally: But *Our Officer* never has any Regard to Interest, nor allows it as of Course. *The* COURT *themselves* have sometimes indeed ordered Interest to be computed on the Sum liquidated by the Judgment below: *One* Instance of this was in the Case of the *Bishop of London and Lewen*, against *the Mercers Company*, and is mentioned in 2 *Strange* 931. That was a Writ of Error upon a *Quare Impedit*; And the Judgment below was for 70*l.* for half a Year's Value of the Church, and for a Writ to the Bishop: Which Judgment having been affirmed here, the Defendants in Error moved, in *Easter* Term 5 *G.* 2. for Costs and Damages on 3 *H.* 7. *c.* 10. And they would have had the Damages computed according to the Value of the Church, during the Time of their being kept out of their Presentation. The Court, after Deliberation, agreed that it was in their DISCRETION, to settle the *Quantum* of Damages: But They did not think it right, to give Damages to the *Patron*, in Proportion to the Profits of the Benefice; because He himself would not have been intitled to receive them. They declared therefore that the *Measure* they went by, was the *Interest* of the Money recovered, the legal Interest from the Time of bringing the Writ of Error to the Time of affirming the Judgment. And They directed the Master to compute the Damages ac-

 cordingly,

cordingly, *viz.* legal Intereſt upon the 70*l.* recovered; and to add it to the Coſts.

So here, in the preſent Caſe, Intereſt ought to be paid after the Rate of 9 *per Cent.* according to the *Indian* Allowance, *till* the Aſcertainment of the Sum to be paid, by *ſigning the Judgment*; and *from that* Time, till the *actual Payment* of the Money, after the Rate of 5 *per Cent.* only, upon the accumulated Sum aſcertained by the Judgment: For *that* is the *real Damage* which the Plaintiff has ſuſtained by the Delay of his Execution and the Detention of his Debt.

The *Juſtice* of the Caſe is plain: And the *Law* is agreeable to it.

Mr. *Morton* agreed that his Client, the Defendant, had better acquieſce in paying the Plaintiff what was *juſtly* and *fairly* due to Him, voluntarily and without further Litigation, than to render himſelf liable to the Coſts of another Action.

Wherefore He *gave up* his preſent Motion: And no Rule was taken upon it.

Bondfield, qui tam &c, *verſ.* Milner.

IN a *qui tam* Action, for Uſury, Mr. *Stowe* ſhewed Cauſe againſt making abſolute a Rule of Mr. *Yates*'s, for diſcharging a Rule which had been before obtained by Mr. *Stowe* Himſelf, for AMENDING THE DECLARATION, in altering the *Date* of the Note; (all being *in Paper*.) He cited *Griffith qui tam &c* v. *Hollyer*, *Trin.* 29, 30 *G.* 2. *B. R.* Where the Plaintiff had Leave to amend his Declaration, by laying the *Venue* at *Alceſter* in *Warwickſhire*, inſtead of *Woodſtock* in *Oxfordſhire*; And the Court were clear "that it "might be done at any Time whilſt the Proceedings were in "Paper:" And Mr. Juſtice DENISON declared and repeated "that "it was an Amendment at *Common* Law."

Mr. *Norton*, and Mr. *Yates*, *contra*—The laſt Day of laſt Term, this Motion was * *denied* to Mr. *Stowe*. Here is *Iſſue joined*, and entered on the Roll; And *many Terms* have elapſed ſince the Commencement of this Action: And the Amendment propoſed is to vary the Count, to add a *new* Count, which is a new kind of Action; For it is to *alter the Date* of the Notes.

* *Hodſon, qui tam &c.* v. *Milner*, *Trin.* 1760. (a Caſe very like this; though not preciſely the ſame.)

The *Statutes* do not extend to *penal* Actions: And at *Common* Law, they come too late.

In

In Sir *William Turner*'s Case, * it is not allowed *after Issue joined*: And Mr. *Stowe*'s former Rule was † *discharged* on that Authority, upon Mr. *Altham*'s Motion.

* 2 *Mod.* 144.

† *Hodgson, qui tam &c.* v. *Milner, Trin.* 1760.

Lord MANSFIELD—The Rule is, "That whilst All is *in Paper*, "You may amend." Here, he has only mistaken the *Date*. In the *Exchequer*, they amend *penal* Informations. To be sure, the STATUTES of Amendment do not extend to *penal* Actions. This is an Amendment at *Common* Law.

Mr. Just. DENISON—There is no Difference between *Civil* and *Penal* Actions; where they apply as for an Amendment at *Common* Law, and All is *in Paper*.

|| *Per Cur.* unanimously,

Mr. *Yates*'s Rule, to shew Cause "Why upon Payment of the "Plaintiff's Costs of making the former Rule of last Term "absolute, together with the Costs of this Application, the "said former Rule (of *Wednesday prox. post tres Trin.*) should "not be discharged," was now itself DISCHARGED.

|| Note—The present Resolution (though Contrary to Sir *William Turner*'s Case) is agreeable to many later Determinations; particularly, to *D'Oyley* v. *Daniel, Tr.* 1732. 5, 6 *G.* 2. *Strode* v. *Tilly, H.* 15 *G.* 2. *Rivet* v. *Cholmeley, H.* 17 *G.* 2. *Hallet* v. *Hallet, Tr.* 21 *G.* 2. and *Griffith* v. *Hollier, Tr.* 1756: All which were *qui tam* Actions, and All in this Court. (*Hodson qui tam* v. *Milner* was in the Hurry of the last Day of a Term; and only two Judges in Court.)

Sir William Yea *vers.* Fouraker.

Monday 24th *November* 1760.

IN an Action upon a Promissory Note, tried before Mr. Just. *Noel* upon the Western Circuit, It was there ruled by Him, and confirmed by this Court, without Argument, upon a Motion here for a New Trial, "That an Acknowledgment of the Debt, *after* the Commencement of the Action, takes it *out* of the *Statute of Limitations*."

Rex *vers.* Peter Wright, Robert Voss, et al'.

ON the Motion of Mr. *Norton*, who moved on behalf of the Relations and Friends of one Mrs. *Frances Savage*, a Woman addicted to and almost destroyed by Liquor, representing that She was in the Hands of very improper Persons, who were suspected to be using Artifices with Her, in Order to the obtaining a Will from Her, when She was under very improper Circumstances of Mind to make One; and was too much under their Influence, even if

 her

her Underſtanding and Memory had been more perfect, and leſs diſordered by intemperate Drinking; A Rule was made upon the Defendants to ſhew Cauſe Why an Information ſhould not be exhibited againſt them for the Miſdemeanors charged in the Affidavits.

☞ It was alſo added to the Rule, *at firſt* (and *without* any Rule to ſhew Cauſe, as to this part of it,) " That *Frank Nichols Dr.* of Phy-" ſic, *Robert Halifax Apothecary*, *Catharine Forcer* Widow (who " was *Mother-in-Law* to Mrs. *Savage*, then a *Widow*,) *Thomas* " *Lloyd* Gentleman (*Attorney* for Mrs *Forcer*,) *John Little* and *Anne* " his Wife (*Relations* to Mrs. *Savage*,) *Margaret Francis*, a *Nurſe*, " and *Jane Francis* a *Maid-Servant*, ſhould at all proper Times and " ſeaſonable Hours, reſpectively be admitted and have free Acceſs " to the ſaid Mrs. *Frances Savage*, Widow, Daughter-in-Law of the " ſaid *Catharine Forcer*, at the Dwelling-houſe of the ſaid *Robert* " *Voſs* (One of the Defendants) in *Furnival's Inn Court Holbourne*, " to conſult with, adviſe, and aſſiſt the ſaid *Frances Savage*."

N.B. It was repreſented, that She was too infirm and weak, to be brought into Court by an *Habeas Corpus:* (And in Fact, She died the next Day.)

Tueſday 25th *November* 1760.

Doe, ex dimiſſ. Long, *verſ.* Laming.

THIS was a Special Caſe, which aroſe upon an Ejectment brought for GAVEL-KIND Lands in *Kent*, tried before Lord *Mansfield* at *Niſi prius*.

The Ejectment was brought by the Heir at Law of One *Martin Long*, for an undivided fourth Part of One Meſſuage &c, in the Pariſh of *St. John the Baptiſt* in the Iſle of *Thanet* in *Kent*.

Special Caſe ſtated for the Opinion of the Court—

Martin Long, being ſeiſed in Fee &c, made his Will &c; and thereby deviſed thus—" I give and deviſe One equal undivided fourth " Part &c, unto my Nephew *Martin Read*, and to the *Heirs of his* " *Body* lawfully to be begotten, as well Females as Males, *and to* " *their Heirs and Aſſigns for ever*, to be divided equally, Share and " Share alike, as Tenants in Common and not as Joint-tenants. " Alſo I give and deviſe one Other equal undivided fourth Part " &c, unto my *Niece in Law Grace Read*, *Widow* of my *late Ne-* " *phew Edward Read deceaſed*; and to the *Heirs of her Body* law-" fully begotten, as well Males as Females, and to *their Heirs and* " *Aſſigns for ever*, to be divided equally Share and Share alike,

" as Tenants in Common and not as Joint-tenants. Alſo I give and " deviſe one Other equal undivided fourth Part &c, unto *my Niece* " ANNE, now Wife of *William Corniſh*, and to the HEIRS OF HER " BODY lawfully begotten or to be begotten, *as well* FEMALES as " Males, and TO THEIR HEIRS AND ASSIGNS FOR EVER, to be " divided *equally* Share and Share alike, as *Tenants in Common* and " not as Joint-tenants. Alſo I give and deviſe One other equal undi- " vided fourth Part, &c, unto my Niece *Sarah* now Wife of *S.* " *Hooper*, and to the *Heirs Females and Males of her Body* lawfully " begotten or to be begotten, to be divided (as before,) and *to their* " *Heirs and Aſſigns for ever.*"

There were likewiſe in this Will, other Deviſes of other Eſtates; *viz.* " I give and deviſe unto my Nephew *J. Tickner* his *Heirs and* " *Aſſigns for ever*, All that &c &c." " I give and deviſe my Farm " &c, unto my Siſter *Catharine*, Wife of *William Abbot*, and to her " *Aſſigns*, for and during the *Term of her natural Life*; and from " and after her Deceaſe, I give the ſame unto my Nephew her Son " *William Abbot* and the *Heirs of his Body* lawfully to be begotten, " *for ever*: And for want of ſuch *Iſſue*, I give and deviſe the ſame " to the *right Heirs* of Me, for ever."

" And as concerning my Meſſuages &c, I give and deviſe the " ſame to *Elizabeth Long*, *her Heirs and Aſſigns for ever.*"

" And as concerning &c, I give and deviſe the ſame to my Siſter " *Sarah Tailor* and her *Aſſigns*, during her *natural Life*, provided " She keep the ſame in Repair: And from and after her Deceaſe, " I give the ſame to my Siſter *Elizabeth Long* her *Heirs and Aſſigns* " *for ever.*"

" Alſo I give and bequeath to my Niece *Sarah* now Wife of " *William Long*, and to the *Heirs of her Body*, the *Sum of* 150*l.* " of like Money to be divided between them equally."

The Teſtator lived two Years after making this Will: He died in *May* 1751.

At the *Time* of making the ſaid Will, the Teſtator's ſaid Niece ANNE CORNISH, Wife of *Thomas Corniſh*, had *two Daughters* (by her ſaid Huſband) then living; *viz. Elizabeth* and *Anne*.

ANNE CORNISH, the Teſtator's Niece, died *after* the Time of *Making the Will*; but in the *Life-time of the Teſtator*: And her two *Daughters*, *Elizabeth* and *Anne*, *ſurvived* both their ſaid *Mother* and alſo the *Teſtator Martin Long*.

The Whole Premiffes are *Gavel-kind*.

The Queftion fubmitted to the Court is—" Whether, by the " DEATH of ANNE CORNISH (the Mother) in the Life-time of " the Teftator, the Devife, as to her One fourth Part, was VOID " or LAPSED: Or Whether the faid One fourth Part devifed as " above, or *any* and *what Part* thereof, on the Teftator's Death, " DESCENDED to the Leffor of the Plaintiff, as *Heir at Law* to the " Teftator.

Mr. *Filmer* Junior, argued this Cafe for the Plaintiff.

He endeavoured to maintain that Either the *Whole* of the One fourth Part devifed to *Anne Cornifh* was *lapfed* by her dying in the Teftator's Life-time; Or, at leaft, that fome *Part* of it was fo; and that what was lapfed would confequently *defcend* to the Leffor of the Plaintiff, as Heir at Law to the Teftator.

ANNE CORNISH, the Teftator's Niece would have taken, He faid, if She had furvived the Teftator, an Eftate in TAIL *General*; Or, if not fo, then She muft have taken *One third* Part of the *Fee Simple*, as Tenant in Common with her two Daughters: If the former, the Whole is lapfed; If the latter, One third only.

But He conceived that She would have taken an Eftate in *general Tail*, by PURCHASE, under this Devife.

The Word " *Heirs*," (in the *plural* Number,) is a Word of *legal Limitation*: And there is no Inftance, in Cafe of a *mere* LEGAL Eftate, where " *Heirs* of the Body" have been conftrued to be Words of *Purchafe*. The Cafe of *Bagfhaw* v. *Spencer* was a TRUST.

The Court will keep to the *legal technical* Interpretation.

The Cafe of *Goodright* v. *Pulleyn et al'*, *M.* 11 *G.* 1. *B. R.* reported in 2 *Ld. Raym.* 1437. is material to this Point.

There was likewife a Cafe before the Council, on 18th *March* 1730, at which Ld. *Raymond* and Ld. Ch. J. *Eyre* were Both prefent. It was between *Morris*, on the Demife of *William Andrews*, and *Ifaac Le Gay* and *John Wood*; upon an Appeal from *Barbadoes*. It was a Devife " to *Lucretia*, for Life; then to *Heirs* of the Body " of *Lucretia*, and their Heirs; and if She died without fuch *Heir* " of her Body, then over." This was holden to be an Eftate Tail in *Lucretia*.

There were also two late Cases in Chancery; *viz. Wright* v. *Pearson, June 6th* 1758, *Trin.* 31 *G.* 2. Where *Thomas Raleigh* was holden to take an Estate Tail: (This Case was upon a Trust-Estate.) The Other was *King* v. *Burchell,* 20th *November* 1759, before the Lord Keeper *Henley. John Blunt* devised to his Wife, for her Life; then to *John Harris,* for Life; then to the *Heir* Male of *John Harris,* and his Heirs; And for want of such Issue, then over. *John Harris* was holden to have taken an Estate Tail; though there were Words of Limitation over. An Appeal was brought; but afterwards deserted.

The Word "*Heirs,*" in the *Plural,* with Words of Limitation added to it, has *never* been construed to be a Word of *Purchase:* But the Word "*Heir,*" in the *singular,* has been construed to be a Word of *Limitation.*

An Estate *Tail* to *Anne Cornish* best answers the apparent *Intention* of the Testator.

But if "the Heirs of her Body" are to be here construed as Words of *Purchase*; Then *Anne Cornish and her two Daughters* must take an Estate in *Fee Simple,* as Tenants in *Common* and not as Joint-tenants; *Each* of them *One third* of the whole One fourth Part: And consequently, as She was (in *that* Construction of the Devise) made Tenant in Common, in *Thirds,* with her two Daughters, but died before the Testator; her *One third lapsed* by her Death, and *descends* to the Plaintiff as Heir at Law.

Mr. *Thomas Clarke* (of *Lincoln's Inn*) argued for the Defendant.

He proposed to consider the Question, under two general Heads; 1st, The *Intention* of the Testator, to be collected from the whole Will; 2dly. The *Operation of Law,* to effectuate such Intention.

First—The *Intention* of the Testator plainly was, "That *All the* "*Children* of his Niece *Anne Cornish,* both Sons and Daughters "should *take*; and *they only:* Though it is not indeed so clear, Whether He meant that they should take as Tenants in Common *with* their Mother; or *after* her Death. He probably meant it as a Description of Heirs in Gavel-kind: But He certainly meant, that they should take *as* Purchasers; and that they should take an Estate in *Fee*; and not that *Anne Cornish* should take an Estate Tail.

This Intention is plainly to be collected, He said, from several other Clauses in the Will. The several other Devises shew, that, by "Heirs of the Body," the Testator meant *Children:* Particularly,

larly, the Bequeſt to *Sarah* the Wife of *William Long*, and to the *Heirs of her Body*, of the *Sum of* 150 *l.* to be divided between them equally; which can be taken in no other Senſe. And in the Deviſe to *William Abbot* and the Heirs of his Body, He explains his Meaning, by adding "and for Want of ſuch *Iſſue*."

Secondly—The *Operation of Law* will *effectuate* the Intention of the Teſtator, where it is *plain* and *manifeſt*. And here is a plain manifeſt Intention of the Teſtator, "That his Deviſees ſhould take "by *Purchaſe*, and *not* by Deſcent."

And "Heir*s* of the Body," (in the *plural*) may be Words of PURCHASE, where the *Intention* of the Teſtator is clear and evident. There is *no* ſuch Diſtinction as that which Mr. *Filmer* has laid down, "That where the Words of Limitation are grafted upon the Word "Heir in the *ſingular* Number, that Word ſhall be conſtrued a "Word of *Purchaſe*; But where the Words of Limitation are graft-"ed upon the Word Heir*s* in the *plural*, that plural Word Heirs "ſhall *always* be conſtrued a Word of *Limitation*."

* *Mich.* 1748, 22 *G.* 2. *in Canc'.*
† *V. poſt*

In the Caſe of * *Bagſhaw* v. *Spencer*, "Heir*s* of the Body," were conſtrued to be Words of *Purchaſe*. And in that Caſe, Lord *Hardwicke* mentioned a Caſe of † *Liſle* v. *Gray*; where the Word was *plural*, and the ſame Determination was made: And that Caſe of *Liſle* v. *Gray*, was upon a *Deed*, and at *Common* Law.

‡ *Fitz-Gibbon* 112, and 2 *Ld. Raym.* 1561.

Law v. *Davis et al'*, ‡ *M.* 3 *G.* 1. *B. R.* was a Deviſe "to *Benjamin Jevon* and the Heir*s* of his Body lawfully to be begotten;" And Words of Limitation were ſuperadded: Yet it was holden to be an Eſtate for Life; not in Tail.

‖ See it alſo, in *Viner's Abr.* Tit. *Remainder*, *Pa.* 393. Note on Letter G. *pl.* 7.

All the Parts of a Deviſe ought to be taken into the Conſtruction: And the Intention of this Teſtator was, "That all the Devi-"ſees ſhould here take by Purchaſe." And the Words are ſufficient and apt enough for that Purpoſe. In Proof of his Allegation, He cited 1 *Co.* 95. *Shelley*'s Caſe, cited in 1 *Ld. Raym.* 205. by Ld. Ch. J. *Treby*, and confirmed by Him. 1 *Ld. Raym.* 203. *Luddington* v. *Kime*: And *Clerk* v. *Day*, or *Cheeke* v. *Day*, there cited, in *Pa.* 205. ‖ 1 *Inſt.* 26. *b.* Deviſe "to *Roberge*, and to the Heir*s* "of *John Mandevile* her late Huſband, on her Body begotten," was adjudged only an Eſtate for Life in *Roberge*; And that the Eſtate Tail veſted in her Son; "Heirs of the Body of his Father," being a *good* Name of *Purchaſe*.

If it be objected "That this Intention could not operate to the "Daughters of *Anne Corniſh* as *Heirs* of the Body of *Anne Corniſh* "who was *then living*, (For that Nemo eſt Hæres *viventis*;") The Caſe

Case of *Burchett* v. *Durdant*, 2 *Ventr*. 211. (which was Six Times determined, under different Names,) is a full Answer to that Objection; and shews that Persons *may* take an immediate and vested Estate, under the Denomination of "Heirs of the Body of a Person "*living*."

Upon the Whole, The Court will *depart* from the strict Rules of Words of *rigid* legal Limitation, where the *Intention* of the Testator is manifest: And it is here sufficiently plain and clear, to induce the Court to do so in the present Case.

N.B. This Argument was begun upon the 21st of *November*; from which Day, it was Adjourned to the present 25th. And now—

Mr. *Filmer* replied—He denied, that the Testator's *Intention* was clear plain and manifest; either upon the particular Clause in question, or upon the whole Will taken together. The Intention supposed by Mr. *Clarke* is opposite to the Testator's plain positive Words. The plain Words must be adhered to; And the impertinent or inconsistent Words, rejected. *Shelley*'s Case, 1 *Co*. 89.

But *if* the Intention was clear and plain, yet there is a *Difference* between LEGAL Estates, and TRUSTS: In *Bagshaw* v. *Spencer*, Ld. *Hardwicke made this Distinction*; which He founded on the Case of *Coulson* v. *Coulson*. And even in Chancery, there is a Distinction (upon this Point) between what they call a Trust *executed*, and a Trust *executory*.

As to the Word "Heirs" (in the Plural,) being descriptive of the Person, although *Nemo est Hæres Viventis*—He observed that Mr. Justice *Fortescue*, in the Case of *Goodright* v. *Pullyn et al'*, thought that the Word "*his*" [Heirs] would, in grammatical Construction, properly refer to * *Nicholas*. * See 2 *Ld. Raym*. 1440.

In all Mr. *Clarke*'s Cases, except *Law* v. *Davis*, there was a Limitation for Life: And that Case stands upon it's own Circumstances. The Words "Heirs of the Body" were there explained by the following Words, "*that is to say*, to his 1st, 2d, 3d, and every "other Son and Sons successively &c."

So, in *Lisle* v. *Gray*, "Heirs Male" had a plain Reference to the Four Sons.

The Quotation from *Shelley*'s Case, 1 *Co*. 95. *b*. is only a Case put by *Anderson*, *arguendo*: The *Resolution* is contrary.

As to *Luddington* v. *Kime*—It only proves That "*Issue*" may be a Word of Purchase: But it does not prove, That "*Heirs* of the "Body," may be so.

Upon the Whole, *Anne Cornish* must have taken an Estate *Tail*; not an Estate for her Life only: But, *at least*, She was to have taken *One third of the Fee Simple*, as Tenant in *Common* with her two Daughters; For a Devise "to *A. et liberis suis*, and to their Heirs," is a *Joint-Fee* to *All*. So is *Co. Litt.* 9. *a.* expres: Which is allowed and affirmed in the Case of *Oates*, *on the Demise of Elizabeth Hatterley*, v. *Jackson*, 2 *Strange* 1172.

Lord MANSFIELD—The Words are—"to my Niece *A. C.* and "to the HEIRS OF HER BODY lawfully begotten or to be begotten, "*as well Females* as Males, *and to their Heirs and Assigns for ever*; "to be divided *equally*, Share and Share alike, as Tenants in *Com-* "*mon*, and not as Joint-tenants."

The Question is, "Whether it be contrary to the Rules of Law, to understand, in this Case, "*Heirs of the Body* of *A. C.*" as a De- "scription of CHILDREN: For that such was the INTENTION *of* "*the Testator*, there can be little Doubt.

It is to be lamented, that Questions of this kind have occasioned so much Litigation and Expence. The best way to settle them, is, to reduce the Matter, if possible, to some *certain Rules*.

It is clear, that where an Estate is given to the Ancestor "*and* "*his Heirs*" (either general or special,) the Term denotes the *Quantity* of the Estate which the Ancestor takes; *viz.* either Fee Simple, or Fee Tail.

It is clear too, that a Person to take as a Purchaser, may be described from *every* Course of Descent; as Heir at Law, Heir in Borough-English, Heir or Heir-Male of the Body.

By an ancient Maxim of Law, although the Estate be limited to the Ancestor, *expressly* "FOR LIFE, *and after his Death to his* "*Heirs*, (general or special,) the Heir shall take by *Descent*, and the Fee shall vest in the *Ancestor*.

This Maxim was originally introduced in favour of the *Lord*, to prevent his being deprived of the Fruits of the Tenure; and likewise for the Sake of *Specialty-Creditors*.

The Ancestor, had the Limitation been construed a contingent Remainder, *might* have *destroyed* it for his own Benefit. *If* he did *not* destroy it, the Lord would have lost the Fruits of his Tenure; and the Specialty-Creditors, their Debts. Therefore the Law said, "Be the *Intention* as it may, where an Estate is given to the An- "cestor *and his Heirs*, The *Fee* shall *vest in* HIM."

The *Reason* of this Maxim has long *ceased*; because Tenures are now abolished, and Contingent Remainders may be preserved from being defeated before they come *in Esse*: Yet, having become a *Rule of Property*, it is *adhered to* in all Cases *literally within it*, although the Reason has ceased. But where there are Circumstances which take the Case OUT *of the Letter* of this Rule, it is *departed from*, in *favour of Intention*; because the *Reason* of the Rule has *ceased*.

In the Case of *King* v. *Melling*, (1 *Vent*. 231.) a Case was cited by Ld. Ch. J. *Hale*, where a Man devised "to his Eldest Son for "Life, *et non aliter*; and after his Deceafe, to the Sons of his "Body:" It was holden to be but an Estate for Life, by reason of the Words * "ET NON ALITER." Yet the "*non aliter*" was im- "plied, if it had not been expressed: But it shewed the *clear Intention* of the Testator; and the Construction was made so as to *effectuate* that Intention.

* See this cited Case discussed at large, in the Case of *Robinson* v. *Robinson*, P. 1756, 29 G. 2. *B. R.* ante pa. 38.

And in a later Case of *Backhouse* v. *Wells*, *M.* and *H.* 12 *Ann*. Where the Devise was "to *J. B.* for his *Life* ONLY, without Im- "peachment of Waste; and from and after his Death, then to the "Issue Male of his Body lawfully to be begotten; with Remainder "to the Heirs Males of the Body of that Issue;" The whole Court were of Opinion, That the Devisee, was, by that Devise, made Tenant for Life, with Remainder to the Issue in Tail. They † held, that the Words "for Life *only*," clearly and expressly shewed the *Intention* of the Testator; and thereby took the Case *out* of the General Rule, and turned the Words *commonly* used as Words of *Limitation*, into Words of *Purchase*.

† *V. Lucas's Rep.* 181 to 184. *Fortescue's Rep.* 139. and *Abr. of Cases in Equity* 184. *pl.* 27.

Indeed such a Construction as this, cannot be made, but in Cases where it is *agreeable to the clear Intention* of the Testator, that this should be the Construction. For though the Devise be "for Life "*only*," yet if the Intention of the Testator should appear, upon the whole Will taken together, to be manifestly *otherwise*; It shall, in *such* Case, be construed an Estate Tail: As in the Case of ‖ *Robinson* v. *Robinson*, *M.* 1756, 30 *G.* 2. *B. R.*

‖ *V. ante, pa.* 38. (*ut supra.*)

In the Case of ‡ *Lisle* v. *Gray*, (which was upon a *Deed*) the Words "Heirs Male of the Body", were, by the *necessary Construction* arising from the Context, turned into Words of ‡ Purchase.

‡ *V.* Sir *Tho. Jones* 114. 2 *Lev.* 223. *Pollexf.* 582. *Raym.* 278, 302, 315.

In the Case of *Allgood* v. *Withers*, * Where One *Isaac Allgood* had by *Deed* conveyed his Freehold Land to Trustees and their Heirs, and his Leasehold to Trustees and their Executors, Upon Trust that they should apply the Rents and the Benefit of Redemption,

* In Chancery, on 4th *July* 1735.

to

to the Plaintiff *Hannah Withers for Life*; and after her Death, to the *Heirs of the Body* of the said *Hannah Withers* and of *Isaac Allgood* (since deceased) and of *Hannah Glass* and *Mary Allgood*, their Heirs Executors and Assigns, during the Continuance of the Estate in the Premisses; The Question was Whether *Hannah Withers* took for Life, or in Tail: And Ld. *Talbot* held "That She took an Estate "for *Life*; and that the Heirs took as Purchasers."

In the Case of *Bagshaw* and *Spencer*, *All* the Cases upon this Subject were ransacked and thoroughly considered: And Lord *Hardwicke* held "that *Heirs of the Body*, (after an Estate for Life to the "Father,) should be construed Words of *Purchase*."

To take off the Authority of Decisions in *Chancery*, It was contended at the Bar, "That as to this Point, there was a *Distinction* "between a TRUST and a LEGAL *Estate*; and that even in *Chan-* "*cery*, there was a Distinction upon this Point, between what they "call a Trust *executed*, and a Trust *executory*."

It is true, These Distinctions are to be met with, and have often been mentioned: But there don't seem to be much Solidity in Either.

ALL Trusts are *executory*: They are to be executed by a *Conveyance*; And the Parties have a Right to apply to a Court of Equity, for such Conveyance.

In *Bagshaw* and *Spencer*, the Trust was *executed*, in the Sense of the Distinction, and as contrasted with a Trust executory.

There seems to be as little Ground, in respect of *this* Point, for the *other* Distinction between a *Trust* and a *legal* Estate.

A Court of EQUITY is *as much bound by positive Rules and general Maxims concerning Property* (though the Reason of them may now have ceased,) as a Court of LAW is.

Whatever is sufficient, upon a Devise, to make an Exception out of the Rule, holds in the Case of a *legal* Estate, as well as in the Case of a *Trust*. If the *Intention* of the Testator be *contrary* to the Rules of Law, it can no more take Place in a Court of Equity, than in a Court of Law: If the Intention be illegal, it is *equally void* in *both*. A Court of Equity can't support an Intention in the Testator, to create a Perpetuity, or to limit a Fee upon a Fee, or to make a Chattel descend to Heirs, or Land to Executors. On the other hand, *If* the Intention be *not* contrary to Law, a Court of *Common* Law is as much bound to construe and effectuate the Will *according* *to that Intention* of the Testator, as a Court of Equity can be. Upon the very Point now in question, the Determinations have been agreeable to this Reasoning. Therefore where the *Trust* of a Real Estate was devised " to *A. for Life*, and after his Death to " the Heirs of his Body," Lord *Hardwicke* decreed a Conveyance to *A. in Tail*; although the Estate devised to *A.* expressly " for " Life, left no Room to doubt of the Testator's *Intention*: But the Rule of Law said, " The Heir of the Body should take by Descent, " and not by Purchase;" and he thought, the Rule bound a *Trust*, as well as a legal Estate. *

* *Garth* against *Baldwin*, in Chancery, 18th *July* 1755.

Where there are Circumstances which take a Case *out of* the Rule, the Exception holds upon a *legal* Estate, *as much* as upon a *Trust*.

The Case of *Lisle* v. *Gray* was a *legal* Estate, upon a Deed: And the Judgment was *affirmed*, (though, by Mistake, it is said in Sir *Thomas Jones*, to have been *reversed*.)

Sir *Joseph Jekyll*'s Decree in *Papillon* and *Voyce*, was upon a *legal* Estate: And Lord *King*, after considering, did not differ from Him; but reversed the Decree, expressly upon a *new* Point, upon the Discovery of Articles in 1697.

Some of the other Cases I have mentioned, were likewise upon *legal* Estates.

It is true, Ld. *Hardwicke*, in *Bagshaw* and *Spencer*, laid Hold of this Distinction, to avoid expressly over-ruling the Certificate in *Coulson* and *Coulson*: But He certainly did not agree in Opinion with that Certificate. In speaking of it, when he delivered his Judgment in *Bagshaw* and *Spencer*, He expressed Himself thus— " IF " *that Case be Law*:" And One of the last Things he did in the Court of Chancery was, to send a like Case to this Court for their Opinion; And He told Me, " He did it, to have *Coulson* and *Coul-* " *son reconsidered*."

IT APPEARS therefore from All that I have been saying, That there is NO such *fixed invariable* Rule as has been supposed, " That " Words of Limitation shall NEVER in any Case be construed as " Words of Purchase."

And the present Case is the strongest that I can form any Imagination of, to justify a Construction, " that the Heirs of the Body " of *Anne Cornish shall here* take as PURCHASERS." The Devise can not take Effect *at all*, but must be *absolutely void*, unless the Heirs of her Body take as *Purchasers*.

It *must be observed*, that the Lands devised by this Will are Gavel-kind. The Testator had Nephews and Nieces, and great Nephews and great Nieces: And He provides for them, by 4 distinct Clauses in his Will, according to the 4 distinct Stocks.

It is agreed, that where Words of Limitation are grafted upon the Word "*Heir*" in the *singular* Number, *such Heir shall take by* Purchase. This is *settled* * in *Archer*'s Case, and was *admitted* in the Case of *Dubber, on the Demise of Trollope*, v. *Trollope*, *P.* 8 *G.* 2. *B. R.* (though that Case was distinguished from *Archer*'s Case, by having † *no* Words of Limitation superadded to the Words "first "Heir Male.") The Distinction is, That where it appears to be the *Intention* of the Testator, that there should be a *Succession in Tail*, it would totally *defeat* that Intention, if All were to vest in the *first* Son: But where it does *not* appear that the Testator intended a Succession in Tail, there indeed the Using the Word "*Heir*" in the *singular* Number, may be a Circumstance of great Weight.

* 1 *Co.* 66.

† *V. Robinson on Gavel kind*, *pa.* 95. and *Abridgment of Cases in Equity, Vol.* 2. *pa.* 317. *pl.* 31.

Now the Term "*Heirs*," (in the *plural*,) in the Case of Gavel-kind Lands, *answers* to the Term "*Heir*" (in the *singular*) in the common Case of Lands which are *not* Gavel-kind: For the Word "Heir" (in the *singular*) would *not serve* for *Gavel-kind* Lands; It *must* be "Heirs" (in the *plural*.)

Therefore All the Arguments and Reasonings that are applicable to the Word "*Heir*" (in the singular,) in the *common* Case of Lands *not* being Gavel-kind, hold with equal Strength and Propriety, when applied to the *plural* Termination "*Heirs*," when the Lands *are Gavel-kind.*

And it is manifest that the Testator does not here mean, that this One Fourth should go in a *Course of Descent* in Gavel-kind; For He gives it to the Heirs of her Body, *as well Females*, as Males; and mentions *Females*, not only expressly and particularly, but even prior to Males. Therefore they can *not take otherwise* than as Purchasers. It would be a *void* Devise, if the Words were to be construed as Words of *Limitation:* For He breaks the Gavel-kind Descent, by giving it to *Females* as well as Males. It can not *descend* to Females as well as Males, by the Rules of Gavel-kind: And yet He seems to lay the chief Stress upon the Word "*Females*." He adds likewise, "and to their Heirs and Assigns for ever, to be *divided* "*equally Share and Share alike:*" Nay, He goes further—"as *Tenants* "*in Common* and not as Joint-tenants." But this could not be, if they were to take in the Course of *Gavel-kind Descent:* For in such Case, they must take as *Co-parceners.*

The Testator's Disposition of *One* of the Proportions of his Estate shews his Intent as to the *rest*: I mean the Devise of the One Fourth to the *Widow* of his deceased Nephew *Edward Read*, and to the Heirs of her Body &c; which can receive no other Construction, but that *those* Heirs of the Body must *take as* PURCHASERS. For though this Nephew was dead, yet He uses the very same Words in this Devise as in the rest: But He could not mean that his Nephew's *Widow* should take an Estate *Tail* in that *whole* One Fourth, or a *joint Fee* with her Children in any *Part* of it. Therefore the *necessary* Construction of *that* Devise is a strong Argument of his *Intention and Meaning* as to the *rest*.

As to *Anne Cornish's* taking a FEE *jointly with her two Daughters*, in *Thirds*, as Tenants in Common; There can be no Ground for *such* a Construction. For it is clearly the Testator's Intention, that the Heirs of *Anne Cornish*'s Body should not take till *after her Death*: And as the Devise to *Her* has no Words of Limitation added to it, It is of Course a Devise to Her *for her Life*; and what She would have taken, if She had survived the Testator would have been an Estate for *Life*.

Upon the Whole, As no Man can doubt of this Testator's INTENTION; And as this is the ONLY *Method of* EFFECTUATING *it*; And as there is *no Rule of Law* that prevents Heirs taking *as Purchasers*, where the Intention of the Testator *requires* that they should do so; I am of Opinion that Judgment ought to be given for the Defendant.

Mr. Just. DENISON concurred with His Lordship in Opinion, "That Courts of LAW (as well as Courts of Equity) will always "construe Wills agreeably to the *Intention* of the Testator, if such "Intention be *not contrary* to and *inconsistent* with the Rules of Law:" And He shewed that the Intention of the Testator, in the present Case, must have been, "that the Heirs of the Body of his Niece "*Anne Cornish* should take as *Purchasers*;" making the like Observations as his Lordship had done, upon the Lands being *Gavel-kind*, and their being devised to the Heirs *Female* as well as Male.

And He held, that it is *not* disagreeable to or inconsistent with the Rules of Law, That "*Heirs of the Body*" should, in *some* Cases, be construed as *Designatio Personæ*: (a Position, not to be disputed, at *this* Time, after so many concurring Resolutions.) And this Case now before the Court is *One* of the Cases where they must be so construed. Therefore the Heirs of the Body of *A. C.* must here take *by* PURCHASE: They can take no other way.

And

And there is no Foundation for ſuppoſing that *Anne Corniſh*, if She had ſurvived her Uncle, could have taken any Eſtate *jointly with her Daughters*, as Tenants in *Common*.

(Mr. Juſt. FOSTER was abſent.)

Mr. Juſt. WILMOT premiſed, That the Court were obliged to the Gentlemen who had argued this Caſe at the Bar, for declining to go into that long String of Caſes uſually cited upon this Subject. For the Principle that muſt govern all Caſes of this kind, is the INTENTION of the Teſtator, *provided* it be not inconſiſtent with the Rules of Law. And all Caſes which depend upon the Intention of the Teſtator (which is the Pole-Star for the Direction of Deviſes) are beſt determined upon comparing all the Parts of the Deviſe itſelf, without looking into a Multitude of other Caſes: For Each ſtands pretty much upon its own Circumſtances; And One is no Rule for Another, or very ſeldom at leaſt.

Here, the Teſtator *intended*, beyond all Doubt, That the *Children* of his Nephews and Nieces ſhould take the *Inheritance in Fee Simple*, both Males and Females, *per Capita*, as Tenants in Common. And this is a legal Intention.

But this Intention can not *take Effect* by giving an Eſtate in *Tail* or in *Fee* to the *firſt* Taker: For the Intention of the Teſtator muſt be *ſubſervient to the Law*; and not the Law to the Intention of the Teſtator. Now a Teſtator, be his Intention what it will, can not make an Eſtate deſcend to Males and Females All together; nor Gavel-kind Lands to deſcend to them as Tenants in Common. The Teſtator's Intention can not, therefore, *take Place*, by giving *Anne Corniſh* an Eſtate *Tail*.

Well then! What is to be done? Why (as my Lord *Coke* ſays) You are to *mould* the barbarous Words and Expreſſions of the Teſtator, ſo as to *effectuate* his Intention; *if* you can do ſo, *without* going contrary to the Rules of Law: But you cannot do this, *contrary* to the Rules of Law.

The Queſtion therefore, in the preſent Caſe, comes to this; "Whether it be *abſolutely neceſſary*, that the Words *Heirs*, or *Heirs* "*Male*, or *Heirs of the Body*, muſt be, in *all* Caſes, and under *all* "Circumſtances, Words of *Limitation*."

Now it is certain, that in *ſome* Caſes and under *ſome* Circumſtances, they *may* be conſtrued Words of *Purchaſe*; either upon a *Will*, or upon a *Deed*. The Caſe of * *Liſle* v. *Gray* was upon a

* *V. ante, pa.* 1107.

Deed. And there is a Case in *Palm.* 359. *Waker* v. *Snowe,* which was likewise upon a *Deed:* " *Edward Egerton* conveyed Lands by " Fine, to the Use of Himself for Life, Remainder to his first Son " and the Heirs Male of his Body begotten *&c*; and so to his Six " Sons; Remainder to the right Heir Male of the said *Edward* " *Egerton* to be begotten after the said sixth Son, and of his Heirs " Male. This was holden to be only a *contingent* Estate, and " *not an Estate Tail* in *Edward Egerton*; because it was limited to " particular Persons." They are *not* to be construed as Words of *Limitation,* either upon a *Will* or upon a *Deed,* when the *manifest Intention* of the Testator or of the Parties is declared to be, or clearly appears to be, " that they shall *not* be so construed."

Now it is plain, in the present Case, that the Testator did *not* mean to use Words " Heirs of the Body," *as* Words of *Limitation:* It is as clear as if He had expressly said, " I do *not* intend these " Words in that Sense."

And as to *Anne Cornish*'s taking an *equal* Share in Fee Simple, in *Common* with her Daughters—*That* Construction can never hold: For it is most certain, that the Testator did not intend the Division into equal Shares to be *made* till *after Anne Cornish*'s DEATH.

This same Construction is further confirmed by the Clause which devises One Fourth to his *Niece in Law Grace Read,* the *Widow* of his deceased Nephew, and to the Heirs of *her* Body, in the *same* Form of Expression. For it can never be imagined, that it was his Intention to give *Her,* (who was only the Widow of his Nephew,) an *equal* Share of the *Fee Simple and Inheritance,* with his *natural* Relations.

Per Cur. unanimously,
JUDGMENT for the DEFENDANT.

Haward *vers.* Bankes Esq.

Wednesday 26th November 1760.

MR. Serj. *Hewitt,* supported by Mr. *Aspinall,* Mr. *Campbell,* and Mr. *Winn,* moved in *Arrest of Judgment,* after a Verdict for the Plaintiff.

This was an Action *upon the Case,* (or at least, it was *so laid,*) for Damage done to the Plaintiff's Colliery, by what the Defendant had done *in his own* Colliery and within his *own Soil:* Which Colliery belonging to the Defendant lay *near* to that of the Plaintiff, and COMMUNICATED *with it,* though not immediately but *mediately,* there being some other Collieries lying between them.

 The

The Declaration consisted of *three Counts*, all laid as in Trespass *upon the Case*. A Verdict passed for the Plaintiff: And the Judgment was taken as an ENTIRE *Judgment* on all the *three* Counts.

The Objection now made by the Defendant's Counsel, in Arrest of Judgment, was, That two of these 3 Counts are *really* and *essentially* in TRESPASS, (though they are *laid as in Case*;) And that *Trespass* and *Trespass on the Case* can NOT *be* JOINED in the *same Action*. *Hardress* 60, *Preston* v. *Mercer*. 2 *Ld. Raym.* 1399. *Reynolds* v. *Clarke*. 1 *Ld. Raym.* 272. *Courtney* v. *Collett*. *Carthew* 436. S. C. *Courtney* v. *Connett*. *Register of Writs* (two Places) *De fossato terra et fimo impleto*; *per quod &c.*

* *V. ante pa.* 1087, 1088. The DISTINCTION between * *Trespass* and *Case*, they said, was This: IMMEDIATE Damage to the Plaintiff's Property, is a Ground for *Trespass*; CONSEQUENTIAL Damage to it, is a Ground for *Case*. Now two of these 3 Counts are *immediate Acts*, ("that the "Defendant CAUSED great Quantities of Water to be conveyed, "through divers other Collieries, into the Plaintiff's Colliery; "whereby *&c*;") and they are therefore, properly, in Trespass *vi et armis*: But the 3d Count lays the Damage to be *consequential*; and is therefore rightly laid in *Case*. So that it appears upon the Face of the Declaration, "That Trespass and Case ARE here *joined* "*together*."

The Plaintiff's Counsel *agreed* the LAW; but *denied the Fact*: For they insisted, "That *All* the *three* Counts were strictly and properly Trespass upon the CASE, and laid the Damage to be *consequential*, and *not* immediate."

THE COURT (without hearing the Plaintiff's Counsel,) overruled the Objection.

The Plaintiff describes, in his Declaration, a Fact which, *as it comes out* at the Trial, *may*, or *may not*, be a proper strict Trespass: It might, at the Trial, be proved to be *either* Trespass, or Case; either One or the Other of them, *according to the Evidence*. And it appears, that it *was here proved* at the Trial, to be Trespass *upon the Case*. IF it had been proved to be Trespass *vi et armis*, the Plaintiff must in *that* Event, have been *non-suited*. *Before* the Trial, it stood *indifferent*, Whether it would come out to be the One, or the Other. However, in the *Nature* of the Thing, it must be a *consequential* Damage; as the Act complained of was done upon the Plaintiff's *own* Soil.

Let the PLAINTIFF be at Liberty to enter up his Judgment.

The End of * *Michaelmas* Term 1760, 1 *G.* 3.

* Mr. *Justice* FOSTER was at *Bath* during this whole Term.

Hilary

Hilary Term

1 Geo. 3. B. R. 1761.

The Court was now *full* again.

Rex *verſ.* Turlington.

Wedneſday 28th *January* 1761.

ON *Saturday* laſt, the 24th of *January*, a Motion was made for a *Habeas Corpus* to be directed to *Turlington*, the Keeper of a private *Mad-houſe*, commanding him to bring up the Body of Mrs. *Deborah D'Vebre*, who was confined there by her own Huſband.

The Court thought it fit to have a previous Inſpection of Her, by proper Perſons, Phyſicians and Relations; and then to proceed, as the Truth ſhould come out upon ſuch Inſpection. And a Caſe was hinted at where an Inſpection was ordered, in the * laſt Term.

* *Rex* v. *Pt Wright et al'*, 24th *November* 1760. *V. ante* 1100.

A Rule was accordingly made, "That Doctor *Robert Monroe*, "† *Peter Bodkin*, and || *Edmund Kelly* ſhall at all proper Times "and ſeaſonable Hours, reſpectively be admitted and have free Ac- "ceſs to Mrs. *Deborah D'Vebre*, the Wife of *Gabriel D'Vebre*, in "the Affidavit mentioned, at the Mad-houſe kept by *Robert Tur-* "*lington*, at *Chelſea*, in order to conſult with adviſe and aſſiſt the "ſaid *Deborah D'Vebre*."

† Her neareſt Relation.

|| Her Attorney.

On *Monday* the 26th, An Affidavit of Dr. *Monroe*'s was read; and Dr. *Monroe* alſo perſonally aſſured the Court, "That He had "ſeen and converſed with this Woman, and examined her Nurſe; "and ſaw no ſort of Reaſon to ſuſpect that She was or had been "diſordered in her Mind: On the Contrary, He found Her to be "very ſenſible, and very cool and diſpaſſionate."

Lord Mansfield—Take a Writ of *Habeas Corpus:* And if this ſhould appear to be the Caſe, We ought to go further.

Mrs. *D'Vebre* was now brought into Court by Mr. *Turlington*. But no Return was indorſed upon the Writ.

She

She appeared to be absolutely free from the least Appearance of Insanity.

She was prepared to have sworn Articles of the Peace against her Husband; and they were offered in Court, ready ingrossed; But not being stamped, they could not be read.

She was permitted to go away with her Attorney, to his House; He undertaking to produce Her here to Morrow Morning.

Note—She desired not to go back to the Mad-house: And the Court would not permit her Husband to take Her, under the present Circumstances of Danger apprehended by Her from Him.

It afterwards ended in a Compromise, and an Agreement to separate.

Thursday 29th *January* 1761.

Sprightly, on the Demise of John Collins, *vers.* Humphry Dunch.

In Ejectment—

ON Mr. *Clayton*'s Motion, supported by Mr. *Gould*, who cited 2 Cases out of *Barnes*; (Vol. 2. *Supplement* 23. * 26. †) And on Affidavit "That *Boggust*, the Tenant in Possession *absconded*; and that the Plaintiff had personally *served his Niece*, "who was the only *Manager of this House*, and resided in it; and "had also *fixed up another Copy* of the Declaration upon the Premisses;"

* *H.* 26 *G.* 2. *Roe, ex dimiss. Fernley and Tancred,* v. *Doe.*

† *Tr.* 27, 28 *G.* 2. *Fenn, ex dimiss. Knight,* v. *Dean.*

Note—These Cases are not in the 1st Edit. 1754.

The Court, perceiving the Inconvenience that Landlords might suffer by being kept out of Possession, thought it reasonable to make a Rule upon the Tenant in Possession to shew Cause "Why "Judgment should not be entered up against the casual Ejector;" and accordingly did make such Rule: And they further Ordered that Notice of the present Rule, being given to *any* Person in the House, should be sufficient; And if no Person was in the House, then to be *affixed to the Door &c.*

On *Wednesday* 11*th February* This Rule was made absolute without Defence; on Affidavit of Notice being given to the *Niece*, and also *affixed* to the Door of the House. ||

|| *V. post* S. P. *accord*': *Goodright, ex dimiss. Methold,* v. *No-Right*; 23d *May* 1761; and *Fenn, ex dimiss. Tyrrell et al'*, v. *Denn*; 26th *May* 1761.

Rex *verſ.* John Gardner Eſq.

Thurſday 5th February 1761.

THE Affirmation *of a Quaker*, (namely, *John Lewis* of *Lantriſhent* in *Monmouthſhire*) was offered, in *Exculpation of Mr. Gardner the Defendant*, upon ſhewing Cauſe why an Information ſhould not be exhibited againſt Mr. *Gardner* for a Miſdemeanour.

The Reading of this Affirmation was objected to, by the Proſecutor's Counſel; and not much inſiſted upon, by the Counſel for the Defendant.

The Court held clearly, That a Quaker's Affirmation could *not* be read, in *Support* of a *Criminal* Charge: But They thought that an Affirmation *might* be read in *Defence* of a criminal Charge, if the Perſon charged was *Himſelf* a Quaker, in order to exculpate *Himſelf.*

In this *third* Caſe of a Quaker's *collateral* Evidence, in Aſſiſtance of the Exculpation of another Perſon, when the Quaker himſelf was *not charged* at all, They thought his Affirmation *ought not* to be read: And accordingly, It was withdrawn.

Biddlecombe *verſ.* Kervell.

Friday 6th February 1761.

THIS was an Action of Replevin, upon a Diſtreſs of Hogs taken in the New Foreſt in *Hampſhire.* The Defendant makes Conuſance, as Bailiff to the King; and juſtifies the taking the Hogs *&c*, as *Damage feaſant* in the ſaid New Foreſt in the King's Soil.

Plea in Bar—For that, though the Soil is the King's, Yet the King (5 *Ja.* 1.) granted to the Earl of *Southampton &c*, a *Right of Common* for *&c*, and Pannage *for Hogs &c*, within the ſame Foreſt *&c*, at all *Times of the Year*, as well in the Fence Month, as at other Times *&c*; Except *&c*. Then it deduces the Title to *&c*; in Whom the Right was, at the Time of making the * Statute of 9 & 10 *W.* 3. *c.* 36. Intitled "An Act for the Increaſe and Preſervation of Timber in the New Foreſt in the County of *Southampton*:" and ſets forth That Incloſures of 1000 Acres were made, agreeable to the Act; but not of any more than *One* thouſand Acres.

* This Statute (§ 1.) gives the King Liberty to incloſe *two* Thouſand Acres; (1000 immediately, and the other 1000 at a ſpecified Time;) † and afterwards, 200 in each Year, for 20 ſucceſſive Years.

† See the Note in next Page.

It then deduces the Title down to the Duke of *Montagu*; and ſhews a Demiſe from him to the Plaintiff, under which, He claims a *Right of Common* and Pannage in *thoſe* Parts of the new Foreſt which are *not* incloſed; and ſhews Enjoyment thereof accordingly: And therefore concludes that the Defendant took them *de injuria ſuâ propria, &c.*

The Replication of the Avowant admits the *Original Right* of Common and Pannage to have been as ſtated; But relies on the * Clauſe in the Act, "That Every Perſon having any Right of "Common of Paſture or Pannage, or any Privileges within the ſaid "Foreſt or any Part thereof, ſhould enjoy the ſame for the future, "in MANNER FOLLOWING; *viz.* their ſaid Right of PANNAGE, "*between 14th September and 11th November yearly*, from and after "*Michaelmas* 1716, and not before; *on Forfeiture* of any Hog Pig "or Swine that from and after the Feaſt of *St. Michael* next, and "before the Time aforeſaid ſhall be found in the *Waſtes* of the ſaid "Foreſt: And their ſaid Right of Common of Paſture ſhall be and "is hereby continued to them in and through ſuch of the ſaid Waſte "Ground of the ſaid Foreſt, at ſuch Time and Times as the ſame "ſhall not be incloſed as aforeſaid; the Time of the Fence-Month, "(*viz.* 15 Days before and 15 Days after the Feaſt of *St. John the Baptiſt*, yearly) and the Time of the Winter-Heyning, (*viz.* from "the 11th *November* to the 23*d* of *April* yearly) excepted."

* Sect. 9.

Then it ſtates, that the Hogs *&c* were found Damage feaſant, between the 11th of *November* and 23d *April &c*, *within* the Time of the Winter Heyning; And therefore He had a Right to take them Damage feaſant *&c*, and did ſo: Which He avows and juſtifies.

The Rejoinder ſtates That ſuch a Time (ſpecifying the Day) was the firſt Seſſion of Parliament held after the Year 1699; † And that at the End of that Seſſions, the *remaining* One thouſand Acres were NOT admeaſured ſet out or incloſed, *nor are yet* admeaſured *&c*; and avers that even at this Time, 100 Acres and no more are incloſed.

† Note. The particular Time ſpecified by the Statute (§ 1.) for admeaſuring ſetting out and incloſing the *ſecond* Thouſand Acres, was "from and *immediately after* the Determination of the firſt "Seſſions of Parliament which ſhould be held after the Year of our Lord 1699."

To this Rejoinder, the Avowant demurs.

Mr. *Huſſey* argued for the Avowant; and undertook to maintain, That the Act of 9 & 10 *W.* 3. *c.* 36. *meant* to *reſtrain* the Right of Common and of Pannage; *whether the Incloſure* of the remaining thouſand Acres was ‡ ever made, or not.

‡ Note—In Fact, the Incloſure of 1000 Acres was made: And the other thouſand were not incloſed.

The Question depends chiefly on * the 9th Section of this Act: Which Mr. *Hussey* discussed and argued upon, at large. * V. 9, 10 W. 3. c. 36. § 9.

Mr. *Burland contra*—for the Plaintiff in Replevin.

The 1st Question is, Whether the Proviso ever *intended* to *take away* the Plaintiff's *Right*.

2d Question—Whether (if it did,) the Plaintiff's Right is taken away, by inclosing 1000 *Acres* ONLY.

First—It only meant to take away *Prescriptive* Rights of Common: *V.* 20 *C.* 2. *c.* 3. for the Increase and Preservation of Timber within the Forest of *Dean*; (from whence this Proviso is literally † transcribed.) And He cited Sir *Francis Barrington*'s Case, 8 *Co.* 136. † V. § 11. of that Act of 20 C. 2.

Secondly—This Right could not be taken away by a *partial* Inclosure.

Mr. *Hussey*, in Reply—(1st) *Hogs* can not be within a *Prescriptive* Right: The Right for *them* must depend upon *Grant*. And This is a *distinct independant* Provision. (2d) *Some* Part must be many Years before it could be inclosed. It was not necessary to inclose the Remainder, at the precise Time mentioned in the Act.

Lord MANSFIELD held it clear, that the Statute meant that the Right of COMMON in the *inclosed* Parts, should be restrained ABSOLUTELY, so long as they should *remain inclosed*; but be continued in the UN*inclosed Parts only*, under certain *Limitations* and Exceptions: But the Right of PANNAGE is *absolutely* taken away, for *Eighteen* Years; and after that, *restrained to a particular limited Time*; And these Hogs were there found, at a Time when they ought *not* to have been there.

2d. The Inclosure of the *Whole* is not necessary: It is *not* a Condition *precedent*, "That the Whole shall be first inclosed, before "the Restriction of Common shall at all take Place."

Mr. Just. DENISON and Mr. Just. FOSTER agreed with His Lordship in Opinion.

Mr. Just. WILMOT—1st. This is a Common appendant by Grant. The present Question only respects *Pannage*: The Action is brought for taking *Hogs* only. The Act gives the Crown the Power of inclosing 6000 Acres in the Whole, for the Sake of increasing and preserving the Growth of Timber; And this is to be always

always free from Common and all Rights &c, whilſt it remains incloſed: But as to the *uninclosed*, the Right remains as it was, under certain Limitations and Exceptions.

But the Right of PANNAGE is quite taken away for Eighteeen Years; and is even then reſtrained to a certain limited Time, *viz.* between 14th *September* and 11th *November*.

2dly. And theſe are two diſtinct Clauſes. The Incloſure is not a Condition precedent. Sir *Francis Barrington*'s Caſe does not prove any thing in the preſent Caſe, nor interfere with any thing that I have ſaid.

Per Cur. JUDGMENT for the DEFENDANT, (Mr. *Hussey*'s Client.)

Hallet Eſq; and Others *verſ.* Eaſt-India Company.

Tueſday 10th *February* 1761.

UPON ſhewing Cauſe againſt a Rule Why the Defendants ſhould not have Leave to bring 2670*l.* *into Court*, upon two of the aſſigned Breaches only, * (*viz.* for *Freight* and for *Demorage*,) in an Action of *Covenant* brought upon a Charter-Party, by the Owners of a Ship, againſt the *Eaſt-India* Company who had taken it up in their Service; and that the ſaid 2670*l.* ſhould be ſtruck out of the Declaration; (in which Several other Breaches were aſſigned, as well as theſe two;)

* See the very *Words* of this Rule, *infra* 1121. together with an Explanation of it's *Meaning*.

Lord MANSFIELD obſerved, that in Motions of this kind, where the Defendant applies to pay Money into Court, and to have the Demand thereupon ſtruck out of the Declaration, the *Law* ariſes upon the FACT; And the true and ſenſible Diſtinction is, "That "where the Sum demanded is a *Sum certain*, or capable of being "*aſcertained by mere Computation*, without leaving any other Sort of "Diſcretion to be exerciſed by the Jury, It is right and reaſonable "to admit the Defendant to pay the Money into Court and have ſo "much of the Plaintiff's Demand upon Him ſtruck out of the De"claration; And that if the Plaintiff will not accept it, He ſhall "proceed at his Peril."

In the preſent Caſe, it being eaſy to *aſcertain by mere Computation* the Demorage at ſo much *per Day*, and the Freight at ſo much *per Tun*, (notwithſtanding that different Sorts of Goods are to pay different Rates *per* Tun;) and to ſettle the Account very exactly, from *Facts that muſt be notoriouſly known* in the Ship; And Nothing elſe remaining to be ſettled, nor any thing further being left for the Judgment and Diſcretion of the Jury to be exerciſed upon; the Defendants ought, in the present Case, to be at Liberty to pay the Money into Court, upon these two Counts: But then, on the other hand, the Plaintiffs ought to have INSPECTION of the Ship's Papers, now remaining in the Hands of the Company; in Order to enable them to judge Whether it will be prudent and adviseable for them to *accept* the Money so brought in; or to *proceed* in their Cause. And this Method will be most advantageous to both Sides.

This Proposal was readily agreed to, on both Sides: And a Rule was made accordingly.

The Original Rule was made on the Motion of Mr. *Norton* and Mr. *Winn*, on behalf of the Defendants, and was worded thus, "That the Plaintiffs should shew Cause Why the Defendants should "not have Leave to bring into Court the Sum of 2670*l.* with Re- "spect to the *Freight* and *Demorage* in this Cause: And thereupon, "unless the Plaintiffs shall accept thereof, with Costs to be taxed by "Mr. *Owen*, in full Discharge of the several Breaches assigned in this "Suit, on account of Non-Payment of *Freight* and *Demorage*; the "said 2670*l.* shall be struck out of the Plaintiffs Demands on that "Account, and paid out of Court, to the Plaintiffs or their Attor- "ney; And upon the Trial of the Issue, the Plaintiffs shall not be "permitted to give Evidence for the same."

Note—The Meaning of this Rule is—That if the Plaintiffs do not accept the Sum brought into Court, the same is to be struck out of the Declaration; and the Plaintiffs, upon the Trial, are not admitted to give Evidence for the Sum brought into Court: And if the Plaintiffs, upon the Trial, do not prove more due to them than the Money brought into Court, there must be a Verdict for the Defendants. But the Plaintiffs are at Liberty to accept the Sum brought into Court, in respect to the Breaches assigned for Non-Payment of Freight and Demorage, and to proceed as to any other Breaches mentioned in the Declaration (excepting those two,) if they think proper.

This RULE was made absolute: And it was now further added, "That a *true Freight-Note* be delivered to the Plain- "tiffs; And that the Plaintiffs shall have *Inspection* of all "Papers Books &c that may ascertain the Ship's Freight and "Earnings."

Rex *verſ.* John Perrott.

THE Defendant being brought up from *Newgate*, by HABEAS CORPUS, appeared upon the Return to have been committed by *Commiſſioners of* BANKRUPTCY, to be ſafely kept and detained, without Bail or Mainprize, "UNTIL *ſuch Time as He ſhall* SUBMIT "*Himſelf to the ſaid Commiſſioners* or the major Part of them, and "FULL *Anſwer* make to *their Satisfaction* to the *Queſtion* ſo put by "them to him as aforeſaid:" Which Queſtion was ſpecified in their Warrant, to have been put to him by them in Writing, upon the LAST Day of his Examination, after his having obtained 46 Days beyond the ordinary Time; and to have been propounded to him in theſe Words, *viz.* "As you do admit that you have ſpent the laſt "Week previous to this your Examination with Mr. *Maynard* (one "of your Aſſignees) to ſettle and adjuſt your Accounts and to draw "up a true State thereof, to enable you to cloſe ſuch your Exami-"nation; and do likewiſe admit, that upon ſuch State thereof, it "appears that after giving you Credit for all Sums of Money paid "by you, and making you Debtor for all Goods ſold and delivered "to you, from your firſt entering into Trade to the Time of your "Bankruptcy, it appears that there is a Deficiency of the Sum of "13513 *l.* Give a true and *particular* Account *what is become* of "the ſame; And *how and in what Manner* you have *applied and* "*diſpoſed* thereof." To which Queſtion ſo put by the Commiſ-"ſioners as aforeſaid, The ſaid *John Perrott* did wilfully and obſti-"nately refuſe to give any other than the following GENERAL *An-ſwer*, (that is to ſay) "That on Goods ſold this laſt Year, I have "loſt upwards of 2000 *l.* And by Mournings, I have loſt upwards "of 1000 *l.* And that for 9 or 10 Years, I have (and I am ſorry "to ſay it) been EXTREAMLY EXTRAVAGANT, and *ſpent* LARGE "*Sums* of Money. *John Perrott.*" Which Anſwer of the ſaid *John Perrott* NOT *being* SATISFACTORY to Us the ſaid Commiſ-ſioners—Theſe are therefore to will require and authorize you immediately upon Receipt hereof to arreſt *&c*, and him ſafely to convey *&c*, and to deliver *&c*, ſafely to keep and detain, without Bail or Mainprize, UNTIL ſuch Time as he ſhall *ſubmit* himſelf to Us the ſaid Commiſſioners or to the major Part of the ſaid Commiſ-ſioners by the ſaid Commiſſion named and authorized, and FULL *Anſwer make* to our or their *Satisfaction, to the Queſtion ſo put to him* by Us as aforeſaid.

Two Reaſons were urged on the Part of the Defendant, why he ought to be diſcharged from this Impriſonment. 1ſt. That the Anſwer which He had already given was a *full ſufficient* and *ſatiſ-factory* Anſwer, and the *beſt and only One* that could be given by an idle

idle extravagant Man who had never kept any Accounts; And, consequently, that the Imprisoning him *until* he should give a *more* full and satisfactory Answer to the Question, was an *Imprisonment for Life.*

The 2d Reason was, That the *Power and Jurisdiction* of the Commissioners, *to take* the Bankrupt's Examination and Disclosure, was *temporary* and *limited*, and *confined* to the Time allowed to the Bankrupt to come in and surrender himself and submit to be examined; *After* which limited Time, the Commissioners had *no Power to examine him at all:* Consequently, they had no Jurisdiction to commit him for any LONGER *Time* than their own Power to examine him lasted; which did not exceed the Time allowed him to come in and surrender himself and submit to be examined. And his Counsel compared it to a Commitment by the House of Commons; which ended with their Session.

In Support of these Objections, they relied upon the Construction of the Bankrupt-Acts; and particularly of 5 *G.* 2. *c.* 30. § 1, 2, 3.

On the other Side, it was insisted—1st. That the Bankrupt's Answer was *nugatory* and *insufficient*; and 2dly. That the Power and Jurisdiction of the Commissioners to examine the Bankrupt, and obtain a Disclosure and Discovery of his Estate and Effects and the Manner in which He had disposed of them, was *not limited and confined* to the last Minute allowed him for his Surrender and Submission; but might be pursued and proceeded upon at *any* SUBSEQUENT *Time.* And for this, they relied on the End and Intention and genuine Construction of all the Bankrupt-Acts, and particularly of 1 *J.* 1. *c.* 15. § 7, 8. and 5 *G.* 2. *c.* 30. § 16.

Lord MANSFIELD—If the Question put was improper; or if the Question be proper, and the Answer satisfactory, the Man ought to be discharged. But this is a *proper* Question; And the Answer is very *insufficient and unsatisfactory.*

The Construction offered by the Counsel who object to this Commitment, is founded upon mere arbitrary Implication: The Legislature say no such Thing. On the Contrary, The 5 *G.* 2. *c.* 30. § 16. gives Power to the Commissioners to commit the Bankrupt UNTIL he shall submit himself, and *full Answer make to their Satisfaction:* And Section 17th gives Power to the Court or Judge, to recommit him to the same Prison, there to remain as aforesaid, UNTIL He shall conform as aforesaid.

The *Examination* is *not confined* to be *within* the Time limited for the Bankrupt to come in and surrender and submit to be examined.

The

The Bankrupt muſt indeed *ſurrender* within the limited Time; and he muſt *ſubmit* within the limited Time, to be examined from Time to Time; And he muſt, upon his Examination, diſcloſe and diſcover and deliver up his Eſtate and Effects: But the Act does not
* V. 5 G. 2. require the Examination to be full and perfect and * completed with-
c. 30. § 1. in the limited Time; Nor is it proper that it ſhould be ſo. A Man's Memory may fail him at one Time, and be refreſhed at another; Or his firſt Anſwer may be equivocal, or imperfect: And Why ſhould he not be called upon to explain and complete it? The Power of the Commiſſioners is *general*, and not limited to the Compaſs of Time given to the Bankrupt to come in.

The laſt Examination within the limited Time is material indeed to the *Bankrupt himſelf*, (Becauſe He can not afterwards contradict himſelf:) But he may be compelled by the Commiſſioners to make *further* Anſwer, *after* that Time. The Bankrupt may omit to come in, till the very laſt Minute of his Time; And if He then ſurrenders and ſubmits to be examined, this will *ſave his Felony:* But it may be abſolutely *impoſſible* for him to make a full Diſcovery and Diſcloſure of his Eſtate and Effects, or to give full Anſwers to proper Queſtions within *this Space* of Time.

But here, the Commiſſioners have, *within* the limited Time, *required* a further Anſwer to their Queſtion, and committed him for refuſing to give it. This Commitment was *legal*, at the Time when it was made: And I am clearly ſatisfied, that he can not redeem himſelf from his Impriſonment, but on giving a *full* Anſwer to the Queſtion. If he ſhould give a full Anſwer, and the Commiſſioners not be ſatisfied with it, He will then be intitled to his proper Remedy.

The Objection has been ſtrongly argued: But there is no Caſe to ſupport it. It is a new Invention, and would entirely defeat the End and Intention of the Bankrupt-Acts.

The Three Judges were All equally clear That the Man ought to be remanded.

Mr. Juſt. Foster added, that the Powers under the Statute of 1 *Ja.* 1. *c.* 15. continues ſtill in Force, notwithſtanding the ſubſequent Statutes; And that None of them preclude a further Examination.

Mr. Juſt. Wilmot alſo concurred in this; and ſaid, that All the Bankrupt-Acts ought to be taken *together*, ſo as to anſwer the great general End and Intention of the Legiſlature: The Clauſes operate together, and are auxiliary to each other; And they certainly give a

Power of further Examination. There are vast Numbers of Questions that may be asked under the Examination, more than can be under the mere Surrender and Submission; that may require further Time, or even arise afterwards. The Submission *alone* is not enough: He must submit to be *examined from Time to Time*; And he ought not to be discharged till he has fully answered. His present Answer is most clearly deficient.

Per Cur. unanimously,
The DEFENDANT was REMANDED.

V. post. Monday 8th *June* 1761.

Rex *vers.* Wheatly.

Thursday 12th *February* 1761.

MR. *Norton*, for the Prosecutor, shewed Cause why Judgment should not be arrested; A Rule for that Purpose having been obtained, upon a Motion made by Mr. *Morton* on *Monday* 26th *January* last, in Arrest of Judgment upon this Indictment for knowingly selling Amber-Beer short of the due and just Measure, (whereof the Defendant had been convicted.)

The Charge in the Indictment was, " That *Thomas Wheatly* late " of the Parish of *St. Luke* in the County of *Middlesex* Brewer, being " a Person of evil Name Fame and of dishonest Conversation, and " *devising and intending to deceive and defraud One Richard Webb of* " *his Monies*, on &c, at &c, *falsely fraudulently and deceitfully* did " *sell and deliver* and cause to be sold and delivered to the said *Richard Webb* 16 Gallons and no more of a certain Malt Liquor commonly called Amber, FOR AND AS 18 Gallons of the same Liquor; " Which said Liquor so as aforesaid sold and delivered did then " and there *want Two Gallons of the due and just Measure of* 18 *Gallons*, FOR WHICH *the same was sold and delivered* as aforesaid; (the " said *Thomas Wheatly* then and there *well knowing* the same Liquor " so by him sold and delivered to want 2 Gallons of the due and " just Measure as aforesaid;) And He the said *Thomas Wheatly* did " *receive* of the said *Richard Webb* the Sum of 15 *Shillings* &c for " 18 Gallons &c *pretended* to have been sold and delivered &c; al- " though there was *only* 16 Gallons so as aforesaid delivered: And " he the said *Thomas Wheatly* Him the said *Richard Webb* of 2 Gallons of &c *fraudulently and unlawfully* did *deceive* and *defraud*; " To the great Damage and Fraud of the said *Richard Webb*, To " the evil Example of others in the like Case offending, and against " the Peace of our Sovereign Lord the King his Crown and Dignity."

Mr. *Morton* and Mr. *Yates*, who were of Counsel for the De-"fendant, (to arrest the Judgment,) objected that the Fact charged was Nothing more than a *mere Breach of a* CIVIL CONTRACT; not an indictable Offence. To prove this, they cited *Rex* v. *Combrun*, *P.* 1751, 24 *G.* 2. *B.R.* Which was exactly and punctually the same Case as the present, only *mutatis mutandis*. And *Rex* v. *Drisfield*, *Tr.* 1754, 27, 28 *G.* 2. *B.R.* S. P. An Indictment for a Cheat, in selling Coals as and for Two Bushels, whereas it was a Peck short of that Measure: There the Indictment was quashed on Motion. *Rex* v. *Hannah Heath*—An Indictment for selling and delivering 17 Gallons 3 Quarts and ½ Pint of *Geneva*, (and the like of Brandy,) as and for a greater Quantity, was quashed on Motion.

In 1 *Salk.* 151. *Nebuff's* Case, *P.* 4 *Ann. B. R.* A *Certiorari* was granted to remove the Indictment from the *Old Bailey*; because it was not a Matter Criminal: It was "borrowing 600*l.* and promi-"sing to send a Pledge of fine Cloth and Gold Dust; and sending "only some coarse Cloth, and no Gold Dust."

* *V. Tremaine's Pleas of the Crown, pa.* 85 *to* 111.

In *Tremaine*, * Title *Indictments for Cheats*,—All of them either lay a *Conspiracy*, or shew Something amounting to a *false Token*.

A *mere Civil Wrong* will not support an Indictment. And here is no *Criminal* Charge: It is not alledged "That he used false Mea-"sures." The Prosecutor should have examined and seen that it was the right and just Quantity.

Mr. *Norton*, *pro Rege*, offered the following Reasons why the Judgment should not be arrested.

The Defendant has been *convicted* of the Fact. He may bring a Writ of Error, if the Indictment is erroneous.

This *is* an *indictable Offence*; 'Tis a *Cheat*, a *public Fraud*, in the Course of his *Trade*: He is stated to be a *Brewer*. There is a Distinction between *private* Frauds, and Frauds in the *Course of Trade*. The same Fact may be a Ground for a private Action, and for an Indictment too.

None of the cited Cases were *after Verdict*. It *might* here (for ought that appears to the Contrary) have been *proved* "That he "sold this less Quantity, *by false Measure*:" And Every Thing shall be *presumed* in favour of a Verdict. And here is a *false Pretence*, at least: And it appeared upon the Trial to be a very foul Case.

The

The Counsel for the Defendant, in Reply, said that Nothing can be intended or *presumed*, in a Criminal Case, but *secundum allegata et probata*: It *might* happen without his own *personal* Knowledge. And they denied any Distinction between this being done privately, and its being done in the Course of Trade.

Lord MANSFIELD—The Question is, Whether the Fact here alledged be an *indictable* Crime or not. The Fact alledged is—

(Then His Lordship stated the Charge, * *verbatim.*) * *V. ante* 1125.

The Argument that has been urged by the Prosecutor's Counsel, from the present Case's coming before the Court *after a Verdict*, and the Cases cited being only of quashing upon Motion *before* any Verdict, really turns the *other* Way: Because the Court may use a *Discretion*, "Whether it be right to quash upon Motion, or put the Defendant to demur;" But after Verdict, they are *obliged* to arrest the Judgment if they see the Charge to be insufficient. And in a *Criminal* Charge, there is NO *Latitude of Intendment*, to include any thing *more* than is charged: The Charge must be explicit enough to *support itself.*

Here, the *Fact* is allowed; but the *Consequence* is denied: The Objection is, that the Fact is *not an Offence indictable*, though acknowledged to be true as charged.

And that the Fact here charged should not be considered as an indictable Offence, but left to a Civil Remedy by an Action, is reasonable and right in the Nature of the Thing: Because it is only an Inconvenience and Injury to a *private* Person, arising from that private Person's own Negligence and *Carelessness* in not measuring the Liquor, upon receiving it, to see whether it held out the just Measure or not.

The Offence that is indictable must be such a one as affects the PUBLIC. As if a Man *uses false Weights and Measures*, and sells *by them* to all or to many of his Customers, or uses them in the *general* Course of his Dealing: So, if a Man defrauds Another, under *false Tokens.* For these are Deceptions that *common* Care and Prudence are not sufficient to guard against. So, if there be a *Conspiracy* to cheat: For *ordinary* Care and Caution is no Guard against this.

Those Cases are much more than mere private Injuries: They are *public Offences.* But here, it is a mere *private* Imposition or Deception: No false Weights or Measures are used; No false Tokens

2 kens

kens given; No Conspiracy; Only an Imposition upon the Person he was dealing with, in delivering him a less Quantity instead of a greater; which the other carelessly accepted. 'Tis only a Non-performance of his Contract: For which Non-performance, He may bring his Action.

The Selling an unsound Horse, as and for a sound One, is not indictable: The Buyer should be more upon his Guard.

The several Cases cited are alone sufficient to prove, That the Offence here charged is *not* an *indictable* Offence. But besides these, My Brother *Denison* informs Me of another Case, that has not been mentioned at the Bar. It was *M.* 6 *G.* 1. *B. R.* * *Rex* v. *Wilders*, a Brewer: He was indicted for a Cheat, in sending in, to Mr. *Hicks* an Ale-house keeper, so many Vessels of Ale *marked* as containing such a Measure, and writing a *Letter* to Mr. *Hicks*, assuring him that they did contain that Measure; when in Fact they did not contain such Measure, but so much less &c. This Indictment was quashed on Argument, upon a Motion: Which is a stronger Case than the present.

* I have a like Account of this Case. The Court said that the Prosecutor could not have been imposed upon, without his own Carelessness; and instanced the Case of selling an unsound Horse, affirming Him to be sound: And they held that such private unfair Dealings, which did not affect the Public, were not indictable Crimes; unless accompanied with false Tokens, or Conspiracy, or Selling by false Weights or Measures.

Therefore the Law is clearly established and settled; and I think, on *right* Grounds: But on whatever Grounds it might have been originally established, yet it ought to be adhered to, after it is established and settled.

Therefore, (though I may be sorry for it in the present Case as circumstanced;) The Judgment must be arrested.

Mr. Just. Denison concurred with His Lordship.

This is nothing more than an Action upon the Case turned into an Indictment. 'Tis a *private Breach of Contract*. And if this were to be allowed of, it would alter the Course of the Law; by making the injured Person a *Witness* upon the Indictment, which He could not be (for himself) in an Action.

Here are no false Weights, nor false Measures; nor any false Token at all; nor any Conspiracy.

In the Case of *The Queen* v. *Maccarty et al'* † there were false Tokens, or what was considered as such. In the Case of ‖ *The Queen* v. *Jones*, 1 *Salk.* 379. the Defendant had received 20*l.* pretending to be sent by One who did not send him—*Et per Cur.* "It is not "indictable,

† 6 *Mod.* 301. 2 *Ld Raym.* 1179.

‖ 2 *Ld. Raym.* 1013. and 6 *Mod.* 105. S. C.

" indictable, unless he came with false Tokens: We are not to " indict one Man for making a Fool of another; Let him bring his " Action."

If there were *false Tokens* or a *Conspiracy*, it is another Case. *The Queen* v. *Maccarty* was a * Conspiracy, as well as false Tokens. *Rex* v. *Wilders* was a much stronger Case than this; and was well considered: That was an Imposition in the *Course of his Trade*; and the Man had *marked* the Vessels, as containing more Gallons than they did really contain, and had written a *Letter* to Mr. *Hicks*, attesting that they did so.

* V. ut supra, and 6 Mod. 302. particularly.

But the present Case is no more than a *mere Breach of Contract*: He has not delivered the Quantity which He undertook to deliver.

The Court use a *Discretion* in quashing Indictments on *Motion*: But they are are *obliged* to *arrest Judgment* when the Matter is *not indictable*. And *this* Matter is *not* indictable: Therefore the Judgment ought to be *arrested*.

Mr. Just. Foster—We are obliged to follow settled and established Rules already fixed by former Determinations in Cases of the same kind.

The Case of *Rex* v. *Wilders* was a strong Case; (too strong perhaps; for there were false Tokens, the Vessels were *marked* as containing a greater Quantity than they really did.)

Mr. Just. Wilmot concurred. This Matter has been fully settled and established, and upon a reasonable Foot. The true Distinction that ought to be attended to in all Cases of this kind, and which will solve them all, is this—That in such Impositions or Deceits where common Prudence may guard Persons against their suffering from them, the Offence is not indictable, but the Party is left to his Civil Remedy for the Redress of the Injury that has been done him: But where false Weights and Measures are used, or false Tokens produced, or such Methods taken to cheat and deceive, as People can not, by any ordinary Care or Prudence be guarded against, there it is an Offence indictable.

In the Case of *Rex* v. *Pinkney*, *P.* 6 *G.* 2. *B. R.* upon an Indictment " for selling a Sack of Corn (at *Rippon* Market) which " he falsely affirmed to contain a *Winchester* Bushel, *ubi revera et* " *in facto plurimùm deficiebat &c,*" The Indictment was quashed upon Motion.

In the Cafe now before Us, the Profecutor might have meafured the Liquor, before He accepted it: And it was his own Indolence and Negligence if He did not. Therefore common Prudence might have guarded him againft fuffering any Inconvenience by the Defendant's offering him lefs than he had contracted for.

This was the Cafe of *Rex* v. *Pinkney*: And it was there faid, That if a Shop-keeper who deals in Cloth, pretends to fell Ten Yards of Cloth, but inftead of Ten Yards bought of him, delivers only Six, Yet the Buyer can not indict him for delivering only Six; Becaufe He might have meafured it, and feen whether it held out as it ought to do, or not. In this Cafe of *Rex* v. *Pinkney*, and alfo in that Cafe of *Rex* v. *Combrun*, a Cafe of *Rex* v. *Nicholfon*, at the Sittings before Ld. *Raymond* after *Michaelmas* Term, 4 *G*. 2. was mentioned; Which was an Indictment for felling Six Chaldron of Coals, which ought to contain 36 Bufhels each, and delivering Six Bufhels fhort: Lord *Raymond* was fo clear in it, that He ordered the Defendant to be acquitted.

Per Cur. unanimoufly,
The JUDGMENT muft be * ARRESTED.

* See the next Cafe, S. P. *accord*.

Rex *verf.* Dunnage.

† *V. ante, pa.* 1125. (the laft preceding Cafe)

THIS Cafe was exactly the fame Point with that of *Rex* v. *Wheatly*, which was determined this very Morning. †

The Defendant ftood indicted for knowingly felling and delivering Three Bufhels and a half of Oats, as and for Four Bufhels, which wanted half a Bufhel of the juft and due Meafure; with Intent to deceive and defraud &c.

Upon Mr. *Stowe*'s Motion to quafh this Indictment, and Mr. *Norton*'s agreeing that it could not be fupported, fince the Determination of the Court this Morning, in the Cafe of *Rex* v. *Wheatly*,

This INDICTMENT was alfo QUASHED;—the Rule for fhewing Caufe why it fhould not be fo, being made abfolute without Argument.

The

The following Case may be considered as One of this Term; because the Certificate bears Date in the Vacation next following it, and nearer to *Hilary* Term than to *Easter* Term.

Selwyn Esq; *vers.* Selwyn Widow and Others.

THIS Case came out of Chancery, for the Opinion of the Court of King's Bench.

It was twice argued here, and both Times very elaborately and well; first, by Mr. *Sewell*, for the Plaintiff, and Mr. *Charles Yorke*, Solicitor General, for the Defendants, in *Easter* Term 1760, 33 *G.* 2. and again in *Michaelmas* Term 1760, 1 *G.* 3. by Mr. *De Grey*, for the Plaintiff, and Mr. *Norton* for the Defendants.

The Causes in Chancery were thus intitled—

Between	*George Augustus Selwyn* Esq; now the Eldest Son and Heir of *John Selwyn* Esq; deceased	Plaintiff;
	Mary Selwyn Widow and Administratrix with the Will annexed of the said *John Selwyn*, and Others	Defendants.

And

Between	The said *Mary Selwyn* Widow,	Plaintiff;
	The said *George Augustus Selwyn* and Others	Defendants.

The Case stated several Family-Settlements and Transactions: By which it appeared that the Premisses were limited in strict Settlement to *John Selwyn* the Elder for Life; Remainder to his first and every other Son by his Wife *Mary*, successively, in Tail Male; Remainder to *John Selwyn* the Elder and his Heirs.

John Selwyn the Younger was the Eldest Son; And, as such, seised of the Remainder in Tail Male.

By Bargain and Sale, dated 20th *April* 1751, inrolled in the Common Pleas, between the said *John Selwyn* the Elder and *John Selwyn* the Younger of the first Part, *John Wakelin* Gent. of the second Part, and *Francis Donce* Gent. of the third Part, It is Witnessed that for barring All Estates Tail Remainders and Reversions of and in in the Messuages Farms Lands and Hereditaments after mentioned, and for settling and limiting the same to and for the Uses Intents and Purposes and in Manner after mentioned, the said *John Selwyn* the Elder and *John Selwyn* the Younger did Grant Bargain and Sell unto the said *John Wakelin* and his Heirs, All those two Farms Lands and Hereditaments in the Possession of the said *John Harris* and *William Harris* mentioned in the said Bargain and Sale of the 12th of *June* 1750 with the Appurtenances, and the said 4 Farms in the Indentures of Lease and Release of the 1st and 2d of *April* 1751, then in the several Tenures of *William Gascomb*, *John Print*, *Mary Print*, and *Jane Cannon*, with their Appurtenances, and the Reversion and Reversions &c: To hold to and to the Use of the said *John Wakelin* and his Heirs, To the Intent He might become Tenant of the Freehold, to the End a Common Recovery might be suffered of the Premisses comprized in that Indenture of Bargain and Sale: For which Purpose, it was agreed that the said *Francis Donce* should, on this Side or before the End of *Easter* Term then next, or of some subsequent Term, prosecute a Writ of Entry upon Disseisin of the same Premisses, against the said *John Wakelin*; who was to appear and vouch over to Warranty the said *John Selwyn* the Elder, who was to appear and vouch the said *John Selwyn* the Younger, who was to vouch the Common Vouchee. And it was thereby declared and agreed that from and immediately after the suffering the said Common Recovery so as aforesaid or in any other Manner or at any other Time suffered or to be suffered, the said Common Recovery and All and Every other Common Recovery or Recoveries then-tofore or then-after to be had or suffered of the said Premisses between the said Parties, should enure, and the Recoverors stand seised of the Premisses, to the Uses aftermentioned, *viz.* To the Use of the said *John Selwyn* the Elder for Life, without Impeachment of Waste, with Power to grant Leases for any Term not exceeding 21 Years; Remainder to the Use of the said *John Selwyn* the Younger, his Heirs and Assigns for ever.

Easter Term ended on the 20th of *May* 1751.

On the 30th of *May* 1751, The Writ of Entry was sued out.

This Writ of Entry was returnable in 15 Days from the *Holy Trinity*; which was the 16th Day of *June* in the said Year 1751. *Trinity* Term begun on the 7th of *June* 1751.

On the 8th of *June* 1751, *John Selwyn* the Younger made his Will in the Words or to the Effect following, *viz.* " This is the " last Will and Testament of me *John Selwyn* the Younger; which " I now make and publish in Order to settle my Real Estate in such " prudent Manner as to continue the same in my own Family.

"And for that Purpose, I do hereby give and devise unto my Honoured Father *John Selwyn* Esq; All that my Manor or Lordship of *Luggershall* in the County of *Wilts*, and all my Manor of *Matson* in the County of *Gloucester*, with the Rights Members and Appurtenances thereunto belonging, and all other my Manors Messuages Farms Lands Tenements Rectories Advowsons Rents and Hereditaments whatsoever, and all the Freehold and other Estate of Inheritance whereof I the said *John Selwyn* the Younger or any Person or Persons whatsoever In Trust for or to my Use are or is seised or possessed either in Possession Reversion Remainder or Expectancy, and all my Estate Right Title and Interest therein; To hold the same unto and to the Use of my said Father his Heirs and Assigns for ever."

On the 12th of *June* 1751, the Bargain and Sale of the 20th of *April* 1751, was acknowledged by *John Selwyn* the Elder before Mr. Just. *Gundry* in Court, and afterwards inrolled.

The Writ of Entry *sur Disseisin en le Post* was returnable on the 26th of *June* in the same Year.

The Writ of *Seisin* was tested 19th *June*; returnable forthwith.

The Sheriff executed the Writ of Seisin, on the 22d of *June* 1751: And on the 26th of the same *June*, He made his Return on the above Writ.

Trinity Term ended on the *26th* of *June*.

John Selwyn the Younger died, on the *27th* of *June* 1751, without altering or re-publishing his Will.

On the Hearing of these Causes before the Right Honourable the Lord Keeper of the Great Seal of *Great Britain*, on the 11th of *December* 1758, His Lordship Ordered that a Case should be made for the Opinion of the Judges of the Court of King's Bench upon the following

Question—Whether the several Lands Tenements and Hereditaments comprized in the *Deed of the 20th of April* 1751, PASSED *by the Will of John Selwyn the Son.*

The Question turned upon two Points;

1st. Whether *John Selwyn* the Younger, at the Date of his Will, had any Use Estate or Interest in the Premisses, to devise:

2d. If He had, Whether the subsequent Recovery was a Revocation.

 "The

The Certificate returned to the Court of Chancery was dated on 2d *March* 1761; and was in the following Words, *viz.*

"Having heard Counsel, and considered this Case, (which the "Parties, by Agreement between themselves, delayed arguing,) "We are of Opinion That the several Lands Tenements and Here-"ditaments comprized in the Deed of the 20th of *April* 1751, "PASSED by the Will of *John Selwyn* the Son."

"MANSFIELD.
"T. DENISON.
"M. FOSTER.
"E. WILMOT.

Agreeable to ancient Usage, Upon Cases referred out of Chancery, The Court did *not* give the *Reasons* of their Opinion, nor mention the *Grounds* upon which they formed it. Therefore I have omitted the Arguments at the Bar; which were very elaborate, very learned, and very ingenious: Because they took in many Topics which the *Court* might not form their Judgment upon.

In the Course of the Arguments, The Court repeatedly expressed their Approbation of the Case of Sir *John Ferrers and Sir John Curson* against *Sir Richard Fermor and Others.* * And therefore it is likely that they considered the Whole as *One Conveyance*, which must relate to the Date of the Bargain and Sale; Which was perfected, made absolute, and delivered from Objections, by the subsequent Ceremonies.

* Cro. Jac. 643.

It is probable too, from some Expressions dropped, They might think that *John Selwyn* the Younger, by virtue of the Bargain and Sale, had a voidable contingent executory Use, to arise out of the subsequent Common Recovery;—That such a Use was devisable;—And that the subsequent Recovery executed such Use, and made it absolute.

Note—It had been at first urged, on behalf of the Defendants, against the Plaintiff the Heir at Law, "That the Will was made "*subsequent* to the Recovery: For that the Will was made on the "8th of *June* 1751, And the Term begun upon the 7th. And the "Recovery shall *relate* to the *first* Day of the Term, as the Whole "Recovery is, both in Law and in Fact, the Transaction of *One* "Day; And therefore the Judgment in the Recovery shall be con-"sidered as *prior* to the Return of the Writ of Entry, and to the "making of the Will; And that there is Nothing appearing upon "the Record, to prevent the Court from considering it in this Light."

But Mr. *Norton* gave up this Point, (and the Court had hinted at the Difficulty of Supporting it,) as this was a Case that came out of Chancery upon Facts particularly stated; And it is † here stated expressly "that this Writ of Entry was returnable in 15 Days from "the *Holy Trinity, which was the* SIXTEENTH Day of *June*:" So that if this must be taken as the Fact, "that the Writ of Entry "was returnable on the *second* Return of the Term," and there can be no Judgment till after Appearance, Then the Relation to the first Day of the Term is out of the Case, And the Recovery cannot be till the second Return of that Term.

† *V. ante pa.* 1132.

The End of *Hilary* Term 1761, 1 *G.* 3.

Easter

Easter Term

1 Geo. 3. B.R. 1761.

Wednesday April 1761.

Zouch, ex dimiss. Woolston, *vers.* Woolston et al'.

THIS was a Case upon a Special Verdict in Ejectment. The Question arose upon a Devise by the Will of *Christopher Woolston*, who died seised in Fee of Lands in *Staverton*, *Broadhempston*, and *Westogell*, in *Devonshire*. All the Defendants, except *Elizabeth Woolston*, were found Not guilty, generally: And She also was found Not guilty, *as to* the Lands in *Staverton*; But, as to the *Residue* of the Trespass, relating to the Lands in *Broadhempston* and *Westogell*, the Jury found specially.

The special Finding was as follows—

Christopher Woolston being seised in Fee, on the 11th of *August* 1707, of the Lands &c in the Declaration described, in the Parishes of *Staverton*, *Broadhempston*, and *Westogell* in the County of *Devon*, and of other Lands in *Tor-Newton* and *Tor-Bryan*, did, by Will of that Date, devise to his Wife *Mary*, *Benjamin Abraham*, and *John Pope*, and their Heirs, All his Messuages &c in those Parishes, to the following Uses. As to the Lands in *Tor-Bryan*, To the Use of the said Trustees, for 40 Years after his Decease: And as to the Messuages &c in *Staverton*, *Broadhempston* and *Westogell*, To the Use of his Eldest Son *James*, for Life; Remainder to Trustees, to preserve contingent Remainders; Remainder to the first and every other Son of *James*, in Tail Male; And in Default of such Issue, the like Limitations to his (the Testator's) Son *John* &c; Remainder to the Daughters of *James*, in Tail; with like Remainders to the Daughters of *John*, and the like to the Testator's own Daughters; Remainder, as to *Westogell*, To the Use of his own right Heirs; And as to *Staverton* and *Broadhempston*, To his Cousin ——— *Woolston* in Tail, with Remainder to his own right Heirs. And as to the Lands Messuages &c in *Tor-Newton* and *Tor-Bryan*, subject to the

Term of 40 Years, He limited them, first to his Son *John*, and then to his Son *James*, first for Life, and then with Limitations over, (like to the preceding Ones;) with Remainder to his own right Heirs: And the Trust of the Term was declared to be, to raise 1000*l.* out of the Rents and Profits of the Premisses in *Tor-Bryan*, for his Daughter *Elizabeth*; payable, One Moiety at her Marriage, and the Residue within 3 Months after; and in the mean Time 30*l.* a Year for Maintenance; And then the Term to cease.

Then comes this Proviso, *viz.*

" *Provided* always, and it is my Will Intent and Meaning, That " the said *James Woolston* and *John Woolston*, severally and respectively, " when they or either of them shall have an Estate in Possession, to " his or their respective proper Use or Uses, of and in the aforesaid " Messuages Lands Tenements and Hereditaments, for his or their " Life or Lives, by virtue of the several Limitations herein before " mentioned, shall have full Power Liberty and Authority, *from* " *Time to Time* during his or their respective Life or Lives, by Deed " *or Deeds* Writing *or Writings* to be by him or them respectively " subscribed and sealed in the Presence of two or more credible " Witnesses, *to assign limit or appoint*, to or to the Use of or in Trust " for any *Woman or Women that shall be his or their respective Wife* " *or Wifes*, for and during the natural Life and Lives of such Wo- " man or Women, for or in the Name or in lieu of their Jointure " or Jointures, *All or any Part* of the several Messuages Lands Te- " nements and Hereditaments to Him or Them the said *James* " *Woolston* and *John Woolston* herein before respectively limited as " aforesaid."

The Testator died on the 12th of *August* 1707.

James entred into *his* Part, under the Devise; And *John* also, into *his* Part.

John died seised, leaving only One Son, named also *John*; who is the Lessor of the Plaintiff.

James, being so seised, took to Wife the Defendant, then *Elizabeth Bogan*; And, previous to the Marriage, by Indenture dated 31st *May* 1712, duly executed, between the said *James Woolston* of the first Part, *William Bogan* of *Gatcomb* in the said County Esq; and *John Legassic* Clerk of the second Part, and the said *Elizabeth Bogan* (Sister to the said *William Bogan*) of the third Part, (*Reciting the said Will* as to the Devise to *James, and the Proviso,*) In Consideration of the intended Marriage, and in Part-performance of certain Articles of Agreement (of the Day before) between the said Parties, *James Woolston*, having by virtue of his Father's Will an Estate in Possession to his own proper Use for his Life in the several Messuages &c so devised, Doth ACCORDING TO THE POWER TO HIM GIVEN, AND BY VIRTUE THEREOF *and of all and every other* Power and Powers and Authorities which to him doth or may belong, *assign limit* and *appoint* to the said *William Bogan* and *John Legassic* and the Survivor of them and his Heirs, All that Capital Messuage &c and all other Messuages Lands &c in *Staverton*, and his Messuages and all other his Lands in *Westogell*, and the Reversion and Reversions &c: To hold, as to the Lands in *Staverton*, to the Trustees, to the Use of *Elizabeth Bogan for Life, for and in the Name and in lieu of her Jointure*, (to commence from and after the Marriage and the Death of *James*;) And as to the other Premisses in *Westogell*, to the Use of the said *Elizabeth Bogan during* the JOINT-LIVES of *Herself* and of *Prudence Woolston* Widow of the Testator's eldest Brother, *for and in the Name and in lieu of her Jointure*, (to commence from and after the Marriage and the Death of *James*.)

In this Indenture is contained a *Proviso*, That if the said *Elizabeth Bogan* do not, within 3 Months after Request made, at the Costs of such Person as shall then be Tenant of the Freehold or be seised of all or any Part of the Messuages Lands &c whereof the said *James Woolston* shall during the Coverture be seised of any Estate of Inheritance, RELEASE *all and every Dower and Claim of Dower, and all her Right and Interest unto the several Messuages Lands &c* (her said Jointure excepted,) Every Thing contained in this Indenture should be *void*.

There was also in this Indenture, a *Covenant* from *James Woolston* with the Trustees, That He has *full Power thus to appoint* the Premisses in *Staverton* and *Westogell*; And that the said *Elizabeth* and his Sons by her *shall enjoy* according to the Intent of this Deed *and of the Will*, free from all Incumbrances except an Annuity of 50*l*. *per Annum* payable (out of *Blacker*) to the said *Prudence*: And He covenants to make further Assurance, within ten Years, if required.

AFTERWARDS, *during the Coverture*, *James*, by Deed Poll dated the 15th of *February* 1738, (containing a Recital of the abovementioned Devise to him, and of the said Indenture tripartite of 31st *May* 1712, and of the Proviso therein contained and abovementioned, and that the then intended Marriage took Effect,) for and in Consideration of the great *Love and Affection* which He bore to the said *Elizabeth* now his Wife, and *for a* BETTER *Provision and Maintenance for Her*, RELEASES to *Norton Nelson* and *Margaret* his Wife Executrix of *William Bogan* the surviving Trustee in the Indenture of 31st *May* 1712, the PROVISOES contained in the said Indenture and in the Articles of Agreement therein mentioned.

AFTER-

AFTERWARDS, by Indenture dated 3d *October* 1751, Reciting to the same Effect as is recited in the Deed Poll of 15th *February* 1738, and also reciting that the said *Prudence Woolston* (the Widow) was dead, and that *James Woolston* had received the Sum of 600 *l.* and upwards which had fallen to his Wife *Elizabeth* since their Marriage, so that the Jointure made for her by the said Indenture tripartite of 31st *May* 1712, was no Way equivalent to the Fortune He had received with Her, He the said *James Woolston*, in Consideration of the Premisses and of Love and Affection to the said *Elizabeth* his Wife, as an INCREASE to her Jointure, (being then in Possession &c *ut supra*,) *assigns limits* and *appoints*, *in Pursuance and by Virtue of the* POWER GIVEN HIM BY THE WILL, and of all other Powers and Authorities that were in Him, All the Messuages Lands &c devised to him by his Father's Will, in the several Parishes of *Westogell Broadbempston* and *Staverton* (specifying them particularly) to Trustees, to the Use of the said *Elizabeth* and her Assigns for her Life, *as an* AUGMENTATION *of her Jointure.*

The Jury then find the Value of all the Lands devised to *James Woolston* to be 196 *l.* 10 *s.* *per Annum*; *viz.* *Staverton* 90 *l.* *Broadbempston* 60 *l.* *Westogell* 46 *l.* 10 *s.* And that the Lands devised to *John* were of the yearly Value of 230 *l.*

James died on 30th *November* 1756, without Issue Male; leaving only One Daughter now living; and Ten Grand-children by another Daughter, Nine of which are now living.

Elizabeth entered into *all* the Premisses devised by the Will of *Christopher* and *comprised in the said Indentures*; and is still possessed thereof.

John, the Son of *John* and Lessor of the Plaintiff, is, and has been ever since the Death of *John* his Father, seised of the *Rest.*

Prudence died before *James*, and before his Making the Deed dated 3d *October* 1751.

The Lessor of the Plaintiff entered into the Premisses in *Broadbempston* and *Westogell* on 30 *June* 31 *G.* 2. and demised to the Plaintiff &c. But whether, upon the whole Matter, the said *Elizabeth* be guilty of the Trespass as to the Premisses in *Broadbempston* and *Westogell*, the Jury know not; but pray the Advice of the Court: And if it shall seem to the Court "that She is guilty thereof," then they find Her guilty; but if &c, then Not guilty.

The

The Question arose upon the PROVISO in the Will of *Christopher Woolston*, *impowering* his two Sons to make Jointures, and upon the EXECUTION *of that Power*.

It was argued, on *Friday* last, the 10th of *April* 1761, by Mr. *Gould* for the Plaintiff;, and now by Mr. *Dunning* for the Defendant.

Mr. *Gould*—The Question (in a narrow Compass) is Whether *James Woolston* had not *completely* EXHAUSTED *his Power*, by executing his Indenture of 31st *May* 1712: Or Whether *any Power* REMAINED in him *after* the Making of that Deed.

* 1 *Salk*. 240. *Lucas* 31. 2. *Peere Wms*. 149. 8 *Rep*. 69. *b*. 2 *Strange* 992.

He begun with laying down some of the * General Rules as to the Execution of Powers; And then proposed to consider 1st. The *Sense* and Substance of the *present Power*; 2dly. Whether it was *exhausted*.

First—The *Intent* was to enable *James* to make a Jointure on his future Wife or Wives as often as He should marry.

Secondly—It has been *completely exhausted* with respect to *this* Wife, by the *first Deed*; which has *no express Reservation*; nor *intended* any. It is like the Case of Powers of Revocation; which can be executed but once, and not *toties quoties*. This was settled in the Case of *Hele* v. *Bond*, *Prec. in Chancery* 474.

The Lands in *Staverton* were charged with an Annuity of 50 *l*. *per Annum* to *Prudence*: And the Intention was, "That *Staverton*, when clear of that Annuity, should be her Jointure;" And She and her Issue were to enjoy those Lands in *Staverton*.

He said He could find no Cases that were quite applicable to the present. *Harvey* v. *Harvey*, † *in Canc*. is not.

† 12th *November* 1739. and 22d *July* 1740. See *Equity Cases Abridged*, *Vol*. 2. *pa*. 669, 670. *pl*. 20, 21, 22.

Mr. *Dunning* now argued for the Defendant—He entered into the Origin, and went through the History of *Powers*: Which He divided into three Sorts;

1st. *Naked* Powers, unaccompanied with any Interest: (Which He allowed, were to be construed strictly.)

2d. Powers given to *Donees in particular Estates*: (Which, though to be construed strictly in favour of Remainder-men; yet are extended by Ld. *Harcourt*, in the Case of *Beale* v. *Beale*, 1 *Peere Wms*. 244.)

3d. Powers *reserved by the Donor*, for the Benefit of himself, or of his Heir who would have been intitled to the Fee, if it had not been limited by the Donor's Act. Of this *last* Sort, is the present Power: Where the Donor *reserved* a Power to the Tenant for Life, which would otherwise have descended with the Fee; And is *part of the old Dominion* the Donor had over his own Estate.

These have received *liberal* Constructions. *Hob.* 312. *Kibbet* v. *Lee*, *Tr.* 17 *Jac.* 1. *Orby* v. *Mohun*, *Eq. Cases Abr.* 343. *pl.* 5. 2 *Vern.* 531. *Prec. in Chancery* 257. 3 *Chanc. Rep.* 102. *Rep. Eq.* 45. *Lady Coventry* v. *Earl of Coventry et al'*: *Eq. Ca. Abr.* 348. *Pl.* 19. *Lucas* 463. 9 *Modern* 12. *Viner's Abr.* Tit. *Powers*, 477. A. 13. *pl.* 4.

The Point is—Whether the *second* Deed of Appointment in this Case is well *warranted* by the Power.

The Objection can only be to the *Manner* of executing it; *viz.* doing it by *two* Deeds instead of *One*: For it is admitted " It might " have been done by *One* Deed."

But the Words of the Power are, " by Deed or *Deeds*:" Which warrants the Doing it by *Two*. Powers of leasing, jointuring, selling, revoking &c, may be executed at *different Times*, and by *different Deeds*: As was Lady *Jane Coke*'s Case, (then Lady *Jane Holt*.)

As to the Case of *Hele* v. *Bond*, *Prec. in Chancery* 474—That Determination was right: For there the Power of Revocation was executed over the whole Estate.

He denied that there was any Thing in the *first* Appointment, which *takes away* or bars *James's Right* to make a *Second*: Though He admitted that He might *not at that Time* have any formed positive Intention to do so.

The Proviso in the Indenture of 31st *May* 1712, " that *Eliza-* " *beth Bogan* should release all Claim to Dower," was to bar Her, *not Him*. And He has released that Proviso.

Besides, She never could have Dower out of *these* Lands. And the *Covenant* " *to enjoy*" is only an *Expressio eorum quæ tacitè insunt*: It does not include nor relate to the *Remainder*-men; but is only a Transaction between the Husband and Wife and her Issue; and is only for Enjoyment according to the Intent of the Deed and *Chri-*

"*stopher*'s Will." So that this Covenant would not extinguish the Power, or release it, or extend to the Remainder-man; but leaves the Matter just as it found it: It only operated on the Subject Matter of that particular Deed.

Therefore these *two* Appointments are not at all incompatible; but are agreeable to the Intent of the Power and of the Parties.

And there was even a *pecuniary* Consideration for the second Jointure; *viz.* her additional Fortune: (though Love and Affection alone were sufficient.)

As to Authorities—The only One, He said, that seems to impeach the Liberality He contended for, is the Case of *Rattle* v. *Popham*, 2 *Strange* 992. *M.* 8 *G.* 2. *B. R:* And there indeed, the Court looked upon themselves to be bound down to a strict Construction, by *Whitlock*'s Case, 8 *Rep.* 69. *b.*

But *Harvey* v. *Harvey*, in * *Barnardiston's Rep. in Chancery* 103, 109. was *since* that Case. He then cited it from a *Manuscript*; and argued from it to the present Case. He also mentioned the Case of *Scrope* v. *Offley*, *in Dom' Proc'* 25*th March* 1736: which He said was unlike to the present Case and also to that of *Harvey* v. *Harvey*; For the latter is in Point, and proves "That such a Power as this is "*may* be executed at several Times." If the Settlement in 1712, was *not intended* to be a *full* and *complete* Execution of the Power, it shall not prevent the making a further Provision afterwards. Here, the Remainder-Man is a *meer Volunteer*; there, he was a *Purchaser*.

* Ld. *Mansfield* absolutely forbid the citing that Book: For it would be only misleading Students, to put them upon reading it He said it was marvellous, however, to those who knew the Serjeant and his manner of taking Notes, that he should so often *stumble* upon what was right: But yet, that there was not one Case in his Book, which was so throughout.

That Case was indeed in a Court of *Equity*. But the Constructions of *this* Court, and of a Court of *Equity*, ought to be the *same:* Else, a *defective* Execution of a Power would be in a better Case than a *legal* Execution of it.

Mr. *Gould*, in Reply—The Power was *exhausted* by the first Deed, according to the *substantial* Intent of the Power given by the Will. The Husband had Power, it is true, to limit *from Time to Time* upon *different* Wives; or upon *One* Wife, at *several Times* and by *different Deeds*. But upon *this* Deed, it manifestly appears *to be*, and to be INTENDED *to be a* COMPLETE *Jointure* by this first Deed of 1712: And no subsequent Event (as the not having Issue Male, for instance,) can make any Alteration.

The *contracting Parties*, her *own* Relations and Friends, *intended* that the Lands in *Staverton* should be the *full* and *whole* Provision for the Jointure of the Defendant *Elizabeth:* But as there was an

 Annuity

Annuity of 50*l.* a Year issuing out of those Lands during the Life of *Prudence*, *therefore* the Farm called *Metley*, lying in *Westogell*, was also settled upon her during the *Joint* Lives of Her and *Prudence*, as a Security against that Incumbrance upon *Staverton*. And She was obliged by the Proviso, to release all Right and Title of Dower to *James's Lands of Inheritance*.

The Covenant from *James* is confined, "According to the Limitations in the *Will*:" And The Power given by the Will was, "To make a Jointure of *all or any Part* of the Lands."

I admit that if *James* had *declared* this to be *only in* PART of her Jointure, or *expressly reserved* a Power to add any more, He *might afterwards have augmented it*: But *not* having made any such Declaration or Reservation, the Power is exhausted. And it is just like the Case of *Hele* v. *Bond*, (a Case very solemnly determined.)

As to the Case of *Harvey* v. *Harvey*—There, the Power *never was executed at all*. That Power was to settle *Lands*: He settled a *Rent-Charge*. It was, at Law, *no* Execution of the Power. It came into Chancery, to supply the Defect, and *make* it good, which it was *not* before. And the third Deed there shewed the Intention "That it should be *according to the Power* reserved to *Edward Harvey* by the Deed of 1715."

The * Case of *Scrope* v. *Offley* is strong for the Plaintiff here.

* *In Dom' Proc.* 24th *March* 1735.

Lord MANSFIELD—The material Facts stated, are, The Devise by *Christopher* to his two Sons, in strict Settlement; and the Power given them "to settle Jointures," Which Power *James* made Use of, upon his Marriage in 1712, by settling Lands in *Staverton*, with a provisional Addition during two joint Lives, of Lands in *Westogell*, (there being an Annuity of 50*l.* *per Annum* payable to the Testator's elder Brother's Widow out of *Staverton*.) In this Deed of Settlement, there is a Proviso for the Wife's releasing Dower, and also a Covenant from *James*, "That he had Power to make the Appointment," and for Enjoyment under it. He afterwards releases her Agreement to give up her Claim to Dower. Then comes the Indenture of *October* 1751, in Augmentation of her Jointure. There is Nothing stated in the Verdict, nor any Question made, about the *Dower*.

The single Question is Whether the *additional* Jointure is *warranted by the Power*, and is a *good Execution* of it; Or whether the Power was totally *exhausted* by the Settlement in 1712.

This

This Question depends upon two Points: 1st. What is the *Original Construction* of the Power; 2d. Whether the Settlement of 1712 has *barred James* the Husband from making any *further* Settlement upon the *same* Wife; (provided it be such as is warranted by the Original Construction of the Power.)

The First Point is—Whether it be necessary that this Power must be executed *all at once*; Or whether it may be executed at *different* Times.

The Proviso in *Christopher*'s Will which gives this Power, gives it *at large*, without any Restraint: All is left in the Discretion of the Husband. It is no Bar of *Dower*; because 'tis only "for or in the "Name or in lieu of *Jointure*:" (which does not bar Dower.) The only Limitation to it is, that She can not enjoy it *longer than her Life*.

It looks as if the Drawer of the Clause in the Will, which gives this Power, had it in View, "that it *might* be done at different "Times, and repeated more than once." For the Words are that the Husband shall have Power "*from Time to Time* during his "Life, by Deed or *Deeds*, Writing or *Writings*, to limit *all or any* "*Part* of the Estate to any Woman or Women that shall be his "Wife or Wives, for and during their Life or Lives:" And it has no Meaning other than by applying these Words to *each respective* Wife that he might marry, and construing them to impower the Husband to make different Settlements upon the *same* Wife.

The Answer given to this is, "That this Manner of Expression "is meant to take in the Case of marrying *different* Wives, one "after another."

But that might have been done without these *particular* Words, and by a more general Manner of Expression than is here used.

So that upon the very *Frame* and *Creation* of the Power, it is to be executed at *different* Times, if it shall be so thought proper.

The Power in the Case of *Harvey* v. *Harvey* was in different Words from these, and not so strong as these: The Power there was "To settle so much of the Premisses as should be of the yearly "Value of 603*l.* for *a* Jointure and Provision for such *Wife* during "*her* natural Life." That was for A Jointure; *One* specific *entire*

2 Thing:

Thing: Not "upon a Wife * or Wives;" Not "*from Time to* "*Time*;" Nor "by Deed *or Deeds*, Writing *or Writings*." It was there urged "That the Power was EXECUTED." The Lord Chancellor (Lord *Hardwicke*) was clear That he might execute the Power at *different* Times; *less* than the Whole, *at first*; and then more. It was in that Case admitted by Mr. *Wilbraham*, "That it "might be executed at *different* Times." And so Lord *Hardwicke* again held at the Re-hearing.

* The Words were, "that if *Edward* marries any other Wife, that then *and so often Edward* may settle &c."

This Case now before Us is infinitely stronger than that of *Harvey* v. *Harvey*: And it is certain, that in the present Case, the Power might have been executed at *different* Times, upon the *original Construction* of it.

Second Point—This being so, It brings Us to the *Operation* of the Deed of Settlement in 1712; and leads Us to inquire, in the first Place, What *James intended* by this Deed, which limits the Lands in *Staverton* and the Farm in *Westogell* to the Use of the Defendant *Elizabeth*.

It is urged that they are given Her "for and in the Name and in "Lieu of her Jointure;" And that there is a Covenant, "That "She and his Sons by Her shall enjoy."

Now if this was a Dispute with the Son of the Marriage, I should, even in *that* Case, think that *James* had *not* exhausted his Power by this first Deed, so as to bar himself from adding a further Provision. For this is *not* said to be *in full* of her Jointure, or *in Bar* of any further Provision, or in *full* Satisfaction of it, or any such Thing: And the *Covenant* relates to *Christopher*'s Title and Power of Devising; and is for Enjoyment *according to the Will*, and to support the Title to the Estate *under the Will*. So that this Covenant does not carry the Thing further than if there had been no such Covenant in the Deed: It is only *Expressio eorum quæ tacitè insunt*.

He might, notwithstanding that Covenant, have executed the Power for the Benefit of *another* Wife, if he had married One. And it is not natural to suppose that *Elizabeth*'s Friends should tie Him up against *Her*, and *not* against a *future* Wife, who would be a Step-mother to her Children.

The Case of *Scrope* v. *Offley* is not like *this* Case. That Case turned upon the Words—"To be thereafter made committed or "done by them or either of them:" And there could be no Incumbrance but the second Jointure.

But if there could have been a Doubt, if the Dispute had been with the Son or other Issue of the Marriage; Yet *this* is a Dispute with the *Remainder-Man:* And it can not be imagined that it could be the Intention of *James* Himself or of any of the Parties to this Deed, "That He should preclude Himself from making a further "Provision for his Wife, for the Benefit of the *Remainder-Man*, "who was no Party to the Deed, but a mere Stranger to it, and "enjoyed a good Estate under the Will." The Remainder-Man could never be in the Contemplation of the Parties who made this Deed.

And as to this Point—The Case of *Harvey* v. *Harvey* is very applicable. That was "*in full* for her Jointure, and *in full* Recompence and Satisfaction of Dower or Thirds at Common Law:" And that Power was a Power "to settle *a* Jointure;" And He had by the Deed directed ALL *the Residue to be paid over* to the Remainder-Man. But Lord *Hardwicke* observed, that though the Husband barred *Her* to CLAIM, yet He did not bar *Himself* to GIVE.

He was, in that Case, clear That the former Settlement was no Bar against the Husband's making an *additional* Provision for his Wife under the Power: And so am I, here. There might be many Reasons very sufficient to induce Him to make an additional Provision for Her. For Instance, Alterations might have happened to his Family or Fortune, subsequent to the former Settlement. Here is a Circumstance recited and not contradicted, though not expressly found; An *Additional Fortune* came to his Wife since the former Settlement was made: So that it became really his *Duty* to make an additional Provision for Her; as He had no Issue Male. And there is Nothing in the Settlemenent of 1712, to prevent it.

There is good Sense in what Mr. *Dunning* said, "That Executions of Powers should have the *same* Construction Force and Effect in Courts of *Law*, which they have in Courts of Equity:" Because the Statute of Uses transferred that Mode of Real Property, from Equity to the Common Law. Whatever is a good Power or Execution in Equity, the Statute makes good at Law.

But in some of the early Cases, they reasoned in Courts of *Law*, upon these Equitable Powers, from Notions applicable to naked Authorities Unconnected with any Interest, or to mere legal Powers introduced by other Statutes, (such as Leases by Ecclesiastical Persons, or Tenants in Tail;) instead of adopting the Liberality of Courts of Equity, and considering these Powers brought into the Common Law by the Statute of Uses, merely as a MODE *of Ownership or Property*.

Considering them in *this* Light, No Doubt could ever have been made " Whether a Man might not do *less* than his Power;" Or if he did more, " Whether it should not be good to the *Extent* of his " Power."

Courts of *Equity* reasoned as they would have done if the Statute had not been made; and were forced to assume a Jurisdiction to correct the too strict and narrow Construction put upon Powers and the Execution of them.

And yet whatever is an *Equitable* OUGHT to be deemed a *Legal* Execution of a Power: For there can be no Circumstances to affect a Remainder-Man personally in Conscience, when a *Power* is not duly executed, any more than the Issue in Tail or the Successor of an Ecclesiastical Person if a *Lease* is not duly made.

In the Case of * *Rattle* v. *Popham*, THIS Court thought themselves bound by † *Whitlock*'s Case; and held the Lease *not* to be warranted by the Power. The Widow brought her Bill in the Court of Chancery. And Lord *Talbot*, arguing from the same Premisses, the Power and the Lease, without any other Circumstance, held the Lease to *be* warranted by the Power. He said, It was *not a defective*, but a blundering Execution: And He decreed the Defendant to pay all the Costs, both at Law and in Equity.

* *M.* 8 *G.* 2. *B. R.* 2 *Stra.* 992.

† 8 *Co.* 70.

But there are no Precedents which can stand in the Way of our determining *this* Case, as it ought to be determined, liberally, equitably and according to the true Intention of the Parties.

Mr. Just. DENISON declared Himself satisfied with these Reasons so fully given by Lord *Mansfield*; and that He was of the same Opinion.

Mr. Just. WILMOT—Courts of *Law* and Courts of *Equity* ought to *concur* in supporting the Execution of these Powers, which are very convenient to be inserted in Marriage Settlements, and are very useful to Families: And they ought not to listen to nice Distinctions that savour of the Sophistry of Schools; but to be guided by true good Sense and manly Reason.

After the Statute of *Uses*, it is much to be lamented that the Courts of Common Law had not adopted all the Rules and Maxims of Courts of Equity, by which they were guided in their Determinations upon them. This would have prevented the Absurdity of the same Party's *receiving* Costs in *one* Court, and *paying* them in *Another*, upon the very same Litigation.

But

But the *present* Case wants no Support. Here, the two Points are, 1st. Whether this Power was, in it's *original Creation*, *intended* to be such as might be executed at different Times, and consequently might be so, if the Tenant for Life thought proper to use it in that Manner: 2dly. Whether the *Deed* in 1712 *prevented and barred* the Tenant for Life from repeating it a second Time.

First—The *Intention* is clear, That it was originally intended to be executed at *different* Times, even upon the same Woman.

Then it is to be inquired Whether it might be so executed, within the *Rules of Law*.

* Precedents in Chancery 474. The Determination in the * Case of *Hele* v. *Bond* was certainly right. There, the Power of Revocation was executed over the *whole* Estate. The Power reserved to *A.* was "to revoke the Uses "of the Settlement, and declare new Ones:" And He did revoke the old Uses, and limit new Ones, without annexing any *new* Power of Revocation to these *new* Uses. There, the first Power of Revocation did not ride over the *new* Uses: It was executed over the *whole* Estate.

Here, the Question is, Whether this Power be so *indivisible*, that it can be only executed *once*.

Digges's Case is in Point, "That a Person who has such a Power "of Revocation may revoke *Part* at *one* Time and *Part* at *another*; "but not the same Part twice, unless he reserves a *new* Power of "Revocation." 1 *Co.* 173. *b.*

And this Power in the present Case relates *to all and* EVERY PART of the Estate, by the express Terms of the Proviso. It can not therefore be necessary to be all done *uno Flatu*; but may be executed at *different* Times: And it is highly reasonable that it should be so. There may be many cogent Reasons to render it convenient: As Children being more or less numerous; A Wife's additional Fortune, or her good Behaviour and Merit; or many other Circumstances of a Family. And what is such a Power, but a Mode of Conveyance putting the Tenant for Life into the same Condition as if he was Tenant in *Fee*, quoad *hoc*? Therefore it may be executed at different Times.

Second Question—Then the only Question is, Whether the *Deed* in 1712 *prevents* this, and *bars James* from making any further Provision for his Wife.

Now

Now as to the Frame of the Deed, it must be observed that the PRACTICE in Conveyancing is, *to release* the Power and all further Claim to it, whenever the Power is completely executed, and there is *no Intention to go any further* in the Exercise of it.

And as to the Covenant—This Covenant means no more than the usual Covenant for Enjoyment *according to the Limitations in the Will*; "that his Wife and her Issue shall enjoy it, *subject* to the Power given by his Father's Will."

Therefore even *if* there had been Issue Male, and this a Litigation with that Male Issue of the Marriage, I should still have been of this Opinion that I have now declared: But, as there is *no* Issue Male, it would be absurd to make the Husband stipulate that He should not provide for his Daughter or Daughters and their Children.

And the Proviso "that the Wife should release her Claim to Dower," does not stand in the Way; nor the Release of that Proviso: For though the Husband might mean to bind *Her* from CLAIMING any more, Yet he did not mean to bind *Himself* from GIVING Her more, if He should think fit. It would be absurd to suppose that the Parties to the Deed understood or meant it in that Light. Therefore no Inference can be drawn from this Proviso.

Per Cur. unanimously,
JUDGMENT for the DEFENDANT.

Rex *vers.* Sir Willoughby Aston Bart. and John Dodd Esq; et al'. *Thursday* 6th *April* 1761.

MR. *Aston* and Mr. *Schutz* shewed Cause against a Rule obtained in the last Term upon the Motion of Mr. *Norton*, for Sir *Willoughby* and Mr. *Dodd* (as Justices of the Peace for the County of *Berks*) and Mr. *James Head* (Treasurer of the said County) to shew Cause Why a Writ or Writs of *Mandamus* should not be awarded, directed to them All, Requiring them the said Justices to make an Order or Orders upon the said Treasurer, to *re-imburse* the Parishioners of the Parish and Burrough of *Newbury* in the same County the Sum of 114*l.* 1*s.* expended by the Officers of that Parish, *for the Relief of the Wives and Children* of several MILITIA-MEN ordered out into *actual Service*, in Pursuance of Orders of the said two Justices made for that Purpose in the Months of *August September* and *November* in the Year 1759; and requiring him the said Treasurer to pay the same.

Mr. *Aston* made a Doubt Whether the *Direction* of the Writ was rightly prayed; Or whether it ought not rather to have been prayed to be *directed* to the * *Sessions:* But however, He said the Justices at Sessions were very ready to make any Order that the Court should think right; assoon as they should be informed what the Opinion or Sense of the Court is; And that they would do this voluntarily, without being compelled by *Mandamus:* But that at present, and until they should know the Sense of the Court, They were of Opinion

* V. Peat's Case, 6 Mod. 228, 310.

1st. That a *Substitute* of a Militia-man is not properly a *Militia-man* within the Meaning of 31 *G.* 2. *c.* 26. § 28.

2dly. That as the Town of *Newbury* does *not contribute* to the County-Stock, but have a *separate Stock* of their own (which was admitted to be true;) they were not intitled to be re-imbursed out of the *County*-Stock for the weekly Allowance made to the Families of *any Newbury Men* who served as Substitutes: But that such Allowance ought to be paid out of the *Newbury* Stock, and not out of the *County*-Stock.

Mr. *Norton, contra,* insisted, 1st. That a *Substitute* was properly a *Militia-man,* within the Meaning of the Act of 31 *G.* 2. *c.* 26. § 28.: Especially, *since the Construction* which the *Legislature themselves* have put upon it, by the subsequent Act of 33 *G.* 2. *c.* 22. § 1, 6. And particularly by the Preamble of this latter Statute.

2dly. That the Parish of *Newbury* have a great many of their Inhabitants who are willing to serve as Substitutes for Others; And that many *Newbury*-men serve as Substitutes for other *Newbury*-men; and many of them, as Substitutes for such Militia-men as are resident *out* of *Newbury,* and Inhabitants of *other Parts* of the County. And He thought his Request was very fair and equitable; for that He did not desire to be re-imbursed out of the County-Stock, for the Allowances made to the Families of any *Newbury*-men that had served as Substitutes for *other Newbury-men,* but of those *Newbury*-men *only,* who had been *ordered out into actual Service,* as Substitutes for *such* Militia-men as were *not* Inhabitants of *Newbury,* but of *other* Parts of the *County at large;* pursuant to 31 *G.* 2. *c.* 26. § 28. whereby it is enacted " That when any Militia-man shall be ordered out into actual Service, leaving a Family not of Ability to " support themselves during his Absence, the Overseer or Overseers " of the Parish where such Family shall reside shall allow to such " Family such weekly Allowance for their Support, until the Re-" turn of such Militia-man, as shall be ordered by any One Justice " of the Peace; such Allowance to be *re-imbursed out of the County-*

" *Stock,*

" *Stock*, by the Treaſurer of the County: And ſuch Treaſurer ſhall " be allowed the ſame in his Accounts."

Lord MANSFIELD was clear in his Opinion againſt that of the Juſtices, in both Points.

1ſt. A Subſtitute muſt, *ſince* the Act of 33 *G.* 2. *c.* 22. be conſidered as a Militia-man within the 31 *G.* 2. *c.* 26. For though there might have been a Doubt upon the former Act (at the firſt making of it) " Whether a Subſtitute was a Militia-man for this " Purpoſe;" Yet this Doubt is removed by the latter Act, which is a plain *declaratory* legiſlative Expoſition of the former: The Preamble recites this very Clauſe, and puts this Conſtruction upon it " That Subſtitutes *are* Militia-men within it."

2dly. As to the Re-imburſment out of the County-Stock, for the Allowances made (under a proper Order) to the Families of ſuch *Newbury*-men as have been Subſtitutes for Inhabitants of the *other* Parts of the County—It is very reaſonable and equitable: And they do not claim it for the Family of any One who was Subſtitute for a Perſon drawn out of the Liſt for their *own Diſtrict*.

Mr. Juſt. DENISON and Mr. Juſt. WILMOT were of the ſame Opinion.

However, as this Queſtion was a very general One, and might affect other Parts of the Kingdom as well as this County of *Berks*, They offered Mr. *Aſton* to conſider further of it, if He had any Doubt about their preſent Opinion.

But Mr. *Aſton* declared He had not: And He anſwered for the Juſtices, that they would conform themſelves to the Opinion of the Court; which they were only deſirous to be appriſed of, in Order to make it the Rule of their Conduct.

Upon which Declaration, THE COURT thought it unneceſſary to make any Rule or Order in Form, upon the preſent Occaſion.

Bevan *verſ.* Protheſk.

IN a long Motion about the Stay of Proceedings in an Inferior Court—

THIS COURT held, That the Delivery of a *Recordari facias loquelam*, to the Clerk of a County-Court, *after Interlocutory Judgment*

ment and *before final* Judgment, is a Stop to all further Proceedings in that Court.

They likewise held, That the Officer of the inferior Court can not refuse paying Obedience to the Writ, under Pretence of his *Fees* not being paid to him: For He is *obliged to obey the Writ*; and has a *proper Remedy*, which He may take, for such Fees as are due to Him.

Tuesday 21st *April* 1761.

Stevens *verſ.* Evans et al'.

THIS was an Action of Trover, for Cattle: In which, a Special Case was agreed upon, for the Court's Opinion.

The Special Case states, That on the *12th* of *April* 1759, an Assessment was made and allowed at a Vestry of the Inhabitants of the Parish of *Wix* in *Essex*, to *re-imburse* to *Stephen Durant*, the Overseer, the Monies laid out in the Half Year ended on *Easter Monday* then next ensuing the Date, for the necessary Relief of the Poor of the said Parish of *Wix*, by the said *Stephen Durant* the Overseer &c. Which Assessment was in due Manner allowed and confirmed by two Justices of the Peace &c, and published in the Church &c. That *William Vesey* was therein assessed 9*l.* 11*s.* That afterwards, *viz.* on 18th *July* 1759, *William Vesey died, intestate.* That on 12 *December* 1759, ADMINISTRATION of his Goods &c was granted to *John Stephens, the Plaintiff*; who possessed Himself of his personal Estate, and particularly of the Cattle in the Declaration mentioned.

That on the 14th of *January* 1760, two Justices of Peace executed a Warrant; in which Warrant, the said Rate or Assessment is recited; And the Warrant also recites That whereas it appeared on the Oath of *Stephen Durant* the late Overseer, "that the said "9*l.* 11*s.* had been lawfully *demanded of the said William Vesey de-*"*ceased*, and of his *Widow and Representative Susannah Vesey*, since "his Decease, who have refused and doth refuse to pay the same"; It requires the Church-Wardens Overseers and Constables &c. to make *a Distress of the* GOODS AND CHATTELS OF THE LATE WILLIAM VESEY; And if within six Days next after such Distress, the said Sum of 9*l.* 11*s.* and also reasonable Charges of the Distress, rendering the Overplus to Her the said *Susannah Vesey*, be not paid on Demand, then to sell &c: And if no Distress be to be had, then to certify the same; so that such further Proceeding may be had therein, as to the Law doth appertain.

By Virtue of this Warrant, the Defendant *Goby* (then Constable) and the other Defendant *Durant* (the late Overseer) at *Wix* aforesaid on the 19th of *January* 1760, *distrained the Cattle, and sold them* for 15*l*: Which Cattle so distrained, were the Cattle of the said *William Vesey* in his Life-time, and at his Death, and were distrained on the Lands in the said Parish of *Wix*, occupied by the said *William Vesey* in his Life-time.

That the Overplus, after Payment of the Rate, was tendered back.

That Notice of the Action was given to the Justices.

The Question upon this Case, is Whether the Distraining and Taking and Selling the Cattle which were the Goods of *William Vesey*, in *the Hands* of the Plaintiff, his ADMINISTRATOR, by virtue of the said Warrant, was lawful, or not.

This Case stood now in the Paper, for Argument.

Mr. *Norton*, on Behalf of the Plaintiff, argued that it was *not* lawful: And an Action of Trover is maintainable against the Parish Officers, for taking them.

1st Objection. It is a *bad Rate*, and *illegal*.

First—It is a Rate made to *re-imburse* an Overseer: Which is a bad Rate, as was settled in *Tawney*'s Case, 2 *Ld. Raym.* 1009. and 6 *Mod.* 97. *Domina Regina* v. *Paroch' de Littleport*, S. C. and 2 *Salk.* 531. S. C. *Tawney*'s Case. For the Overseer was not obliged to advance the Money without a previous Rate: And He may re-imburse Himself out of the next, made in his own Time.

Secondly—It is a Rate made for *Half a Year* ending on *Easter-Monday* next: Whereas a Rate can not be made for longer than a *Month*. 6 *Mod.* 98. *Tawney*'s Case, *ut supra*; but called there *Domina Regina* v. *Par. de Littleport*. The Case of *Tracey* v. *Talbot*, * in 2 *Salk.* 532. is in point. * The 2d Resolution.

2d Objection. There was *no Refusal by the Representative* to pay the Money. Now there can be no Distress, without a *previous Demand and Refusal*. The Refusal was really by *Vesey*, who is dead; and by the Widow who was *not* in Fact, (though She is in the Case stated to be) his *Representative*.

But supposing these Objections not to hold, and that the Rate and Warrant are *good*; Yet the Goods of *Vesey* are *not* distrainable, in the *Hands of his personal Representative*, for a Rate made *upon Vesey* Himself. There is no Instance of it, nor any Case to sup-

 port

port this: Therefore it ought not to be supported. Nor is there any Neceffity for it; For the *Poor* can *not fuffer* by the Non-Payment of this Money. There are other Provifions for raifing the Money.

This is a *Cafus omiffus:* And *Lex non curat de minimis*, (as this is.) The Acts of Parliament give *no fuch Power* to the Juftices, as to grant fuch a *Warrant:* And Nothing can be *intended* in Favour of their Jurifdiction. It is for this Reafon, that with regard to the Wages of Servants they are confined to Wages of Servants in *Hufbandry* only, and can not exercife fuch Jurifdiction in refpect to the Wages of other Servants.

As to any *inferred* Power, (for there is no exprefs Power,) None can be pretended, but from 43 *Eliz. c.* 2: For 17 *G.* 2. *c.* 38. makes no Alteration in the Method of compelling Payment of the Rate.

It is not the *Thing* that is rated by 43 *Eliz. c.* 2. § 1. but only the *Perfon*, (the Occupier;) And Section 4 gives the Means of compelling it: And the *Occupier* alone is the Perfon there meant; And the Refufal to contribute according to the Affeffment made upon Him, is treated as an *Offence*; And the *Offender* is to be fent to Gaol. But the *Executor* or *Adminiftrator* is *not* an *Offender:* It is a *perfonal* Charge. An Overfeer could not bring an *Action* for it, even againft the *Perfon charged:* He muft purfue the *particular* Remedy appointed by the Act. And if fo, the Court will never *extend* the Remedy, againft a *Reprefentative*.

If an Adminiftrator fhould pay this Rate, He might be guilty of a *Devaftavit*. And the Compulfion by Diftrefs will not alter the Cafe, or be an Excufe for a *Devaftavit*.

In what *Courfe* of Debt is this Rate to be ranked? How is the Adminiftrator to know what *Preference* it is to have?

There is indeed a *legiflative Expofition* made, upon this head, in *another* Statute relating to the Poor Laws: I mean 17 *G.* 2. *c.* 38. § 3: Which provides a Remedy for the Cafe of the Death of an Overfeer who has Parifh-Money in his Hands; and gives the Preference of this Sort of Debt to all others; directing the Executors or Adminiftrators of the Overfeer to pay it out of the Affets, "before *any* of his other Debts are paid and fatisfied."

Therefore, as the Legiflature have made a Declaration in *that* Cafe, and *not* in *this*, It is plain that they did *not mean* fo in this Cafe, but meant to leave it to the *ordinary* Courfe of Adminiftration.

2 Mr.

Mr. *Bishop*, *contra*, for the Justices of Peace, and for the Parish Officers.

1st. The Court will not now enter into any Objection to the *Rate*.

The only Questions therefore are as to the *Warrant*, and as to the *Assets being distrainable* in the Hands of the *Representative*.

As to the Demand of the Money upon *Vesey Himself*, It *was* made upon *Him*; and is so stated: And as to the Demand upon the *Representative*, The End and Intention of this Special Case, was to settle the material Point, the real Question "Whether the Goods "of the Person rated are or are not distrainable in the Hands of the "*Representative*."

The *Practice* is with Us, That they *are*. It is no Answer, to say That *other* People are *liable* to pay, if the Person rated *does not*. The Question is, Whether the Representative of the Person rated, is or is not liable.

The Authority to make this Warrant, and to make the Distress in Obedience to it, is founded upon the Stat. of 43 *Eliz*. *c*. 2. § 4. which gives this Remedy by Warrant and Distress, upon Refusal to pay.

The *Demand* of the Money is to be made, and in the present Case was actually made *upon the Person assessed*: And that made it a *Debt* from *Him*. There was *no Need* of a Demand upon the *Representative*: The *Assets* were already *become liable*, and *remained* so in his Hands.

As to the Danger of a *Devastavit*—A Representative could not be guilty of a *Devastavit*, even by paying a simple Contract-Debt before a Bond-Debt, *if He had no Notice* of the Bond-Debt: And the Distress made upon Him would be a Justification to Him for paying it under the Compulsion of such Distress. The Act of 17 *G*. 2. *c*. 38. § 3. makes a Debt of this Sort, payable before any other Debts of the deceased Overseer.

I do not say, That the Executor or Administrator could be *sent to Gaol*, for Non-payment of this Debt: But yet, the *Assets* in his Hands are *distrainable*, as the *proper Fund out of which* it is to be paid; Especially, as *no Action* would lie for it (as Mr. *Norton* agrees.)

Mr. *Norton*, in Reply—No Answer at all has been given to my Objection to the *Rate itself*.

And

And I say, that even if the Administrator were admitted to be liable to pay, yet still there ought to have been a previous *Demand* upon *Him*.

No such *Practice* as what Mr. *Bishop* speaks of, is *stated* in the Case; And therefore the Court will intend That there is none such: And I believe there *is None*. I never heard of it before: I take it to be directly the other Way.

And, at *all* Events, the *Poor* can not suffer: For there are other Persons who must make up the Deficiency, in Case this Man do not pay.

This is scarce a *solvent* Estate; because the Widow has renounced Administration, and it is granted to a Creditor.

This is a *Charge* upon the *Person*, which *dies with Him*: Like *Costs* payable by One who dies; (for which a Bill, in the Court of Chancery, can not be revived; And so in this Court, upon Informations, they are gone by the *Death* of the Party.)

And the Administrator can not possibly know in *what Course* of Administration to pay this Rate. If an Executor or Administrator pays a Debt of a lower Nature, at that Time *knowing* of others of an higher, it is undoubtedly a *Devastavit*: And here there *may* be Debts of an higher Nature, which the Administrator may know of. And if He is obliged to pay it *under Compulsion*, He ought to pay it *without* Compulsion; And *vice versâ*.

* Mr. *Bishop* denied this.

It is a *Charge* imposed; not a Debt. The Case was * left open upon its being stated at the Trial, to all or any other Objections that could be made upon the Face of it. There were Other Debts beside this.

Mr. Just. Denison.—That makes no Difference.

The Question is stated particularly upon this Case; and is *confined* to the levying the Money upon the *Representative* of the Person charged.

I should think, the Event must have *often* happened, in Fact and Experience.

The *Practice* is *not stated*: But however, the Question is What the *Law* is; *not* What the *Practice* is.

2 It

REPRESENTATIVE ought to have been *convened* before the Justices, and asked "What HE had to say Why he should not pay the Rate "assessed upon *Vesey* his Intestate." This Case seems to be like a *Scire facias* upon a Judgment; upon which, Execution can not be sued out against the Representatives, without asking them what they have to alledge why it should not be taken out.

At the Time of the Teste, they were the *bona et catalla* of the Representative. If the Teste had been prior to the Death, they would have been *bona et catalla* of the Deceased: But if tested after his Death, they are not his *bona et catalla*; but the *bona et catalla* of the Representative.

Therefore *if* the Money *had been demanded of the Representative*, I should have had great Doubt Whether this Warrant and Distress would not have been good: For I can not think that by the Death of the Person charged with this Rate, the Assessment before made upon Him and demanded of Him would have been quite gone and lost to the Parish, and could not have been any Way come at. For though it may be a Charge upon the *Person*, (as has been objected,) Yet it is a Charge upon Him *in respect of the Thing* occupied: And though He be called an *Offender*, if He refuse to pay it, yet He can be *no otherwise* considered as an Offender, than every other Debtor who refuses or neglects to pay his Debts, and thereby renders his Person and Goods liable to be taken in Execution, is so far treated as an Offender, till he shall comply with the Judgment awarded.

And in Experience, I know it to be the Case, that these Payments by Executors or Administrators are often allowed, (I dare say I have known it done 50 Times) to go in Discharge of the Assets of the Testator or Intestate. I do not say, in *what Course* of Administration of Assets: But it has been very often allowed, I am sure; though I do not remember that it has been settled in what Course of Administration. Indeed it might be of too much Consequence, to put it into the Power of Justices of Peace to determine upon the Administration of Assets, as to the Course in which they were to be administered.

In a Case of *Wallis, Administrator* v. *Hewit*, at *Guildhall*, at the Sittings after *Hil.* Term 5 *G.* 2. before Ld. Ch. Just. *Eyre*, in an Action of Trespass, Two Aldermen of *London* had made a Warrant to distrain a Man for a Poor-Rate. The Man died intestate; But before that, there had been a Demand made upon Him and Refusal by Him, and a Warrant of Distress granted upon his Refusal: And then He died—*Eyre* Ch. J. held that a Distress could not be made after his Death; Or if it could, yet the Representative ought to have

He agreed the State of the Case to be, that the *Placita* were of *Hilary* Term in the first Year of *George* the *Third*; And that it was alledged in the Declaration, that the Defendant entered &c, "against "the Peace of our *said* Lord the King;" And that it lays the *Demise* to have been made on the 30th of *May* in the *thirty-third* Year of His SAID Majesty.

But He answered and observed, 1st. That this is *after a Verdict*: 2dly. That it is *aided* and assisted by some or One of the Statutes of *Jeofails*; and therefore shall not be regarded by the Court, but altogether *disregarded* and over-looked.

First—An Ejectment being a *fictitious* Action, and the Defendant confessing Lease Entry and Ouster, He consequently confesses a Lease SUFFICIENT *to bring the Title in Question*: And it must be a Lease of a *subsisting* Term. But as there could be *no* 33d Year of THIS King; therefore the Court will apply those Words, "the "33d Year," *secundùm subjectam materiam*, when it comes before them AFTER *a Verdict*.

In 2 *Strange* 1011. *Rex* v. *Bishop of Landaff*, in a *Quare Impedit*; a Verdict was solemnly determined to have cured the Want of alledging a Presentation. And if this be considered as an *impossible* Day, then the Lease took Effect from the *Delivery* of the Deed. In the Case of *Acton* v. *Eels*, 2 *Salk*. 662. It was held to be a Time impossible, and as if no Day at all had been alledged: And Judgment was given for the Plaintiff.

Secondly—It is aided by the Statutes of *Jeofails*. The 32 *H*. 8. *c*. 30. § 1. cures it, as a Jeofail; being after a Verdict. This can be no more than a mere *Jeofail*; 'Tis a mere Misprision of the Clerk: Therefore the Court will overlook it, and give Judgment *without any regard* to it. 2 *Strange* 1011. *Rex* v. *Bishop of Landaff*, is in Point so.

Besides, it may be AMENDED. In the Case of *Muttit* v. *Denny*, 2 *Strange* 807. A Declaration in Ejectment was amended after a Verdict for the Plaintiff; though there was Nothing to amend by; on the Authority of *Cro. Jac*. 306. and 1 *Salk*. 48. *pl*. 5. Bishop of *Worcester*'s Case. And if it may be amended without any Thing to amend by, the Court will surely *over-look* it, and not arrest Judgment upon such a trifling Objection.

Mr. *Norton* and Mr. *Burland* were of Counsel for the Defendant. They insisted that this *Title*, made upon the Plaintiff's own Declaration, is such as he *can not recover upon*: For it appears upon the very Face of it, "that He has *No* Title at all."

The

If the Demise had been laid "in the 33d Year of his *late* Majesty," undoubtedly in that Case, the Court would have *supplied* the Words "King *George* the Second." And this seems to be just such a *Kind* of Defect as that would have been.

This is *not an uncertain* Description; but only a Title *defectively set out*, by the mere *Mistake of the Clerk*. And being in *Ejectment*, there is the more Reason for our over-ruling this nice Objection.

I think there is *no Need of any Amendment* at all.

Mr. Just. Wilmot was very clear in the same Opinion: And He said, It was so plain a Case, that there was no Occasion to use many Words about it. Therefore He would only declare his entire Concurrence, that the Rule should be discharged.

Per Cur. Rule was discharged.

Rex *vers.* Palmer and Baine Esquires et al'.

Wednesday 22d April 1761.

UPON shewing Cause Why an Information should not be granted against two Justices of Peace and Others, for a Misdemeanour, relating to the Conviction of a Poacher, and the Circumstances attending it;

The Court thought proper, upon fully hearing and considering all the Affidavits and what was urged by the Counsel on both Sides, to *discharge* the Rule, as to *All* the Defendants; with Costs *to be paid to the* Justices, but without Costs as to the *Others*.

And They were, upon this Occasion, most explicit in their Declaration, "That even where a Justice of Peace acts *illegally*," (which, however, was not the present Case,) "Yet if He has acted *honestly* "and candidly, *without* Oppression, Malice, Revenge, or any bad "View or *ill Intention* whatsoever, The Court will never punish "Him in this *extraordinary* Course of an Information; but "leave the Party complaining, to their *ordinary* legal Remedy or "Method of Prosecution, by Action or by Indictment."

Rex

Mr. Serj. *Davy*, on Behalf of the Defendants, objected to it;

1st. That *No Evidence* is stated to have been *given in the* PRESENCE *of the Defendants*; Only, the Charge was READ *to them*, in the Presence of the Prosecutor *Thomas Eaton*, the Witness; But it was not made out and proved by him *vivâ voce* before them, though they *personally appeared*, and consequently had a Right of *Cross-examining* the Witnesses, upon their giving verbal Evidence Face to Face: Nor indeed is any Evidence at all *set out* with sufficient Particularity and Preciseness.

2d Objection—This *Fact*, as charged, is NOT *an Offence within* the * Statute. These People were All of them *Journey-men to the same Master* at Home; and *not* Persons assembled and FORMED *into* UNLAWFUL CLUBS *or* UNLAWFUL SOCIETIES † abroad: Which He would have had it understood that the Statute required. And there was *no* WRITTEN Agreement, no Resolution "not to work "with Him or any *other* Master for such Wages."

* See the Preamble and the whole first Section.

† But the Words of the Charge are "that; they had agreed one amongst another AND WITH OTHER Journey-men Wool-combers." *Vide ante* 1163.

3d Objection. Here is *no Judgment*: It is only said "That they "are *convicted* for unlawfully entering into such Combination." It ought to proceed "*quod forisfaciat*," and expressly ADJUDGE *the Forfeiture*. So is 2 *Strange* 858. 3 *G.* 2. in ‡ *Rex* v. *Hawks*; Where a Conviction for killing a Deer was quashed, because it was only "*convictus est*;" without any Judgment "*quod forisfaciat*."

‡ *V. Fitz-G.* 124. S. C.

They ought to have awarded the particular Punishment; as the Act does not fix the Duration of the Punishment, but leaves the Time of the Imprisoment quite discretionary, "for any Time not "exceeding 3 Months." Therefore this Case differs widely from Cases where the Punishment is *ascertained* and *necessarily flows from* the Conviction.

THE COURT over-ruled the 2d Objection, as a frivolous One, and not to be seriously supported.

Mr. *Caldecott*, *contra*, for the Plaintiff, applied Himself to answer the first and third Objections.

1st. It sufficiently appears on the Face of the Conviction, that the Defendants HEARD the ‖ Evidence. However, it is *not necessary* that the Evidence should be *given in the* PRESENCE *of the Defendants*: For which, He cited *Rex* v. *Baker*, 2 *Strange* 1240. in Point, as *He* said, *for* Him; but quite otherwise as the Serjeant * alledged,

‖ But the Words are only, "having heard the said CHARGE."

* Notwithstanding this Allegation and Explanation, the Cases seem very much alike: And One of the Judges expresly said "that He knew no Law that *required* the Presence of the Witness Face to Face;" And another said that "perhaps it had been sufficient without either of the Words *read*, or heard, It being "alledged that the Matter was *fully understood* by the Defendant."

1st. Because the General Rule of estimating should be the Difference between the *Price the damaged Goods sell for*, and the *prime Cost* (or Value in the Policy.) Here, the damaged sold at 20*l.* 0*s.* 8 *d.* *per* Hogshead: And the Under-Writer should make it up 30 *l.*

Answ. It is impossible this should be the Rule. It would involve the Under-Writer in the *Rise* or *Fall* of the *Market:* It would subject him in some Cases to pay *vastly more than the Loss*; in Others, it would deprive the Insured of *any Satisfaction, though there was a Loss.*

For Instance,—Suppose the prime Cost or Value in the Policy 30*l.* *per* Hogshead; the Sugars are injured; the Price of the Best is 20*l.* a Hogshead; the Price of the damaged is 19*l.* 10*s.*—The Loss is about a fortieth, and the Insured would be to pay above a third.

Suppose they come to a rising Market, and the sound Sugars sell for 40*l.* a Hogshead, and the damaged for 35*l*, the Loss is an Eighth; yet the Insurer would be to pay Nothing.

The 2d Ground upon which the Plaintiff contends that the 30*l.* should be made up, is, that it appears the Sugars *would* have sold for that Price, if the Damage from the Sea-Water had not made an immediate Sale necessary.

The Moment the Jury brought in their Verdict, I was satisfied that they did right, in totally disregarding the particular Circumstances of this Case: And I wrote a Memorandum at *Guild-hall* in my Note-Book, " that the Verdict seemed to me to be right."

As I expected the other Cause would be tried, I thought a good Deal of the Point, and endeavoured to get what Assistance I could by conversing with some Gentlemen of Experience in Adjustments. The Point has now been very fully argued at the Bar; and the more I have thought, the more I have heard upon the Subject, the more I am convinced that the Jury did right to pay no Regard to these Circumstances.

The Nature of the Contract is, that the Goods shall come safe to the Port of Delivery; or if they do not, to indemnify the Plaintiff to the Amount of the prime Cost, or Value in the Policy. If they arrive, but lessened in Value through Damages received at Sea, the Nature of an Indemnity speaks demonstrably, that it must be by putting the Merchant in the *same* Condition, (Relation being had to the prime Cost or Value in the Policy,) which He would have been

County, *Edward Burrow* Esq; Collector of His Majesty's Subsidies and Customs within the Port of the said Town and County, and *an Inhabitant* thereof, cometh in his own proper Person before *John Wood* and *William Cogan* Esquires, two Justices of our said Lord the King assigned to keep the Peace of our said Lord the King within the said Town and County; and, suing as well for the Poor of the Parish of *St. Trinity* in the said Town and County as for Himself in this Behalf, giveth the said Justices to be informed and to understand, That certain *Butter*, to wit, 547 Barrels thereof, containing All together in Weight 301 Hundred-Weight, was on the 8th Day of *July* last past *imported into this Kingdom*, to wit at the Port of the said Town and County, the same Butter and every Part thereof having been exported *from out of the Kingdom of Ireland* TO LISBON in the Kingdom of *Portugal*, and having been FROM THENCE *imported* into *this* Kingdom, to wit at the Port aforesaid, *in* FRAUD *of the Revenue* of our said Lord the King, and contrary to the Form of the Statutes in that Case made and provided; And that the said Butter had been duly and legally SEIZED, at and in the said Town, on the 28th Day of *July* aforesaid, between the Hours of Ten and Twelve in the Forenoon, and duly and legally preserved and kept from that Time to the Time of exhibiting this Information; And that the *Owner or Owners of the said Butter* or any Part thereof, or any Person for or on the Behalf of him them or any of them, *had not made it appear* unto any Justice of the Peace of and for the said Town and County, by the Oath of two credible Witnesses or otherwise howsoever, "That the said Butter was *not* imported, in "Manner and Form aforesaid, *from* the said Kingdom of IRELAND "into this Kingdom." Whereupon the said Justices did, on the said 2d Day of *August*, duly and legally order *Mr. Richard Bell* of the said Town and County Merchant, the *Consignee and apparent Owner* of the said Butter and every Part thereof, to be summoned to appear before them at the House of *Archibald Brown*, at the Sign of the *Dog and Duck* in the said Town and County, on the 5th Day of the said Month of *August*, then and there to answer the said Information and Premisses. At which Time and Place, come before them the same Justices, as well the said *Edward Burrow* as the said *Richard Bell*: And the said *Richard Bell* having heard the said Information read to Him, and being asked by the said Justices, "Why the said Butter should not be *forfeited*," saith, "That He "hath *Nothing to object* against the *Truth* of the said Premisses con- "tained in the said Information." Whereupon, and upon the Examination of a credible Witness in that Behalf, in the Presence of the said *Richard Bell*, and because the said *Richard Bell* hath Nothing to say nor can say any Thing touching the said Premisses, but doth acknowledge the same to be true as the same are charged in the said Information; It appears unto them the said Justices, That the said Information and every Part thereof is true: And they the portation of Pig and Bar Iron from His Majesty's Colonies in *America*;) And 32 *G.* 2. *c.* 11, 12.

However, This Conviction was unnecessary, and only *ex majori cautela:* For the Goods were *actually and ipso facto forfeited*, by not being claimed and proved, *&c.* within 48 Hours.

Mr. *Morton* was going to reply—

But Lord MANSFIELD said it was needless.—Here is no Suspicion of Fraud. If there had, it might be a different Case. It would not be worth while to go round by *Lisbon*, to evade the Act; and to pay 7 *s.* 8 *d.* to avoid paying 4 *d.* And if it be within the Prohibition, it is within the Permission.

His Lordship however proposed to the Parties, That the Officer of the Customs (Mr. *Edward Burrow*, Collector at *Hull*) should pay the Proprietor, (the Consignee,) the Value of the Butter at the Time of the Seizure, together with the Costs.

And, in Order to compromise the Matter, and save the bringing an Action, He ordered it to stand over from *Saturday* last to this Day.

A Third Person having now named 26 *s. per* Barrel as the Price that Mr. *Burrow* ought to refund to the Consignee of it; And Mr. *Norton* thinking that too much; the Compromise came to Nothing: For Mr. *Norton* thought it better for his Client, to stand an Action, and suffer Judgment to go by Default, and leave the Matter to a Jury, upon a Writ of Inquiry of the Damages sustained by the Seizure.

Whereupon *Per Cur.*
CONVICTION WAS QUASHED.

The End of *Easter* Term 1761, 1 *G.* 3.

Trinity

It is not to be conceived that the Legiſlature intended to put the Parties to the Expence of 40*l.* or 50*l.* in taking out *Office*-Copies; only for the ſake of raiſing 18*d.* or (upon the firſt Act) only a Penny to the Crown.

Mr. *Aſton* obſerved that ſuch a Conſtruction would greatly leſſen the Revenue. At this Rate, *One* Three Penny Stamp would do for a whole Bill.

Mr. Juſt. WILMOT—So You would have FORTY 3*d.* Stamps for this *One* Copy of the Original Bill.

Mr. *Aſton*—Yes: This is what I inſiſt on.

Lord MANSFIELD—The Act of Parliament did not mean to alter the Rule, as to the giving Copies *in Evidence:* If it had, it would have been a heavy Charge upon the Suitor. The *Practice* of a Party's giving the Office Copies in Evidence, very often, is to be accounted for, by their having thoſe Office-Copies in their Poſſeſſion already: So that it is in ſuch Caſe even cheaper to them, to uſe theſe than any Others.

Mr. *Norton* who was retained for the Defendant, urged the Loſs that the Stamp Duty would ſuffer, if this Queſtion ſhould be determined againſt them.

It was therefore Ordered to be ſet down for further Argument on the firſt Day of this Term; with a particular Clauſe in the Rule (by Conſent) to prevent the Plaintiff's being delayed in bringing a new Ejectment, in Caſe the Court's Opinion ſhould be againſt him.

Which Day being now come, and the Cauſe called,

Mr. *Norton* ſaid He ſhould have hoped to have been able to have ſupported the Objection, if it had come out, upon Inquiry, that the *Uſage* of the Stamp-Office had been uniform and conſiſtent, ever ſince the making of the Act, in requiring cloſe Copies to be ſtampt in this Manner.

But He acknowledged, that upon Examination into the Facts, it appeared that there had been no ſuch uniform Uſage; but, on the contrary, different Uſages, and even different Opinions amongſt the Commiſſioners themſelves. Therefore unleſs the Court would couple ſome of the Sections with each Other, He was afraid He could not pretend to ſupport the Objection.

" could not be served; whereupon a Copy of the Rule was fixed " on the Door of the House;" And moreover, " that at a subsequent Day," (upon a Doubt Whether what had been already done, was sufficient,) " the Maid being at Home and opening the " Window, but refusing to open the Door, and denying that her " Mistress was at Home, *Another Copy was affixed* on the Door, " and the Maid was told the Effect of it; and *another Copy was* " *thrown in* at the Window; and the Original Rule was *shewn* to " the Maid."

Per Cur. RULE made ABSOLUTE.

Wednesday 27th May 1761.

Rex *vers.* Darbyshire.

THIS was a Case from *Warwickshire* Assizes.

The Defendant was originally indicted at the Quarter-Sessions holden at *Warwick* on the 4th of *April* 1758, for refusing to take upon Himself the Office of Constable of and for the MANOR *of Birmingham*, having been duly nominated and elected thereto. And The Indictment set forth, That at a Court Leet holden on the 18th of *October* 31 *G.* 2. in and for the MANOR of *Birmingham*, The Defendant, according to the Custom of the same Manor, was duly nominated and elected by the Jury One of the Constables of the said MANOR of *Birmingham* for the Year then next ensuing; He then being an Inhabitant and Resiant of and within the said Manor, and being a fit Person so to be nominated and elected, and a Person liable to be nominated and elected to the said Office. That the Defendant had Notice *&c.* That the Steward certified his Appointment to a Justice of Peace; by whom He was summoned to appear on *&c* at *&c*, to take the Oath of Office as Constable nominated and elected of and for the said *Manor* of *Birmingham* as aforesaid. That although He personally appeared according to the Summons, and was then and there required by the said Justice to take the said Oath of Office of Constable of and for the said *Manor* of *Birmingham* according to the Nomination and Election aforesaid, He unlawfully wilfully and contumaciously did neglect and refuse to take it, and to be duly sworn into the said Office, and to take it upon Him. There was a second Count in the Indictment, alledging that He was personally present in Court at the Leet; and being required by the Steward to be sworn and take the Office upon him, neglected and refused *&c.*

This Indictment being removed hither by *Certiorari*, the Defendant pleaded " Not guilty:" And the Cause was tried at *Warwick* Summer-Assises in *August* 1759, before Ld. Ch. B. *Parker.*

It

Parish of *Birmingham:* Therefore this is not a PARISH Office. And there is no such Division in this Place, as a *Ward:* Therefore no WARD Officer.

But a CONSTABLE is *not a Parish*-Officer at all. It was a Common-Law Office, before Parishes existed. Constables were, by Common Law, Conservators of the Peace. " The Office is as ancient as Turns or Leets;" 4 *Inst.* 265. Therefore *more* ancient than *Parishes.*

A Parish is not a *Common-Law Division*; but an *Ecclesiastical* One: And so it was asserted, in *Freeman's Rep.* 228. in the Case of *Adeson* v. *Sir John Otway*, by Mr. Justice *Atkins.* And in *Mich.* 10 *W.* 3. An Appointment of a Constable was * quashed, because it was not alledged in the Order, " That He was an Inhabitant of " the *Liberty*," but only " of the *Parish.*" *Cases temp. W.* 3. 256. *Anonymous.*

* *Absente Holt.*

Here, this Man is appointed Constable in and for the MANOR of *Birmingham.*

The Office of Constable is always annexed to a *Vill, not* to a *Parish.* But the *Felony*, in this Case, was committed in the *Parish of Birmingham*, not in the Vill of *Deritend.*

Mr. *Caldecott*, for the Defendant.—He is *at least* a PARISH-*Officer*, (whatever more He may be;) because his Office *extends throughout* the *whole* Parish of *Birmingham:* And He is an Inhabitant of the Parish of *Birmingham.* Therefore, though He be *also* Constable of the MANOR which *includes the Parish*; yet He is certainly a *Parish* Officer, notwithstanding that greater Extent of his Jurisdiction or Power.

This Act is to be construed *favourably.* And it has been determined on † 3, 4 *W.* & *M. c.* 11. " That serving the Office of " Constable for a City at large, (though he was appointed by the " Corporation, and exercised it throughout the whole City,) gained " a Settlement in the Parish where he inhabited." 2 *Strange* 1014. *Between the Parishes of St. Maurice* and *St. Mary Calendar in Winchester.*

† It was on 9, 10 *W.* 3. *c.* 11. (See Serjeant *Hewitt's* Reply.)

P. 29 *G.* 2. *B.R. Rex* v. *Davis, Collector of the Rates and Duties of the Highways of the Parish of St. Leonard Shoreditch*, Who was appointed by the Trustees under the Act of Parliament, and *not chosen by the Parish:* Yet it was holden to be a *Parish-Office*; and " That this Act ought to receive the *most liberal* Construction.

In

of the Functions are to be exercised *out of the Limits of the Parish.*

This Man cannot be esteemed a *Parish*-Officer, either from the *Origin* of his Office, or the *Nature*, or the *Exercise* of it.

Mr. Just. DENISON—*If* it had been stated "That the Manor of "*Birmingham* and Parish of *Birmingham* were *co-extensive*," this Certificate might have been a sufficient Discharge. But this is stated quite otherwise, namely "That the Jurisdiction of the Constables "elected for the Manor generally, extends *not only* throughout "the Town and Parish, but ALSO *within and throughout the Ham-* "*let of Deritend.*"

The Act only meant to excuse the Proprietor of the Certificate, from serving Parish and Ward Offices *within* the Parish or Ward where the Felony was committed; and not from Offices to be exercised *out* of the Parish or Ward. If so, this is *not* an Office within the Words or Meaning of the Act of Parliament, upon this State of the Case now before Us: For this is not an Office of Constable in and for the *Parish*; but in and for the MANOR, which is *more extensive* than the Parish is; and a different Species of Division too, One being Ecclesiastical, the other Civil.

Mr. Just. WILMOT—The Act of Parliament means these Certificates to be Exemptions from such Offices only, the Functions of which are *confined within* that Sort of Division which is now called a *Parish*; which is not a Civil, but an * Ecclesiastical Division. No such Species of Division was known at * Common Law: The Temporal or Civil Division was into *Vills*, not into Parishes.

* *V. Freeman's Reports* 228. *per Atkins, accord'.*

And this Office now under our Consideration, as the Case is stated, could be only a *partial* Exercise of the Functions of this Office, *within the Parish of Birmingham*: For He could only exercise within the Parish of *Birmingham*, the Functions of *such Part* of the Jurisdiction as the *Limits of the Parish extended to*; but *not* those of the *Rest* of his Jurisdiction which lay *beyond* the Limits of it. Consequently, the Exemption He could pretend to claim under this Certificate could be, as this Case is stated, *only partial*: But it would be *absurd* to construe the Act to *exempt* him from serving the same identical Office within the *Parish*, and yet leave him *liable* to serve it in the *Vill.*

Mr. *Caldecott's* Case cited from 2 *Strange* is very strong for the present Opinion of the Court. That Case was upon the Certificate-Act of 9, 10 *W.* 3. *c.* 11. The Question was "Whether executing "the Office of Constable for the City at large gave a Certificate-man "a

Mr. *Yates*, *contra*, for the Plaintiff, insisted that it was *right and regular*, in true and even * *strict* Computation: And, were it otherwise, Yet as it was an *Execution* and not upon mesne Process, the Writ of *Ca. sa.* would *not be void*, but only liable to be set aside upon *Motion*, for Irregularity. And He cited the Case of *Shirley* v. *Wright*, 1 *Salk*. 273. Where it was holden "That the Sheriff who had let "his Prisoner escape, should not take Advantage of the Want of a "*Scire facias* to ground the *Ca. Sa.* upon which had issued *post* "*diem et annum*."

* It was so. For the Purification fell on *Monday*: So that, either Way, the *Thursday* next after 8 Days from it, or the *Thursday* next after the Octave of it, was the 12th of *February*.

The Whole Court were very clearly and unanimously with Mr. *Yates*, in *both* Points; and accordingly gave

Judgment for the Plaintiff.

Sarah Nickleson *vers.* Stephen Croft.

THIS was a Question, (upon the Master's Report,) "Whe- "ther there were, or were not, *more Counts* inserted in the "Declaration, than were necessary."

It was a *Declaration upon a Policy of Insurance*, consisting of *Seven* Counts; 1st. for a *total* Loss on a Policy *subscribed by the Defendant Himself*; 2d. for an *Average* Loss, (averred to amount to 63*l.* 4*s.* 6*d.*) on a Policy *subscribed by the Defendant himself*; 3d. for 6*l. per Cent.* to be returned, (it being averred "That the Ship departed with "Convoy;") on a Policy *subscribed by the Defendant himself*; 4th, 5th and 6th, exactly the same with 1st, 2d and 3d (respectively,) with *this Difference only*, that these three last Counts alledged the Policy to have been *subscribed* by One *Manoel Francis Silva, the Defendant's then Agent Factor or Servant* in that Behalf by Him duly authorized appointed and deputed for that Purpose; 7th. for Money had and received to the Plaintiff's Use. The Master (Mr. *Owen*) thought that *Four* Counts were sufficient; *viz.* either the Three first with the last; or else the 4th, 5th and 6th, together with the last.

The Court agreed with Him in Opinion.

Lord Mansfield—On a Declaration for a *total* Loss, You may *recover an Average Loss*: Yet I *would not tie the Plaintiff down* to declare *only* for a total Loss; but leave the Plaintiff at Liberty to declare *both* Ways. And the latter Method is often of Service to a Defendant, by pointing out the particular Average that the Plaintiff goes for.

Friday 5th June 1761.

John Enys Esq; Executor of Samuel Enys Esq; *verſ.* Iſaac Donnithorne, Executor of Nicholas Donnithorne.

THIS was an Action of COVENANT brought by the *Executor* of the Leſſor, againſt the *Executor* of a deceaſed *Joint*-Leſſee.

The Declaration ſets forth an Indenture made on the 10th of *October* 1735, between the ſaid *Samuel Enys* (the Plaintiff's Teſtator) of the one Part, and the ſaid *Nicholas Donnithorne* deceaſed, and *One Joſeph Donnithorne* on the other Part, (the Counterpart of which Indenture, ſealed &c, he brings into Court,) whereby the ſaid *Samuel Enys*, for and *in Conſideration* of the Sum of Twenty Guineas paid to him by the ſaid *Nicholas Donnithorne* and *Joſeph D.* or One of them, and *alſo for and in Conſideration* of the yearly Rent and other Reſervations COVENANTS *and Agreements* therein after mentioned and compriſed on the Parts and Behalf of the ſaid *Nicholas D.* and *Joſeph D.* and *Either* of them, their or *Either* of their Executors Adminiſtrators and Aſſigns, to be paid *obſerved and performed*, Did demiſe unto the ſaid *Nicholas Donnithorne* and *Joſeph D.* their Executors Adminiſtrators and Aſſigns, All that &c, *then in the Tenure and Occupation of the ſaid Nicholas D. and Joſeph D. or One of them*, their or One of their Agents or Servants; HABENDUM to the ſaid *Nicholas D.* AND *Joſeph D.* their Executors Adminiſtrators and Aſſigns, FROM *the firſt Day of March* LAST PAST, for 50 Years *then next enſuing*, if the ſaid *Samuel Enys* and *Richard Plint* or Either of them ſhould happen ſo long to live, and the then preſent Term and Eſtate of the ſaid *Samuel Enys* therein ſhould ſo long continue; THE SAID TERM TO COMMENCE AND BEGIN *from and immediately after the Surrender Forfeiture or other Determination of the ſaid Leaſe or Demiſe of the ſaid Premiſſes made and granted by him the ſaid Samuel Enys to them the ſaid Nicholas D. and Joſeph D. and bearing Date* the 27th Day of *February* 1728; They the ſaid *N. D. and J. D.* their Executors Adminiſtrators and Aſſigns yielding and paying therefore Yearly and every Year during the ſaid Term hereby granted, AFTER *the Commencement thereof*, unto the ſaid *Samuel Enys* his Executors Adminiſtrators and Aſſigns the yearly Rent &c, at &c; The *firſt Payment* thereof to be made at or upon *ſuch* of the ſaid Days as ſhould *firſt and next happen* AFTER *the* COMMENCEMENT *of the ſaid Term.* And the ſaid *Nicholas Donnithorne* and *Joſeph D.* did in and by the ſaid Indenture, for themſelves *and Either* of them, their or *Either* of their Executors and Adminiſtrators, COVENANT *promiſe and agree* unto and with the ſaid *Samuel Enys* his Executors Adminiſtrators and Aſſigns, That they the ſaid *Nicholas D. and Joſeph Donnithorne or One* of them, their

2 *or*

thereof *possessed for the said Term so as aforesaid demised by the said Indenture now brought into Court*, in Form aforesaid, determinable as aforesaid; the *Reversion* thereof with the Appurtenances for the Residue of the aforesaid Term of 99 Years, belonging to the said *Samuel Enys* and his Assigns. That, being so possessed, the said *Samuel Enys* afterwards, to wit on the first Day of *November* 1755, made his last Will and Testament in Writing, and thereby appointed the said *John Enys* (the Plaintiff) Executor thereof; and afterwards, to wit on the same Day and Year, *died* so possessed of and in his said Reversion with the Appurtenances in Form aforesaid: And the said *John Enys* (the Plaintiff) duly proved the said Will of the said *Samuel*, and took upon Himself the Execution of it, and thereby became and was possessed of and in the said Reversion with the Appurtenances, for the Rest and Residue of the said Term of 99 Years then to come and unexpired, determinable as aforesaid; and still is thereof possessed. That the said *James Donnithorne*, after the Death of the said *Nicholas*, to wit on the 1st of *December* 1755, *died*: And the said *Isaac Donnithorne* (the Defendant) thereby became and is the *sole surviving Executor* of the said last Will and Testament of the said *Nicholas*. Then the Plaintiff *John Enys* says that *He* being so possessed of the said Reversion with the Appurtenances as aforesaid, afterwards, to wit on 12*th December* 1759, (being 1*st December* 1759. O. S.) 240*l.* of the said yearly Rent of 80*l.* for three Years of the said Term of 50 Years, elapsed and run out *since the Death of the said Samuel Enys*, and ended at and upon that Day in the Year last mentioned, at that Day in the Year last mentioned became due owing and in Arrear *to* the said *John Enys* the *Executor* and now Plaintiff, AS EXECUTOR, in Form aforesaid: And that the said *Nicholas* and *Joseph*, in the Life-time of the said *Nicholas*, or the said *Joseph* since the Death of the said *Nicholas*, or the said *James* in his Life-time, or the said *Isaac* so *being the* EXECUTOR of the last Will and Testament of the said *Nicholas* as aforesaid, have not, nor hath Any or Either of them or any other Person or Persons paid the aforesaid 240*l.* or any Part thereof to the said *John Enys according to the Form and Effect of the aforesaid Covenant of the said* NICHOLAS *by* HIM *made* in Form aforesaid; But the Payment thereof They and Each and Every of them have hitherto wholly neglected and refused, And the said 240*l.* and every Part thereof still remain and are in Arrear due owing and unpaid to the said *John Enys*, contrary to the Form and Effect of the said Indenture and *of the aforesaid* COVENANT of the said *Nicholas* on this behalf as aforesaid. The Declaration then sets forth that in the said Demise of the Premisses made on 11th of *January* 1711, by *Hugh* Lord *Falmouth* to the said *Samuel*, and under which the said *Samuel* was possessed and intitled at the Time of the making of the Indenture now brought into Court, there is a Reservation of the yearly Rent of 5*l.* payable yearly during the said Term of 99 Years deter-

Mr. *Walker*, in Reply—(1st.) This Lease was so uncertain in the Time it was to commence, that it could not be reduced to a Certainty: Neither does it distinguish when the Computation shall commence, and when the Interest or Possession shall take Effect.

2dly. Upon a joint Lease, the Covenants shall operate *only jointly* not severally. *Yelv.* 177. * *Rolls Administrator of Rolls* v. *Yate*: Therefore this Action could only be brought against the *Survivor*. The Case of *Lilly* v. *Hodges*, 1 *Strange* 553. does † not impugn what I say. But 1 *Saunders* 155. *Eccleston et Ux' Executor of Castle*, v. *Clipsham*, is to the Purpose, and shews that the Covenant shall *go along with* the *Interest*.

* This Case does not at all prove his Position.

† It does, very strongly.

3dly. The Plaintiff's Demand appears to be for Injuries in his *own Time*. Therefore he can not sue for them, as *Executor*.

4thly. The Law operates upon Him as Assignee.

However, He chiefly relied on the first and second Objections.

Lord Mansfield and Mr. Just. Foster were Both absent at this Time.

Mr. Just. Denison thought the second Objection (which goes to the Point of the Action,) deserved further Consideration; *viz.* "Whether where there is a *Joint Lease*, and where the Interest "*must in its Nature survive*, the Covenants, though joint and several, must not be construed to *run with the Land*." It looks very odd, that when One of the Lessees dies, and the Interest survives to the longer Liver of them; yet the Other's Representatives should be bound by the Covenants, though *no Benefit remains to them*. And especially it is right to consider fully of the Objection in a Case where the Plaintiff would otherwise ‡ lose his Action.

‡ Note—In this Case, the Survivor happened to be insolvent.

I would look into || *Slingsby*'s Case.

|| 5 *Co.* 18. *b.*

Mr. Just. Wilmot also was willing to hear it argued again; as He thought that there might perhaps be *some* Weight in the *second* Objection; though little or none in the *Rest*.

Yet there seems to be a Doubt, Whether (as Mr. *Gould* says,) *One* Lessee may not very reasonably covenant *for Another*, as well as a *Stranger* might covenant *for Both*.

On the other hand, perhaps the Subject-Matter of the Covenant may make it reasonable that it should rather be construed as a *Joint Covenant only*, since the *Interest* and *Benefit survives*.

4 Whereupon,

17 G. 2. intitled "An Act to amend and make more effectual the "Laws relating to Rogues Vagabonds and other idle and disorderly "Persons, and to Houses of Correction."

V. 12 G. 2. c. 29. § 6. and 17 G. 2. c. 5. § 1, 4, 16, 17.

He insisted that the SESSIONS have a Jurisdiction to *examine into the Accounts* of the Constables: Whereas these are only allowed by a *single Justice*.

Mr. *Norton*, *contra*, for the *Mandamus*, denied that the Sessions have any Jurisdiction to over-hale the Constable's Accounts.

This is the only Remedy We have. They may return what they think proper, if they think their Point maintainable.

Here is no Chief Constable in this Burrough: Therefore We are obliged to apply to the Treasurer.

Lord MANSFIELD—They are obliged by the Act to apply to the *Quarter-Sessions*; and the *Surplus* only is to be paid over: Which shews that the *Sessions have a Jurisdiction* to make Deductions.

There is Waste enough, upon these Occasions, already.

Discharge the Rule.

The RULE was accordingly DISCHARGED.

Monday 8th June 1761.

Hamilton *vers.* Mendes.

THIS was a Special Case reserved at *Guild-hall*, at the Sittings there before Lord *Mansfield* after *Michaelmas* Term 1760, in an Action brought against the Defendant as One of the Insurers, upon a Policy of *Insurance* from *Virginia* or *Maryland* to *London*, of A SHIP *called the Selby* and of Goods and Merchandize therein, until She shall have moored at Anchor 24 Hours in good Safety.

The Case stated for the Opinion of the Court was as follows—

Facts stated.

That the Ship *Selby*, mentioned in the Policy, being valued at 1200*l*, and the Plaintiff having Interest therein, caused the Policy in Question to be made; and the same was accordingly made, in the Name of the said *John Mackintosh*, on behalf and for the Use and Benefit of the Plaintiff, and which was subscribed by the Defendant, as stated, for the Sum of 100*l*.

2 That

That the whole Cargo of the said Ship *Selby* was delivered to the Freighters, at the Port of *London*; who paid the Freight to *Benjamin Vaughan*, without Prejudice.

The Question therefore submitted to the Opinion of the Court in this Case, is, —" Whether the Plaintiff, on the said 26th Day of " *June*, had a *Right to* ABANDON, and hath a Right to recover as " for a *Total* Loss." If He is intitled to recover for a *Total* Loss; then the Jury find a Verdict for the Plaintiff, Damages 98*l*. Costs 40*s*. But if the Court shall be of Opinion, that he had *no* Right to abandon on the said 26th Day of *June*, or he ought only to recover an *Average* Loss; then the Jury find a Verdict for the Plaintiff, Damages 10*l*. Costs 40*s*.

Flet. Norton, for Plaintiff.
H. Gould, for Defendant.

This Case was first argued on *Friday* 10*th April* last by Mr. *Morton* for the Plaintiff, and Mr. *Aston* for the Defendant.

Mr. *Morton*—The Question is, Whether, by Law, the Insurers are subject to a TOTAL, or only to an AVERAGE Loss.

The CAPTURE of the Ship by an Enemy does amount to a *total* Loss of it. *Roccius Pa.* 282. *Respons.* 34. And upon a *total* Loss, the Ship being *in this Country*, the Insured may always abandon. On 13*th December* 1759, in the Case of *Gardiner* v. *Brosnall* before Lord *Mansfield* at *Guild-hall*, it was so settled, " That on a *total* Loss, " the Insured may always abandon, *if in our* OWN Country:" (though there indeed the Ship was in a *foreign* Port.)

This is a *valued* Policy: And the Insurer having received a sufficient Premium, the Insured ought, in Point of Justice and Equity, to have a Right of *Election* whether to keep or to abandon the Thing insured. And when the Insured has once had his Election to demand the Money insured, no *subsequent* Event can take it from Him. For the Peril insured against having actually happened, the Condition of the Contract is broken, on the *Insurer*'s Part: And when a Condition is once broken, no *subsequent* Event can hinder the other Party from insisting upon it. Nor can an Abandonment be partial.

In the Case of *Fitzgerald* v. *Pole*, in the House of Lords, many Cases are * cited in the Margin, where the Plaintiffs had Judgment as for a total Loss, though the Ships remained in being.

* See *Cases in Dom' Proc' Wednesday* 13th *February* 1754.

Lord MANSFIELD—But they were absolutely denied by the other Side.

Mr.

only be a Loss in *Proportion* to the Damages. *Roccius ut supra*. A Ship cannot be abandoned, so long as it will swim.

The Case of *Goss* v. *Withers* turned upon *particular Circumstances*: But the general Doctrine of that Case is with Us. There, the Loss was total *at the Time* of abandoning: Here, it was not. There, the Ship was disabled to pursue her destined Voyage; The Goods were perishable, and the *Lent*-Season for the Sale of the Fish was over: But here, the Ship was perfectly *safe*, and *able to pursue* her Voyage, at the Time of abandoning; She was *completely redeemed* from her Peril, *undamaged*; and came Home so, to her destined Port.

The Case of *Gardiner* v. *Brosnall* turned upon other Questions.

There is *no Difference* between a *valued*, and an *open* Policy, where the Loss is only *partial*, and not total: For the *Value* must be *proved* in the Case of a partial Loss; And the *Interest* must be *proved*, if it was a *total* Loss.

In Order to give the Insured a Right to abandon, the Peril must *subsist* at the Time of abandoning.

Therefore here, the Insured are only intitled to an *Average*-Loss.

Mr. *Morton*, in Reply—This is an Insurance against the Taking of a Ship: Which Ship *has been* taken. The Facts stated amount to a *Breach* of the Insurer's Contract: And *Subsequent Events* can not alter the Case. The Voyage was *delayed* and *defeated*, for a *Month*; the Ship was *without Sailors*; and it was brought into a Port We were Strangers to.

The Case of *Goss* v. *Withers* was particularly circumstanced; yet the * *General Doctrine* was laid down, "that if an insured Ship "be taken, the Assured may demand as for a *total* Loss, and may "*abandon* to the Insurer." Here, as well as there, the *Views* of the Insured were *defeated*.

* *V. ante* 696, 697.

The Insurer *might* possibly have been a Gainer by the Ship being abandoned to Him, under his Right of Salvage.

Note—

It was admitted on both Sides, that there was no Case where there had been an † Adjustment of a *partial* Loss upon a *valued* Policy; nor any Determination that it's being a VALUED Policy turned it into

† It must be observed that at this Time, the Case of *Lewis* v. *Rucker* (reported *ante* 1167.) had not received it's Determination; nor had even been mentioned in Court: The very first Motion in that Case was made upon the next Day after this first Argument of the present Case; and it was determined on 2d *May* 1761.

any Inſtance of a total Loſs in *this* Senſe of the Term, where there is not Something ſaved.

In the Caſe of a *Capture*, the Thing itſelf is as far from being really *deſtroyed* or *annihilated*, as it was when in the Hands of the Owner: But yet it is totally loſt *to* the Owner; His *Dominion* over it is totally gone. There may be an Abandonment even upon an *Embargo*, if the Cargo be periſhable.

This Objection being cleared I come to the two Propoſitions before ſtated.

Firſt—Here did *once exiſt* a total Loſs; and conſequently there exiſted, at that Time, a Right of abandoning.

* V. ante 696, 697. Since the Caſe of * *Goſs* v. *Withers*, It ſtands ſettled "that where "the Hope of Recovery is gone, a *Capture* makes a *total* Loſs, *as* "*between Inſurers and the Inſured.*" If carried *infra Præſidia Hoſ-*
† V. ante 693. *tium*, then even the Right of † *Property* is altered: So alſo, if all Hope of Recovery is gone.

Now here were no Hopes of Recovery left: This Ship was 17 Days in the Hands of the Enemy; and only One Man and One Boy left on Board. The Inſured might *then* have called upon the Inſurer for a *Total* Loſs; and He could have had no Excuſe. It will perhaps be ſaid, that it was *not a* CONTINUING Loſs upon the 26th of *June*, becauſe the Ship was before that Time retaken and ſafe. But the Anſwer to that is "that it was total ſo long as it con-"tinued."

I will therefore now conſider the ſecond Queſtion.

Second Queſtion—Whether the *ſubſequent Events* have *taken away* the Inſured's Right to abandon: As the Inſurance is only an Indemnity for the Ship's ſafe Arrival at it's deſtined Port; and as the Ship arrived at that Port, without having ſuſtained any Damage from the Capture; and the Inſurer is content to pay the Salvage and all Coſts.

Notwithſtanding all this, I ſay that where there was ONCE a *total* Loſs, or a Loſs of ſuch a kind as is *in it's Nature total*, the Inſured have a Right to abandon, *although* there be a ſubſequent Re-Capture: For when once the Inſured had a Right to abandon veſted in Him, ſuch Right *continued* in Him and could not be taken away from Him.

‖ V. ante ut ſupra. And ‖ ſo I underſtood it to be laid down, in the Caſe of *Goſs* v. *Withers*.

A Right of Action once *veſted* cannot be diveſted.

2 This

It has been ſaid "That it would *introduce Fraud.*"

But Fraud is *not to be preſumed.*

I hope therefore that this Court will concur with foreign Writers, That there is no Inſtance where, in Caſe of a Capture and Recapture, and the Loſs total in it's Nature, there may not be an Abandonment. And So it was determined in the Caſe of *Goſs* v. *Withers.*

Here, the total Loſs *veſted a Right* to abandon; which Right could not be deveſted by the Recapture: And no Injury is done to the Inſurer; nor can any Inconvenience ariſe.

Therefore the Plaintiff ought to recover the 98*l.* as for a total Loſs. This is a firm ſtable Ground to go upon, in Caſes of Capture: And unleſs this fixed Rule be eſtabliſhed, there muſt be infinite Uncertainty and Diſpute in every Caſe of Capture and Recapture.

Mr. *Gould, contra,* for the Defendant.—Every thing was ſaid laſt Term, in the Argument for the Defendant, that poſſibly could be urged upon the Subject.

Mr. *Aſton* did not inſiſt That a total Loſs muſt be an abſolute Annihilation of the Thing inſured.

The Determination in the Caſe of *Goſs* v. *Withers* was founded upon the particular Circumſtances of that Caſe; and the Doctrine was not laid down ſo generally as Mr. *Norton* cites it.

As to it's having been *once* a total Loſs, and *continuing* ſo till 26th of *June*, and the *Spes recuperandi* being utterly gone by the Capture; the Point was ſettled in that Caſe of *Goſs* v. *Withers.* *

* *V. ante* 693 to 698.

Mr. *Norton* admits that both in the Caſe of a *valued* and of an *open* Policy, the Inſurance is to be conſidered only as an INDEMNITY. Whereas his Argument would prove the Inſurer to be liable to have the Ship abandoned to Him, though retaken within an Hour.

The ſubſtantial Inquiry is, "Whether any of the Perils inſured "againſt, have happened, *to the Detriment* of the Ship, so FAR "as to intitle the Inſured to abandon, *within the true Intent of the* "*Policy.*"

Roccius, 204, (cited by Mr. *Aſton*) proves that *Reſtoration* before Payment is ſufficient, and the Inſurer is clear:—"Acetiam quia Con-"tractus Aſſecurationis eſt conditionalis &c, reperiantur. Non au-"tem

Roccius 204. is a general Assertion; which may depend upon Circumstances, and is not applicable to the present Case. The General Position is not Law.

My Argument *ab inconvenienti* has Weight, if this be a *total* Loss; as it certainly is, and was determined to be so, in the Case of *Goss* v. *Withers*.

The Case of *Dean* v. *Dicker* is not applicable to this Case.

Cur. advis'.

Lord Mansfield now delivered the Resolution of the Court; having first stated the Case, as settled at *Nisi Prius*.

The Plaintiff has averred in his Declaration, as the Basis of his Demand for a *total* Loss, "that by the Capture the Ship became "wholly lost *to Him*."

The General Question is, Whether the Plaintiff, who at the Time of his Action brought, at the Time of his Offer to abandon, and at the Time he was first apprized of any Accident having happened, had only, in Truth, sustained an Average-Loss, ought to recover for a *Total* One.

In Support of the Affirmative, the Counsel for the Plaintiff insisted upon the four following Points;

1st. That by this Capture, the *Property was changed*, and therefore the Loss total for ever.

2dly. If the Property was not changed, yet the Capture was a *total* Loss.

3dly. That when the Ship was brought into *Plymouth*, particularly *on the 26th of June*, the Recovery was not such as, in Truth, *changed* the Totality of the Loss into an Average.

4thly. Supposing it did, yet, the Loss having *once* been total, a Right *vested* in the Insured to recover the Whole upon abandoning; which Right could never afterwards be *divested or taken from him* by any subsequent Event.

1st Point. As to the *first Point*—If the Change of Property was at all material *as between the Insurer and Insured*, it would not be applicable to the present Case; Because by the marine Law received and

If they differed about the Value, the Court of Admiralty would have ordered a Commiſſion of Appraiſement. In this Caſe, it was the *Intereſt* of the Owner of the Ship, the Owners of the Cargo, and the Re-captor, that She ſhould forthwith *proceed* upon her Voyage from *Plymouth* to *London*. But, had the Re-captor oppoſed it, or affected Delay, the Court of Admiralty would have made an *Order* for bringing her immediately to *London*, her Port of Delivery, upon reaſonable Terms.

Therefore it is moſt clear, that upon the 26th of *June*, the Ship had ſuſtained no other Loſs by reaſon of the Capture, than a *ſhort temporary Obſtruction*, and a Charge which the Defendant had *offered to pay* and ſatisfy.

4th Point. This brings the Whole to the fourth and laſt Point.

The Plaintiff's Demand is for an *Indemnity*. His Action then muſt be founded upon the *Nature of his Damnification*, as it really is, at the *Time* the Action is brought. It is repugnant, upon a Contract of *Indemnity*, to recover as for a *total* Loſs when the final Event has decided that the Damnification, in Truth, is an *Average* or perhaps *no* Loſs at all.

Whatever undoes the Damnification, in whole or in part, muſt operate upon the Indemnity in the *ſame Degree*. It is a Contradiction in Terms, to bring an Action for Indemnity, when, upon the whole Event, *no* Damage has been ſuſtained. This Reaſoning is ſo much founded in Senſe and the Nature of the Thing, that the Common Law of *England* adopts it; (though inclined to Strictneſs.) The Tenant is obliged to indemnify his Landlord from *Waſte*: But if the Tenant do or ſuffer Waſte to be done in Houſes; yet, if he *repair before any Action brought*, there lies no Action of Waſte againſt him. * But he can not plead "*non fecit* vaſtum;" but the Special Matter. The Special Matter ſhews, that the Injury being repaired before the Action brought, the Plaintiff had *no Cauſe* of Action: And whatever takes away the *Cauſe*, takes away the *Action*.

* *Co. Lit.* 53. a.

Suppoſe a *Surety*, ſued to Judgment; and afterwards, before an Action brought, the Principal pays the Debt and Coſts, and procures Satisfaction to be acknowledged upon Record: the Surety can have no Action for Indemnity; becauſe he is indemnified before any Action brought. If the Demand or Cauſe of Action does not ſubſiſt *at the Time* the Action is brought, the having exiſted at any *former* Time can be of no Avail.

But,

The present Attempt is the first that ever was made to charge the Insurer as for a total Loss, upon an Interest-Policy, after the Thing was recovered. And it is said the Judgment in the Case of *Goss* v. *Withers* gave Rise to it.

It is admitted, that Case was no Way similar. Before that Action was brought, the whole Ship and Cargo were literally lost; At the Time of the Offer to abandon, a Fourth of the Cargo had been thrown over-board; The Voyage was entirely lost; The Remainder of the Cargo was Fish perishing, and of no Value at *Milford Haven*, where the Ship was brought in; The Ship so shattered, as to want great and expensive Repairs; The Salvage was one Half, and the Insurer did not engage to be at any Expence; It did not appear that it was worth while to try to save any Thing; And the Recaptor, (though intitled to one half, as well as the Owner of the Ship and Cargo,) left the Whole to perish, rather than be at any further Trouble or Expence.

But it is said, " Though the *Case* was entirely different, some part " of the *Reasoning* warranted the Proposition now inferred by the " Plaintiff from it."

The great Principle relied upon, was, " that as between the In- " surer and Insured, the Contract being an Indemnity, the *Truth*, " of the Fact ought to be regarded; And therefore there might be " a total Loss by a Capture, which could not operate a Change of " Property; And a Re-capture should not relate by Fiction (like the " *Roman Jus Postliminii*) as if the Capture had never happened, *un-* " *less* the Loss was in Truth recovered."

This Reasoning proved *è converso*, That if the Thing *in Truth was safe*, no artificial Reasoning should be allowed to set up a total Loss.

The *Words* quoted at the Bar were certainly used, " That there is " no Book, ancient or modern, which does not say *That in Case of* " *the Ship being taken, the Insured may demand as for a total Loss,* " *and abandon.*" But the Proposition was *applied* to the Subject Matter; and is certainly true, provided the Capture, or the total Loss occasioned thereby, *continue to the Time of abandoning and bringing the Action.*

The Case *then* before the Court did not make it necessary to *specify all the Restrictions.* But I will read to You, *verbatim*, from my Notes of the Judgment then delivered, what was said; to prevent any Inference being drawn beyond the Case then determined. I said

2 " In

The *Insurer*, by the Marine Law, ought never to *pay less*, upon a Contract of Indemnity, than the *Value of the Loss*: And the *Insured* ought never to *gain more*. Therefore if there was Occasion to resort to that Argument, the *Consequence* of the Determination would alone be sufficient upon the present Occasion.

But, upon *Principles*, this Action could not be maintained as for a *total* Loss, if the Question was to be judged by the strictest Rules of *Common* Law: Much less can it be supported for a *total* Loss, as the Question ought to be decided, by the large Principles of the *Marine* Law, according to the substantial Intent of the Contract and the real Truth of the Fact.

The daily Negociations and Property of Merchants ought not to depend upon *Subtleties* and *Niceties*; but upon Rules, easily learned and easily retained, because they are the Dictates of common Sense, drawn from the Truth of the Case.

If the Question is to depend upon the *Fact*, Every Man can judge of the Nature of the Loss, before the Money is paid: But if it is to depend upon *speculative Refinements*, from the Law of Nations or the *Roman Jus Postliminii* concerning the Change or Re-vesting of Property; no Wonder *Merchants* are in the dark, when *Doctors* have differed upon the Subject, from the Beginning, and are not yet agreed.

To obviate too large an Inference being drawn from this Determination; I desire it may be understood, that the Point here determined is, "*That the Plaintiff, upon a Policy, can only recover an Indemnity according to the Nature of his Case at the Time of the* ACTION BROUGHT; *or (at most) at the Time of his* OFFER TO ABANDON."

We give no Opinion, how it would be, in Case the Ship or Goods be restored in Safety, BETWEEN *the Offer to abandon*, and the *Action* brought; or BETWEEN *the Commencement* of the Action, and the *Verdict*. And particularly I desire, that no Inference may be drawn, "that in Case the Ship or Goods should be restored *after the Money paid as for a total Loss*, the Insurer could compel the Insured to *refund* the Money and take the Ship or Goods:" That Case is totally different from the present, and depends, throughout, upon different Reasons and Principles.

Here, the Event had fixed the Loss to be an Average only, *before* the Action brought; *before* the Offer to abandon; and *before* the Plaintiff had Notice of any Accident; Consequently *before* He could make an Election.

Therefore,

Mr. *Gould*, Mr. Serj. *Davy*, Mr. *Coxe*, and Mr. *Stowe* argued that he ought now to be discharged, as having given a *full and complete* Answer to the Questions propounded to him: And it is not material, in the present Respect, whether it be true or false; or whether his Conduct was prudent or imprudent. If he be not now discharged, He must be imprisoned for Life.

Mr. Serj. *Hewitt*, and Mr. *Norton*, *contra*, insisted that this Answer was still *incomplete and unsatisfactory*; and that the Defendant can not be indicted for Perjury upon it. He was bound down by what was already proved upon him and traced to him, to account for a very great Sum of Money which appeared to have come to his Hands in this *particular* Year: And this is by no Means a satisfactory Account of the Disposition of it, nor at all probable in itself. He lets the Commissioners into no Sort of Light whereby to trace this Money, or to discover what is become of it: It is not to be imagined or conceived that 4, 5, 6 or 7 hundred Pounds in a Month could be paid Her for Maintenance and Expences only; especially as it appears (as it does by what He himself has represented in one Part of his Examination) that She had only a Man-Servant and two Maids, whilst She was at *Bath*. It might have been repaid to him or to some One in Trust for him; or laid out in Stocks, and those Stocks transferred in Trust for him.

The COURT held his Answer to be incomplete and unsatisfactory; and ORDERED Him to be REMANDED. *

* This Man was afterwards convicted and executed for concealing his Effects.

Edie and Another *vers.* East-India Company.

THIS was an Action, brought by the Indorsees, upon two *foreign Bills of Exchange* drawn by Colonel *Clive*, then in the *East-Indies*, upon the *East-India* Company, and accepted by them, payable to Mr. *Campbell* or Order, then also in *India*, and indorsed by Mr. *Campbell* to Mr. *Robert Ogilby*. One of these Bills was by such Indorsment directed to be paid to *Robert Ogilby or Order*, in the usual Way of Indorsing; And no Dispute or Question arose upon it. The other Bill was also indorsed by Mr. *Campbell* to *Robert Ogilby*: but the Words "*or Order*" were originally OMITTED in *this Indorsement*; and afterwards put in, by another Hand, before the Trial.

These Bills *thus* indorsed by Mr. *Campbell* to Mr. *Ogilby*, (without adding the Words " or Order," in the Indorsement of the latter,) were by Him indorsed to the Plaintiffs *Edie* and *Lard* or Order.

Ogilby

Words: And if it be given in Blank, it may be filled up by the Indorsee or by any One else, even in the Face of the Court, *at the Trial.* *

* See *Comyns* 312. *accord'.* *V. post*

Having thus established this Principle, "That the Bill of Ex-"change being *originally made assignable and negotiable*, and being *in* "*it's own Nature assignable* must continue *always* so, And that the "Law will interpret the Assignment to be made in the *same* Man-"ner in which the Bill is drawn, although the Words *or Order* be *omitted*;

They grounded their Motion for a New Trial upon these two Foundations;

1st. That the Jury have found directly contrary to this settled Law, and have founded their Verdict upon the CUSTOM OF MERCHANTS, which they suppose to be quite to the contrary; and Of which Custom of Merchants, *Evidence* was permitted to be given at the Trial: which *Evidence* should not have been allowed. For the Custom of Merchants is part of the Law of *England:* And the Law of *England* being already fully settled on this Point, no Evidence in *Contradiction* to it ought to have been *admitted*; nor can any Finding of a Jury *alter* it.

2dly. That *if* the Counsel for the Plaintiff had *apprehended* that such Sort of Evidence would have been gone into at the Trial, they could and would have produced better and fuller Evidence than they did, to prove that the Custom of Merchants was really and in Truth and Fact *agreeable* to the Law as settled: And they alledged That *no Fact* of Usage was proved at the Trial, to support a Notion "that the Acceptor was not liable upon such an Indorsement as "this."

Mr. *Norton* and Mr. *Wedderburn*, *contra* for the Defendants, insisted that the present Verdict was right, and ought to stand.

It has been urged, 1st, "That this Bill is *in it's nature negotiable*; and 2dly. "That being so, it can not be *restrained* by this or any "other Indorsement."

As to the first—They agreed a Bill of Exchange to be negotiable in it's *Nature.* But it does not follow, they said, that because it was *once* so, it must therefore *always continue* so. For the Payee has the *absolute* Property in it; He is the Purchaser of it: And why should not He *limit* the Payment of it as He pleases? No Man can be *injured* by this; No Man can be *deceived* by it; It cannot be attended with the least Inconvenience.

No

and experienced Perſons at the Trial, was agreeable to the Finding. And if they *could* have encountered it; Why did they not? Their Omitting to do ſo, is ſurely no Ground for a New Trial.

Mr. *Morton* and Mr. *Yates*, in Reply—

They admit the Queſtion to be, "What is the true Conſtruction "of ſuch a reſtrained Indorſement as this is." And certainly this Sort of Indorſement makes or rather continues a Bill of Exchange generally negotiable. Meſſieurs *Edie* and *Lard* are in the Caſe of every common Indorſee.

The Caſes that We have cited are plain and clear, on our Side: On the other Side, They ſuppoſe imaginary Circumſtances, which did not really exiſt in them.

The Determinations upon Promiſſory Notes prove "That the "Law was likewiſe ſo, upon Foreign Bills of Exchange."

The *Fact* of Uſage that would have been cogent and binding, if proved, ſhould have been a *Refuſal* to negotiate a Bill with ſuch a limited and reſtrained Indorſement.

If this Bill was to go back to *India*, proteſted by Meſſieurs *Edie* and *Lard* for Non-Payment by the Company and the Indorſers, undoubtedly the Drawer would be liable to Mr. *Edie* and Mr. *Lard*, for the Payment of it.

Lord Mansfield—I thought, at the Trial, that the Defendants *might* be at Liberty to go into the *Uſage of Merchants* upon this Occaſion.

And Mr. *Race*, Caſhier of the Bank of *England*, gave Evidence "That the Bank, if they ever diſcounted theſe Bills not indorſed "to Order, did it *only* upon the *Credit of the Indorſer*; but that "otherwiſe they would not take them, *not* conſidering them as be-"ing negotiable."

Mr. *Simon*, a very eminent and experienced Merchant, depoſed That He conſidered the Omiſſion of theſe Words as *reſtrictive* of the Indorſement to the particular individual Perſon ſpecified in the Indorſement: And He added, That it was, in his Opinion, merely in the Nature of a *perſonal Authority* "to receive the Money;" and was not negotiable.

So Mr. *Grant*, another Witneſs on the Part of the Defendants, declared his Opinion alſo to be.

2 So

Who it was that *gave the Trust to Ogilby:* For He that gives the Trust, ought to run the Risque of his Credit.

I observed that this Indorsement was made by Mr. *Campbell*, the Payee, to this *Ogilby:* And if *He* meant to trust *Ogilby*, it was but reasonable that He should be the Person to suffer by *Ogilby*. And it was clear that He meant to trust *Ogilby* with the Money: For it is acknowledged on all Hands, that *Ogilby* Himself had a Right to receive it of the Company; whether he had a Right to indorse the Bill to another Person, or not.

The Jury staid out a considerable Time; and then brought in a Verdict for the Plaintiffs, upon the Bill indorsed to *Ogilby or Order*, (which was not disputed:) But They gave their Verdict for the *Defendants*, upon that Count which declared upon the second Bill (for 2000 *l*,) which was indorsed to Him WITHOUT adding the Words "*or Order*."

In the whole Course of the Evidence, *No One Fact* was proved, where the Indorsee to whom a Bill was indorsed, without adding the Words "or Order," *ever actually* LOST *the Money*; so as to put Him upon *disputing* the Point.

Since the Trial, I have looked into the Cases, and have considered the Thing with a great deal of Care and Attention, and thought much about it: And I am very clearly of Opinion that I *ought not* to have admitted any Evidence of the particular *Usage* of Merchants in such a Case. Of this, I say, I am now satisfied; For the *Law* is already SETTLED.

I lay the Case of *Evans* v. *Cramlington* out of the Way; as I do not see that it is much applicable to the Case now before Us.

But I go upon the two Cases of *More* v. *Manning*, and *Acheson* v. *Fountain*. The former was an *Assumpsit* upon a Promissory Note given by *Manning* to *Statham* or Order: *Statham* assigned it to *Witherhead*; and *Witherhead*, to the Plaintiff. Upon a Demurrer to the Declaration, Exception was taken, "Because the Assignment "was made to *Witherhead without* saying to Him *and Order*; and "then He *can not assign it over*." But it was resolved by the whole Court, That it was *good:* For *if* the *Original* Bill was assignable, then, to whomsoever it is assigned, He has *all* the Interest in the Bill, and may assign it as he pleases. And very right that was: For the main Foundation is, "What the Bill is in its *Origin*." And accordingly, as that Note was *originally* made payable to *Statham and Order*, they held the Assignment of it to *Witherhead* to be an *absolute* Assignment to Him, which comprehended his Assigns. It

The Words "*or Order*" are not neceſſary to be *inſerted in the Indorſement*, any more than the Words "*Executor's or Adminiſtrators*" are neceſſary to be added to it.

The Point now in Queſtion has been already *ſolemnly ſettled* both in the Court of King's Bench and Common Pleas, by the two Adjudications that have been mentioned: And therefore Witneſſes ought *not* to have been examined to the *Uſage*, after ſuch ſolemn Determinations of what was the Law.

Therefore there ought to be a New Trial.

As to the Coſts—I think there ſhould be None, in this Caſe. For the Verdict muſt be ſet aſide *generally*, not in part only. Yet this Verdict is agreed to be right upon the *firſt* Count; and that is found for the *Plaintiffs*. Therefore there ought to be no Coſts upon granting a new Trial in the preſent Caſe: Since the Merits were *always* clear for the Plaintiffs, on the *firſt* Count; And it *now* appears that Nothing remained to be tried, on the *Second*.

Mr. Juſt. DENISON concurred, *in toto*.

This Verdict upon the ſecond Count is not well founded. The Point in Queſtion is not Matter of *Fact*; but Matter of *Law*.

I never before heard of this Notion of a *reſtrictive* Aſſignment of a *negotiable* Bill.

Where a Bill is originally made payable to *A.* or Order, it is of Courſe and in its very Eſſence negotiable from hand to hand. An Inland Bill of Exchange is aſſignable in its Nature, *toties quoties:* And Promiſſory Notes are now put upon the ſame Foot with them. Foreign Bills of Exchange are equally ſo, by the Law of Merchants, and by the ſettled Determinations of Courts of Law in *England*.

This is a Matter of *Law:* And the Law is clearly and fully fixed. There is no Inſtance of a *reſtrictive Limitation*, where a Bill is *originally* made payable to a Man *or Order*.

I never heard of an Indorſement to *A. only*. In general, the Indorſement follows the Nature of the Thing indorſed; and is equally negotiable.

But at leaſt, *here* is no ſuch Reſtraint as *that:* Here is Nothing from whence to collect an *Intent* to limit and reſtrain it. The Law has

Much has been ſaid about the *Cuſtom of Merchants.* But the *Cuſtom of Merchants*, or Law of Merchants, is the Law of the Kingdom; and is *part of the Common Law.*

People do not ſufficiently diſtinguiſh between Cuſtoms of different Sorts. The true Diſtinction is between *general* Cuſtoms, (which are *part* of the Common Law,) and *local* Cuſtoms (which are not ſo.) This Cuſtom of Merchants is the *general* Law of the Kingdom, part of the Common Law; and therefore *ought not* to have been left to the Jury, *after* it has been already ſettled by judicial Determinations.

But there ſhould be *no Coſts* paid upon this Occaſion; becauſe the Verdict is both againſt Law and againſt the Opinion and Direction of my Ld. Ch. Juſtice, upon the ſecond Count; and is with the Plaintiffs, on the firſt.

Mr. Juſt. WILMOT was of the ſame Opinion.

The *Law*, with regard to this Point, is *ſettled* and fully *eſtabliſhed*, by the two Caſes which have been cited; and upon right and proper Principles.

This Original Contract is, "to pay to ſuch Perſon or Perſons, "as the Payee or his Aſſignees or their Aſſignees ſhall direct:" And there is as much Privity between the laſt Indorſer and the laſt Aſſignee, as between the Drawer and the firſt Payee.. When the Payee aſſigns it over, He does it by the Law of Merchants; being a Choſe in Action, not aſſignable by the general Law. And the Indorſement is *part* of the Original Contract, and is *incidental and appurtenant* to it in the Nature of it; and muſt be underſtood and interpreted to be made in the *ſame Manner* as the Bill was drawn. And the Indorſee holds it in the ſame Manner, and with the ſame Privileges Qualities and Advantages, as the Original Payee held it; that is, as an aſſignable negotiable Note, which He may indorſe over to Another, and that Other to a third, and ſo on, at Pleaſure.

There is a great deal of Difference between giving a naked Authority "to receive it," and transferring it over *by Indorſement*. And I doubt Whether He *can* limit his Indorſement of it by Way of Aſſignment or Transfer to Another, ſo as to *preclude* his Aſſignee from aſſigning it over as a Thing negotiable. For the Aſſignee purchaſes it for a *valuable Conſideration*; and therefore purchaſes it with all its Privileges Qualities and Advantages; One of which, is it's Negotiability.

The *Custom of Merchants* is *Part* of the *Law of England*: And Courts of Law must take Notice of it as such.

There may indeed be *some* Questions depending upon Customs amongst Merchants, where, *if* there be a DOUBT *about the Custom*, it may be fit and proper to take the Opinion of Merchants thereupon: Yet that is only where the *Law* remains *doubtful*. And even there, the Custom must be proved by *Facts*, not by OPINION only; And it must also be subject to the Control of Law: And so was the Case of *Hawkius* v. *Cardy*, reported in *Carthew* 466, and in 1. *Salk*. 65. There the Defendant had given a Note under his Hand, "to pay "unto *E. G.* or Order a certain Sum of Money:" "*E. G.* by Indorsement on this Note, ordered PART *of the Money* to be paid to "the Plaintiff. Upon which, this Action was brought: and a "special *Custom* amongst Merchants was laid in the Declaration, "according to the Plaintiff's Case." Upon a Demurrer to this Declaration, It was adjudged "that this is a *void* Custom; because by "means of such Division, the Defendant would be subject to as "many Actions, as the Person to whom the Note was given should "think fit; and this upon a *single Contract* which subjected Him to "One Action only." This warrants what I said, "That the *Original Contract* must be looked into." Here, the Original Contract is a *negotiable* Bill; and the Indorsee is in the *Place* of the Original Payee.

The two Cases of *More* v. *Manning*, and *Acheson* v. *Fountain*, serve to prove "That there is NO *such Custom of Merchants*, as the "Defendants pretend:" For they could not have been so determined as they were, *if* there *had* been such a Custom of Merchants.

Therefore these *judicial* Determinations of the Point are the LEX MERCATORIA, as to *this* Question: For they settle what *is* the Custom of Merchants; which Custom is the *Lex Mercatoria*, which is part of the Law of the Land. But this Finding of the Jury in the present Case, is directly *contrary* to the *Lex Mercatoria* so fully settled and established by legal Adjudications.

Therefore the Verdict ought to be set aside: but it should be without Costs, for the Reasons already specified.

Per Cur. unanimously,
The VERDICT was set aside, And a NEW TRIAL ordered; (but without Costs.)

Baskerville

can not be set off, in an Action tried *after* that Verdict had been given.

To this, it was answered by Mr. *Morton* and Mr. *Stowe*, (in Support of the Rule)—That the Debt remains *unchanged* in its Nature, and *unextinguished*, notwithstanding the Verdict. And it might have been still set off, they said, in the present Action, without any Inconvenience: For if *Brown* should attempt to take out Execution for the *Whole*, in the other Action wherein He was Plaintiff, *after* a Set-off in this Action, Either the Court would set the Matter right, (even with Costs,) or *Baskerville* might have Redress by an *Audità Querela*. But *Brown* was *obliged*, they said, to take his Verdict for the *Whole* of his Demand: For He could not be sure that *Baskerville* would try his Cause at all; and then *Brown* would have entirely *lost* this Sum of 11 *l.* 18 *s.* *Brown* did all He could to come at a fair Balance: He could do no more than plead it, or give Notice to set it off, *as it stood* at the *Time* of the Plea pleaded. The *Fault* was in *Baskerville*. He ought to have set off his Demand upon *Brown* of 11 *l.* 18 *s.* against *Brown*'s Demand upon Him of 30 *l.* And then complete Justice had been done easily and at once. He *ought not* to have brought his Action against *Brown*, *at all*.

Cur. advis'.

Lord Mansfield now delivered the Resolution of the Court.

* See the Stat. of 2 G. 2. c. 22. § 13. for setting off mutual Debts, one against the other.

The Meaning of the * Act of Parliament, He said, was, that in all Cases of mutual Debts, the less Sum should be deducted out of the greater, *if the Defendant desires it*.

But *Brown could not compel Baskerville* to set off his less Demand upon *Brown*, against *Brown*'s greater Demand upon him: Nor could *Brown* have safely taken his Verdict for less than his *whole* Demand. Yet *Baskerville* Himself might have done this without Prejudice, and with perfect Safety: And he ought to have done it. But he declined doing it; and at the same Time brings his Action against *Brown*, for what he might, without Prejudice, have set off against *Brown*'s Demand upon him.

Therefore it was litigious and vexatious in him not to do it, when he might safely and easily have done it; but chose, instead of it, to commence an Action against *Brown*.

Both Actions stood together for Trial: But it happened that the Cause of *Brown* v. *Baskerville* stood first. *Brown* took his Verdict for the *whole* Demand upon the two Notes; there being no Plea nor Notice of any Set-off in *this* Cause wherein *Brown* was Plaintiff.

Then

But it would be strange, if the mere Accident of the Priority of Trial should, by his Cause's happening to stand first in the Paper, preclude Him from taking the Benefit of the Act, according to his Notice rightly and truly given at the *Time* when it was given.

Per Cur. unanimously,
VERDICT set aside; And the Defendant to have Costs of a Non-suit: And *Brown* to remit so much of his Damages recovered in the other Action, as exceed the Balance of the mutual Debts.

Sir John Astley Bart. *vers.* Young.

THE Plaintiff's Declaration consisted of *two Counts*. The Defendant *demurred to the One*, and obtained Judgment thereupon. To the *Other*, *He pleaded*: and upon Trial of the Issue joined, the Verdict was *for the Plaintiff*. The Question was, In *what Manner* the COSTS ought to be taxed.

Note—These were *single* Pleas, at Common Law. (As to *double* Pleas pleaded by Leave of the Court under the 4, 5 *Ann.* c. 16. § 4. See a former Case, of *Cooke* v. *Sayer*, *Friday 9th February* 1759, *ante pa.* 670 to 672.)

The COURT were All, except Mr. Justice *Foster* who was gone, unanimous That in the present Case, the Plaintiff was intitled to Costs upon his Verdict; and the *Defendant* to *None* upon his Demurrer: For that the Plaintiff having prevailed upon One of his Counts, had a Right to have his Costs upon *that* Count, without any Deduction to be made on Account of the Defendant's having gotten Judgment upon his Demurrer to the *other* Count.

Rex *vers.* Higginson.

ON *Monday* 13th of *April* last, Mr. *Morton* moved in Arrest of Judgment; the Indictment upon which the Defendant had been convicted, being (as He alledged) *too general:* And He obtained a Rule to shew Cause why it should not be quashed. It was in these Words—*Middlesex*—The Jurors for our Lord the King upon their Oath present, That *Thomas Higginson* of *James Street* in the Parish of *St. Martin in the Fields* in the County of *Middlesex* Yeoman, on the sixth Day of *November* in the first Year of the Reign of

A. *in the Court of Conscience*, on each of the 4 Notes, as Indorser; and received 6 *l.* of Him, under the Order of that Court; though *A.* tendered and offered to prove to them the said Indemnity and Agreement signed by *C.*: Which the Commissioners thought *They* had *no Power to judge of*, and that it was therefore *no sufficient Bar* to the Suit in *their* Court. They therefore decreed for C. in one of the Causes; and *A.* paid in the Money, upon the 3 Others: And C. *took out* the Whole, *by Order* of the Commissioners. It was resolved—

1st. That *A.* may recover *this Money* from C. in the *present Form of Action, viz.* "*for Money had and received to his Use. Page* 1012. He may *wave* any Demand upon the Foot of the Indemnity, for the *Costs* he had been put to; and bring this Action to *recover the* 6 *l.* which C. *got* and *kept* from him iniquitously. *ibid.*

2d. An Action of *Assumpsit* will lie in many Cases where *Debt does lie*, and in many where Debt does *not* lie. 1008.

3d. A main Inducement, originally, for *encouraging Actions of Assumpsit*, was, *to take away the Wager of Law. ibid.*

4th. *If* the Defendant be under an *Obligation from the Ties of natural Justice*, "TO REFUND;" the *Law implies a Debt* and *gives this Action. ibid.*

5th. *This Species of Assumpsit* lies in many Instances, for Money received from a *third* Person, under *lawful Authority*. 1008, 1009.

6th. Though the *Merits* of a *regular Judgment* can *never be overhaled by an original Suit*, yet the Ground of this Action is *consistent* with the Judgment of the Court of Conscience. 1009.

7th. *That Court acted right*, in refusing to go into the collateral Matter. *ibid.*

8th. The Ground of the present Action is "That the Defendant "ought not to KEEP the Money." *ibid.*

9th. This Action is *beneficial* both to *Plaintiff* and *Defendant*. 1010.

1st. The Plaintiff may *declare generally*, and make out his Case at the Trial. 1010.

2dly. The Defendant can be *liable no further than the Money He has received*; and against *that*, may go into an *equitable Defence* upon the general Issue; *claim every equitable Allowance*; prove a *Release*, *without* pleading it; and defend Himself by *whatever* may shew that the Plaintiff, *ex æquo et bono*, is *not intitled* to the *Whole* or any *Part* of his Demand. 1010.

10th. *This* Action is a *Bar* to the Plaintiff's bringing an Action *upon the Agreement* (though He might *recover more* in *that* Action, than in *this*. 1010.

11th. *This* Action *lies* only for Money which the Defendant *ex æquo et bono*, *ought not to* KEEP. 1011, 1012.

12th. It *lies not* for Money *paid* as due in *Honour and Honesty*; though *not recoverable by Law*. 1012: as

1st. Payment of a Debt *barred* by the *Statute of Limitations*. *ibid.*

2dly. Or *contracted during Infancy*. *ibid.*

3d. There is no Difference between an Amendment in *Civil* Actions and in *Penal*; when an Amendment at *Common* Law is applied for, and all is in Paper. *Page* 1098, 1099.

4th. But the *Statutes* of Amendment do *not* extend to *penal* Actions. *ibid.*

A *Declaration* in a *Qui tam* Action for Usury, was amended, in *altering the Date* of the Note; All being *in Paper*. *ibid.*

In *Ejectment*—is now carried *much further* than formerly; and, *after* Verdict, is *not necessary* to be *applied for* or *actually made*, in Cases of mere *Mistake of the Clerk*; but the Court will *overlook* the Exception. 1162. See *Ejectment*.

Ancient Demesne

May be pleaded in *Ejectment*, by *Leave* of the Court, and upon a *proper Affidavit*. 1047, 1048.

But the Court will not oust themselves of Jurisdiction, in Favour of such a *strange wild Jurisdiction* as this, without a *very sufficient Affidavit*. *ibid.*

Such *Affidavit* must shew " That the Lands are holden of a Manor, " *which* MANOR is itself Ancient Demesne; and that the Matter " *can be tried* in the Court of that Manor; and that there *are* " *Suitors there*:" And it must shew " That the Demandant has " a Freehold." *ibid.*

Domesday-Book will not shew whether the *particular Lands* are Ancient Demesne: It will only shew whether the *Manor* is so, or not. 1048.

Arbitration, Arbitrators.

The Act of 9, 10 *W.* 3. *c.* 15. " for determining Differences, by Arbitration," was made, to put Submissions where *no Cause* was depending, upon the *same Foot* with those where there *was* a Cause depending: And it is only declaratory of what the Law was before, in the *latter Case*. 701.

Articles of the Peace

Ought to be exhibited in the *Neighbourhood*; that the Security may be given there: And accordingly, a Man residing at the *Devizes*, and coming hither to exhibit Articles against another Man residing also at the *Devizes*, was rejected here, and referred to his own Neighbourhood. 780. *V. infra* 1039.

The *Facts sworn* must be taken to be TRUE; And the Court *cannot* give the Defendant Leave to *dispute* them; (as the Court declared in Ld. *Vane*'s Case in *H.* 1743. 17 *G.* 2.) Yet one *Robert Parnell* having sworn the Peace against Sir *Thomas Allen* and his

not relevant, nor do the legal Consequences depend upon the *Truth* of it, but upon the *Rule of Law*. Page 967.
Of the WANT *of Qualifications*—Where necessary or not necessary in an *Indictment*. 1036, 1037. See *Indictment*.

Bail

COmmon—*Special*—The *Affidavit* to hold to Special Bail must be POSITIVE: *A positive Oath of the Debt* is required both by the *Act of Parliament* and by the *Established Rule* of the Court. 655.
1st. By 12 *G.* 1. *c.* 29. § 1, 2. No Person shall be held to *Special* Bail, for any Cause of Action under 10 *l.* in a *superior* Court, and 40 *s.* in an *inferior* Court. Of which Cause of Action, *Affidavit* shall be made and filed; and the Sum therein specified, indorsed on the Writ or Process: For which *indorsed Sum*, the Officer shall take Bail, and *for no more*. 655, 656.
2dly. Swearing *only to* BELIEF, though with a *Reference to Accounts* sent from abroad, where the Debt arose, will not do. 655. *Sed v. infra, sub pa.* 1032.
Common—Special—A Debtor regularly *discharged* of an old Debt, but conscientiously making a *new Acknowledgment* of it and a *new Promise* to pay it, shall be discharged upon *Common* Bail, and *not* holden to *Special*. 737, 738. See *Bankrupt*.
Upon Writs of *Error*, on 3 *J.* 1. *c.* 8. (on Bonds conditioned for Payment of Money *only*.) 746, 747. See *Error*.
It is the *Duty* of Sheriff's Officers to take it, in Actions on the Case: And they are punishable if they take Money for doing it. 926 to 929. See Statutes (23 *H.* 6. *c.* 10.)
Common—Special.—The *Affidavit* to hold to Special Bail was only "That the Defendant was indebted to the Plaintiff in &c, AS HE COMPUTES IT: Yet it was thought sufficient, by the only two Judges then in Court. 1032. *Sed v. supra* 655.

Bailiff

To Sheriff. See *Sheriffs and their Bailiffs*: Also *Statutes* (under 23 *H.* 6. *c.* 10.)

Baker.

Baking *Puddings*, *Pies*, and *such Things* for Dinner on a *Sunday*, is *not* an Offence meant by 29 *C.* 2. *c.* 7: But is within the *Equity* of the Proviso in the 3d Section of it, as a *Cook's Shop*; and within the Exception of Works of *Necessity* and *Mercy*. 787, 788.

Ballast—

3

of *W*'s Debt, it was to be *in Trust for L Himself*, as to the Residue. A Defeazance, in a separate Deed, was soon after executed, making the Assignment void, upon Payment of *all* the Money due to *W* (who had been concerned with *L* in circulating Notes, many of which were outstanding :) But *neither* the Assignment nor Defeazance *particularly liquidated* HOW MUCH *Money was due* from *L* to *W*. The Deed of Assignment *recited L*'s being " *obliged*, upon urgent and necessary Business, *to leave London*;" and " that He *could not raise Money soon enough* to answer *all the* " *Demands* that *W* had upon him." There was *no Counterpart* of this Deed: And the Original *remained in the Keeping of L* the Assignor. No *Possession* was delivered: Only, *L* gave a *Letter of Attorney* to *B. his* OWN *Clerk*, (a Person privy to the Whole,) to collect receive dispose &c; *the Goods still continuing in L's House*. *No Notice* was given to *L's Debtors*. *Page* 827. *V. supra* 467 to 485. almost S. P.

1st. This DEED *alone* is *itself* an *Act of Bankruptcy*; 'Tis *within* 21 *J.* 1. *c.* 19. § 2. and, if permitted, would *defeat* the whole System of the Bankrupt Laws. 829 to 833. *V. supra* 467 to 485.

2dly. The CIRCUMSTANCES confirm this: Particularly, there being NO *visible Change of Possession*, a *secret Transaction*, *no Notice* &c. 830.

3dly. It was resolved,—

1st. That a Trader (even *before* Bankruptcy,) *can not* PREFER One or more Creditor or Creditors to the *Rest*, by a Conveyance of his WHOLE Estate and Effects. 829 to 833. *V. supra* 484.

2dly. But He may *pay* a particular Creditor; or He may *mortgage* a PART of his Estate or Effects (at least) to a particular Creditor, provided He *delivers Possession* at the same Time. 831. *V. supra* 484.

3dly. Yet a COLORABLE *Exception of a small Part* would not (*per* Lord *Mansfield*) help the Matter: For the Court would not suffer such an *Evasion* to prevail. 832.

4thly. The *System* of the Bankrupt Laws is " That the Bankrupt's " Effects shall be taken OUT *of his* OWN *Possession and Manage-* " *ment*, and put under that of the *Commissioners*; and be divi- " ded *equally*, *i. e.* proportionally, amongst all his Creditors, 829, 830.

5thly. Therefore *L became a Bankrupt* the *Moment He executed this Deed*, which puts his WHOLE Estate under the Management of *his* OWN *Trustee*, instead of the Commissioners; and assigned it ALL to One Creditor, leaving *Nothing* for the Rest. 830.

A *Mortgage* by a Trader, of *Ships abroad*, or of *Cargoes upon the high Seas*, is good (notwithstanding the Clause in 21 *J.* 1. *c.* 19.) though Possession be not actually delivered. 941.

Berwick—

8. A

"found upon such Trial to be, and in Fact was *utterly ignorant* "*of it*," was allowed. *Page* 892 to 897.

Capiatur—

THE Award "*quod capiatur*"—is only to bring the Defendant in, to receive Sentence; but is *not* the *final* Judgment. 801. See *Practice*, *Judgment*.

Cases doubted or denied.

Lambert v. *Oakes*, 1 *Ld. Raym.* 433. 1 *Salk.* 126. *pl.* 6. 12 *Mod.* 244. and 1 *Salk.* 127. *pl.* 9. (there called *Lambert* v. *Pack*,) *discussed*, *denied*, and *explained*. 677, 678. See *Bill of Exchange*, *Promissory Notes*.

Seymour's Case, 10 *Co.* 95. *not* denied; on the contrary, *affirmed*, as the Facts were there expressly found, (which shewed that the Bargain and Sale was totally *unconnected* with the Fine:) But *distinguished* from a Case where a Lease and Release and a Fine were all *intended* to be, and were accordingly adjudged to be, All together, *One entire Assurance*. 711 to 716. See *Discontinuance*.

1 *Salk.* 78. *Queen* v. *Darby* 801. See *Practice*, *Capiatur*, *Judgment*.

7 *Co.* 23. *b.* concerning *Berwick* 858, 859. See *Berwick* (*pa.* 858, 859.)

Hale's Hist. Com. Law 184. concerning *Berwick*. *ibid.* See *Berwick*, (*ibid.*)

Rex v. *Clendon*, 2 *Strange* 870. 2 *Ld. Raym.* 1572. "That an "Indictment will *not* lie, for an Assault upon *Two*"—denied. 984. See *Information*.

Rattle v. *Popham*, (2 *Strange* 992.) 1147. See *Powers*.

Certificate

Of having *apprehended prosecuted and convicted* a *Felon*, under 10, 11 *W.* 3. *c.* 23. § 2. 1182 to 1188.

1st. Is *assignable* over, once and no more; provided it has not been used before. *V.* the Act, § 2, 3.

2d. Exempts from all *Parish* and *Ward* Offices, within the Parish or Ward wherein the Felony was committed. 1183.

3d. But it will not serve to exempt the *Constable of a Manor* which comprehends the whole Town and Parish where the Felony was committed, *and* MORE. 1185 to 1188.

Condition precedent

Must be *averred* to be *performed*, or that the Plaintiff was *ready* to perform it. 900.

The *Want* of such Averment may be *helped by a* VERDICT; but not by a Judgment by *Default*. *ibid.*

In Consideration that the Plaintiff, at the Request of the Defendant, *would execute* to the Defendant a General Release, the Defendant promises to pay: This is a Condition precedent, "to *give* or "*tender* a Release executed." *ibid.*

Consent

Cannot *give* Jurisdiction to a Court that has none. 746.

Consideration

Illegal—shall *not* be *assisted* by the Court, nor *helped by Verdict* (where it appears upon the Face of the Declaration to be illegal.) 926 to 928.

A Promise to pay Money to a Sheriff's Officer, in Consideration "That He would *accept* of the Promiser and *A. R.* to be *Bail* for the Person arrested," is an *illegal* Consideration. *ibid.* See *Statutes* (23 *H.* 6. *c.* 10.)

Conspiracy. See *Indictment* 999. *Judgment villainous* 996.

To *charge with a Capital Crime*. 993 to 1000. See *ut supra*.

The *Punishment* of it. *ibid.* and 1027.

Constable—

Of the *Night* is guilty of a *Misdemeanour*, if He suffers a Street-Walker delivered to his Custody by One of the nightly Watch, to escape. 866, 867. See *Indictment*.

Of a *Manor* including a Parish, but *more extensive*, is not exempt from serving *this* Office, by having a Certificate under 10, 11 *W.* 3. *c.* 23. § 2, 3: For this is *not* a PARISH-Office within that Act. 1182 to 1188. See *Certificate*.

Conveyance. See *Common Recovery*.

Where a *Deed* or *Deeds*, and a *Fine*, shall be considered as *unconnected* and having *distinct Operations*: And where they shall be considered

the Butter had been firſt exported from *Ireland* to *Liſbon*, and *from* LISBON hither. *Page* 1176.

Copies

Of *Proceedings*—are of two Sorts; *viz.* *Office* Copies, and *Cloſe* Copies:

1ſt. *Office* Copies, in the *ſame Court* and in the *ſame Cauſe*, are *equivalent to the Record* itſelf. 1179, 1181.

2dly. In *another Court*, or in *another Cauſe* in the ſame Court, the Copy muſt be *proved.* 1179.

3dly. Each Party in a Cauſe in Chancery, though He muſt take an Office-Copy of the adverſe Pleadings, may *read the* DRAUGHT *of his own. ibid.*

4thly. Copies to be *given in Evidence* in another Court may be written as *cloſe* as the Writer pleaſes. Thus the *Stamp-Acts* found it: And they did not mean to alter the Manner of making them, or to fix *them* to ſo many Words in a Sheet. They only meant to prevent any Fraud upon the Stamp-Duties, with Regard to the *Office*-Copies: And the 64th Clauſe of 9, 10 *W.* 3. *c.* 25. (which Clauſe is intended to prevent Colluſion and Fraud) does not ſay a Word about *Copies.* 1177, 1181.

5thly. A *Cloſe* Copy of a Bill in Chancery, written on only *two* Sheets of Paper Each ſtampt with a triple Sixpeny Stamp only, was holden to be *properly ſtampt* ſo as to intitle the Plaintiff to have it *read in Evidence*; although it contained the Quantity of 40 Office-Copy Sheets. *ibid.*

6thly. So alſo was a like *cloſe* Copy of an amended Bill containing 44 Office-Copy Sheets, written on 3 Sheets of Paper Each ſtampt with a triple Sixpeny Stamp. *ibid.*

Copyhold.

Copyhold Land *mortgaged in Fee*, and become a *forfeited Mortgage* at Law, was *deviſed by the Mortgagee*, by *general* Words in his Will; but had been *particularly* deſcribed in the previous *Surrender to the Uſe of his Will.* The Deviſe was of *All* the Teſtator's Lands &c &c. (See the Words *pa.* 971, 972.) "to *H. W.* his "Son *and Anne his Wife*, and to the *Heirs of the Body* of the ſaid "*H. W.* by the ſaid *Anne*." By the Cuſtom of the Manor, intailed Copyhold Lands are *barrable by* SURRENDER. *H. W. alone*, WITHOUT *his Wife*, *ſurrendered* this mortgaged Land. Two Queſtions were made; 1ſt. Whether any Eſtate *Tail* was hereby *created*; 2dly. If there was, then whether *barred* by the Surrender of *H. W.* alone, *without* his Wife.

1ſt. *If* the Teſtator *meant* to deviſe this as *Land*, it ſhall *paſs as Land*: If as *Money*, then it ſhall paſs *as Money*. 978.

Covenant

Court

Damages

" lemnization of the Marriage, and at the Request &c, *at or after* " *such Time* as Dr. *W.* should settle *his* Estate to the same Uses, " *settle and convey* &c, so Trustees &c, (naming them,) To hold " &c, To the Use &c." Part of the Uses were To the Dr. for Life; Remainder to Trustees &c; Remainder to *Anne* for Life; Remainder to the first and every other Son of their Bodies, and the Heirs of the Body of such first and other Son &c; Remainder to their first and every other Daughter, and the Heirs of their Bodies &c; Remainder to the Use of the Aunt Mrs. *S. M. her Heirs and Assigns for ever*. The Marriage took Effect. Afterwards, the Aunt made her WILL, (*Reciting the Articles*, and " that the " Premisses so *agreed* to be settled by Her are, after her Death and " the Deaths of Dr. *W.* and his Wife and in Default of Issue of " their two Bodies, limited *or agreed* to be limited to Her and " her Heirs;") and *devises the absolute Inheritance thereof* " To the " Use and Behoof of the HEIRS OF THE BODY *of her said Niece* " *Anne Wynn by any* OTHER *Husband* lawfully to be begotten; " and for want of such Issue, then to the Use and Behoof of her " Nephew CHARLES LLOYD and the Heirs of his Body; with " several Remainders over;, Remainder to her own right Heirs." The Aunt died seised, leaving the said *Anne Wynn* her Heir at Law. Dr. *W.* and *Anne* his Wife entered, and regularly suffered a COMMON RECOVERY; in which They were vouched &c: And They afterwards declared the Uses of this Recovery; the last of which was " to the *right Heirs of the said* ANNE, for ever." And it was UNDER *the* HEIR AT LAW *of the said* ANNE WYNN, that *Goodman et al'* (the Defendants below) claimed, Dr. *Wynn* and his Wife *Anne* being Both *dead without Issue*. The *Lessors* of the Plaintiff below were *Annabella*, the *only Daughter and Heir* of CHARLES LLOYD, and her Husband. 874 to 879.

1st. The Question depends upon the *Intention* of the Testatrix, " Whether She meant to give *Charles Lloyd* an *Estate* IN POSSES- " SION," or not. For *if She did not*, neither He nor those claiming under Him can have any Title. 877: Because the Devise to Him could not be good any other Way than either as a *contingent Remainder* or as an *Executory Devise*; And it is *not good*, in *either* Way, 877, 878.

2d. It is NOT *a* PRESENT Devise: For neither the *Words* nor the *Nature of the Provision* will admit of *this* Construction. *ibid.*

3d. It is a FUTURE Devise, to take Place after an *indefinite* Failure of Issue: Which is *too remote*, as it far exceeds the utmost Limits allowed to Executory Devises, namely, the Compass of a *Life or Lives in being*, AND 21 *Years after*. 878, 879.

4th. The *Articles* can not be considered as EXECUTED. (Yet this was not given as a direct Opinion.) 879.

5th. An Executory Devise too remote in it's *Creation* cannot be made good by any subsequent *Event*. 878.

might, *by Sale* of ſuch of the ſaid Lands *&c*, raiſe ſo much Money as ſhould be ſufficient to diſcharge ſuch of his DEBTS as ſhould not be diſcharged out of his perſonal Eſtate: And as to ſo much Part of the ſaid Lands and Tenements as ſhould *remain unſold*, To the Uſe of his Son *Audley Mervyn*, in Tail Male; and ſo to his three other Sons in Tail Male; with ſeveral Remainders over. The Will referred to an Eſtate ſettled upon his Eldeſt Son *Henry*, on his Marriage, with the Reverſion in Fee to the Teſtator; and gave an Annuity to his ſaid Wife *Olivia*, out of the deviſed Lands, and ſeveral Powers of Leaſing, Jointuring, and committing Waſte; and contained ſeveral Clauſes which it would be tedious to particularize. The two Queſtions upon this Will were, 1ſt. Whether the REVERSION *of the ſettled Lands* paſſed by it, or not: 2d. *If* it *did paſs*, then whether the Leſſors of the Plaintiff, who *claimed under Thoſe in Remainder*, (the four Sons being All dead without Iſſue,) had *any Title*. *Page* 912

1ſt. The Court were unanimous, upon the firſt Queſtion (which went to the Fundamental Merits,) That the REVERSION *did* NOT *paſs* by the Will; as appeared upon the *whole Tenor and Complexion* of the Will, conſidered in *all it's Parts* and *taken all together*: Which is the Way to diſcover the *Intention* of the Teſtator; and which ſhall be equally regarded, if it can be *clearly and plainly collected from the Will*, as if it had been directly expreſſed. 920, 923, 924.

2dly. As the Reverſion was holden NOT *to paſs*, by the clear *Intention* of the Teſtator, the Court thought it unneceſſary to give any Opinion "whether the Deviſe over could *take Effect*, *in Point of* LAW; which depended upon *nice Queſtions of Law*. 918, 923, 924.

By Mortgagee, of LANDS HOLDEN IN MORTGAGE. 969 to 980. See *Copyhold*, *Mortgage*.

Deviſe "that the *Executors ſhall ſell* the Teſtator's Land, for the Payment of his Debts," does *not*, in general, *paſs the Eſtate* to the Executors. 1030, 1031.

Deviſe "*that his Executors ſhall and may* ABSOLUTELY SELL *mortgage* "*or otherwiſe diſpoſe of his Freehold Eſtate*, for the Payment of "ſuch of his Debts Legacies and Funeral Expences as his Leaſe-"hold Eſtate ſhould not be ſufficient to diſcharge," is ONLY *a* POWER *to ſell &c*: And NO ESTATE *paſſes* to the Executors. *ibid.* and 1032.

"To the poor Priſoners and inſolvent Debtors in the MARSHALSEA-"*Priſon* in the Burrough of *Southwark*—"means the Priſon of the *Palace-Court*, not of the *King's Bench*. 1038, 1039.

"To my dear Wife," of his Farm at *B. in the Tenure of J. S.* "ſub-"ject to her Diſpoſal in *as full and abſolute a Manner* as *I* could "diſpoſe of the ſame if living"—*paſſes* to the Wife, as well ſuch *Woods and Woodlands Hedge-Rows Timber and Trees*, as ſtood

7th. The ancient Maxim of the Law was, "That although the "Estate be limited to the Anceſtor expreſſly *for Life*, and "after his Death *to his Heirs* (general or ſpecial,) yet the *Heir* "ſhall take by *Deſcent*, and the Fee ſhall veſt in the *Anceſtor*." *Page* 1106.

1ſt. This Maxim was *originally introduced* in *Favour of the Lord* (to prevent his being deprived of the Fruits of the Tenure,) and likewiſe for the Sake of *Specialty-Creditors. ibid.*

2dly. The *Reaſon* of it has now *ceaſed.* 1107.

3dly. Yet, having become a Rule of Property, it is adhered to in all Caſes *literally* within it. *ibid.*

4thly. But where there are Circumſtances which take the Caſe OUT *of the Letter* of this Rule, it is departed from, in Favour of the *Intention. ibid.*

8th. There is *no ſolid Diſtinction* (as to the Point in queſtion in this Caſe) between a TRUST and a LEGAL *Eſtate*, or between a *Truſt* EXECUTED and a *Truſt* EXECUTORY. 1108.

1ſt. A *Court of* EQUITY is as much *bound* by *poſitive Rules* and *general Maxims* concerning Property as a Court of *Law* is. *ibid.*

2dly. If the *Intention* of the Teſtator be *contrary to the Rules of Law*, it can no more take Place in a *Court of* EQUITY, than in a Court of *Law. ibid.*

3dly. On the other hand, If the Intention be *not contrary to Law*, a *Court of* COMMON *Law* is as much bound to conſtrue and effectuate the Will *according to that Intention*, as a Court of Equity can be. 1108, 1109.

John Selwyn the Elder being Tenant for Life, with Remainder to *John Selwyn* his Son in Tail Male, They both joined in a Bargain and Sale to *J. W.* and his Heirs, to the Intent He might become Tenant of the Freehold, to the End a Common Recovery might be ſuffered To the Uſe of the ſaid *J. S.* the Elder for Life &c, Remainder to the Uſe of the ſaid *J. S.* the Younger his Heirs and Aſſigns for ever. A Writ of Entry was ſued out, returnable (as is expreſſly ſtated) "in 15 Days from the Holy "*Trinity, which was the 16th Day of June* 1751." *Trinity* Term 1751 begun on *7th* of *June*. On the *8th* of *June* 1751, *John Selwyn* the Younger made his Will, and died on the 27th without altering it or *republiſhing* it. Queſtion, "Whether the ſe- "veral Lands Tenements and Hereditaments comprized in the "Deed of Bargain and Sale (which was dated on 12th of *April* "1751,) PASSED *by the Will of John Selwyn the Son*." The Court of King's Bench certified their Opinion to the Court of Chancery, "That they DID *paſs* thereby." 1134.

Diſcontinuance.

A Fine *with* Proclamations, (as well as a Fine at Common Law, *without* Proclamations,) levied by Tenant in Tail in Poſſeſſion, will

4thly. Such a *general Allegation* needs not therefore to be traversed. *Page* 731, 733.

If the *whole* Body of a Corporation meet upon a Day NOT *a Charter* or *Prescription-Day*, and amove a Member, it is as necessary that *Each* individual Member should be summoned and have *Notice* of the *particular Business* intended to be proceeded upon, as it is in the Case of a *select* Number. 741 to 745. *V. supra, the last Case.*

Previous Conviction at Common Law—Where necessary; where not necessary; is a Point *not settled*; (as was alledged, *arguendo*:) See it discussed, *arguendo*. 742 to 745. *Sed. v. supra, pa.* 538, 539.

Ejectment.

THE *Nominal* Plaintiff, and the *Casual* Ejector are *judicially* to be considered as the *fictitious Form* of an Action *really* brought by the *Lessor* of the Plaintiff against the *Tenant in Possession*. 667, 668.

This Action is an Invention for the *Advancement of Justice*, and to force the Parties to go to Trial upon the *Merits*. *ibid.*

The *Lessor* of the Plaintiff, and the *Tenant in Possession*, are, substantially and in Truth, the only *Parties* to the Suit. *ibid.*

There is *no Distinction* between a Judgment in Ejectment upon a *Verdict*, and One by *Default*: In the former, the Plaintiff's Right is found; In the other, confessed. *ibid.*

An *Action* for the *mesne Profits* may be brought either in the *Name* of the *Lessor* or of the *Lessee*: It is equally the Action of the *Lessor* of the Plaintiff. *ibid.*

The *Tenant* is *concluded* by the Judgment; and can *not controvert* the Plaintiff's *Title* nor *Possession*. *ibid.* But the Judgment proves Nothing *beyond the Time laid* in the Demise. *ibid.* It proves Nothing as to *Length of Time the Tenant has occupied*; nor as to the *Value*: Both these must be *proved*, in an Action for the *mesne Profits*. *ibid.*

A *Landlord* was *made Defendant*, according to 11 *G.* 2. *c.* 19. § 13. on the *Tenant's Non*-Appearance; and entered into the Common Rule; and thereupon, a *Stay of Execution* against the Casual Ejector was ordered, until the Court should make *further Order*.

1st. A *Writ of Error* brought by the Landlord, is a sufficient Reason against taking out Execution. 757.

2dly. But the *proper Opportunity* for the Landlord to make his *Stand* against the Execution is by shewing this as *Cause* against the Plaintiff's Motion *for Leave* to take it out. *ibid.*

3dly. If He *omits this Opportunity*, the Execution (regularly issued) shall *not* be set aside. *ibid.*

Ancient

Error.

Evidence

Execution—

1st. If a freighted Ship becomes *disabled* on it's Voyage, *accidentally and without any Fault* of the Master, the *Master has his* OPTION, either to *refit* it (in convenient Time,) or to procure *another* Ship to carry the Goods. If the Freighter disagrees to this, and will not suffer it, the Master shall yet be intitled to his WHOLE Freight, as of the *full* Voyage. *Page* 887, 888.

2d. But the Master (if in no Fault) is, at *all* Events, and *though* He neither refits his own Ship nor procures another, intitled to Freight PRO RATA ITINERIS, i.e. *in Proportion to such former Part* of the Voyage as He has *already* performed. 888 to 891.

3d. In this Case, He had performed [illegible] Parts of it: And therefore [illegible] of the whole Freight had been the *rateable Proportion*, had the whole Cargo been saved. 888.

4th. But here was *Salvage* paid for *Half*: Therefore *Half* must be considered *as lost*; and *Half*, as *saved*. Consequently, the *rateable Proportion* is [illegible] of *Half* of the full Freight. 888, 890.

5th. The *Value* of the Goods, or what they sold for, or whether they are spoiled or not, was Nothing to the Master; because the Freighter *took* them; And He must take *All* that are saved, *or None*: But the Master had *earned* his Freight by carrying them. 887, 888.

6th. *If* He had *abandoned all*, He had been *excused* Freight. *ibid.*

7th. The Master is not bound to *deliver* the Goods, *till* AFTER *He is paid* his Freight. 890.

Gaming.

Action upon the Case on several Promises: 3 Counts; 1st. upon a *Bill of Exchange* drawn *at* PARIS, by the Intestate Sir *John Bland*, upon *Himself* in ENGLAND, for 672*l*, payable to the Plaintiff's Order, *ten Days after Sight*, Value received, and accepted by Sir *John Bland*; 2d Count—for 700*l.* lent and advanced by the Plaintiff to Sir *John Bland*; 3d Count—for 700*l.* had and received by Sir *John*, to the Plaintiff's Use. General Issue. Verdict for the Plaintiff, for 672*l*, Damages, subject to the Opinion of the Court, on the following Facts proved and admitted: *viz.* The *Bill of Exchange* was *given at* PARIS for 300*l.* there LENT by the Plaintiff to Sir *John*, at the *Time and Place of Play*; and for 373*l*, more LOST at the *same Time and Place*, by Sir *John* to the Plaintiff, at Play. But the Play was very *fair*; and *no Imputation* on the Plaintiff's Behaviour: And several other Persons of Fashion were then and there at Play. That Sir *John* and the Plaintiff were *Both Gentlemen*. That *in* FRANCE, Money LOST at *Play*, between *Gentlemen*, may be *recovered*, as a Debt of *Honour*, before the MARSHALS OF FRANCE; Who can enforce Obedience to their Sentences, by *Imprisonment*: Though such Money

1st. This is agreeable to *natural Justice*. *Page* 1081, 1086.
2dly. And to *Law*, both *Statute* and *Common*. 1086, 1087.
3dly. And to the Practice of the Court of *Chancery* and of *all other Courts*. 1087.

Grand Jury

Ought not to consist of more than 23 actually sworn upon it. 1088.

Habeas Corpus

FOR a PRISONER OF WAR taken on Board of an Enemy's Privateer Ship, and alledging and proving by Affidavit, "That "He was a *Foreigner*, Subject of a *Neutral* Power, taken by a "*French* Privateer, in an *English* Ship as He was coming to "*England* to enter into our *English* Merchant's Service, and "detained *by Force* and *against his Will* to serve on Board the "*French* Privateer"—*This Court* will not take upon themselves to set Him at Liberty: The Application must be to the *Crown*. 765, 766.

A Person *extremely weakened* in Body and Mind being got into bad Hands, and *too infirm* to be brought into Court by *Habeas Corpus*, a Rule was made, in the first Instance (without Time to shew Cause) for a Doctor, Apothecary, Nurse, Relations and Attorney to have *Access*, to advise and assist Her. 1099, 1100.

Habeas Corpus *cum* Causa. See *Procedendo*.

When to be *delivered* (pursuant to 21 *J.* 1. *c.* 23. § 1, 2.) 759. See *Statutes*.

A *By-Law* shall not be objected to, in a *summary* Way, upon *Motion*, on the *Return*; *except* in Cases from LONDON. 779. In all *other* Corporations, the Plaintiff must *declare here*: And if the Defendant has any Objection to the By-Law, He may demur. *ibid.* And this, though the By-Law has *negative* and *exclusive* Words, "that the Action for the Penalty shall be brought in the "Corporation Court, and *not elsewhere*." *ibid.*

Heriots

Are *not assessable* to the *Poor*-Rates. 991, 992. See *Manor*, *Statutes* (43 *Eliz.* *c.* 2. § 1.) *Quit-Rents*.

On 22 *C.* 2. *c.* 12. § 9. For not ſending a Cart and Men to the Highways. *Page* 832.

1ſt. "*Being* then Surveyors"—is a *ſufficient Averment* "That "they *were* ſo." 834.

2dly. It is *not* neceſſary to alledge *when* or *by whom* the Surveyors were appointed. *ibid.*

3dly. This was an Offence *indictable* BEFORE *this Act*: And therefore the *particular Remedy* given by it is CUMULATIVE. 834. *V. ſupra* 545. and 803 to 806.

Lies againſt a Conſtable, for a Miſdemeanour in *wilfully ſuffering a looſe idle lewd and diſorderly* Woman, taken up by One of the nightly Watch as a Common Street-Walker and *delivered to Him* for ſafe Cuſtody, to *eſcape* out of his Cuſtody, before She could be carried before a Magiſtrate. 866, 867.

For a CONSPIRACY "to indict for a *Capital* Offence," was laid, "That the Defendants did wickedly and maliciouſly (*omitting* "the Word *falſely*) conſpire to indict and cauſe to be indicted "*W. G.* for A Crime or Offence (*omitting* to ſpecify WHAT "Crime) liable by the Laws of this Kingdom to be puniſhed "capitally: And that they, ACCORDING TO *the Conſpiracy aforeſaid* between them as aforeſaid before had, DID afterwards "FALSELY *wickedly and maliciouſly indict* Him &c;" *ſpecifying* the *very Indictment itſelf*; which *appears to be for a Capital Crime.* This is a *good* Indictment; although the Word "FALSELY" is not added to the *firſt Charge* of the Conſpiring, nor the *particular Crime* there ſpecified. 999. And although it is *not* laid "that the ſaid *W. G.* was *acquitted* of it. 998, 999. Note—The *Sentence* was *not the* VILLAINOUS *Judgment*; though the Indictment concluded "*contra Formam Statuti.*" *ibid.* and 1027. It was a *long Impriſonment*; *Pillory, twice*; a *Fine*; and *Security for good Behaviour.* 1027.

On 5 *Eliz. c.* 4. § 31. for exerciſing the Occupation of a TANNER, not having ſerved an *Apprenticeſhip for ſeven* Years therein—is ſufficient WITHOUT *ſpecifying and averring the Want of other* Qualifications allowed by *ſubſequent* Statutes: For ſuch other Qualifications or Exceptions ought to be ſhewn *by the Defendant.* 1036, 1037.

For where an Indictment is brought *upon* a Statute which has *general Prohibitory Words* in it, it is ſufficient to charge the Offence *generally*, in the Words of it: And if a *ſubſequent* Statute, or even a Clauſe of *Exception* in the *ſame* Statute, excuſes or excepts Perſons particularly circumſtanced, out of the general Words, ſuch *Excuſe* or *Exception* muſt come by Way of *Plea* or *Evidence. ibid.*

But where the Words of a Statute are *deſcriptive of the Nature of the Offence*, or the *Purview* of the Statute, or are *neceſſary to give a ſummary Juriſdiction*, the Indictment muſt in ſuch Caſes *ſpecify* in it's particular Words. 1037.

But

Judgment in it, It ſhall be *included*. *Page* 1086, 1087. See *Gaming*.

In the *Eaſt-Indies*, the allowed Intereſt is *Nine per Cent.* A Bond was given there, where both Parties then reſided, conditioned for Payment *with that Intereſt*. An Action was brought upon it here: And Verdict for the Plaintiff. The Defendant affected very great *Delay*, in various Methods; particularly, by bringing a *Writ of Error* in the Exchequer-Chamber, and alſo in the Manner of proceeding upon it. It is both Law and Juſtice, that the Plaintiff ſhould recover the Sum lent, together with INDIAN *Intereſt* up to the Time of *ſigning the Judgment*; but with *only the* LEGAL *Intereſt* of *this* Country, upon the *accumulated* Sum liquidated and aſcertained by the Judgment, *from* the Time of ſigning the Judgment TILL *actual Payment* of the Money: For that is the *Real Damage* which the Plaintiff has ſuſtained by the Delay of the Execution and the Detention of his Debt. 1096 to 1099.

1ſt. He may *either* bring an *Action of Debt on the Judgment*, and have Damages *pro Detentione Debiti*: 1096.

2dly. *Or* He is intitled to a Satisfaction for this Damage, under 13 *C.* 2. *Stat.* 2. *c.* 2. (§ 8, 9, 10.) which obliges the Plaintiff in Error to give *Security* as well for *Damages* as Coſts. *ibid.*

3dly. And there are *four* Courts, to which Writs of Error may be made returnable: *viz.* The Houſe of *Lords*; The Court before the *Lord Chancellor Treaſurer and Judges* (under 31 *E.* 3.) The *Exchequer-Chamber*, before the *Judges of C. B. and Barons* (under 27 *Eliz. c.* 8.) And *this* Court of *King's Bench*. *ibid.*

1ſt. The *Lords* give Coſts according to their *Diſcretion*. 1097.

2d. In the 2d—It is done by the Lord Chancellor or Lord Keeper, perſonally: And the Practice is, to give *Intereſt* from the Day of *ſigning the Judgment* to the Day of *affirming* it there; computed according to the *Current* Rate of Intereſt, *not* according to the *ſtrictly legal* Rate. *ibid.*

3d. In the 3d (the Exchequer-Chamber) The Officer ſettles it, unleſs there be particular Directions given by the Court: And He, in taxing the Coſts, allows *double* the Money out of Pocket or thereabouts, but NO *Intereſt*. *ibid.*

4th. In *this* Court, the *Officer* taxes theſe Coſts of Affirmance, ſomewhat more *liberally* than other Coſts; but has *never any Regard to* INTEREST, nor allows it as of Courſe: But the *Court themſelves* have ſometimes *ordered Intereſt* to be computed on the *Sum liquidated* by the Judgment below. *ibid.*

Ireland.

ſhall be left to his *ordinary* Remedy. 1162. And where They are complained of without Reaſon, they ſhall have *Coſts*. *Page* 1162.

Latin

IS neceſſary to be underſtood by a Perſon put APPRENTICE *to a* SURGEON *of London*. 892 to 897. See *By-Law*.

Latitat—

Where the *true* Time of ſuing it out is *material*, It may be *ſhewn*; notwithſtanding the *Teſte*. 963 to 967. See *Pleading* 950 to 969.

It was not ſettled, till many Years after the Statute of 21 *J.* 1. *c.* 16. "That the Plaintiff *might* reply a *Latitat*." 961.

And now, though the *Latitat* is holden to ſave the Bar, within the *Equity* and *Reaſon* of the Statute, yet it muſt be taken out *with Intent to declare in that Action*, and muſt be *continued* to the Filing of the Bill. *ibid.*

The *Teſte* of a *Latitat* ſued out in Vacation *muſt* be of the preceding Term. 964.

A *Latitat* is a *good Commencement* of a *Penal* Action. 964.

A *Latitat* may bear *Date before* the Cauſe of Action, if *really* proſecuted *after* it. 967.

Leaſes.

A Leaſe "for 7, 14, OR 21 Years, *as the Leſſee ſhall think proper*;" (upon which the Leſſee enters, and continues in Poſſeſſion;) is undoubtedly a *good* Leaſe for *ſeven* Years; whatever may be it's Validity as to the two other eventual Terms, of 14 and 21 Years. 1034.

A Leaſe may *commence* at one Day, in Point of *Computation*; and at another Day, in Point of *Intereſt*: And ſuch a Leaſe, "*Habendum* "*from* a Day paſt, for 50 Years then next enſuing; the ſaid Term "to *commence and begin* from and immediately *after the Deter-* "*mination* of an exiſting Leaſe of the ſame Premiſſes," ſhall *not* be eſteemed uncertain in it's Commencement. 1190 to 1198.

Libel, Libellous.

Words ſpoken or ſworn in a Man's *own Defence* againſt a Complaint in a *Court* of Juſtice, are *not actionable*; becauſe 'tis in a *legal* and *judicial* Way: The Words were—"which Sir *J. A.* hath *ſo* "*falſely ſworn* againſt Him." 809 to 813. See *Affidavit*.

Licence—

Manor—

Marriage—

Navigation

MAY not be *obstructed* by casting *Rubbish*, or unlading *Ballast*, in any Havens, Roads, Channels &c; but ONLY *upon the* LAND, where the Tide never flows: By 34, 35 *H.* 8. *c.* 9. and 19 *G.* 2. *c.* 22. *Page* 656 to 661.

1st. The Unloading it *into a Hopper*, with *Intent* to carry it *out to Sea*, is an Offence against the *express* Provision of the latter Act, which says "That it shall *not* be discharged, *but* ONLY *upon Land.* 659, 660.

2dly. But putting it into the Hopper, *in Order to carry it upon Land*, would *not* be so. *ibid.*

3dly. Nor *Shifting* it out of one Ship into Another, without Intention *to drop it* ANY *where*. 660.

New Forest.

The Statute of 9, 10 *W.* 3. *c.* 36. for the Increase and Preservation of the Timber therein, (*V.* § 1. and § 9.) gives the Crown Power to inclose 2000 Acres, (*viz.* 1000 immediately, and 1000 at a *specified Time*;) and afterwards to inclose more; freed and discharged of all Manner of Rights &c.

1st. By the 9th Section, the Right of COMMON is,

1. In the *inclosed* Parts, restrained *absolutely*, so long as they *remain inclosed.* 1119, 1120.

2. In the UN*inclosed* Parts, It is *continued*, under certain *Limitations* and Exceptions. *ibid.*

2dly. But the Right of PANNAGE is (by that Section) *absolutely taken away*, for 18 Years; and is, even after that, *restrained* to a limited Time (*viz.* between 14th *September* and 11th *November.*) *ibid.*

3dly. These Restrictions take Place, though 1000 *Acres* ONLY be yet inclosed: It is not a Condition precedent, "that the "*Whole* shall be first inclosed." *ibid.*

New Trial

Shall *not* be granted, even where the Jury have found for the Defendant *against Evidence*; if the Plaintiff appears to have received NO REAL *Injury*, and the Damages (if the Verdict had been found for the Plaintiff) could have been but a MERE *Trifle.* 665. *V. next Case below.*

Though the Ground of a Verdict for a Plaintiff be wrong, yet if *no Injustice* be done to the Defendant; or if the Plaintiff can, by *another Form of Action*, recover as much; *No* new Trial shall be granted: *Contra*, where *Injustice is done* Him by it; and if it be

 not

2dly. NEITHER the *Lessees*, (who are merely nominal uninterested Trustees,) nor the *Servants*, much less the *Lunatics* themselves, are rateable *as* OCCUPIERS. *Page* 1064, 1065.

3dly. THIS is *not* like the Case of Hospitals of Royal Foundation where the Officers have APARTMENTS which they use *as Dwelling-Houses* (as in *Chelsea* and *Greenwich* Hospitals) where They *and their Families* reside: For it has been determined "that All those *large distinct Apartments* ought to be taxed to "the *Window-Lights* as *Dwelling-Houses*; and that the said "Officers *are* rateable, for them, to that Tax." 1063, 1064.

Orders of Removal—

A Pauper cannot be removed from *his* OWN; though He came originally into the Parish by Certificate. 702. *V. supra*, under *pa.* 507.

Apprentice to a Certificate-Man does *not* gain a Settlement, where the Master (being *uncertificated* at the Time of *Binding*) obtains and delivers a Certificate, *before* the Apprentice has served Him 40 *Days*: For, by 12 *Ann. Stat.* 1. *c.* 18. § 2. it is a *Condition* PRECEDENT to the Apprentice's gaining a Settlement, "That He "must have been bound to and served *for* 40 *Days*, a Master "who did not either *come* into, OR RESIDE IN the Parish by Li-"cence of a Certificate." 752, 753.

Thomas Lymer, legally settled in *Shenston*, took a House in *Gratwich* at 30*s. per Annum*; and afterwards took 2 Acres of Land in *King's Bromley*, for the growing of POTATOES, from CANDLEMAS to MICHAELMAS, for 9*l.* and also ½ an Acre there, at 40*s.* for the *like Term*; and paid his Rent for all the Premisses, which were of the VALUE aforesaid. He entered, and enjoyed the Lands during the Term; and *lodged above* 40 *Days in K. B.* (where the Land lay,) for the Convenience of digging up and disposing of the Potatoes. 760.

1st. It was agreed, That *if* the Taking be sufficient, this *Residence* would gain Him a Settlement in the Parish *wherein He resided.* 761, 763, 764.

2dly. This Taking, of above 10*l. per Annum Value*, in the *Manner stated*, is sufficient. 763, 764.

3dly. For the *Criterion* of the Act of 13, 14 *C.* 2. *c.* 12. is the *Credit* and *Ability* of being trusted with and using a Tenement or Tenements, in the same Parish or in different Parishes, of the yearly VALUE of 10*l. Such* a Person not being considered by the Legislature, as a Vagrant. *ibid.*

4thly. And a Taking "for a *whole* Year" is *not necessary*: The *Value* is the Thing to be regarded; *not the Duration* of the Tenure. 763, 764, 765.

5thly.

Parish-Office—

CONSTABLE of a MANOR including the Parish, but *more extensive*, is not a PARISH-Officer within 10, 11 *W.* 3. *c.* 23. § 2, 3. 1182 to 1187. See *Certificate*.

Pauper—

Upon an *Attachment for a Contempt*, The Defendant can not be admitted to defend *in Forma Pauperis.* 1039.

Perjury—

In an *Answer in Chancery*—No Need to prove *Identity of Person*, nor *actual* Swearing. 1189. See *Proof.*

Pillory.

Dr. *Shebbeare*, convicted of writing and publishing a Treasonable Libel, was ordered (as One part of his Sentence) to be set IN and upon the Pillory, at *Charing Cross.* The Under-Sheriff of *Middlesex* (Mr. *Arthur Beardmore*) suffered Him to stand UPON it *only*, in a Sort of Triumph, *without* putting his Head, Neck, Arms, or Hands THROUGH the respective Holes; a *Servant* in Livery holding an *Umbrella over his Head.* And although the Under-Sheriff shewed that *his* officiating that Day was *quite accidental*; and though He produced many Affidavits to shew that it was *not usual*, in *Middlesex*, to put the Head, Neck or Arms or Hands *through*; and though He swore positively to the *Innocence and Uprightness* of his INTENTION, and that He did, according to the *best of his Judgment*, *fully and duly execute* the Sentence of the Court in the USUAL *and* COMMON *Manner*; Yet an *Attachment* issued against him for this Contempt: And He afterwards was *fined* 50*l.* and *committed* to the Custody of the Marshal, for 2 Months. 794 to 798.

Play—

Money *lost* or *lent* at Play; And *Securities* given for the same. 1077 to 1088. See *Gaming.*

Pleading.

Defendant pleads TWO PLEAS (by Leave, under 4, 5 *Ann. c.* 16.) 1. *Not guilty*; 2dly. *Not guilty within* 6 *Years:* On the former of

"was not made within six Years next before the *exhibiting of the* " *Bill*," The Plaintiff replies " that *on 28th of November* 32 *G.* 2. " (within 6 Years &c) He *sued out a* LATITAT, with *Intent* " to exhibit his Bill thereupon, and accordingly did exhibit his " Bill thereupon, in *Hilary* Term 32 *G.* 2; And that the Promise " was made *within six Years next before the* SUING OUT *of this* " LATITAT." The Defendant rejoins, " That by the *Course* " *and Custom of this Court* of *B. R.* a *Latitat* sued out *after the* " *End of any Term* is *supposed* to have issued within the Term " preceding: But that *this Latitat* was REALLY *and* TRULY *sued* " *out* AFTER *the said* 28*th of November*, *viz.* on the 8TH OF " DECEMBER in that Year, and on the *same* Day and Year was " *signed* according to the Statute; and that the Promise was *not* " made within six Years next before the said 8TH OF DECEM- " BER, on which Day the *Latitat* was so REALLY *and in* " TRUTH *sued out*." The Plaintiff demurred to this Rejoinder. But the Court were All clear " That the *Averment* therein " contained, *ought*, by Law, to be ADMITTED:" And in Consequence of that Opinion, They *over-ruled the Demurrer*, and gave *Judgment for the* DEFENDANT. *Page* 950 to 969. See *Averment*, *Latitat*, *Limitation*, *Teste*.

Where there is an *Affirmative and a Negative*, the CONCLUSION must be to the *Country*. 1022. *V. supra* 774.

In Debt on Bond conditioned " for *G's* rendering an Account within " 30 Days after *any* Demand in Writing," The Defendant (*protestando* " that no Demand in Writing was made") pleads " that " *G. did render an Account* within 30 Days after *any* Demand in " Writing:" The Plaintiff replies " that a Demand in Writing " was made *on a particular Day* (specifying the Day;) And yet " no Account was rendered by *G.* within 30 Days after it;" and *concludes* to the COUNTRY. *ibid.* and 1023.

1st. This *Plea* " that *G.* rendered &c within &c after *any* Demand" must be understood as if it had been worded, " after " *every* Demand." 1023, 1024.

2d. The *Replication* is *rightly* concluded to the *Country*. *ibid.*

In Covenant—Breach assigned in Non-Payment of Rent *to a Wife and her* SECOND *Husband*, upon a Lease made by her FIRST *Husband and Her*, for 7, 14 OR 21 Years, *as the Lessee should think proper*. The Lessee had covenanted to pay the Rent to them and their Executors Administrators and Assigns, during the SAID TERM: And *He* had *entered*, and was possessed, and *continued in Possession*. The *second* Husband and the *Wife* (the former Husband being dead) assign the Breach in Non-Payment TO THEMSELVES of Rent incurred within the *first seven Years*. General Demurrer to this Declaration. Joinder in Demurrer. Judgment for the Plaintiffs. 1034.

 On

The

10thly. Where He has an *Election*, No Right to sue as for a total Loss can *vest* in Him *till* He has *made* that Election. *Page* 1211.

Poor-Tax. See *Orders*, *Statutes*, (43 *Eliz.* *c.* 2. § 1.) *Manors*, *Quit-Rents*, *Heriots*, *Hospitals*, *Rates*.

Powers—

To make a JOINTURE—*C. Woolston*, having devised his Lands in *S.* and in *B. H.* and in *W. O.* to the Use of his Eldest Son *James* for Life, with Remainder in Tail Male to *James*'s Sons; and in default of such Issue, the like Limitations to his (the Testator's) Son *John*; with several Remainders over; and having devised other Lands to the Use of his Son *John*, and then to his said Son *James*, in much the same Manner; inserted a Proviso in his Will, " That *James* and *John*, when They should come into Possession " of their Estate for Life, should respectively have full Power Li- " berty and Authority, FROM TIME TO TIME *during his or* " *their respective Life or Lives*, by Deed *or Deeds* Writing *or* " *Writings* to be by Him or Them respectively subscribed and " sealed in the Presence of two or more credible Witnesses, to " *assign limit or appoint* to or to the Use of or in Trust for any " *Woman or Women* that shall be his or their respective *Wife* " *or Wives*, for and during the natural Life and Lives of such " Woman or Women, for or in the Name or in Lieu of their " Jointure or Jointures, ALL *or any Part* of the several Mes- " suages Lands Tenements and Hereditaments to Him or Them " (the said *J. W.* and *J. W.*) herein before respectively limited " as aforesaid." JAMES *made Use of this Power*, upon his Marriage in 1712, by settling Lands in *S.* with a provisional Addition (during two Joint Lives) of Lands in *W. O.* (there being an Annuity payable to a Widow out of *S*:) In which Deed of Settlement there is a *Proviso* for his Wife's *releasing Dower*; and also a *Covenant* from *James*, " That He had Power to make such Ap- " pointment, and that his said Wife and his Sons by Her shall " *enjoy according to the Intent* of the said Deed and of his *Father's* " *Will*." In 1738, *James* RELEASES *this Proviso* " that his " Wife shall release her Claim to Dower out of his Estate:" And in 1751, by Indenture, reciting " That the Annuitant-Widow " was dead," and " that He had received an *additional For-* " *tune* of above 600 *l.* which had fallen to his Wife since their " Marriage," He, as an INCREASE *to his Jointure*, assigns, limits, and appoints, *in* PURSUANCE *and* BY VIRTUE *of the* POWER *given Him by his Father's Will*, and of all other Powers and Authorities that are in Him, ALL the Messuages Lands &c devised to Him by his Father's Will, in *W. O.* *B. H.* and *S.* to Trustees, to the

 Use

"The MARSHALSEA-*Prison* in the Burrough of *Southwark*"—Is a Description (in a Will, at least,) of the *Palace-Court* Prison, *not* of the King's Bench Prison. *Page* 1037 to 1039.

The Method of *Charging them in Custody*; and the whole Practice of it, (both ancient and modern, and both in Term-time and in Vacation.) 1049 to 1053. See *Practice*.

Procedendo

Granted to a *Quarter-Sessions*; because the *Certiorari* had not issued, till *after* the Defendants had CONFESSED the Assault *below*. 749.

To the *Sheriff's Court in London*. 758, 759. See *Statutes*.

To a *Corporation* whose *By-Law* directed a Penalty to be sued for *in their own Court* and *not elsewhere*. 775 to 780. See *Habeas Corpus cum Causa*.

Process

May be *served* at *any* Time of the Return-Day, although it be AFTER the *Rising* of the Court. 812, 813.

Prohibition—

To the *Spiritual Court*—shall *not* be granted, where they *have Jurisdiction* and have *pronounced Sentence*; (For in such Case, the Remedy must be by *Appeal*:) But if They proceed where they have NO *Jurisdiction* at all, a Prohibition may be applied for, AFTER *Sentence*. 813.

Promissory Note. See *Bill of Exchange*.

An original *unindorsed* Promissory Note has no Resemblance to a Bill of Exchange. But when once *indorsed*, it has an exact *Analogy* to a *Bill of Exchange*. The *Indorser* then resembles the *Drawer* of a Bill; The *Maker*, the Accepter of a Bill; and the *Indorsee*, the *Payee* of a Bill. And Promissory Notes, and *Inland Bills of Exchange*, are just upon the same Footing. 676, 677. A Confusion has arisen from Calling the Maker of a Note "the *Drawer*." *ibid.* and 678.

The *Indorsee* is bound to apply to the MAKER of the Note: And if He is guilty of a *Neglect*, and the Maker becomes insolvent, the Indorsee loses the Money, and can not come upon the Indorser at all. 676. And if the Indorsee of a Note brings an Action against the Indorser, He (the Plaintiff) *must prove a Demand* of, *or due Diligence* used to have gotten the Money from the MAKER of the Note. 676, 677, 678.

Bills of Exchange, and *Promissory Notes* are under the SAME *Rules of Determination*. 1224, 1227. See *Bill of Exchange*.

1ſt. There may be a Doubt whether ſuch a Diſtreſs would be lawful, after a *previous Demand* of the Money made *upon the Repreſentative*. *Page* 1157, 1158, 1159.

2dly. But it is clearly bad, WITHOUT ſuch a *Demand* upon Him. 1159.

Recordari facias Loquelam

Stays all further Proceeding in a County Court, if delivered after interlocutory but *before final* Judgment. 1151, 1152.

The Officer of the inferior Court can not refuſe Obedience to the Writ, under Pretence of his *Fees* not being paid Him. 1152.

Relation. See *Fiction*, *Teſte*, *Pleading*, *Declaration*.

Of a *Bankrupt's Certificate* (when allowed,) to the *Time of Signing*. 716 to 719. See *Bankrupt*.

Of a Bankruptcy ariſing from *lying* 2 *Months in Priſon*, to the *Time* of the *firſt* Arreſt. 817 to 820. See *Bankrupt*.

Where a Deed of *Bargain and Sale* " to make a Tenant to the *Præcipe*," and a *Common Recovery*, when Both are completed, ſhall be conſidered as ONE *Conveyance* and to *relate* to the Date of the *former*. 1134. See *Deviſe*.

Repleader.

The COSTS *of the* AMENDMENT of a Plea, which requires ſuch a ſlight Alteration in it and in all the ſubſequent Pleadings, as *not to deface the Record*, ſhall be allowed in Proportion to NECESSARY *Alterations only*, and no more. 757, 758.

The Expence of *adviſing* whether to *reply de novo*, ſhall in all Events be allowed to the Proſecutor; and He is at Liberty to do it if He pleaſes: But *if* He does *not* judge proper to do ſo, He muſt *not* have Coſts as if He actually had. 758.

Return

Of *Nulla Bona*, upon Executions againſt *Bankrupts*. 817 to 820. See *Bankrupt*.

Richmond-Park—

FOOT-*Ways* through *Richmond-Gate* and through *Eaſt-Sheen-Gates*, acroſs it, were eſtabliſhed: *Contra*, for CARRIAGES, or for HORSE-People. 908, 909.

Sentence (pronounced on Criminals convicted.)

An *Under-Sheriff* of *Middlesex*, instead of setting Dr. *Shebbeare* (who had been convicted of writing and publishing a Treasonable Libel) IN and upon the Pillory, according to his Sentence, suffered Him to stand *in a sort of Triumph, Erect* upon the Pillory, *without* putting his Head, Neck Arms or Hands *through* the Holes; with a *Servant* in Livery holding an *Umbrella* over his Head. An Attachment issued for this, as for a Contempt: And He was *fined* 50 *l.* and committed to the Marshal for 2 *Months*, *Page* 794 to 798. See *Pillory*.

For *gross and malicious* PERJURY in *Articles of the Peace*—Pillory once; and TRANSPORTATION for *seven* Years. 806. See *Articles of the Peace*.

For a CONSPIRACY to indict for a *Capital* Crime. 996, 1027. See *Indictment, Judgment Villainous*.

Service

Of *Process*—May be at *any* Time of the Return-Day; although it be long AFTER *the Rising of the Court*. 812, 813.

Set-off (of mutual Debts.)

Is extremely *beneficial* to the Subject. 823.

It was *first given* by 2 *G.* 2. *c.* 22. § 13. a *temporary* Act. But 8 *G.* 2. *c.* 24. § 5. *perpetuates* this Clause of 2 *G.* 2. (which enacts generally, " That where there are *mutual Debts* between the Parties, One may be set against the other:") And as Doubts had arisen upon the former Act, about the *different Natures* of Debts, the Latter makes a *general* Provision (*viz.* " *notwithstanding* such " Debts are deemed in Law to be of a different Nature,") without Exception, " *unless* in Cases where Either of the said Debts " shall accrue by reason of a *Penalty* contained in any Bond or Specialty;" In which Cases, the Debt intended to be set off shall be *pleaded in Bar*, and the Plea shall shew how much is *truly and justly due* on either Side, and Judgment (if the Plaintiff recovers) shall be entered for *no more* than shall appear to be *truly and justly due* to the Plaintiff. 822, 826.

Since these two very beneficial Acts, *Stoppage* or *Setting-off* of mutual Debts is *become equivalent to actual Payment*; and a *Balance shall be struck*, as in Equity and Justice it ought to be. 825.

But at COMMON LAW, *before* these Acts, If the Plaintiff was *even more* indebted to the Defendant than the Defendant to Him, He could only go into a Court of Equity. 826.

of the Damages recovered *by Him* against *Baskerville* in the other Action, as *exceeded* the Balance of the mutual Debts between them. 1229 to 1232. Resolved as follows—

1. A Plaintiff cannot *compel* a Defendant to set off. *Page* 1230.
2. *Brown* had a Right, *at the Time* when He gave the Notice, to give it. 1231.
3. His Right to make the Set-off *remained* in Him *after his own Verdict*; Which neither extinguished his Debt, nor changed it's Nature, (for Judgment was not signed,) but only amounted to conclusive Evidence of it. 1231.
4. *Brown* could not, with Safety, have taken his Verdict for *less*. *ibid.*

Sheriffs and their Bailiffs—

Are obliged to let Persons out *upon Bail*, upon reasonable Sureties of sufficient Persons. 926.

It is *Oppression*, to take *Money* for doing it; and *punishable* by *Attachment* or Indictment. *ibid.* and 927, 928.

Ship. See *Policy*, *Insurance*.

Capture of it. 690 to 698. See *Policy*.

Recapture of a taken Ship. *ibid.* And see *Policy*, *Statutes*.

Mortgage of it. 941. See *Bankrupt*, *Mortgage*.

Stamps.

Upon Copies *of Bills in Equity*. 1177 to 1181. See *Copies*, *Statutes*.

Statutes. See *Construction*.

22, 23 *C.* 2. *c.* 25. § 7. against *Stealing Fish*. 682. See *Conviction*.

29 *G.* 2. *c.* 34. § 24. (the *Prize*-Act) concerning *Ships taken* by the Enemy, and RETAKEN by Men of War or Privateers. 683 to 698. See *Policy of Insurance*.

9, 10 *W.* 3. *c.* 15. " for determining Differences by Arbitration"—was made to put Submissions to Arbitrations, where *no Cause* was depending, upon the *same Foot* as those where there *was* a Cause depending: And it is only *declaratory* of what the Law was before, in the *latter* Case. 701.

12 *Ann.* *c.* 16. 716. and 891, 892. See *Usury*.

3, 4 *W.* & *M.* *c.* 12. § 9. concerning Surveyors of Highways. 745, 746. See *Orders*.

3 *J.* 1. *c.* 8. (to avoid unnecessary Delays of Executions.) 746, 747. See *Bail*, *Error*.

If a Statute *creates* a NEW Offence, and prescribes a *particular Method of Proceeding*, Such *particular Remedy* must be *specifically pursued*, and an *Indictment at Common* Law will *not* lie: But if it was an Offence *punishable* BEFORE the Making of the Statute which prescribes the particular Method of Proceeding, In *such* Case the particular Remedy is CUMULATIVE, and does *not* take away the former Remedy; but an *Indictment at Common* Law will lie. *Page* 805. See *Indictment*. 545, 805.

13, 14 *C.* 2. *c.* 12. } An Overseer *refusing to receive a removed*
3, 4 *W.* & *M. c.* 11. } *Pauper*, is an Instance of this. 803, 804.

43 *Eliz. c.* 2. § 7, 11. A Grandfather refusing to obey an Order of Sessions "to provide for his Grandsons"—is Another. 803 to 806. See *Indictment* 803 to 806.

8, 9 *W.* 3. *c.* 11. § 8. } Most clearly and excellently explained.
2 *G.* 2. *c.* 22. § 13. } 824 to 827. See *Set-off*. See also *supra*
8 *G.* 2. *c.* 24. § 5. } 747, 748. and 799.

22 *C.* 2. *c.* 12. § 9. (about sending Men and Teams to the Highways.) 832. See *Indictment*.

9 *Ann. c.* 20. § 4. An Information against a *whole* Corporation *as a* BODY must be brought by the *Attorney General*, on Behalf of the *Crown*. 869. See *Information*.

26 *G.* 2. *c.* 33. § 11. (for the better preventing of *Clandestine Marriages*,) is made against *Both* Parties: And a Marriage contrary to it is ABSOLUTELY *void*. 898, 899.

32 *G.* 2. *c.* 28. § 13. (for *Relief of Debtors* with Respect to the Imprisonment of their Persons &c) was *favourably construed*, so as to obviate any Inconvenience from the Chasm of 14 Days, and to serve the *Intention* of the Act, which did not design this Omission. 901. See *above* 799.

23 *H.* 6. *c.* 10. though a PRIVATE Act, so far that it must be *pleaded* in Cases arising immediately and directly upon it, yet does not prevent a Court of Justice from taking *judicial* Notice "That a "Sheriff's Officer is *obliged to admit to Bail*, in an *Action upon* "*the Case*, provided that unexceptionable Bail be offered Him:" And He is punishable if He *takes Money* for so doing; because it is his *Duty* to do it. 926, 927, 928.

21 *J.* 1. *c.* 16. § 3. Of *Limitations*—The TRUE *Time of suing out a* LATITAT may be *shewn*, where it is *material*; notwithstanding the *Teste*. 966. See *Pleading*, 950 to 969. See *Latitat* 961 to 967.

43 *Eliz. c.* 2. § 1. Neither *Quit-Rents*, nor *Heriots*, or other *Casual* Profits of a Manor, are *rateable* to the *Poor-Tax*. 999.

13, 14 *C.* 2. *c.* 1. }
1 *W.* & *M. c.* 18. § 13. }
7, 8 *W.* 3. *c.* 34. } 1002, 1003. See *Quakers*.
8 *G.* 1. *c.* 6. }
22 *G.* 2. *c.* 46. § 36, 37. }

26 *G.* 2.

17 *G.* 2. *c.* 5. "to amend and make more effectual the Laws relating to *Rogues and Vagabonds &c*" § 1, 4, 16, 17. The *Quarter-Sessions* have Jurisdiction to *overbale the Constable*'s Accounts. *Page* 1198.

29 *G.* 2. *c.* 34. § 24. (the Act for the Encouragement of Seamen, and the more speedy and effectual Manning his Majesty's Navy.) 1209. See *Policy of Insurance.*

2 *G.* 2. *c.* 22. § 13. (about Setting One *mutual Debt* against Another.) 1229 to 1232. See *Set-off.*

Surgeon—

Understanding LATIN is a previous Qualification to being even put *Apprentice* to a *London* Surgeon. 896. See *By-Law.*

Surrender—

Of a *Life-Estate*, by Tenant for Life, to impower a *Remainder-Man in Tail* to suffer a Recovery—In what Cases an *actual* Surrender shall be PRESUMED to have been made: In what, not. 1072 to 1077. See *Tenant in Tail.*

Tanner—

EXERCISING the Occupation, without 7 Years Apprenticeship. 1035 to 1037. See *Indictment.*

Tenant in Tail. See *Common Recovery.*

May turn his Estate into a *Fee*, or *alienate* it for his own Benefit, by DULY *suffering a Common Recovery.* 1072.

But He must have a *sufficient Estate and Power*, to qualify Him to suffer it. *ibid.* He must either be the Tenant in Tail in *Possession*; Or He must have the *Concurrence of the Freeholder* who claims *prior* to Him under the *same* Settlements. *ibid.*

This Principle is adhered to, by 14 *G.* 2. *c.* 20: Which Act means to preserve the same Negative to Persons *claiming under the Family-Settlement*, as they had before, *ibid.* and 1075.

Where a Person has POWER *to suffer* a Common Recovery, *Omnia præsumentur* ritè et solenniter acta, until the Contrary appears: But if the *Contrary appears*, there is an *End* of the *Presumption.* 1073, 1074.

1st. Where the Freeholder is a *Trustee* for the Tenant in Tail and *under his Direction*, it is a Cause for presuming "that Every "thing was rightly transacted." 1073.

So all *local* Matters in *Wales*. So, as to *Ireland*. So, as to the *Cinque-Ports*. So, as to the Isle of *Ely*. *Page* 859.

Turkey-Company—

Admission into it. See *Quakers*, *Mandamus*.

Verdict—

VERDICTS are to be taken *favourably*, not strictly (like Pleadings:) And if the Court can *collect* the clear Meaning of the Jury, They will work it into *Form*, and make it serve. 699, 700. See *Error*.

A Verdict shall not help, where the *Consideration* manifestly appears, upon the *Face of the Declaration*, to be illegal. 926 to 929.

May be set aside WITHOUT *Costs*, upon Circumstances. 1224, 1228. See *Bill of Exchange*.

University of Cambridge

Has a *concurrent* Right with the King's Printer, to PRINT *Acts of Parliament* and *Abridgments of Acts of Parliament* within the University, upon the Terms in their Letters Patent. 664. See *Printing*.

Usury.

A *Real bonâ fide* WAGER, not at all intended as a Loan, is *not* an Usurious Contract: But an *Usurious* LOAN, *disguised as a Wager* (with Intent to have a Shift,) *is* so. 716.

A *Bond* in the Penalty of 200*l.* was conditioned for the Performance of Articles. The Articles recited that the Obligee had lent the Obligor 100*l.* to be repaid at the End of 4 Years, WITHOUT *Interest*; But in Consideration that the Obligor his Executors and Administrators should *find and provide* for the *Obligee's Daughter*, *Meat and Drink* in his House for 4 Years, and also *Board*; And that She should be *Co-partner with his Wife* in the Business of a Milliner, and *equally Share* in the *Profits*, and bear Half the Losses, Charges (except House-keeping,) *Shop-Rent*, and *Materials* (which the Obligor agreed to provide;) And also that the Obligor should *lodge the Obligee*, She *paying Him* 10*l. a Year*: And at the End of the 4 Years, the Obligor to repay the 100*l.* Principal Money; And *in Case of the Death* of the Obligee's said Daughter, to repay to the Obligee the said Principal Sum of 100*l.* TOGETHER *with lawful Interest* for the same. 891, 892. This is *not*

Milton Keynes UK
Ingram Content Group UK Ltd.
UKHW020922111023
430351UK00005B/63